MODELING AND SIMULATION IN ENGINEERING

Edited by **Catalin Alexandru**

Modeling and Simulation in Engineering
Edited by Catalin Alexandru

Published by InTech
Janeza Trdine 9, 51000 Rijeka, Croatia

Publishing Process Manager Vedran Greblo

Technical Editor Teodora Smiljanic

Cover Designer InTech Design Team

Modeling and Simulation in Engineering, Edited by Catalin Alexandru
p. cm.
ISBN 978-953-51-0012-6

For EU product safety concerns:
IN TECH d.o.o., Prolaz Marije Krucifikse Kozulić 3, 51000 Rijeka, Croatia,
info@intechopen.com or visit our website at intechopen.com.

Meet the editor

Dr Cătălin Alexandru is a Professor at the Transylvania University of Braşov (Romania). His focus is on Product Design, Mechatronics, and the Environment Department. His teaching and research activity centers on the dynamic modeling and simulation and the mechanical and mechatronical systems. His experience in this field can be summarized as follows:

- PhD Supervisor in Mechanical Engineering;
- Co-ordination of the virtual prototyping laboratory at the Product Design for Sustainable - Development Research Center;
- Bachelor and Master Degrees with emphasis on virtual prototyping tools, virtual prototyping, modeling and simulation in engineering, and virtual prototyping of renewable energy systems;
- Publication of books and scientific papers in international journals and conference proceedings;
- Co-ordination of research projects that address the modeling and simulation in virtual environment for various types of mechanical and mechatronical systems;
- Post-graduate programs in the field of informatics applied in engineering and software solutions for virtual prototyping;
- Member of national and international organization that promotes research in the field of mechanical and mechatronical systems.

Contents

Preface

We are living in a computer-based world. Computer use in various fields has long ceased to be fashionable and has become almost a necessity. Since the early phases of design to the final implementation of a product, the computer has replaced traditional tools, providing efficient and elegant instruments. We can say, without fear of being wrong, that the strides that mankind has taken in recent decades is due largely to computer assistance.

This book provides an open platform from which to establish and share knowledge developed by scholars, scientists, and engineers from all over the world, about various applications of computer aided modeling and simulation in the design process of products in various engineering fields. The book consists of 12 chapters arranged in an order reflecting the multidimensionality of applications related to modeling and simulation. The chapters are in two sections: 3D Modeling (seven chapters), and Virtual Prototyping (five chapters). Some of the most recent modeling and simulation techniques, as well as some of the most accurate and sophisticated software in treating complex systems, are applied.

Modeling is an essential and inseparable part of all scientific activity, being the process of generating abstract, conceptual, graphical, and/or mathematical models. In other words, modeling is a method in science and technology consisting of the schematic representation of an object or system as a similar or analog model. Modeling allows the analysis of real phenomena and predicts the results from the application of one or more theories to a given level of approximation. Simulation is an imitation used to study the results of an action on a product (system), without performing the experiment on the physical/hardware product. So, simulation can be defined as the virtual reproduction of physical systems. A computer simulation is an attempt to model a real-life or hypothetical situation on a computer so that it can be studied to see how the system works. Computer simulation has become a useful part of modeling many systems in engineering, to gain insight into the operation of those systems. The basic goal for a computer simulation is to generate a sample of representative scenarios for a model.

Advances in computer hardware and software have led to new challenges and opportunities for researchers aimed at investigating complex systems. The modern approach of the modeling and simulation process has now shifted from the traditional CAD/CAM/CAE practices, which were focused on a concept referred to as art-to-component, to the system-focused approach, the interaction of form, fit, function, and assembly of all components in a product having a major contribution to overall product quality. Virtual prototyping practices can ensure greater product performance and quality in a fraction of both the time and cost required for traditional approaches.

Virtual prototyping is a computer-aided engineering-based discipline that entails modeling products and simulating their behavior under real-world operating conditions. By using various types of software solutions for evaluating the form, fitting, functionality, and durability of the products in an integrated approach, complex digital prototypes can be created and then used in virtual experiments (lab and field tests) in a similar way to the real circumstances.

Generally, a virtual prototyping platform includes the following software environments: CAD (Computer Aided Design) to create the geometric (solid) model of the system/product; MBS (Multi-Body Systems) – to analyze, optimize, and simulate the system under real operating conditions; FEA (Finite Element Analysis) to capture inertial and compliance effects during simulations, to study deformations of the flexible components, and to predict loads with greater accuracy, therefore achieving more realistic results; DFC (Design for Control) – to create the control/command system model for the mechatronic products; and PDM (Product Data Management) to track and control data related to a particular product, and to promote integration and data exchange among all users who interact with products. Depending on the type of application, other particular software solutions can obviously be used.

One of the most important advantages of this kind of simulation, based on virtual prototyping, is the possibility of performing virtual measurements in any point or area of the system, and for any parameter (motion, force, energy). This is not always possible in the real case due to the lack of space for transducers placement, lack of appropriate transducers, or high temperatures. This helps engineers to make quick decisions on any design changes without going through expensive hardware prototype building and testing. The behavioral performance predictions are obtained much earlier in the design cycle of the products, thereby allowing more effective and cost-efficient design changes and reducing overall risk substantially.

This book collects original and innovative research studies on recent applications in modeling and simulation. *Modeling and Simulation in Engineering* is addressed to researchers, engineers, students, and to all those professionally active and/or interested in the methods and applications of modeling and simulation, covering a large engineering field: mechanical engineering, electrical engineering, biomedical engineering, and others. The book provides a forum for original papers dealing with any aspect of systems simulation and modeling. The basic principle for a successful modeling and simulation process can be formulated in this way: as complex as necessary, and as simple as possible. This is in accordance with the Einstein's principle: "A scientific theory should be as simple as possible, but no simpler". The idea is to manipulate the simplifying assumptions in a way that reduces the complexity of the model (in order to make the real-time simulation), but without altering the precision of the results. In other words, a useful model is a tradeoff between simplicity and realism. All original contributions collected in this book are strictly jointed by this principle.

Prof. Catalin Alexandru
University Transilvania of Brasov, Product Design and Robotics Department,
Romania

Part 1

3D Modeling

1

Image-Laser Fusion for *In Situ* 3D Modeling of Complex Environments: A 4D Panoramic-Driven Approach

Daniela Craciun[1,2], Nicolas Paparoditis[2] and Francis Schmitt[1]
[1]*Telecom ParisTech CNRS URA 820 - TSI Dept.*
[2]*Institut Geographique National - Laboratoire MATIS*
France

1. Introduction

One might wonder what can be gained from the image-laser fusion and in which measure such a hybrid system can generate automatically complete and photorealist 3D models of difficult to access and unstructured underground environments.

Our research work is focused on developing a vision-based system aimed at automatically generating in-situ photorealist 3D models in previously unknown and unstructured underground environments from image and laser data. In particular we are interested in modeling underground prehistoric caves. In such environments, special attention must be given to the main issue standing behind the automation of the 3D modeling pipeline which is represented by the capacity to match reliably image and laser data in GPS-denied and feature-less areas. In addition, time and in-situ access constraints require fast and automatic procedures for in-situ data acquisition, processing and interpretation in order to allow for in-situ verification of the 3D scene model completeness. Finally, the currently generated 3D model represents the only available information providing situational awareness based on which autonomous behavior must be built in order to enable the system to act intelligently on-the-fly and explore the environment to ensure the 3D scene model completeness.

This chapter evaluates the potential of a hybrid image-laser system for generating in-situ complete and photorealist 3D models of challenging environments, while minimizing human operator intervention. The presented research focuses on two main aspects: (i) the automation of the 3D modeling pipeline, targeting the automatic data matching in feature-less and GPS-denied areas for in-situ world modeling and (ii) the exploitation of the generated 3D models along with visual servoing procedures to ensure automatically the 3D scene model completeness.

We start this chapter by motivating the jointly use of laser and image data and by listing the main key issues which need to be addressed when aiming to supply automatic photorealist 3D modeling tasks while coping with time and in-situ access constraints. The next four sections are dedicated to a gradual description of the 3D modeling system in which we project the proposed image-laser solutions designed to be embedded onboard mobile plateforms, providing them with world modeling capabilities and thus visual perception. This is an important aspect for the in-situ modeling process, allowing the system to be aware and to act intelligently on-the-fly in order to explore and digitize the entire site. For this reason, we introduce it as ARTVISYS, the acronym for ARTificial VIsion-based SYStem.

2. The in-situ 3D modeling problem

The *in-situ* 3D modeling problem is concerned with the automatic environment sensing through the use of active (laser) and/or passive (cameras) 3D vision and aims at generating in-situ the *complete* 3D scene model in a step by step fashion. At each step, the currently generated 3D scene model must be exploited along with visual servoing procedures in order to guide the system to act intelligently on-the-fly to ensure in-situ the 3D scene model completeness.

Systems embedding active 3D vision are suitable for generating in-situ *complete* 3D models of previously unknown and high-risk environments. Such systems rely on visual-based environment perception provided by a sequentially generated 3D scene representation. Onboard 3D scene representation for navigation purposes was pioneered by Moravec's back in the 1980s (Moravec, 1980). Since then, Computer Vision and Robotics research communities have intensively focused their efforts to provide vision-based autonomous behavior to unmanned systems, special attention being given to the vision-based autonomous navigation problem. In (Nister et al., 2004), Nister demonstrated the feasibility of a purely vision-based odometry system, showing that an alternative for localization in GPS-denied areas can rely on artificial vision basis. Several research works introduced either 2D and 3D Simultaneous Localization and Mapping (SLAM) algorithms using single-camera or stereo vision frameworks (Durrant-White & Bailey, 2006), (Bailey & Durrant-White, 2006). While gaining in maturity, these techniques rely on radiometric and geometric features' existence or exploit initial guess provided by navigation sensors (GPS, IMUs, magnetic compasses) employed along with dead-reckoning procedures.

Scientists from Robotics, Computer Vision and Graphics research communities were introducing the 3D modeling pipeline (Beraldin & Cournoyer, 1997) aiming to obtain photorealist digital 3D models through the use of 3D laser scanners and/or cameras. Various 3D modeling systems have been developed promoting a wide range of applications: cultural heritage (Levoy et al., 2000), (Ikeuchi et al., 2007),(Banno et al., 2008), 3D modeling of urban scenes (Stamos et al., 2008), modeling from real world scenes (Huber, 2002), natural terrain mapping and underground mine mapping (Huber & Vandapel, 2003), (Nuchter et al., 2004), (Thrun et al., 2006).

Without loss of generality, the 3D modeling pipeline requires automatic procedures for data acquisition, processing and 3D scene model rendering. Due to the sensors' limited field of view and occlusions, multiple data from various viewpoints need to be acquired, aligned and merged in a global coordinate system in order to provide a complete and photorealist 3D scene model rendering. As for SLAM techniques, the main drawback standing behind the automation of the entire 3D modeling process is the *data alignment* step for which several methods have been introduced.

For systems focusing on 3D modeling of large-scale objects or monuments (Levoy et al., 2000), (Ikeuchi et al., 2007),(Banno et al., 2008) a crude alignment is performed by an operator off-line. Then the coarse alignment is refined via iterative techniques (Besl & McKay, 1992). However, during the post-processing step it is often observed that the 3D scene model is incomplete. Although data alignment using artificial markers produces accurate results, it cannot be applied to high-risk environments due to time and in-situ access constraints. In addition, for cultural heritage applications, placing artificial landmarks within the scene causes damages to the heritage hosted by the site. The critical need for an in-situ 3D modeling procedure is emphasized by the operator's difficulty to access too small and too dangerous areas for placing artificial landmarks and by the need to validate in-situ the 3D scene model completeness in order to avoid to return on site to complete data collection.

Existing automatic data alignment methods perform *coarse alignment* by exploiting prior knowledge over the scene's content (Stamos et al., 2008) (i.e. radiometric or geometric features' existence, regular terrain to navigate with minimal perception) or the possibility to rely on navigation sensors (GPS, INS, odometry, etc.). In a second step, a *fine alignment* is performed via iterative methods.

Since in our research work the environment is previously unknown, features' existence cannot be guaranteed. In addition, in underground environments and uneven terrain navigation sensors are not reliable and dead-reckoning techniques lead to unbounded error growth for large-scale sceneries. A notable approach reported by Johnson (Johnson, 1997) and improved by Huber (Huber, 2002) overcomes the need of odometry using shape descriptors for 3D point matching. However, shape descriptors' computation requires dense 3D scans, leading to time consuming acquisition and processing, which does not cope with time and in-situ access constraints.

A main part of this chapter focuses on providing image-laser solutions for addressing the automation of the 3D modeling pipeline by solving the data alignment problem in feature-less and GPS-denied areas. In a second phase, we propose to exploit the world modeling capability along with visual servoing procedures in order to ensure in-situ the 3D scene model completeness.

3. Proposed solution: Automatic 3D modeling through 4D mosaic views

This section resumes how we solve for the automation of the 3D modeling pipeline through the use of 4D mosaics. We start by introducing the hardware design and by summarizing the 4D-mosaicing process. In order to ensure in-situ the 3D scene model completeness, Section 3.3 proposes a 4D-mosaic driven acquisition scenario having as main scope the automatic digitization and exploration of the site.

3.1 Testbed. Hard- and soft-ware architecture

We designed a *dual* system for performing in-situ 3D modeling tasks in large-scale, complex and difficult to access underground environments. Since in such environments navigation sensors are not reliable, the proposed system embeds only 2D and 3D vision sensors, unifying photorealism and high resolution geometry into *4D mosaic views*. Figure 1 illustrates the ARTVISYS's hardware along with the proposed *4D-mosaicing* process. We describe hereafter several ARTVISYS's features and justify the proposed design.

RACL[1] dual-system (Craciun, 2010). The proposed hardware architecture falls in the category of the RACL dual sensing devices, embedding a high-resolution color camera mounted on a motorized pan-tilt unit and a 3D laser-range-finder, which are depicted in Figures 1 a) and b), respectively. There are several reasons for choosing a RACL design:

[1] RACL system: Rigidly Attached Camera Laser system

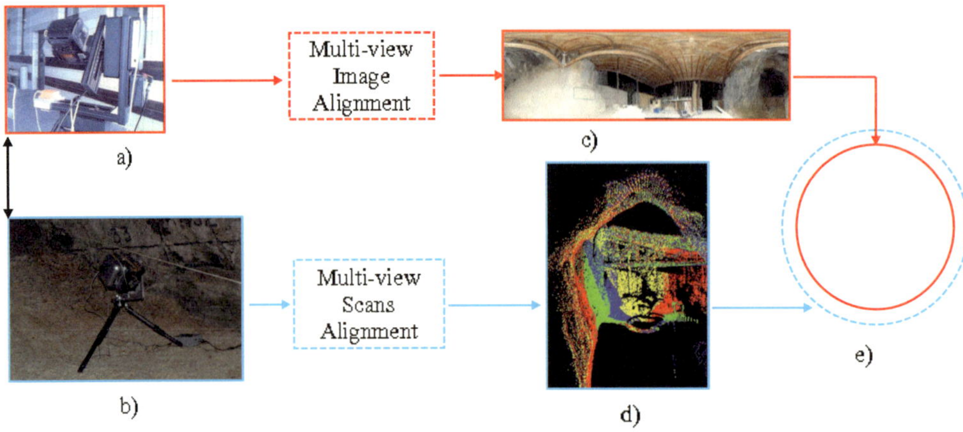

Fig. 1. The 4D-mosaicing process proposed for integration onboard ARTVISYS. a) NIKON D70 ® digital camera mounted on Rodeon ® motorized pan-tilt unit, b) Trimble ® 3D laser-range-finder during a data acquisition campaign undertaken in the Tautavel prehistoric cave (France) by the French Mapping Agency in October 2007, c) a Gigapixel color mosaic resulted from an image sequence acquired in the Tautavel prehistoric cave using an automatic image stitching algorithm which we introduce in Section 5 of this chapter, d) a 3D mosaic resulted from several overlapped scans acquired in the Tautavel prehistoric cave, matched by an automatic multi-view scan-matcher proposed in Section 4, e) alignment the 3D mosaic onto the Gigapixel one to produce the 4D mosaic, process described in Section 6 of this chapter.

- image-laser complementarity has been widely emphasized and investigated by several research works (Dias et al., 2003), (Stamos et al., 2008), (Zhao et al., 2005), (Cole & Newman, 2006), (Newman et al., 2006). There is no doubt that employing the two sensors separately, none can solve for the 3D modeling problem reliably.
- RACL systems overcomes several shortcomings raised by FMCL[2] ones. In particular, image-laser alignment and texture mapping procedures are difficult due to occluded areas in either image or laser data.

Addressing time and in-situ access constraints. An in-situ 3D modeling system must be able to supply fast data acquisition and processing while assuring the 3D scene model completeness in order to avoid to return on site to collect new data.
To this end, we design a *complementary* and *cooperative* image-laser fusion which lead to a *4D mosaicing sensor* prototype. The *complementary* aspect is related to the data acquisition process: in order to deal with time and in-situ access constraints, the proposed acquisition protocol consists in acquiring low-resolution 3D point clouds and high-resolution color images to generate in-situ photorealist 3D models. The use of both sensors rigidly attached leads to a *cooperative* fusion, producing a dual sensing device capable to generate in-situ omnidirectional and photorealist 3D models encoded as 4D mosaic views, which to our knowledge are no achievable using each sensor separately.

[2] Freely Moving Camera Laser system

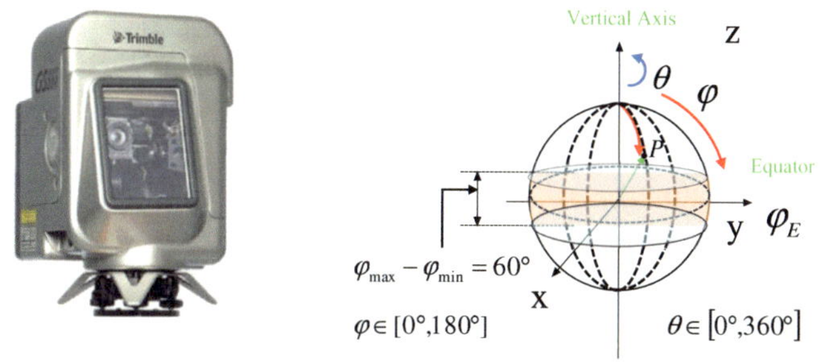

a) b)

Fig. 2. a) Trimble ® laser range finder delivering 5000 points per second with an accuracy of 3mm at 100m. The dimensions of the laser range finders are: 340mm diameter, 270mm width and 420mm height. The weight of the capturing device is 13.6kg. b) the field of view covered by the sensor.

3.2 Introducing 4D mosaic views: omnidirectional photorealist 3D models

In this chapter we solve for the automation of the 3D modeling pipeline by introducing the *4D mosaic views* as fully spherical panoramic data structure encoding surface geometry (depth) and 3-channel color information (red, green and blue). A *4D mosaic* is generated within three steps (process illustrated in Figure 1), each of which being described in Sections 4, 5 and 6 of this chapter and for which we provide a brief description hereafter.

3D Mosaics from laser-range-finders (LRFs). First, a 3D laser scanner acquires several partially overlapped scans which are aligned and merged into a fully 3D spherical mosaic view via a multi-view scan matching algorithm for which a detailed description is provided in Section 4. Figure 1 d) illustrates an example of a 3D mosaic obtained from real data acquired in the Tautavel prehistoric cave. Since our work is concerned with the 3D modeling in unstructured and underground environments, we introduce an automatic scan matcher which replaces the two-post processing steps usually performed by the currently existing scans alignment techniques (coarse alignment via manual or GPS pose and ICP-like methods for fine registration). The proposed method does not rely on feature extraction and matching, providing thus an environment-independent method.

Gigapixel panoramic head. Second, the motorized panoramic head illustrated in Figure 1 a)acquires a sequence of high-resolution images which are further automatically stitched into a Gigapixel color mosaic via a multi-view image matching algorithm for which a description is given in Section 5. Figure 1 c) depicts an example of the obtained optical mosaic. Since the nowadays image stitching algorithms present several limitations when dealing with unstructured environments, one of our main concern in this chapter is the ability to match images in feature-less areas.

4D-Mosaicing. Third, the 3D mosaic and the 2D optical Gigapixel one are aligned and fused into a photorealist and geometrically accurate 4D mosaic. This is the last step of the 4D-mosaicing process corresponding to Figure 1 e) and for which a mosaic-based approach for image-laser data alignment is proposed in Section 6. The estimated pose is exploited to generate in-situ a 4D mosaic (4-channel: red, green, blue and depth) which to our knowledge has not been reported until now.

The proposed 3D modeling pipeline leads to a vision-based system capable to generate in-situ photorealist and highly accurate 3D models encoded as 4D mosaics for each ARTVISYS's spatial position, called *station*. The next section introduces the 4D-mosaic-driven in-situ 3D modeling process performed by ARTVISYS aiming to ensure in-situ the 3D scene model completeness.

3.3 4D Mosaic-driven in situ 3D modeling

When dealing with the in-situ 3D modeling problem in large scale complex environments, one has to generate dynamically 3D scene models and to deal with occluded areas on-the-fly, in order to ensure automatically the 3D scene model completeness. This calls for an intelligent 3D modeling system, which implies the computation of the Next Best View (NBV) position (Dias et al., 2002) from which the new 4D mosaic must be acquired in order to sense the occluded areas. In addition, the system must be able to navigate from it's current position to the next best estimated 3D pose from which the next 4D mosaic must be acquired. This implies path planning, autonomous navigation and fast decision making capabilities. A detailed description on this process can be found in (Craciun, 2010).

4D-mosaic-driven acquisition scenario. Due to occlusions, several 4D mosaics must be autonomously acquired from different 3D spatial positions of the system in order to maximize the visible volume, while minimizing data redundancy. To this end, the 4D mosaicing sensor prototype comes together with a a *4D-mosaic-driven acquisition scenario* performed in a stop-and-go fashion, as illustrated in Figure 3.

The acquisition scenario starts by acquiring a 4D-mosaic which is further exploited to detect the occluded areas. In Figure 3, they corresponds to the blue segments representing depth discontinuities associated to each station. In a second step, the system must estimate the 3D pose from which the next 4D-mosaic must be acquired in order to maximize the visible volume. In a third step, the 4D mosaics are matched and integrated within a global 3D scene model which is further exploited to iterate the two aforementioned steps until the 3D scene model completeness is achieved.

Unambigous wide-baseline data alignment. The main advantage of 4D-mosaic views is represented by the fact that they encode explicit color information as 3-channel components (i.e. red, green and blue) and implicit shape description as depth for a fully spherical view of the system's surroundings. The four dimensional components are required in order to ensure reliably further processing, such as unambiguous data matching under wide viewpoint variation.

4. Multi-view rigid scans alignment for in-situ 3D mosaicing

This section presents the first step of the *4D mosaicing process* introduced in Figure1. We describe a multi-view scans alignment technique for generating in-situ 3D mosaics from several partially overlapped scans acquired from the same 3D pose of the system. We first describe the data acquisition scenario, followed by the global approach and an overview of experimental results obtained on real data gathered in two prehistoric caves are presented.

4.1 3D mosaicing acquisition scenario

In Section 3 we presented the hardware design of the proposed system which includes a Trimble® scanning device illustrated in Figure 2 a) providing a cloud of 3D points and their associated light intensity backscattering, within a field of view of 360° horizontally x 60° vertically, as shown in Figure 2 b). When mounted on a tripod, due to the vertical narrow

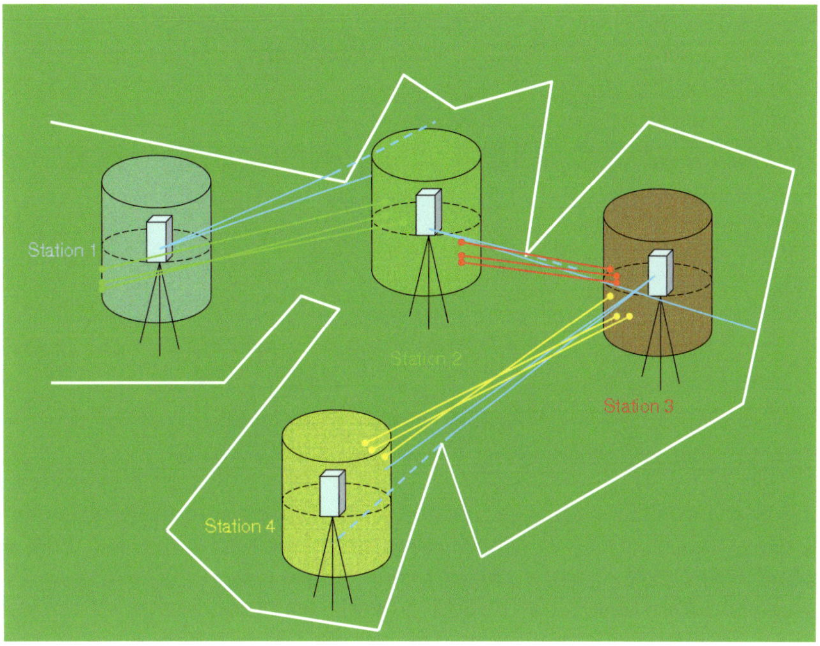

Fig. 3. The 4D-mosaic-driven acquisition scenario performed by ARTVISYS.

field of view, the scanning device is not suitable for the acquisition coverage of ceiling and ground. Therefore, we manufactured in our laboratory a L-form angle-iron shown in Figure 4 a).

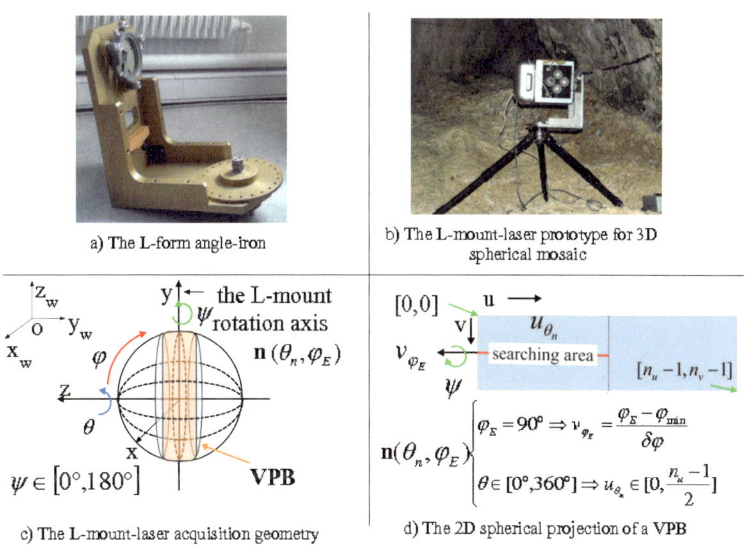

Fig. 4. The 3D mosaicing acquisition geometry.

The L-mount-laser prototype illustrated in Figure 4 b) captures all the area around its optical center within 360° vertically and 60° horizontally as shown in Figure 4 c), which we call a *vertical panoramic band* (VPB). Given a spatial position of the tripod, which we call a *station*, the

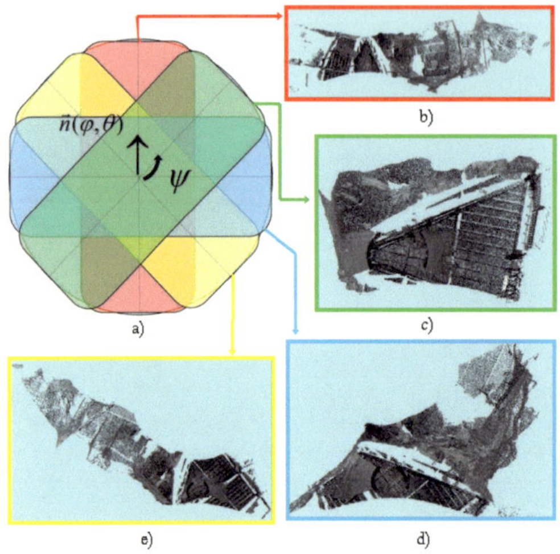

Fig. 5. Example of the 3D mosaicing acquisition scenario performed in the Tautavel prehistoric cave - France. (a)Top view of the acquisition: the laser acquires 4 VPBs as it rotates around its vertical axis $\mathbf{n}(\theta\mathbf{n}, \varphi\mathbf{n})$ with different values of ψ: (b) VBP 1 corresponding to $\psi \approx 0°$, (c) VPB 2 for $\psi \approx 45°$ (d) VPB 3 for $\psi \approx 90°$, (e) VPB 4 for $\psi \approx 135°$.

scenario consists in acquiring multiple overlapping VPBs in order to provide a fully $360° \times 180°$ 3D spherical view. For this purpose, the L-mount-laser is turned around its vertical axis $\mathbf{n}$ (superposed with the scan equator axis, Oy) with different imprecisely known orientations ψ, acquiring one VPB for each orientation, as shown in Figure 5. The L-mount-laser rotation angle ψ may vary within the range of $[0°, 180°]$. For this experiment the L-mount-laser was turned manually, but using a non-calibrated turning device it is straight forward. Generally, $N_{scenario} = 4$ VPBs are acquired to provide a fully 3D spherical view, separated by a rotation $\psi_{max} \simeq 45°$ providing an overlap of $\simeq$ 33% which our algorithm can handle (to be compared to the state of the art (Makadia et al., 2006), for which a minimum overlap of 45% is required).
Minimum overlap guaranteed. The proposed acquisition scenario facilitates considerably the scan matching task providing a constant and minimal overlapping area situated at the bottom (ground) and top (ceiling) areas of the 3D spherical view. This is an important key issue when performing 3D modeling tasks in large-scale environments, where the amount of the acquired and processed data must be minimized.
The following section introduces an automatic scan alignment procedure which aligns 4 VPBs (composing a fully spherical view) wrt a global coordinate system and integrates them into a single 3D entity, providing thus *in situ* a fully 3D spherical view of the system's surrounding.

4.2 Automatic multi-view rigid scans alignment

Let $S_0, ..., S_{N-1}$ be N partially overlapping scans acquired from different viewpoints. Since each scan is represented in the sensor's local coordinate system, the multi-view scan matching problem consists in recovering each sensors' viewpoints with respect to a global coordinate system, thereby aligning all scans in a common reference system. Generally, the first scan in a sequence can be chosen as the origin, so that the global coordinate system is locked to the coordinate frame of that scan. An absolute pose $\mathbf{T}_i, i = \{0, .., N-1\}$ is the 3D linear operator which rigidly transforms the 3D coordinates of a point $\mathbf{p} \in S_i, \mathbf{p} = (p_x, p_y, p_z, 1)^t$ from the

local coordinate system of scan S_i to the global (or world) coordinate system: $\mathbf{p}_w = \mathbf{T}_i\mathbf{p}_i$. In order to estimate the absolute poses $\mathbf{T}_i$, it is necessary to compute the relative poses $\mathbf{T}_{ij}, j = \{0, .., N-1\}$ and the corresponding overlaps $\mathbf{O}_{ij}$ for each pair of scans via a pair-wise scan matching procedure. Due to the mutual dependency which lies between the overlaps $\mathbf{O}_{ij}$ and the relative poses $\mathbf{T}_{ij}$, the multi-view scan matching is a difficult task.
Pair-wise rigid poses. We developed a pair-wise scan matcher algorithm by matching 2D panoramic views, solving *simultaneously* the above interrelated problems using a pyramidal dense correlation framework via quaternions. The pair-wise scan matching procedure exploits either intensity or depth 2D panoramic views, which encode spatial and appearance constraints increasing therefore the robustness of the pair-wise scan matching process. We solve for the pose estimation in two steps, within a hybrid framework: the rotation $\mathbf{R}$ is first computed by matching either intensity or depth data in the 2D panoramic image space, while the residual translation is computed a posteriori by projecting back in the 3D space the rotationally aligned panoramic images.
The proposed method employs an adaptable pyramidal framework which is the key issue for modeling in occluded environments, providing robustness to large-scale sparse data sets and cutting down the combinatory. In addition, the pyramidal structure emphasizes the tradeoff between the two key aspects of any scan matcher, the accuracy and the robustness. In this work, the accuracy is related to the subpixel precision attached to the dense correlation step, while the robustness component is related to the capability of the scan matcher to handle large motions, performing pose estimation in a coarse to fine fashion.
The global *multi-view fine alignment* is built upon a topological criterion introduced by (Sawhney & Ayer, 1996) for image mosaicing and employed by (Huber, 2002) for matching partially overlapped 3D point clouds. We extend this criterion in order to detect scans which do not correspond to the currently processed sequence (introduced in (Craciun et al., 2010) as *alien* scans). Next, the global multi-view fine alignment refines the pair-wise estimates by computing the best reference view which optimally registers all views into a global 3D scene model.
A detailed description of our method and a quality assement using several experiments performed in two prehistoric underground prehistoric caves may be found in (Craciun et al., 2008), (Craciun et al., 2010), (Craciun, 2010).

4.3 Multi-view scans alignment experiments

Data input. We applied the 3D mosaicing scenario described in Section 4.1 in two prehistoric caves from France: Moulin de Languenay - trial 1 and Tautavel - trials 2, 3 and 4. Each trial is composed by sequence of 4-VPBs acquired nearly from the same 3D position. In order to evaluate the robustness of the proposed method wrt different scanning devices and different scans resolutions, we performed several tests on data acquired with different acquisition setups.
Moulin de Languenay - trial 1: time and in-situ access constraints were not noticed and therefore the Trimble® GS100 laser was set to deliver multi-shot and high resolution scans.
Tautavel - trials 2, 3, 4: the experiments were run in a large-scale and "difficult-to-access" underground site. Therefore, the acquisition setup was designed to handle large-scale scenes while dealing with time and in-situ constraints. In particular, Trimble® GS200 was employed to supply accurate measurements at long ranges. In addition, during experiments we focused to limit as much as possible the acquisition time by setting the sensing device to acquire

one-shot and low resolution scans, emphasizing the robustness of our algorithm with respect to sparse large scale data sets caused by depth discontinuities. Figures 6 illustrates the rendering results for trial 2, obtained by passing each 4-VPBs sequence to the automatic intensity-based multi-view scan matcher.

Trial	Mode	$(\bar{\mathbf{r}} \pm \sigma_{\bar{\mathbf{r}}}) \times 10^{-2}$(m)	$(\Delta\bar{\mathbf{r}} \pm \Delta\sigma_{\bar{\mathbf{r}}}) \times 10^{-2}$(m)	♯points, CPU time (min)
Trial 1	Intensity	3.913 ± 15.86	0.793 ± 2.22	1.508×10^6
GS100	Depth	3.12 ± 13.64		16.44
Trial 2	Intensity	1.18 ± 16.14	1.94 ± 0.84	2.5829×10^6
GS200	Depth	3.12 ± 16.98		27.39
Trial 3	Intensity	0.332 ± 4.15	0.021 ± 0.154	2.6079×10^6
GS200	Depth	0.353 ± 4.304		27.66
Trial 4	Intensity	0.184 ± 1.249	0.007 ± 0.884	2.5321×10^6
GS200	Depth	0.191 ± 0.365		26.28

Table 1. Results of the global 3D scene models. The fourth column illustrates that the accuracy may vary following the mode used with an order of 10^{-2} of the pose estimates wrt the mode used. The last column illustrates the number of points and runtime obtained for each trial.

Table 1 provides the global residual errors obtained for all trials. When analyzing the residual mean errors, we observe the inter-dependency between the alignment accuracy and the number of points provided by the capturing device for pose calculation. The experiments demonstrates the robustness and the reliability of our algorithm in complex environments where depth discontinuities lead to large scale sparse data sets. The fourth column of Table 1 illustrates that following the scan matcher mode, the results' accuracy may vary between $[10^{-2}, 10^{-3}]$.

Runtime. The experiments were run on a 1.66 GHz Linux machine using a standard CPU implementation. The last column of Table 1 shows that the proposed approach exhibits robustness to registration errors with a reasonable computation time. Nevertheless, since the algorithm was originally designed in a multi-tasking fashion, it allows for both sequential and parallel processing on embedded platforms. In (Craciun, 2010) we provide the embedded design for parallel implementation on a multi-core embedded platform.

5. Automatic gigapixel optical mosaicing

The second step in the 4D mosaicing process illustrated in Figure 1 is represented by multi-view image alignment for generating in-situ a fully spherical panoramic view of the system's surroundings. We describe hereafter the Gigapixel mosaicing system designed to be integrated within the proposed in-situ 3D modeling process driven by 4D mosaic views. Further reading on the research work presented in this section can be found in (Craciun et al., 2009), (Craciun, 2010).

5.1 Gigapixel mosaicing system

The inputs of our algorithm are several hundreds of ordered high resolution images acquired from a common optical center. The capturing device illustrated in Figure 7 is previously parameterized with the field of view to be cover and the desired overlap between adjacent images. The method proposed in this paper uses the complementarity of the existing image

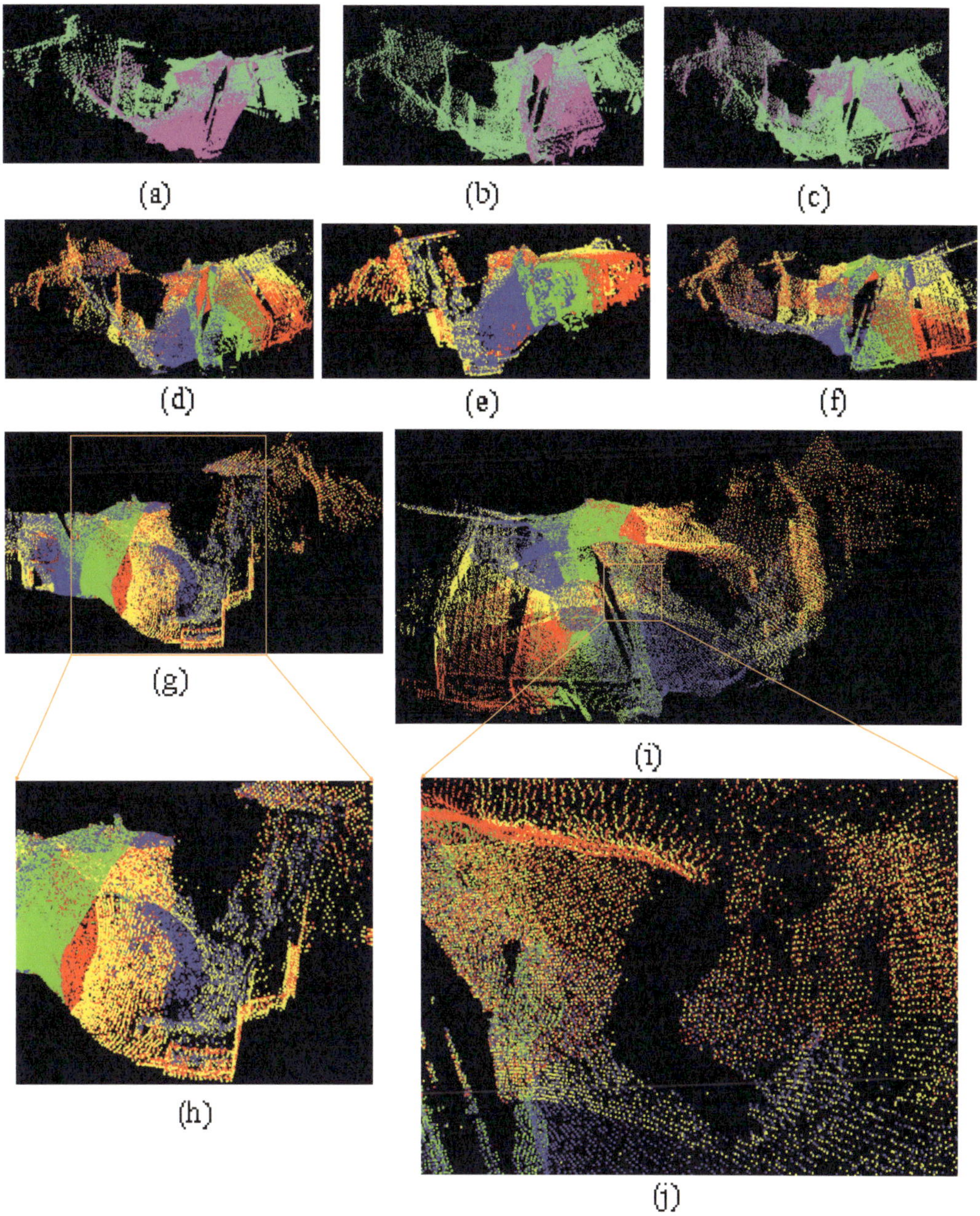

Fig. 6. Multiview Scan Matching results on data sets acquired in Tautavel prehistoric cave, France - Trial 2. (a) S_1 - green, S_2 - magenta, (b) S_{12} - green, S_3 - magenta, (c) S_{123} - green, S_4 - magenta, (d) Multiview scan alignment - Top-down view, S_1 - yellow, S_2 - blue, S_3 - green, S_4 - red, (e) Front-left view, (f) Top view, (g) Front-right view, (h) Zoom-in outdoor front-right view, (i) Bottom-up view, (j) Zoom-in cave's ceiling.

alignment techniques (Snavely et al., 2006), (direct vs. feature-based) and fuses their main advantages in an efficient fashion.

First, a global-to-local pairwise motion estimation is performed which refines the initial estimates provided by the pan-tilt head. We solve for rotation using a pyramidal patch-based correlation procedure via quaternions. The pyramidal framework allows to handle very noisy initial guess and big amounts of parallax.

In order to provide robustness to deviations from pure parallax-free motion[3], the global rotation initializes a patch-based local motion estimation procedure. The pairwise procedure outputs a list of locally matched image points via a translational motion model. Since the matched points do not correspond to any corner-like features, we introduce them as *anonymous features* (AF).

Second, the multi-view fine alignment is achieved by injecting the AF matches in a bundle adjustment engine (BA) (Triggs et al., 1999).Comparing to Lowe's method(Brown & Lowe, 2007), the proposed algorithm can deal with feature-less areas, providing therefore an environment-independent method for the image alignment task.

The following sections describe the overall flow of processing. First, we briefly introduce the camera motion parametrization. Second, we introduce the global-to-local pairwise motion estimation, followed by the multi-view fine alignment description.

(a) (b)

Fig. 7. Mosaicing acquisition System: a NIKON® D70 digital camera (a) with its optical center fixed on a motorized pan-tilt head (Rodeon manufactured by Clauss®) attached to a tripod base (b).

5.2 Camera motion parametrization

Assuming that the camera undergoes purely rotations around it's optical center the camera motion can be parameterized by a 3×3 rotation matrix $\mathbf{R}$ and the camera calibration matrix $\mathbf{K}$. Under the pinhole camera model, a point in space $\mathbf{p} = (p_x, p_y, p_z)^T$ gets mapped to a 2D point $\mathbf{u} = (u_x, u_y)^T$ through the central projection process, which can be written using the

[3] In practice we may notice visible seams due to images' misalignment. One of the main reason is that the motorization of the capturing device yields some vibration noise which is further amplified by the tripod platform. Moreover, unmodeled distortions or failure to rotate the camera around the optical center, may result small amounts of parallax.

homogenous coordinates $(u_x, u_y, 1)^T$ as following:

$$\begin{pmatrix} u_x \\ u_y \\ 1 \end{pmatrix} \cong \mathbf{KR} \begin{pmatrix} p_x \\ p_y \\ p_z \end{pmatrix} \tag{1}$$

where, $\mathbf{K} = \begin{bmatrix} f & 0 & x_0 \\ 0 & f & y_0 \\ 0 & 0 & 1 \end{bmatrix}$ contains the intrinsic parameters, i.e. the focal f and the principal point offset (x_0, y_0). The inversion of Equation 1 yields a method to convert pixel position to 3D-ray. Therefore, using pixels from an image (I_2) we can obtain pixel coordinates in another image (I_1) by applying the corresponding 3D transform and by projecting the transformed points into the I_1's space using equation 1. This principle can be summarized by the warping equation which is expressed as:

$$\hat{\mathbf{u}}_1 \cong \mathbf{K}_1 \mathbf{R}_1 \mathbf{R}_2^{-1} \mathbf{K}_2^{-1} \mathbf{u}_2 \tag{2}$$

Assuming that all the intrinsic parameters are known and fixed for all n images composing the mosaic, i.e. $\mathbf{K}_i = \mathbf{K}, i = 1, .., n$, this simplifies the 8-parameter homography relating a pair of images to a 3-parameter 3D rotation

$$\hat{\mathbf{u}}_1 \cong \mathbf{K} \mathbf{R}_{12} \mathbf{K}^{-1} \mathbf{u}_2 \tag{3}$$

Rotation parametrization. We employ unit quaternions $\mathbf{q}_\theta$, $\mathbf{q}_\varphi$, $\mathbf{q}_\psi$ for representing rotations around the tilt, pan and yaw axis which are denoted by their corresponding vectors $\mathbf{n}_\theta = (1, 0, 0)$, $\mathbf{n}_\varphi = (0, 1, 0)$, $\mathbf{n}_\psi = (0, 0, 1)$. The 4 components of an unit quaternion representing a rotation of angle θ around the n_θ axis are given by $q_\theta = (q_\theta^w, \mathbf{n}_\theta) = (q_\theta^w, q_\theta^x, q_\theta^y, q_\theta^z)^T$.
The orthogonal matrix $\mathbf{R}(\dot{\mathbf{q}})$ corresponding to a rotation given by the unit quaternion $\dot{\mathbf{q}}$ is expressed by:

$$\mathbf{R}[\dot{\mathbf{q}}] = \begin{pmatrix} q_0^2 + q_x^2 - q_y^2 - q_z^2 & 2(q_x q_y - q_0 q_z & 2(q_0 q_y + q_x q_z) \\ 2(q_0 q_z + q_x q_y) & q_0^2 - q_x^2 + q_y^2 - q_z^2 & 2(q_y q_z - q_0 q_x) \\ 2(q_x q_z - q_0 q_y) & 2(q_0 q_x + q_y q_z) & q_0^2 - q_x^2 - q_y^2 + q_z^2 \end{pmatrix} \tag{4}$$

Capture deviations from parallax-free or ideal pinhole camera model. In order to handle deviations from pure parallax-free motion of ideal pinhole camera model we improve the camera motion model by estimating a local motion estimation provided by a patch-based local matching procedure.

5.3 Global-to-local pair-wise motion estimation

The proposed framework starts with the global rotation estimation followed by the parallax compensation which is performed via a patch-based local motion estimation.

5.3.1 Rigid rotation computation

The motion estimation process follows four steps: (i) pyramid construction, (ii) patch extraction, (iii) motion estimation and (iv) coarse-to-fine refinement. At every level of the pyramid $l = 0, ..., L_{max}$ the goal is to find the 3D rotation $\mathbf{R}^l$. Since the same type of operation is performed at each level l, let us drop the superscript l through the following description.
Let $\mathbf{R}(\mathbf{q}_\theta, \mathbf{q}_\varphi, \mathbf{q}_\psi)^{init}$ be the initial guess provided by the pan-tilt head, where $(\theta, \varphi, \psi)_{hard}$ denote the pitch, roll and yaw angles, respectively expressed in the camera coordinate system.

The optimal rotation is computed by varying the rotation parameters (θ, φ, ψ) within an homogeneous *pyramidal searching space*, $\mathcal{P}_{SS}$, which is recursively updated at each pyramidal level. $\mathcal{P}_{SS}$ is defined by the following parameters: θ range $\Delta\theta$, φ range $\Delta\varphi$, ψ range $\Delta\psi$ and their associated searching steps, $\delta\theta, \delta\phi, \delta\psi$.
The rotation angles are computed by applying rotations $\mathbf{R}_{(\theta,\varphi,\psi)}, (\theta, \varphi, \psi) \in \mathcal{P}_{SS}$ to the 3D rays of recovered from pixels belonging to I_2 and matching the corresponding transformed pixels with pixels from I_1. For a given rotation $\mathbf{R}_{(\theta,\varphi,\psi)}, (\theta, \varphi, \psi) \in \mathcal{P}_{SS}$ we can map pixels $\mathbf{u}_2$ from I_2 in the I_1's space using the warping equation expressed in Equation 3.

$$\hat{\mathbf{u}}_1 \cong \mathbf{K}\mathbf{R}_{(\theta,\varphi,\psi)\in\mathcal{P}_{SS}}\mathbf{K}^{-1}\mathbf{u}_2 \tag{5}$$

We obtain the rotated pixel from I_2 warped in the I_1's space which yields an estimate of I_1, noted $\hat{I}_1$. The goal is to find the optimal rotation which applied to pixels from I_2 and warped in the I_1's space minimizes the difference in brightness between the template image I_1 and its estimate, $\hat{I}_1(\mathbf{u}_2; \mathbf{R}_{(\theta,\varphi,\psi)})$.
Since images belonging to the same mosaic node are subject to different flash values, we employ the Zero Normalized Cross Correlation score [4] to measure the similarity robustly wrt illumination changes. The similarity score $\mathcal{Z}$ is given in Equation (6), being defined on the $[-1, 1]$ domain and for high correlated pixels is close to the unit value.

$$-1 \leq \mathcal{Z}(I_1(\mathbf{u}), I_2(\hat{\mathbf{u}})) = \frac{\sum_{\mathbf{d}\in\mathcal{W}}[I_1(\mathbf{u}+\mathbf{d}) - \bar{I}_1(\mathbf{u})][I_2(\hat{\mathbf{u}}+\mathbf{d}) - \bar{I}_2(\hat{\mathbf{u}})]}{\sqrt{\sum_{\mathbf{d}\in\mathcal{W}}[I_1(\mathbf{u}+\mathbf{d}) - \bar{I}_1(\mathbf{u})]^2 \sum_{\mathbf{d}\in\mathcal{W}}[I_2(\hat{\mathbf{u}}+\mathbf{d}) - \bar{I}_2(\hat{\mathbf{u}})]^2}} \leq 1 \tag{6}$$

The global similarity measure is given by the mean of all the similarity scores computed for all the patches belonging to the overlapping region. For rapidity reasons, we correlate only border patches extracted in the overlapping regions.

$$\mathbf{E}[\mathbf{R}_{(\theta,\varphi,\psi)}] = \frac{1}{N_w} \sum_{j=0}^{N_w - 1} \Phi_j \mathcal{Z}(I_1(\mathbf{u}^j), I_2(\hat{\mathbf{u}}^j_{\mathbf{R}_{(\theta,\varphi,\psi)}})) \tag{7}$$

Φ_j defines a characteristic function which takes care of "lost"[5] and "zero"[6] pixels and N_w denotes the number of valid matches belonging to the overlapping area.
The global dissimilarity score $\mathbf{E}(\mathbf{R}_{(\theta,\varphi,\psi)})$ is defined on the interval $[0, 1]$. The optimal rotation $\hat{\mathbf{R}}_{(\theta,\varphi,\psi)}$ is obtained by maximizing the global similarity score $\mathbf{E}[\mathbf{R}_{(\theta,\varphi,\psi)}]$ over the entire searching area $\mathcal{P}_{SS}$.

$$\hat{\mathbf{R}}_{(\theta,\varphi,\psi)} = \arg \max_{(\theta,\varphi,\psi)\in\mathcal{P}_{SS}} \mathbf{E}[\mathbf{R}_{(\theta,\varphi,\psi)}] \tag{8}$$

5.3.2 Non-rigid motion estimation

In order to handle deviations from pure-parallax motions or from ideal pinhole camera, we use the rotationally aligned images to initialize the local patch matchingprocedure. Let $\mathbf{P}_1 =$

[4] For each pixel, the score is computed over each pixel's neighborhood defined as $\mathcal{W} = [-w_x, w_x] \times [-w_y, w_y]$ centered around $\mathbf{u}_2$ and $\hat{\mathbf{u}}_1$ respectively, of size $(2w_x + 1) \times (2w_y + 1)$, where $w = w_x = w_y$ denote the neighborhood ray.

[5] the pixel falls outside of the rectangular support of I_2

[6] missing data either in $I_1(\hat{\mathbf{u}}^j_{\mathbf{R}})$ or $I_2(\hat{\mathbf{u}}^j_{\mathbf{R}})$, which may occur when mapping pixels $\hat{\mathbf{u}}^j_{\mathbf{R}}$ in the I_2's space

$\{\mathcal{P}(\mathbf{u}_1^k)|\mathbf{u}_1^k \in I_1, k = 1, ..., N_1\}$ and $\mathbf{P}_2 = \{\mathcal{P}(\mathbf{u}_2^k)|\mathbf{u}_2^k \in I_2, k = 1, ..., N_2\}$ be the patches extracted in image I_1 and I_2 respectively, which are defined by a neighborhood $\mathcal{W}$ centered around $\mathbf{u}_1^k$ and $\mathbf{u}_2^k$ respectively. For each patch $\mathcal{P}(\mathbf{u}_1^k) \in \mathbf{P}_1$ we search for its optimal match in I_2 by exploring a windowed area $\mathbf{W}^{\mathbf{SA}}(\mathbf{u}_2^k; \hat{\mathbf{R}})$ centered around $(\mathbf{u}_2^k; \hat{\mathbf{R}})$, where **SA** denotes the searching area ray.
Let $\mathbf{P}_2^{k,\mathbf{SA}} = \{\mathcal{P}(\mathbf{u}_2^m)|\mathbf{u}_2^m \in \mathbf{W}^{\mathbf{SA}}(\mathbf{u}_2^k; \hat{\mathbf{R}}) \subset I_2, m = 1, .., M\}$ be M patches extracted from the warped image's searching area centered around $(\mathbf{u}_2^k; \hat{\mathbf{R}})$, with 1-pixel steps. For each patch $\mathcal{P}(\mathbf{u}_2^m)$ we compute the similarity score $\mathcal{Z}(I_1(\mathbf{u}^k), I_2(\mathbf{u}^m))$ and we perform a bicubic fitting in order to produce the best match with a subpixel accuracy and real time performances. The best match is obtained by maximizing the similarity score $\mathcal{Z}$ over the entire searching area $\mathbf{W}^{\mathbf{SA}}$.

$$\mathcal{P}(\hat{\mathbf{u}}_2^k) = \arg \max_{\mathbf{u}_2^m \in \mathbf{W}^{\mathbf{SA}}(\mathbf{u}_2^k; \hat{\mathbf{R}})} \mathcal{Z}(I_1(\mathbf{u}^k), I_2(\mathbf{u}_2^m)) \tag{9}$$

In order to handle "lost" or "zero" pixels, patch matches corresponding to uncomplete warped patches are discarded. This yields a list of matched patches $\mathcal{P}(\mathbf{u}_1^k)$ and $\mathcal{P}(\hat{\mathbf{u}}_2^k)$ which gives the possibility to compute a local translational model for each patch: $\mathbf{t}^k = \|\mathbf{u}_1^k - \hat{\mathbf{u}}_2^k\|$ and compensates eventual parallax motions or deviations from the ideal pinhole camera model. Moreover, the local motion allows the possibility to establish a mean translational motion model over the entire image space, noted $\bar{\mathbf{t}}$. The list of the patch matches are further injected into a bundle adjustment engine for multi-view fine alignment and gap closure.

5.3.3 Experimental results

Figures 8 and 9 illustrate the results obtained by running the global-to-local image motion estimation procedure on an image pair gathered in the Tautavel prehistoric cave, France. The capturing device was set to acquire high resolution images of size 3008×2000 with an overlap of $\simeq 33\%$. In order to evaluate our technique with respect to a feature-based method, we show the results obtained on an image pair for which the SIFT detection and matching failed. The rotation computation starts at the lowest resolution level, $L_{max} = 5$ where a fast searching is performed by exploring a searching space $P_{SS}^{L_{max}} = 5°$ with 1-pixel steps in order to localize the global maximum (Fig. 8c). The coarse estimation is refined at higher resolution levels $l = L_{max} - 1, .., 0$ by taking a P_{SS} of 4 pixels explored with 1-pixel steps. Since deviations from parallax-pure motion are negligible we speed up the process by computing the local motion directly at the highest resolution level, $l = 0$ (Fig. 9). The residual mean square error ($\bar{\mathbf{r}}$) and the standard deviation ($\sigma_{\mathbf{r}}$) of the pairwise camera motion estimation $[\hat{\mathbf{R}}, \mathbf{t}^k]$ are computed using the reprojection error in the 2D space given by:

$$\bar{\mathbf{r}}_{2D} = \frac{1}{N} \sum_{k=1}^{k=N} \|\mathbf{u}_i^k - \mathbf{K}\hat{\mathbf{R}}_{ij}^T \mathbf{K}^{-1}(\hat{\mathbf{u}}_j^k - \mathbf{t}^k)\| \tag{10}$$

5.4 Multi-view fine alignment using the existent BA solutions

Given the pairwise motion estimates $\hat{\mathbf{R}}_{ij}$ and the associated set of AF matches $\mathbf{P}(i,j) = \{(\mathbf{u}_i^k \in I_i; \hat{\mathbf{u}}_j^k \in I_j)|i \neq j, j > i\}$, we refine the pose parameters jointly within a bundle adjustment process (Triggs et al., 1999). This step is a critical need, since the simple concatenation of pairwise poses will disregard multiple constraints resulting in mis-registration and gap. In order to analyze the behavior of the existent BA schemes when consistent matches are injected into

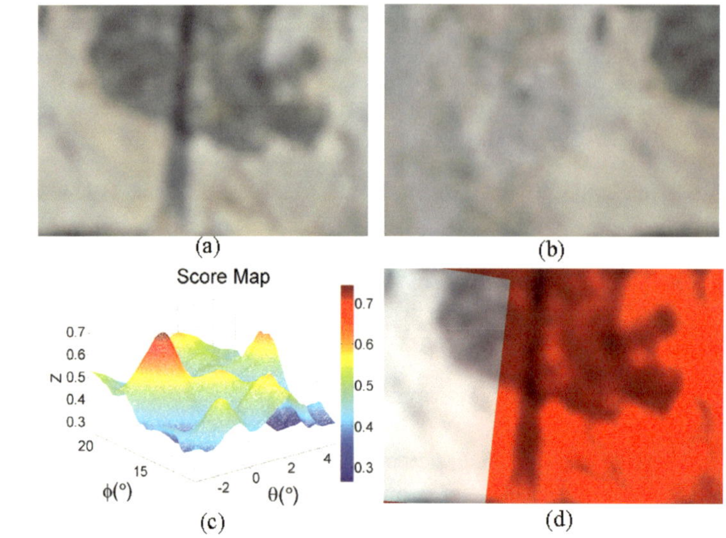

Fig. 8. Rigid Rotation Estimation.(a)origin I_1, (b)image to align I_2, (c)global maximum localization at level $L_{max} = 5$, (d)rotationally aligned images at level $l = 0$: I_1-red channel, the warped image $I_2(\mathbf{u}; \hat{\mathbf{R}})$-green channel, $\hat{\mathbf{R}}(\theta, \varphi, \psi) = (17.005°, 0.083°, 0.006°)$.

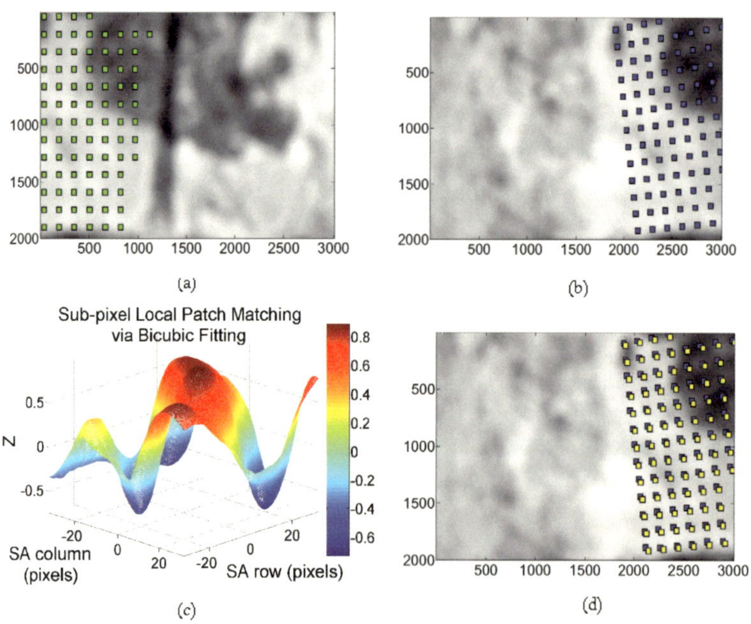

Fig. 9. Anonymous Features Matching Procedure. $\mathcal{W} = 15$ pixels, 85 AF matches. (a)$\mathcal{P}(\mathbf{u}_1^k)$, (b)$\mathcal{P}(\mathbf{u}_2^k)$ extraction in I_2 using the rotation initialization, (c)Bicubic fitting for an arbitrary patch: $\mathbf{SA} = 32$ pixels, matching accuracy: 0.005 pixels, (d)AF-based optical flow: $\mathcal{P}(\mathbf{u}_2^k)$ blue, $\mathcal{P}(\hat{\mathbf{u}}_2^k)$ yellow, $\bar{\mathbf{t}} = [1.6141, 1.0621]$ pixels. $\bar{\mathbf{r}} \pm \sigma_{\mathbf{r}} = 0.08 \pm 0.01$

it, we run the BA step integrated within the Autopano Pro v1.4.2 (Kolor, 2005) by injecting AF pairings pre-computed by the proposed global-to-local pair-wise image alignment step described in Section 5.3.
As in (Brown & Lowe, 2007), the objective function is a robust sum squared projection error. Given a set of N AF correspondences $\mathbf{u}_i^k \longleftrightarrow \hat{\mathbf{u}}_j^k, k = 0, .., N-1$ the error function is obtained by summing the robust residual errors over all images:

$$e = \sum_{i=1}^{n} \sum_{j \in I(i)} \sum_{k \in \mathbf{P}(i,j)} h(\mathbf{u}_i^k - \mathbf{K}\hat{\mathbf{R}}_{ij}^T \mathbf{K}^{-1} \hat{\mathbf{u}}_j^k) \tag{11}$$

where n is the number of images, $I(i)$ is the set of adjacent images to image I_i and $h(\mathbf{x})$ denotes the Huber robust error function (Huber, 1981) which is used for outliers' rejection. This yields a non-linear least squares problem which is solved using the Levenberg-Marquardt algorithm. A detailed description of this approach may be found in (Brown & Lowe, 2007).
Trial Tautavel Prehistoric Cave. Since our research work is focused on generating *in situ* complete and photorealistic 3D models of complex and unstructured large-scale environments, the Gigapixel mosaicing system was placed in different positions in order to generate mosaics covering the entire site. We illustrate in this section two examples of high-resolution mosaic views acquired from different spatial poses of the system corresponding to the cave's entrance and center.
Autopano Pro and AF matches. Figures 10 (a), (b) and Table 2 illustrate the mosaicing results obtained by injecting the AF pairings into the BA procedure integrated within the AutopanoPro v1.4.2 which took in charge the rendering process using a spherical projection and a multi-band blending technique. The mosaic's high photorealist level is emphasized by a high-performance viewer which allows for mosaic visualization using 4-level of detail (LOD), as shown in Figures 10 (c)-(f).
Residual errors. The BA scheme includes a self-calibration step and minimizes an error measured in the 2D image space, causing the rejection of correct AF matches and leading to relatively high mis-registration errors, as shown by the fourth row of Table 2. In practice we observed that this shortcoming can be overcome by injecting a high number of AF matches. However, this may be costly and when a low number of matches are used, there is a high probability that all of them to be rejected, producing the BA's failure. Since we can not afford this risk, our first concern is to improve the multi-view fine alignment process by simultaneously computing the optimal quaternions using a criterion computed in the 3D space in order to reduce the residual error when using a minimum number of AF correspondences. To this end, we propose an analytical solution for the multi-view fine alignment step (Craciun, 2010) .
Runtime. For this experiment we employed the original Rodeon® platform, i.e. without the improvements. Therefore, the searching range for the rotation refinement was considerably high, i.e. $\pm 5°$, leading to a computationally expensive rotation estimation stage. The upgraded-Rodeon® (Craciun, 2010) reduces the computational time by a factor of 5.83 for an experimental version of the implementation, i.e. without code optimization. Moreover, the number of images to be acquired is reduced to $N_{im} = 32$ which decreases by a factor of 4 the acquisition time.

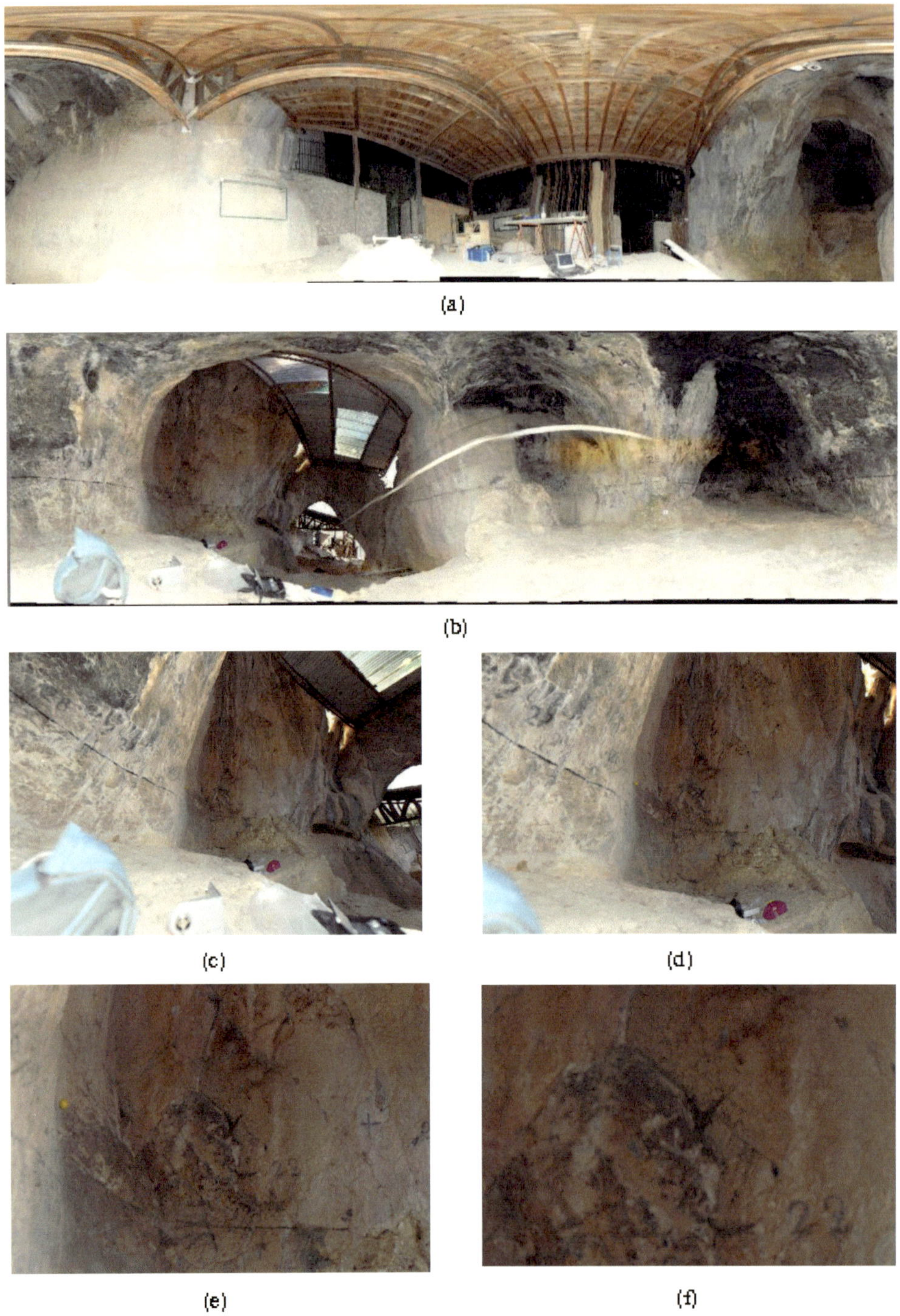

Fig. 10. Mosaicing tests on data sets acquired in Tautavel prehistoric cave using the Rodeon® platform. The mosaics were generated by injecting the AF matches into the BA process integrated within Autopano Pro v1.4.2. (a) - cave's entrance, (b) - cave's center, (c)-(f) 4-LODs corresponding to the right part of mosaic (b).

Mosaic	Figure 10 (a)	Figure 10 (b)
$\#N_{station}$	272	168
FOV(°)	360 × 108.4	360 × 105.37
Size(pixels)	43365 × 13057(567 Mp)	43206 × 12646 (546 Mp)
e(pixels)	1.93	1.76
# AF matches	21840	13440
CPU (time)	8h 12min	5h 33min

Table 2. Qualitative results corresponding to mosaics generated using Autopano Pro and AF matches when running on a 1.66 GHz Linux machine equipped with 2Gb of RAM memory. The mosaics illustrated in Figures 10 (a) and 10 (b) correspond to the cave's entrance, center respectively.

6. Generating 4D dual mosaic views from image and laser data

The last stage of the 4D mosaicing process illustrated in Figure 1 consists in aligning the 3D mosaic onto the 2D color one, unifying them in a photorealist and geometrically accurate 3D model. This section describes a mosaic-based approach for image-laser data alignment. The reconstruction of the 3D scene model is performed within two steps: (i) an integration step exploits the 3D mosaic to generate 2D meshes and (ii) a texture mapping procedure enables the photorealist component of the 3D scene model.

6.1 Data input and problem statement

Figure 11 illustrates the two inputs of the image-laser alignment procedure. In order to facilitate the visualization of the FOV[7] imaged by each sensor, Figure 11 depicts both the 3D spherical and the 2D image projections associated to each input, i.e. the 3D mosaic generated by the laser and the 2D mosaic obtained from the Gigapixel camera which was down-sampled to meet the 3D mosaic resolution. It can be observed that both sensors are capturing the same FOV, having their optical centers separated by a 3D rotation and a small inter-sensor parallax. In order to build photorealistically textured panoramic 3D models, one must register the 3D spherical mosaic M_{BR-3D} and the color Giga-mosaic M_{HR-RGB} in a common reference coordinate system in order to perform the texture mapping stage.

Pose estimation under calibration constraints. Since the two capturing devices (laser scanner and camera) are supposing to acquire the same FOV, they can be either rigidly attached or used successively, one after another. However, in both cases, it is difficult to calibrate the system such that the parallax is completely eliminated. Consequently, it is possible to model the transformation between the two sensors through a 3D Euclidian transformation with 6-DOF (i.e. three for rotation and three for translation) as illustrated in Figure 11. The following section is dedicated to the description of the image-alignment algorithm allowing to compute transformation relating their corresponding optical centers.

6.2 Automatic pyramidal global-to-local image-laser alignment

We employ a direct correlation-based technique within a feature-less framework. In order to cope with time and in-situ access constraints, we cut down the pose estimation combinatory using a pyramidal framework.

[7] Field of View

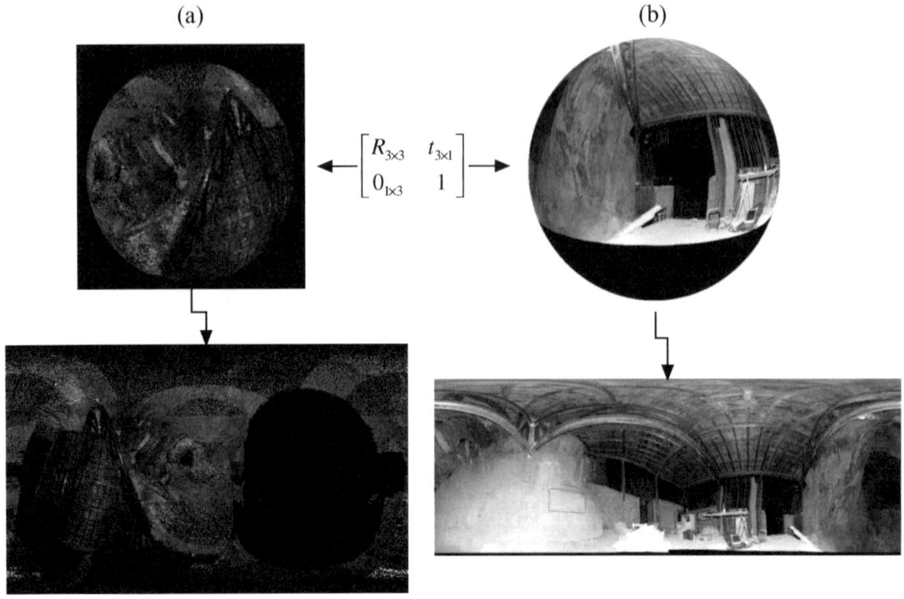

Fig. 11. The two inputs of the panoramic-based image-laser alignment procedure exemplified on a data set acquired in Tautavel prehistoric cave. We illustrate the spherical and image plane projections associated to each input. (a) M_{BR-3D} - the scan matcher output by the 3D mosaicing process described in Section 4. FOV $360° \times 180°$, size: 2161×1276, angular steps $[\delta\theta, \delta\varphi]_{BR-3D} = [0.002906°, 0.00246°]$, (b) the optical mosaic obtained using the algorithm described in Section 5. FOV: $360° \times 108.4°$

Figure 12 illustrates the image-laser fusion pipeline which can be split in two main processes, each of which being detailed through the following description. Since the entire pose estimation method is very similar to the pair-wise global-to-local alignment described in Section 5.3, the following subsections resume several specifications related to its appliance on fully spherical mosaic views.

6.2.1 Pre-processing

The proposed image-laser alignment method correlates the reflectance acquired by the LRF with the green channel of the optical mosaic M_{HR-G}. To do so, we first recover automatically the parameters of the spherical acquisition through a 2D triangulation procedure in order to compute the 2D projection of the 3D mosaic. This stage of the algorithm is very important as it provides the topology between the 3D points and allows fast interpolation.

Generating pyramidal structures for each input: M_{BR-G} **and** M_{BR-3D}. We generate pyramidal structures of $L_{max} = 3$ levels for both inputs $M_{BR-3D} = \{M^l_{BR-3D} | l = 0, .., L_{max-1}\}$ and $M_{BR-G} = \{M^l_{BR-G} | l = 0, .., L_{max-1}\}$, where the mosaic size ranges from $[2162 \times 1278]$ up to $[270 \times 159]$ corresponding to levels $l = 0, .., L_{max}$.

6.2.2 Pose estimation

The pose estimation procedure employs a hybrid scheme, the 3D rotation is computed by minimizing a radiometric criterion in the 2D mosaic space, while the translation is computed by back-projecting the rotationally aligned mosaics in the 2D space via a local patch matching

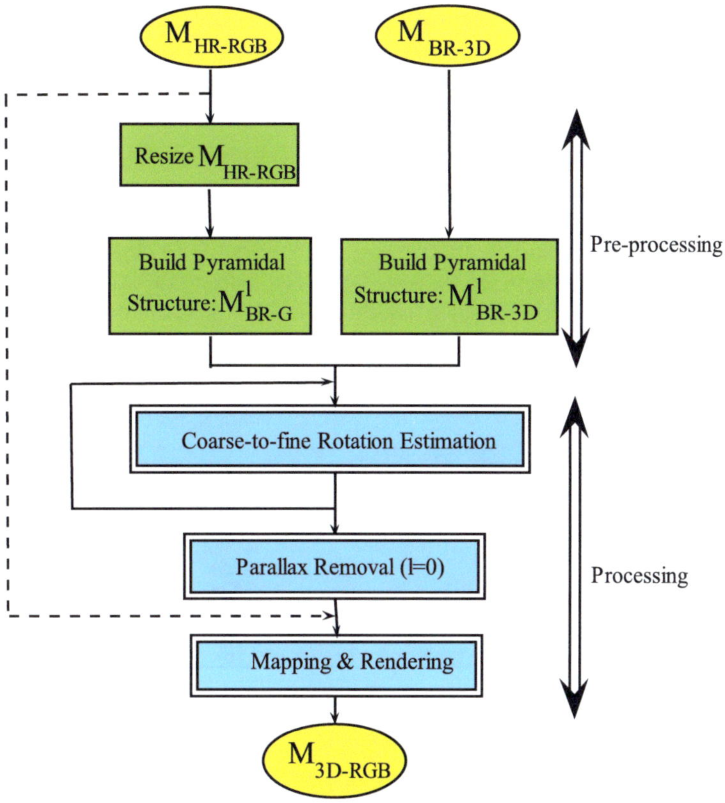

Fig. 12. Image-laser fusion pipeline. Inputs: 3D mosaic M_{HR-RGB} and 2D Giga-pixel color mosaic M_{BR-3D} illustrated in Figures 11 (a) and (b), respectively. The pre-processing and processing steps are highlighted in green and blue, respectively.

procedure. The proposed approach lead to a two-steps rigid transformation computation process: first, the 3D global rotation $\mathbf{R}_{(\theta,\varphi,\psi)}$ is computed in a pyramidal fashion, while the second step is dedicated to the inter-sensor parallax compensation being performed only at the highest resolution level.

Correction of 3D mosaic distortions. As mentioned in Section 4, the 3D mosaic acquisition combines several bands acquired through laser's rotations which may introduce wavy effects within the 3D mosaic geometry. These effects are captured within the inter-sensor parallax computation step which is performed through a non-rigid motion estimation procedure. Consequently, in order to correct the 3D mosaic's geometry, the alignment procedure is performed by aligning the 3D mosaic onto the 2D optical one, M_{BR-G}.

Figure 13 (a) shows that the superposition of the two images does not result in grey-level due to the different responses given by the sensing devices. Figure 13 (b) illustrates a close-up view of the superposed mosaics showing that the global rotation does not model completely the motion separating the camera and the laser, and consequently the inter-sensor parallax must be introduced within the estimated motion model.

Parallax removal. As for the local patch matching procedure described in Section 5, this stage of the algorithm uses the rotationally aligned mosaics. We recover the parallax between the laser's and the optical mosaicing platform by performing a local patch matching procedure at the highest resolution of the pyramidal structure.

The patch matching procedure outputs a 2D translational motion for each patch, estimating a non-rigid motion over the entire mosaic space. This vector field is used for the parallax removal stage. In addition, the non-rigid motion allows to compute a mean translation motion model defined over the entire mosaic space $\bar{\mathbf{t}}_{2D}$. The parallax is removed in the 2D image space by compensating each $\bar{\mathbf{t}}_{2D}$, obtaining therefore the warped 3D mosaic $\hat{M}_{BR-3D}$ aligned onto the 2D mosaic. Figure 13 (c) depicts the result of the laser-camera alignment procedure.

Accuracy. Although the Giga-pixel mosaic produced using the Autopano Pro software (details are presented in Section 5) has a residual error of 3.74 pixels, it becomes negligible in the down-sampled mosaic M_{BR-G} used for the registration process. A sub-pixel accuracy can be achieved by using a bicubic fitting, as described in Section 5.

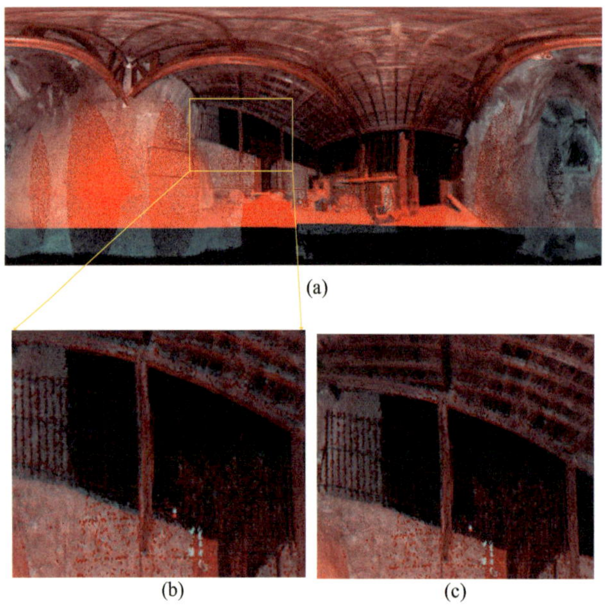

Fig. 13. Experimental results of the parallax removal procedure obtained on data sets acquired in Tautavel prehistoric cave: (a) Superposed aligned mosaics: M_{BR-G} - red channel, $\hat{M}_{BR-3D}$ - greed channel. (b) zoom in - before parallax removal, (c) zoom in - after parallax removal. The compensated parallax amount: $\bar{\mathbf{t}}_{2D} = [-1.775, -0.8275]^T$ pixels.

6.3 Texture mapping and rendering

Since the main goal of our research work is concerned with the in-situ 3D modeling problem, we are mainly interested in producing a fast rendering technique for visualization purposes in order to validate in-situ the data acquisition correctness. To this end, a simple point-based rendering procedure may suffice. Nevertheless, off-line a more artistic rendering can be performed by sending data to a host wirelessly connected to the target.

In-situ point-based visualization. The employed method simply associates the RGB-color to its corresponding 3D coordinate. In order to emphasize the photorealist rendering results obtained when using high-resolution texture maps, Figure 14 compares the rendering results

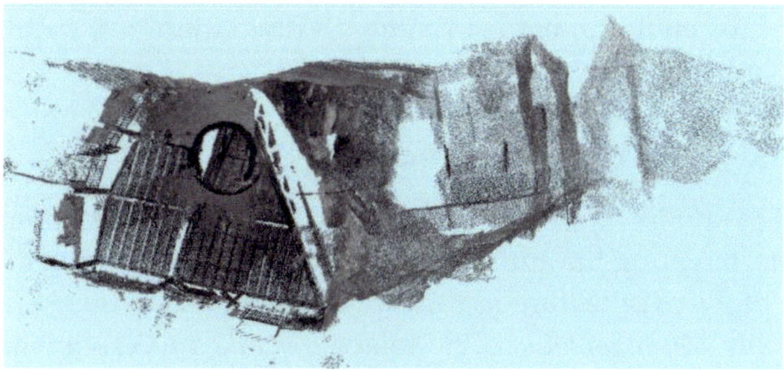

(a)

(b)

Fig. 14. Texture mapping results. (a) The 3D point cloud displayed using the intensity acquired by the LRF. (b) The colored 3D point cloud using the down-sampled optical mosaic M_{BR-RGB}.

obtained by first using the intensity acquired by the 3D scanning device illustrated in Figure 14 (a), while the rendering using the texture maps obtained from the color mosaic is shown in Figure 14 (b).

Off-line mesh-based rendering. We apply an existing 2D meshing algorithm developed in our laboratory by Mathieu Brèdif which assigns to each polygon the RGB-color corresponding to its 3D coordinates. Figures 15 illustrates the rendering results showing that the complex

(a)

(b)

Fig. 15. Mesh-based rendering of the Tautavel prehistoric cave. (a) Outdoor view. (b) Indoor view of the 3D model.

surface geometry of the environment lead to depth discontinuities, requiring for a meshing algorithm robust to missing data.

7. Conclusions and future research directions

This chapter aimed at providing solutions for in-situ 3D modeling in complex and difficult to access environments, targeting the automation of the 3D modeling pipeline, and in particular the data alignment problem in feature-less areas. We proposed an image-laser strategy which lead to a *4D mosaicing sensor prototype* able to acquire and process image and laser data to generate in-situ photorealist omnidirectional 3D models of the system's surroundings.
2D, 3D and 4D mosaic views. We propose hardware and software solutions for generating in-situ 2D, 3D and 4D mosaic views in feature-less and GPS-denied areas, making them suitable for map-building and localization tasks. In addition, they provide long-term features tracking, ensuring reliable data matching in feature-less environments. The aforementioned advantages are exploited within a *4D-mosaic-driven acquisition scenario* aiming to ensure the 3D scene model completeness.
Automatic data alignment in feature-less areas. This leads to a two-steps strategy which addresses the automation of the 3D modeling pipeline by solving for its main data alignment issues through the image-laser fusion. We first address a simple problem, i.e. *same viewpoint and small-parallax data alignment*, resulting in automatic 2D and 3D mosaicing algorithms, to provide in a second step image-laser solutions, i.e. the *4D mosaic views*, to solve for *wide-baseline* 3D model alignment using a joint 2D-3D criterion to disambiguate feature matching in feature-less areas.
In our research work, we integrate the 4D mosaicing sensor within a vision-based system designed to supply site surveys and exploration missions in unstructured and difficult to access environments.

8. References

Bailey, T. & Durrant-White, H. (2006). Simultaneous localization and mapping: Part II, *In Proceeding of IEEE Robotics and Automation Magazine* 13(2): 99–110.

Banno, A., Masuda, T., Oishi, T. & Ikeuchi, K. (2008). Flying Laser Range Sensor for Large-Scale Site-Modeling and Its Applications in Bayon Digital Archival Project, *In International Journal of Computer Vision* 78(2-3): 207–222.

Beraldin, J.-A. & Cournoyer, L. (1997). Object modeling creation from multiple range images: Acquisition, calibration, model building and verification, *In Proceedings of International on Recent Advances on 3-D Digital Imaging and Modeling* pp. 326–333.

Besl, P. J. & McKay, N. D. (1992). A method for registration of 3d-shapes, *In IEEE Transactions on Pattern Recognition and Machine Intelligence* 14(2): 239–256.

Brown, M. & Lowe, D. G. (2007). Automatic panoramic image stitching using invariant features, *In International Journal on Computer Vision* 74: 59–73.

Cole, D. M. & Newman, P. M. (2006). Using laser range data for 3d SLAM in outdoor environments, *In Proceedings of IEEE International Conference on Robotics and Automation (ICRA'06)* .

Craciun, D. (2010). Image-laser fusion for 3d modeling in complex environments, *Ph D Thesis Telecom ParisTech* .

Craciun, D., Paparoditis, N. & Schmitt, F. (2008). Automatic pyramidal intensity-based laser scan matcher for 3d modeling of large scale unstructured environments, *In Proceedings of the Fifth IEEE Canadian Conference on Computer and Robots Vision* pp. 18–25.

Craciun, D., Paparoditis, N. & Schmitt, F. (2009). Automatic Gigapixel mosaicing in large scale unstructured underground environments, *In Tenth IAPR Conference on Machine Vision Application* pp. 13–16.

Craciun, D., Paparoditis, N. & Schmitt, F. (2010). Multi-view scans alignment for 3d spherical mosaicing in large scale unstructured environments, *In Journal Computer Vision and Image Understanding* pp. 1248–1263.

Dias, P., Sequeira, V., Gonï£¡laves, J. G. M. & Vaz, F. (2002). Automaic registration of laser reflectance and colour intensity images for 3d reconstruction, *Robotics and Autonomous Systems* 39(3-4): 157–168.

Dias, P., Sequeira, V., Vaz, F. & Goncalves, J. (2003). Underwater 3D SLAM through entropy minimization, *In Proceedings of the 3D Digital Imaging and Modeling (3DIM03)* pp. 418–425.

Durrant-White, H. & Bailey, T. (2006). Simultaneous localization and mapping: Part I, *In Proceeding of IEEE Robotics and Automation Magazine* 13(2): 99–110.

Huber, D. (2002). Automatic Three-dimensional Modeling from Reality, *Ph. D. thesis, Robotics Institute, Carnegie Mellon University,Pittsburgh, PA* .

Huber, D. & Vandapel, N. (2003). Automatic 3d underground mine mapping, *The 4th International Conference on Field and Service Robotics* .

Huber, P. J. (1981). *Robust Statistics*, John Wiley & Sons, New York.

Ikeuchi, K., Oishi, T., Takamatsu, J., Sagawa, R., Nakazawa, A., Kurazume, R., Nishino, K., Kamakura, M. & Okamoto, Y. (2007). The Great Buddha Project: Digitally Archiving, Restoring, and Analyzing Cultural Heritage Objects, *In International Journal of Computer Vision* 75(1): 189–208.

Johnson, A. (1997). Spin-images: A representation for 3-d surface matching, *PhD thesis, Robotics Institute, Carnegie Mellon University* .

Kolor (2005). Autopano pro, *http://www.autopano.net/en/* .

Levoy, M., Pulli, K., Curless, B., Rusinkiewicz, S., Koller, D., Pereira, L., Ginzton, M., Anderson, S., Davis, J., Ginsberg, J., Shade, J. & Fulk, D. (2000). The Digital Michelangelo Project: 3D Scanning of Large Statues, *In Proceedings of the 27th Annual Conference on Computer Graphics and Interactive Techniques* pp. 131–144.

Makadia, A., Patterson, A., & Daniilidis, K. (2006). Fully automatic registration of 3d point clouds., *In Proceedings of Compute Vision and Pattern Recognition CVPR'06* pp. 1297–1304.

Moravec, H. P. (1980). Obstacle avoidance and navigation in the real world by a seeing robot rover, *Ph. D. thesis, Stanford University, Stanford, California* .

Newman, P., Cole, D. & Ho, K. (2006). Outdoor SLAM using visual appearance and laser ranging, *In Proceedings of International Conference on Robotics and Automation* .

Nister, D., Naroditsky, O. & Bergen, J. (2004). Visual odometry, *In Proceeding of IEEE Computer Society Conference on Computer Vision and Pattern Recognition (CVPR 2004)* pp. 652–659.

Nuchter, A., Surmann, H. & Thrun, S. (2004). 6D SLAM with an application in autonomous mine mapping, *In Proceedings of the IEEE International Conference on Robotics and Automation (ICRA'04)* .

Sawhney, H. S. & Ayer, S. (1996). Compact representation of video thourgh dominant multiple motion estimation, *In IEEE Transactions on Pattern Recognition and Machine Intelligence* 18(8): 814–830.

Snavely, N., Seitz, S. M. & Szeliski, R. (2006). Photo tourism: exploring photo collections in 3d, *In Proceedings of ACM SIGGRAPH'06* .

Stamos, I., Liu, L., Chen, C., Wolberg, G., Yu, G. & Zokai, S. (2008). Integrating Automated Range Registration with Multiview Geometry for the Photorealistic Modeling of Large-Scale Scenes, *In International Journal of Computer Vision* 78(2-3): 237–260.

Thrun, S., Montemerlo, M. & Aron, A. (2006). Probabilistic terrain analysis for high-speed desert driving, *In Proceedings of Robotics: Science and Systems* .

Triggs, B., McLauchlan, P., Hartley, R. & Fitzgibbon, A. (1999). Bundle adjustment - a modern synthesis, *In Proceedings of the of the International Workshop on Vision Algorithms: Theory and Practice* pp. 298–372.

Zhao, W., Nister, D. & Hsu, S. (2005). Alignment of Continuous Video onto 3D Point Clouds., *In IEEE Transactions on Pattern Analysis and Machine Intelligence* 27(8): 1308–1318.

2

DART: A 3D Model for Remote Sensing Images and Radiative Budget of Earth Surfaces

J.P. Gastellu-Etchegorry, E. Grau and N. Lauret
CESBIO - CNES, CNRS (UMR 5126), IRD, Université de Toulouse, Toulouse, France

1. Introduction

Knowledge of the radiative behavior and the energy budget of land surfaces is essential for studying the functioning of natural and urban surfaces with remotely acquired information. Account of their 3D nature is often essential because in most cases these surfaces are not isotropic. For example, it has long been known that the albedo of a canopy with anisotropic Bi-directional Reflectance Factors (BRF) may be underestimated by as much as 45% if it is computed with nadir reflectance only (Kimes and Sellers, 1985). Radiative transfer (R.T.) models have the potential for correcting this type of error provided they account for the three dimensional (3D) nature of Earth surfaces. Neglect of the 3D structure of canopies can lead to large errors on the 3D radiation budget and remote sensing measurements. For example, for vegetation BRF and directional brightness temperature (DTDF) distribution functions, errors can be as large as 50%, depending on instrumental (*e.g.*, view and sun directions) and experimental (*e.g.*, vegetation heterogeneity) conditions (Gastellu-Etchegorry et *al.*, 1999). The problem is similar for urban canopies due to their strong spatial heterogeneity. The application of R.T. modeling to urban surfaces is important in the context of the advent of satellite sensors with spatial and spectral resolutions that are more and more adapted to urban characteristics such as building dimensions and temperature spatial variability. It explains the numerous works conducted in the field of remote sensing of urban surfaces (Soux *et al.*, 2004; Voogt and Oke, 1998). The use of descriptions with qualitatively based land use data instead of more fundamental surface descriptors is a source of inaccuracy for modeling BRFs and DTDFs (Voogt and Oke, 2003).

R.T. models are essential tools for assessing accurately radiative quantities such as the exitance, the irradiance and remote sensing measurements in the optical and thermal domains. However, in order to meet this objective, models must account for the three dimensional (3D) nature of Earth surfaces. Here, we consider vegetation canopies and urban canopies. This consideration of the 3D architecture of Earth surfaces is possible with the so-called 3D models. Generally speaking, the latter ones are intended to be accurate, robust and more comprehensive than other models. Ideally, they should be used in place of other models. However, they are often more difficult to manage, both in terms of computation time and landscape description. Moreover, when dealing with specific situations, one needs that the model be accurate and robust, but one does not necessarily need that the model be comprehensive. This explains that in many cases, the objective of 3D models is to calibrate models that are simpler to manage in terms of landscape description, computation time, etc. Once calibrated, these models can meet the required accuracy levels.

These remarks stress the usefulness of 3D R.T. models. A number of 3D models is being developed by the scientific community (Widlowski *et al.*, 2007). Usually, they are designed for a given type of landscape (*e.g.*, natural or urban), with or without topography and atmosphere, for a specific type of application (*e.g.*, remote sensing or radiation budget), and for a given spatial resolution of analysis (*e.g.*, simulation of a tree crown with or without branches). Moreover, remote sensing models are usually designed for a given spectral domain (*e.g.*, sun reflected spectral domain or thermal infrared spectral domain).

A common problem when designing a R.T. model is to assess to which level of detail landscapes must be taken into account. This is very especially important in term of landscape simulation. However, it affects also the mathematical formulation of R.T. Generally speaking, one should take into account all landscape elements that have a significant influence on the application we are dealing with (*i.e.*, landscape radiative budget or remote sensing measurement). In practice, the answer can be complex. For example, when simulating remote sensing measurements of heterogeneous Earth surfaces in the visible spectral domain, is it necessary to simulate the atmosphere within a unique "Earth - Atmosphere" system in order to simulate with a good accuracy its complex interaction with earth surfaces?

Some of these aspects are discussed here with the brief presentation of DART (Discrete Anisotropic Radiative Transfer) model. This is one of the most complete 3D models designed for simulating the radiative budget and the satellite observations of the land surfaces in the visible, near infrared and thermal infrared of land surfaces. It was originally developed (Gastellu-Etchegorry *et al.*, 1996) for simulating remote sensing images of 3D vegetation canopies in the visible / near infrared (NIR) spectral domain. Afterwards, it was extended to the thermal infrared domain and to the simulation of any landscape: urban or natural, with atmosphere and topography. As a result, the present DART model simulates the radiation budget and remote sensing images of vegetation and urban canopies, for any experimental (sun direction, canopy heterogeneity, topography, atmosphere, etc.) and instrumental (view direction, spatial resolution, etc.) configuration.

After a brief presentation of DART, two types of applications are discussed: urban and forest canopies. This is followed by the presentation of three recent improvements:

- Account of the Earth / Atmosphere curvature for oblique remote sensing measurements.
- Possibility to import 3D objects simulated as the juxtaposition of triangles and to transform them into 3D turbid objects.
- Possibility to simulate landscapes that have a continuous topography and landscapes that are non repetitive.

Finally, preliminary results concerning two application domains are discussed. 1) 2D distributions of reflectance, brightness temperature and radiance of the African continent that would be measured by a geostationary satellite. 2) Radiative budget of urban (Gastellu-Etchegorry, 2008) and natural (Belot, 2007) canopies. They are simulated with a DART energy budget (EB) component, called DARTEB, under development.

2. DART model

DART was originally developed for simulating BRFs (Bi-directionnal Reflectance Factor), remote sensing images and the spectral radiation budget of 3D natural (*e.g.*, trees, roads, grass, soil, water) landscapes in the visible and short wave infrared domains. Since its first release in 1996, it was successfully tested, in the case of vegetation canopies, against reflectance measurements (Gastellu-Etchegorry *et al.*, 1999) and against a number of 3-D reflectance models (*e.g.*, *Flight* (North, 1996), *Sprint* (Thompson and Goel, 1998), *Raytran* (Govaerts and Verstraete, 1998)), in the context of the RAMI (RAdiation transfer Model Intercomparison) experiment (Pinty *et al.*, 2001; Pinty *et al.*, 2004; Widlowski *et al.*, 2007; Widlowski *et al.*, 2008). Only BRFs could be compared because DART was the only 3-D model that simulates images.

DART was successfully used in many scientific domains: impact of canopy structure on satellite images texture (Pinel and Gastellu-Etchegorry, 1998) and reflectance (Gastellu-Etchegorry *et al.*, 1999), 3D distribution of photosynthesis and primary production rates of vegetation canopies (Guillevic and Gastellu-Etchegorry, 1999), influence of Norway forest spruce structure and woody elements on LAI retrieval (Malenovský *et al.*, 2005) and canopy reflectance (Malenovský *et al.*, 2008), determination of a new hyperspectral index for chlorophyll estimation of forest canopy (Malenovský *et al.*, 2006), study of tropical forest texture (Barbier *et. al.*, 2010; Barbier *et. al.*, 2011; Proisy C. *et al.*, 2011).

DART simulates R.T. in heterogeneous 3-D landscapes with the exact kernel and discrete ordinate methods. It uses an iterative approach: radiation intercepted in iteration "i" is scattered in iteration "i+1". Any landscape is simulated as a rectangular matrix of parallelepipedic cells. Figure 1 illustrates the way urban and natural landscapes are

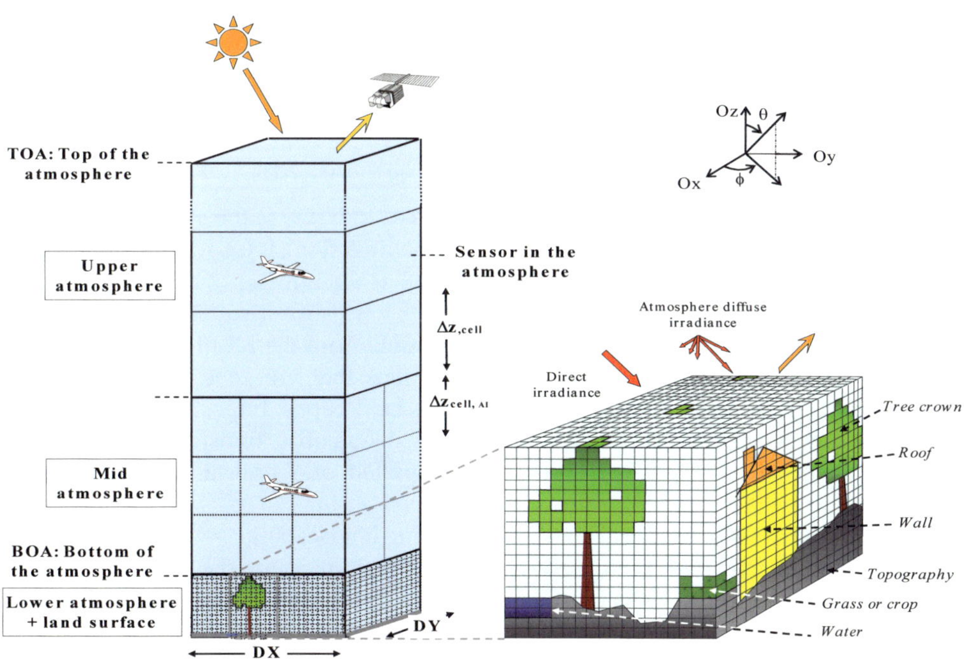

Fig. 1. DART cell matrix of the Earth / Atmosphere system.

simulated, possibly with topography and atmosphere. The atmosphere is made of cells the size of which increases with altitude. Radiation is restricted to propagate in a finite number of directions (Ω_i) with an angular sector width ($\Delta\Omega_i$) (sr). Any set of N discrete directions can be selected ($\sum_{n=1}^{N} \Delta\Omega_n = 4\pi$). A radiation that propagates along direction (Ω_i) at a position r is called a source vector $W(r,\Omega_i)$. It has 3 components: total radiation W, radiation unrelated to leaf mesophyll and polarization degree associated to first order scattering.

The atmosphere has 3 levels: upper (*i.e.*, layers with any depth), mid (*i.e.*, cells with any size) and lower (*i.e.*, cells identical to land surface cells) atmosphere. Land surface elements are the juxtaposition of triangles and/or turbid cells.

DART can work in 3 operating modes: flux tracking, Lidar and Monte Carlo. Only, the flux tracking mode is considered here. This mode tracks emitted and scattered radiation fluxes (*i.e., watts*) within angular cones. The Monte Carlo mode tracks individual photons that are emitted by the sun or a sensor. It is a reference tool for testing the accuracy of the flux tracking mode. The Lidar mode uses the Monte Carlo mode and keeps track of the path length (*i.e.*, time) of each single photon.

For the flux tracking mode, there are 3 sub modes:

- Mode reflectance (R): sun is the only source of radiation. Atmosphere is a secondary source.
- Mode temperature (T): the atmosphere and the land surfaces are the sources of radiation. They depend on temperature and wavelength, using either the Planck's law or the Boltzmann law. Boltzmann law is especially useful for simulation radiation budget over the whole spectrum.
- Mode (R + T): the sun, atmosphere and land surfaces are the radiation sources. This mode is very useful for simulating remote sensing measurements in the 3-4μm spectral domain.

For the 3 modes, the atmosphere can be treated as a propagating medium or as an interface. In any case, landscape irradiance has 2 components: direct sun $W(\Omega_s,x,y)$ and atmospheric $W_a(\Omega_n,x,y)$ source vectors. $W(\Omega_s)$ propagates along direction (Ω_s). $W(\Omega_s)$ and $W_a(\Omega_n)$ are simulated from a fictitious cell layer on top of the scene (Figure 1), with values equal to:

$$W(\Omega_s) = E_s(\Omega_s).|\mu_s|.\Delta x.\Delta y \quad \text{and} \quad W_a(\Omega_n) = L_a(\Omega_n).|\mu_n|.\Delta x.\Delta y.\Delta\Omega_n$$

where $\Delta x.\Delta y$ is the area of the cell face, $\mu_s=\cos\theta_s$, $\mu_n=\cos\theta_n$, $E_s(\Omega_s)$ is the solar constant at the top of the scene, and Ω_s denotes the solar incident direction. $L_a(\Omega_n)$ is the atmospheric radiance along direction (Ω_n), with $n\in[1\ N']$, where N' is the number of downward discrete directions. It is null at the top of the atmosphere.

DART landscape modeling is as independent as possible from the RT modeling in order to allow DART to simulate RT on landscapes simulations that are generated by any other model. It can combine them with its own simulated landscapes. Imported landscapes and landscape elements can be edited to some extent. Geometric transformations (*i.e.*, 3D translation, 3D homothety, 3D rotation) can be applied and optical properties can be assigned.

DART uses 2 complementary approaches for simulating landscapes:

- Juxtaposition of cells that contain one or several turbid medium (*i.e.*, cloud of infinitely small planar elements). This is useful for simulating volumes of foliar elements such as grass and tree crown. A turbid medium is characterized by its volume density, an angular distribution and optical properties (*i.e.*, abaxial reflectance, adaxial reflectance, transmittance).

- Juxtaposition of translucent triangles. This is useful for simulating the ground, the branches, the urban surfaces (*i.e.*, walls and roofs) and also foliar elements. A single cell can contain several turbid medium and several triangles or part of them.

In addition to the atmosphere and to the ground and its topography, DART simulates 4 types of landscape elements:

- Trees with exact or random locations and specific optical properties. Each tree is made of a trunk, possibly with branches, simulated as triangles, and a tree crown simulated as the juxtaposition of turbid cells. Tree crown can have a number of predefined shapes (*e.g.*, ellipsoid, cone, trapezoid, etc.), with specific vertical and horizontal distributions of leaf volume density. Trees with different geometric and optical properties can be mixed.
- Grass or crops. They are simulated as a volume of turbid medium. This volume can located anywhere in space (x,y,z).
- Urban elements (*i.e.*, houses, roads,...). The basic element is a house with walls characterized by the location of their 4 upper corners and roofs characterized by their 4 upper corners.
- Water elements (*i.e.*, river, lake). They are simulated as surfaces with any optical property (*e.g.*, anisotropic reflectance possibly with specular component).

Generally speaking, two types of radiation interaction take place. (1) Volume interaction within turbid cells (Gastellu-Etchegorry *et al.*, 2004). (2) Surface interaction on triangles (Gastellu-Etchegorry, 2008). First scattering order is exactly computed in turbid cells, using 2 points on the ray path within the cell: one point for upward scattering and one point for downward scattering. As expected, simplifying hypotheses are used for simulating multiple scattering in turbid cells. Its computation uses a much faster method than the initial "harmonic expansion" method: it uses the energy intercepted within a finite number of incident angular sectors $\Omega_{sect,k}$ that sample the 4π space of directions ($\Sigma\, \Omega_{sect,k} = 4\pi$). An angular sector Ω_{sect} is a set of close discrete directions. Their number can be as large as the number of directions of ray propagation, but a number equal to 6 leads to very accurate results, with relative errors smaller than 10^{-3} (Gastellu-Etchegorry *et al.*, 2004). Actually, these points are computed for each sub-face of each cell face f ($f \in [1\ 6]$) that intercepts incident rays, and for each angular sector "incident" on the cell face (Martin, 2006; Grau, 2011). This implies that intercepted vector sources $W_{int}(s,f,\Omega_{sect,k})$ are stored per sub face s of cell face f and per incident angular sector $\Omega_{sect,k}$. Thus, we have: $W_{int}(s,f,\Omega_{sect,k}) = \Sigma\Omega_s\, W_{int}(s,f,\Omega_s)$, with directions ($\Omega_s$) within ($\Omega_{sect,k}$). For the case "direct sun illumination", there is 1 sector only.

Atmospheric R.T. modeling is implemented for any spectral band in the optical domain from the ultraviolet up to the thermal infrared (Gascon, 2001; Grau and Gastellu-Etchegorry, 2011). It simulates the atmospheric backscattering phenomenon, which avoids the need to couple DART with an atmospheric model. Atmospheric optical properties are characterized by the molecular $P_m(\lambda,\Omega',\Omega)$ and aerosol $P_p(\lambda,\Omega',\Omega)$ phase functions and by a number of profiles (molecular extinction coefficient $\alpha_e^m(\lambda,z)$ and spherical albedo $\omega_m(\lambda,z)$, aerosol extinction coefficient $\alpha_e^p(\lambda,z)$ and spherical albedo $\omega_p(\lambda,z)$). These quantities are specified by the operator or come from a data base ([0.3μm 30μm]) pre-computed with the Modtran atmospheric model (Berk *et al.*, 1989), for a few predefined atmospheres. DART TOA (Top Of the Atmosphere) reflectance, transmittance and brightness temperature values are very close to Modtran simulations for any atmosphere, any BOA (Bottom Of the Atmosphere) surface and sun / view configuration (Grau, 2011).

Several tools are integrated in the DART model for facilitating the task of the users. Major tools are listed below:

- Sequencer of simulations: it runs a set of simulations where a predefined number of DART input variables vary. For example, one can run $A_1^{N1} . A_2^{N2} . A_3^{N3} . A_4^{N4}$ ... simulations where DART input variables A_1, A_2, A_3,.. take N_1, N_2, N_3,..., values, respectively. Results are stored in a LUT (Look Up Table) for further display and / or processing.
- Manipulation of DEM (Digital Elevation Model): this is used for importing, creating and resampling DEMs.
- Simulation of foliar spectra with the Prospect model (Jacquemoud and Baret, 1990).
- Simulation of scene spectra (reflectance, brightness temperature, radiance). It can be computed using a single DART simulation that is conducted with N spectral bands, or with the help of the sequencer for running N DART simulations with 1 spectral band each.
- Simulation of broadband reflectance, brightness temperature, radiance, irradiance,... It is the sum of a few DART simulated narrow spectral bands, possibly weighted by sensor spectral sensitivity.
- Importation of land cover maps for a direct simulation of DART scenes.

DART models and tools are managed with a user friendly Graphic User Interface (GUI: Figure 2) to input all necessary parameters (*e.g.*, view and illumination conditions) and to specify the required products. They can be also managed with command lines such as scripts written in Python programming language. DART computation code is written in C++ language (more than 300 000 lines of code). The GUI is written in Java language.

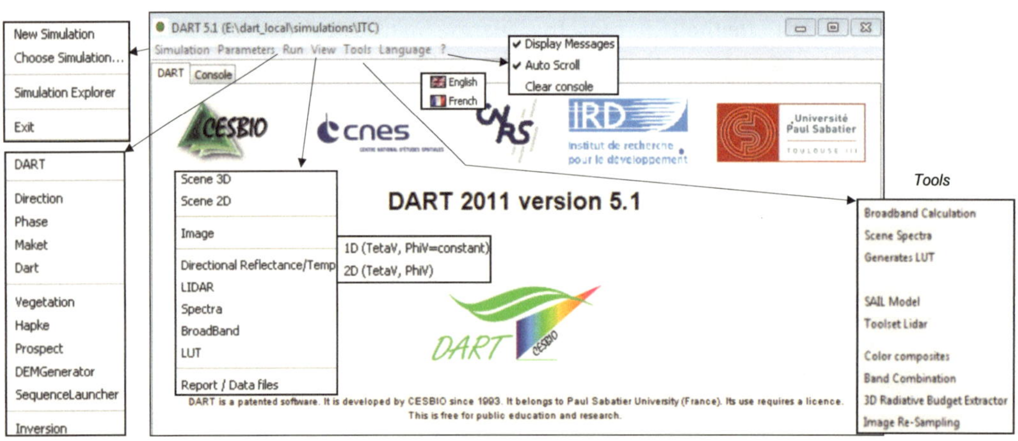

Fig. 2. Graphic User Interface of DART.
'Simulation': creation of simulation folders. 'Parameters': input of DART parameters. 'Run': simulation of scene and RT. 'View': display of results. 'Tools': for deriving products from DART simulations.

DART provides two major types of products:

- Remote sensing measurements at 3 altitude levels: BOA, TOA and atmosphere level. Measurements are essentially images for the "Flux tracking" mode and waveforms for the "Lidar" mode. Images are simulated in the focal plane of the satellite sensor. The cross section of the emitters and scatterers at the origin of the signal are taken into account for improving the image quality, especially for scenes with marked 3D architectures (urban elements, topography). A bi-linear interpolation method is used for projecting the horizontal upper grid of the scene onto an over sampled grid in the sensor plane, at any altitude (BOA to TOA).

- Radiative budget: 3D, 2D and 1D distribution of the radiation that is intercepted, scattered, emitted and absorbed.

3. Examples of DART simulations

DART potential for simulating remote sensing images of urban and forest canopies is illustrated here with 2 examples.

3.1 Urban canopy

The example shown here is derived from the CAPITOUL project of Meteo France (Masson *et al.*, 2007) that took place over the city of Toulouse, France, from February 2004 to February 2005. Study of urban energy balance was one of the objectives. For that, different types of measurements took place: acquisition of TIR airborne images, in-situ measurements of turbulent fluxes, surface energy balance, surface temperatures, etc. DART was used for simulating remote sensing images and the radiative budget (Gastellu-Etchegorry, 2008). First, we developed a specific program for creating a DART scene from the urban database (Autocad format) and digital elevation model (DEM) of the Toulouse town hall (France). This led to the creation of DART objects (*e.g.*, houses, trees). The fact that urban elements in the data base are not individual houses or buildings but unrelated walls and roofs was a difficulty. Figure 3 shows nadir (a) and oblique (b) color composites of the St Sernin district of Toulouse city. They were created with DART simulations in the blue, green and red spectral bands. Simulations stress that urban reflectance and brightness temperature values display a marked angular heterogeneity. This heterogeneity is illustrated here with the angular distribution of NIR reflectance values of St Sernin district (*Figure* 4).

Figure 3.c and d display DART remote sensing images of St Sernin basilica, in the center of district. They are simulated for a sensor at the bottom of the atmosphere (*i.e.*, BOA image) and for a sensor at the top the atmosphere (TOA). The bluish tone of the TOA image, compared to the BOA image, is due to the fact that atmosphere scatters more in the blue than in the red spectral domain. DART images realism is very useful for verifying that the land surface is correctly simulated. Moreover, it helps also for testing the coherence of the RT. For example, at the 1st scattering order, the reflectance of shadows is null.

3.2 Forests

One considers here DART simulations of the reflectance of a tropical forest (Sumatra, Indonesia) in the visible (VIS), near infrared (NIR) and short wave infrared (SWIR) spectral domains. Optical and geometric characteristics are given in Gastellu-Etchegorry *et al.*, 1998. Sun direction is characterized by a 35° off-nadir angle (θ_s) and a 200° azimuth angle (ϕ_s). Figure 5 shows DART VIS images for three viewing directions: nadir viewing direction (θ_v=0°), sun backscattering viewing direction (θ_v=35°, ϕ_v=200°), also called hot spot configuration, and specular configuration (θ_v=35°, ϕ_v=20°).

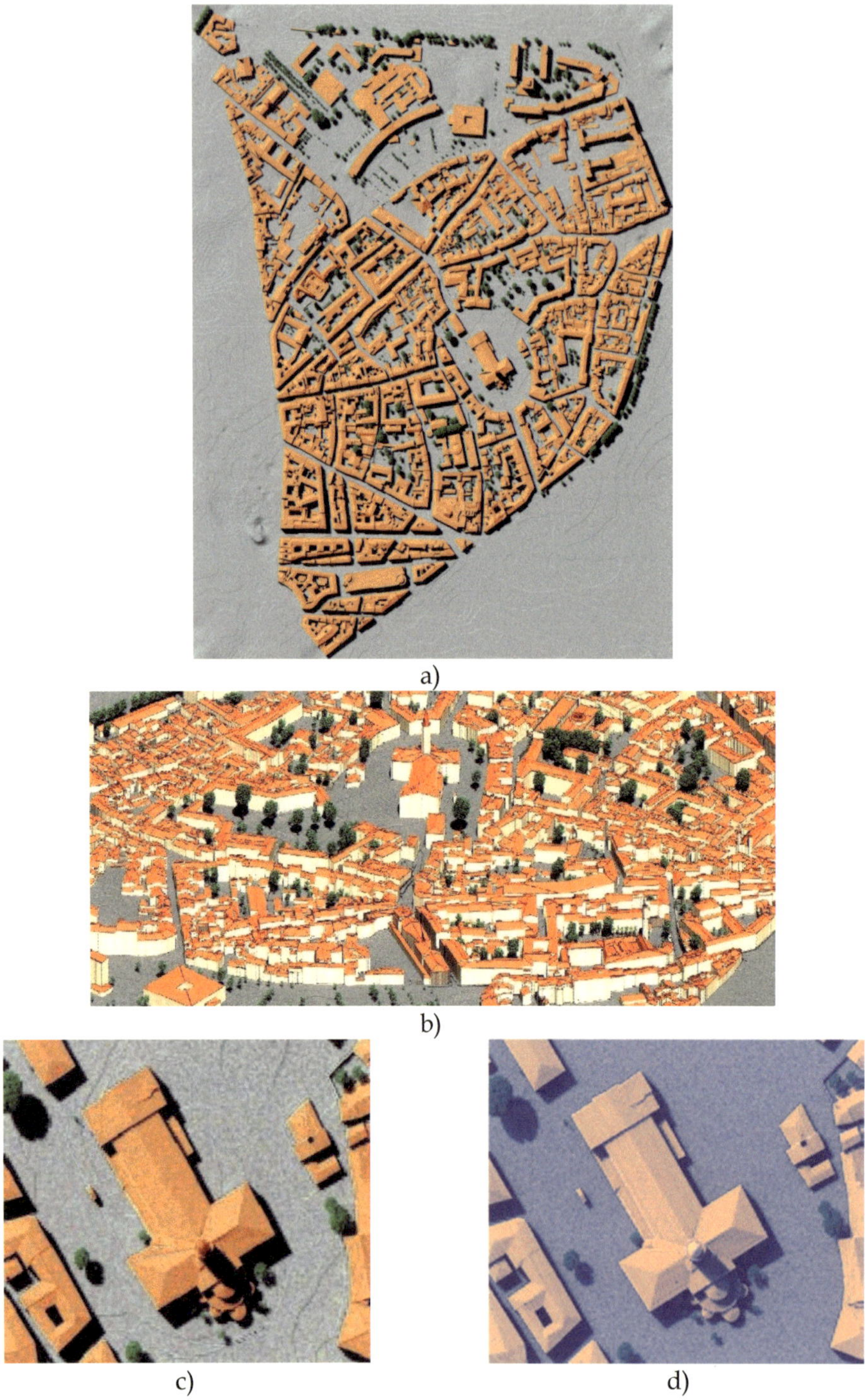

Fig. 3. DART simulated nadir (a) and oblique (b) images of St Sernin district. They are color composites made with blue, green and red DART simulated images. c) Zoom of central part of a): St Sernin basilica. d) Top of the atmosphere simulation.

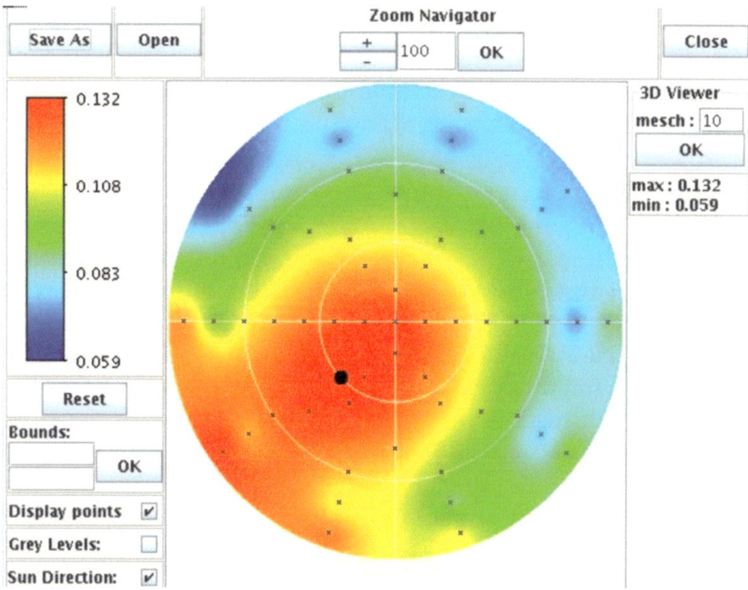

Fig. 4. Example of near infrared BRF of St Sernin district.
It is computed with simulated reflectance values (crosses), for a sun direction shown by a black circle. Distance from the circle centre gives the view zenith angle ([0 90°]) and the anti clockwise angle from the horizontal axis gives the azimuth view angle ([0 360°]).

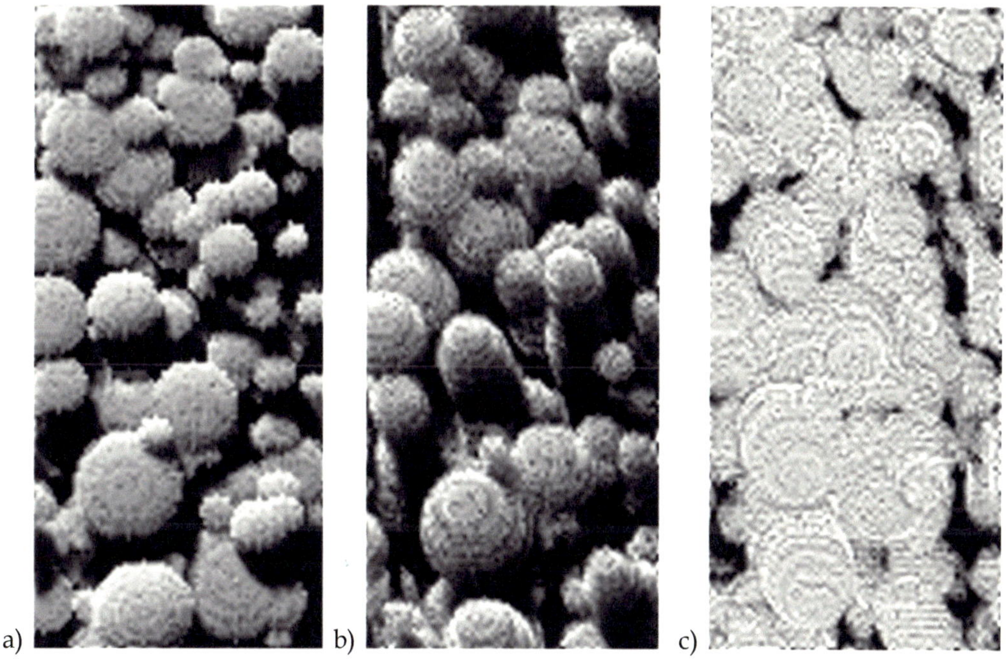

Fig. 5. VIS DART images of tropical forest (Sumatra, Indonesia). Sun direction: θ_s=35°, ϕ_s=200°. (a) Nadir ($\rho \approx 0.031$), (b) specular (θ_v=35°, ϕ_v=20°: $\rho \approx 0.023$), and (c) hot spot ($\rho \approx 0.091$) viewing directions. SKYL=0.

- Nadir viewing direction (Figure 5.a). Mean canopy reflectance is ($\rho_{vis}\approx0.031$, $\rho_{nir}\approx0.376$, $\rho_{swir}\approx0.143$). Illuminated and shaded tree crowns have very different reflectances, shown here with gray tones. Only trees of the upper canopy are easily distinguished. Surfaces with a reflectance smaller than 0.02, *i.e.* shaded crowns and understory, represent 36% of the total scene area. Reflectance of illuminated crown is $\rho_{vis}\approx0.048$ ($\rho_{nir}\approx0.55$, $\rho_{swir}\approx0.21$).
- Specular direction (Figure 5.b), *i.e.* (θ_v=35°, ϕ_v=20°). Mean canopy reflectance is ($\rho_{vis}\approx0.023$, $\rho_{nir}\approx0.344$, $\rho_{swir}\approx0.119$). The reflectance difference between nadir and specular directions stresses the non lambertian nature of forest BRF. Vertical sides of tree crowns can be observed, which explains why trees appear with larger dimensions, compared to nadir viewing direction. This forward scattering configuration is mainly characterized by the important proportion of dark shadows, *i.e.* light trapping, due to the 3-D distribution of trees. Surfaces with a reflectance smaller than 0.02, *i.e.* shaded crowns and understory, occupy 50% of the total scene area. Reflectance of illuminated crown is ($\rho_{vis}\approx0.037$, $\rho_{nir}\approx0.51$, $\rho_{swir}\approx0.18$). Thus, crown VIS, NIR and SWIR reflectance is smaller than in the nadir configuration. This is explained by the fact the sunlit crown fraction and the leaf scattering phase function $\frac{1}{4\pi}.P(\Omega_s,\Omega_v)$ are smaller.
- hot spot configuration (Figure 5.c), *i.e.* (θ_v=35°, ϕ_v=200°). The absence of shade in this configuration explains the strong canopy reflectance in all spectral domains, *i.e.* $\rho_{vis}\approx0.091$ ($\rho_{nir}\approx0.684$, $\rho_{swir}\approx0.341$). Darkest areas correspond to the low reflecting understory. Their reflectance is less than 0.03 and occupy about 5% of the total scene area. Crown reflectance is ($\rho_{vis}\approx0.1$, $\rho_{nir}\approx0.74$, $\rho_{swir}\approx0.4$).

Figure 6 shows DART NDVI (Normalized Vegetation Index) and VIS / NIR / SWIR reflectance values in the principal and perpendicular solar planes, for several sun off-nadir directions. Reflectance values share some similar characteristics: (1) a well marked bowl shape in the principal solar plane with a spectrally dependent minimum for a direction between the specular and nadir directions, (2) a strong maximum in the hot spot direction, more marked in the VIS than in the NIR and SWIR, (3) a systematic increase of reflectance if view zenith angles exceed a threshold value (*e.g.* ≈50° in the VIS if θ_s=0°), which depends on the spectral domain and the sun direction, (4) an azimuth symmetry relative to the principal solar plane, and (5) a relatively small variability in the perpendicular solar plane.

Reflectance is maximal at hot spot (ρ_{vis}=0.073, ρ_{nir}=0.615, ρ_{swir}=0.324) and minimal for directions between nadir and specular configurations (ρ_{vis}=0.025, ρ_{nir}=0.354, ρ_{swir}=0.12), whereas NDVI is minimal (≈0.79) in the hot spot direction and maximal (≈0.87) in the specular direction.

In addition to DART simulations, Figure 6 shows reflectance simulations carried out with the well known SAIL model (Verhoef, 1984). For this model, vegetation is an homogeneous turbid medium. Figure 6 allows one to stress the role of canopy architecture on forest reflectance. Its neglect by the SAIL model explains that DART reflectance is much smaller. Reflectance differences depend a lot on view direction. Smaller differences occur in the hot spot directions because no shadows occur for these viewing directions. Outside the hot spot configuration, for θ_s=0°, mean relative reflectance difference is around 60-70% in the VIS, 50% in the SWIR and 25% in the NIR. Differences tend to increase with sun off-nadir angle.

The bowl shape of VIS and SWIR reflectance is more marked with SAIL than with DART. It corresponds to the fact that in the forward principal plane, for large off-nadir viewing angles θ_v, an increase of θ_v implies that DART reflectance increases less than SAIL reflectance, especially for large off-nadir sun angles. Indeed, the canopy 3-D heterogeneous structure ensures that an increase of θ_v leads to an increase of the proportion of shaded tree crowns that are viewed in the principal plane. This effect tends to be less marked in the NIR than in the VIS because the role of shadows is less marked in the NIR, due to the increased occurrence of multiple scattering processes. Moreover, the presence of shadows explains that with oblique sun illumination, minimal values of DART reflectance are more shifted towards the specular direction than those of SAIL. This is also true for NDVI.

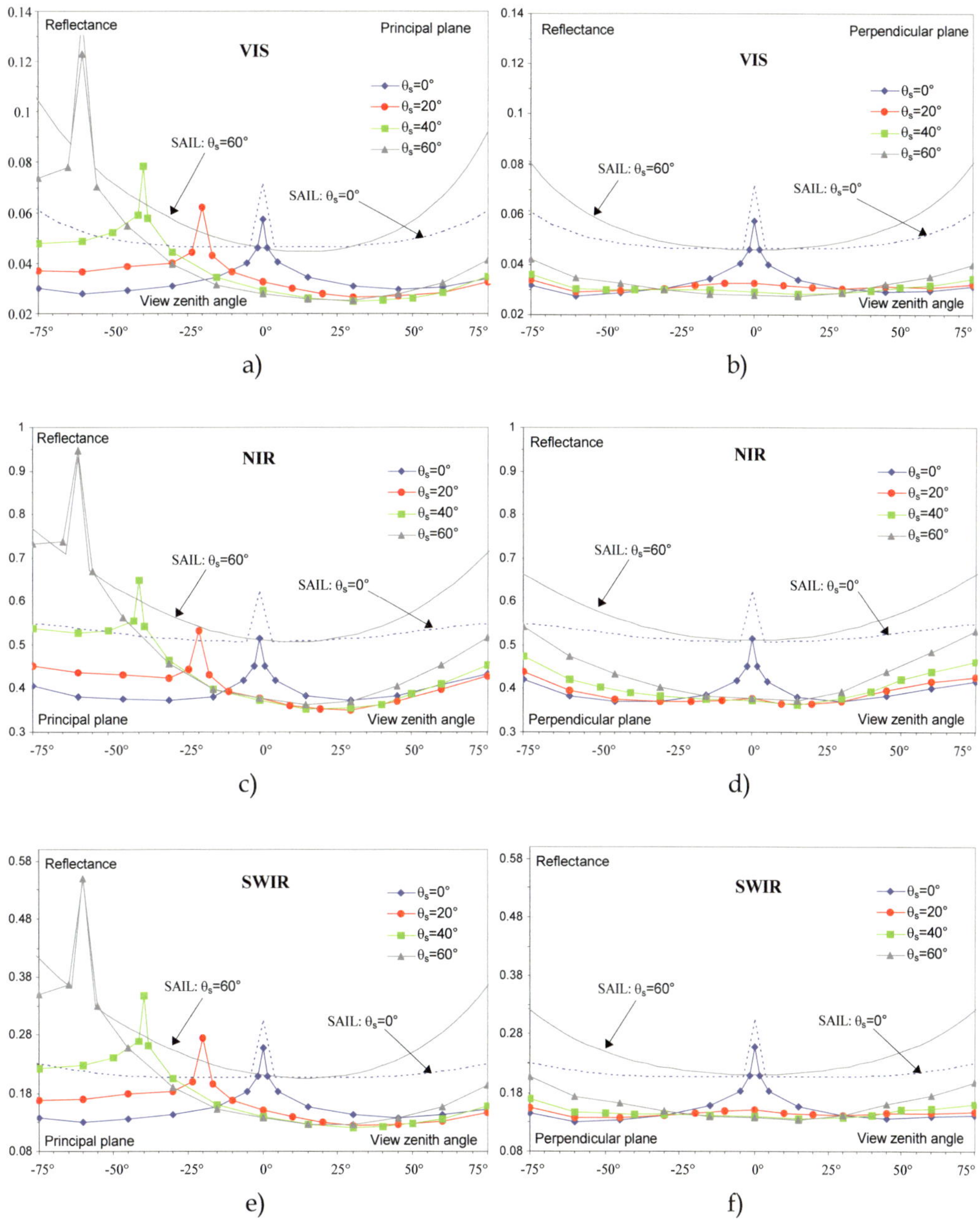

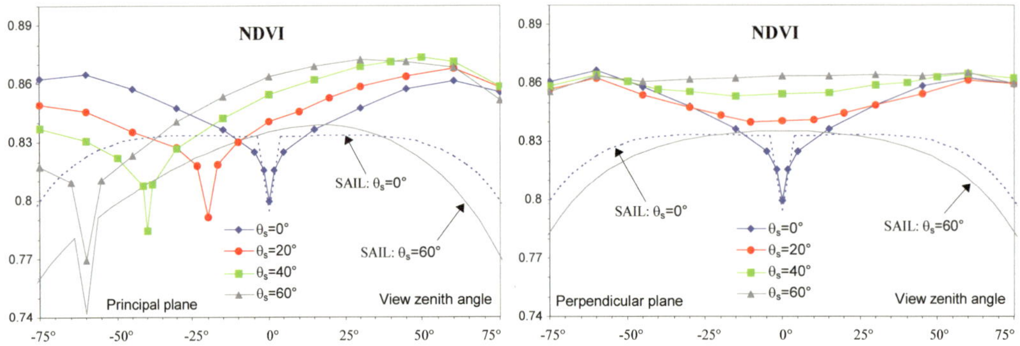

g) h)

Fig. 6. Tropical forest angular DART and SAIL VIS (a, b), NIR (c, d), SWIR (e, f) simulated reflectance and NDVI (g, h) for 4 sun off-nadir directions (0°, 20°, 40°, 60°). Principal (left column) and perpendicular (right column) solar planes. SKYL is 0.3 for VIS, 0.24 for NIR and 0.09 for SWIR. For a better clarity SAIL simulations are for θ_s=0° and 60° only.

Image simulation is very useful for understanding forest reflectance behavior with experimental and instrumental parameters. Here, this is shown for sky radiation. Figure 7 shows DART nadir NIR images of part of the tropical forest, for 2 extreme atmosphere conditions: SKYL equal to 0 and 1, with $SKYL = \frac{Atmosphere\,irradiance}{Total\,irradiance}$. We note that some tree crowns are invisible with SKYL=0 (bottom of Figure 7), because they are shaded, and

a) b)

Fig. 7. NIR DART nadir images of a tropical forest with SKYL equal to 0 (a) and 1 (b). Most crowns of upper trees that are shaded with SKYL=0 are well lit if SKYL=1. Moreover, shaded crowns of a few lower trees that are not viewed with SKYL=0 become visible if SKYL=1. Sun off-nadir angle is 35°.

visible with SKYL=1. It explains that forest reflectance varies with atmosphere radiation. In a first approximation, we can consider that forest reflectance depends on the fraction of illuminated crowns, shaded crowns of upper trees, and shaded lower trees and understory (*i.e.* vegetation smaller than 10m height). With SKYL=0 (SKYL=1), fractions of these 3 classes are around 48% (68%), 37% (12%) and 15% (20%), respectively, whereas their apparent NIR reflectances are around 0.55 (0.52), 0.27 (0.14) and 0.069 (0.062), respectively. As expected, a SKYL increase implies that the area of illuminated crowns increases whereas their apparent reflectance slightly decreases. Indeed, with SKYL=1 all upper trees are totally illuminated, conversely to the case SKYL=0. On the other hand, a SKYL increase implies that the fraction and reflectance of shaded upper trees regularly decrease, whereas the area and apparent reflectance of the shaded lower trees and understory remain nearly constant if SKYL<0.5. The fraction and reflectance decrease of the shaded upper tree crowns results from two opposite effects: when SKYL increases some crown surfaces, only slightly shaded if SKYL=0, become darker whereas crown surfaces that are initially totally shaded become better lit. Thus, when SKYL increases, tree crowns that are initially shaded with SKYL=0, can become lit enough to belong to the category "illuminated upper trees".

4. Recent and on going improvements

Three recent improvements of DART are briefly described here:

- Earth / Atmosphere curvature. It is important when simulating satellite measurements, because the usual assumption that the Earth is a flat surface is less and less valid with more and more oblique ray directions.
- Transformation of 3D objects made of juxtaposed triangles into 3D turbid objects.
- Finite landscapes and infinite landscapes with a continuous (*i.e.*, not repetitive) topography.
- Simulation of Lidar waveform.

4.1 Earth / Atmosphere curvature

The Earth / Atmosphere curvature has an impact at 2 levels: (1) the incidence angle of sun and view directions of Earth surfaces, and (2) ray path lengths in the atmosphere. Both effects are now taken into account by DART.

View and sun incidence angle:

For a non-horizontal atmosphere, the incidence angle α differs from the satellite sensor off nadir angle β. DART computes α, β and the azimuth view direction in the Earth surface reference system with the locations (latitude, longitude, altitude) of the Earth target T and satellite sensor S, assuming the Earth to be an ellipsoid (*cf.* Annex).
Sun incidence angle at target level and on an horizontal surface below the satellite are computed by DART as a function of time with the equations of the NOAA solar calculator (http://www.esrl.noaa.gov/gmd/grad/solcalc/).

Ray paths in the atmosphere:

For an off-nadir angle θ, an atmosphere path length between altitudes z_a and z_b is smaller than in an horizontal atmosphere (*i.e.*, $\Delta z/|\mu|$, with $\mu=\cos\theta$ and $\Delta z = |z_a - z_b|$). Moreover, gas and aerosol vertical distributions are not constant. Here, atmosphere is assumed to be spherical (Figure 27).

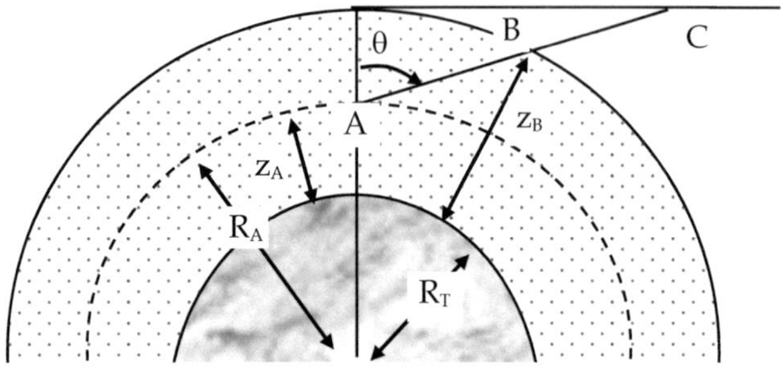

R_T: Earth radius,

R(z): radius of the sphere at the altitude z. $R(z) = R_T + z$

θ: zenith angle of a direction ($\mu = \cos\theta$)

Fig. 8. The atmosphere with the Earth curvature.

$$\mu=\cos\theta > 0\text{: Path } \{\Delta z > 0;\ \mu\} \text{ is } AB = -R_A.\mu + \sqrt{R_A^2.\mu^2 + \Delta z.(\Delta z + 2R_A)}$$

It can be viewed as a path {Δz; μ_{sph}} in an horizontal atmosphere if:

$$\mu_{sph} = \frac{\Delta z}{-R_A.\mu + \sqrt{R_A^2.\mu^2 + \Delta z.(\Delta z + 2R_A)}} \Rightarrow AB = \frac{\Delta z}{\mu_{sph}} < \frac{\Delta z}{\mu}$$

$\mu=\cos\theta < 0$: Path {Δz < 0; μ} is $AB = -R_A.\mu - \sqrt{R_A^2.\mu^2 + \Delta z.(\Delta z - 2R_A)}$
It can be viewed as a path {Δz; μ_{sph}} in an horizontal atmosphere if:

$$\mu_{sph} = \frac{\Delta z}{R_A.\mu + \sqrt{R_A^2.\mu^2 + \Delta z.(\Delta z - 2R_A)}} \Rightarrow AB = \frac{-\Delta z}{\mu_{sph}} < \frac{-\Delta z}{\mu}$$

Note: the 2 expressions of AB and μ_{sph} are identical. Indeed: {μ > 0, Δz > 0} for the 1st one and {μ < 0, Δz < 0} for the 2nd one.
The optical depth of path AB is:
$\Delta\tau(z_A, \Delta z, \mu) = \int_0^{\Delta l = AB} \alpha(t).dl = \int_{z_A}^{z_B} \alpha(t).\frac{R_A + t}{\sqrt{R_A^2.\mu^2 + t.(t + 2R_A)}}.dt$, with t the altitude relative to z_a and l the path length from A, we have: $l = -R_A^2.\mu + \sqrt{R_A^2.\mu^2 + t.(t + 2R_A)}$l if $\mu > 0$ and: $l = -R_A^2.\mu - \sqrt{R_A^2.\mu^2 + t.(t - 2R_A)}$ if $\mu < 0$.
The computation of $\Delta\tau(z_a,\Delta z,\mu)$ could be solved with an integration by parts:

$$\int_{Z_A}^{Z_A+\Delta z} \alpha(t).\frac{R_A + t}{\sqrt{R_A^2.\mu^2 + t.(t + 2R_A)}}.dt$$

$$= \left[\alpha(t).(R_A.\mu + \sqrt{R_A^2.\mu^2 + t.(t + 2R_A)}\right]_{Z_A}^{Z_A+\Delta z} - \int_{Z_A}^{Z_A+\Delta z} \alpha'(t).\left(-R_A.\mu + \sqrt{R_A^2.\mu^2 + t.(t + 2R_A)}\right).dt$$

This approach requires the derivative $\alpha'(z)$ of the extinction coefficient. However, $\alpha'(z)$ is known only for an ideal case such as an exponential atmosphere. In order to work with any atmosphere (*e.g.*, non exponential vertical profile of O_3), $\Delta\tau(z_a,\Delta z,\mu)$ is computed with: $\Delta\tau(z_A,\Delta z,\mu) = \overline{\alpha(z)}.AB = \overline{\alpha(z)}.|\frac{\Delta z}{\mu_{sph}}|$, with $\overline{\alpha(z)}$ the mean extinction coefficient within [z_a $z_a+\Delta z$]

Thus, before simulating the atmosphere RT, DART computes $\mu_{sph}(z_i,\mu_j)$ for all I atmosphere layers and all J discrete directions, including the sun direction, with $i \in [1\ \ I]$ and $j \in [1\ \ J]$.

$$\left|\mu_{sph}(z_i,\mu_j)\right| = \frac{\Delta z}{-(R_T+z_i)^2.\left|\mu_j\right| + \sqrt{(R_T+z_i)^2.\mu_j^2 + \left|\Delta z\right|.\left(\left|\Delta z\right| + 2.(R_T+z_i)\right)}}$$

The use of $\mu_{sph}(z_i,\mu_j)$ allows one to treat the atmosphere as an horizontal plane for simulating the atmosphere RT: any path $\delta r(z_i,\mu_j)$ that is computed for an horizontal atmosphere layer $[z_i z_i + Dz]$ is replaced by $\delta r_{sph}\left(z_i,\mu_j\right) = \delta r\left(z_i,\mu_j\right).\frac{\mu_j.\left(z_i,\mu_j\right)}{\mu_{sph}.\left(z_i,\mu_j\right)}$.

We have: $\delta r_{sph}\left(z_i,\mu_j\right) \le \delta r_{sph}\left(z_i,\mu_j\right) \le \frac{\Delta z}{\mu_j}$

4.2 Transformation of "3D triangle objects" into "3D turbid objects"

As already mentioned DART can import 3D objects (Figure 9) that are simulated as groups of triangles. In many cases, especially for vegetation, these objects are simulated with tremendous numbers of triangles (*e.g.*, 10^6 triangles). This is very costly is terms of computation time and volume memory, especially if we work with forests... In order to solve this problem, we designed a module that transforms 3D objects simulated as triangles (*i.e.*, 3D triangle objects) into 3D objects simulated as turbid medium (*i.e.*, 3D turbid objects). Figure 10 shows the schematic approach. It is reminded that a cell filled with turbid medium is characterized by its LAI (Leaf Area Index), its leaf angle distribution (LAD) and the leaf optical properties (e.g., transmittance and adaxial and abaxial reflectance, possibly with specular parameters). The "transformation" module computes the LAI and LAD of all leaf

Fig. 9. Examples of 3D trees that are imported by DART.

elements within each cell of a 3D cell matrix. This is done for all or part of the groups of triangles of the "3D triangle" object. Optical properties of the turbid medium are those of the triangles. On the other hand, the LAD is either the one that is computed or a predefined LAD. The possibility to use a predefined LAD is well adapted to the case of 3D triangle objects with low volume densities of triangles.

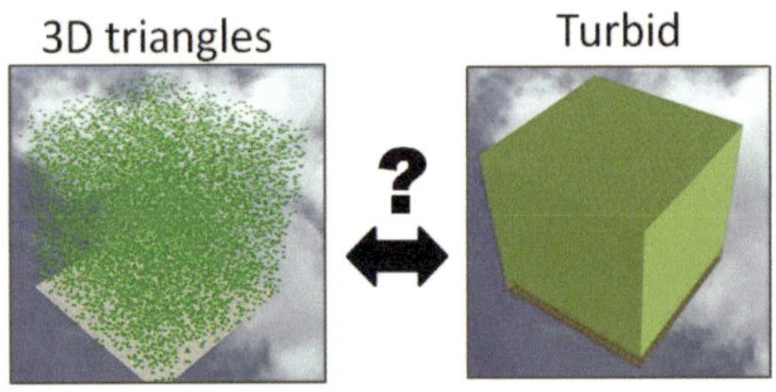

Fig. 10. Schematic representation of the transformation of a "triangle cell" into a "turbid cell".

Here, the transformation of a 3D triangle scene into a turbid 3D turbid scene is illustrated by DART color composite images of the citrus tree "3D triangle scene" and "3D turbid scene" (Figure 11). The associated 2D reflectance polar plots are shown also. For these 2 cases, RT was simulated in the blue, green and red spectral bands. Results are very encouraging: reflectance values are very close. Actually, reflectance values of the 3D triangle and turbid scenes are much closer than the 3D triangle objects contain a lot of triangles. It can be noted that DART images in Figure 11 b and e are duplicated 2 x 2 times. This mode of representation of images is often useful for better interpreting simulated images where objects (*e.g.*, trees) and their shadows cross the scene boundaries.
Compared to the usual simulation of trees with classical tree crown shapes such ellipsoids or cones, the transformation of 3D triangle tree crowns into 3D turbid tree crowns is very interesting for keeping the 3D architecture of trees.

a) b) c)

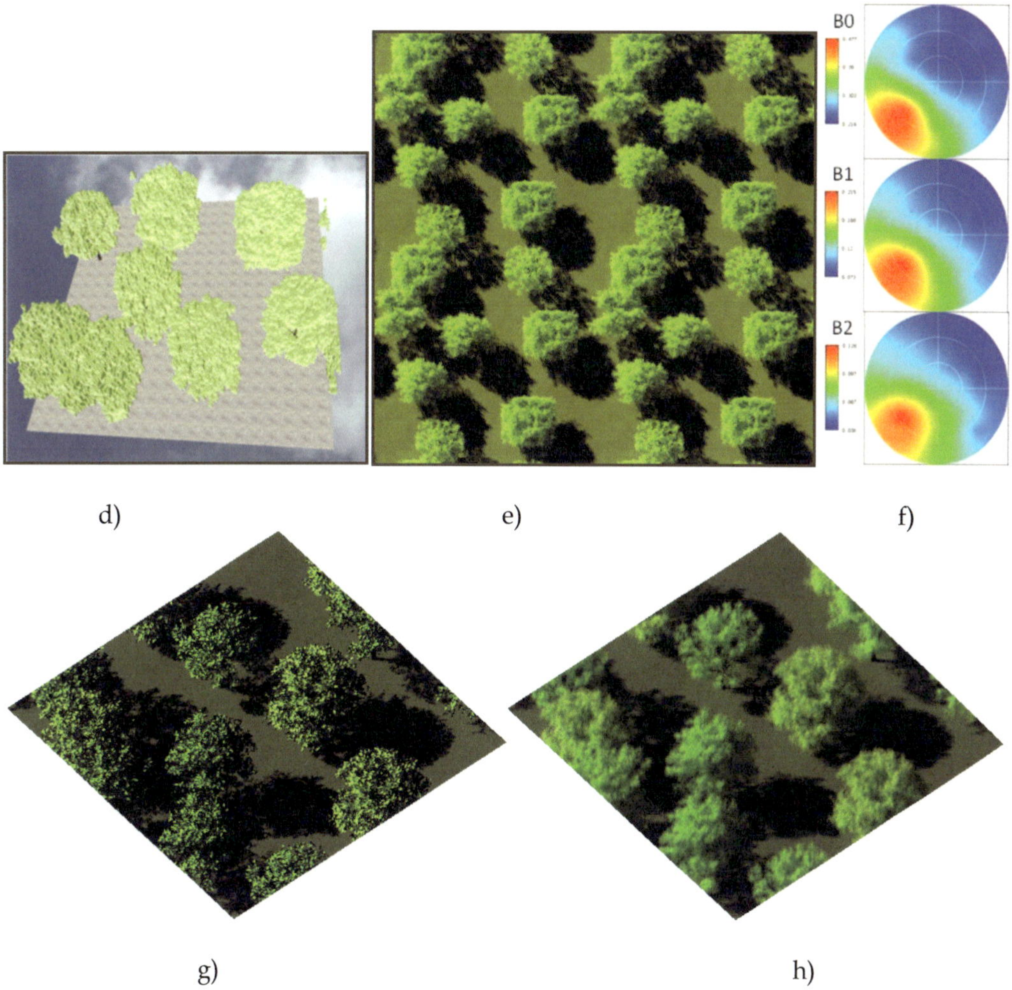

Fig. 11. 3D triangle and turbid simulations in the blue (B0), green (B1) and red (B2) spectral bands of the citrus plot. a) 3D triangle scene. d) Derived 3D turbid scene. Associated triangle and turbid nadir (b, e) and oblique (g, h) color composite of the DART simulated images. c, f) Associated 2D reflectance polar plots.

4.3 Finite landscapes and continuous infinite landscapes topography

DART was designed to operate with infinite scenes that are made of a DART simulated pattern that is periodic. When a ray exits the scene, it re-enters the scene by the scene opposite side. This is the so-called "repetitive topography" method. This approach is used in most 3D models. It works very well with landscapes without topography or if the topography is identical on the landscape opposite sides. Thus, it is erroneous in presence of any topography. It is also erroneous if one wants to simulate a finite landscape without interaction with their neighborhood. We solved these 2 problems by introducing 2 new landscape modeling methods, called "Continuous topography" and "Isolated landscape", respectively. This implied to adapt the 3 DART RT modeling modes (*i.e.*, flux tracing, Monte Carlo and lidar). In short, landscapes can be simulated with 3 methods (Figure 12):

- Repetitive topography: the landscape and the topography are periodic. It that case, a landscape with a simple slope is actually simulated as a series of periodic slopes, which implies undesirable illumination (Figure 12.a) and view (Figure 12.b) effects.
- Continuous topography: repetitive landscape with a continuous topography. It allows one to simulate more realistic landscapes such as infinite slopes. This method is well adapted to landscapes such as mountain slopes.
- Isolated landscape: no influence of the neighborhood.

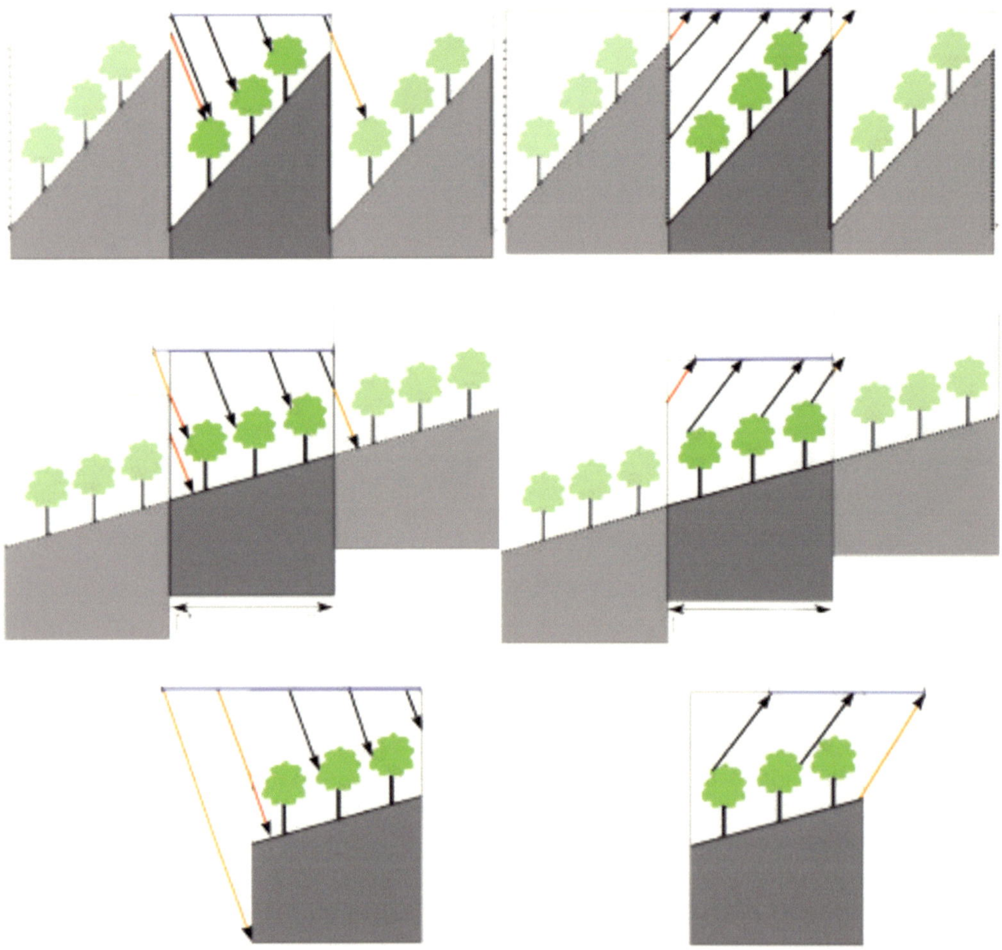

Fig. 12. The 3 methods of landscape simulation in DART. Top: Repetitive landscape. Middle: Continuous topography. Bottom: Isolated landscape. Left and right columns illustrate the illumination and view configurations.

Figure 13 illustrates the 3 methods for simulating landscapes. In the image simulated with the repetitive method, shadow is not continuous on the scene edges, due to the discontinuity of the slope. It would have been continuous in the absence of topography. On the other hand, as expected, shadow is continuous with the "Continuous method". As expected, for the "Isolated landscape", shadow is not continuous (no adjacency effects).

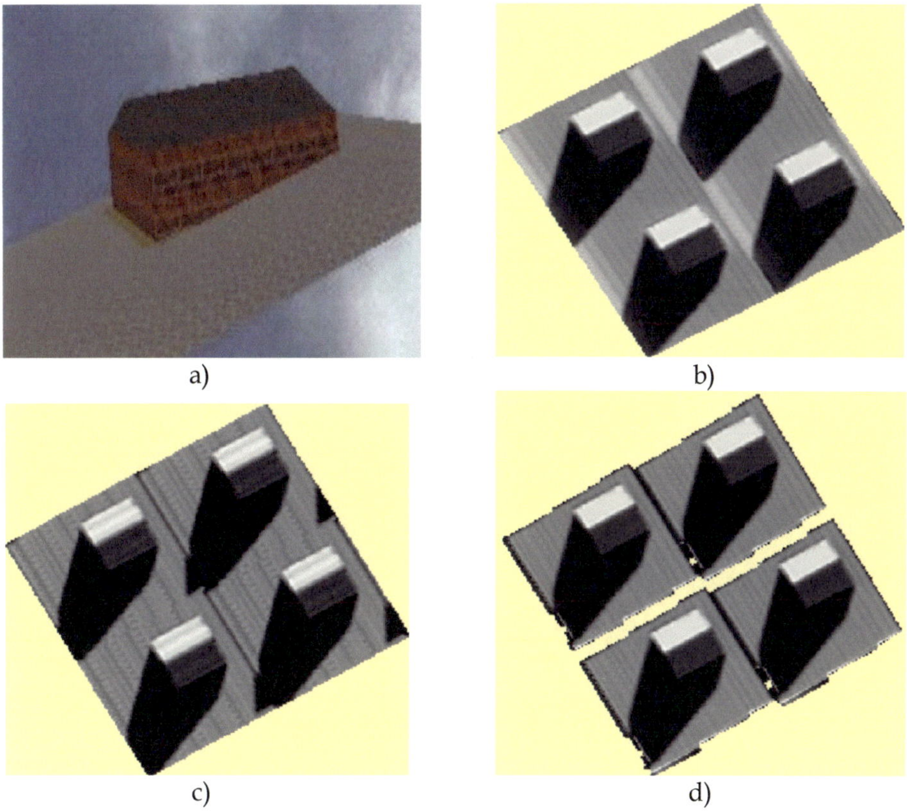

Fig. 13. Simulation of a house on a slope.
a) Scene. b) Repetitive topography. c) Infinite (i.e., continuous) slope. The shadow is not continuous, due to the discontinuity of the slope. d) Isolated scene (no adjacency effects).

4.4 Radiative budget

Different modules and tools were added to DART for better simulating and managing the 3D radiative budget. DART computes the different terms of the radiative budget: absorbed energy per cell, intercepted energy per cell, scattered energy per cell and downward and upward energy on top cell faces. Here, this is illustrated by a schematic tree landscape (Figure 14). DART simulation was conducted in the near infrared with a SKYL equal to 0.2 and a sun direction ($\theta_s = 160°$, $\phi_s = 90°$). The possibility to obtain 2D and 3D displays is very helpful for understanding the radiation interaction within the tree canopy. For example, here, larger downward radiation occurs in the air cells that are directly illuminated by the sun. This quantity can be larger than 1 because tree crowns scatter radiation through these air cells. Larger interception occurs on the illuminated tree crowns and the ground that is directly illuminated by the sun. Larger scattering occurs where interception is maximal and where local reflectance / albedo is maximal. This explains that scattering by illuminated tree crowns is larger than scattering by the illuminated ground. Indeed, in the near infrared, leaf albedo is larger than ground reflectance. It is interesting to note that the "Broadband" module of DART computes broadband radiation budget with the DART simulated narrow band radiation budgets.

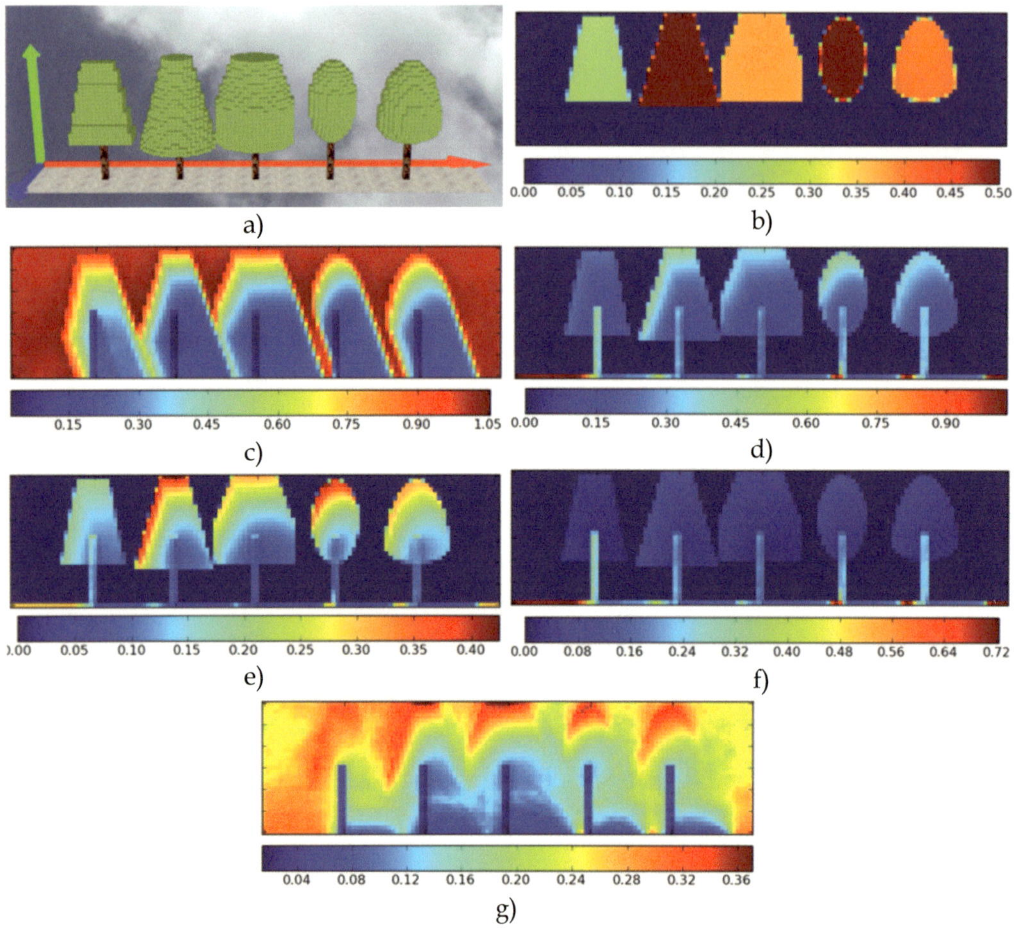

Fig. 14. 3D radiative budget of a schematic tree cover. Spatial resolution is Δx=0.5m. Ox axis is in blue color in a). Figures b to g) show 2D distributions in the plane x=5m of the ratio "Radiometric quantity / Irradiance on the top of the landscape. b) LAI_{cell}. Leaf volume density is LAI_{cell}. Δx. c) Downward energy. d) Intercepted energy. e) Scattered energy. f) Absorbed energy. g) Upward energy.

4.5 Lidar

DART simulates lidar waveforms of urban and natural landscapes. For that, it uses a Monte Carlo method that is adapted for taking into account the usually strong anisotropy of the phase function of landscape elements. In short, the occurrence probabilities of scattering events that have the same order of magnitude are grouped for obtaining groups that have cumulated probabilities with the same order of magnitude (Gastellu-Etchegorry *et al.*, 2010). The Monte Carlo mode in the DART model was initially developed for assessing the accuracy of DART flux tracing method, using the same simulations of landscapes. Indeed, flux tracing RT modelling requires some simplifying hypotheses for representing multiple scattering. The associated inaccuracy depends on the trade-off between the expected accuracy and computational time of simulations. The advantage of the Monte Carlo approach is to simulate multiple scattering processes as a succession of exactly modelled single scattering processes.

In order to simulate Lidar waveforms, the DART Lidar module works with a Gaussian spatial distribution for illumination, and a Gaussian (time) laser pulse. It is suited for small and large footprints. It is very flexible because it inherits major features of the DART model: urban and natural scenes, with topography, atmosphere, etc. Examples of waveforms are presented here for urban and natural scenes.

Figure 15 illustrates lidar modelling of a urban area that is the St Sernin district (Figure 3). It shows the image that is simulated with the flux tracing mode and the waveform that is simulated with the lidar module. As expected, the horizontal axis of the waveform gives the altitude of scene elements (buildings, vegetation, ground).

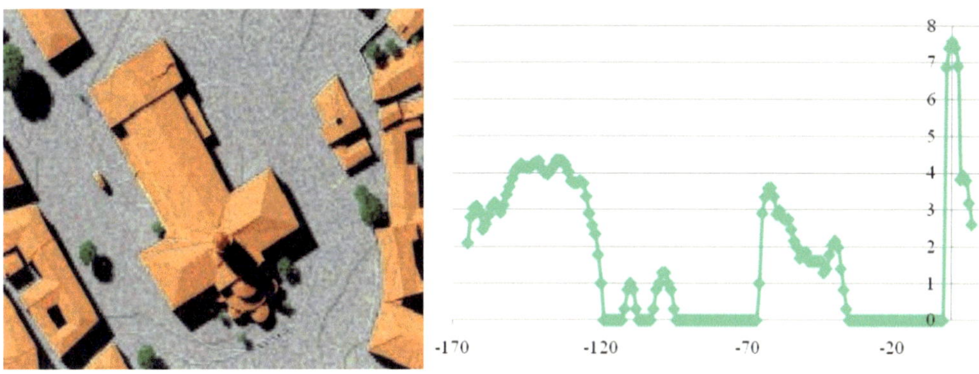

a) b)

Fig. 15. DART lidar simulation of the St Sernin district. a) Image simulated with the flux tracing mode. b) Waveform (Ox: time (ns), Oy: power (logarithmic). Ground gives the larger peak. Top point (Basilique) gives the 1st signal.

Lidar simulation of a plot of citrus trees is shown here (Figure 20.a). Figure 20 b and c show the DART images simulated with the Monte Carlo mode and with the flux tracing mode. The 2 images are very similar. Actually, the degree of similarity depends on the number of photons that are used. As expected, the Monte Carlo mode is usually much more expensive in terms of computation time. An interesting point is that DART simulates the images of the illuminated and view footprints (Figure 20 d and e). This is very useful for interpreting the simulated waveform (Figure 20 f). As expected, the latter one shows a peak that corresponds to the ground and a peak that corresponds to the tree crowns.

The citrus waveform (Figure 16.f) being related to the LAI (Leaf Area Index) vertical profile, Ueberschlag (2010) assessed the potential of DART for retrieving the LAI of forests with an inversion procedure. Results were encouraging. As expected, similarly to the lidar response, the LAI retrieval depends a lot on the location of trees within the footprint, except if the lidar signal is uniform. For a Gaussian lidar signal, Figure 17 shows that in the case of a tree cover the LAI of which is 0.5, the retrieved LAI can vary from 0.33 up to 0.70, depending on the tree location within the footprint.

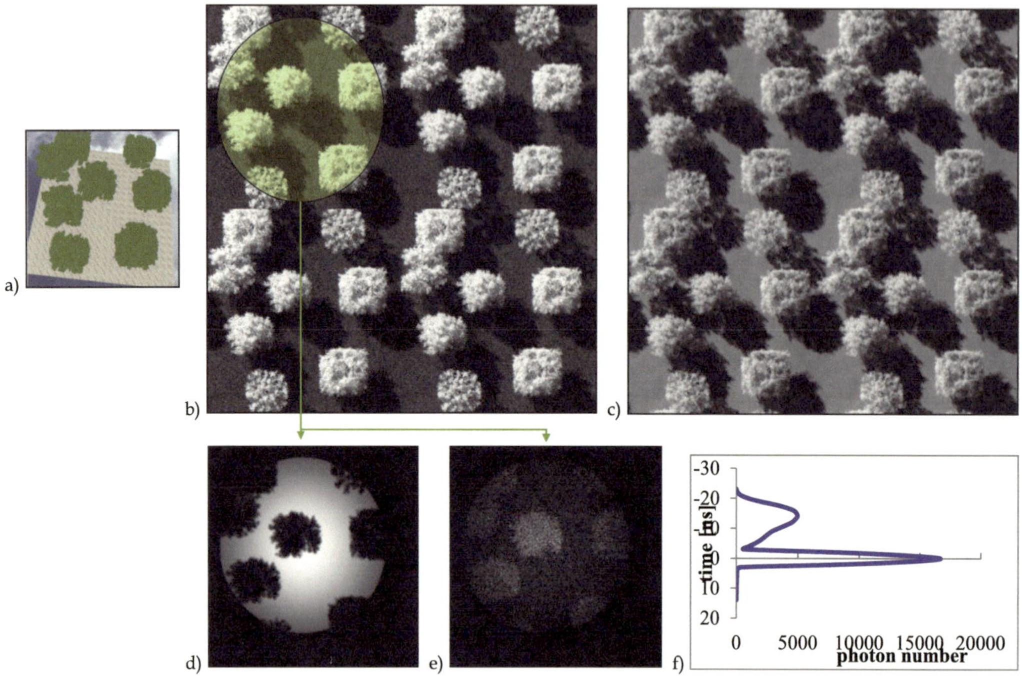

Fig. 16. Lidar simulation of citrus trees (a). Images simulated with the Monte Carlo mode (b) and the flux tracing mode (c). Images of Lidar ground (d) and view area (e) footprint. Waveform (f). The lidar has a 3ns pulse duration, a 0.5ns acquisition rate, a 4m footprint radius and a 0.368 Gaussian illumination parameter.

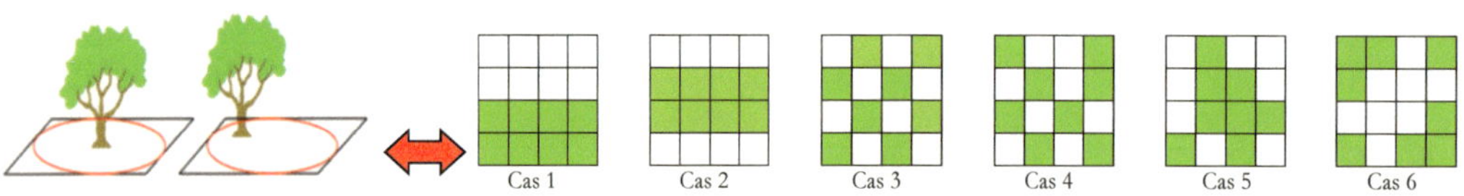

Case	1	2	3	4	5	6
Theoretical LAI	0,5	0,5	0,5	0,5	0,5	0,5
Retrieved LAI - Gaussian signal	0,52	0,70	0,50	0,45	0,64	0,33
Absolute error (%) - Gaussian signal	4,5	40,1	-0,2	-10,4	28,2	-33,8
Retrieved LAI - Uniform signal	0,5	0,5	0,5	0,5	0,5	0,5
Absolute error (%) - Uniform signal	0	0	0	0	0	0

Fig. 17. Influence of vegetation location in the lidar footprint for retrieving forest LAI with DART.

The potential of altitude mapping was assessed. Figure 18.a shows an altitude map where the altitude of each pixel is the local higher altitude. This is called the Lidar first return altitude map. Figure 18.b is an interpolation of Figure 18.a for obtaining a 3D display.

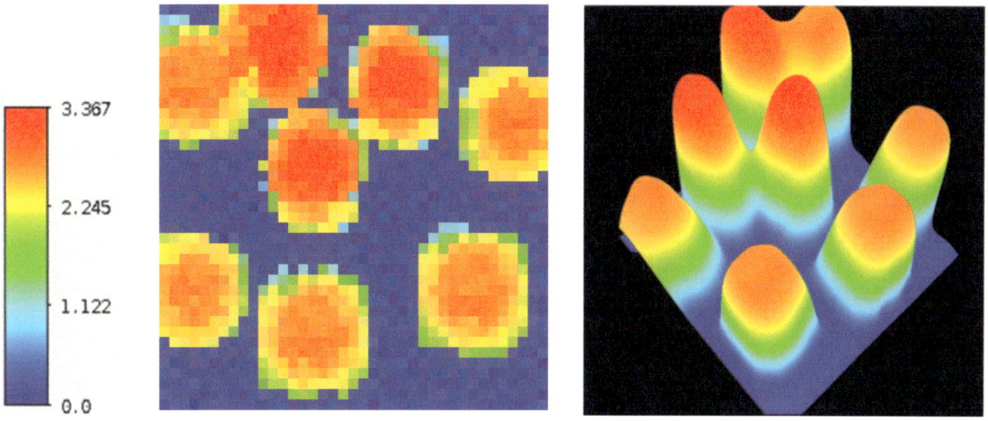

Fig. 18. Altitude mapping from DART waveforms. a) Height scale. b) Lidar first return altitude map: resolution 0.25*0.25m. c) Lidar interpolated altitude 3D map

5. Examples of applications

5.1 Radiance and radiative budget at continental scale

A method was developed to create automatically for every spectral band, any date and any land area, maps of radiometric products (*i.e.*, radiance, reflectance, brightness temperature) at a continental scale. For that, it realizes a spatial interpolation on a set of georeferenced DART products that are created by running the DART "sequencer" module with time, wavelength and land surface location used as variable parameters.

Results shown here are for the African continent, with a geostationary satellite (35800km altitude, 0° N, 17° E) for 2 spectral bands (550nm: Figure 19 and Figure 20; 900nm: Figure 21 and Figure 22) at 4 dates: March 21 2011 (spring equinox), June 21 2011 (summer solstice), September 21 2011 (autumn equinox) and December 21 2011 (winter solstice), at 3 daytimes (8hUTC, 12hUTC, 16hUTC). The atmosphere is defined by a US Standard gas model and rural aerosols with a 23km visibility. Simulations were carried out with the ground horizontal Lambertian "Brown to dark brown gravelly loam" from the USDA Soil Conservation Service): $\rho_{ground,550} = 0.061$ and $\rho_{ground,900} = 0.351$.

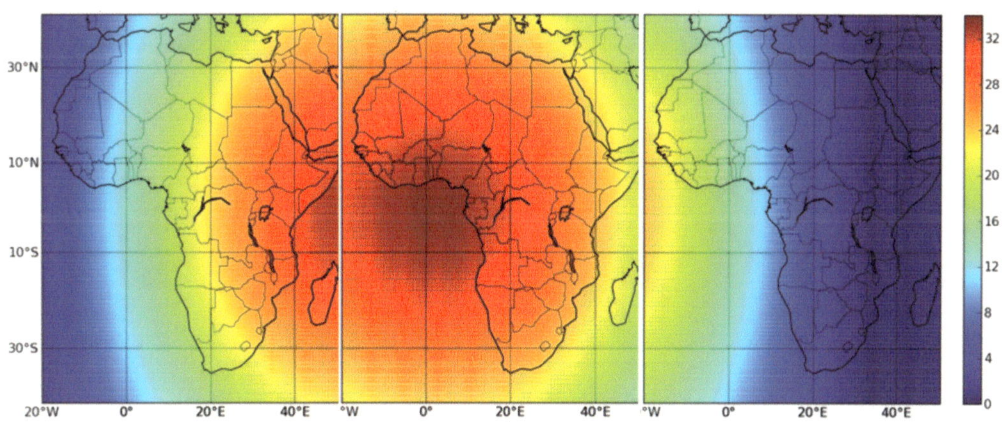

a)

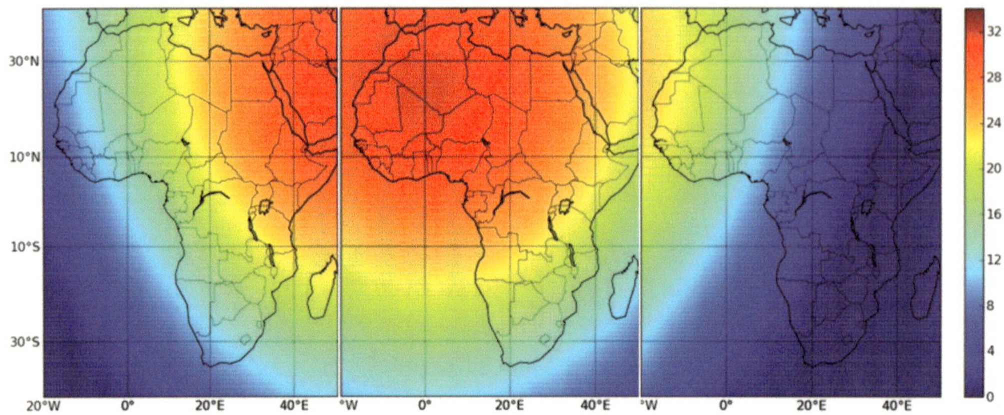

b)

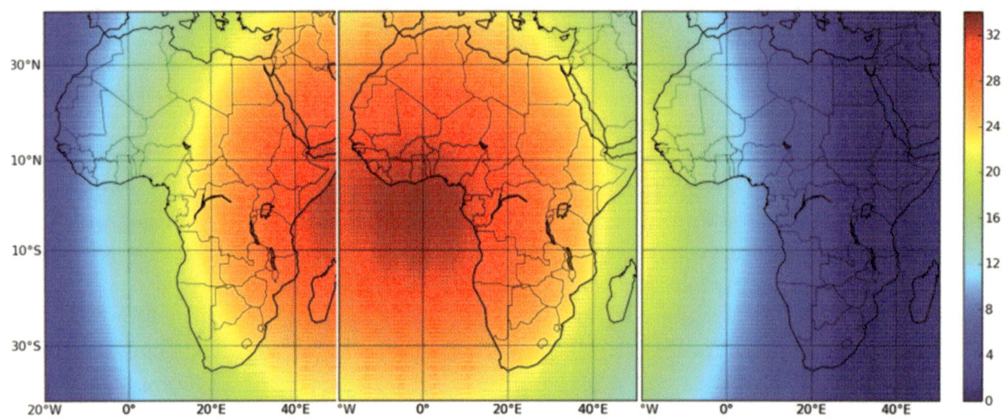

c)

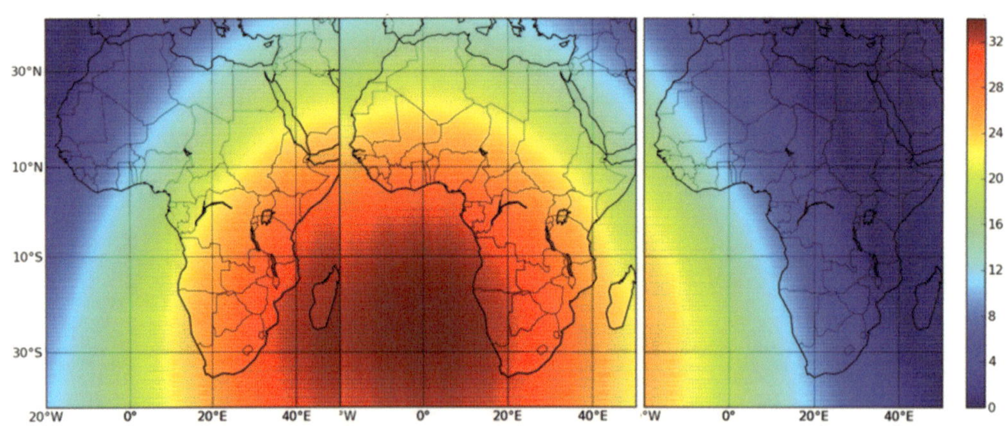

d)

Fig. 19. Seasonal 550nm BOA radiance at 8, 12 and 16h UTC. a) Spring (J=80). b) Summer (J=172). c) Autumn (J=264). d) Winter (J=355). J stands for Julian day.

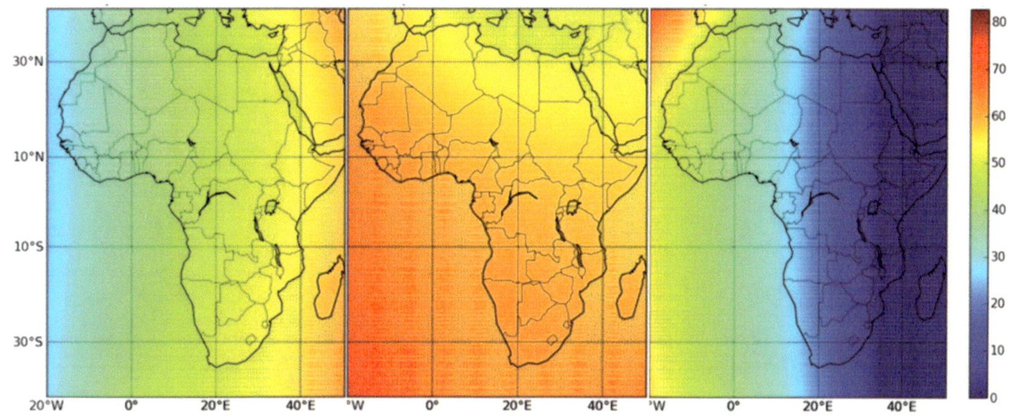
30°N
10°N
10°S
30°S
20°W
0°
20°E
40°E
80
70
60
50
40
30
20
10
0

a)

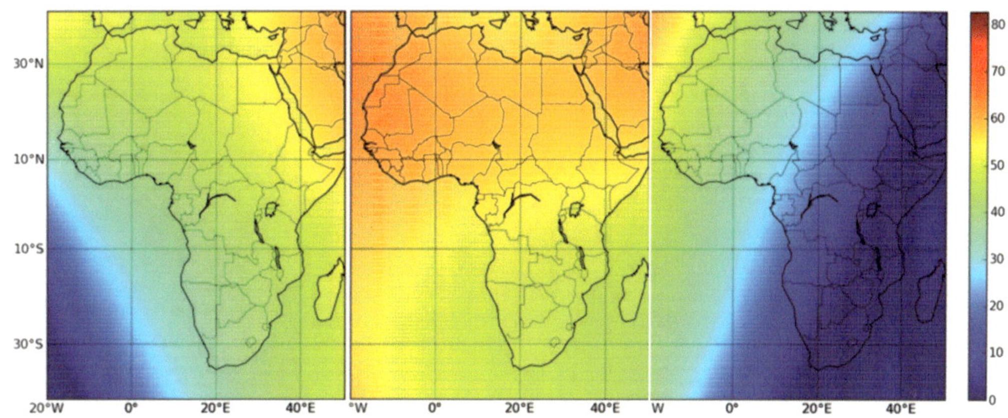
30°N
10°N
10°S
30°S
20°W
0°
20°E
40°E
80
70
60
50
40
30
20
10
0

b)

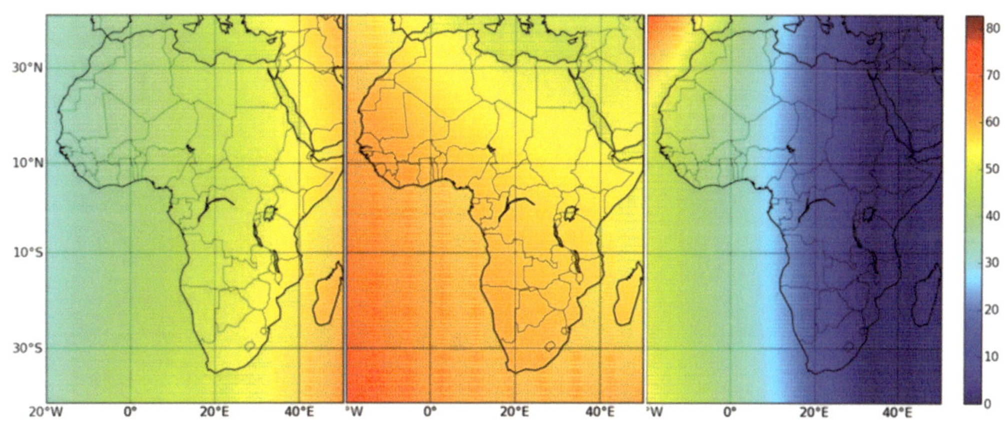
30°N
10°N
10°S
30°S
20°W
0°
20°E
40°E
80
70
60
50
40
30
20
10
0

c)

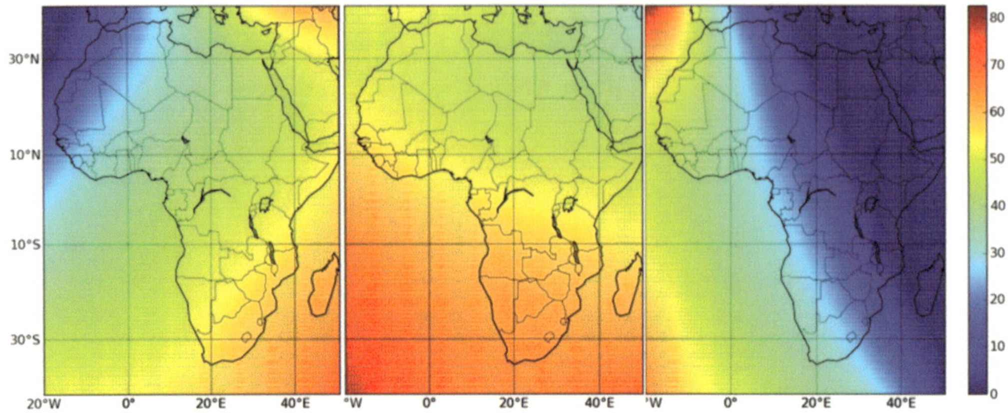

d)

Fig. 20. Seasonal TOA 550nm radiance at 8, 12 and 16h UTC.
a) Spring. b) Summer. c) Autumn. d) Winter.

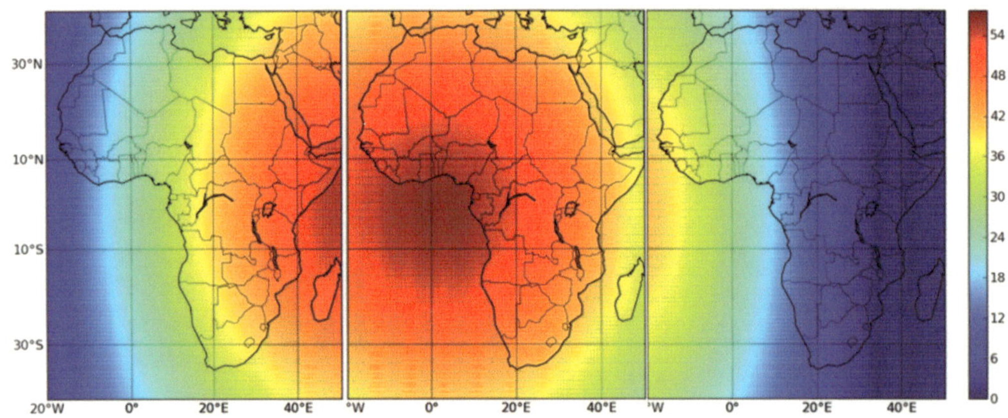

a)

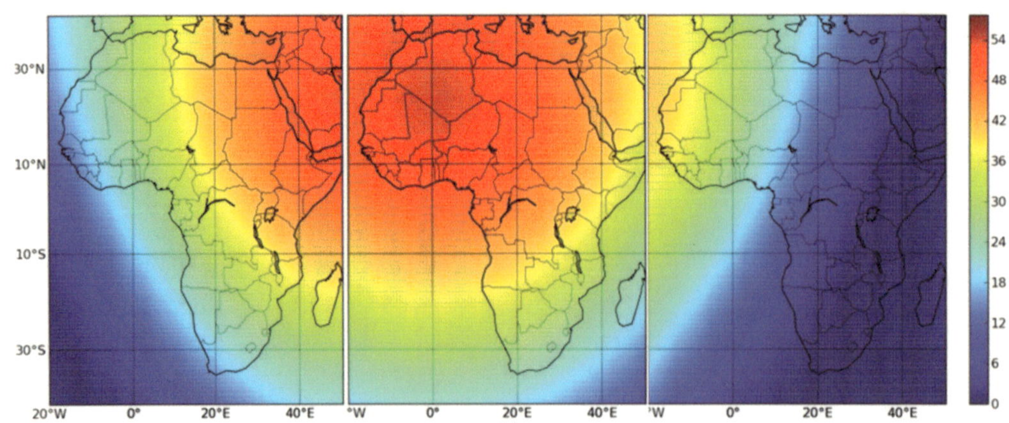

b)

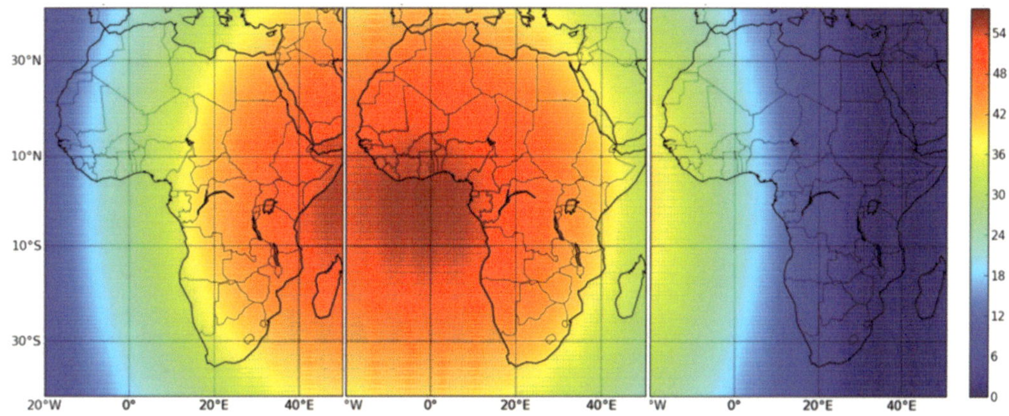

c)

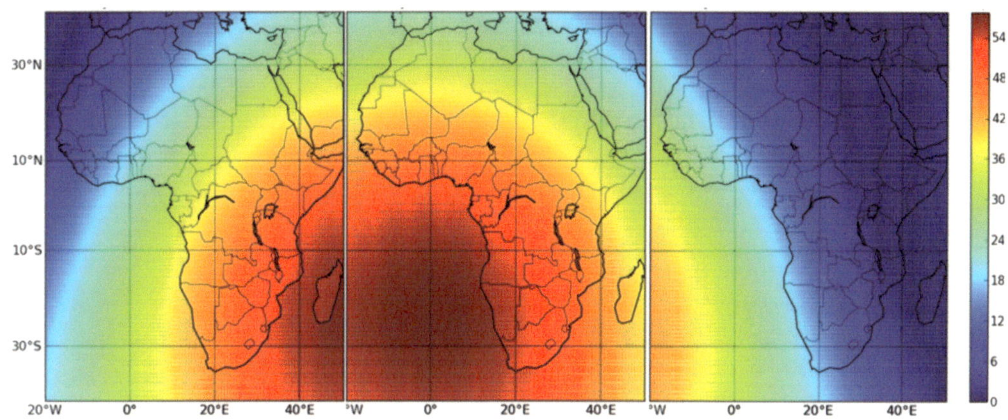

d)

Fig. 21. Seasonal BOA 900nm radiance at 8, 12 and 16h UTC. a) Spring (J=80). b) Summer (J=172). c) Autumn (J=264). d) Winter (J=355). J stands for Julian day.

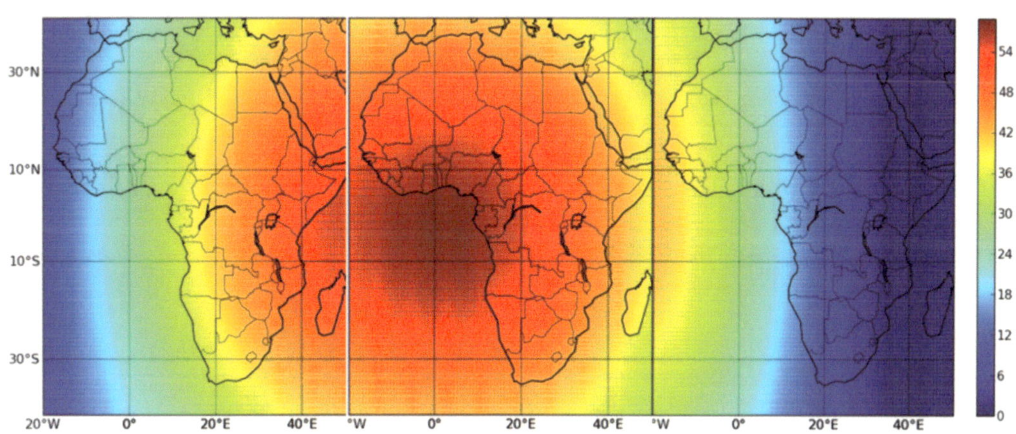

a)

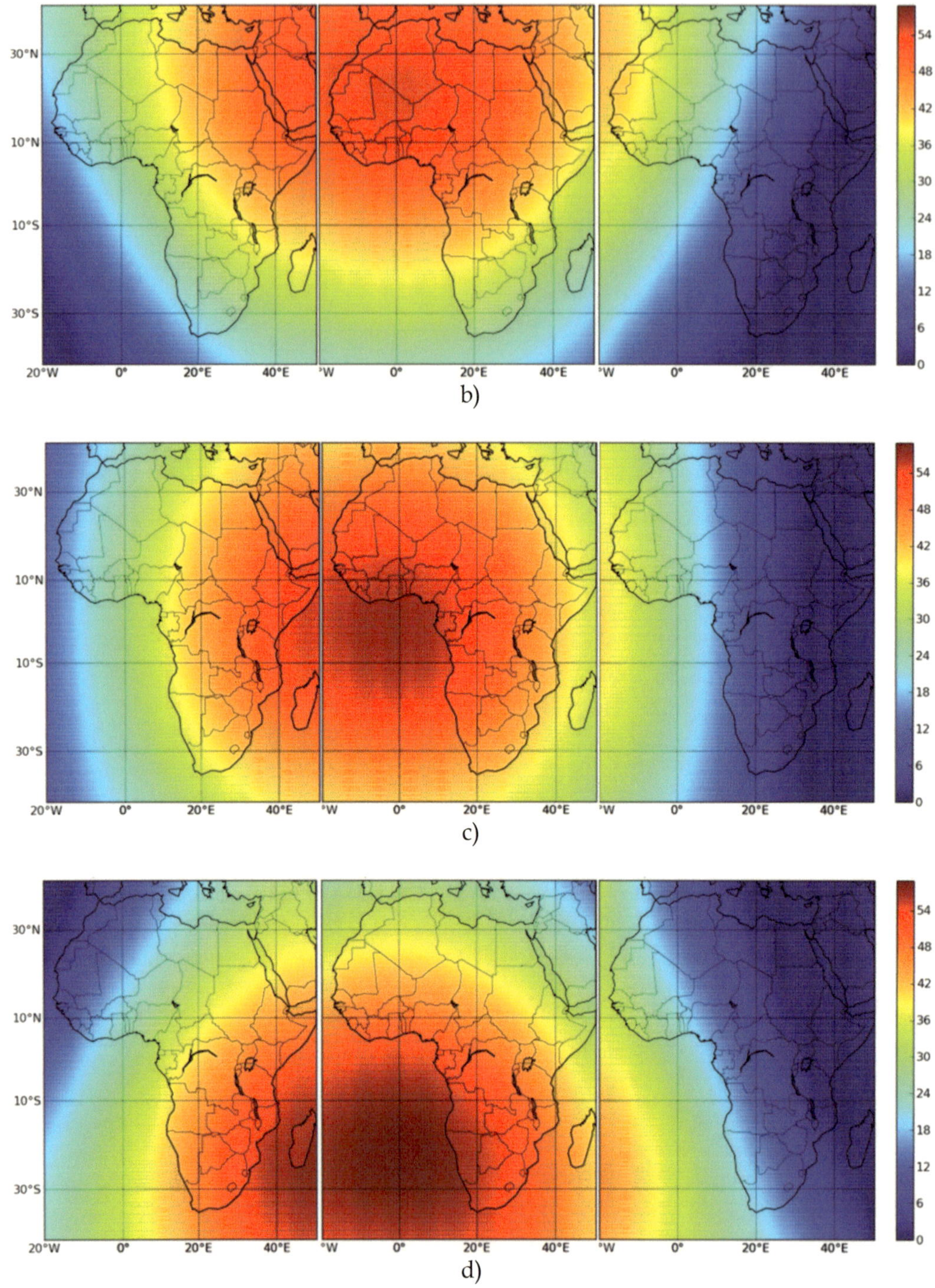

Fig. 22. Seasonal TOA 900nm radiance at 8, 12 and 16h.
a) Spring (J=80). b) Summer (J=172). c) Autumn (J=264). d) Winter (J=355).
J stands for Julian day.

In a 1st step, the tool "Sequencer" created a grid of 20x20 DART simulations at 5 wavelengths (0.4µm, 0.55µm, 0.67µm, 0.9µm, 1.65µm, 11µm), with an automatic computation of the sun and view sensor angles in the local reference system, as a function of the date, time and coordinates. The grid covers almost all of the African continent: "40° S - 44° N" in latitude (step of 4.2°) and "20° W - 54° E" in longitude (step of 3.7°). In a 2nd step, the grid of DART products is interpolated (Python script and Numpy module). Results are displayed with a Python script and the module Basemap.
Logically, TOA radiances differ a lot from BOA radiances, because of the atmosphere. Moreover, one can note:

- BOA radiances are maximal in the East in the morning and West in the evening. During summer, they are larger in the Northern Hemisphere and lower in the Southern hemisphere. The situation is reversed in winter.
- TOA radiances tend to be maximal in the East in the morning and in the West in the evening. This effect is less clear than for BOA radiances. During summer, TOA radiances are larger in the Northern Hemisphere and lower in the southern hemisphere. The situation is reversed in winter.

The impact of atmosphere on TOA radiances depends on its optical thickness and phase function and on the sun and view directions. The analysis of DART images allows one to verify that this impact is not symmetric from the point of view of the satellite sensor.
The Figure 11 and Figure 12 show the maps of luminance to 900nm of the African continent to 4 dates (spring, summer, autumn, winter) and 3:00 (UTC 8h, 12h UTC 16h UTC) defined above. As Figure 9 and Figure 10, this is 100 * 100 maps obtained by interpolation of DART simulations performed for 400 geographical sites, with a Lambertian soil (ρ = 900 0351: "Brown to dark brown gravelly loam" of USDA Soil Conservation service) and an atmosphere "US Standard" with aerosols 23km visibility. Logically, the TOA radiances and reflectances are much less affected by the atmosphere in the near infrared than in the field of green. The spatial variability of radiances is mainly due to the spatial variability of the illumination of the land surface. The geometric configuration "Sun - Earth" plays a much more important role than the geometric configuration "Sensor - Sun-Atmosphere". This is particularly the case of the phase function of gases and aerosols. This explains the much larger symmetry of the near-infrared maps of luminance.
Figure 23 shows the annual evolution of BOA (a) and TOA (b) radiances of 6 cities: Algiers (36.42 ° N, 3.13 ° E, UTC +1), Cairo (30.2 ° N, 31.13 ° E; UTC +2), Dakar (14.4 ° N, 17.25 ° W, UTC), Pretoria (25.45 ° S, 28.11 ° E, UTC +2), Mogadishu (2.02 ° N 45.21 ° E, UTC +3), Luanda (8.50 ° S, 13.14 ° E, UTC +1). The evolution of the radiance $L_{ref}(t)$ at the nadir of the satellite sensor is used as a reference. Any radiance L(t) larger than $L_{ref}(t)$ indicates that the sensor receives light above this reference.
Figure 24 shows the 11µm TOA radiance, and its associated Brightness temperature, of the African continent. It was obtained with a ground surface characterized by an emissivity equal to 1 and a 300K thermodynamic temperature, a US standard atmosphere and an atmosphere water vapor thickness equal to 1.4cm. The simplicity of this configuration explains the spatial symmetry of brightness and temperature. Indeed, one should take into account the actual local emissivity and thermodynamic temperature.

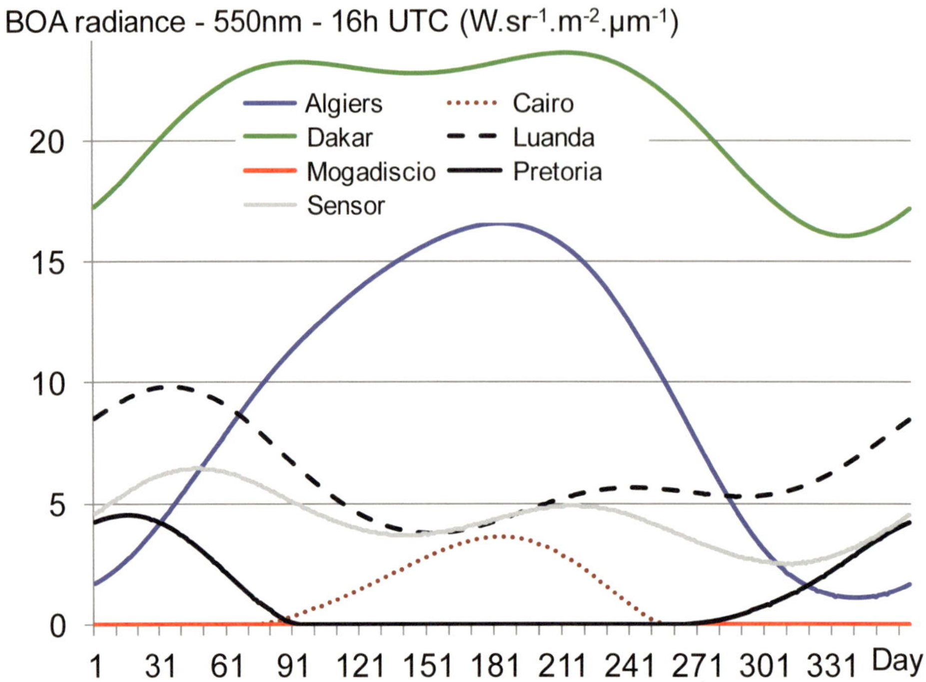

a)

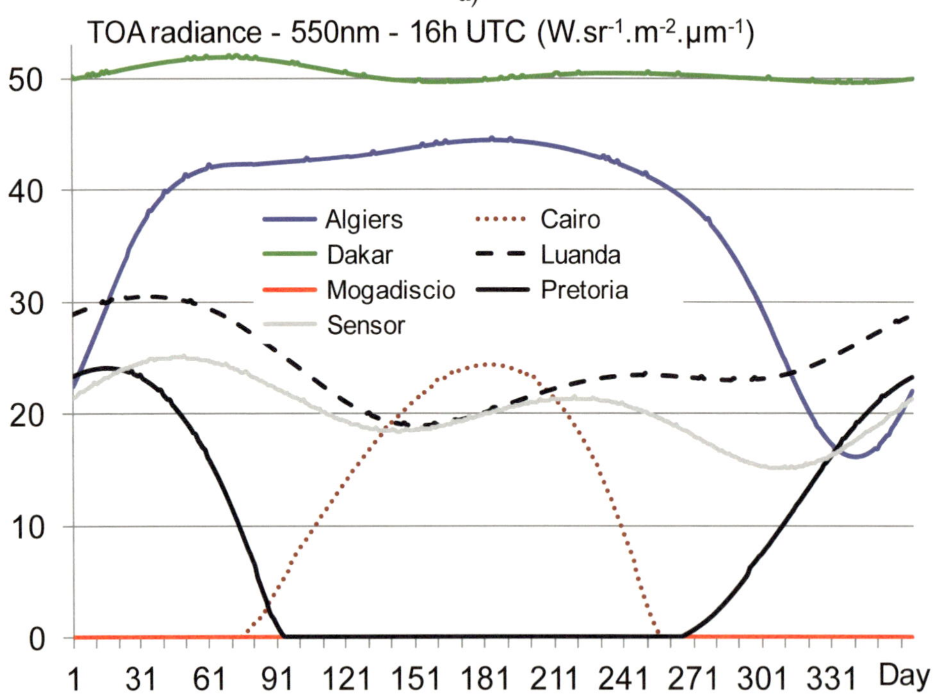

b)

Fig. 23. 550nm BOA (a) and TOA (b) radiance of 7 cities at 16h UTC over 1 year.

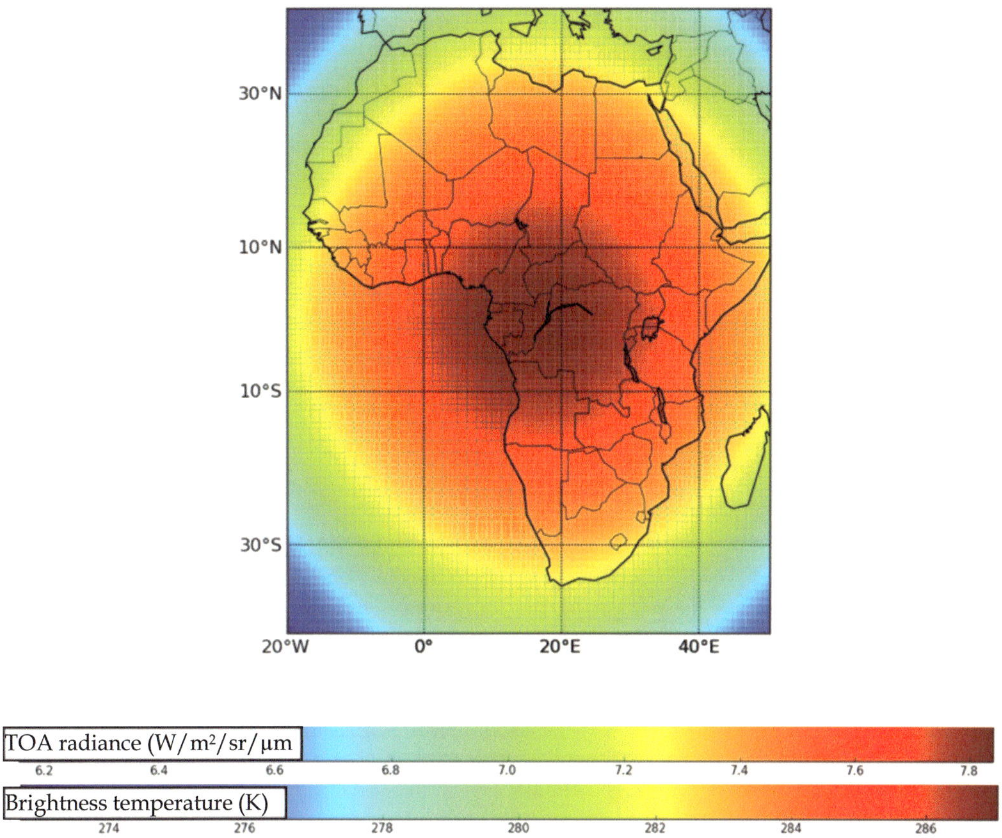

Fig. 24. 11µm TOA radiance (a) and associated brightness temperature (b).

5.2 DARTEB energy budget simulation

Energy budget modeling is essential for many application domains such as the functioning of land surfaces. It is also essential for obtaining realistic simulations of satellite measurements in the thermal infrared. Indeed, it allows one to obtain the 3D distribution of thermodynamic temperature. This explains present efforts for developing a model, called DARTEB (DART Energy Budget), that simulates the 3D radiative budget of urban and vegetation surfaces, possibly with topography and atmosphere. DARTEB uses the 3-D DART radiative budget and it models all physical phenomena, other than radiation, that contribute to the energy budget: heat conduction, turbulent momentum and heat fluxes, water reservoir evolution, vegetation photosynthesis, evapotranspiration. The example shown here is for a urban canopy. In that case, non-radiative mechanisms that contribute to the energy budget are simulated with the equations of the TEB urban surface scheme (Masson, 2000). This scheme works with a canyon geometry. For example, turbulent fluxes and conduction are computed with classical boundary-layer laws using equations of TEB.

Conversely to the TEB scheme, DARTEB uses a 3-D cell discretization, in addition to the layer discretization of roofs, walls and roads: modeling is conducted on a DART cell per cell basis. As a result, fluxes are computed for each point of the 3-D scene. The transfer coefficients for turbulent heat and moisture fluxes are identical; they differ from the transfer coefficients for momentum fluxes. For DARTEB, the urban canopy is simulated as the juxtaposition of urban street canyons. Here, we worked with a single urban canyon, for remaining in the validity domain of TEB equations (Masson, 2000). Each surface type (wall, soil, roof) is discretized into several layers for simulating the conduction fluxes to or from the ground and building interiors. The number of layers for road, wall and roof can differ. A minimal number of three layers is advised because temperature gradients can be large and because of the multi-layer structure of the walls and roofs.

DARTEB uses a prognostic approach for assessing the 3D radiative budget distribution, and consequently the 3D temperature distribution. Temperature values at time "k - 1" are used for computing the 3D TIR and energy budgets at time "k", which allows one to compute the 3D temperature distribution at time "k", using the 3D visible and NIR radiation budget at time "k" (Figure 25). DART simulations in the short wave domain are conducted during the day period only.

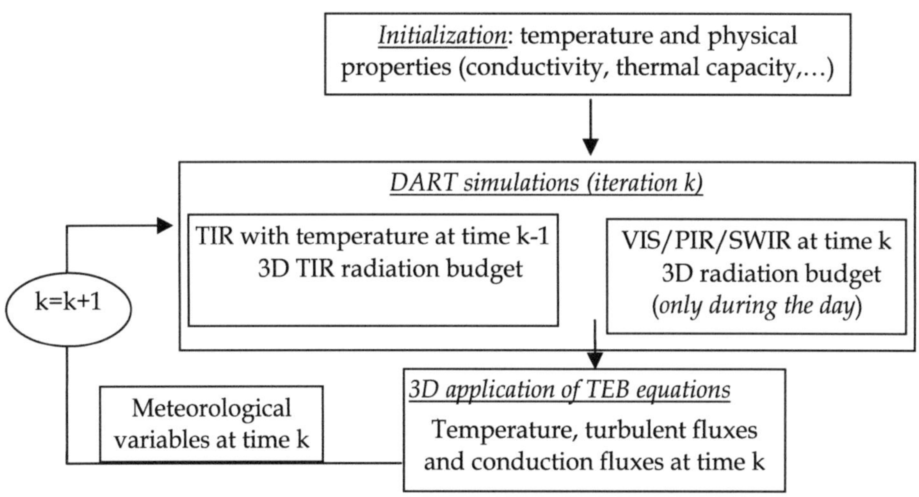

Fig. 25. Diagram of DARTEB model.

The validity of DARTEB was tested against TEB simulations and against in situ temperature measurements during the Capitoul campaign (Albinet, 2008). DARTEB proved to be coherent with TEB and with measurements. Here, this is illustrated by the comparison of simulated and measured temperatures during 3 days, from July 14 to July 17, 2004, for the Alsace Lorraine street (South-North orientation) and La Pomme street (South East - North West orientation) in Toulouse.

The simulated and measured road temperature curves are very similar (Figure 26.a). As expected, road temperature values increase during the day. There are 3 major differences

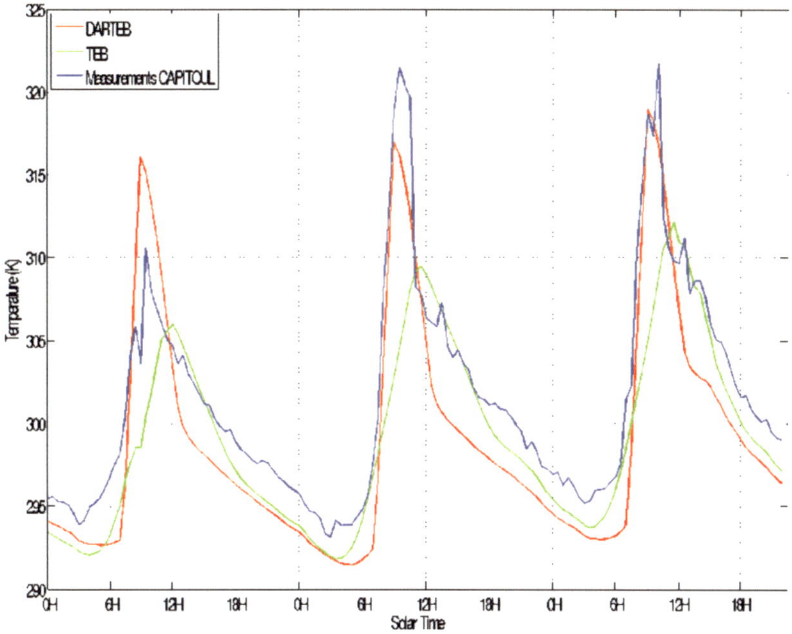

a)

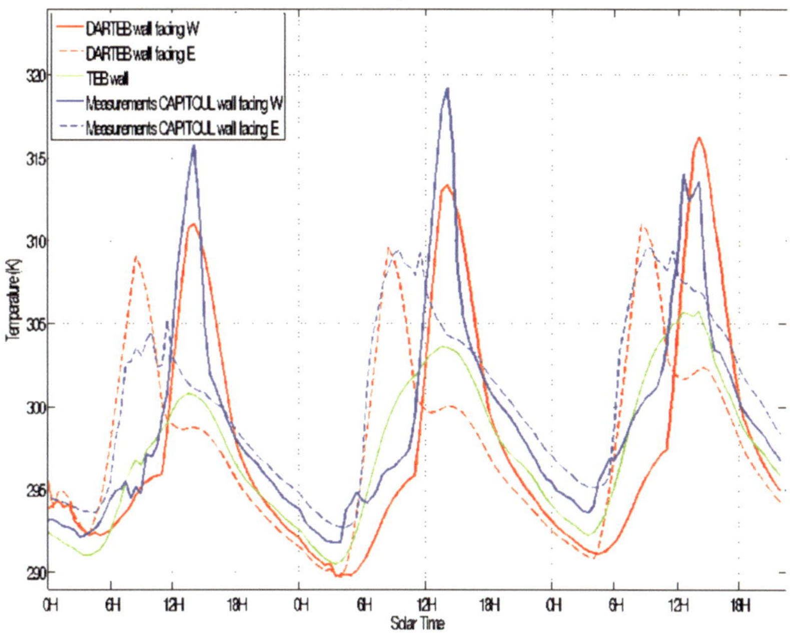

b)

Fig. 26. Comparison of temperature measurements (blue) with DARTEB (red) and TEB (green) simulations. July 14-16 2004. a) Road of La Pomme street (Toulouse) with a south East - North West orientation. b) Walls of Alsace Lorraine street (Toulouse) with a South-North orientation. The 2 walls are facing West and East directions, which implies different thermal behaviors.

between DARTEB and TEB simulations. (1) Maximal DARTEB temperatures are larger than maximal TEB temperatures. (2) Maximal DARTEB temperatures occur before midday conversely to maximal TEB temperatures that occur at midday. (3) DARTEB curves are smoother than TEB curves. These differences are mostly explained by the fact that DARTEB takes into account the 3-D nature of the canyon geometry, conversely to TEB. Indeed, the TEB model works with a mean canyon that corresponds to an azimuthally averaged street direction. Thus, TEB temperatures are mean values, which explains that their time variations are smoothed, with maximal values at midday. Actually, due to the South East - North West orientation of La Pomme street, the maximum road illumination occurs before midday and the maximal road illumination is larger than the mean road illumination for all possible canyon orientations. This is well simulated by DARTEB. Each morning, the measured and DARTEB temperature values display nearly the same sharp increase. However, each afternoon, DARTEB temperature values decrease faster than TEB and the observed temperature values. Several factors can explain the differences between the DARTEB and observed temperature values. For example, an inaccurate road heat capacity implies an inaccurate conduction flux, and an inaccurate road roughness length tends to imply an inaccurate heat flux, which tends to lead to inaccurate road temperature values. Another possible explanation can come from an inaccurate simulation of the proportions of the 2 components of the canyon illumination: sun and sky illumination. Here, these components are driven by the atmosphere optical depth and sun zenith angle. However, in the absence of measurements, the atmosphere optical depth is assumed to be constant.

The wall (Figure 26.b) DARTEB and measured temperature values tend to be very close, both for the wall facing West, and for the wall facing East. They differ from TEB temperature values because TEB gives a mean value for the 2 walls of the canyon. Account of wall orientation is important because walls with different sun illumination have different temperature values, with larger values during daytime for walls with best sun orientation. As expected, DARTEB maximal temperature values occur in the morning for the wall facing East, and in the afternoon for the wall facing West. This is not the case with TEB maximal temperature values; they occur at midday due to the fact that TEB works with azimuthally averaged canyons. This explains also that TEB temperature values are too small. These examples stress the impact of 3-D architecture on temperature distributions.

6. Concluding remarks

Some major and recent improvements of DART radiative transfer model are presented in this paper. After years of development DART has reached the stage of a reference model in the field of remote sensing in the optical domain. It was patented (PCT/FR 02/01181) in 2003. It is used in more than 80 Space Centers, Universities and Research Centers: NASA GSFC (USA), the King's College (UK), Research center of Meteo France, IRD (France), Virginia University (USA), Instituto de Agricultura Sostenible (Spain), etc. Paul Sabatier University (France) provides free licenses for scientific works (www.cesbio.ups-tlse.fr), for windows and Linux systems. Its domains of application are centered on remote sensing applications for land surfaces (forestry, agriculture, urbanism,...), on the preparation of future satellite sensors and on the improvement of the use of already available satellite data. It is also more and more used for radiation budget in urban and natural environments, with the objective to couple it with functioning models. Moreover, DART is also more and more used in the field of education for teaching the physical bases of remote sensing and radiative budget. Generally speaking, the possibility to create very easily urban and natural landscapes is very interesting for scientists who want assess remote sensing measurements in any experimental and instrument conditions.

Today, work continues for improving DART, for both the physics, functionalities and computer science aspects. Present ongoing improvements concern the storing and manipulation of LUTs as actual databases, the inversion of satellite images, the Lidar and the design of a new GUI. Planned improvements concern the modeling of the Earth-Atmosphere system in presence of clouds. DART will not simulate RT within clouds. These will be considered as interfaces with specific optical properties and geometric dimensions. Other major planned improvements will be the simulation of RT adapted to water bodies and to fire.

7. Acknowledgement

This work was supported by Region Midi Pyrénées and by the Centre National d'Etudes Spatiales (CNES) in the frame of the project "High spatial resolution of the land surfaces with a geostationary satellite". Authors are also thankful to the CESBIO (Space Center for Biosphere Studies) research team that contributes to the development of DART.

8. Annex: Computation of view incidence angle

For an Earth target T and a satellite sensor S, DART computes the local incidence angle α, the sensor off-nadir direction β and the sun azimuth angle in the Earth surface reference system as a function of the locations (latitude, longitude, altitude) of T and S, with the assumption that the Earth is an ellipsoid.

Let us note O the Earth center and Oz the "South - North" axis perpendicular to the equatorial plane. The axis Ox is perpendicular to Oz and is in the plane $\{\overrightarrow{OT}, Oz\}$. The plane that contains the target T and the vertical Oz is an ellipse defined by $\frac{x^2}{a^2}+\frac{z^2}{b^2}=1$, with a=6378.136km and b=6356.751km. The earth eccentricity is: $e=\frac{\sqrt{a^2-b^2}}{a}$e. At local latitude Lat, the local Earth radius is: $R(Lat)=\frac{b}{\sqrt{1-e^2.cos^2(Lat)}}$

Any point M on the ellipsoid is characterized by (Lat_m, $Long_m$) or by the angles (γ_m, ϕ_m) in the Earth spherical coordinate system (Figure 26):

Lat ∈ [90°S 90°N] ⇔ $\gamma \in [0\ 180°]$ ($\gamma = 0$ ⇔ Lat = 90°N)

Long ∈ [0 360°] ⇔ $\phi \in [0\ 360°]$

Let R_{target} and R_{sat} be the Earth radius at points t and s that are the vertical projection on the Earth ellipsoid of target T and satellite S respectively. Points t and s are defined by:

- t: Lat_t, $Long_t$. Target T altitude is H_{target} above the Earth surface
- s: Lat_{sat}, $Long_{sat}$. Satellite altitude is H_{sat} above the Earth surface

Zenith angles of vectors $\overrightarrow{OS}$ and $\overrightarrow{OT}$, with s and t the vertical projections of points S and T, are:

$$\gamma_{sat} = \frac{\pi}{2} - Lat_{sat} \text{ and } \gamma_t = \frac{\pi}{2} - Lat_t \quad \text{respectively (in radians)}$$

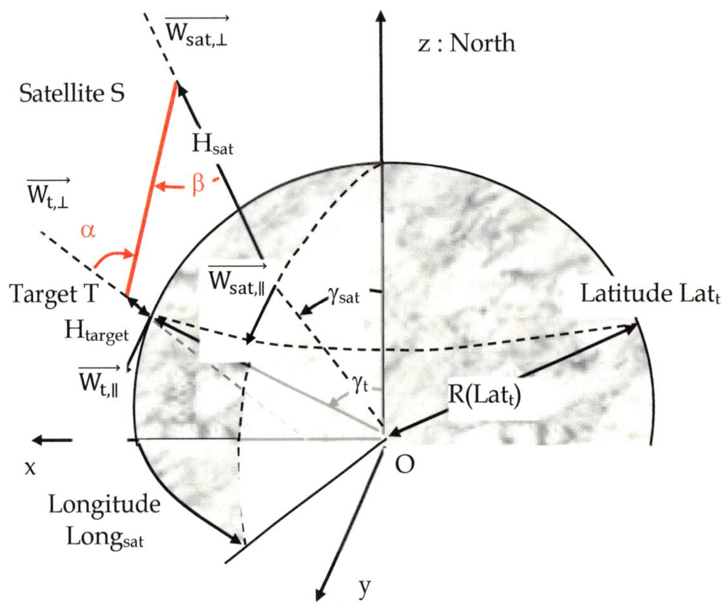

Fig. 27. Geometric configuration "Satellite - Earth scene", for an ellipsoidal Earth.

In the pre-defined Earth system, point t is defined by $\overrightarrow{OT}$ $\{R_t(\gamma_t).\sin(\gamma_t),\ 0,\ R_t(\gamma_t).\cos(\gamma_t)\}$. The unit vector $\overrightarrow{W_{t,\parallel}}$ of the tangent to the ellipse along the axis Ox at point t is defined by:

- $z_t \neq 0$: $\overrightarrow{W_{t,\parallel}}\left\{1,0,-\frac{b^2}{a^2}\frac{x_t}{z_t}\right\}.\frac{1}{\sqrt{1+\left[\frac{b^2 x_t}{a^2 z_t}\right]^2}}$ We note that $\overrightarrow{W_{t,\parallel}}$ $\{0, 0, 1\}$ if x_t=0 (i.e., z_t = b)
- z_t =0 (i.e., x_t = a): $\overrightarrow{W_{t,\parallel}}\{1, 0, 0\}$

The unit vector $\overrightarrow{W_{t,\perp}}$ perpendicular to the ellipse at point t is: $\overrightarrow{W_{t,\perp}}\left\{1,0,-\frac{a^2}{b^2}\frac{z_t}{x_t}\right\}.\frac{1}{\sqrt{1+\left[\frac{a^2 z_t}{b^2 x_t}\right]^2}}$

Let γ_t^* be the zenith angle of $\overrightarrow{W_{t,\perp}}$ in the Earth system. It allows one to compute $\overrightarrow{OT}$:
$\overrightarrow{OT} = \overrightarrow{Ot} + \{h_t.\sin(\gamma_t^*), 0, H_t.\cos(\gamma_t^*)\}$ with $\cos(\gamma_t^*) = \overrightarrow{W_{t,\perp}}.\overrightarrow{W_z}$ and $\gamma_t^* \in [0\ \ \pi]$
Similarly, for point s, we have: $\overrightarrow{Os}$ $\{R_{sat}.\sin(\gamma_{sat}).\cos(Long_{sat} - Long_t),\ R_{sat}.\sin(\gamma_{sat}).\sin(Long_{sat} - Long_t),\ R_{sat}.\cos(\gamma_{sat})\}$

Let $\overrightarrow{W_{sat,\perp}}$ be the perpendicular to the ellipse at point s in the Earth system. In the local reference:

$$(Z - Z_{sat}) = \frac{a^2.z_{sat}}{b^2.X_{sat}}(X - X_{sat}) \Rightarrow \overrightarrow{W_{sat,\perp}}\left\{1,0,-\frac{a^2}{b^2}\frac{z_{sat}}{X_{sat}}\right\}.\frac{1}{\sqrt{1+\left[\frac{a^2.z_{sat}}{b^2.X_{sat}}\right]^2}} \text{ if } X_{sat} \neq 0.$$

with $X_{sat}^2 = x_{sat}^2 + y_{sat}^2 = R^2(Lat_{sat}).\sin^2(\gamma_{sat})$, $x_{sat} = R(Lat_{sat}).\sin(\gamma_{sat}).\cos(Long_{sat} - Long_t)$ and $y_{sat} = R(Lat_{sat}).\sin(\gamma_{sat}).\sin(Long_{sat} - Long_t)$

Thus, we have: $\overrightarrow{W_{sat,\perp}}\left\{cos(Long_{sat} - Long_t), sin(Long_{sat} - Long_t), \frac{a^2}{b^2}\frac{z_{sat}}{X_{sat}}\right\}.\frac{1}{\sqrt{1+\left[\frac{a^2.z_{sat}}{b^2.X_{sat}}\right]^2}}$

It implies: $-\overrightarrow{OS} = \overrightarrow{Os} + \{H_{sat}.sin(\gamma_{sat}^*).cos(Long_{sat} - Long_t), H_{sat}.sin(\gamma_{sat}^*).sin(Long_{sat} - Long_t), H_{sat}.cos(\gamma_{sat}^*)\}$

This allows one to compute the incidence angle α, the sensor off-nadir angle β and the satellite azimuth ϕ_{sat} in the local system:

$$cos(\alpha) = \frac{\overrightarrow{TS}.\overrightarrow{W_{t,\perp}}}{||\overrightarrow{TS}||.||\overrightarrow{W_{t,\perp}}||} \Rightarrow \alpha = acos(\frac{\overrightarrow{TS}.\overrightarrow{W_{t,\perp}}}{||\overrightarrow{TS}||.||\overrightarrow{W_{t,\perp}}||}) \text{ with } \alpha \in [0 \ \ 90°] \text{ and } \overrightarrow{TS} = \overrightarrow{OS} - \overrightarrow{OT}$$

$$cos(\beta) = \frac{\overrightarrow{TS}.\overrightarrow{W_{sat,\perp}}}{||\overrightarrow{TS}||.||\overrightarrow{W_{sat,\perp}}||} \Rightarrow \beta = acos(\frac{\overrightarrow{TS}.\overrightarrow{W_{sat,\perp}}}{||\overrightarrow{TS}||.||\overrightarrow{W_{sat,\perp}}||}) \text{ with } \beta \in [0 \ \ 90°]$$

$\overrightarrow{W_{t,\perp}}.\frac{\overrightarrow{TS}}{||\overrightarrow{TS}||} = -\sin(\alpha).\cos(\varphi_{sat}) \Rightarrow \varphi_{sat} = acos(-\overrightarrow{W_{t,\perp}}.\frac{\overrightarrow{TS}}{||\overrightarrow{TS}||}.\frac{1}{\sin(\alpha)})$ with $\varphi_{sat} = 2\pi - \varphi_{sat}$ if $Long_t < Long_{sat}$

8. References

Albinet C. (2008). Modélisation 3D des flux et du bilan d'énergie des zones urbaines Modélisation des échanges d'énergie des milieux urbains. M2 report. Paul Sabatier University, Toulouse, France. 57p.

Barbier, N.; Couteron, P.; Proisy, C.; Yadvinder, M. & Gastellu-Etchegorry, J-P. (2010). The variation of apparent crown size and canopy heterogeneity across lowland Amazonian forests. Global Ecology and Biogeography, DOI: 10.1111/j.1466-8238.2009.00493.

Barbier, N.; Couteron, P.; Gastellu-Etchegorry J.P. & Proisy, C. (2011), Linking canopy images to forest structural parameters: potential of a modeling framework, Annals of Forest Science, DOI 10.1007/s13595-011-0116-9

Berk, A.; Bernstein, L.S. & Robertson, D.C. (1989). MODTRAN: A Moderate Resolution Model for LOWTRAN 7, GL-TR-89-0122, Geophys. Lab., Bedford, MA, USA 38pp.

Gascon, F. (2001). Modélisation Physique d'Images de Télédétection Optique. PhD Thesis. Université Paul Sabatier, Toulouse, France.

Gastellu-Etchegorry, J.P.; Demarez, V.; Pinel V. & Zagolski F. (1996). Modeling radiative transfer in heterogeneous 3-D vegetation canopies, Remote Sensing of Environment, 58: 131-156.

Gastellu-Etchegorry, J.P.; Guillevic, P.; Zagolski, F.; Demarez, V.; Trichon, V.; Deering, D. & Leroy, M. (1999). Modeling BRF and radiation regime of tropical and boreal forests - BRF. Remote Sensing of Environment, 68: 281-316.

Gastellu-Etchegorry, J.P.; Martin, E. & Gascon, F. (2004), DART: a 3-D model for simulating satellite images and surface radiation budget, 2004, International Journal of Remote Sensing, 25 (1): 75-96.

Gastellu-Etchegorry, J.P. (2008). 3D modeling of satellite spectral images - Radiation budget and energy budget of urban landscapes, Meteorology and Atmosphere Physics, Vol. 102, N 3-4, pp187-207

Gastellu-Etchegorry, J.P.; Grau, E.; Rubio, J.; Ueberschlag, A.; Sun, G.; Brut, A.; Cros, J. & Lauret, N. (2010). 3-D Monte Carlo radiative transfer with DART model - An application to Lidar modeling. Third International Symposium Recent Advances in Quantitative Remote Sensing, 27 September to 1 October 2010. Torrent-Valencia, Spain.

Govaerts, Y. & Verstraete, M.M. (1998). Raytran: A Monte Carlo ray tracing model to compute light scattering in three-dimensional heterogeneous media. IEEE Transactions on Geoscience and Remote Sensing, 36, 493-505.

Grau, E. (2011). Modélisation 3D optique d'images de télédétection et du bilan radiation des paysages terrestres. PhD thesis. Paul Sabatier University.

Guillevic, P. & Gastellu-Etchegorry, J.P. (1999). Modeling BRF and radiation regime of tropical and boreal forests - PAR regime. Remote Sensing of Environment, 68: 317-340.

Jacquemoud, S. & Baret, F. (1990). PROSPECT: a model of leaf optical properties spectra, Remote Sensing of Environment, 34(2):75-91.

Kimes, D.S. & Sellers, P.J. (1985). Inferring hemispherical reflectance of the Earth's surface for global energy budgets from remotely sensed nadir or directional radiance values. Remote Sensing of Environment, 18: 205-223.

Malenovský, Z.; Martin, E.; Homolová, L.; Gastellu-Etchegorry, J.-P.; Zurita-Milla, R.; Schaepman, M.E.; Pokorný, R.; Clevers, J.G.P.W. & Cudlín, P. (2008). Influence of woody elements of a Norway spruce canopy on nadir reflectance simulated by the DART model at very high spatial resolution. Remote Sensing of Environment. 112:1-18.

Malenovský, Z.; Ufer, C.; Lhotakova, Z.; Clevers, J.G.P.W.; Schaepman, M.E.; Albrechtova, J. & Cudlin, P. (2006). A new hyperspectral index for chlorophyll estimation of a forest canopy: Area under curve normalised to maximal band depth between 650-725 nm, EARSeL eProceedings 5 (2). p. 161 - 172.

Malenovský, Z.; Martin, E.; Homolova, L.; Pokorny, R.; Schaepman, M.E.; Gastellu-Etchegorry, J.-P.; Zurita Milla, R.; Clevers, J.G.P.W. & Cudlin, P. (2005). Influence of forest canopy structure simulated using the Discrete Anisotropic Radiative Transfer (DART) model on the retrieval of spruce stand LAI. In: 9th International Symposium on Physical Measurements and Signatures in Remote Sensing (ISPMSRS), Beijing, 17-19 October 2005. Beijing: ISPRS WG VII/1, p. 3.

Martin, E. (2006). DART: Modèle 3D Multispectral et Inversion d'Images Optiques de Satellite - Application aux couverts forestiers. PhD thesis. Paul Sabatier University.

Masson, V. (2000). A physically-based scheme for the urban energy budget in atmospheric models, Boundary-layer Meteorology, 94:357-397.

Masson, V.; Gomes, L.; Pigeon, G.; Liousse, C.; Pont, V.; Lagouarde, J.-P.; Voogt, J. A.; Salmond, J.; Oke, T. R.; Legain, D.; Garrouste, O.; Lac, C.; Connan, O.; Briottet, X. & Lachérade, S. (2007). The Canopy and Aerosol Particles Interaction in Toulouse Urban Layer (CAPITOUL) experiment. Meteorology and Atmospheric Physics. , Vol. 102, N 3-4, pp137-157

North, P.R.J. (1996). Three-dimensional forest light interaction model using a Monte Carlo method, IEEE Transactions on Geoscience and Remote Sensing, 34, 946-956.

Pinel, V. & Gastellu-Etchegorry, J.P. (1998). Sensitivity of Texture of High Resolution Images of Forest to Biophysical and Acquisition Parameters. Remote Sensing of Environment. 65: 61-85.

Pinty, B.; Gobron, N.; Widlowski, J.L.; Gerstl, S.A.W.; Vertraete, M.M.; Antunes, M.; Bacour, C.; Gascon, F.; Gastellu-Etchegorry, J.P.; Jacquemoud, S.; North, P.; Qin, W. & Thompson, R. (2001). Radiation transfer model intercomparaison (RAMI) exercise, Journal of Geophysical Research, 106, D11, 11937-11956.

Pinty, B.; Widlowski, J-L.; Taberner, M.; Gobron, N.; Verstraete, M. M.; Disney, M.; Gascon, F.; Gastellu-Etchegorry, J.-P.; Jiang, L.; Kuusk, A.; Lewis, P.; Li, X.; Ni-Meister, W.; Nilson, T.; North, P.; Qin, W.; Su, L.; Tang, S.; Thompson, R.; Verhoef, W.; Wang, H.; Wang, J.; Yan, G. & H. Zang (2004). RAdiation transfer Model Intercomparison (RAMI) exercise: Results from the second phase, Journal of Geophysical Research, 109, D06210 10.1029/2003JD004252.

Soux, C.A.; Voogt, J.A. & Oke, T.R. (2004). A model to calculate what a remote sensor 'sees' of an urban surface, Boundary Layer Meteorology, 111:109-132.

Thompson, R.L. & Goel, N.S. (1998). Two models for rapidly calculating bidirectional reflectance: Photon spread (ps) model and statistical photon spread (sps) model. Remote Sensing Reviews, 16, 157-207.

Ueberschlag, A. (2010). Etude des couverts forestiers par inversion de formes d'onde Lidar à l'aide du modèle de transfert radiatif DART, XYZ, 126: 22-26.

Voogt, J.A. & Oke, T.R. (1998). Effects of urban surface geometry on remotely sensed surface temperature, Int. J. Remote Sensing, 19: 895-920.

Voogt, J.A. & Oke, T.R. (2003). Thermal remote sensing of urban climates, Remote Sensing of Environment, 86:370-384.

Widlowski, J.L.; Taberner, M.; Pinty, B.; Bruniquel-Pinel, V.; Disney, M.; Fernandes, R.; Gastellu-Etchegorry, J-P.; Gobron, N.; Kuusk, A.; Lavergne, T.; Leblanc, S.; Lewis, P. E.; Martin, E.; Mottus, M.; North, P. R. J.; Qin, W.; Robustelli, M.; Rochdi, N.; Ruiloba, R.; Soler, C.; Thompson, R.; Verhoef, W.; Verstraete, M.M. & Xie, D. (2007). The third RAdiation transfer Model Intercomparison (RAMI) exercise: Documenting progress in canopy refectance models, J. Geophysical Research, 112, D09111, doi: 10.1029/2006JD007821

Widlowski, J-L; Robustelli, M.; Disney, M.; Gastellu-Etchegorry, J.-P.; Lavergne, T.; Lewis, P.; North, P.R.J.; Pinty, B.; Thompson, R. & Verstraete, M.M. (2008). The RAMI On-line Model Checker (ROMC): A web-based benchmarking facility for canopy reflectance models, Remote Sensing of Environment, 112:1144-1150.

3

3D Modelling from Real Data

Gabriele Guidi[1] and Fabio Remondino[2]
[1]*Politecnico di Milano*
[2]*Fondazione Bruno Kessler, Trento*
Italy

1. Introduction

The genesis of a 3D model has basically two definitely different paths. Firstly we can consider the CAD generated models, where the shape is defined according to a user drawing action, operating with different mathematical "bricks" like B-Splines, NURBS or subdivision surfaces (mathematical CAD modelling), or directly drawing small polygonal planar facets in space, approximating with them complex free form shapes (polygonal CAD modelling). This approach can be used for both ideal elements (a project, a fantasy shape in the mind of a designer, a 3D cartoon, etc.) or for real objects. In the latter case the object has to be first surveyed in order to generate a drawing coherent with the real stuff.

If the surveying process is not only a rough acquisition of simple distances with a substantial amount of manual drawing, a scene can be modelled in 3D by capturing with a digital instrument many points of its geometrical features and connecting them by polygons to produce a 3D result similar to a polygonal CAD model, with the difference that the shape generated is in this case an accurate 3D acquisition of a real object (reality-based polygonal modelling).

Considering only device operating on the ground, 3D capturing techniques for the generation of reality-based 3D models may span from passive sensors and image data (Remondino and El-Hakim, 2006), optical active sensors and range data (Blais, 2004; Shan & Toth, 2008; Vosselman and Maas, 2010), classical surveying (e.g. total stations or Global Navigation Satellite System - GNSS), 2D maps (Yin et al., 2009) or an integration of the aforementioned methods (Stumpfel et al., 2003; Guidi et al., 2003; Beraldin, 2004; Stamos et al., 2008; Guidi et al., 2009a; Remondino et al., 2009; Callieri et al., 2011). The choice depends on the required resolution and accuracy, object dimensions, location constraints, instrument's portability and usability, surface characteristics, working team experience, project's budget, final goal, etc.

Although aware of the potentialities of the image-based approach and its recent developments in automated and dense image matching for non-expert the easy usability and reliability of optical active sensors in acquiring 3D data is generally a good motivation to decline image-based approaches. Moreover the great advantage of active sensors is the fact that they deliver immediately dense and detailed 3D point clouds, whose coordinate are metrically defined. On the other hand image data require some processing and a mathematical formulation to transform the two-dimensional image measurements into metric three-dimensional coordinates. Image-based modelling techniques (mainly

photogrammetry and computer vision) are generally preferred in cases of monuments or architectures with regular geometric shapes, low budget projects, good experience of the working team, time or location constraints for the data acquisition and processing.
This chapter is intended as an updated review of reality-based 3D modelling in terrestrial applications, with the different categories of 3D sensing devices and the related data processing pipelines.

2. Passive and active 3D sensing technologies

In the following sections the two most used 3D capturing techniques, i.e. photogrammetry (section 2.1) and active range sensing (section 2.2 and 2.3) are reported and discussed.

2.1 Passive sensors for image-based 3D modelling techniques

Passive sensors like digital cameras deliver 2D image data which need to be transformed into 3D information. Normally at least two images are required and 3D data can be derived using perspective or projective geometry formulations (Gruen & Huang, 2001; Sturm et al., 2011). Images can be acquired using terrestrial, aerial or satellite sensors according to the applications and needed scale. Terrestrial digital cameras come in many different forms and format: single CCD/CMOS sensor, frame, linear, multiple heads, SLR-type, industrial, off-the-shelf, high-speed, panoramic head, still-video, etc. (Mass, 2008). Common terrestrial cameras have at least 10–12 Megapixels at very low price while high-end digital back cameras feature more than 40 Megapixel sensors. Mobile phone cameras have up to 5 Megapixels and they could be even used for photogrammetric purposes (Akca & Gruen, 2009). Panoramic linear array cameras are able to deliver very high resolution images with great metric performances (Luhmann & Tecklenburg, 2004; Parian & Gruen, 2004). The high cost of these sensors is limiting their market and thus panoramic images are also generated stitching together a set of partly overlapped images acquired from a unique point of view with a consumer or SLR digital camera rotated around its perspective centre. This easy and low-cost solution allows to acquire almost Gigapixel images with great potential not only for visual needs (e.g., Google Street View, 1001 Wonders, etc.), but also for metric applications and 3D modelling purposes (Fangi, 2007; Barazzetti et al., 2010).
An interesting and emerging platform for image acquisition and terrestrial 3D modelling applications is constituted by Unmanned Aerial Vehicles (UAVs). UAVs can fly in an autonomous mode, using integrated GNSS with Inertial Navigation Systems (INS), stabilizer platform and digital cameras (or even a small range sensor) and can be used to get data from otherwise hardly accessible areas (Eisenbeiss, 2009).

2.1.1 Photogrammetry

Photogrammetry (Mikhail et al., 2001; Luhmann et al., 2007) is the most well-known and important image-based technique which allows the derivation of accurate, metric and semantic information from photographs (images). Photogrammetry thus turns 2D image data into 3D data (like digital models) rigorously establishing the geometric relationship between the acquired images and the scene as surveyed at the time of the imaging event. Photogrammetry can be done using underwater, terrestrial, aerial or satellite imaging sensors. Generally the term Remote Sensing is more associated to satellite imagery and their use for land classification and analysis or changes detection (i.e. no geometric processing).

The photogrammetric method generally employs minimum two images of the same static scene or object acquired from different points of view. Similar to human vision, if an object is seen in at least two images, the different relative positions of the object in the images (the so-called parallaxes) allow a stereoscopic view and the derivation of 3D information of the scene seen in the overlapping area of the images.

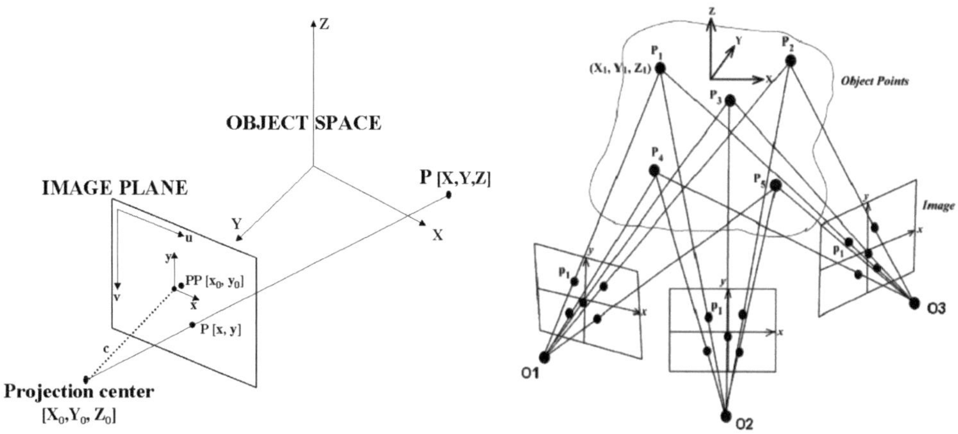

Fig. 1. The collinearity principle established between the camera projection center, a point in the image and the corresponding point in the object space (left). The multi-image concept, where the 3D object can be reconstructed using multiple collinearity rays between corresponding image points (right).

Photogrammetry is used in many fields, from the traditional mapping, monitoring and 3D city modelling to the video games industry, from industrial inspections to the movie production, from heritage documentation to medical field. Photogrammetry was always considered a manual and time consuming procedure but in the last decade many developments lead to a great improvement of the technique and nowadays many semi- or fully-automated procedures are available. When the project's goal is the recovery of a complete, detailed, precise and reliable 3D model, some user interaction in the modelling pipeline is still mandatory, in particular for geo-referencing and quality analysis. Thus photogrammetry does not aim at the full automation of the image processing but it has always as first goal the recovery of metric and accurate results. On the other hand, for applications needing 3D models for simple visualization or Virtual Reality (VR) uses, fully automated 3D modelling procedures can also be adopted (Vergauwen & Van Gool, 2006; Snavely et al., 2008).

The advantages of photogrammetry stay in the fact that (i) images contain all the information required for 3D modelling and accurate documentation (geometry and texture); (ii) photogrammetric instruments (cameras and software) are generally cheap, very portable, easy to use and with very high accuracy potentials; (iii) an object can be reconstructed even if it has disappeared or considerably changed using archived images (Gruen et al., 2004). But a large experience is required to derive accurate and detailed 3D models from images. This has limited a lot the use of photogrammetry in favour of the more powerful active 3D sensors, which allow easily the derivation of dense and detailed 3D point clouds with no user processing.

2.1.2 Basic principles of the photogrammetric technique

The basic principle of the photogrammetric processing is the use of multiple images (at least two) and the collinearity principle (Fig. 1). Such principle establishes the relationship between image and object space defining a straight line between the camera perspective center, the image point P(x, y) and the object point P(X, Y, Z). The collinearity model is formulated as:

$$x = -f\frac{r_{11}(X - X_0) + r_{21}(Y - Y_0) + r_{31}(Z - Z_0)}{r_{13}(X - X_0) + r_{23}(Y - Y_0) + r_{33}(Z - Z_0)} + x_0$$

$$y = -f\frac{r_{12}(X - X_0) + r_{22}(Y - Y_0) + r_{32}(Z - Z_0)}{r_{13}(X - X_0) + r_{23}(Y - Y_0) + r_{33}(Z - Z_0)} + y_0 \quad (1)$$

with:

f	… camera constant or focal length	} interior orientation parameters
x_0, y_0	… principal point	
X_0, Y_0, Z_0	… position of the perspective center	} exterior orientation parameters
r_{11}, r_{12}, … r_{33}	… elements of the rotation matrix	
x, y	… 2D image coordinates	
X, Y, Z	… 3D object coordinates	

All measurements performed on digital images refer to a pixel coordinate system while collinearity equations refer to the metric image coordinate system. The conversion from pixel to image coordinates is performed with an affine transformation knowing the sensor dimensions and pixel size.

For each image point measured in at least two images (generally called tie points), a collinearity equation is written. All the equations form a system of equations and the solution is generally obtained with an iterative least squares method (Gauss-Markov model), thus requiring some good initial approximations of the unknown parameters. The method, called *bundle adjustment*, provides a simultaneous determination of all system parameters along with estimates of the precision and reliability of the unknowns. If the interior orientation parameters are also unknowns, the method is named *self-calibrating bundle adjustment*.

The system of equations is iteratively solved with the least squares method and after the linearization and the introduction of an error vector *e*, it can be expressed as:

$$-e = A \cdot x \cdot l \quad (2)$$

with:

e = error vector;

A = design matrix n x m (numb_observations x numb_unknonws, n>m) with the coefficients of the linearized collinearity equations;

x = unknowns vector (exterior parameters, 3D object coordinates, eventually interior parameters);

l = observation vector;
Generally a weight matrix P is added in order to weight the observations and unknown parameters during the estimation procedure. The estimation of x and the variance factor s is usually (not exclusively) attempted as unbiased, minimum variance estimation, performed by means of least squares and results in:

$$\hat{x} = (A^T PA)^{-1} \cdot A^T Pl \tag{3}$$

with the residual v and the standard deviation a posteriori (s_0) as:

$$v = A \cdot \hat{x} - l \tag{4}$$

$$\sigma_0 = \sqrt{\frac{v^T Pv}{r}} \tag{5}$$

with r the redundancy of the system (numb_observations - numb_unknonws).
The precision of the parameter vector x is controlled by its covariance matrix $C_{xx} = \sigma_0^2 (A^T PA)^{-1}$.
For ($A^T PA$) to be uniquely invertible, as required in (Eq. 3), the network needs to fix an external "datum" i.e. the seven parameters of a spatial similarity transformation between image and object space. This is usually achieved by introducing some ground control points with at least seven fixed coordinate values. Another possibility is to solve the system (Eq. 2) in a free-network mode providing at least a known object's distance to retrieve the correct scale.
Depending on the parameters which are considered either known or treated as unknowns, the collinearity equations may result in different procedures (Table 1).
As previously mentioned, the photogrammetric reconstruction method relies on a minimum of two images of the same object acquired from different viewpoints. Defining B the baseline between two images and D the average camera-to-object distance, a reasonable B/D (base-to-depth) ratio between the images should ensure a strong geometric configuration and reconstruction that is less sensitive to noise and measurement errors.
A typical value of the B/D ratio in terrestrial photogrammetry should be around than 0.5, even if in practical situations it is often very difficult to fulfil this requirement. Generally, the larger the baseline, the better the accuracy of the computed object coordinates, although large baselines arise problems in finding automatically the same correspondences in the images, due to strong perspective effects. According to Fraser (1996), the accuracy of the computed 3D object coordinates (s_{XYZ}) depends on the image measurement precision (s_{xy}), image scale and geometry (e.g. the scale number S), an empirical factor q and the number of images k:

$$\sigma_{XYZ} = \frac{qS\sigma_{xy}}{\sqrt{k}} \tag{6}$$

The collinearity principle and Gauss-Markov model of the least squares are valid and employed for all those images acquired with frame sensors (e.g. a SLR camera). In case of linear array sensors, other mathematical approaches should be employed. The description of such methods is outside the scope of this chapter.

The entire photogrammetric workflow used to derive metric and accurate 3D information of a scene from a set of images consists of (i) camera calibration and image orientation, (ii) 3D measurements, (iii) structuring and modelling, (iv) texture mapping and visualization. Compared to the active range sensors workflow, the main difference stays in the 3D point cloud derivation: while range sensors (e.g. laser scanners) deliver directly the 3D data, photogrammetry requires the mathematical processing of the image data to derive the required sparse or dense 3D point clouds useful to digitally reconstruct the surveyed scene.

Method	*Observations*	*Unknowns*
General bundle adj.	tie points, evt. datum	exterior param., 3D coord.
Self-calibrating bundle adj.	tie points, evt. datum	interior and exterior, 3D coord
Resection	tie points, 3D coord.	interior and exterior param.
Intersection	tie points, interior and exterior param.	3D coord.

Table 1. Photogrammetric procedures for calibration, orientation and point positioning.

2.1.3 Other image-based techniques

The most well-known technique similar to photogrammetry is computer vision. Even if accuracy is not the primary goal, computer vision approaches are retrieving interesting results for visualization purposes, object-based navigation, location-based services, robot control, shape recognition, augmented reality, annotation transfer or image browsing purposes. The typical computer vision pipeline for scene's modelling is named "structure from motion" (Pollefeys et al., 2004; Pollefeys et al., 2008; Agarwal et al., 2009) and it is getting quite common in applications where metrics is not the primary aim.

Other image-based techniques allowing the derivation of 3D information from a single image use object constraints (Van den Heuvel, 1998; Criminisi et al., 1999; El-Hakim, 2000) or estimating surface normals instead of image correspondences with methods like shape from shading (Horn & Brooks, 1989), shape from texture (Kender, 1978), shape from specularity (Healey and Binford, 1987), shape from contour (Meyers et al., 1992), shape from 2D edge gradients (Winkelbach & Wahl, 2001).

2.2 Triangulation-based active range sensing

Active systems, particularly those based on laser light, make the measurement result nearly independent of the texture of the object being photographed, projecting references on its surface through a suitably coded light. Such light is characterized by an intrinsic information content recognizable by an electronic sensor, unlike the environmental diffuse light, which has no particularly identifiable elements. For example, an array of dots or a series of coloured bands are all forms of coded light. Thanks to such coding, active 3D sensors can acquire in digital form the spatial behaviour of an object surface. The output attainable from such a device can be seen as an image having in each pixel the spatial coordinates (x, y, z) expressed in millimetres, optionally enriched with colour information (R, G, B) or by the laser reflectance (Y). This set of 3D data, called "range image", is generally a 2.5D entity (i.e. at each couple of x,y values, only one z is defined).

At present, 3D active methods are very popular because they are the only ones capable to acquire the geometry of a surface in a totally automatic way. A tool employing active 3D techniques is normally called range device or, referring in particular to laser-based equipment, 3D laser scanner. Different 3D operating principles may be chosen depending on the object size hence on the sensor-to-object distance. For measuring small volumes, indicatively below a cubic meter, scanners are based on the principle of triangulation. Exceptional use of these devices have been done in Cultural Heritage (CH) applications on large artefacts (Bernardini et al., 2002; Levoy et al. 2000).

2.2.1 Basic principles

The kind of light that first allowed to create a 3D scanner is the laser light. Due to its physical properties it allows to generate extremely focused spots at relatively long ranges from the light source, respect to what can be done, for example, with a halogen lamp. The reason of this is related to the intimate structure of light, which is made by photons, short packets of electromagnetic energy characterized by their own wavelength and phase. A laser generates a peculiar light which is monochromatic (i.e. made by photons all at the same wavelength), and coherent (i.e. such that all its photons are generated in different time instants but with the same phase). The practical consequence of the first fact (mono-cromaticity) is that the lenses used for focusing a laser can be much more effective, being designed for a single wavelength rather than the wide spectrum of wavelengths typical of white light. In other words with a laser it is easier to concentrate energy in space. On the other hand the second fact (coherence) allows all the photons to generate a constructive wave interference whose consequence is a concentration of energy in time. Both these factors contribute to make the laser an effective illumination source for selecting specific points of a scenery with high contrast respect to the background, allowing to measure their spatial position as described below.

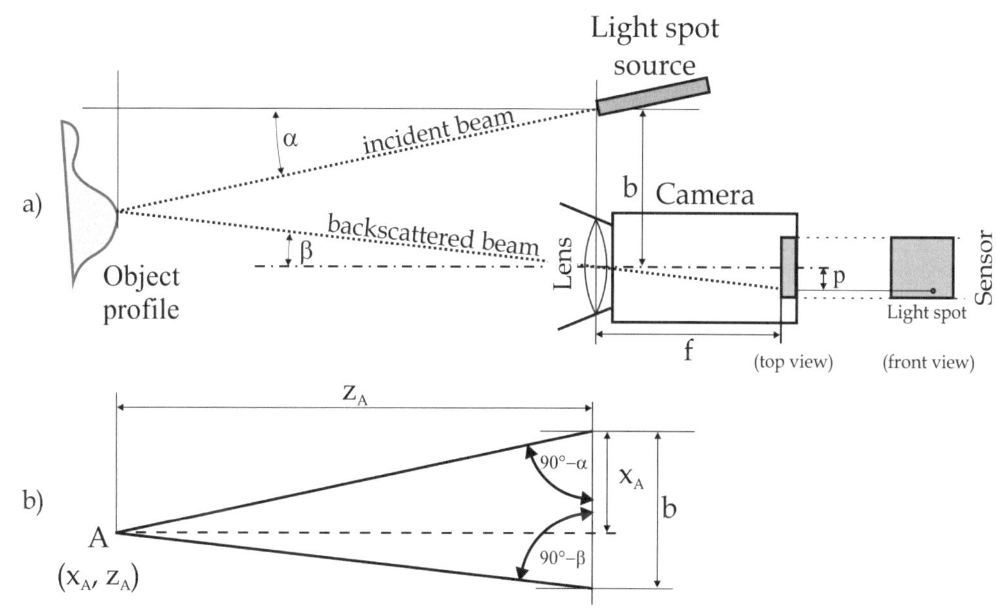

Fig. 2. Triangulation principle: a) xz view of a triangulation based distance measurement through a laser beam inclined with angle α respect to the reference system, impinging on the surface to be measured. The light source is at a distance b from the optical centre of an image capturing device equipped with a lens with focal length f; b) evaluation of x_A and z_A.

Let's imagine to have a range device made by the composition of a light source and a planar sensor, rigidly bounded each other. The laser source generates a thin ray producing a small light dot on the surface to be measured. If we put a 2D capture device (e.g. a digital camera) displaced respect to the light source and the surface is enough diffusive to reflect some light also toward the camera pupil, an image containing the light spot can be picked up. In this opto-geometric set-up the light source emitting aperture, the projection centre and the light spot on the object, form a triangle as the one shown in fig. 2a, where the distance between image capture device and light source is indicated as baseline b. The lens located in front of the sensor is characterized by its focal length f (i.e. distance in mm from the optical centre of the lens to the focal plane). On the collected image, a trace of the light spot will be visible in a point displaced with respect to the optical centre of the system.
Depending from the position of the imaged spot respect to the optical axis of the lens, two displacement components will be generated along the horizontal (x) and vertical (y) directions. Considering that the drawing in fig. 2a represents the horizontal plane (xz) we will take into account here only the horizontal component of such displacement, indicated in fig. 2a as p (parallax). If the system has been previously calibrated we can consider as known both the inclination a of the laser beam and the baseline b. From the spot position the distance p can be estimated, through which we can easily calculate the angle b:

$$\tan\beta = \frac{p}{f} \tag{7}$$

As evidenced in fig. 2b, once the three parameters b, α and β are known, the aforementioned triangle has three known elements: the base b and two angles (90°-α, 90°-β), from which all other parameters can be evaluated. Through simple trigonometry we go back to the distance z_A between the camera and point A on the object. This range, which is the most critical parameter and therefore gives name to this class of instruments (range devices), is given by:

$$z_A = \frac{b}{\tan\alpha + \tan\beta} \tag{8}$$

Multiplying this value by the tangent of α, we get the horizontal coordinate x_A.
In this schematic view y_A never appears. In fact, with a technique like this, the sensor can be reduced to a single array of photosensitive elements rather than a matrix such as those which are equipped with digital cameras. In this case y_A can be determined in advance by mounting the optical measurement system on a micrometric mechanical device providing its position with respect to a known y origin. The Region Of Interest (ROI), namely the volume that can be actually measured by the range device, is defined by the depth of field of the overall system consisting of illumination source and optics. As well known the depth of field of a camera depends on a combination of lens focal length and aperture. To make the most of this area, it is appropriate that also the laser beam is focused at the camera focusing distance, with a relatively long focal range, in order to have the spot size nearly unchanged within the ROI. Once both these conditions are met, the ROI size can be further increased by tilting the sensor optics, as defined by the principle of Scheimpflug (Li et al, 2007).

2.2.2 3D laser scanner

The principle described above can be extended by a single point of light to a set of aligned points forming a segment. Systems of this kind use a sheet of light generated by a laser reflected by a rotating mirror or a cylindrical lens. Once projected onto a flat surface such light plane produces a straight line which becomes a curved profile on complex surfaces.

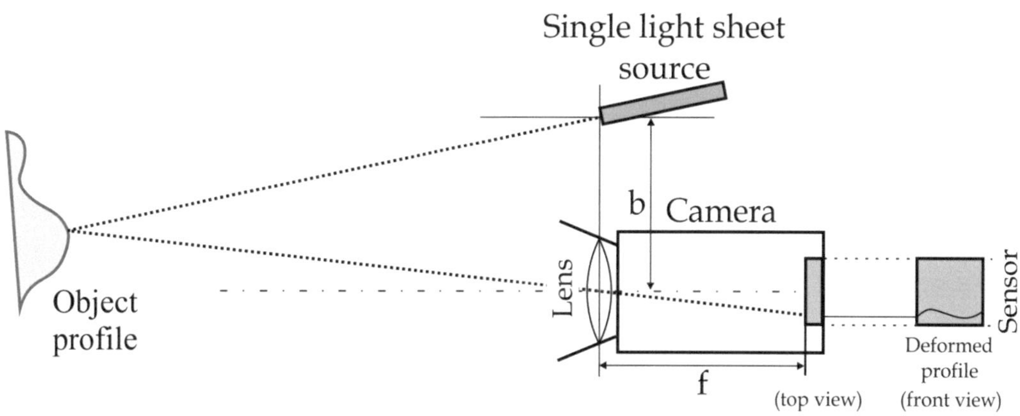

Fig. 3. Acquisition of coordinates along a profile generated by a sheet of laser light. In a 3D laser scanner this profile is mechanically moved in order to probe an entire area.

Each profile point responds to the rule already seen for the single spot system, with the only difference that the sensor has to be 2D, so that both horizontal and vertical parallaxes can be estimated for each profile point. Such parallaxes are used for estimating the corresponding horizontal and vertical angles, from which, together with the knowledge on the baseline b and the optical focal length f, the three coordinates of each profile point can be estimated.

This process allows therefore to calculate an array of 3D coordinates corresponding to the illuminated profile for a given light-object relative positioning.

By displacing the light plane along its normal of a small amount Dy, a different strip of surface can be probed, generating a new array of 3D data referred to an unknown geometrical region close to the first one. The 3D laser scanner is a device implementing the iteration of such process for a number of positions which generates a set of arrays describing the geometry of a whole area, strip by strip. This kind of range image (or range map), is indicated also as structured 3D point cloud.

2.2.3 Pattern projection sensors

With pattern projection sensors multiple sheets of light are simultaneously produced thanks to a special projector generating halogen light patterns of horizontal or vertical black and white stripes. An image of the area illuminated by the pattern is captured with a digital camera and each Black-to-White (B-W) transition is used as geometrical profile, similar to those produced by a sheet of laser light impinging on an unknown surface. Even if the triangulating principle used is exactly the same seen for the two devices mentioned above, the main difference is that here no moving parts are required since no actual scan action is performed. The range map is computed in this way just through digital post-processing of the acquired image.

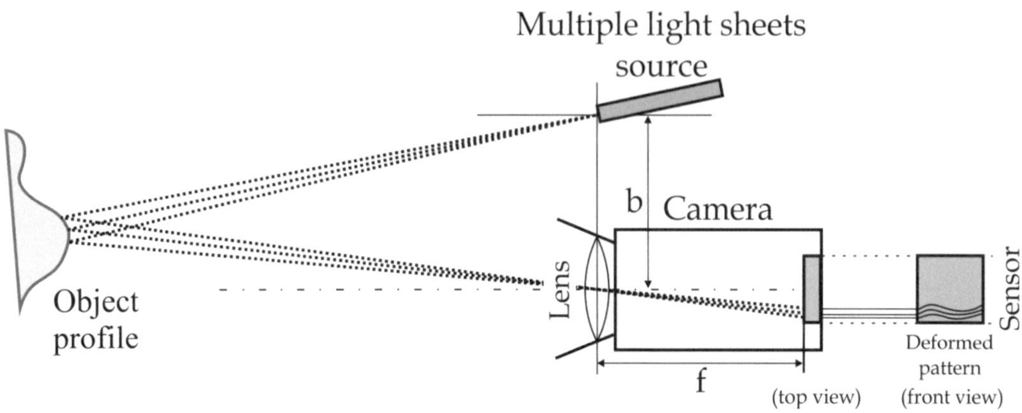

Fig. 4. Acquisition of coordinates along a different profiles generated by multiple sheets of white light.

The more B-W transitions will be projected on the probed surface, the finer will be its spatial sampling, with a consequent increase of the geometrical resolution. Therefore the finest pattern would seem the most suitable solution for gaining the maximum amount of data from a single image, but, in practical terms, this is not completely true. This depends by the impossibility to identify, in an image of an unknown surface with striped patterns projected on it, each single B-W transition, due to the possible framing of an unknown subset of the projected pattern (e.g. for surfaces very close to the camera), or for the presence of holes or occlusions generating ambiguity in the stripes order.
In order to solve such ambiguity this category of devices uses a sequence of patterns rather than a single one. The most used approach is the Gray coded sequence, that employs a set of patterns where the number of stripes is doubled at each step, up to reaching the maximum number allowed by the pattern projector. Other pattern sequences have been developed and implemented, such as phase-shift or Moirè, with different metrological performances.
In general the advantage of structured-light 3D scanners is speed. This makes some of these systems capable of scanning moving objects in real-time.

2.3 Time Of Flight (TOF) active range sensing

With active range sensing methods based on triangulation, the size of volumes that can be easily acquired ranges from a shoe box to a full size statue. For a precise sensor response the ratio between camera-target distance and camera-source distance (baseline), has to be maintained between 1 and 5. Therefore framing areas very far from the camera would involve a very large baseline, that above 1 m becomes difficult to be practically implemented. For larger objects like buildings, bridges or dams, a different working principle is used. It is based on optically measuring the sensor-to-target distance, having the *a priori* knowledge of angles through the controlled orientation of the range measurement device.

2.3.1 Base principles

Active TOF range sensing is logically derived from the so-called "total station". This is made by a theodolite, namely an optical targeting device for aiming at a specific point in space, coupled with a goniometer for precisely measuring horizontal and vertical orientations, integrated with an electronic distance meter. TOF, or time of flight, is referred to the method used for estimating the sensor-to-target distance, that is usually done by measuring the time needed by light for travelling from the light source to the target surface and back to the light detector integrated in the electronic distance meter.

Differently from a total station, a 3D laser scanner does not need that a human operator take aim at a specific point in space, therefore it does not have such sophisticate crosshair. On the other hand it has the capability to automatically re-orient the laser on a predefined range of horizontal and vertical angles, in order to select a specific area in front of the instrument. The precise angular estimations are then returned by a set of digital encoders, while the laser TOF gives the distance. As exemplified in fig. 5, showing a schematic diagram of a system working only on the xz plane analogously to what shown for triangulation based systems, it is clear that if the system return the two parameter distance (r) and laser beam orientation (a), the Cartesian coordinates of A in the xz reference system are simply given by:

$$x_A = \rho \sin \alpha \tag{9}$$

$$z_A = \rho \cos \alpha \tag{10}$$

In case of a real 3D situation, in addition to the vertical angle an horizontal angle will be given, and the set of coordinate (x_A, y_A, z_A) will be obtained by a simple conversion from polar to Cartesian of the three-dimensional input data.

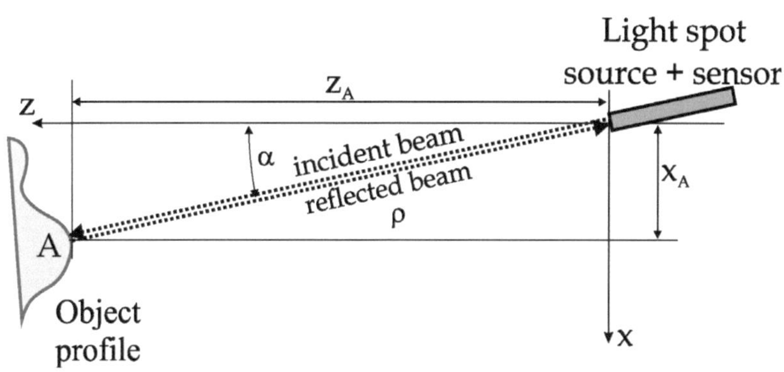

Fig. 5. Acquisition of coordinates of the point A through the *a priori* knowledge of the angle α, and the measurement of the distance r through the Time Of Flight of a light pulse from the sensor to the object and back.

Systems based on the measurement of distance are in general indicated as LiDAR (Light Detection And Ranging), even if in the topographic area this acronym is often used for indicating the specific category of airborne laser scanner. The most noticeable aspect of such devices is in fact the capability to work at very long distance from the actual scanning surface, from half meter up to few kilometres, making such devices suitable also for 3D acquisition from flying platforms (helicopters or airplanes) or moving vehicles (boats or cars).

For ground based range sensors the angular movement can be 360° horizontally and close to 180° vertically, allowing a huge spherical volume to be captured from a fixed position. As

for triangulation based range sensors the output of such devices is again a cloud of 3D points originated by a high resolution spatial sampling an object. The difference with triangulation devices is often in the data structure. In TOF devices data are collected sampling an angular sector of a sphere, with a step not always fixed. As a results the data set can be formed by scan lines not necessarily all of the same size. Therefore the device output may be given by a simple list of 3D coordinates not structured in a matrix.
In term of performances, contributions to measurement errors may be given by both angular estimation accuracy and distance measurements. However, due to the very high speed of light, the TOF is very short, and this involves that the major source of uncertainty is due to its estimation that becomes a geometrical uncertainty once time is converted in distance. For this reason angle estimation devices implemented in this kind of laser scanners are similar each other. But different strategies for obtaining distance from light have been proposed for minimizing such uncertainty, all derived by approaches originally developed for radars.
An interesting sensor fusion is given by the Range-Imaging (RIM) cameras which integrate distance measurements (based on the TOF principle) and imaging aspects. RIM sensors are not treated in this chapter as not really suitable for 3D modeling applications.

2.3.2 PW laser scanner

Distance estimation is here based on a short Pulsed Wave (PW) of light energy generated from the source toward the target. Part of it is backscattered to the sensor, collected and reconverted in an electric signal by a photodiode. The transmitted light driving pulse and the received one are used as start/stop command for a high frequency digital clock that allows to count a number of time units between the two events. Of course the higher is the temporal resolution of the counting device, the finer will be the distance estimation. However, frequency limitations of electronic counting does not allow to go below a few tens of ps in time resolution, corresponding to some millimetres.
Considering that the speed of light is approximately $c=3 \cdot 10^8$ m/s, and that the TOF is related to a travel of the light pulse to the surface and back (double of the sensor-to-target distance), the range will be given by:

$$r = \frac{TOF \cdot c}{2} \tag{11}$$

Therefore a small deviation in estimating TOF, for example in the order of 20 ps, will give a corresponding range deviation $Dr=1/2 \cdot (20 \cdot 10^{-12}) \cdot (3 \cdot 10^8)$ m = 3 mm.
For some recent models of laser scanner based on this principle (Riegel, 2010), the device is capable to detect multiple reflected pulses by a single transmitted pulse, provided by situations where multiple targets are present on the laser trajectory (e.g. a wall behind tree leaves). In this case the cloud of points is not anymore a 2.5D entity.

2.3.3 CW laser scanner (phase shift)

In this case distance is estimated with a laser light whose intensity is sinusoidally modulated at a known frequency, generating a Continuous Wave (CW) of light energy directed toward the target. The backscattering on the target surface returns a sinusoidal light wave delayed respect to the transmitted one, and therefore characterized by a phase difference with it. Similarly to the previous approach, the distance estimation is based on a comparison between the signal applied to the laser for generating the transmitted light wave:

$$s_{TX} = cos(\omega_0 t) \tag{12}$$

and the signal generated by re-converting in electrical form the light backscattered by the surface and received by the range sensor:

$$s_{RX} = cos(\omega_0 t + \varphi) \tag{13}$$

A CW laser scanner implement an electronic mixing the two signals, that corresponds to a multiplication of these two contributions. It can be reduced as follows:

$$cos(\omega_0 t) \cdot cos(\omega_0 t + \varphi) = \frac{1}{2} cos(2\omega_0 t + \varphi) + \frac{1}{2} cos(\varphi) \tag{14}$$

The result is a contribution at double the modulating frequency, that can be cut through a low-pass filter, and a continuous contribution, directly proportional to phase difference f, that can be estimated. Since this angular value is directly proportional to the TOF, from this value the range can be evaluated similarly to the previous case. This indirect estimation of TOF allows a better performance in term of uncertainty for two main reasons: a) since the light sent to the target is continuous, much more energy can be transmitted respect to the PW case, and the consequent signal-to-noise ratio of the received signal is higher; b) the low-passing filtering required for extracting the useful signal component involves a cut also on the high frequency noise, resulting in a further decrease of noise respect to signal.
A peculiar aspect of this range measurement technique is the possibility to have an ambiguous information if the sensor-to-target distance is longer than the equivalent length of a full wave of modulated light, given by the ambiguity range r_{amb}=pc/w_0, due to the periodical repetition of phase. Such ambiguity involves a maximum operating distance that is in general smaller for CW devices rather than PW.

2.3.4 FM-CW laser scanner (laser radar)

In CW systems the need of a wavelength long enough for avoiding ambiguity, influence the range detection performance which is as better as the wavelength is short (i.e. as w_0 grows). This leaded to CW solutions where two or three different modulation frequencies are employed. A low modulating frequency for a large ambiguity range (in the order of 100m), and shorter modulation frequencies for increasing angular (and therefore range) resolution.
By increasing indefinitely the number of steps between a low to a high modulating frequency, a so-called chirp frequency modulation (FM) is generated, with a linear growing of the modulating frequency in the operating range. As light is generated continuously, this kind of instruments are indicated as FM-CW. Since this processing is normally used in radars (Skolnik, 1990), this devices is also known as "laser radar". The peculiar aspect of this approach is the capability to reduce the measurement uncertainty at levels much lower than that of PW laser scanners (typically 2-3 mm), and lower than that of CW laser scanners (less than 1mm on optically cooperative materials at the proper distance), competing with triangulation laser scanners, capable to reach a measurement uncertainty lower than 100 mm. Such devices have therefore the advantage of the spherical acquisition set-up typical of TOF laser scanners, with a metrological performance comparable to that of triangulation based devices, at operating distances from 1 to 20 meters, far larger than the typical triangulation devices operating range (0.5 to 2 m). For this reason such instruments have been experimented in applications where a

wide area and high precision are simultaneously required, like in industrial (Petrov, 2006) and CH (Guidi et al., 2005; Guidi et al., 2009b) applications.

3. Digital camera calibration and image orientation

Camera calibration and image orientation are procedures of fundamental importance, in particular for all those geomatics applications which rely on the extraction of accurate 3D geometric information from images. The early theories and formulations of orientation procedures were developed many years ago and today there is a great number of procedures and algorithms available (Gruen and Huang, 2001).
Sensor calibration and image orientation, although conceptually equivalent, follow different strategies according to the employed imaging sensors. The camera calibration procedure can be divided in geometric and radiometric calibration but in this chapter only the geometric calibration of terrestrial frame cameras is reported.

3.1 Geometric camera calibration

The geometric calibration of a camera (Remondino & Fraser, 2006) is defined as the determination of deviations of the physical reality from a geometrically ideal imaging system based on the collinearity principle: the pinhole camera. Camera calibration continues to be an area of active research within the Computer Vision community, with a perhaps unfortunate characteristic of much of the work being that it pays too little heed to previous findings from photogrammetry. Part of this might well be explained in terms of a lack of emphasis and interest in accuracy aspects and a basic premise that nothing whatever needs to be known about the camera which has to be calibrated within a linear projective rather than Euclidean scene reconstruction. In photogrammetry, a camera is considered calibrated if its focal length, principal point offset and a set of Additional Parameters (APs) are known. The camera calibration procedure is based on the collinearity model which is extended in order to model the systematic image errors and reduce the physical reality of the sensor geometry to the perspective model. The model which has proved to be the most effective, in particular for close-range sensors, was developed by D. Brown (1971) and expresses the corrections (Dx, Dy) to the measured image coordinates (x, y) as:

$$\Delta x = -\Delta x_0 + \frac{\bar{x}}{f}\Delta f + \bar{x}S_x + \bar{y}a + \bar{x}r^2k_1 + \bar{x}r^4k_2 + \bar{x}r^6k_3 + 2P_1\overline{xy} + (2\bar{x}^2 + r^2)P_1 + 2\overline{xy}P_2 \quad (15)$$

$$\Delta y = -\Delta y_0 + \frac{\bar{y}}{f}\Delta f + \bar{x}a + \bar{y}r^2k_1 + \bar{y}r^4k_2 + \bar{y}r^6k_3 + 2P_1\overline{xy} + (2\bar{y}^2 + r^2)P_2 \quad (16)$$

with:

$$\bar{x} = x - x_0;$$
$$\bar{y} = y - y_0;$$
$$r^2 = \bar{x}^2 + \bar{y}^2;$$

Brown's model is generally called "physical model" as all its components can be directly attributed to physical error sources. The individual parameters represent:

Dx_0, Dy_0, Df = correction for the interior orientation elements;
K_i = parameters of radial lens distortion;
P_i = parameters of decentering distortion;
S_x = scale factor in x to compensate for possible non-square pixel;
a = shear factor for non-orthogonality and geometric deformation of the pixel.
The three APs used to model radial distortion Δr are generally expressed via the odd-order polynomial $\Delta r = K_1r^3 + K_2r^5 + K_3r^7$, where r is the radial distance. A typical Gaussian radial distortion profile Δr is shown in fig. 6a, which illustrates how radial distortion can vary with focal length. The coefficients K_i are usually highly correlated, with most of the error signal generally being accounted for by the cubic term K_1r^3. The K_2 and K_3 terms are typically included for photogrammetric (low distortion) and wide-angle lenses, and in higher-accuracy vision metrology applications. The commonly encountered third-order barrel distortion seen in consumer-grade lenses is accounted for by K_1.

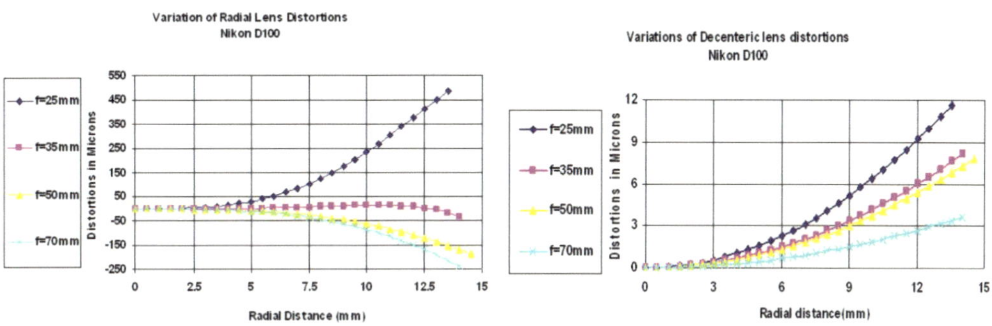

a) b)

Fig. 6. Radial (a) and decentering (b) distortion profile for a digital camera set at different focal length.

Decentering distortion is due to a lack of centering of lens elements along the optical axis. The decentering distortion parameters P_1 and P_2 are invariably strongly projectively coupled with x_0 and y_0. Decentering distortion is usually an order of magnitude or more less than radial distortion and it also varies with focus, but to a much less extent, as indicated by the decentering distortion profiles shown in fig. 6b. The projective coupling between P_1 and P_2 and the principal point offsets (Dx_0, Dy_0) increases with increasing focal length and can be problematic for long focal length lenses. The extent of coupling can be diminished, during the calibration procedure, through both use of a 3D object point array and the adoption of higher convergence angles for the images.
The solution of a self-calibrating bundle adjustment leads to the estimation of all the interior parameters and APs, starting from a set of manually or automatically measured image correspondences (tie points). Critical to the quality of the self-calibration is the overall network geometry and especially the configuration camera stations. Some good hints and practical rules for camera calibration can be summarized as follows:

- acquire a set of images of a reference object, possibly constituted of coded targets which can be automatically and accurately measured in the images;

- the image network geometry should be favourable, i.e. the camera station configuration must comprise highly convergent images, acquired at different distances from the scene, with orthogonal roll angles and a large number of well distributed 3D object points;
- the accuracy of the image network (and so of the calibration procedure) increases with increasing convergence angles for the imagery, the number of rays to a given object point and the number of measured points per image (although but the incremental improvement is small beyond a few tens of points);
- a planar object point array can be employed for camera calibration if the images are acquired with orthogonal roll angles, a high degree of convergence and, desirably, varying object distances;
- orthogonal roll angles must be present to break the projective coupling between IO and EO parameters. Although it might be possible to achieve this decoupling without 90° image rotations, through provision of a strongly 3D object point array, it is always recommended to have 'rolled' images in the self-calibration network.

Nowadays self-calibration via the bundle adjustment is a fully automatic process requiring nothing more than images recorded in a suitable multi-station geometry, an initial guess of the focal length and image sensor characteristics (and it can be a guess) and some coded targets which form a 3D object point array.

3.2 Image orientation

In order to survey an object, a set of images needs to be acquired considering that a detail can be reconstructed in 3D if it is visible in at least 2 images. The orientation procedure is then performed to determine the position and attitude (angles) where the images were acquired. A set of tie points needs to be identified (manually or automatically) in the images, respecting the fact that the points are well distributed on the entire image format, non-coplanar nor collinear. These observations are then used to form a system of collinearity equations (Eq. 1), iteratively solved with the Gauss-Markov model of least squares (Eq. 2).

A typical set of images, acquired for 3D reconstruction purposes, forms a network which is generally not suitable for a calibration procedure. Therefore it is always better to separate the two photogrammetric steps or to adopt a set of images suitable for both procedures.

4. Characterization of 3D sensing devices

When a range sensor has to be chosen for geometrically surveying an object shape, independently of its size, the first point to face regards which level of detail has to be recognizable in the final 3D digital model that will be built starting from the raw 3D data, and the acceptable tolerance between the real object and its digital counterpart. These matters are so important that influence all the technological and methodological choices for the whole 3D acquisition project.

The main metrological parameters related to measurement are univocally defined by the International Vocabulary of Metrology (VIM), published by the Joint Committee for Guides in Metrology (JCGM) of ISO (JCGM, 2008). Such parameters are basically Resolution, Trueness (Accuracy) and Uncertainty (Precision).

Although the transposition of these concepts to the world of 3D imaging has been reported in the reference guide VDI/VDE 2634 by the "Association of German Engineers" for pattern projection cameras, a more general international standard on optical 3D measurement is still in preparation by commission E57 of the American Society for Testing Material (ASTM, 2006). Also the International Standard Organization (ISO) has not yet defined a metrological standard for non-contact 3D measurement devices. In its ISO-10360 only the methods for characterizing contact based Coordinate Measuring Machines (CMM) has been defined, while an extension for CMMs coupled with optical measuring machines (ISO 10360-7:2011) is still under development.

4.1 Resolution

According to VIM, resolution is the "smallest change in a quantity being measured that causes a perceptible change in the corresponding indication". This definition, once referred to non-contact 3D imaging, is intended as the minimum geometrical detail that the range device is capable to capture. This is influenced by the device mechanical, optical and electronic features. Of course such value represents the maximum resolution allowed by the 3D sensor. For its 3D nature it can be divided in two components: the axial resolution, along the optical axis of the device (usually indicated as z), and the lateral resolution, on the xy plane (MacKinnon et al., 2008).

For digitally capturing a shape, the 3D sensor generates a discretization of its continuous surface according to a predefined sampling step adjustable by the end-user even at a level lower than the maximum. The adjustment leads to a proper spacing between geometrical samples on the xy plane, giving the actual geometrical resolution level chosen by the operator for that specific 3D acquisition action. The corresponding value in z is a consequence of the opto-geometric set-up, and can't be usually changed by the operator.

In other words it has to be made a clear distinction between the maximum resolution allowed by the sensor, usually indicated as "resolution" in the sensor data sheet, and the actual resolution used for a 3D acquisition work, that the end-user can properly set-up according to the geometrical complexity of the 3D object to be surveyed, operating on the xy sampling step.

The latter set-up is directly influenced by the lens focal length and the sensor-to-target distance for triangulation devices, using an image sensor whose size and pixel density is known in advance. In that case the sampling step will be attainable for example dividing the framed area horizontal size for the number of horizontal pixels. Since most cameras has square pixels, in general this value is equivalent to (vertical size)/(vertical number of pixels). For TOF devices the sampling can be set-up on the laser scanner control software by defining the angular step between two adjacent point on a scan line, and between two adjacent scan-lines. Of course, in order to convert the angular step in a linear step on the surface, such angle expressed in radians has to be multiplied for the operating distance. Some scanner control packages allow to set directly the former value.

The sampling should be made according to a rule deriving directly by the Nyquist-Shannon sampling theorem (Shannon, 1949), developed first in communication theory. Such theorem states that, if a sinusoidal behaviour has a frequency defined by its period T, that in the geometrical domain becomes a length (the size of the minimal geometrical detail that we intend to digitally capture), the minimal sampling step suitable for allowing the reconstruction of the same behaviour from the sampled one, is equal to T/2. Of course it is not generally true that the fine geometrical details of a complex shape could be considered as made by the extrusions of sinusoidal profiles, but at least this criteria gives a "rule of the thumb" for estimating a minimum geometrical sampling step below which it is sure that the smaller geometrical detail will be lost.

4.2 Trueness (accuracy)

VIM definition indicates accuracy in general as "closeness of agreement between a measured quantity value and a true quantity value of a measurand". When such theoretical entity has to be evaluated for an actual instrument, including a 3D sensor, such value has to be experimentally estimated from the instrument output. For this reason VIM also define trueness as "closeness of agreement between the average of an infinite number of replicate measured quantity values and a reference quantity value". It is a more practical parameter that can be numerically estimated as the difference between a 3D value assumed as true (because measured with a method far more accurate), and the average of a sufficiently large number of samples acquired through the range device to be characterized. Such parameter refers therefore to the systematic component of the measurement error with respect to the real data (fig.7), and can be minimized through an appropriate sensor calibration. For 3D sensors, accuracy might be evaluated both for the axial direction (z) than for a lateral one (on the xy plane). In general, accuracy on depth is the most important, and varies from few hundredths to few tenths of a millimetre for triangulation based sensors and FM-CW laser scanners, it is in the order of 1mm for CW laser scanners, and in the order of 5 mm for PW laser scanners.

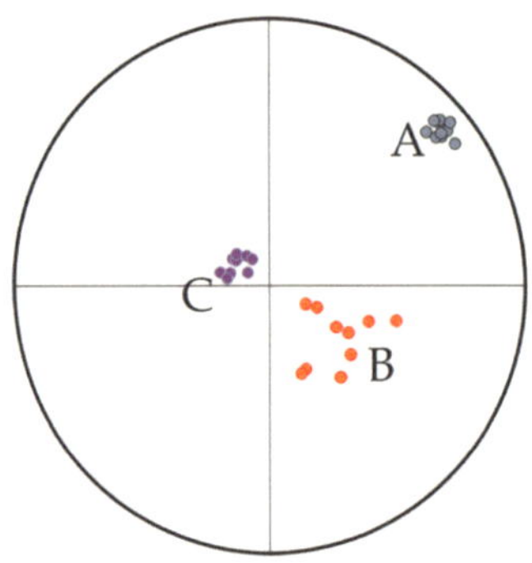

Fig. 7. Exemplification of the accuracy and precision concepts. The target has been used by three different shooters. The shooter A is precise but not accurate, B is more accurate than A but less precise (more spreading), C is both accurate and precise.

4.3 Uncertainty (precision)

Precision is the "closeness of agreement between indications or measured quantity values obtained by replicate measurements on the same or similar objects under specified conditions" (JCGM, 2008). A practical value for estimating such agreement is to calculate the dispersion of the quantity values being attributed to a measurand through the standard deviation of the measured values respect to their average (or a multiple of it), defined by VIM as uncertainty (fig.7).

As accuracy is influenced by systematic errors, precision is mostly influenced by random errors, leading to a certain level of unpredictability of the measured value, due to thermal

noise in the sensor's detector, and, in case of laser based devices, by the typical laser speckle effect (Baribeau & Rioux 1991).
For a 3D sensor such estimation can be done acquiring several times the same area and analysing the measured value of a specific point in space as a random variable, calculating its standard deviation. This would involve a very large number of 3D acquisitions to be repeated, namely from 10000 to one million, in order to consider the data statistically significant. For this reason a more practical approach (even if not as theoretically coherent with the definition) is to acquire the range map of a target whose shape is known in advance, like for example a plane, and evaluate the standard deviation of each 3D point respect to the ideal shape (Guidi et al., 2010). Since a range map can be easily made by millions of points the statistical significance is implicit.
Precision of active 3D devices ranges from a few tens of micrometres for triangulation based sensors, with an increase of deviation with the square of sensor-to-target distance. It has similar values for FM-CW laser scanners with a much less significant change with distance. For CW laser scanners it has values starting from below 1mm up to a few mm as the sensor is farer from the target, and not less of 2 mm for PW laser scanners (Boehler et al., 2003) with no significant change with distance (Guidi et al., 2011).
For modelling applications the uncertainty level of the range sensor should not exceed a fraction of the resolution step for avoiding topological anomalies in the final mesh (Guidi & Bianchini, 2007). A good rule of the thumb is to avoid a resolution level smaller than the range device measurement uncertainty.

5. Photogrammetric 3D point clouds generations

Once the camera parameters are known, the scene measurements can be performed with manual or automated procedures. The measured 2D image correspondences are converted into unique 3D object coordinates (3D point cloud) using the collinearity principle and the known exterior and interior parameters previously recovered. According to the surveyed scene and project requirements, sparse or dense point clouds are derived (fig. 8).
Manual (interactive) measurements, performed in monocular or stereoscopic mode, derive sparse point clouds necessary to determine the main 3D geometries and discontinuities of an object. Sparse reconstructions are adequate for architectural or 3D city modelling applications, where the main corners and edges must be identified to reconstruct the 3D shapes (fig. 8a) (Gruen & X. Wang, 1998; El-Hakim, 2002). A relative accuracy in the range 1:5,000-15,000 is generally expected for such kinds of 3D models.
On the other hand, automated procedures ("image matching") are employed when dense surface measurements and reconstructions are required, e.g. to derive a Digital Surface Model (DSM) to document detailed and complex objects like reliefs, statues, excavations areas, etc. (fig. 8b). The latest development in automated image matching (Pierrot-Deseilligny & Paparoditis, 2006; Hirschmuller, 2008; Remondino et al., 2008; Hiep et al., 2009; Furukawa & Ponce, 2010) are demonstrating the great potentiality of the image-based 3D reconstruction method at different scales of work, comparable to point clouds derived using active range sensors and with a reasonable level of automation. Overviews on stereo and multi-image image matching techniques can be found in (Scharstein & Szeliski, 2002; Seitz et al., 2006). Recently some commercial, open-source and web-based tools were released to derive dense point clouds from a set of images (Photomodeler Scanner, MicMac, PMVS, etc.).

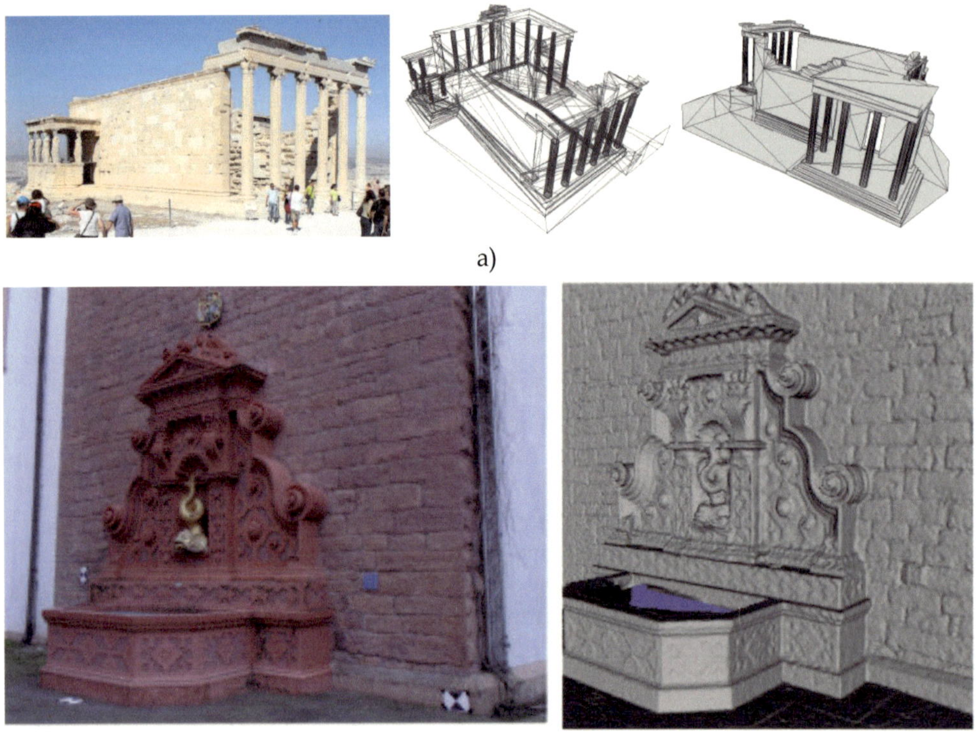

a)

b)

Fig. 8. 3D reconstruction of architectural structures with manual measurements in order to generate geometrical models with the main geometrical features (a). Dense point clouds produced using automated image matching (b).

6. Acquisition and processing of 3D point clouds with active sensors

Independently of the active 3D technology used, a range map is a metric representation of an object from a specific point of view through a set of 3D points properly spaced apart, according to the complexity of the imaged surface.

In order to create a model, several views have to be taken for covering the whole object surface. This operation leads to a set of measured points that can be used as nodes of a mesh representing a 3D digital approximation of the real object. Hence, for going from the raw data to the final 3D model, a specific process has to be followed (Bernardini & Rushmeyer, 2002; Vrubel et al., 2009), according to the steps described in the next sections. Many of these steps have been implemented in 3D point cloud processing packages, both open source, like Meshlab (ISTI-CNR, Italy), Scanalize (Stanford University, USA), and commercial, as Polyworks (Innovmetric, Canada), RapidForm (Inus Technology, South Corea), Geomagic Studio (Geomagic , USA), Cyclone (Leica, Switzerland), 3D Reshaper (Technodigit, France).

6.1 Project planning

The final scope of the digital model is the first matter to be considered for properly planning a 3D acquisition project. Applications of 3D models may span from a simple support for multimedia presentations to a sophisticate dimensional monitoring. In the former case a visually convincing virtual representation of the object is enough, while in the latter a strict metric correspondence between the real object and its digital representation is absolutely mandatory. Since parameters as global model accuracy and geometrical resolution have a considerable cost in terms of acquired data and post-processing overhead, a choice coherent with the project budget and final purpose, is a must. Once such aspects have been clearly identified, the object to be acquired has to be analyzed in terms of size, material and shape.

6.2 Acquisition of individual point clouds

Once the planning has been properly examined, the final acquisition is rather straightforward. In addition to basic logistics, possible issues may be related with sensor positioning and environmental lighting. Camera positioning for small objects can be solved either by moving the object or the sensor, but when the object is very large and heavy (e.g. a boat), or fixed into the ground (e.g. a building), the only possibility is obviously to move the range sensor. In that case a proper positioning should be arranged through scaffoldings or mobile platforms, and the related logistics should be organized. Another aspect that might influence a 3D acquisition is the need of working in open air rather than in a laboratory where lighting conditions can be controlled. In the former case it has to be considered that TOF laser scanners are designed for working on the field and are therefore not much influenced by direct sunlight. Triangulation based range sensors employ much less light power per surface unit and for this reason give worst or no results with high environmental light. In this case a possible but logistically costly solution is to prepare a set with tents or shields for limiting the external light on the surface to be acquired. However in that conditions a more practical approach for obtaining the same high resolution is dense image matching, that, being a passive technique, works well with strong environmental lighting (Guidi et al., 2009a).

6.3 Point clouds alignment

In general each range map acquired from a specific position is given in a coordinate system with the origin located into the range sensor.

Taking range data of a scene or object from different points of view means gathering 3D data representing the same geometry by different reference systems whose mutual orientation is generally unknown. For such reason it is necessary to align all 3D data into the same coordinate system. The process can be achieved in three different ways.

6.3.1 Complementary equipment

This approach requires the measurement of the range device position and orientation with a complementary 3D measurement device like a CMM, giving such data in its coordinate system which is assumed as the global reference. These 6 pieces of information (position and orientation) can be used for calculating the roto-translation matrix from the range device coordinate system to the global one. Applying systematically such roto-translation to any 3D point measured by the range device allows to find immediately its representation in the global reference system even for different device-to-target orientations. Although the working volume is limited by the CMM positioning range, such approach is very accurate. This is why it is used in equipment typically employed in high-accuracy industrial

applications with articulated arms (contact CMM) or laser trackers (non-contact CMM) coupled with triangulation based scanning heads (Pierce, 2007; Peggs et al., 2009).
In case of long-range active range sensors (e.g. TOF laser scanners) the complementary device can be represented by a GNSS which is used, for every acquisition, to measure the position of the range sensor in a global reference system.

6.3.2 Reference targets

Measuring some reference points on the scene with a surveying system like for example a total station, allows to define a global reference system in which such targets are represented. During the 3D acquisition campaign the operator captures scenes containing at least three targets which are therefore represented in the range device reference system for that particular position. Being their positions known also in a global reference system, their coordinates can be used to compute the roto-translation matrix for re-orienting the point cloud from its original reference system to the global one. The operation is of course repeated up to the alignment of all 3D data of the scene. This approach is used more frequently with TOF laser scanners thanks to their large region of interest.

6.3.3 Iterative Closest Point (ICP)

Using as references natural 3D features in the scene is a possible alternative somehow similar to the previous one. The only difference is that no special target has to be fixed on the scene and individually measured by the operator. On the other hand for allowing a proper alignment, a considerable level of overlapping between adjacent range maps has to be arranged, resulting in a large data redundancy and long computational time.
The algorithm for aligning this kind of 3D data sets involves the choice of a range map whose coordinate system is used as global reference. A second data set, partially overlapping with the reference one, is manually or automatically pre-aligned to the main one choosing at least three corresponding points on the common area of both range maps (fig. 9a). This step allows to start an iterative process for minimizing the average distance between the two datasets, initiated by a situation of approximate alignment (fig. 9b) not too far from the optimized one (fig. 9c), that can be reached after a number of iterations as large as the initial approximation is rough. For this reason this class of algorithms is called "Iterative Closest Point" (ICP).
The most critical aspect is that the range maps to be aligned represent different samplings of the same surface, therefore there is not exact correspondence between 3D points in the two coordinate systems. Several solutions have been proposed by considering the minimization of Euclidean distances between points as much corresponding as possible, but it is highly time consuming due to the exhaustive search for the nearest point (Besl & McKay, 1992), or between a point and a planar approximation of the surface at the corresponding point on the other range map (Chen & Medioni, 1992). In both cases the algorithm core is a nonlinear minimization process, being based on a nonlinear feature such as a distance. For this reason the associated cost function has a behaviour characterized by several confusing local minima, and its minimization needs to be started by a pre-alignment close enough to the final solution in order to converge to the absolute minimum.
Once the first two range maps of a set are aligned, ICP can be applied to other adjacent point clouds up the full coverage of the surface of interest. This progressive pair-wise alignment may lead to a considerable error propagation, clearly noticeable on closed surfaces when the

first range map has to be connected with the last one. For this reason global versions of ICP have been conceived, where the orientation of each range map is optimized respect to all neighbour range maps (Gagnon et al., 1994).

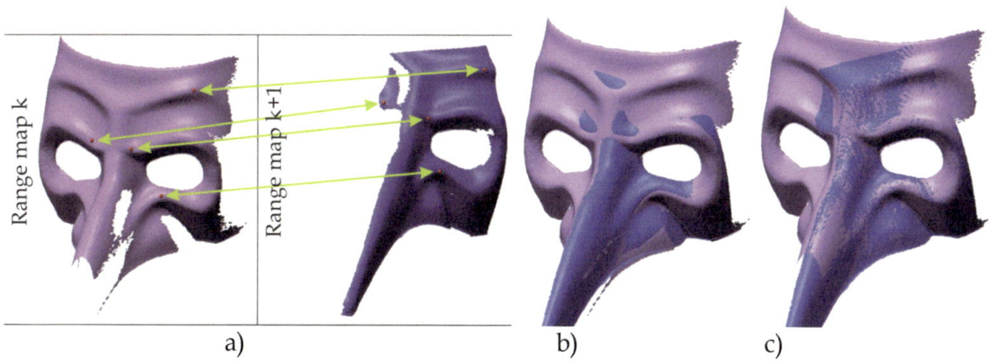

Fig. 9. ICP alignment process: a) selection of corresponding points on two partially superimposed range maps; b) rough pre-alignment; c) accurate alignment after a few iterations.

Several refinements of the ICP approach have been developed in the last two decades for pair-wise alignment (Rusinkiewicz & Levoy, 2001), with the introduction of additional non-geometrical parameters as colour, for solving alignment of object with rich image content but poor 3D structure like flat or regular texturized surfaces (Godin et al., 2001b), and for managing possible shape changes between different shots due to non-rigid objects (Brown & Rusinkiewicz, 2007). A quantitative test of different alignment algorithm has been recently proposed in term of metric performances and processing time (Salvi et al., 2007). For a widespread updated state of the art about alignment algorithms see (Deng, 2011).

7. Polygonal model generation

Once a point cloud from image matching or a set of aligned point clouds acquired with an active sensor are obtained, a polygonal model ("mesh") is generally produced. This process is logically subdivided in several sub-steps that can be completed in different orders depending by the 3D data source (Berger et al., 2011).

7.1 Mesh generation for structured point clouds

The regular matrix arrangement of a structured point cloud involves an immediate knowledge of the neighbour potential mesh connection for each 3D point, making the mesh generation a rather straightforward procedure. This means that once a set of range maps is aligned, it can be easily meshed before starting the final merge.

This is what is done for example by the Polyworks software package used to create the alignment and meshing shown in fig. 10. For carrying out the following merge, the meshes associated to the various range maps have to be connected with the neighbour meshes. This can be achieved with two different approaches: (i) the so-called *zippering* method (Turk & Levoy, 1994) which selects polygons in the overlapping areas, removes redundant triangles and connects meshes together (zipper) trying to maintain the best possible topology. An optimized version that uses Venn diagrams for evaluating the level of redundancy on mesh overlaps has been proposed (Soucy & Laurendeau, 1995). Other approaches work by triangulating union of the point sets, like the Ball Pivoting algorithm (Bernardini et al., 1999), which consists of rolling an imaginary ball on the point sets and creating a triangle for each triplet of points supporting the ball. All methods based on a choice of triangles from a certain mesh on the overlapping areas may get critical in case of large number of overlapped range maps; (ii) a *volumetric* algorithm which operates a subdivision in voxels of the model space, calculates an average position of each 3D point on the overlapping areas and re-samples meshes along common lines of sight (Curless & Levoy, 1996). In this case areas with possible large number of overlapped range maps are evaluated more efficiently than with the zippering method, with a reduction of measurement uncertainty by averaging corresponding points.

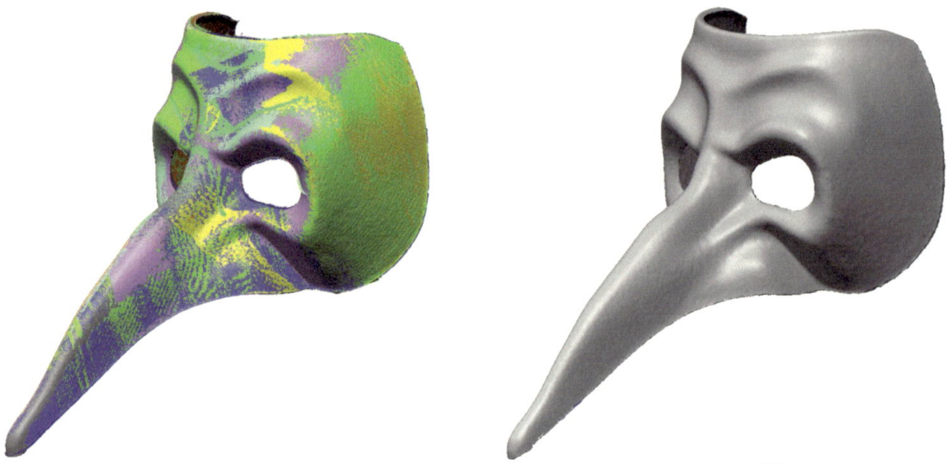

a) b)

Fig. 10. Mesh generation: a) set of ICP aligned range maps. Different colours indicate the individual range maps; b) merge of all range maps in a single polygonal mesh.

7.2 Mesh generation for unstructured point clouds

While meshing is a pretty straightforward step for structured point clouds, for an unstructured point cloud it is not so immediate. It requires a specific process like Delaunay, involving a projection of the 3D points on a plane or another primitive surface, a search of the shorter point-to-point connection with the generation of a set of potential triangles that are then re-projected in the 3D space and topologically verified. For this reason the mesh generation from unstructured clouds may consist in: a) merging the 2.5D point clouds reducing the amount of data in the overlapped areas and generating in this way a uniform resolution full 3D cloud; b) meshing with a more sophisticate procedures of a simple Delaunay. The possible approaches for this latter step are based on: (i) *interpolating surfaces* that build a triangulation with more elements than needed and then prune away triangles not coherent with the surface (Amenta & Bern, 1999); (ii) *approximating surfaces* where the output is often a triangulation of a best-fit function of the raw 3D points (Hoppe et al., 1992; Cazals & Giesen, 2006).

Dense image matching generally consist of unstructured 3D point clouds that can be processed with the same approach used for the above mentioned laser scanner unstructured point clouds. No alignment phase is needed as the photogrammetric process deliver a unique point cloud of the surveyed scene.

7.3 Mesh editing and optimization

Mesh editing allows to correct all possible topological incoherence generated after the polygonal surface generation. Generally some manual intervention of the operator is required in order to clean spikes and unwanted features and to reconstruct those parts of the mesh that are lacking due to previous processing stages or to an effective absence of 3D data collected by the sensor.
These actions are needed at least for two purposes: (i) if the final 3D model has to be used for real-time virtual presentations or static renderings, the lacking of even few polygons gives no support to texture or material shading, creating a very bad visual impression and thwarting the huge modelling effort made until this stage; (ii) if the model has to be used for generating physical copies through rapid prototyping, the mesh has to be watertight.
Several approaches have been proposed for creating lacking final mesh as much agreement as possible with the measured object, like radial basis functions (Carr et al., 2001), multi-level partition of unity implicits (Ohtake et al., 2003) or volumetric diffusion (Davis et al., 2002; Sagawa & Ikeuchi, 2008).
In some cases, like for example dimensional monitoring applications, mesh editing is not suggested for the risk of adding not existing data to the measured model, leading to possible inconsistent output.
Optimization is instead a final useful step in any applicative case, where a significant reduction of the mesh size can be obtained. After the mesh generation and editing stages, the polygonal surface has a point density generally defined by the geometrical resolution set by the operator during the 3D data acquisition or image matching procedure. In case of active range sensing as specified in sect. 4.1, the resolution is chosen for capturing the smaller geometrical details and can be therefore redundant for most of the model. A selective simplification of the model can thus reduce the number of polygons without changing significantly its geometry (Hoppe, 1996). As shown in fig. 11a, the point density

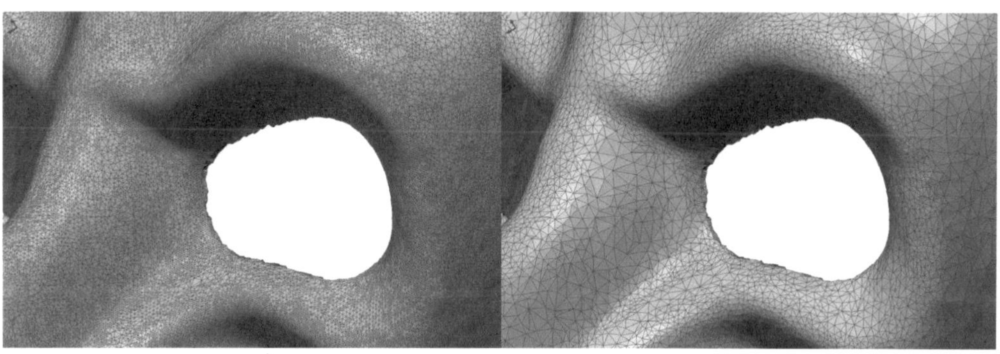

a) b)

Fig. 11. Mesh optimization: a) mesh with polygon sizes given by the range sensor resolution set-up (520,000 triangles); b) mesh simplified in order to keep the difference with the unsimplified one, below 50mm. The polygon sizes vary dynamically according to the surface curvature and the mesh size drops down to 90,000 triangles.

set for the device appears to be redundant for all those surfaces whose curvature radius is not too small.
A mesh simplification that progressively reduces the number of polygons eliminating some nodes, can be applied up to reaching a pre-defined number of polygons (useful for example in game applications where such limitation holds), or, as an alternative, checking the deviation between simplified and un-simplified mesh and stopping at a pre-assigned threshold. If such threshold is chosen in the order of the 3D sensor measurement uncertainty, this kind of simplification does not practically influence the geometric information attainable by the model (fig. 11b), with a strong data shrinking (nearly six time in the example). Mesh simplification algorithms have been extensively examined and compared by Cignoni et al. (1998).

8. Texture mapping and visualization

A polygonal 3D model can be visualized in wireframe, shaded or textured mode. A textured 3D geometric model is probably the most desirable 3D object documentation by most since it gives, at the same time, a full geometric and appearance representation and allows unrestricted interactive visualization and manipulation at a variety of lighting conditions. The photo-realistic representation of a polygonal model (or even a point cloud) is achieved mapping a colour images onto the 3D geometric data. The 3D data can be in form of points or triangles (mesh), according to the applications and requirements. The texturing of 3D point clouds (point-based rendering techniques (Kobbelt & Botsch, 2004) allows a faster visualization, but for detailed and complex 3D models it is not an appropriate method. In case of meshed data the texture is automatically mapped if the camera parameters are known (e.g. if it is a photogrammetric model and the images are oriented) otherwise an interactive procedure is required (e.g. if the model has been generated using range sensors and the texture comes from a separate imaging sensor). Indeed homologue points between the 3D mesh and the 2D image to-be-mapped should be identified in order to find the alignment transformation necessary to map the colour information onto the mesh. Although some automated approaches were proposed in the research community (Lensch et al., 2000; Corsini et al., 2009), no automated commercial solution is available and this is a bottleneck of the entire 3D modelling pipeline. Thus, in practical cases, the 2D-3D alignment is done with the well-known DLT approach (Abdel-Aziz & Karara, 1971), often referred as Tsai method (Tsai, 1986). Corresponding points between the 3D geometry and a 2D image to-be-mapped are sought to retrieve the interior and exterior unknown camera parameters. The colour information is then projected (or assigned) to the surface polygons using a colour-vertex encoding, a mesh parameterization or an external texture.
In Computer Graphics applications, the texturing can also be performed with techniques able to graphically modify the derived 3D geometry (displacement mapping) or simulating the surface irregularities without touching the geometry (bump mapping, normal mapping, parallax mapping).
In the texture mapping phase some problems can arise due to lighting variations of the images, surface specularity and camera settings. Often the images are exposed with the illumination at imaging time but it may need to be replaced by illumination consistent with the rendering point of view and the reflectance properties (BRDF) of the object (Lensch et al., 2003). High dynamic range (HDR) images might also be acquired to recover all scene details

and illumination (Reinhard et al., 2005) while colour discontinuities and aliasing effects must be removed (Debevec et al., 2004; Umeda et al., 2005).
The photo-realistic 3D product needs finally to be visualized e.g. for communication and presentation purposes. In case of large and complex model the point-based rendering technique does not give satisfactory results and does not provide realistic visualization. The visualization of a 3D model is often the only product of interest for the external world, remaining the only possible contact with the 3D data. Therefore a realistic and accurate visualization is often required. Furthermore the ability to easily interact with a huge 3D model is a continuing and increasing problem. Indeed model sizes (both in geometry and texture) are increasing at faster rate than computer hardware advances and this limits the possibilities of interactive and real-time visualization of the 3D results. Due to the generally large amount of data and its complexity, the rendering of large 3D models is done with multi-resolution approaches displaying the large meshes with different Levels of Detail (LOD), simplification and optimization approaches (Dietrich et al., 2007).

9. Conclusions

This chapter reported an overview of the actual optical 3D measurements sensors and techniques used for terrestrial 3D modelling. The last 15 years of applications made clear that reality-based 3D models are very useful in many fields but the related processing pipeline is still far from being optimal, with possible improvements and open research issues in many steps.
First of all automation in 3D data processing is one of the most important issues influencing efficiency, time and production costs. At present different research solution and commercial packages have turned towards semi-automated (interactive) approaches, where the human capacity in data interpretation is paired with the speed and precision of computer algorithms. Indeed the success of fully automation in image understanding or 3D point clouds processing depends on many factors and is still a hot topic of research. The progress is promising but the acceptance of fully automated procedures, judged in terms of handled datasets and accuracy of the final 3D results, depends on the quality specifications of the user and final use of the produced 3D model. A good level of automation would make also possible the development of new tools for non-expert users. These would be particularly useful since 3D capturing and modelling has been demonstrated to be an interdisciplinary task where non-technical end-users (archaeologists, architects, designers, art historians, etc.), may need to interact with sophisticate technologies through clear protocols and user-friendly packages.
Sensor fusion has been experimentally demonstrated to be useful for collecting as many features as possible, allowing the exploitation of each range sensing technology capability. Currently available packages allows the creation of different geometric levels of detail (LoD) at model level (i.e. at the end of the modelling pipeline), while this could be performed also at data-level with the development of novel packages capable to deal simultaneously with different sensors and data. Such novel feature should allow also to include new sensors and 3D data in the processing pipeline taking into account their metrological characteristics.
For this reason also the adoption of standards for comparing 3D sensing technologies would help. At present even no common terminology exists for comparing sensors performances.

A smooth connection between a data base and reality-based 3D models is another issue that has to be faced when the model becomes a "portal" for accessing to an informative system associated to the modelled object. Although some experimental systems have been developed, no simple tools suitable for non-expert users are available yet.
The latter open issue is connected with the problem of remotely visualize large 3D models, both for navigation and data access. Despite 3D navigation through the internet has been attempted both with local rendering of downloaded 3D models (possible large initial time lag and poor data security), or with remote rendering and streaming to the client of a sequence of rendered frames (good security but poor real-time navigation), a complete and reliable user oriented solution is still lacking.

10. Acknowledgment

The authors would like to thank J. Angelo Beraldin for many useful discussions.

11. References

Abdel-Aziz Y.I. & Karara, H.M. (1971). Direct linear trans-formation from comparator coordinates into object space coordinates in close-range photogrammetry, *Proc. of the Symposium on Close-Range Photogrammetry*, Falls Church (VA) USA, pp. 1–18.

Agarwal, S.; Snavely, N.; Simon, I.; Seitz, S.; Szelinski, R. (2009). Building Rome in a Day, *Proceedings of the IEEE 12th International. Conference on Computer Vision*, pp. 72-79.

Akca, D. & Gruen, A. (2009). Comparative geometric and radiometric evaluation of mobile phone and still video cameras. *The Photogrammetric Record*, Vol. 24, pp. 217-245.

Amenta, N. & Bern, M. (1999). Surface reconstruction by Voronoi filtering, *Discrete and Computational Geometry* Vol. 22, No. 4, pp. 481–504.

ASTM International (2006). Committee E57 on 3D Imaging Systems; West Conshohocken, PA, USA.

Barazzetti, L.; Fangi, G.; Remondino, F.; Scaioni, M. (2010). Automation in Multi-Image Spherical Photogrammetry for 3D Architectural Reconstructions, *Proceedings of VAST 2010*, Paris, France, pp. 75-81.

Baribeau, R. & Rioux, M. (1991), Influence of speckle on laser range finders, *Applied Optics*, Vol. 30, No. 20, pp. 2873-2878.

Beraldin, J.-A., (2004). Integration of laser scanning and close-range photogrammetry the last decade and beyond, *Proc. IAPRS*, Vol.35, No.5, pp. 972-983.

Berger, M.; Levine, J.A.; Nonato, L.G.; Taubin, G.; Silva, C.T. (2011). An End-to-End Framework for Evaluating Surface Reconstruction, *SCI Technical Report*, No. UUSCI-2011-001, SCI Institute, University of Utah. Available from: www.sci.utah.edu/publications/SCITechReports/UUSCI-2011-001.pdf

Bernardini, F. & Rushmeier, H. (2002). The 3D Model Acquisition Pipeline, *Computer Graphics Forum*, NCC Blackwell, Vol. 21(2), pp. 149-172.

Bernardini, F., Mittleman, J., Rushmeier, H., Silva, C. & Taubin, G. (1999). The ball-pivoting algorithm for surface reconstruction. *IEEE Transactions on Visualization and Computer Graphics*, Vol. 5, pp. 349–359.

Bernardini, F.; Rushmeier, H.; Martin, I.M.; Mittleman, J.; Taubin, G. (2002). Building a digital model of Michelangelo's Florentine Pieta, *IEEE Computer Graphics Application*, vol. 22, pp. 59–67.

Besl, P.J. & McKay, N. (1992). A Method for Registration of 3-D Shapes, *IEEE Trans. On Pattern Analysis and Machine Intelligence*, Vol. 14-2, pp. 239-256.

Blais F. (2004). Review of 20 Years of Range Sensor Development, *Journal of Electronic Imaging*, Vol 13-1, pp. 231-240.

Boehler, W.; Bordas V.M. & Marbs, A. (2003). Investigating laser scanner accuracy. *Proceedings of the XIXth CIPA Symposium*, pp. 696-702.

Brown, B. & Rusinkiewicz, S. (2007). Global non-rigid alignment of 3-D scans. *ACM Transactions on Graphics*, Vol. 26, No. 3, Article 21.

Brown, D.C. (1971). Close-range camera calibration. *PE&RS*, Vol. 37(8), pp. 855-866

Callieri, M.; Chica, A.; Dellepiane, M.; Besora, I.; Corsini, M.; Moyé S, J.; Ranzuglia, G.; Scopigno, R.; Brunet, P. (2011). Multiscale acquisition and presentation of very large artifacts: The case of Portalada, *Journal of Computing and Cultural Heritage*, Vol.3, No.4, Article number 14.

Carr, J. C.; Beatson, R. K.; Cherrie, J. B.; Mitchell, T. J.; Fright, W. R.; McCallum, B. C. & Evans, T. R. (2001). Reconstruction and representation of 3D objects with radial basis functions, *Proc. SIGGRAPH*, pages 67–76.

Cazals, F. & Giesen, J. (2006). Delaunay triangulation based surface reconstruction. In: *Effective Computational Geometry for Curves and Surfaces*, J.-D. Boissonnat and M. Teillaud, Eds. Springer-Verlag, Mathematics and Visualization, pp. 231–276.

Chen, Y. & Medioni, G. (1992). Object modeling by registration of multiple range images, *Image and Vision Computing*, Vol 10-3, pp. 145-155.

Cignoni, P., Montani, C. & Scopigno, R. (1998). A comparison of mesh simplification algorithms. *Computers & Graphics* Vol. 22, No. 1, pp. 37–54.

Corsini, M.; Dellepiane, M.; Ponchio, F. & Scopigno. R. (2009). Image-to-geometry registration: a mutual information method exploiting illumination-related geometric properties. *Computer Graphics Forum*, Vol. 28(7), pp. 1755-1764.

Criminisi A.; Reid, I. & Zisserman A. (1999). Single view metrology. *Proc. International Conference on Computer Vision*, pp. 434–442.

Curless, B. & Levoy M. (1996). A Volumetric Method for Building Complex Models from Range Images, *Proc. SIGGRAPH96*, pp. 303-312.

Davis, J.; Marschner, S. R.; Garr, M. & Levoy, M. (2002). Filling holes in complex surfaces using volumetric diffusion. *Proc. 3DPVT*, pp. 428–438.

Debevec, P. ; C. Tchou, A. Gardner, T. Hawkins, C. Poullis, J. Stumpfel, A. Jones, N. Yun, P. Einarsson, T. Lundgren, M. Fajardo, and P. Martinez. (2004). Estimating surface reflectance properties of a complex scene under captured natural illumination. *USC ICT Technical Report ICT-TR-06.*

Deng, F. (2011). Registration between Multiple Laser Scanner Data Sets, *Laser Scanning, Theory and Applications*, Chau-Chang Wang (Ed.), ISBN: 978-953-307-205-0, InTech.

Dietrich, A.; Gobbetti, A. & Yoon S.-E. (2007). Massive-model rendering techniques: a tutorial. *Computer graphics and applications*, Vol. 27, No. 6, pp. 20–34.

Eisenbeiss, H. (2009). *UAV Photogrammetry*. Ph.D. Thesis, Institute of Geodesy and Photogrammetry, ETH Zurich, Zurich, Switzerland, p. 235.

El-Hakim. S. (2000). A practical approach to creating precise and detailed 3D models from single and multiple views. *Int. Arch. Photog. & Rem. Sens.*, Vol. 33(B5), pp. 122–129.

El-Hakim. S. (2002). Semi-automatic 3D reconstruction of occluded and unmarked surfaces from widely separated views. *International Archives of Photogrammetry, Remote Sensing and Spatial Information Sciences*, Vol. 34(B5), pp. 143–148.

Fangi, G. (2007). The Multi-Image Spherical Panoramas as a Tool for Architectural Survey, *Proceedings of the XXI International CIPA Symposium*, Vol. 36, Part 5/C53.

Fraser, C.S., 1996: Network design. In: *Close-range Photogrammetry and Machine Vision*, Atkinson (Ed.), Whittles Publishing, UK, pp.256-282.

Furukawa, Y. & Ponce, J. (2010). Accurate, dense and robust multiview stereopsis, *IEEE Trans. Patt. Anal. Mach. Intell.* Vol. 32, pp. 1362-1376.

Gagnon, H.; Soucy, M.; Bergevin, R. & Laurendeau, D. (1994). Registration of multiple range views for automatic 3D model building, *Proc. of IEEE Conf. on CVPR*, pp. 581-586.

Godin, G.; Beraldin, J.-A.; Rioux, M.; Levoy, M. & Cournoyer, L. (2001a). An Assessment of Laser Range Measurement of Marble Surfaces, *Proc. of the 5th Conference on Optical 3-D Measurement Techniques*, Vienna, Austria, pp. 49-56.

Godin, G.; Laurendeau, D.; Bergevin, R. (2001b). A Method for the Registration of Attributed Range Images. *Proc. of Third Int. Conference on 3D Digital Imaging and Modeling (3DIM2001)*, pp. 179-186.

Godin, G; Borgeat, L.; Beraldin, J.-A.; Blais, F. (2010). Issues in acquiring, processing and visualizing large and detailed 3D models, *Proceeding of the 44th Annual Conference on Information Sciences and Systems (CISS 2010)*, pp. 1-6.

Gruen A. & Wang X. (1998). Cc-modeler: a topology generator for 3d city models, *ISPRS Journal of Photogrammetry and Remote Sensing*, Vol. 53, pp. 286–295.

Gruen, A. & Huang, T.S. (2001). *Calibration and Orientation of Cameras in Computer Vision*, Springer: Berlin/Heidelberg, Germany, p. 239.

Gruen, A.; Remondino, F.; Zhang, L. (2004). Photogrammetric reconstruction of the Great Buddha of Bamiyan. *The Photogrammetric Record*, Vol. 19, pp. 177-199.

Guidi, G.; Beraldin, J.-A.; Ciofi, S. & Atzeni, C. (2003). Fusion of range camera and photogrammetry: a systematic procedure for improving 3D models metric accuracy, *IEEE Trans. on Systems Man and Cybernetics Part B*, Vol. 33-4, pp. 667- 676.

Guidi, G.; Beraldin, J.-A. & Atzeni, C. (2004). High accuracy 3D modeling of Cultural Heritage: the digitizing of Donatello's "Maddalena", *IEEE Transactions on Image Processing*, Vol. 13-3, pp. 370-380.

Guidi, G.; Frischer, B.; Russo, M.; Spinetti, A.; Carosso, L. & Micoli, L. L. (2005). Three-dimensional acquisition of large and detailed cultural heritage objects, *Machine Vision and Applications*, Special issue on 3D acquisition technology for cultural heritage, Vol. 17-6, pp. 347-426.

Guidi, G.; Remondino, F.; Morlando, G.; Del Mastio, A.; Uccheddu, F.; Pelagotti, A. (2007). Performance evaluation of a low cost active sensor for cultural heritage documentation, *VIII Conference on Optical 3D Measurement Techniques*, Ed. Gruen/Kahmen, Vol.2, Zurich, Switzerland, pp. 59-69.

Guidi, G. & Bianchini, C. (2007). TOF laser scanner characterization for low-range applications. *Proceedings of the Videometrics IX – SPIE Electronic Imaging*, San Jose, CA, USA, 29–30 January 2007; SPIE: Bellingham WA, USA; pp. 649109.1-649109.11.

Guidi, G.; Remondino, F.; Russo, M.; Menna, F.; Rizzi, A. & Ercoli, S. (2009a). A multi-resolution methodology for the 3D modeling of large and complex archaeological areas, *International Journal of Architectural Computing*, Vol. 7-1, pp. 40-55.

Guidi, G.; Spinetti, A.; Carosso, L. & Atzeni, C. (2009b). Digital three-dimensional modelling of Donatello's David by frequency modulated laser radar, *Studies in Conservation*, Vol. 54, pp. 3-11.

Guidi, G.; Russo, M.; Magrassi, G. & Bordegoni, M. (2010). Performance Evaluation of Triangulation Based Range Sensors, *Sensors*, Vol. 10-8, pp. 7192-7215.

Guidi, G.; Russo, M.; Magrassi, G.; Bordegoni, M. (2011). Low cost characterization of TOF range sensors resolution, *Proc. IS&T/SPIE Electronic Imaging*, Vol. 7864, pp. D0-D10.

Healey G. & Binford, T.O. (1987). Local shape from specularity. *Proc. ICCV*, London, UK.

Hiep, V.H.; Keriven, R.; Labatut, P.; Pons, J.-P. (2009). Towards high-resolution large-scale multi-view stereo, *Proceedings of IEEE Conference on CVPR*, pp. 1430-1437.

Hirschmuller, H. (2008). Stereo processing by semi-global matching and mutual information. IEEE Trans. Patt. Anal. Mach. Intell., 30, 328-341

Hoppe, H. (1996). Progressive meshes, *SIGGRAPH96*, pages 99–108.

Hoppe, H.; Derose, T.; Duchamp, T.; Mcdonald, J. & Stuetzle, W. (1992). Surface reconstruction from unorganized points, *SIGGRAPH92*, Vol. 26, No. 2, pp. 71-78.

Horn B.K.P. & Brooks. M.J. (1989). *Shape from Shading*. MIT Press, Cambridge.

JCGM (2008). International vocabulary of metrology – Basic and general concepts and associated terms (VIM), Bureau International des Poids et Mesures (BIPM), France.

Kender. J.R. (1978). Shape from texture. *Proc. DARPA IU Workshop*.

Kobbelt L. & M. Botsch. (2004). A survey of point-based techniques in computer graphics. *Computers and Graphics*, Vol. 28, No. 6, pp. 801–814.

Lensch, H.; W. Heidrich, and H. Seidel. (2000). Automated texture registration and stitching for real world models. *Proc. 8th Pacific Graph. Conf. CG and Application*, pp. 317–327.

Lensch, H.P.A.; J. Kautz, M. Goesele, W. (2003). Heidrich, and H.-P. Seidel. Image-based reconstruction of spatial appearance and geometric detail, *ACM Transaction on Graphics*, Vol. 22, No. 2, pp. 234-257.

Levoy, M.; Pulli, K.; Curless, B.; Rusinkiewicz, S.; Koller, D.; Pereira, L.; Ginzton, M.; Anderson, S.; Davis, J.; Ginsberg, J.; Shade, J.; Fulk, D. (2000). The Digital Michelangelo Project: 3D Scanning of Large Statues, *SIGGRAPH00*, pp. 131-144.

Li, J.; Guo, Y.; Zhu, J.; Lin X.; Xin Y.; Duan K. & Tang Q. (2007). Large depth of view portable three dimensional laser scanner and its segmental calibration for robot vision, *Optics and Laser in Engineering*, Vol. 45, pp. 1077-1087.

Luhmann, T.; Robson, S.; Kyle, S.; Hartley, I. (2007). *Close Range Photogrammetry: Principles, Techniques and Applications*, Whittles: Dunbeath, UK, p. 528

Luhmann, T.; Tecklenburg, W. (2004). 3-D Object Reconstruction from Multiple-Station Panorama Imagery. *Proc. of ISPRS Workshop on Panorama Photogrammetry*, Vol. 34, Part 5/W16.

Maas, H.-G. (2008). Close-range photogrammetry sensors, *ISPRS Congress*, CRC, pp. 63-72.

MacKinnon, D.; Beraldin, J.-A.; Cournoyer, L.; Blais, F. (2008). Evaluating Laser Spot Range Scanner Lateral Resolution in 3D Metrology. Proceedings of the 21st Annual IS&T/SPIE Symposium on Electronic Imaging. San Jose. January 18-22, 2008.

Meyers, D.; Skinner, S. & Sloan, K. (1992). Surfaces from contours. *ACM Transactions on Graphics*, Vol. 11, No. 3, pp. 228–258.

Mikhail, E.; Bethel, J.; McGlone, J.C. (2001). *Introduction to Modern Photogrammetry*, Wiley.

Ohtake, Y.; Belyaev, A.; Alexa, M.; Turk G. & Seidel, H. P. (2003). Multi-level partition of Unity Implicits, *ACM Trans. on Graphics*, Vol. 22, No. 3, pp. 463–470.

Parian, J.A. & Gruen, A. (2004). An Advanced Sensor Model for Panoramic Cameras, *Proc. of XXth ISPRS Congress*; Vol. 35, Part 5, pp. 24-29

Peggs, G. N.; Maropoulos, P. G.; Hughes, E. B.; Forbes, A. B.; Robson, S.; Ziebart, M.; Muralikrishnan, B. (2009). Recent developments in large-scale dimensional metrology, *Journal of Engineering Manufacture*, Vol. 223, No. 6, pp. 571-595.

Petrov, V.; Kazarinov, A.; Cherniavsky, A.; Vorobey, I.; Krikalev, S.; Mikryukov, P. (2006), Checking of large deployable reflector geometry, *Proc. EuCap 2006 - European Space Agency Special Publication,* Vol. ESA SP-626, 4p.

Pierce, J. (2007). Wider view, *Engineer*, Volume 293, Issue 7735, Pages 36-40.

Pierrot-Deseilligny, M. & Paparoditis, N. (2006). A Multiresolution and Optimization-Based Image Matching Approach: An Application to Surface Reconstruction from SPOT5-HRS Stereo Imagery. *ISPRS Conf. Topographic Mapping From Space*, Vol. 36 1/W41.

Pollefeys, M., Nister, D., Frahm, J.-M., Akbarzadeh, A., Mordohai, P., Clipp, B., Engels, C., Gallup, D., Kim, S.-J., Merrell, P., Salmi, C., Sinha, S., Talton, B., Wang, L., Yang, Q., Stewenius, H., Yang, R., Welch, G. and Towles, H. (2008). Detailed Real-Time Urban 3D Reconstruction From Video, *International Journal of Computer Vision*, Vol. 78, No. 2, pp. 143-167.

Pollefeys, M.; van Gool, L.; Vergauwen, M.; Verbiest, F.; Cornelis, K.; Tops J. & Kock, R. (2004). Visual modelling with a hand-held camera. *International Journal of Computer Vision*, Vol. 59, No. 3, pp. 207-232.

Reinhard, E.; Ward, G.; Pattanaik, S. & Debevec, P. (2005). *High dynamic range imaging: acquisition, display and image-based lighting*. Morgan Kaufmann Publishers.

Remondino, F., El-Hakim, S., Girardi, S., Rizzi, A., Benedetti, S., Gonzo, L., (2009). 3D Virtual reconstruction and visualization of complex architectures - The 3D-ARCH project. *ISPRS*, Vol. 38(5/W1).

Remondino, F. & El-Hakim, S. (2006). Image-based 3D modelling: A review, *The Photogrammetric Record* Vol. 21, pp. 269-291.

Remondino, F.; El-Hakim, S.; Gruen, A.; Zhang, L. (2008). Turning images into 3D models—Development and performance analysis of image matching for detailed surface reconstruction of heritage objects, *IEEE Sig. Process. Mag.* Vol. 25, pp. 55-65.

Remondino, F. & Fraser, C. (2006). Digital camera calibration methods: considerations and comparisons, *ISPRS*, Vol. XXXVI, part 5, pp. 266-272.

Riegl (2010). VZ400 Terrestrial Laser Scanner with on-line waveform processing, Data Sheet, www.riegl.com/uploads/tx_pxpriegldownloads/10_DataSheet_VZ400_20-09-2010.pdf

Rusinkiewicz, S. & Levoy, M. (2001). Efficient variants of the ICP algorithm, *Proceedings of 3DIM2001*, IEEE Computer Society, pp. 145-152.

Sagawa R. & Ikeuchi K. (2008). Hole filling of a 3D model by flipping signs of a signed distance field in adaptive resolution, *IEEE Trans. PAMI*, Vol. 30, No. 4, pp. 686–699.

Salvi, J.; Matabosch, C.; Fofi, D. & Forest J. (2007). A review of recent range image registration methods with accuracy evaluation. *Image and Vision Computing*, Vol. 25, No. 5, pp. 578–596.

Scharstein, D. & Szeliski, R. (2002). A taxonomy and evaluation of dense two-frame stereo correspondence algorithms. *Intl. Journal of Computer Vision*, Vol. 47, pp. 7–42.

Seitz, S.M.; B. Curless, J. Diebel, D. Scharstein, and R. Szeliski. (2006). A comparison and evaluation of multi-view stereo reconstruction algorithm. *Proc. CVPR*, pp. 519–528.

Shan, J. & Toth, C. (2008). *Topographic Laser Ranging and Scanning: Principles and Processing*, CRC, p. 590.

Shannon, C. E. (1949). Communication in the presence of noise, *Proc. Institute of Radio Engineers*, vol. 37, no.1, pp. 10–21, Jan. 1949. Reprint as classic paper in: Proc. IEEE, Vol. 86, No. 2, (Feb 1998).

Skolnik M.I. (1990). *Radar Handbook*, chapt. 14, McGraw-Hill.

Snavely, N.; Seitz, S.; Szeliski, R. (2008). Modelling the world from internet photo collections. *Int. J. Comput. Vis.*, Vol. 80, pp. 189-210.

Soucy, M. & Laurendeau, D. (1995). A general surface approach to the integration of a set of range views, *IEEE Trans. on PAMI*, Vol. 17, No. 4, pp. 344-358.

Stamos, I.; Liu, L.; Chen, C.; Wolberg, G.; Yu, G.; Zokai, S. (2008). Integrating automated range registration with multiview geometry for the photorealistic modelling of large-scale scenes. *Int. J. Comput. Vis.*, Vol. 78, pp. 237-260.

Stumpfel, J.; Tchou, C.; Yun, N.; Martinez, P.; Hawkins, T.; Jones, A.; Emerson, B.; Debevec, P. (2003). Digital reunification of the Parthenon and its sculptures. *Proceedings of VAST*, pp. 41-50

Sturm, P.; Ramalingam, S.; Tardif, J.-P.; Gasparini, S.; Barreto, J. (2011). Camera models and fundamental concepts used in geometric Computer Vision. *Foundations and Trends in Computer Graphics and Vision*, Vol. 6, Nos. 1-2, pp.1-183

Tsai. R.Y. (1986). An efficient and accurate camera calibration technique for 3d machine vision, *Proc. CVPR 1986*, pp. 364–374.

Turk, G. & Levoy, M. (1994). Zippered polygon meshes from range images, *Proceedings of the ACM SIGGRAPH Conference on Computer Graphics*, pp. 311-318.

Umeda, K.; M. Shinozaki, G. Godin, and M. Rioux. (2005). Correction of color information of a 3d model using a range intensity image, *Proc. of 3DIM2005*, pp. 229-236.

Van den Heuvel, F.A. (1998). 3D reconstruction from a single image using geometric constraints, *ISPRS Journal for Photogrammetry and Remote Sensing*, Vol. 53, No. 6, pp. 354–368.

Vergauwen, M. & Van Gool, L. (2006). Web-based 3D reconstruction service, *J. Mach. Vis. Appl.*, Vol. 17, pp. 411-426.

Vosselman, G. & Maas, H.-G. (2010). *Airborne and Terrestrial Laser Scanning*, CRC, p. 318.

Vrubel, A.; Bellon, O.R.P.; Silva, L. (2009). A 3D reconstruction pipeline for digital preservation, *Proceedings of IEEE Conference on CVPR*, pp. 2687-2694.

Winkelbach S. & F.M. Wahl. (2001). Shape from 2D Edge Gradient, *Lecture Notes in Computer Science*, Vol. 2191, pp. 377-384

Yin, X.; Wonka, P.; Razdan, A. Generating. (2009). 3D building models from architectural drawings. *IEEE Comput. Graph. Appl.*, Vol. 29, pp. 20-30.

4

3D Modeling of a Natural Killer Receptor, Siglec-7: Critical Amino Acids for Glycan-Binding and Cell Death-Inducing Activity

Toshiyuki Yamaji[1,2], Yoshiki Yamaguchi[1], Motoaki Mitsuki[1,3], Shou Takashima[1,4], Satoshi Waguri[5,6], Yasuhiro Hashimoto[5,6,*] and Kiyomitsu Nara[5]
[1]RIKEN Insitute,
[2]National Institute of Infectious Diseases,
[3]Pharmaceuticals and Medical Devices Agency,
[4]The Noguchi Institue,
[5]Fukushima Medical University,
[6]Fukushima Industry-University-Government Research Center
Japan

1. Introduction

Siglecs comprise a family of sialic acid-binding Ig-like lectins, expressed mainly on hematopoietic cells (O'Reilly and Paulson 2010; Angata 2006; Crocker, Paulson et al. 2007). More than ten Siglecs of human orgin have been cloned, all of which bind sialoglycans. Structural commonalities include an extracellular N-terminal V-set Ig-like domain, a sialoglycan-binding domain followed by variable numbers of C2-set Ig-like domains, a transmembrane domain, and a cytoplasmic signaling domain. Each member is expressed in a cell-specific manner, e.g., Siglec-1 on macrophages, Sigelc-2 on B cells, Siglec-7 on natural killer cells, and Siglec-9 on myelocytic cells.

Even though Siglecs bind terminal sialic acids on glycoconjugates, each member preferentially binds different oligosaccharide ligands. The nature of a specific sialic acid, its linkage to substituted sugars, and underlying neutral oligosaccharides can all influence Siglec recognition (see Table 1). For instance, Siglec-1 binds a terminal NeuAcα2-3Gal, but not a NeuAcα2-6Gal residue. In contrast, Siglec-2 preferentially binds a terminal NeuAcα2-6Gal residue (Blixt, Collins et al. 2003; Blixt, Han et al. 2008). Siglec-9 binds both of the structures equally. Siglec-7 binds tumor-associated glycans such as so-called "melanoma antigen" (disialyl glycan; NeuAcα2-8NeuAcα2-3Gal) and the branched α2-6sialyl glycan (Galβ1-3[NeuAcα2-6]GlcNAc) (Yamaji, Teranishi et al. 2002; Miyazaki, Ohmori et al. 2004). The binding of Siglec-7 to unique sialoglycans may be associated with tumor recognition by NK cells. In this context, it is notable that antibody-crosslinking of Siglec-7 on NK cells attenuates the cytotoxicity of NK cells against FcγR+ P815 murine mastocytoma cells (Nicoll,

* Corresponding author

Avril et al. 2003). The inhibitory signal of Siglec-7 is transduced by its cytoplasmic signaling domain containing immune receptor tyrosine-based inhibitory motifs (ITIMs) (Ikehara, Ikehara et al. 2004; Yamaji, Mitsuki et al. 2005), which have been described as suppression motifs for a variety of immunocytes.

2. The 3D mapping of critical amino acids for glycan-binding and inibitory activity

We first developed assays for glycan-binding activity and immunosuppressive activity. To identify influential amino acids, we constructed a series of mutants and tested for their activities. Amino acids of significance were mapped on a 3D model of Siglec-7.

2.1 The mapping of important amino acids for recognizing tumor-associated glycans

2.1.1 Overexpression of Siglec-7 on cultured cells

We used two types of cells for overexpressing Siglec-7: hematopoietic U937 monocytic leukemia cells and Chinese hamster ovary (CHO) cells. Each type of cell was transfected with Siglec-7 cDNA and then stable transformants were isolated (U937-WT7 or CHO-WT7). Mock transfection cells were also prepared (U937-Mock or CHO-Mock). Expression levels of Siglec-7 on transformants were estimated by immunoblotting and/or flow cytometry using specific antibodies against Siglec-7 (Yamaji, Mitsuki et al. 2005). Prior to binding assays, the cells were treated with sialidase to remove endogenous sialic acid.

We also prepared Siglec-7 ligand-expressing cells, i.e., human erythroleukemia K562 cells were transfected with cDNA of α2-8sialyltransferase, ST8SiaVI, which biosynthesizes NeuAcα2-8NeuAcα2-3Gal epitope, a preferred ligand of Siglec-7. The isolated stable transformants (K562-ST) were examined for their epitope expression by flow cytometry using S2-566 antibody, which recognizes the disialyl epitope.

2.1.2 Binding activity of Siglec-7 expressed on U937 cells

Siglec-7 binds to melanoma antigen (α2-8disialyl epitope: NeuAcα2-8NeuAcα2-3). We therefore used NeuAcα2-8NeuAc-polyacrylamide (disialo-PAA) as a probe for characterizing

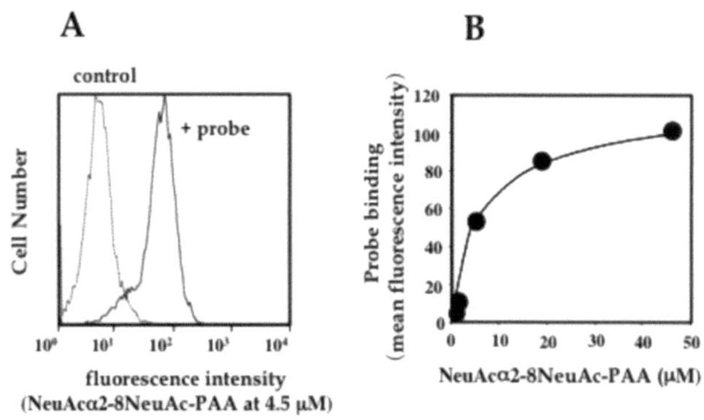

Fig. 1. Binding of a disialyl probe (NeuAcα2-8NeuAc-PAA) to U937-WT7 cells, which overexpress Siglec-7. U937-WT7 cells were incubated with biotinylated NeuAcα2-8NeuAc-PAA. After the cells were incubated with FITC-streptavidin, fluorescnce intensity was detected by flow cytometry (A). Mean fluorescnce intensity increases in a saturable manner in a range of 1-45 μM probe concentration (B).

glycan-binding activity of Siglec-7 on U937-WT7 cells (Fig. 1A). The probe bound to U937-WT7 cells in a saturable manner showing a less than 10 μM of the K_d value (Fig 1B)(unpublished data, Yamaji et al.).
To examine whether Siglec-7 mediates cellular binding, U937-WT7 cells were co-cultured with K562-ST cells, which express α2,8disialyl epitopes. U937-WT7 cells formed aggregates with K562-ST (Fig. 2A) but not with K562-Mock cells (Fig. 2B), suggesting that the cell-cell interaction depends on α2,8disialyl epitopes on K562-ST cells. In this model system Siglec-7 binds α2,8disialyl epitopes on the target cells in a trans-acting manner.

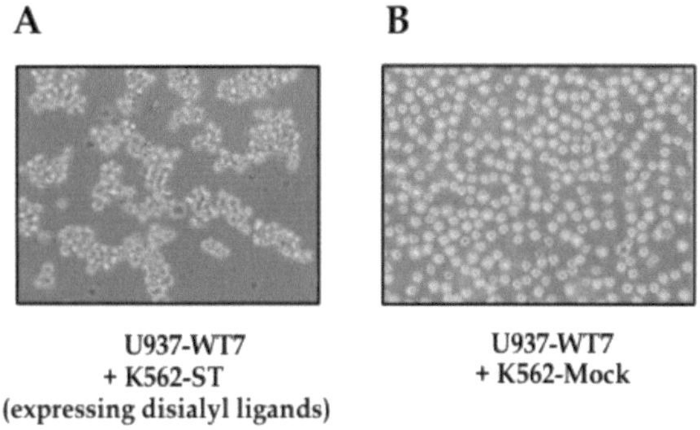

Fig. 2. U937-WT7 cells form aggregates with K562-ST cells (A), which express α2,8disialyl epitopes, but not with K562-Mock cells (B).

Siglec-7 functions as a negative regulator in various immuno-responses. Upon activation of Siglec-7, cytoplasmic immune receptor tyrosine-based inhibitory motifs (ITIMs) are phosphorylated and transduce the inhibitory signal. Co-cultivation of U937-WT cells with K562-ST cells induced tyrosine phosphorylation of Siglec-7, whereas that with K562-mock cells did not (data not shown), suggesting that interaction of Siglec-7 with ligands on opposing cells transduces inhibitory signalling (unpublished data, Yamaji et al.).

2.1.3 Binding specificity of Siglec-7 expressed on CHO cells

To characterize the glycan-binding specificity of Siglec-7, a high-throughput sensitive assay was developed (Yamaji, Nakamura et al. 2003). For the assay we prepared a streptavidin-based neoglycoprotein as a glycoprobe (Hashimoto, Suzuki et al. 1998). Briefly, streptavidin was coupled with oligosaccharides by reductive amination (Mahoney and Schnaar 1994). The synthsized oligosaccharyl streptavidin was mixed with biotinylated BSA, yielding a "polymer" that carries 10-11 molecules of oligosaccharyl streptavidin with more than 100 oligosaccharides (Fig. 3). The multivalency of oligosaccharide ligands increased binding "avidity" of the probe (O'Reilly and Paulson 2010). Radioiodination of biotinylated BSA before mixing gave a radioiodinated glycoprobe. The binding specificity of Siglec-7 on CHO-WT7 cells was examined by utilizing a set of glycoprobes, such as GD3-, GM1-, GD1a-, GT1b-, LSTa-, LSTb-, and LSTc-polymers (Table 1).
GD3-polymer bound to CHO-WT7 cells more effectively than GD1a-polymers (Fig. 4A), suggesting that α2-8disialyl epitopes (NeuAc α2-8 NeuAc α2-3Gal) of the GD3-polymer were more potent ligands than the terminal α2-3-linked sialyl residues of the GD1a-polymer. The GT1b-polymer bound well to CHO-WT7 cells because GT1b contains the α2-8disialyl residue attached to the internal galactose. LSTb-polymer containing the branched α2-6sialyl residue (Galβ1-3[NeuAcα2-6]GlcNAc) also bound well to CHO-WT7 cells. LSTa-,

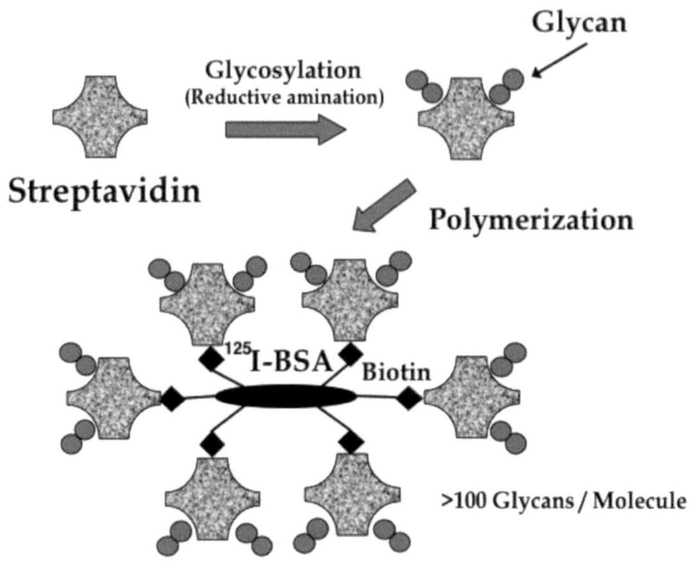

Fig. 3. Preparation of a streptavidin-based glyco-probe.

	Glycochain structures	Siglec-7	Siglec-9
GD3[a]	Siaα2-8Siaα2-3Galβ1-4Glc	++	-
GM1[a]	Galβ1-3GalNAcβ1-4[Siaα2-3]Galβ1-4Glc	-	-
GD1a[a]	Siaα2-3Galβ1-3GalNAcβ1-4[Siaα2-3]Galβ1-4Glc	±	++
GT1b[a]	Siaα2-3Galβ1-3GalNAcβ1-4[Siaα2-8Siaα2-3]Galβ1-4Glc	++	++
LSTa	Siaα2-3Galβ1-3GlcNAcβ1-3Galβ1-4Glc	-	+
LSTb	Galβ1-3[Siaα2-6]GlcNAcβ1-3Galβ1-4Glc	++	-
LSTc	Siaα2-6Galβ1-4GlcNAcβ1-3Galβ1-4Glc	±	++

[a] The nomenclature is based on that of Svennerholm (*J. Neurochem.* **10**, 613, 1963).

Table 1. Glycan structures of oligosaccharides and their recognition by Siglecs.

and LSTc-polymers containing α2-3/6-linked sialyl residue did not bind to the cells. The apparent K_d and B_{max} values of the GD3-polymer to CHO-WT7 cells were about 10 nM and 70 fmol/2 x 10^4 cells, respectively. Next we examined the binding specificity of Siglec-9 (Fig. 4B), which has the highest sequence similarity to Siglec-7 (83% identity) among all Siglecs reported. CHO-WT9 bound poorly to GD3- and LSTb-polymers, but did bind well to GD1a-, LSTa-, GT1b-, and LSTc-polymers, suggesting that Siglec-9 recognizes a terminal NeuAcα2-3(or 6) Gal residue and its binding specificity is distinguished from that of Siglec-7 (Fig. 4).

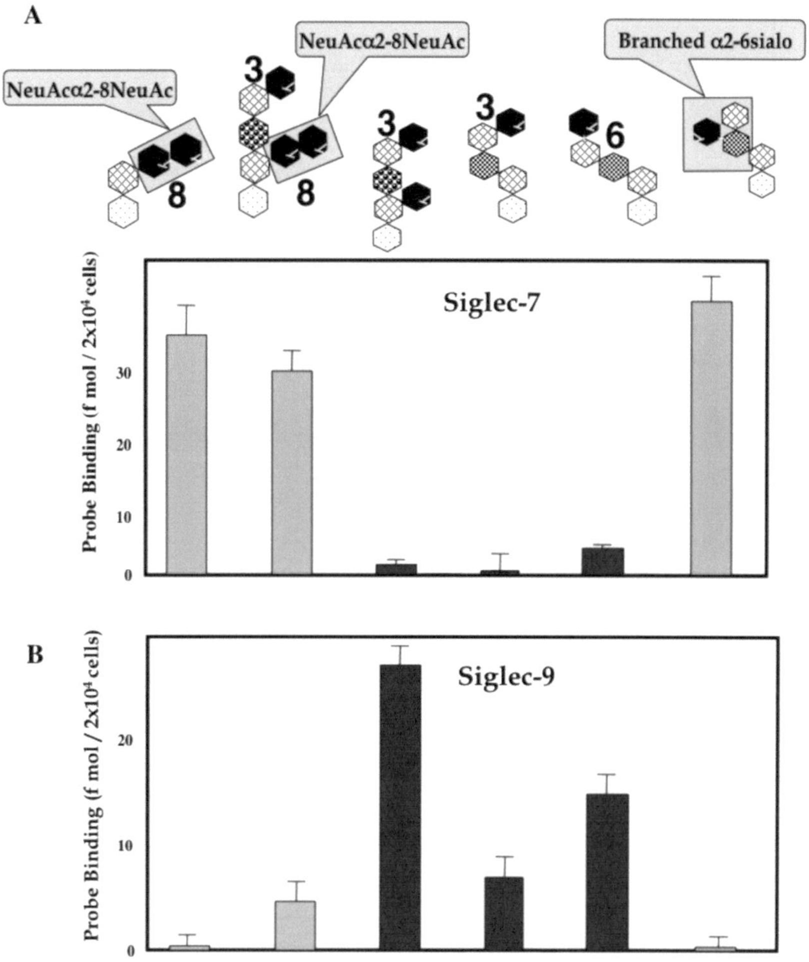

Fig. 4. The glycan-binding specificity of Siglec-7 (A) and Siglec-9 (B).

2.1.4 Mapping of critical amino acids for recognizing tumor-associated glycans

The differences in glycan-binding specificity of the two Siglecs appeared to be attributable to sequence differences in the glycan-binding V-set domains. To identify amino acid(s) responsible for these specificity differences, we prepared a series of shuffling chimeras in the V-set domain between Siglecs-7 and -9. We eventually found that substitution of a small region, Asn70-Lys75, of Siglec-7 with the equivalent region of Siglec-9, Ala66-Asp71 (6 a.a. chimera) resulted in the loss of Siglec-7-like binding specificity and the acquisition of the Siglec-9-like binding property (Fig. 5), suggesting that only the six amino acid sequence in the glycan-binding domain is important for determining the binding specificity of Siglec-7 and -9. None of single amino acid mutants changed binding specificity, suggesting that all of the six amino acids, or possibly a certain combination among these amino acids, is responsible for Siglec-7-like binding specificity (Yamaji, Teranishi et al. 2002).

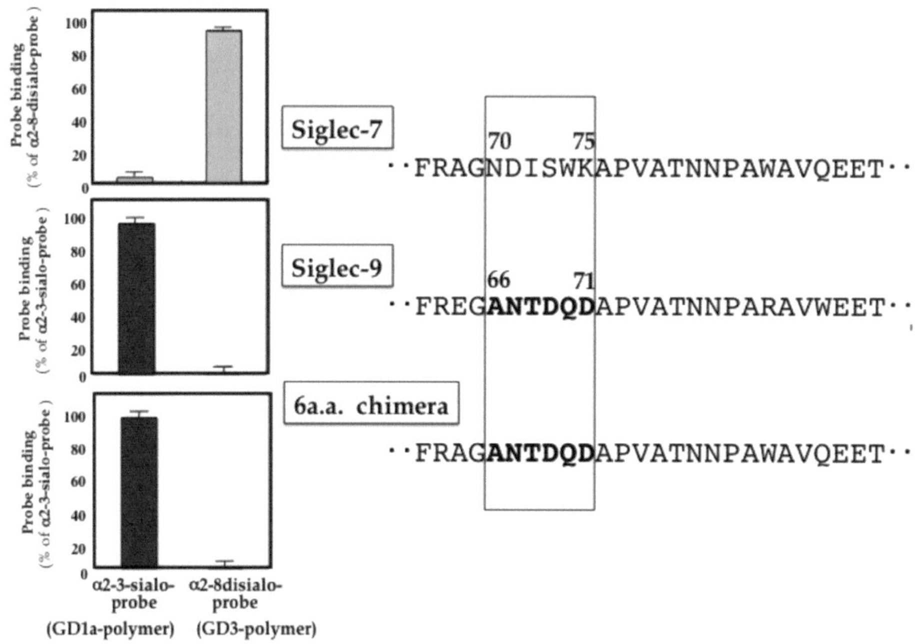

Fig. 5. Siglec-7 binds well to α2-8disialo-probe (Siaα2-8Siaα2-3Gal) whereas Siglec-9 does α2-3sialo-probe (Siaα2-3Gal). Replacement of six amino acids (Asn70-Lys75) of Siglec-7 results in Siglec-9-like binding specificity (6 a.a. chimera).

2.1.5 The 3D mapping of the six amino acid in Siglec-7 V-set domain

To date, crystal structures of Siglec domains have been reported including mouse Siglec-1 V-set domain, human Siglec-5 V-set plus C2-set domain and human Siglec-7 V-set domain (Fig. 6).

Structural information on Siglecs is thus accumulating, and the basis for the recognition of a terminal sialic acid is becoming established. The interaction is highlighted by a conserved arginine residue that forms a crucial salt bridge with the sialic acid carboxylate.

Crystal structures of Siglec-7 V-set domain have been reported so far with or without sialosides (Alphey, Attrill et al. 2003; Dimasi, Moretta et al. 2004; Attrill, Imamura et al. 2006; Attrill, Takazawa et al. 2006). The structure of unliganded Siglec-7 V-set domain is an Ig-like β-sandwich fold formed by two β-sheets (strands A′GFCC′ and ABED) (Fig. 7, left) (Alphey, Attrill et al. 2003). The conserved Arg124, which is the key ligand-binding residue, is solvent-exposed and is located on the center of A′GFCC′ face.

Six amino acid residues (Asn70 to Lys75), which determine the binding preference for disialo-glycans (Yamaji, Teranishi et al. 2002), are located on the tip of the C-C′ loop. The crystal structure of Siglec-7 V-set domain in complex with α(2-8)disialylated glycan reveals how this important family of lectins binds the structurally diverse sialosides (Fig. 7, right). The terminal sialic acid is the major determinants of ligand binding, making several hydrogen bonds with the protein. A key salt bridge is formed between the Arg124 guanidinium group and the terminal sialic acid carboxylate. The C-C′ loop, a region implicated in ligand-binding specificity, undergoes a drastic conformational shift, allowing it to interact with the underlying neutral glycan core. The ligand-induced conformational change observed in the C-C′ loop may be characterstic of Siglec-7.

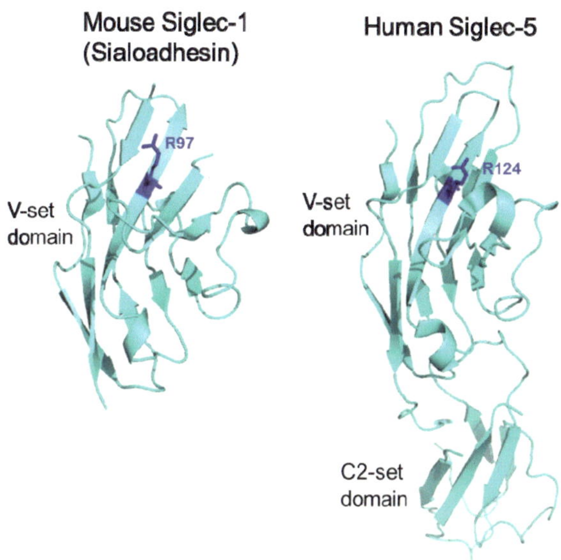

Fig. 6. Crystal structures of Siglec domains reported to date. Mouse Siglec-1 (left, PDB code 1QFO), human Siglec-5 (center, PDB code 2ZG1) and human Siglec-7 (right, PDB code 1O7V) are shown with ribbon representation. Conserved arginine residue is highlighted in dark blue.

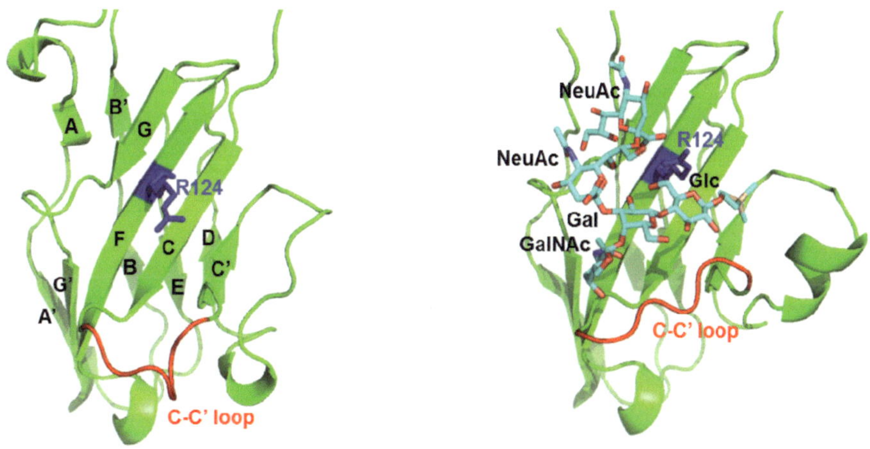

Fig. 7. Dynamic conformational shift of the C-C′ loop of Siglec-7 at the binding pocket. Crystal structures of unliganded (left) (Alphey, Attrill et al. 2003) and liganded (right) (Attrill, Imamura et al. 2006). Siglec-7 V-set domains are shown in ribbon diagrams. In both structures, a conserved Arg124 residue is highlighted in blue with stick representation. Six amino acid residues, Asn70 to Lys75 in the C-C′ loop, are colored in red. Disialylated GT1b glycan is shown with stick representation (right).

2.2 The 3D mapping of critical amino acids for cell death-inducing activity

2.2.1 Cell death-inducing activity of Siglec-7

To analyze effects of Siglec-7 on a cellular function, Siglec-7 on U937-WT7 cells was ligated with an $F(ab')_2$ fragment of anti-Siglec-7. The ligation of Siglec-7 with the specific antibody, 13-3-D, increased cell death at 30-50% (Fig. 8A). Control $F(ab')_2$ fragments of irrelevant antibody showed a subtle effect on the cell death under our experimental conditions. Figure 6B shows a graph of percentage of Annexin V-positive cells in the Annexin V-positive window in Figure 8A. The cell death of Siglec-7-expressing cells was time-dependent and dose-dependent of incubation with the $F(ab')_2$ fragment. A pancaspase inhibitor, Z-VAD-FMK, did not inhibited Siglec-7-dependent cell death, suggesting that caspases are not involved in the cell death. In addition, we could not detect DNA ladder formation in the cell death process (Mitsuki, Nara et al. 2010).

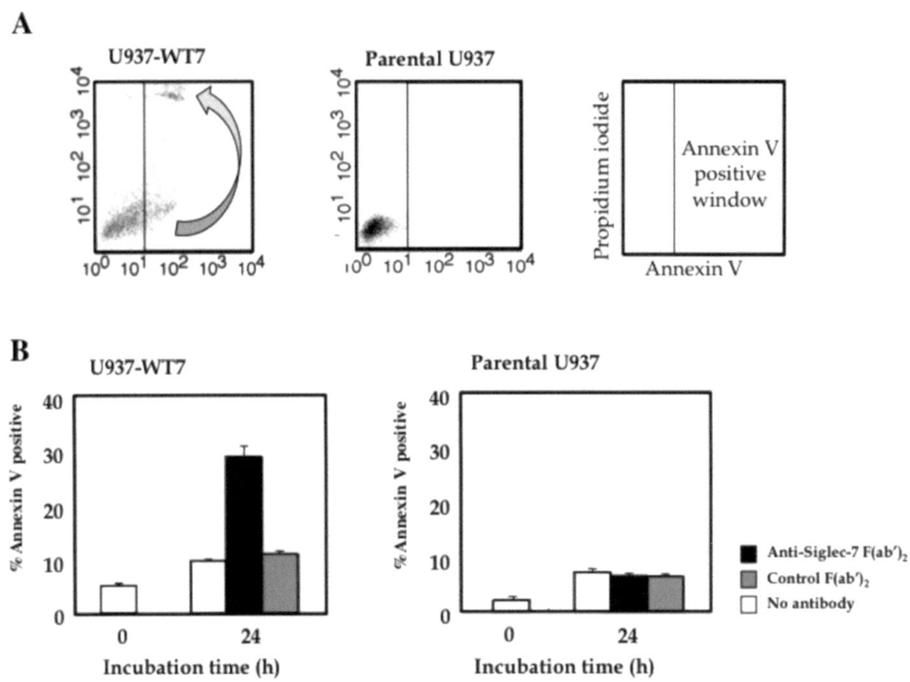

Fig. 8. Ligation of Siglec-7 elicits death of U937-WT7.

2.2.2 Morphological changes of death-induced U937-WT7

Electron microscopy revealed that ligation of Siglec-7 induced some chromatin condensation in the nucleus, but did not induce nuclear condensation and fragmentation (Fig. 9). It was noted that Siglec-7 ligation induced a number of vacuoles, which were associated with "ribosome-like granules", suggesting that the vacuoles are derived from rough endoplasmic reticulum. Neither nuclear condensation nor fragmentation was detected in the cell death, suggesting that Siglec-7 induces non-apoptotic cell death.

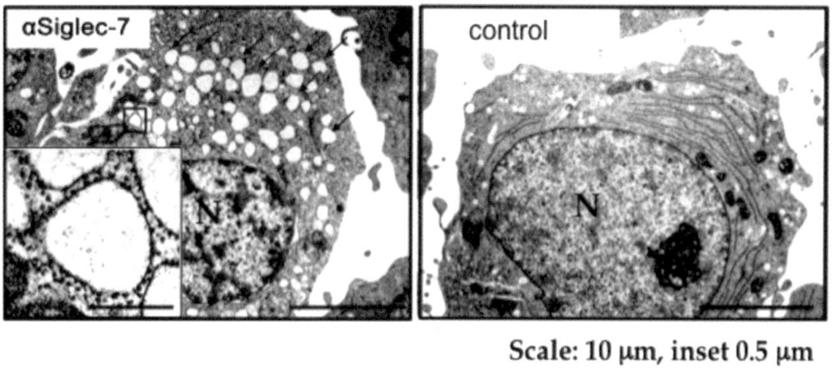

Fig. 9. Electron micrograph of U937-WT cells, which are treated with (αSiglec-7) or (control) an F(ab')$_2$ fragment of anti-Siglec-7. Siglec-7 ligation induces some chromatin condensation and formation of vacuoles with "ribosome-like granules"(inset).

2.2.3 Mapping of important amino acids for inducing cell death

To test the involvement of ITIM for signaling, we deleted the cytoplasmic portion of Siglec-7 and expressed it in U937 cells (U937-7Δcytosol). Unexpectedly, U937-7Δcytosol without cytosolic domain elicited cell death (Fig. 10A), indicating that cell death does not involve

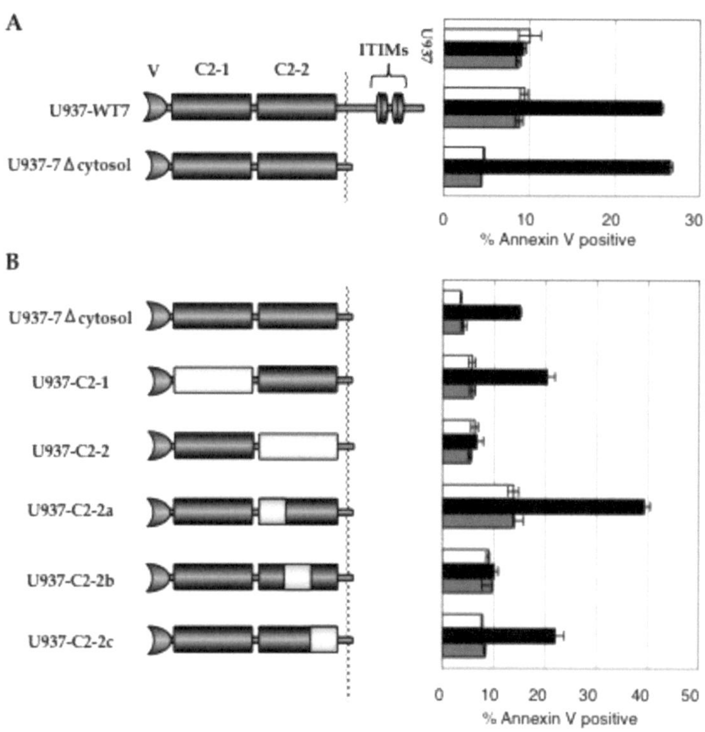

Fig. 10. Shuffling chimeras in C-set domains between Siglec-7 (gray bar) and -9 (white bar). Replacement of C2-2 or C2-2b domain abolishes cell death-inducing activity.

ITIMs. Since U937-WT9 did not show cell death, we prepared a series of domain shuffling chimeras between Siglecs-7 and -9 to identify domain(s) responsible for the cell death.
Each domain of U937-7Δcytosol was replaced with the corresponding domain of Siglec-9. Assays for death inducing activity of the chimeras revealed that replacement of the membrane-proximal C2-set domain abolished cell death activity (U937-C2-2), indicating that C2-2 domain is important for the cell death (Fig. 10B)(Mitsuki, Nara et al. 2010). To narrow down the region responsible for cell death, we prepared additional chimeric mutants. The C2-2 domain was tentatively divided into three portions; C2-2a, C2-2b, and C2-2c regions. When C2-2b region was replaced with the corresponding region of Siglec-9, cell death was completely abolished (U937-C2-2b) (Fig. 10B). Neither replacement of C2-2a nor C2-2c had any effect. These results suggest that the C2-2b region contributes most to cell death.
Six amino acids differ between Siglec-7 and -9 in the C2-2b region, prompting us to prepare single amino acid mutants using U937-7Δcytosol cDNA as a parental construct. Five of six possible mutants were established as stable cell lines. Four of the five mutants (W288L, T289S, S292G, and L304G) showed marked decreases in cell death activity (Fig. 11), suggesting that the four amino acids are critical for inducing the cell death.

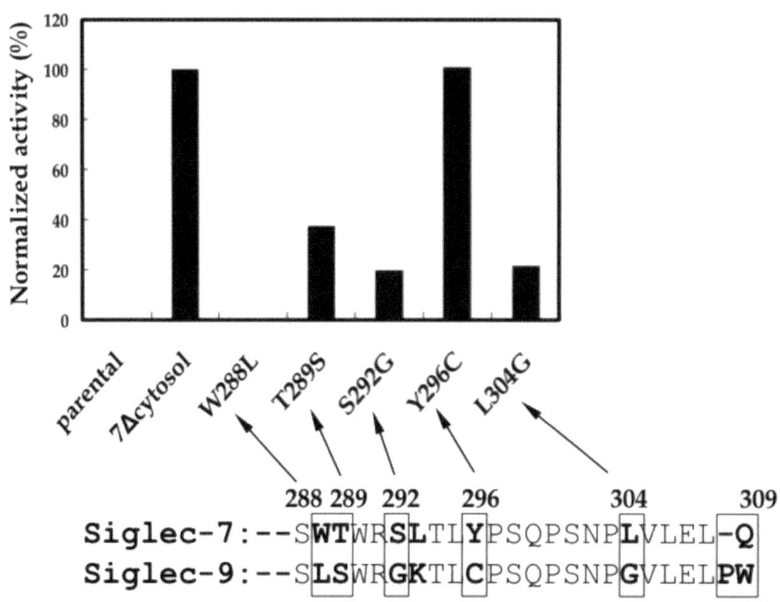

Fig. 11. Single amino acid mutants of Siglec-7 and their cell death-inducing activity. Four mutants (W288L, T289S, S292G, and L304G) show marked decrease in the cell death activity.

2.2.4 The 3D mapping of critical amino acids for cell death-inducing activity

Although structural information on the V-set domain is available for some of Siglecs, little is known about the Siglec C2 domains. We therefore built models of C2-2 domains of Siglec-7 and -9 (Fig. 12). A homology search based on Smith-Waterman algorithm was performed using SSearch (Smith and Waterman 1981) to identify sequences that are homologous with the human Siglec-7 C2-2 domain. The second immunoglobulin domain of human paladin (PDB code 2dm3) was selected as a template among those with low *E* values. The positions of the cysteine residues are conserved between Siglec-7/-9 C2-2 domains and second Ig domain of paladin. The qualities of the resultant protein structures were checked using the Procheck program (Laskowski, MacArthur et al. 1993), which gives Ramachandran plots and a quantitative distribution of the geometric parameters within the allowed conformational space. Importantly, the model of Siglec-7 C2-2 domain suggests that the four amino acid residues (L304, W288, T289 and S292) were proximal to one another (Fig. 12). The close location of these four residues tempted us to speculate that they would be involved in interactions with other adjacent molecules to transduce the death signal.

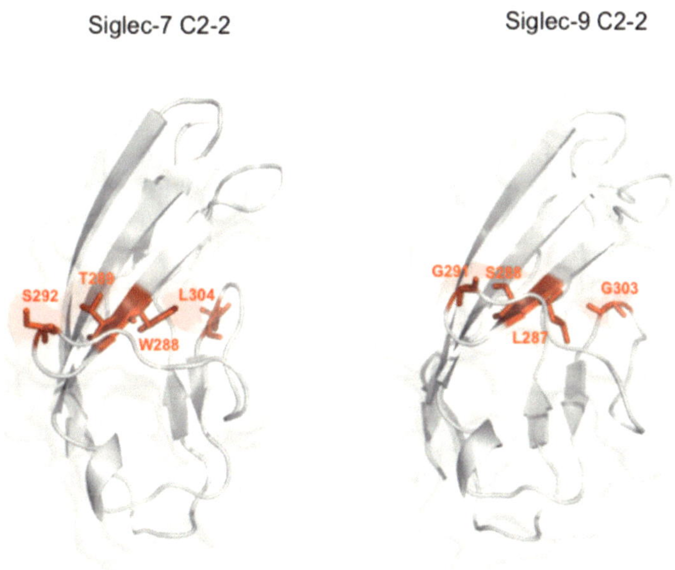

Fig. 12. Computer-assisted homology modeling of the C2-2 domains of Siglec-7 and -9. The models are shown by space filling (transparent) and ribbon representation. Homology modeling was performed using MODELLER version 9.4 software (Sali and Blundell 1993; Fiser, Do et al. 2000; Marti-Renom, Stuart et al. 2000). The four amino acids in Siglec-7 (L304, W288, T289 and S292), which are responsible for the cell death activity, are shown in red with stick representation. The corresponding residues in Siglec-9 (G303, L287, S288 and G291) are also shown in red.

3. Conclusion

We have demonstrated that Siglec-7 may mediate non-apoptotic cell death by signal transduction after binding to tumor-associated glycans such as "melanoma antigen" (α2-8disialyl epitopes). In particular, we have identified amino acid residues responsible for the activity. These residues are mapped on a 3D-structure of Siglec-7 and their functions are discussed from a structural point of view.

Six amino acid residues (Asn70 to Lys75), responsible for the binding preference for α2-8disialyl epitope, are located on the tip of the C-C′ loop and undergoes a drastic conformational shift allowing it to interact with the underlying neutral glycan core. This dynamic comformational change may determine the ligand-binding specificity of Siglec-7. Thus our biochemical data in conjunction with the reported crystallographic data are of great value in understanding the structure-function relationships of Siglecs and other sialoside-binding proteins.

Four amino acid residues (L304, W288, T289 and S292) in the Siglec-7 C2-2 domain, responsible for eliciting cell death, are proximal to one another. It is tempting to speculate that these residues are crucial for interacting with other adjacent molecules to transduce the death signal. These structural models would be useful for developing structure-guided inhibitors or activators of Siglec-7 on NK cells.

4. Acknowledgements

The work was supported by the Core Research for Evolutional Science and Technology (CREST program), funded by the Japan Science and Technology Agency. Yasuhiro Hashimoto was the recipient of grants from the Ministry of Health, Labor and Welfare of Japan [grant number H23-Nanchi-Ippan-018]; the Ministry of Education, Science, Sports and Culture of Japan [grant number 23590367]; and the Naito Foundation. We thank Dr. Kenneth Nollet for editorial advice and proofreading the manuscript, Masaki Kato for helping the modeling of Siglec-7, and Yukari Saito for secretarial assistance.

5. References

Alphey, M. S., H. Attrill, et al. (2003). "High resolution crystal structures of Siglec-7. Insights into ligand specificity in the Siglec family." J. Biol. Chem. 278(5): 3372-7.

Angata, T. (2006). "Molecular diversity and evolution of the Siglec family of cell-surface lectins." Mol. Divers. 10(4): 555-66.

Attrill, H., A. Imamura, et al. (2006). "Siglec-7 undergoes a major conformational change when complexed with the α(2,8)-disialylganglioside GT1b." J. Biol. Chem. 281(43): 32774-83.

Attrill, H., H. Takazawa, et al. (2006). "The structure of Siglec-7 in complex with sialosides: leads for rational structure-based inhibitor design." Biochem. J. 397(2): 271-8.

Blixt, O., B. E. Collins, et al. (2003). "Sialoside specificity of the siglec family assessed using novel multivalent probes: identification of potent inhibitors of myelin-associated glycoprotein." J. Biol. Chem. 278(33): 31007-19.

Blixt, O., S. Han, et al. (2008). "Sialoside analogue arrays for rapid identification of high affinity siglec ligands." J. Am. Chem. Soc. 130(21): 6680-1.

Crocker, P. R., J. C. Paulson, et al. (2007). "Siglecs and their roles in the immune system." Nat. Rev. Immunol. 7(4): 255-66.

Dimasi, N., A. Moretta, et al. (2004). "Structure of the saccharide-binding domain of the human natural killer cell inhibitory receptor p75/AIRM1." Acta Crystallogr. D Biol. Crystallogr. 60(Pt 2): 401-3.

Fiser, A., R. K. Do, et al. (2000). "Modeling of loops in protein structures." Protein Sci. 9(9): 1753-73.

Hashimoto, Y., M. Suzuki, et al. (1998). "A streptavidin-based neoglycoprotein carrying more than 140 GT1b oligosaccharides: quantitative estimation of the binding specificity of murine sialoadhesin expressed on CHO cells." J Biochem. 123(3): 468-78.

Ikehara, Y., S. K. Ikehara, et al. (2004). "Negative regulation of T cell receptor signaling by Siglec-7 (p70/AIRM) and Siglec-9." J. Biol. Chem. 279(41): 43117-25.

Laskowski, R. A., M. W. MacArthur, et al. (1993). "PROCHECK: A program to check the stereochemical quality of protein structures." J. Appl. Crystallogr. 26: 283-291.

Mahoney, J. A. and R. L. Schnaar (1994). "Ganglioside-based neoglycoproteins." Methods Enzymol .242: 17-27.

Marti-Renom, M. A., A. C. Stuart, et al. (2000). "Comparative protein structure modeling of genes and genomes." Annu. Rev. Biophys. Biomol. Struct. 29: 291-325.

Mitsuki, M., K. Nara, et al. (2010) "Siglec-7 mediates nonapoptotic cell death independently of its immunoreceptor tyrosine-based inhibitory motifs in monocytic cell line U937." Glycobiology 20(3): 395-402.

Miyazaki, K., K. Ohmori, et al. (2004). "Loss of disialyl Lewis^a, the ligand for lymphocyte inhibitory receptor sialic acid-binding immunoglobulin-like lectin-7 (Siglec-7) associated with increased sialyl Lewis^a expression on human colon cancers." Cancer Res. 64(13): 4498-505.

Nicoll, G., T. Avril, et al. (2003). "Ganglioside GD3 expression on target cells can modulate NK cell cytotoxicity via siglec-7-dependent and -independent mechanisms." Eur J Immunol. 33(6): 1642-8.

O'Reilly, M. K. and J. C. Paulson (2010) "Multivalent ligands for siglecs." Methods Enzymol. 478: 343-63.

Sali, A. and T. L. Blundell (1993). "Comparative protein modelling by satisfaction of spatial restraints." J. Mol. Biol. 234(3): 779-815.

Smith, T. F. and M. S. Waterman (1981). "Identification of common molecular subsequences." J. Mol. Biol. 147(1): 195-7.

Yamaji, T., M. Mitsuki, et al. (2005). "Characterization of inhibitory signaling motifs of the natural killer cell receptor Siglec-7: attenuated recruitment of phosphatases by the receptor is attributed to two amino acids in the motifs." Glycobiology 15(7): 667-76.

Yamaji, T., K. Nakamura, et al. (2003). "Application of a multivalent glycoprobe: characterization of sugar-binding specificity of Siglec family proteins." Methods Enzymol. 363: 104-13.

Yamaji, T., T. Teranishi, et al. (2002). "A small region of the natural killer cell receptor, Siglec-7, is responsible for its preferred binding to α2,8-disialyl and branched α2,6-sialyl residues. A comparison with Siglec-9." J. Biol. Chem. 277(8): 6324-32.

5

Applications of Computational 3D–Modeling in Organismal Biology

Christian Laforsch[1,2], Hannes Imhof[1,2], Robert Sigl[1,2], Marcus Settles[3], Martin Heß[2,4] and Andreas Wanninger[5]
[1]*Department of Biology II, Ludwig-Maximilians-University Munich,*
[2]*GeoBioCenter, Ludwig-Maximilians-University Munich,*
[3]*Institute of Radiology, Technical University of Munich,*
[4]*Department of Biology I, Ludwig-Maximilians-University Munich,*
[5]*Dept. of Integrative Zoology, Faculty of Life Sciences, University of Vienna,*
[1,2,3,4]*Germany*
[5]*Austria*

1. Introduction

Understanding the interrelations between form, function and evolution has traditionally been a major goal in organismal biology. In former times only line drawings or illustrations have been used to display the fascinating variety of body shape and the underlying functional morphology of living animals. A textbook example for scientific illustrations is still the artwork "Kunstformen der Natur", published by Ernst Haeckel between 1899 and 1904. However, the nature of most of his drawings is art rather than an accurate scientific description of the displayed creatures. When Francesco Stelluti showed details of honey bees in 1625 by using the first simple optical microscope it became obvious that technical improvement leads to substantial progress in elucidating the secrets of nature (Bardell, 1983). Along with the development of photographic and microscopic techniques the quality of biological drawings and illustrations increased, but still only two-dimensional images of dissected or sectioned species were available in order to illustrate the structural nature of organisms. However, to analyse the spatial arrangement of both macroscopic and microscopic three-dimensional biological structures the study of two-dimensional data sets alone is often not sufficient. Given that three-dimensional visualizations facilitate the understanding of the spatial assembly of the object of interest (OOI) and in addition often provide novel information, manual graphical reconstructions were generated prior to the era of computational 3D-imaging (Verraes, 1974). Although scientists gained a deeper understanding about complex morphologies and even the ontogeny of organisms by the application of this labour-intensive approach, it is still limited by the plane of the histological sections. The rapidly advancing field of digital imaging techniques combined with an increase in computational capacity enabled the implementation of computerized 3D-reconstructions, which in turn has opened new avenues in biological sciences (Fig. 1). The entire process of 3D-reconstruction starts from data acquisition by the use of a variety of digital imaging techniques. The obtained image stacks made up of digital pixels are subsequently processed by the appropriate software to model the OOI with high geometric accuracy, resulting in an interactive virtual clone of the selected biological structure. The anatomy of the OOI can be explored by choosing any virtual cutting plane through the raw data stack. Finally, the derived 3D-model can be viewed from different angles and translucent depictions even allow displaying the spatial arrangement of several structures simultaneously. The computerized 3D-models of organs, tissues and cells could then give further insights into the relationship between macroscopic structures such as bones, the connection between microscopic structures such as neuronal networks and the distribution of single components in a tissue such as the distribution of a neurotransmitter in the brain or even the expression pattern of a single gene. In addition, it facilitates precise volume and surface area measurements (Salisbury, 1994).

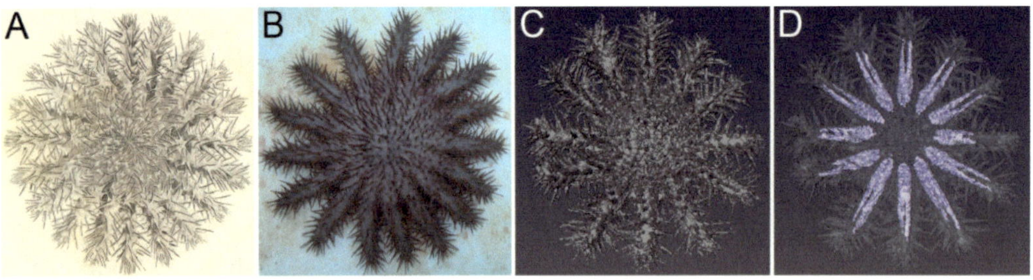

Fig. 1. From drawings to 3D-models, development of imaging techniques.
A Classical drawing of *Acanthaster planci* (Plate 61 of Ellis, J. and Solander, D.: The natural history of many curious and uncommon zoophytes collected from various parts of the globe. Published in 1786 by Benjamin and Son at Horace's Head, Fleet Street.). **B** Digital image of *A. planci*. **C** 3D-model of an *A. planci* individual obtained from MRI-image stacks showing the outer morphology (body wall). **D** 3D-model of an *A. planci* individual obtained from MRI-image stacks offering insights into the inner morphology by showing transparent body wall and pyloric caeca (blue).

State-of-the-art imaging techniques provide not only spatial information but they may also carry multi-dimensional information including time (e.g., live cell imaging) or spectral channels. Another major advantage is that, especially for macroscopic applications, scanner-based non-invasive virtual sectioning techniques (e.g., CT, MRI) have been developed for diagnostics and anatomical investigations.

Depending on the underlying scientific question careful considerations are necessary to choose the appropriate digital imaging method. For instance, soft tissues are best depicted using magnetic resonance imaging (MRI), whereas calcareous and bony structures are best displayed using X-ray computed tomography (CT). For small species or investigations on the cellular level different microscopy techniques such as confocal laserscanning microscopy (CLSM) are frequently used to obtain three-dimensional datasets. For micro-structural and morphological studies, conventional histological sectioning followed by 3D-reconstruction is still an indispensable methodology. Here, a selection of several imaging techniques to generate computerized 3D-reconstructions is presented and their fields of application in organismal biology are illustrated.

2. Histological and ultrastructural analysis based on physical sectioning

The prerequisite for this labour-intensive and time-consuming method is embedding and sectioning of organisms or tissues of interest, after appropriate fixation. Thus, the specimen represents a "snapshot" of the living structure as close to its *in vivo* state as possible. Depending on size and consistency (e.g., transparency, rigidity, biochemical composition, etc.) of the biological objects and according to the requirements of the scientific objectives concerning resolution, contrast and spatial precision, different preparation and imaging methods have to be chosen.

If micro-CT (section 4.1), micro-MRI (section 4.2) or optical sectioning microscopy (CLSM, section 3) are not available or not applicable to achieve the desired quality of data, the volume of interest (VOI) has to be cut physically into a most complete series of plane slices and imaged step by step. Subsequently, these images need to be aligned, segmented and reconstructed.

Generalized flowchart for computer-based 3D-reconstructions from section series

Step 1.	**Procurement** of living biological material (from natural habitat or from culture).
Step 2.	If necessary **dissecting** of the organ/tissue to be investigated (after relaxation and euthanization in case of animals).
Step 3.	Chemical **fixation** (e.g., formalin, glutaraldehyde, osmiumtetroxide); pH and osmolarity have to be adjusted to minimize shrinkage/swellings. **Decalcification** if needed (calcified bones or shells may damage the knifes).
Step 4.	**Embedding** (inclusion or infiltration; e.g., agarose, kryo kits, historesin, epoxy resin).
Step 5.	**Trimming** of the cutting surface, considering the orientation of the structure.
Step 6.	**Cutting** with microtome (using e.g., steel/glass/diamond knifes) or by ion beam milling. **Mounting** slices on glass slides or TEM grids.
Step 7.	**Staining** or "contrasting" slices (e.g., histochemical dyes, immunostaining, heavy metals - in certain cases this step is performed prior to embedding).
Step 8.	**Digital imaging** of slices or of block surfaces (both light or electron microscopy); saving of raw data and generation parameters.
Step 9.	Digital **preprocessing** of the raw data (e.g., autoscaling, unsharp masking, deconvolution).
Step 10.	**Alignment** of image stacks (rigid or elastic registration) and defining voxel size.
Step 11.	**Segmentation** of substructures (manually or semi-automatically, e.g., via thresholding).
Step 12.	**Rendering** (volume rendering or surface rendering after triangulation).
Step 13.	**Morphometry** if required (e.g., volumetry, measuring distances/angles, detecting and counting repetitive structural units).
Step 14.	**Presentation**/publication of selected views or interactively manipulable 3D-models (see e.g., Ruthensteiner & Heß, 2008).

Whereas steps 1-3 are common in invasive visualization techniques, the consecutive steps 4-8 are exclusively applied in histological and ultrastructural analyses based on physical sectioning. The subsequent process from digital processing of the raw data (step 9) to the presentation of a 3D-model (step 14) is identical, regardless which method of data acquisition was applied. Among these steps alignment (step 10) and segmentation (step 11) are crucial to obtain precise volume data from the OOI.

Alignment

For any 3D-reconstruction – in particular when using physical sectioning – image alignment (= image registration) plays a decisive role. To obtain an accurate positioning of all point measurements in the 3D-coordiante system, it is important to match neighbouring 2D image planes as precisely as possible. Simplified, 3 cases can be distinguished: **(1)** Neighbouring planes are correctly aligned *a priori,* because raw data are not acquired in layers (e.g., cone beam micro-CT, MRI with layer selection gradients) or because the acquisition of 2D images is effected without drift from the coherent VOI (e.g., laser scanning microscopy, FIB-FESEM: see section 2.1.2). **(2)** In most cases section series are imaged, whereby the slice orientation with respect to the cutting surface is inevitably lost. Here, subsequent images have to be aligned by transformation and rotation (**rigid registration**). Either this is performed manually by superposition of landmarks in two transparent images (one positive, one negative) until the overlay appears as "flat" as possible, or automatically via iterative shift and cross correlation of two images with an appropriate stop criterion. In this context the correction of some cutting artefacts is possible: by co-embedding tiny polystyrene spheres (e.g., 2 - 20 µm) a compression of slices in cutting direction can be quantified and corrected by unidirectional image stretching, coevally the precise slice thickness can be determined. **(3)** If image distortion is inevitable during raw data acquisition **elastic registration** has to be used. Imaging ultrathin section series by transmission electron microscopy (TEM) may suffer from image distortions generated by electromagnetic lenses, slice compression from cutting and slice deformation in the electron beam. Some partial alignment success can be achieved by computationally intensive image deformation algorithms, such as StackReg in Fiji software (see Thevenaz et al., 1998).

Segmentation

The generation of 3D-views via volume- or surface-rendering requires the identification of structures in the raw data and labelling of the related voxels. This procedure, called "segmentation", can be performed fast and easy in certain cases, either by using the raw data or inverted raw data for volume rendering directly, or by defining thresholds on one or both sides of the relevant intensity range (after contrast enhancement if necessary). The latter enables to extract the structure of interest by a single mouse click (e.g., dark stained object against a bright background in histology, brightly coded bone material against darker soft tissue in CT, fluorescence signal in CLSM). Thresholding, as a rule, produces some artificial border roughness that can be corrected manually or by digital smoothing. Mostly, however, segmentation is a time consuming procedure in which the scientist has to manually label the structures of interest in every single image plane (XY, XZ or/and YZ) using software tools such as a "pencil" or a "polygon lasso". The difficulty in the segmentation of biological structures (e.g., the course of the intestine between adjacent organs or the arborization of a single neuron in the "cable mess" of a brain) lies in the recognition of structure profiles by relative location and inner structure even if contrast is low and in the discrimination from neighbouring structures with similar grey values or without sharp contours. Although some efforts have been made to automatically track structures with adaptive (e.g., Kalman or graph cuts) algorithms having some short-range success (e.g., Jurrus et al., 2006; Yang & Choe, 2009), the human eye and brain seems to be

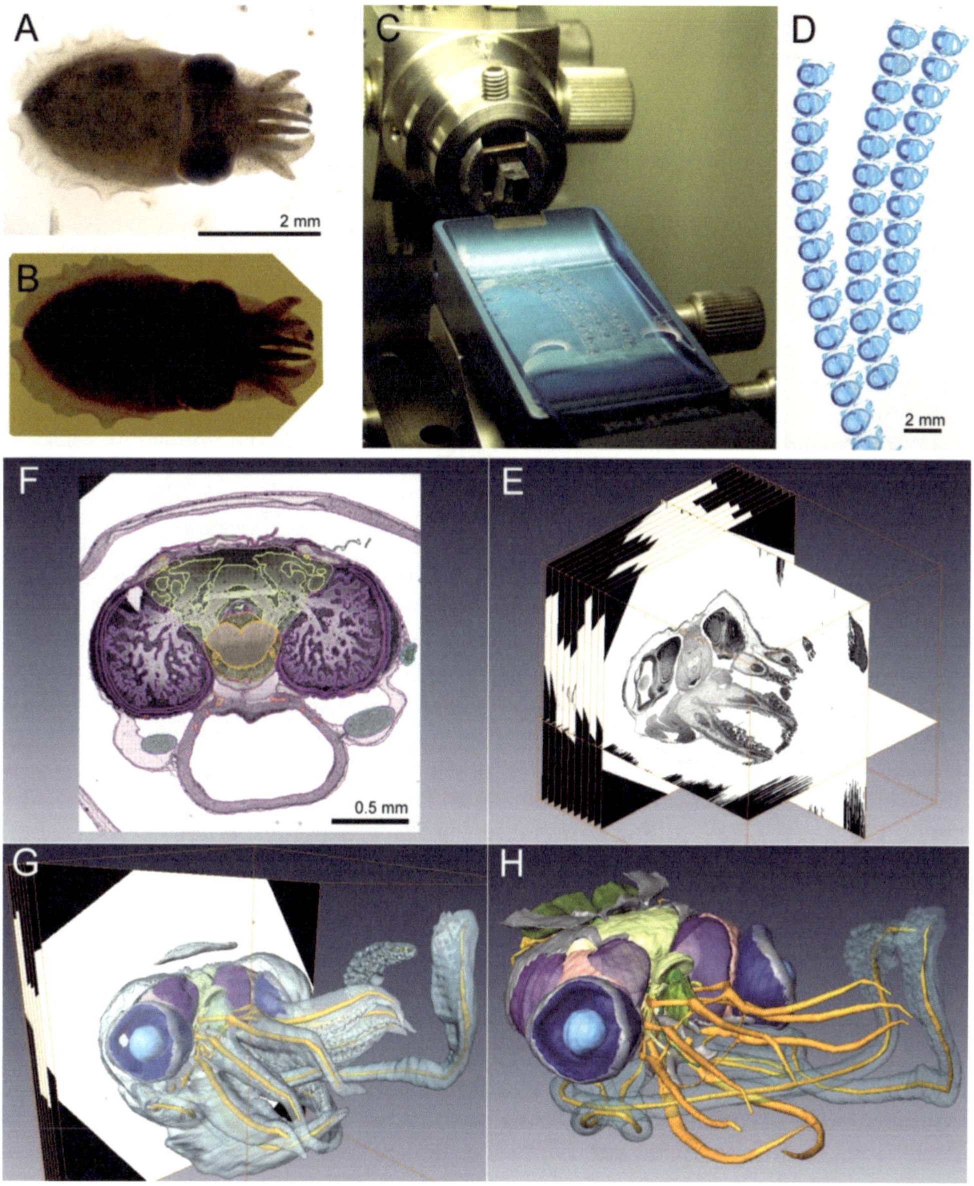

Fig. 2. From organisms to 3D-surface models (based on mechanical slices and light microscopy) **A** *Sepia* hatchling, chemically fixed. **B** *Sepia* hatchling contrasted with OsO_4 and embedded in epoxy resin. **C** Cutting the resin block in slice-ribbons with a diamond knife (1 µm thick). **D** Slice-ribbons stained with toluidine blue on a glass slide ready for light microscopy. **E** Stack of several hundred aligned digital images (= 3D-volume data) with orthogonal virtual reslicing planes. **F** Selected plane after manual segmentation of different tissue domains. **G** Surface rendering of the segmented domains emerging from the 3D-volume data. **H** 3D-surface model of the *Sepia* head in sub-µm resolution, allowing the interactive exploration of shape and constellation of all components, and morphometric analysis (B-D by H. Gensler; F-H by E. Scharpf).

indispensable for this task. To speed up the procedure and to bypass "bad" slices it is possible to interpolate the labels between two more or less distant planes.

2.1 Physical sectioning

Physical sectioning as maximally invasive "opening" of biological structures can be achieved, in principle, by two different approaches. Either the **slices** are collected, contrasted and imaged (commonly applied in transmission light or electron microscopy), or the slices are discarded and the **block-face** is imaged by reflected light microscopy or backscattering electron microscopy. Both approaches have advantages and disadvantages: imaging slices, as a rule, is more flexible concerning different staining protocols for biological tissues and tends to result in better 2D images (resolution and contrast) – imaging block faces, on the other hand, facilitates the alignment of neighbouring image planes for subsequent 3D-reconstruction (circumventing inevitable slice deformations) and avoids the loss of image planes owing to frazzled or furled slices. In the following these two approaches are explained exemplarily.

2.1.1 Imaging slices

There is quite a remarkable number of different possible method combinations for tissue fixation, embedding, cutting, staining and imaging slices. Object size and the desired contrast defines the embedding medium and as a consequence the cutting thickness and eventually the quality of 3D-reconstructions. In any case, one has to take care to obtain smooth, intact slices (single or ribbon) without losing slices or sequence information. In the process of image acquisition (flowchart step 8) one or several digital image stacks (e.g., different stainings on subsequent odd and even slices) are generated. The original specimen in the "refined" physical form of a section series may be stored in an archive or used for further investigations (e.g., cutting ultrathin sections from semithin sections). Four examples may give a glimpse into this broad method spectrum: **(1)** Vibratom sectioning of formalin- or paraformaldehyde-fixed soft tissue enclosed in agarose allows a section thickness down to 25 µm (kryosectioning even 5 – 10 µm) and is often used for fluorescence staining (e.g., lipophile neuron tracers, antibody staining, *in situ* hybridization); the vibratome section series can be imaged on a (fluorescence) stereomicroscope for 3D composition/analysis or single slices may be optically sectioned by CLSM (see section 3). **(2)** Paraffin- or historesin-sections of objects with diameters between 5 and 20 mm can be cut with steel knifes down to 5 µm thickness and subjected to any classical histochemical staining. After imaging with conventional light microscopy, 3D-rendering can be approached (flowchart steps 9 - 12), but artifacts from slice deformation can hamper digital post-processing. **(3)** Semithin section series (thickness 0.5 - 2 µm) cut with glass or diamond knifes from epoxy resin embedded specimens of less than 5 mm diameter provide the best quality for spatially accurate 3D-reconstructions (Fig. 2, see also Heß et al., 2008; Neusser et al., 2009). As a rule the slices are deformed insignificantly, ribboning is easy and minimal unevenness can be compensated by extended focal imaging light microscopy. The lateral resolution of the objective can be fully utilized and also z-resolution is outstanding. One shortcoming is the narrow palette of applicable staining reagents. **(4)** Ultrathin section series: as with semithin sections the resin-embedded material can be cut into so-called "ultrathin" sections of 40 - 100 nm. These flimsy sections are "fished" with grids (tiny metal washers with an central hole spanned by a ultrathin plastic film), contrasted with heavy metals (U, Pb) and imaged under the TEM. Yet, TEM-based 3D-reconstructions are possible (see e.g., Jörger et al., 2009).

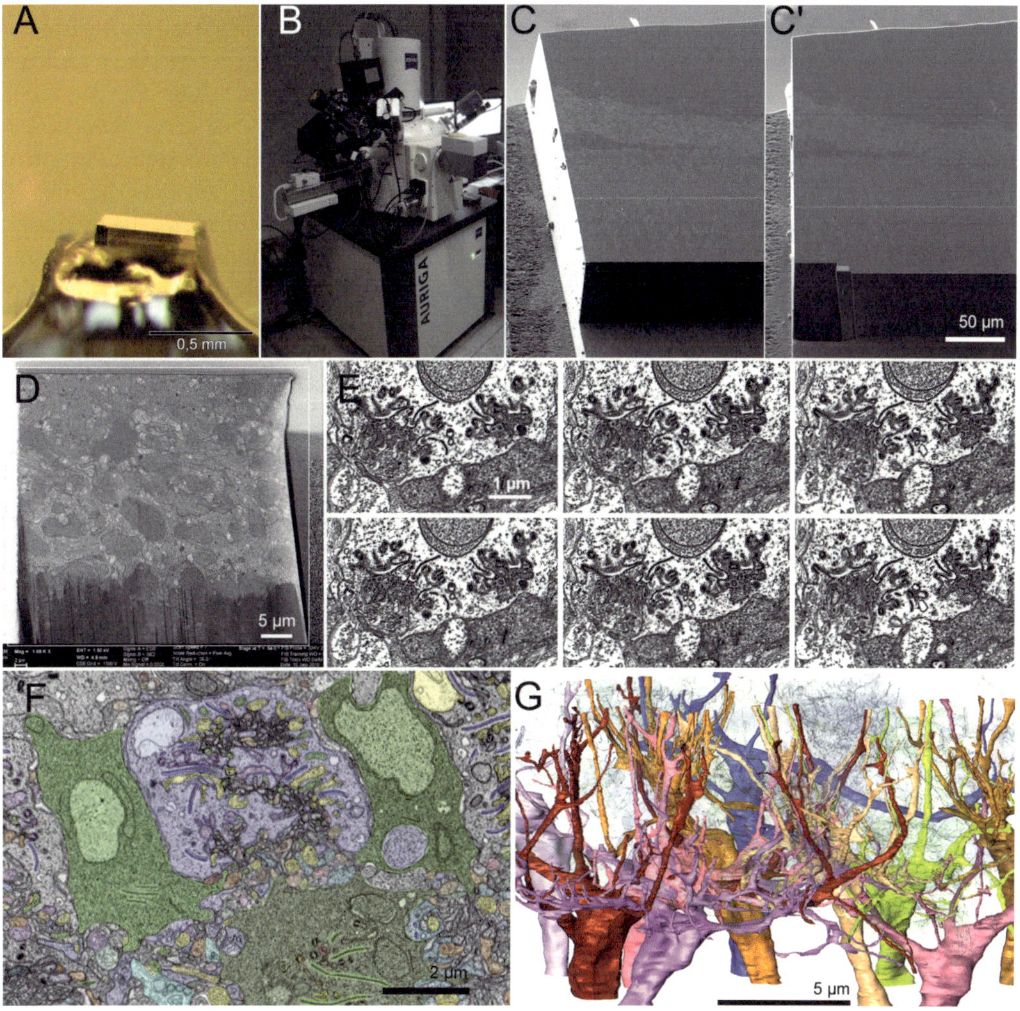

Fig. 3. Reconstructing neuronal nets in <10 nm isotropic resolution (FIB-FESEM-based) **A** Retina sample in epoxy resin trimmed by "mesa"-technique mounted on a minute specimen holder. **B** Zeiss "Auriga" cross beam workstation (FIB-FESEM = focused ion beam milling + field emission scanning electron microscope). **C** SEM image (secondary electron detection) of the mesa before ion beam milling. **C'** SEM picture of the same mesa after milling out a 35 x 15 x 65 µm³ volume of interest. **D** SEM image (back scattering electron detection) of the block surface showing subcellular structures contrasted with OsO_4 and $[UO_2]^{2+}$. **E** Clipping of a FIB image series (showing the cable mess of retinal synapses) with a Z-spacing of 10 nm (columns) and 50 nm (rows). **F** Selected plane after manual segmentation of different neuronal branches (one colour for each cell, continuity retraceable only in 3D). **G** Surface rendering of a subpopulation of branching neurons in the volume of interest in 10 nm isotropic resolution (F, G by P. Koch).

2.1.2 Imaging block faces

On both sides of the size range of biological specimens designated for 3D-reconstruction, e.g. in centimeter- as well as in sub-micrometer dimensions, it can be advantageous (if not the only practicable way) to image block faces instead of slices. **Histological** 10 µm slices of paraffin embedded specimens with a cutting area of several cm^2, e.g., are unstable and not manageable at all. A workaround is discarding the slice and carefully staining the block surface, before taking a macro image and scaling off the next slice. For **3D-electron microscopy**, on the other hand, with cutting areas of several μm^2 only, there is an alternative to TEM-imaging of ultrathin section series (problems see paragraph *alignment*, point 3), namely the "serial block face scanning electron microscopy" (SBF-SEM). Here, the specimen has to be contrasted with heavy metals (Os, U) before embedding in epoxy resin, thoroughly polymerized and carefully trimmed in mesa-shape with perfect object orientation. Then, the sample is cut within the vacuum chamber of a scanning electron microscope with field emission gun (FESEM) and backscattering electron (BE) detector. Two versions of SBF-SEM are currently available (with very few machines up to now): **(1)** the Gatan 3view, in which the sample is cut mechanically with a diamond knife in 25 - 50 nm layers and subsequently imaged with the electron beam using the BE detector. An advantage of this system is the large scanning area that can be achieved by stitching of adjacent fields-of-view without tradeoffs in resolution (max. ca. 20 nm/px). **(2)** crossbeam workstations (e.g., Zeiss Auriga) rest upon a focused (gallium) ion beam for milling off layers of down to less than 10 nm (!) and again BE detection with a scanning electron microscope (FIB-FESEM; see Fig. 3). With a FIB-FESEM an isotropic resolution of 10 nm voxels can be achieved, at the cost of a comparatively small field-of-view (e.g., 35 x 25 µm). SBF-SEM-based data allow for the precise 3D-reconstruction of neuronal networks with all synapses and connectivity rules in the VOI for the first time. Acquisition time (e.g., 75 hrs for 15 µm feed at 3 min/frame) and costs for gallium-emitter consumption are high. As a rule the data will exceed several GB, necessitating powerful imaging computers and graphic cards with sufficient RAM.

As mentioned above, the main drawbacks of physical slicing-based 3D-renderings are the time and effort needed for preparation, imaging, image post-processing and segmentation, as well as the complete destruction of the specimen. Ambitious efforts are undertaken to speed up the procedure, at least in parts. Automatic batch imaging of slice ribbons on several glass slides in combination with extended focal imaging is already available (e.g., Olympus dotSlide). Customized semi-automatic post-processing and 3D-segmentation tools (e.g., Jurrus et al., 2006; Yang & Choe, 2009) may facilitate the work flow in several fields of organismal biology. Additionally, in high-content applications such as 3D-EM analysis of neuronal networks, the KNOSSOS / RESCOPE methodology, in which many persons work together to segment structures in a single 3D-stack, is a promising approach for the future (Helmstaedter et al., 2011).

3. Confocal Laserscanning Microscopy (CLSM)

The accurate three-dimensional depiction of (selected) morphological features of given specimens has been possible for a long time by using serial sectioning techniques combined with light or electron microscopy (see above). However, the resulting obstacle, namely the significant time investment needed to yield these reconstructions, has significantly hampered large-scale comparative analyses. This was at least partly overcome with the introduction of confocal laserscanning microscopy (CLSM) to biological research, whereby pre-aligned optical stacks of digital images through a biological sample may be produced.

These stacks of individual, in-focus images may in a subsequent step be fused into projection images, thus rendering detailed, high resolution representations of the OOI throughout the depth of the sample. In addition, these stacks may be further processed by various imaging software packages to produce three-dimensional, volume and/or isosurface rendered reconstructions, as well as animations, that allow for viewing the given structures from various angles, thus facilitating detailed morphological analyses. This way, complex micro-anatomical structures, such as muscular or neural networks of microscopic animals, may be reconstructed within a few hours, a task that would take weeks or months to complete (if at all possible), if conventional sectioning techniques were to be applied (see Wanninger, 2007).

The breathtaking technological advances in laser technology, scan speed, temporal and spatial resolution of signal detection, *in silico* storage means, as well as software tools have undoubtedly fuelled the rapid establishment of confocal microscopy in the biological sciences since its commercial appearance some 30 years ago. As with numerous other biological research methodologies, the rapid establishment of CLSM as a routine research device after its demonstrated user friendliness in the mid-eighties was intimately linked to its usefulness in cell biological research (see also Amos & White, 2003; Pawley, 2006). The current state-of-the-art allows for high resolution depiction of cellular and subcellular structures unprecedented by light and fluorescence microscopical techniques before. As such, labelling of distinct proteins, cytoskeletal elements, chromosomes, and even single genes within an individual chromosome have rendered confocal applications highly interesting for basic research focusing on cellular ultrastructure, protein distribution, and the like.

3.1 Confocal applications on fixed samples

With the establishment of fluorescence staining procedures as routine laboratory techniques and the advancement and dramatic decrease in costs for computational power, confocal microscopy has significantly broadened organismal biological research. This has led to an explosion of morphological data on microscopic specimens, especially in zoological research (see, among others, Wanninger, 2009 for review). The huge success of confocal applications in this field of research is mainly due to the possibility of selective labelling of individual structures and organ systems such as muscles, neurons (including neuronal subsets such as transmitters and peptides), ciliary bands, or nephridia in entire organisms including individual developmental stages, which can subsequently be analysed using 3D-imaging software (Fig. 4). This has opened the door to explore numerous new pathways focusing on questions concerning the ontogeny and evolution of organ systems, unravelling developmental processes, and injecting entirely novel morphological datasets into issues concerning the interrelationships of animal phyla. Since the evolutionary driving force of character (state) selection takes place at all developmental stages, large-scale comparative, high resolution developmental analyses of organogenesis have generated important data on the microanatomy of developmental - often larval - stages that in such detail had not been available in the pre-confocal era (e.g., Brinkmann & Wanninger, 2008; Hessling, 2002; Hessling & Westheide, 2002; Kristof et al., 2008; Neves et al., 2009). As a most welcomed side effect, the sheer number of significant findings based on these advancements have catapulted evolutionary oriented organismal biological research - a field that often was

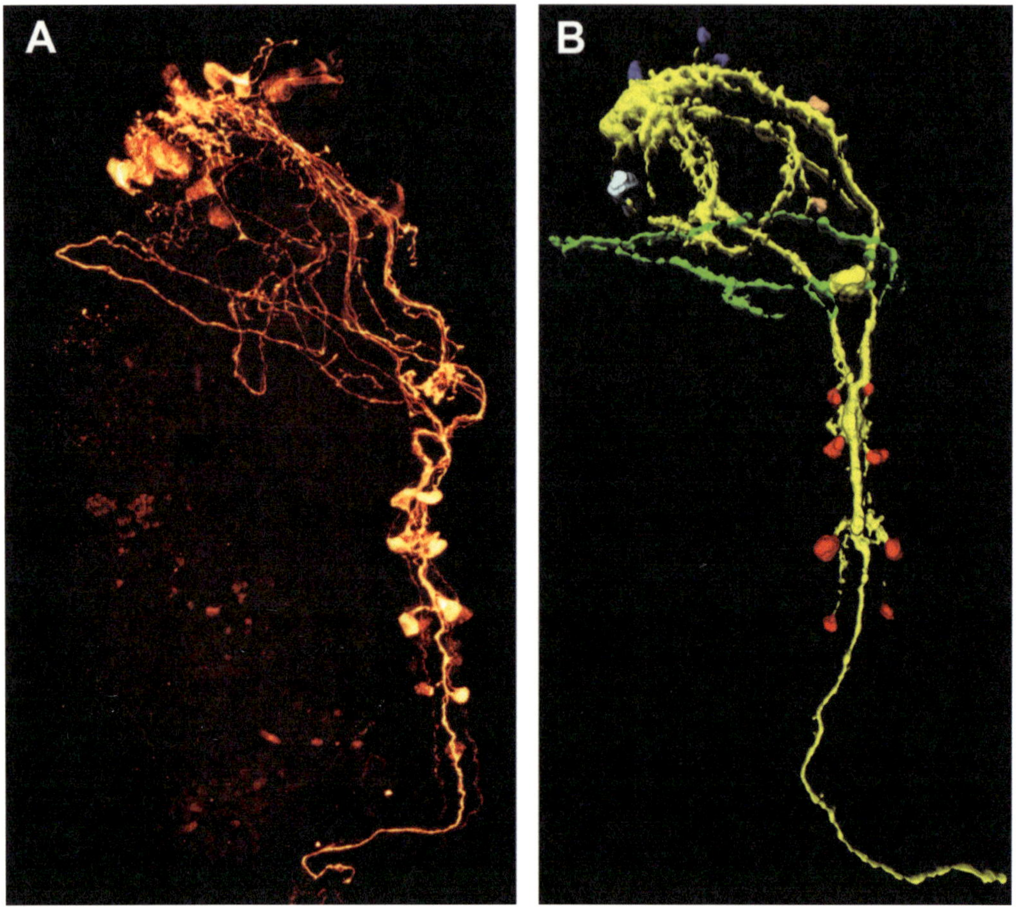

Fig. 4. Depiction of the serotonergic nervous system of a marine invertebrate worm.
A Maximum projection image of a confocal microscopy stack. **B** A stack similar to the one in A has been digitally modified with 3D-imaging software, whereby selective subsets of the immunoreactive parts have been highlighted by different colours. Approximate length of the individuals is 400 µm. (A, B by A. Kristof)

frowned upon as old fashioned and outdated - into the 21st century, and has led to an integration of morphological, developmental, and molecular approaches to solve evolutionary questions. As such, the detailed reconstruction of proliferating cells (by labelling of mitotic cells; Kristof et al., 2011) and gene activity (by *in situ* hybridization; Jékely & Arendt, 2007) using confocal imaging have and undoubtedly further will help to elucidate developmental processes in multicellular animals that entirely rely on fixed material. While classical single-photon confocal microscopy has routinely entered organismal biology, two- or multiphoton applications are yet not that widely spread. Using two- or multiple photon excitation allows for a far greater depth of penetration - up to 1000 µm sample thickness (Helmchen & Denk, 2005) - thus making multiple cellular layers within given, also living, tissues accessible to whole-mount confocal-type analysis. This is due to the fact that the strength of the fluorescence signal increases by the second power if two photons are excited (and is cubed in the case of triple-photon excitation, respectively), thus allowing for significantly higher fluorescence signal than gained by single-photon excitation (Ustione & Piston, 2011). However, in order to generate multi-photon excitation, cost intensive pulsed laser beams need to be applied in order to reach the required photon density. In addition, resolution yielded with this technology is considerably lower than the one obtainable by single-photon confocal microscopy, thus hampering analyses that call for particularly high resolution images. Moreover, due to the higher laser power needed to penetrate the tissue, samples are prone to faster bleaching than in single-photon microscopy applications.

3.2 Live cell imaging

Combining the basic principles of fluorescence microscopy and the high resolution and fast scanning power of confocal laserscanning systems has led to numerous innovations that have enabled confocal recording of live tissue. Accordingly, it is now possible to observe cellular movements or subcellular activities (e.g., protein dynamics) in real time in all three spatial dimensions. Three of the most commonly used techniques in organismal research are thereby FRAP (fluorescence recovery after photobleaching), FLIM (fluorescence lifetime imaging microscopy) and FRET (fluorescence resonance energy transfer).

FRAP experiments involve controlled, irreversible bleaching of a specific area of interest in a living sample. Fluorescence in this region may be recovered by diffusion of fluorescing molecules from the neighbouring, non-bleached areas. This may be combined with GFP application, which allows for non-invasive, long-term studies of living cells and organisms. By measuring the diffusion time of the non-bleached molecules, the mobility rate of the molecule of interest may be inferred in addition to its mere localization. In addition, molecule-molecule interactions as well as signalling events may be followed using FRAP (Reits & Neefjes, 2001).

In FLIM measurements, the lifetime of a fluorescence signal is recorded. Fluorophores exhibit a defined lifetime, which is dependent on certain parameters, including concentrations of specific ions, proteins, oxygen, or the pH in its surrounding medium. Since these values directly correlate with the lifetime of the fluorescence of a given fluorophore, FLIM studies can be used to characterize and detect changes in the environment of living cells with respect to these parameters (Lakowicz et al., 1992). In order to achieve this, two laser pulses are necessary, one to excite the fluorophore at the start of the recording and a second one at the end of its lifetime. Accordingly, FLIM is typically used in combination with multiphoton microscopy, which delivers pulsed laser beams in the required intervals.

Recently, FRET has proven highly efficient to measure the interaction and co-localization of molecules in living systems at particular high temporal (on the nanosecond scale) and spatial (on angstrom level) resolution (Sekar & Periasamy, 2003). Thereby, energy is transferred from a donor to an acceptor fluorophore if their distance is less than 10 nm. While CFP/YFP and FITC/Rhodamine have traditionally been used as FRET pairs, these have nowadays widely been replaced by various GFPs. FRET is often used to measure cellular events such as calcium signalling and protein interactions, which may be particularly well resolved if combined with FLIM (Sekar & Periasamy, 2003). As with FLIM, FRET is often coupled to multiphoton microscopy using a white laser source which enables selection of the excitation wavelength that ideally matches the donor fluorophore.

Despite these obvious advantages, confocal laserscanning microscopy, as any other research tool, is limited by several parameters.

First, and most obvious, albeit a sophisticated device based on laser technology, its basic function still rests on the principles – and limitations - of conventional light microscopy (although these may partly be overcome by specialized application tools such as FRET, see above). Accordingly, if structures other than the very surface of a sample are to be scanned, the laser beam (excitation) as well as the resulting signal (emission) needs to penetrate the sample in order to yield a detectable signal. As a result, electron dense matter may significantly reduce scanning depth, which in many confocal applications generally is limited to the first upper 100 µm of a sample. As mentioned above, this may be increased by multiphoton setups, which penetrate deeper but come at a cost of lower resolution.

Second, and again in contrast to histological analyses, confocal data are typically generated for specifically stained structures (unless autofluorescence is recorded). Hence, and although multicolor staining procedures are often applied, one will never be able to reveal the structural organization of a sample in its entity. Thus, the relative placement or interaction of several, say, organ systems in an animal, are usually not inferable by confocal analysis alone. The otherwise desired high specificity of many agents, such as nucleic acid stains, phalloidin to label F-actin, antibodies against specific neurotransmitters or cytoskeletal components and the like may thus call for additional histology- or tomography-based investigations, especially if functional analyses are sought after.

Third, despite the high specificity of numerous markers, whole-mount preparations in particular are prone to high unspecific signal due to autofluorescence of various molecules at given excitation wavelengths. Chemically, this can be reduced by applying clearing media such as a mixture of benzyl benzoate and benzyl alcohol, which, however, might interfere with some stains (e.g., phalloidin). In confocal analyses, low signal-to-noise ratio might be enhanced by optimizing the excitation wavelengths for the respective fluorochromes by using a white laser which allows for selection of excitation wavelengths that perfectly match a given fluorophore. In addition to more efficient exploitation of the fluorophore, cross-excitation in multicolor experiments is reduced and, due to the lower excitation power needed, the viability of cells in *in vivo* investigations may be significantly increased. This is also true for certain novel, highly sensitive, low-noise detection systems based on single photon counting rather than secondary electron amplification by a photomultiplier tube (PMT) used in more standard confocal setups.

Overall, the strength of confocal applications in biological studies based on fixed samples lies in its high-throughput, high-resolution recording of selected, complex, yet minute microscopical structures. The resulting digital image stacks may subsequently be used for further 3D-processing employing, e.g., volume and surface rendering algorithms. In addition, quantitative studies including volumetrics and measurements of cellular contents can be obtained. In live (cell) imaging experiments, confocal microscopy allows for depictions of cellular processes, including molecular activity. The expected further technological improvement in the sensitivity of detection systems, scan speed and computational power should lead to even higher resolved recordings. It is expected that these further developments will in particular benefit experiments employing live confocal laserscanning imaging, thus moving towards highly resolved real-time recordings of biological processes in spatial resolution (e.g., depiction of organelles, bacteria, cells, organ systems or entire microscopic organisms moving and/or changing over time) – and therefore towards true, live, four-dimensional organismal microscopy.

4. Scanner-based non-invasive virtual sectioning techniques (CT/MRI)

At the end of the 19th century Wilhelm Conrad Roentgens` discovery of "a new kind of light" (Glasser, 1995) heralded a new era: "visualization into the body without painful and often life-threatening surgery" (Robb, 1982). Until now, roentgen radiation (X-ray) has been used as a non-invasive imaging method in diagnostics and was an important step towards the invention of X-ray computed tomography (CT). Another major breakthrough in medical radiology was the development of magnetic resonance imaging (MRI), which is based on the physical phenomenon that nuclei of atoms exposed to a magnetic field absorb and re-emit electromagnetic radiation. The foundation for both, CT and MRI was laid in 1973 and revolutionized non-invasive imaging while offering unprecedented *in vivo* insights into the human body. Increasing computational power set the stage for interactive 3D-models based on virtual sectioning and made medical imaging techniques even more attractive for the application in biological research. This development boosted life science research into a new era, thus enabling to look into an organism and navigating through all its anatomical features from every direction, which in turn provided new insights into morphological and functional coherences.

Both, CT and MRI, have several features in common in creating 3D-models from their recorded data. First, these data are obtained in a standard format for medical imaging (DICOM) that provides not only the image itself but also metadata (e.g., scanning parameters, patient information). Second, each single slice of the image stacks produced by CT and MRI scans consists of gray values that reflect tissue characteristics. Third, the CT and MRI data-sets does not only contain two-dimensional information of each single slice, it consists of three-dimensional pixels, so called "voxels" (= volume elements) which accurately reflect the volume information of a given OOI in isotropic resolution when using appropriate scanning parameters. The last fundamental step is image-based modeling of the data sets by the use of the appropriate computer software (see section 2). In contrast to medical applications, where in some cases automatic segmentation is available for precise 3D-modeling of a specific structure, CT and MRI scans of biological specimens often need intensive manual labour to extract the OOI from the surrounding tissue (see section 2, paragraph *segmentation*).

However, CT- and MRI-based methods not only pioneered medical diagnostics; they offer unique possibilities to unravel scientific questions beyond classical anatomical research in organismal biology. Especially anatomical investigations of rare museum species or species that are difficult to obtain renders scanner-based non-invasive virtual sectioning techniques a perfect tool in contrast to destructive dissections.

4.1 X-ray Computed Tomography (CT)

The invention of computer-based X-ray tomography by Hounsfield (1972, 1973) revolutionized diagnostics in medical radiology. In addition, this technique in combination with all advantages of subsequent 3D-imaging and the possibility of "true" real-time analyses have improved the capacity for innovation in Life Sciences (Schreurs et al., 2003). In general, the process of image acquisition from X-ray computed tomography (CT) is similar to classical radiology, whereby the OOI (e.g., the arm of a patient) is placed in the line between the X-ray source and the detector (e.g., film or digital detector). In this process, the different absorption patterns of the respective tissues are carried in the X-ray beam.

A major disadvantage of conventional radiology is summing up or superimposing of all points along the "single view" line, which leads to a blurry picture (Radon, 1917). Now, scanning around a transaxial plane allows to collect the beam only from a single point of the sample, preventing superposition (Robb, 1982). CT, therefore, produces virtual serial cross-sectional images of a given OOI. The obtained volume of data is a stack of slices, each slice being a digital two-dimensional grey value image. The given grey values basically represent the electron density of an object corresponding to the average attenuation of the X-ray beam which is quantified by the use of the Hounsfield scale (Kak & Slaney, 1988). Hounsfield Units (HU) range from - 1024 to + 3071 and are commonly set at 0 for water and - 1000 for air. Since humans are not capable of distinguishing over 4000 grey values, a process called "windowing" is applied to narrow the range of grey values of a given object for further image processing. A variety of software packages using sophisticated algorithms are available to subsequently reconstruct the scanned OOI in three dimensions. Given that for equivalent X-ray energy a denser structure will attenuate the beam more than a less dense structure, excellent 3D-reconstructions are produced by utilization of the natural contrast when a highly absorbing structure is surrounded by tissues with relatively weak absorbance (e.g., bones in contrast to soft tissues such as muscles; Boistel et al., 2011).

However, if the density of the different soft tissues are similar the use of appropriate contrasting agents is advisable. Conventional clinical CT scanners are designed for objects at the size and density of humans. In addition, non-lethal X-ray energies (~75 kV) are used in medical applications, which in turn foreclose a spatial resolution above 1 - 2 mm (Stuppy et al., 2003). However, with state-of-the-art helical CT scanners and higher X-ray doses, imaging of biological specimens with an isotropic resolution of 0.4 mm^3 (at 140 kV) is possible (Laforsch et al., 2008).

4.1.1 Organismal applications

The rapid advancement in tomographic imaging led to the development of scaled down clinical scanners (Mini-CT) which can provide a dataset of e.g. the torso of a mouse at an image resolution of 50 – 100 µm. Micro-CT scanners, on the other hand, image specimens at spatial resolutions from cellular (20 µm) down to subcellular dimensions (e.g., 1 µm; Dierolf et al., 2010) and fill the resolution-hiatus between optical microscope imaging and mini-CT imaging of intact volumes (Ketcham & Carlson, 2001; Ritman, 2004). However, micro-CT systems suffer from the drawback that high resolution can only be obtained for small samples with a maximum size of 5 – 30 mm (Metscher, 2009). Moreover, it often cannot be used *in vivo* because the applied X-ray doses are lethal (Stuppy et al., 2003). Next to medical applications, CT is often applied in biological studies examining functions of morphological structures or morphological differences between species. The physical properties of the tissue of interest reflected by X-ray attenuation renders mineralized structures such as bones or cartilage particularly suitable for CT (Kruszyński et al., 2007). Hence, studies using CT-based 3D-reconstructions have focused on the depiction of coarse and subtle details of the skeleton in mammals (Marino et al., 2003), fish (Claeson et al., 2007), amphibians (Maddin, 2011) or reptiles (Maisano & Rieppel, 2007). Nevertheless, CT can also be applied to analyse soft tissues. For instance, Wirkner & Prendini (2007) examined the morphology of the hemolymph vascular system in scorpions using micro-CT and 3D-reconstruction.

A further application of CT is centred in Palaeobiology to study fossils in a non-destructive way (Macrini et al., 2007; Rogers, 1999; Vasquez et al., 2008). This facilitates to reveal the nature of the fauna and flora of past ages and therefore boost evolutionary studies.
To illustrate that CT-derived 3D-models offer unique possibilities to unravel scientific questions beyond classical anatomical research, here an example from coral reef ecology will be presented:

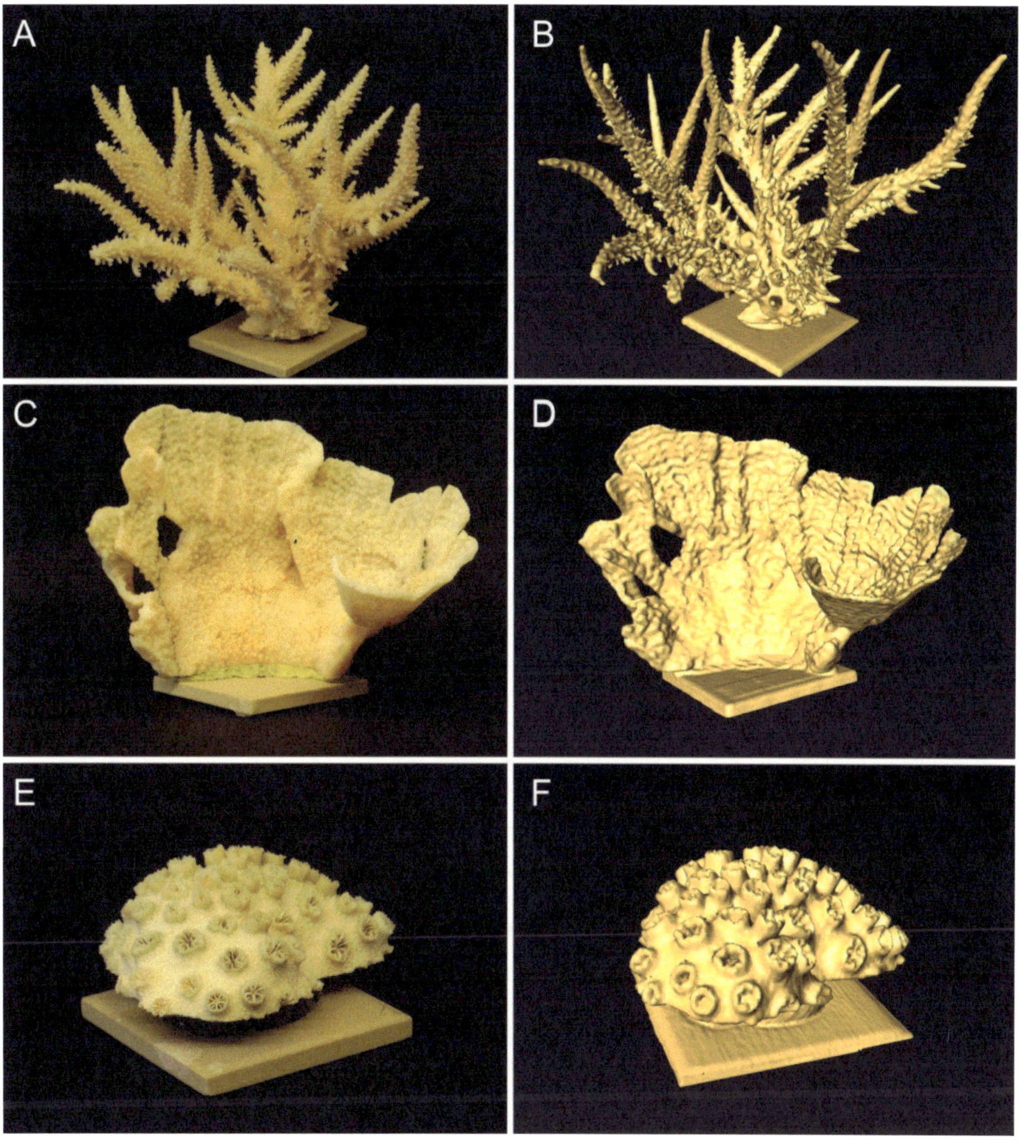

Fig. 5. Coral growth forms imaged with X-ray computed tomography and 3D-reconstruction. Photographies of different coral skeletons (left column) and associated 3D-models based on X-ray computed tomography (right column). **A** & **B** Branching staghorn coral (*Acropora sp.*). **C** & **D** Encrusting coral (*Montipora foliosa*). **E** & **F** Massive-growing coral with large polyps (*Galaxea fascicularis*).

Coral reefs are among the most diverse and productive ecosystems on Earth. Corals occur in a variety of growth forms, and there is strong variation in coral shape even within a single species. Quantifying this variation is relevant for a wide range of ecological studies. Moreover, the question of how to determine the surface area in this phenotypically plastic organism has been of considerable interest in several studies in coral reef science. For instance, the surface area of corals serves as an important reference parameter for the standardization of metabolic processes such as photosynthesis or respiration. Hence, a variety of methodologies have been introduced and applied to determine the morphology, volume and surface area of corals, however, all of them being destructive.

Given the fact that the attenuation of the X-ray beam in calcium carbonate differs extremely from the surrounding medium (e.g., seawater), the shape of the coral skeleton can be easily extracted during image processing with the suitable software (see section 2, paragraph *segmentation*) to generate a virtual clone of the respective coral colony (Kaandorp et al., 2005). Since the calcified skeleton resembles the surface area of the very thin tissue layer of the coral, Laforsch et al. (2008) applied conventional medical CT in living coral colonies, thus enabling highly accurate surface area measurements from the isosurface of the volume data in a non-destructive way (Fig. 5).

A limitation of CT application arises from the fact that it is hardly applicable in the field, although portable CT scanners are already available. Another limitation of CT is the restriction to measurements of the skeleton topography only, while for example coral tissue components remain undetected. To achieve a higher spatial resolution, which in turn enables imaging of delicate details, greater X-ray fluxes are required, hence, evoking an inherent trade-off between image quality and tissue damage (Boistel et al., 2011).

However, sophisticated state of the art technologies in CT in combination with classical methods will enable scientists to improve their knowledge on ecosystem function. Moreover, the breathtaking advancement in CT technology sets the stage for unimagined new possibilities in life science research. Newly developed synchrotron scanners offer a significantly higher resolution, a better signal-to-noise-ratio, and the potential for quantitative reconstructions (Betz et al. 2007) with a resolution down to about 60 - 90 nm (Baruchel et al. 2008).

4.2 Magnetic Resonance Imaging (MRI)

Lauterbur (1973) produced the first 2D-image using MRI-technique depicting two H_2O-filled glass capillaries in a D_2O environment. He paved the way for MRI-based applications in medicine, while today MRI body scanners are standard diagnostic tools in almost every hospital of the developed nations (Glover & Mansfield, 2002). Clinical research on human diseases using small mammals as model systems strongly favoured the invention of small animal MRI and magnetic resonance microscopy (MRM, µMRI, micro-MRI; Benveniste & Blackband, 2002). The difference of MRM to conventional MRI is that the achieved resolution is usually lower than 100 µm and that micro-MRI chambers are typically small (1 cm^3). The higher resolution in micro-MRI is predominantly produced by stronger field strengths of the magnets (e.g., up to 21 Tesla (T) for micro-MRI compared to 1-3 T for conventional MRI).

MRI technique is based physically on the principle of nuclear magnetic resonance (NMR). Since protons and neutrons in a nucleus own a magnetic moment (spin), they behave like a tiny magnet. Exposed to a magnetic field these nuclear magnetic moments align to form a so-called longitudinal magnetization parallel to the external magnetic field. By applying radio-frequency (RF) pulses this longitudinal magnetization is tilted into the plane perpendicular to the magnetic field, forming the so-called transverse magnetization. The latter rotates about the direction of the magnetic field (the so-called precessional motion) and - thus being a temporally varying magnetic field itself - induces an alternating electric current in a receiver coil. This current, the so-called MR-signal, is translated into grey value image stacks containing the accurate volume information. Different grey values reflect the varying properties of water and lipid protons in different tissue types. These properties are mainly the proton density and the so-called relaxation times T1 and T2, which characterize the return of the proton magnetization system back to its equilibrium state after having been disturbed by the RF pulse. Crucial for the discrimination of different tissue types is their difference in grey values, the so-called contrast, which should be maximized for computerized 3D-reconstruction (see also below for the role of image quality). Different MR image contrasts are mainly achieved by varying scanning parameters such as repetition time, echo time or flip angle in order to emphasize one or more of the tissue parameters mentioned above. One then speaks of "proton density weighted", "T1 weighted" or "T2 weighted" images. In addition, mixed forms of image contrast can be achieved by applying appropriate combinations of scanning parameters.

Other crucial parameters for 3D-reconstruction are spatial resolution and image quality. Concerning resolution, the smaller the OOI (e.g., organs of an animal) the higher the spatial resolution of the images has to be in order to minimize the uncertainty when it is about to obtain quantitative data.

Like any other measurable quantity, the signal intensities or grey values of an MR image are not exact but can only be determined within certain error bounds, the so-called image noise. Image quality is usually quantified as so-called „signal-to-noise" ratio (SNR, e.g., grey value divided by the noise figure), whereas it is the so-called '"contrast-to-noise" ratio (CNR) which determines how well two adjacent organs of different tissue type can be discriminated, and is calculated by simply subtracting the signal-to-noise ratios of the tissues under consideration.

Finally, the quantities spatial resolution and SNR cannot be optimized independently from a third important parameter, the net scan duration. The three parameters SNR, the volume measure V of the voxel and the net scan duration T are interlinked via the equation (with 'α' indicating proportionality):

$$\mathrm{SNR} \propto V \cdot \sqrt{T}$$

Thus, if one needs high spatial resolution (small V) and sufficient SNR for 3D-reconstruction of adjacent objects (large CNR) one has to choose a long scan time T. Or, to put it in more physical terms, as the MR signal intensity of a voxel is directly proportional to the number of contributing spins and thus proportional to the volume of the voxel, the weaker signal from a smaller voxel has to be compensated by averaging it over a longer period of time to reduce the root-mean-square deviation of the statistical fluctuations of the signal (for further readings see Vlaardingerbroek & Den Boer, 2003).

4.2.1 Organismal applications

The centrepiece of a conventional MRI scanner is a magnet with a bore diameter that provides enough space to scan a human body. The opening of the magnet bore and the achievable resolution is also what limits the application of conventional MRI to certain biological issues. However, after Aguayo et al. (1986) had published the first MRI image of a toad egg, MRI-based methods became a promising achievement in organismal biology. For microscopic objects, where high resolutions are indispensible, micro-MRI is used, for bigger organisms and where resolutions of less than 100 μm are not required, conventional clinical MRI is applicable. Hence, 3D-models of virtual MRI sections are nowadays important tools in biological disciplines ranging from developmental biology to evolution and ecology, but also increasingly in genetics, physiology and neurobiology. They frequently are applied when it is about to gain a deeper look into preserved or living organisms without being invasive or destructive. A frequent application of MRI is centred in taxonomy. For instance, Ziegler et al. (2008) used micro-MRI-based 3D-models for the systematic comparison of sea urchins. The authors focused on selected soft tissue characteristics to analyse phylogenetic relationships, which would have not been detected by the use of traditional techniques (see section 2).

In line with this, it used to be a frontier for developmental biologists to follow the development of internal soft structures in one and the same individual over time. Traditionally, invasive histological sections that provide high spatial resolution were applied, but with the limitation that tissue preparation may cause artefacts that hamper the interpretation of the data. Furthermore, series of animals preserved in different developmental stages could only provide snapshots of the entire ontogeny. In recent years, researchers have overcome this restriction by the application of MRI-based methods. For instance, Bain et al. (2007) accomplished, by the use of MRI, to display the entire development of a chicken embryo *in ovo* for the first time. In addition, MRI and micro-MRI-based studies followed by 3D-modeling offer the unique possibility to depict intricate morphologies in anatomical atlases within decent time (e.g., Ruffins et al., 2007). Such 3D-atlases not only foster studies on pure anatomical issues, they may provide also an outstanding tool to display molecular pathways and gene expression patterns (Louie et al., 2000).

The rapid advancement of MRI technologies and applications even fuels studies on interrelationships between organisms. Quantitative data derived from 3D-models such as volume and surface areas are often needed in ecological studies and non-destructive MRI-based techniques offer plenty of possibilities to achieve these data *in vivo*. To illustrate the use of MRI derived 3D-models in ecology, an example from the marine system will be presented in the following:

The crown-of-thorns starfish *Acanthaster planci* is one of the most studied organisms in coral reef ecology (Moran, 1986). Due to population explosions they cause fatal damage to coral reefs in the Indo-Pacific region and the Red Sea. The reasons for the emergence of these population explosions are still subject to speculations; therefore, fundamental research on this animal has been a major topic in reef research for many decades. As population explosions, so called outbreaks, are by nature closely related to spawning events, it is indispensible to assess the spawning season of *A. planci*. Therefore, the reproductive status of its gonads has to be quantified, which is done by calculating so-called gonad indices. In this process the size, weight or volume of the organ is determined and set into relation to the respective parameter of the starfish. The bigger the index is, the closer the starfish is to its spawning season. Classical methods to estimate the size of these organs are lethal to the starfish, since *A. planci* has to be dissected for weighting their mass. A novel method has recently been established by Sigl & Imhof (unpublished data) to accurately calculate the volume of the inner organs of *A. planci in vivo*. The MRI-based method enables to determine

Fig. 6. From organisms to 3D-models, based on magnetic resonance imaging (MRI). **A** *Acanthaster planci* individual on the reef. **B** Relaxed *A. planci* individual in a plastic box prepared for scanning using MRI. **C** Plastic box with *A. planci* in the MRI chamber with receiver coil on top. **D** Image stack obtained from MRI scan (3D volume data) with virtual planes (only a few planes are pictured). **E** Horizontal cross-sectional image (MRI-scan) of *A. planci* with outlined (segmentated) organs. **F** 3D-model (volume-rendered) of the starfish and its inner organs (grey: body wall/skeletal elements; purple: pyloric caeca; yellow: gonads; cyan: cardiac stomach).

the indices for a given individual over time, which is a major advantage, since individual differences do not bias the obtained data. Using conventional clinical MRI the organs of *A. planci* can be depicted. The obtained volume data set is subsequently used to render a

3D-model of these organs (Fig. 6). With the aid of these 3D-models and the known size of each voxel it is possible to accurately calculate the volume of these organs, and therefore also to detect size changes, which are a reliable indicator to assess the spawning season.

4.3 Juxtaposition of MRI and CT

Organismal biology benefits significantly from both, virtual sectioning methods, MRI and CT, which offer 3D-data sets in a, at first glance, non-invasive way. Especially for rare specimens, sensitive samples as well as for repeated measures, both techniques seem perfectly suitable.

However, CT uses ionizing radiation and there is direct evidence from epidemiologic studies that the radiation dose of a single common CT-study leads to an increased cancer risk for human adults (Brenner & Hall, 2007). Accordingly, in terms of *in vivo* studies in biological systems, CT clearly is rather non-destructive than non-invasive. Nevertheless, compared to MRI, the scanning times of CT are very low, thus enabling imaging of living organisms without the need of long term anaesthetics which may bias experimental conditions.

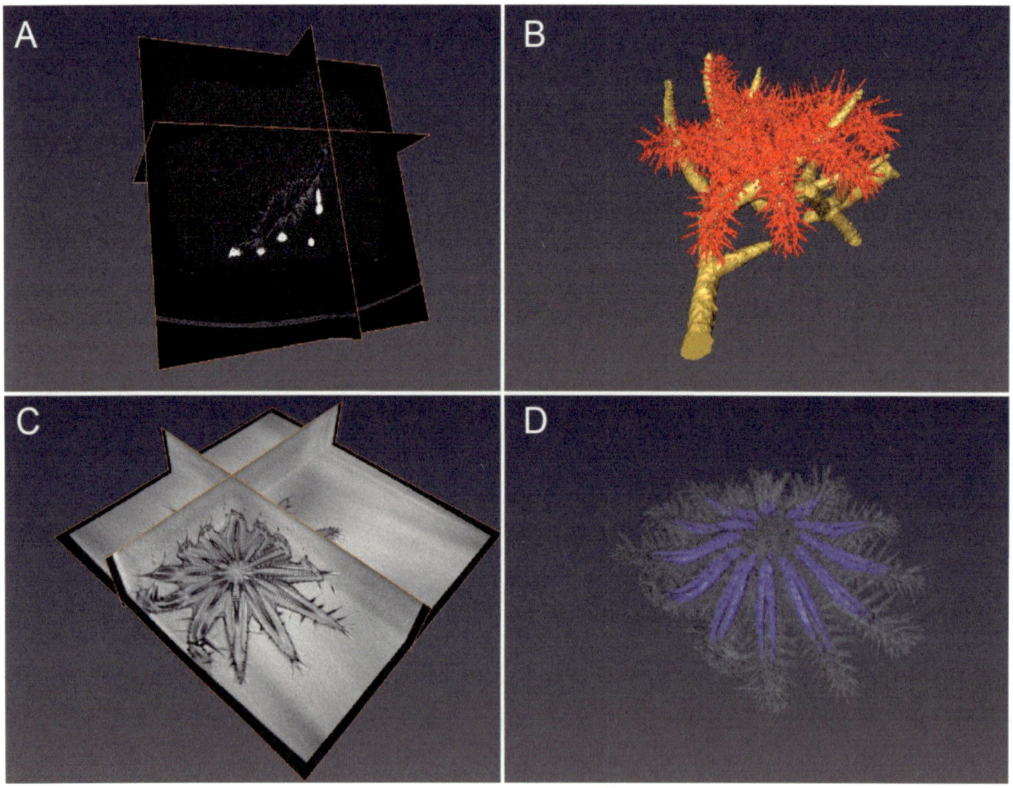

Fig. 7. Comparison of CT & MRI gained data illustrating functional limits of both techniques. **A** Image stack obtained from CT scan (3D volume data) with virtual planes (only a few planes are pictured) of a living *A. planci* individual crawling on a piece of coral. **B** 3D-rendered model of these CT data imaging all calcareous structures (red: starfish; golden: coral). **C** Image stack obtained from MRI scan (3D volume data) with virtual planes (only a few planes are pictured) of a living *A. planci* (anesthetized). **D** 3D-rendered model of these MRI data imaging outer morphology (transparent) and an internal organ (pyloric caeca, blue).

In marked contrast to CT, MRI is based on the detection of proton densities and is therefore advantageous when examining soft tissues. Hence, MRI is supposed to be "a real non-invasive" method, although effects of strong magnetic fields on organisms are by now not fully understood. Further, it offers the possibility for diffusion studies of fluids and the quantification of fluid flows (Walter et al., 2010). In addition, calcified structures can be depicted, but are likely to produce artefacts (Vlaardingerbroek & Den Boer, 2003). These can be suppressed by using certain scanning sequences, however resulting in lower signal-to-noise ratios or longer scanning times. Both methods have their strengths and weaknesses, thus, being mindful of the experimental design and the scientific question, the adequate technique can be selected.

Given that CT and MRI are complementary to each other in a way that CT can produce a distinct contour of mineralized structures such as bones, and MRI can show the adjacent soft tissue (Fig. 7), the development of fusion technologies to depict both data sets in a single 3D-reconstruction are well underway (e.g., Wong and Bishop, 2008). Recent technological progress has led to the development of combined Positron Emission Tomography (PET) and CT or MRI scanners in a single device, providing simultaneous information on metabolic pathways respectively anatomical characteristics in high spatial resolution. Hence, further technical advancement in this field will significantly improve non-destructive 3D live imaging in organismal biology.

5. Conclusion

Although digital imaging and computerized 3D-modeling is a rapidly advancing and promising technique in organismal biology, the interpretation of the visualized data should be handled with care, since the resolution of each acquisition technique differs and therefore relevant details of some biological structures will not be displayed in its entity or may even be entirely lacking. In addition, it has to be considered that there are many pitfalls while converting or even viewing the gathered data, as for example the absolute intensity information is lost in most image viewers, since they rescale the image to cover the maximal dynamic range (Walter et al., 2010).

Nevertheless, if the researcher is aware of those drawbacks, 3D-modeling opens new avenues for a variety of research areas in biology such as functional morphology or evolutionary developmental biology. It may even foster environmental sciences as it allows for accurate biomass calculations or the establishment of taxonomic 3D-libraries in biodiversity research. The latter will enable a high throughout identification, since the 3D-nature of organisms is crucial for a reliable morphological identification (Boistel et al., 2011).

In addition to the described digital imaging techniques there are numerous other 3D-based methods that become increasingly important in biological research. For example, using 3D-ultrasound microscopy at 1,2 Ghz, Laforsch et al. (2004) showed that small planktonic organisms strengthen their armour in the presence of an invertebrate predator and thereby uncovered a hidden inducible morphological defence. This study distinctly shows that imaging techniques are not only crucial to display morphologies in detail but also give striking insights into the ecology and evolution of these organisms.

Hence, the application of further improving techniques such as Atomic Force Microscopy (AFM), Optical Coherence Tomography (OCT) or superresolution light microscopy (e.g., 3D-SIM) are promising tools in organismal biology. With the development of even better imaging techniques and the still increasing computational power, at continuously decreasing acquisition costs, 3D-models will revolutionize several fields in biological science. The current possibility to implement and present interactive 3D-models and animations in online publications and scientific databases offer the unique possibility to share a complete dataset with the scientific community (e.g., https://www.morphdbase.de, http://www.digimorph.org). This enables to interact with the discovered or reviewed issues not only in 2D but rather in 3D/4D. Overall, next to understanding delicate and complex biological structures, 3D-imaging is an outstanding tool to discover and document biological processes down to the molecular level in real-time with precise spatial information.

6. References

Aguayo J. B., Blackband S. J., Schoeniger J., Mattingly M. a. & Hintermann M. (1986). Nuclear magnetic resonance imaging of a single cell. *Nature,* Vol. 322, pp. 190-191

Amos W. & White J. (2003). How the confocal laser scanning microscope entered biological research. *Biology of the Cell,* Vol. 95, No. 6, pp. 335-342, ISSN: 0248-4900

Bain M. M., Fagan A. J., Mullin J. M., McNaught I., McLean J. & Condon B. (2007). Noninvasive monitoring of chick development in ovo using a 7T MRI system from day 12 of incubation through to hatching. *Journal of magnetic resonance imaging,* Vol. 26, pp. 198-201

Bardell D. (1983). The first record of microscopic observations. *BioScience,* Vol. 33, No. 1, pp. 36-38, ISSN: 00063568

Benveniste H. & Blackband S. (2002). MR microscopy and high resolution small animal MRI: applications in neuroscience research. *Progress in Neurobiology,* Vol. 67, pp. 393-420

Boistel R., Swoger J., Kržič U., Fernandez V., Gillet B. & Reynaud E. G. (2011). The future of three-dimensional microscopic imaging in marine biology. *Marine Ecology,* pp. 1-15, ISSN: 1439-0485

Brenner D. J. & Hall E. J. (2007). Computed Tomography — An increasing source of radiation exposure. *New England Journal of Medicine,* Vol. 357, No. 22, pp. 2277-2284, ISSN: 0028-4793

Brinkmann N. & Wanninger A. (2008). Larval neurogenesis in *Sabellaria alveolata* reveals plasticity in polychaete neural patterning. *Evolution & Development,* Vol. 10, No. 5, pp. 606-618, ISSN: 1525-142X

Claeson K. M., Bemis W. E. & Hagadorn J. W. (2007). New interpretations of the skull of a primitive bony fish *Erpetoichthys calabaricus* (Actinopterygii: Cladistia). *Journal of Morphology,* Vol. 268, No. 11, pp. 1021-1039, ISSN: 1097-4687

Dierolf M., Menzel A., Thibault P., Schneider P., Kewish C. M., Wepf R., Bunk O. & Pfeiffer F. (2010). Ptychographic X-ray computed tomography at the nanoscale. *Nature,* Vol. 467, No. 7314, pp. 436-439, ISSN: 0028-0836

Ellis J. & Solander D. (1786). *The natural history of many curious and uncommon zoophytes collected from various parts of the globe.* Benjamin and Son Horace's Head, Fleet Street

Glasser O. (1995). W. C. Roentgen and the discovery of the Roentgen rays. *American journal of roentgenology,* Vol. 165, pp. 1033-1040

Glover P. & Mansfield S. P. (2002). Limits to magnetic resonance microscopy. *Reports on Progress in Physics,* Vol. 65, pp. 1489-1511

Helmchen F. & Denk W. (2005). Deep tissue two-photon microscopy. *Nature Methods,* Vol. 2, No. 12, pp. 932-940

Helmstaedter M., Briggman K. L. & Denk W. (2011). High-accuracy neurite reconstruction for high-throughput neuroanatomy. *Nature Neuroscience,* Vol. 14, No. 8, pp. 1081-1088, ISSN: 1097-6256

Heß M., Beck F., Gensler H., Kano Y., Kiel S. & Haszprunar G. (2008). Microanatomy, shell structre and molecular phylogeny of *Leptogyra, Xyleptogyra and Leptogyropsis* (Gastropoda: Neomphalida: Melanodrymiidae) from sunken wood. *Journal of Molluscan Studies,* Vol. 74, No. 4, pp. 383-401

Hessling R. (2002). Metameric organisation of the nervous system in developmental stages of *Urechis caupo;* (Echiura) and its phylogenetic implications. *Zoomorphology,* Vol. 121, No. 4, pp. 221-234, ISSN: 0720-213X

Hessling R. & Westheide W. (2002). Are Echiura derived from a segmented ancestor? Immunohistochemical analysis of the nervous system in developmental stages of *Bonellia viridis. Journal of Morphology,* No. 252, pp. 100-113

Hounsfield G. N. (1972). *A method of and apparatus for examination of a body by radiation such as X-ray or gammaradiation.* British patent office, No. 12839153. Great Britain.

Hounsfield G. N. (1973). Computerized transverse axial scanning (Tomography). I. Description of system. *British Journal of Radiology,* Vol. 46, No. 552, pp. 1016-1022, ISSN: 0007-1285

Jansen J. F. A., Backes W. H., Nicolay K. & Kooi M. E. (2006). 1H MR spectroscopy of the brain: absolute quantification of metabolites. *Radiology,* Vol. 240, pp. 318-332, ISSN: 2402050314

Jékely G. & Arendt D. (2007). Cellular resolution expression profiling using confocal detection of NBT/BCIP precipitate by reflection microscopy. *BioTechniques,* Vol. 42, pp. 751-755

Jörger K., Heß M., Neusser T. & Schrödl M. (2009). Sex in the beach: spermatophores, dermal insemination and 3D sperm ultrastructure of the aphallic mesopsammic *Pontohedyle milaschewitchii* (Acochlidia, Opisthobranchia, Gastropoda) *Marine Biology,* Vol. 156, No. 6, pp. 1159-1170, ISSN: 0025-3162

Jurrus E., Tasdizen T., Koshevoym P., Fletcher P. T., Hardy M., Chien C.-B., Denk W. & Whitaker R. (2006). Axon tracking in serial block-face scanning electron microscopy. *Proceedings of Workshop on microscopic image analysis with applications in biology,* October 2006

Kaandorp J. A., Sloot P. M. A., Merks R. M. H., Bak R. P. M., Vermeij M. J. A. & Maier C. (2005). Morphogenesis of the branching reef coral *Madracis mirabilis. Proceedings of the Royal Society B: Biological Sciences,* Vol. 272, No. 1559, pp. 127-133

Kak A. C. & Slaney M. (1988). *Principles of computerized tomographic imaging.* IEEE Service Center, Piscataway, NJ, USA

Ketcham R. A. & Carlson W. D. (2001). Acquisition, optimization and interpretation of X-ray computed tomographic imagery: applications to the geosciences. *Computers & Geosciences,* Vol. 27, No. 4, pp. 381-400, ISSN: 0098-3004

Kristof A., Wollesen T., Maiorova A. S. & Wanninger A. (2011). Cellular and muscular growth patterns during sipunculan development. *Journal of Experimental Zoology Part B: Molecular and Developmental Evolution,* Vol. 316B, No. 3, pp. 227-240, ISSN: 1552-5015

Kristof A., Wollesen T. & Wanninger A. (2008). Segmental mode of neural patterning in Sipuncula. *Current Biology,* Vol. 18, No. 15, pp. 1129-1132, ISSN: 0960-9822

Kruszyński K., Kaandorp J. & van Liere R. (2007). A computational method for quantifying morphological variation in scleractinian corals. *Coral Reefs,* Vol. 26, No. 4, pp. 831-840, ISSN: 0722-4028

Laforsch C., Ngwa W., Grill W. & Tollrian R. (2004). An acoustic microscopy technique reveals hidden morphological defences in Daphnia. *Proceedings of the National Academy of Sciences of the United States of America,* Vol. 101, No. 45, pp. 15911-15914

Laforsch C., Wild C., Glaser C. & Niggl W. (2008). A precise and non-destructive method to calculate surface area in living sclerectinian corals using X-Ray computed tomography and 3D modeling. *Coral Reefs,* Vol. 27, pp. 811-820

Lakowicz J. R., Szmacinski H., Nowaczyk K., Berndt K. W. & Johnson M. (1992). Fluorescence lifetime imaging. *Analytical Biochemistry,* Vol. 202, No. 2, pp. 316-330, ISSN: 0003-2697

Lauterbur P. C. (1973). Image formation by induced local interactions: examples employing Nuclear Magnetic Resonance. *Nature,* Vol. 242, pp. 190-191

Louie A., Hüber M., Ahrens E., Rothbächer U., Moats R., Jacobs R., Fraser S. & Meade T. (2000). In vivo visualization of gene expression using magnetic resonance imaging. *Nature Biotechnology,* Vol. 18, pp. 321-325

Macrini T. E., Rougier G. W. & Rowe T. (2007). Description of a cranial endocast from the fossil mammal *Vincelestes neuquenianus* (Theriiformes) and its relevance to the evolution of endocranial characters in Therians. *The Anatomical Record: Advances in Integrative Anatomy and Evolutionary Biology,* Vol. 290, No. 7, pp. 875-892, ISSN: 1932-8494

Maddin H. C. (2011). Deciphering morphological variation in the braincase of caecilian amphibians (Gymnophiona). *Journal of Morphology,* Vol. 272, No. 7, pp. 850-871, ISSN: 1097-4687

Maisano J. A. & Rieppel O. (2007). The skull of the round Island boa, *Casarea dussumieri* Schlegel, based on high-resolution X-ray computed tomography. *Journal of Morphology,* Vol. 268, No. 5, pp. 371-384, ISSN: 1097-4687

Marino L., Uhen M. D., Pyenson N. D. & Frohlich B. (2003). Reconstructing cetacean brain evolution using computed tomography. *The Anatomical Record Part B: The New Anatomist,* Vol. 272B, No. 1, pp. 107-117, ISSN: 1552-4914

Metscher B. (2009). MicroCT for comparative morphology: simple staining methods allow high-contrast 3D imaging of diverse non-mineralized animal tissues. *BMC Physiology,* Vol. 9, No. 1, pp. 11, ISSN: 1472-6793

Moran P. (1986). The Acanthaster phenomenon. *Oceanography and Marine Biology,* Vol. 24, pp. 379-480

Neusser T., Heß M. & Schrodl M. (2009). Tiny but complex - interactive 3D visualization of the interstitial acochlidian gastropod *Pseudunela cornuta* (Challis, 1970). *Frontiers in Zoology,* Vol. 6, No. 1, pp. 20, ISSN: 1742-9994

Neves R. C., Sorensen K. J. K., Kristensen R. M. & Wanninger A. (2009). Cycliophoran dwarf males break the rule: high complexity with low cell numbers. *The Biological Bulletin,* Vol. 217, No. 1, pp. 2-5

Pawley J. B., (Ed(s).). (2006). *Handbook of biological confocal microscopy,* Springer Verlag, ISBN: 038725921X,

Radon J. (1917). Über die Bestimmung von Funktionen durch ihre Integralwerte längs gewisser Mannigfaltigkeiten. *Berichte der Sächsischen Akademie der Wissenschaften,* Vol. 69, pp. 262-278

Reits E. A. J. & Neefjes J. J. (2001). From fixed to FRAP: measuring protein mobility and activity in living cells. *Nature cell biology,* Vol. 3, No. 6, pp. 145-145, ISSN: 1465-7392

Ritman E. L. (2004). Micro-computed tomography-current status and developments. *Annual Review of Biomedical Engineering,* Vol. 6, pp. 185-208, ISSN: 1523-9829

Robb R. A. (1982). X-ray computed tomography: from basic principles to applications. *Annual review of biophysics and bioengineering,* Vol. 11, No. 1, pp. 177-201, ISSN: 0084-6589

Rogers S. W. (1999). Allosaurus, crocodiles, and birds: Evolutionary clues from spiral computed tomography of an endocast. *The Anatomical Record,* Vol. 257, No. 5, pp. 162-173, ISSN: 1097-0185

Ruffins S. W., Martin M., Keough L., Truong S., Fraser S. E., Jacobs R. E. & Lansford R. (2007). Digital three-dimensional atlas of quail development using high-resolution MRI. *TheScientificWorldJournal,* Vol. 7, pp. 592-604

Ruthensteiner B. & Heß M. (2008). Embedding 3D models of biological specimens in PDF publications. *Microscopy Research and Technique,* Vol. 71, No. 11, pp. 778-786, ISSN: 1097-0029

Salisbury J. (1994). Three-dimensional reconstruction in microscopical morphology. *Histology and histopathology,* Vol. 9, No. 4, pp. 773-780, ISSN: 0213-3911

Schreurs G., Hänni R., Panien M. & Vock P. (2003). Analysis of analogue models by helical X-ray computed tomography. *Geological Society, London, Special Publications,* Vol. 215, No. 1, pp. 213-223

Sekar R. B. & Periasamy A. (2003). Fluorescence resonance energy transfer (FRET) microscopy imaging of live cell protein localizations. *The Journal of Cell Biology,* Vol. 160, No. 5, pp. 629-633

Streicher J. & Müller G. B. (2001). 3D modelling of gene expression patterns. *Trends in biotechnology,* Vol. 19, pp. 145-148

Stuppy W. H., Maisano J. A., Colbert M. W., Rudall P. J. & Rowe T. B. (2003). Three-dimensional analysis of plant structure using high-resolution X-ray computed tomography. *Trends in Plant Science,* Vol. 8, No. 1, pp. 2-6, ISSN: 1360-1385

Thevenaz P., Ruttimann U. E. & Unser M. (1998). A pyramid approach to subpixel registration based on intensity. *Image Processing, IEEE Transactions on,* Vol. 7, No. 1, pp. 27-41, ISSN: 1057-7149

Ustione A. & Piston D. W. (2011). A simple introduction to multiphoton microscopy. *Journal of Microscopy,* Vol. 243, No. 3, pp. 221-226, ISSN: 1365-2818

Vasquez S. X., Hansen M. S., Bahadur A. N., Hockin M. F., Kindlmann G. L., Nevell L., Wu I. Q., Grunwald D. J., Weinstein D. M., Jones G. M., Johnson C. R., Vandeberg J. L., Capecchi M. R. & Keller C. (2008). Optimization of volumetric computed tomography for skeletal analysis of model genetic organisms. *The Anatomical Record: Advances in Integrative Anatomy and Evolutionary Biology,* Vol. 291, No. 5, pp. 475-487, ISSN: 1932-8494

Verraes W. (1974). Notes on the graphical reconstruction technique. *Biologisch Jaarboek Dodonaea,* Vol. 42, pp. 182-191

Vlaardingerbroek M. T. & Den Boer J. A. (2003). *Magnetic resonance imaging: theory and practice.* Springer Verlag, ISBN: 3540436812,

Walter T., Shattuck D. W., Baldock R., Bastin M. E., Carpenter A. E., Duce S., Ellenberg J., Fraser A., Hamilton N. & Pieper S. (2010). Visualization of image data from cells to organisms. *Nat Methods,* Vol. 7, No. 3 Suppl, pp. S26-S41

Wanninger A. (2007). The application of confocal microscopy and 3D imaging software in Functional, Evolutionary, and Developmental Zoology: reconstructing myo-and neurogenesis in space and time, In: *Modern Research and Educational Topics in Microscopy,* A., M.-V., et al., pp. 468, Formatex, Bardajoz, Spain

Wanninger A. (2009). Shaping the things to come: ontogeny of lophotrochozoan neuromuscular systems and the Tetraneuralia concept. *The Biological Bulletin,* Vol. 216, No. 3, pp. 293-306

Wirkner C. S. & Prendini L. (2007). Comparative morphology of the hemolymph vascular system in scorpions - A survey using corrosion casting, MicroCT, and 3D-reconstruction. *Journal of Morphology,* Vol. 268, No. 5, pp. 401-413, ISSN: 1097-4687

Yang H. F. & Choe Y. (2009). Cell tracking and segmentation in electron microscopy images using graph cuts. *Proceedings of IEE International Symposium on Biomedical Imaging: from Nano to Macro,* ISBN: 1945-7928, Boston, MA, August 2009

Ziegler A., Faber C., Mueller S. & Bartolomaeus T. (2008). Systematic comparison and reconstruction of sea urchin (Echinoidea) internal anatomy: a novel approach using magnetic resonance imaging. *BMC Biology,* Vol. 6, No. 1, pp. 33, ISSN: 1741-7007

6

Open Source 3D Game Engines for Serious Games Modeling

Andres Navarro, Juan Vicente Pradilla and Octavio Rios
Universidad Icesi,
Colombia

1. Introduction

In this chapter we will review some tools and open source Game Engines used for modeling of real scenarios in serious games for training. One of the typical uses of serious games (3D serious games) is specialized training in dangerous tasks or when the training is quite expensive. However, typical games use artificial scenarios, created by artists and created according to the restrictions imposed by the Game engine used.

In our experience, some tasks require the use of a real scenario like a city, forest area, etc, and most of this information is available as Digital Terrain Models in Geographic Information Systems (GIS). The problem here is that GIS formats are not compatible with 3D formats used in Game engines. Then we have to solve the problem of convert the GIS format to a 3D format supported by the Game Engine.

On the other side of the story, there are different Game Engines in the market and different 3D formats both in the commercial world and in the Open Source world. For working with Open source tools, we have to consider tools like Blender and Game Engines like OGRE or JMonkey. Using these tools, we can model real scenarios based on GIS information, but being aware of some important considerations that will be exposed in the following pages.

During the writing of this chapter, many of the commercial game engines available have released some free versions, in some cases releasing source code for some applications. This is a very important event, because the users can develop serious games and training games using powerful tools according to specific needs. This chapter focuses in free game engines, which may be closed or open source (the code is provided with the software for modification or extension).

In the next pages we will describe some aspects of Serious Games and its importance in this modern time, and then we explain the basics of Open Source Game Engines and the recently released free Game Engines, its characteristics and some basic information about them. After that, we will explain some considerations about the conversion of Digital Terrain Maps in GIS format to 3D models useful for Game Engines. Finally, some conclusions and remarks.

2. The concept of serious games

Serious games have always been an important aspect of human development. They contribute to the acquisition of skills and knowledge that can be applied to daily activities and used to deal with the regular challenges of life.

The game as such doesn't aim anything but "the pleasure of being played" (Huizinga, 1938) any other collateral effect is beyond its goal.
The "serious game" makes reference to any game with a different goal than playing fun. Therefore, when a playful experience is used to teach or train, it can be considered a serious game. This particular kind of games take the consequences in great account, they are training process, development guides (Bruner, 1989).
The concept has received greater attention thanks to the growing interest of education centers for the use of computer games to teach. Nowadays is a common trend for companies to train their employees with help of scenarios simulated with computer games. Teaching institutions are using virtual environments to better impart concepts and procedures.
This is an area where 3D game engines offer a number of tools to achieve greater impact in a multimedia serious game. They support detailed visual representations and real-time interaction with some parts of the game.
They add a multisensory perception of objects that are difficult to access in the real life, and they can shed some light on complex concepts represented as familiar objects at game level.

3. Game engines

Game engines are toolkits aimed to ease the development of videogames, acting as a super-structure of several development efforts. They are also normally packed with a set of tools to be used in the design and coding stages.
A regular game engine provides: scripting, imagery rendering, artificial intelligence, physics, animation, cinematic, network access and resource management.

- Scripting: Let developers to write little pieces of code to control certain parts of the game.
- Imagery rendering: It's the core of visual part of the game. Handles lights, shadows, ray tracing, and rendering of 3D objects.
- Artificial Intelligence: Brings the world and characters of the game to life, through a set of routines that makes possible the interaction with the game environment.
- Animation: Adds behavior to objects, through transformations, skeletons, deformations and dynamics.
- Physics: Provides realistic interaction between objects and with their environment. Plus, character moment, fluid simulation, and "soft bodies".
- Cinematic: Adds the possibility to include video within the game to capture the attention of the player.
- Network access: Provides support to deploy the game in a network environment, be client-server or peer-to-peer.
- Resource management: A fundamental issue for the game engines is the efficient use of the computer resources (CPU, graphics card, memory, storage, hardware) and the load of game related resources (animations, shaders, 3d objects, sound, etc.)

Game engines can be classified according to several criteria, being one of them the type of licensing: commercial and freeware.

4. Open Source Game Engines

There exists different Open Source Game Engines, but perhaps the most popular one is OGRE. Ogre is an open source Game Engine written in C, with different extensions and characteristics.

Other interesting Game Engine that we will revise in deep is JMonkey. This is a Java based Game Engine with similar characteristics as Ogre, but more friendly with some new engineers' generation, familiarized with Java and with the advantages that Java offers.
Currently, serious games are being developed with aid of modeling and simulation tools, in hope of touching the players in a deeper way. This enlarged impact may largely contribute to the goals of the game, while keeping a pleasant visual environment and realistic interaction.

4.1 Jmonkey

JMonkeyEngine - jME (current version 3 alpha 4). It's a free and opensource engine distributed in the terms of BSD licence. It can be used to create games that run in any platform with a Java Virtual Machine (Windows, MAC OS y/o Linux.). It uses a few *native* libraries to improve performance through the Java Native Interface (JNA).
Games are coded in the Java programming language using the Java Standard Edition (J2SE) libraries.
jME is built with a modular architecture on top of OpenGL (Open Graphics Library), version 2, although the development roadmap points for a change to version 3 in the forth version of the engine. The combination of these two technologies offers a huge potential in terms of independence and functionality.
jME provides full scale physics support using jBullet. A shaders pack fully integrated with the engine, along with several other features, offering stunning graphical possibilities.
It also features an integrated system for the creation of Graphic user interfaces (GUI's) using XML (eXtensible Markup Language) through the Nifty GUI, and an advanced resource manager which comes handy to organize materials, textures, models, GUI's, and sound used in the game.
Finally, jME comes bundled with an Integrated Development environment (IDE) based on the Netbeans platform, for easier asset handling, terrain creation, 3D models manipulation, shaders creation, and game coding in Java.

4.2 Ogre (just a render engine)

Web page: http://www.ogre3d.org/
Platforms: Windows, Linux y Mac
Licensing: MIT License
Free: yes
Opensource: yes
None official tool.
Programming language: C++
Alternative programming languages (ports): java (ogre4j), .Net (MOGRE), GM (GMOgre3D), Phyton (Phyton-Ogre)

4.2.1 Ogre3d (just the rendering engine)

Object- Oriented Graphics Rendering Engine - Ogre 3D is not a fully flagged game engine, but a 3D graphics toolkit. Nonetheless, given its relevance in the game developers community, has been included in this chapter.
Ogre 3D is scene oriented and it's coded in C++. The engine provides Libraries to avoid the difficulties associated with the use of OpenGL and Microsoft's Direct3D. Graphic User

Interfaces maybe created in an object oriented manner with the engine's API. Games are coded in C++, but ports had been made for other programming languages such as java (ogre4j), .Net (MOGRE), GM (GMOgre3D) y Phyton (Phyton-Ogre).
Ogre 3D is freeware and open source, it's licensed under the terms of MIT license, and has an active community around its use and development, the result is a continuous improvement. It has a large user-base that creates games for Linux, Mac OS and Windows.
Finally, the engine offers many plugins, provided by the open source community, for quick development of applications. Some of them:
Ogremax (visualization y exporting), MyGui (GUI creation), CrazyEddie's GUI system (GUI widgets creation), OgreSpeedTree (creation of trees and nature elements), NeoaxisEngine (multipurpose 3D engine), ParticleUniverse (a full-flagged system for particle based effects).

4.3 Unity

Web page: http://unity3d.com/
Platforms: Web, iOS, Android, Windows, MAC, Wii, Xbox360 y PlaySatation3
Licensing: Propietary
Free:Yes, the plug-in for end user. Paid for developers
Open source: No
Programming language: C#, javascript, Boo
Additional tools: IDE
Alternative programming languages (ports):
Unity (versión 3), advanced game engine with focus in games with complex graphical content. It offers a high quality editor for design and coding of the game. It support development of games in several platforms: Web (plugin), iOS, Android, Windows, MAC, Wii, Xbox360 y PlaySatation3.
Unity uses a pipeline based deferred rendering method for improved performance. It comes packed with over 100 shaders, ranging from the classics (diffuse, glossy, etc) to the top-notch kind (SelfilluminatedBumpedSpecular)
The engine features a brand-new technology called *surfaceshader*, that permits the creation of new shaders from the scratch, to be used in different applications and renders. This allows the user, by example, to generate an illumination pattern for his game, and being able to reuse it in another.
To minimize computer time for the readers, Unity uses batch processing. The render combines different geometries into parallelizable units; this reduces the load on the graphic drivers and increases flexibility. It is also optimized to work with OpenGL, allowing the user to use shaders on mobile devices.
Besides, the engine features OcclusionCulling, a technology developed by Unity in conjunction with Umbra to function on the Web, mobile devices and game consoles. It reduces the load reducing rendering objects, generated new ones on demand.
Deferred rendering has been added in version 3, it allows the handling of multiple illumination patterns in an efficient way, without the inconvenient of overload.
Real time shadowing is an extremely demanding task for CPU's and graphic cards. The engine uses state of the art techniques to balance the load in a manner it can be processed gracefully by not so last generation equipment.
Unity has a number of tools for modeling and terrain generation within the editor. It can completely generate a terrain from scratch including elements such as trees, bushes, rocks and many types of grass, which give games a much realistic feel.

In the physics department, the engine is based on Nvidia's PhysX, a specialized physics engine that let game creators to focus in design and interaction. It packs default physics for characters and vehicles.

This platform provides last generation tools, which make use of technologies such as FMOD, used to create audio in an interactive way. Application audio can be visualized in real time, filters are provided to improve quality of the final result.

Unity supports 3 scripting languages: Javascript, C#, and a Python dialect called Boo. The three of them can coexist with each other, and make use of .Net libraries for database access, regular expressions, XML, and such. As a high level language, Boo provides syntax for fast prototyping and development of actions an behaviors of objects within the application.

Unlike other engines, Unity offers effortless web deployment, thorough real time network processing, synchronization and remote procedure calls. Multi-player mode is an issue already solved by the engine, which provides a plug-in (add-on) to export the application to any modern web browser, offering unprecedented distribution and interoperability.

4.4 UDK – Unreal Development Kit

Unreal Development Kit - UDK is property of Epic Games Inc, is the well-known game engine behind games such as: Gears of War, X-Men Origins: Wolverine y Unreal Tournament 3. Version 3 has come as a surprise for the game development community, as it will be distributed under a non-commercial free to use license, and with a profit share license for commercial purposes.

UDK is one of the most advanced game engines in use today, and has plenty of tools for easy creation of astounding games, which are coded in the UnrealScript programming language, and can be run on the Xbox/Xbox360 and PlayStation2/3 consoles, and in any computer with Windows, Linux or MAC, and by mobile devices with iOS and Android operating systems.

For animation, the engine uses an "animated skeleton" approach, aiming for detailed control of muscles and movement of characters. It uses a multithreaded processing system called Gemini, making possible the creation of a large number of environment elements with high quality photo-realistic effects. If the application is run on a 64 bits machine, an optimized pipeline rendering system named HDR is used to improve performance.

Physics within the engine are provided by Nvidia's PhsyX, one of the most advanced implementations in the market. It also features illumination and shadowing by the UnrealLightmass application. Kinematics are offered in cinematographic like style by the UnrealSDK, presenting a very realistic game experience. Network layer provides measurement of the gamers game-playing and statistics, providing the necessary information for cooperative, multi-player online deployment.

Finally, UDK features a behavior editor, UnrealEd, for rapid development of complex environments. User can modify terrains, trees and other elements, including sounds and complete scenes of the game.

4.5 Cryengine 3

Web page: http://crytek.com
Platforms: Windows, Xbox 360, PlayStation 3
Licensing: Free for non commercial use.
Free: YES

Open source: NO
Programming language: YES
Additional tools: YES
Alternative programming languages (ports): YES

The CryEngine is property of Crytek Inc, and is one of the most complete and awarded engines available, providing top-notch functionality for the games developed with this technology. It's considered a next generation solution for game development, able to use scalable computing technology. Is expected for version 3 to be free for outside development, but the licensing and business model has not been disclosure yet.

CryEngine technology is build on top of a "sandbox" that permits real time adjustment of parameters and error correction, and optimization as well. The sandbox allows creation and control of the application in real time across multiple platforms in a principle called WYSIWYP (what-you-see is what-you-play). Applications can be deployed directly to the Xbox360 and PlayStation 3 consoles, and to the Windows powered PC's.

CryEngine has a very intuitive interface, which allows closely observing and controlling the event flow in a visual manner, largely avoiding the need for ground zero coding of the application. Generation of terrain and vegetation is carried on by a set of tools that focus in realism and quality.

A real time particle system permits the creation of complex explosions in a few steps, alongside the FX editor, it allows for quick creation of high quality and graphically demanding content. Terrains and rivers can be created with dedicated tools within the engine, and they can be smoothed to any degree, depending on the desired realism level.

The engine offers support for modern multicore computer architectures, largely improving performance through the balanced distribution of the graphics, physics, artificial intelligence, and network tasks across process an threads as well.

Shaders used by CryEngine have been optimized in low level languages, and are compiled and assembled for every specific platform supported. Among the additional tools offered by the engine, we can found EyeAdaptation, that provides a much more realistic feel by the lighting of the scene according to the human eye movement; and High DynamicRange (HDR) Lighting, which permits realistic rendering of high contrast scenes.

Stands out in the CryEngine the generation of very dynamic renders of game characters, the animation is based on a simple skeleton scheme, which permits the creation of very realistic individual moves.

Artificial Intelligence used by the engine response adapting to the given scenario. Dynamic programming is held inside the sandbox, and permits to see changes made to code while the game is running.

Another signature feature of the engine is the extreme realism of water based environments (oceans, rivers, lakes) and high performance of lighting on different environments and natural habitats.

The engine provides a set of tools to measure and evaluate the performance of the applications powered by the engine in a detailed and consistent manner.

The engine has an integrated professional sound edition solution, which permits the edition of ambient soundtrack, event driven sounds and other media, in a very interactive and powerful manner, with a time line familiar to professional sound editors.

Finally, CryEngine offers a number of plug-in and tools that runs on 64 bits architectures, further improving performance. This Engine was released in August 2011 for free use for non-commercial purposes. Source code can be downloaded under specific agreements with Crytek.

4.6 Our recommendation: JMonkey

Selection process between Open Source Game Engines is quite complicated at this time tan some years ago when there were not many options. At this time (2011), the process is quite complicated, but we will try to explain some considerations that we use for our personal selection.

Fig. 1. The JMonkey logo

The choice between an Engine and another requires an exhaustive weighting of factors like: licensing, possibility of code modification, commercial expectation for the development, client computers specifications, platform (Operating System, Console, etc), skills of the development team, Engine support tools, development time, stability of the Engine and target public. In the previous section we have described some Game Engines and its characteristics that can be useful for decision making.

Considering that at the moment of write this lines CryEngine3 has not been released to open source and UDK have only few months under free delivery, we consider some useful aspects for serious games development using JMonkey.

JMonkey is written in Java, giving it a big span in the desktop world, allowing the development for different platforms. The con is that JMonkey does not support consoles or mobile devices. On the other side, is an open source and free game engine with excellent possibilities for Serious Games development.

5. An example of serious game with JMonkey

COMCITY is a simulation and strategy game based on a future chaotic situation where the player has the role of a radio planning agent from an specialized international agency. The player has the task of solve some communications problems occasioned by natural disasters. By means of this interaction, the player learns about the behavior of propagation models and the fulfillment of some basic KPI. The game has been developed especially for technicians, undergraduate students and some decision level personnel with no knowledge of radio planning.

COMCITY could be considered a serious game, because it has been conceived as an educational game; it is supported in real environments and has a mix between reality and entertainment. In COMCITY, game engines capabilities are fully exploited in order to obtain a dynamic environment, with a rich experience, and, at the same time, introduce the student to complex concepts related with wireless planning. In Figure 1, some 3D models used in COMCITY are shown.

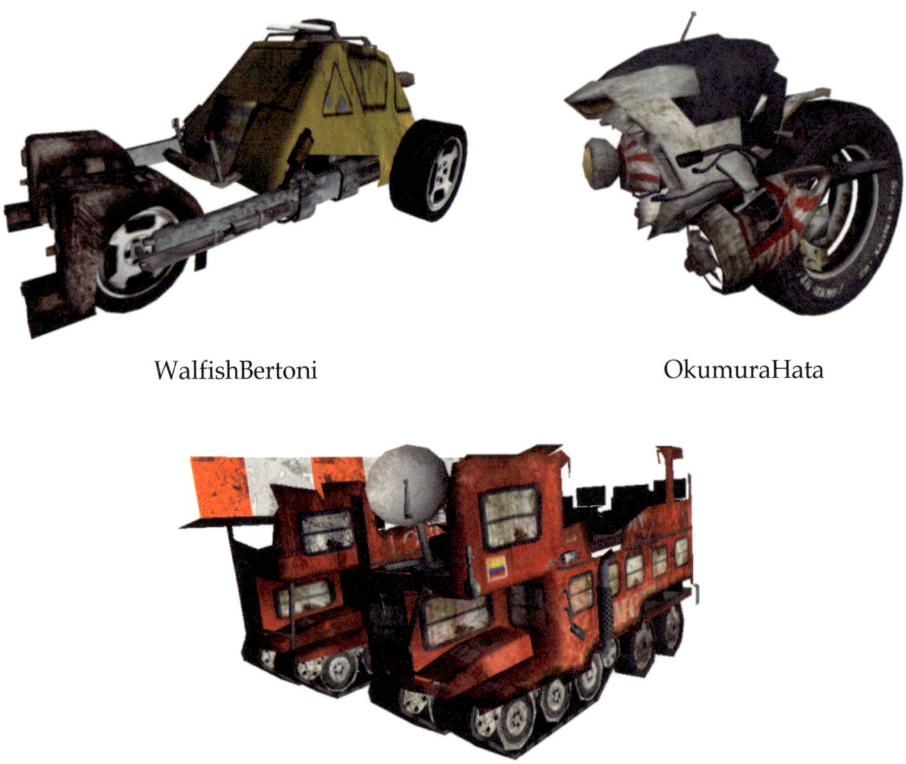

Fig. 2. 3D models for Comcity

TEST is a series of "virtual learning objects" running on a learning platform that combines serious games with training software. The goal of the system is to train people for a specific job and evaluating the most qualified people for the field job. TEST is in part an application of Comcity for specialized training.

In this serious game, we try to reproduce real situations that the apprentice will face in their real activities, preparing them to recognize potentially dangerous situations. Each activity that the player executes is associated with typical activities performed in real situations in remote areas where the trainee will work in a future, if the training is successful.
In this way, the player (trainee) makes associations between real objects that will find in a real situation, but through simulated situations in a 3D environment. In Figure 2, a 3D/2D interface for TEST is shown implemented in the Game Engine.

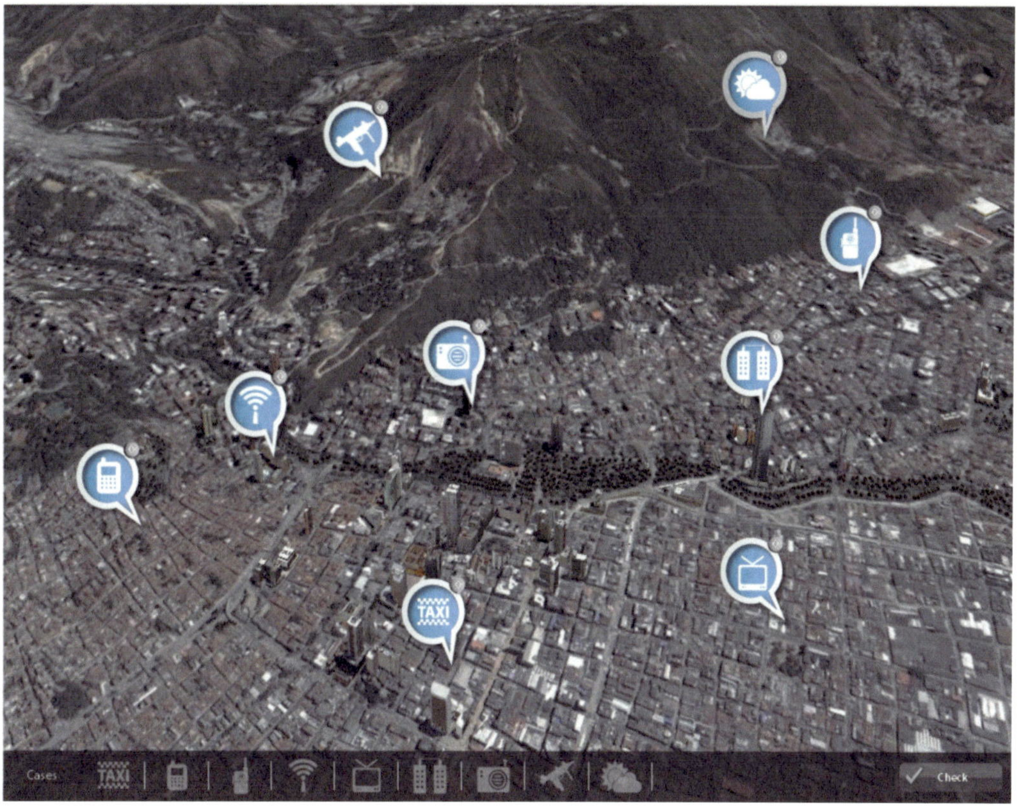

Fig. 3. An interface developed for TEST

6. Considerations for 3D modeling of real scenarios in game engines

The use of Game engines imposes some restrictions to the scenarios and the "3D world" typically used in a training system. Besides the current generation of graphics cards have a high processing capacity and video memory, there exist important restrictions that we have to consider when model different scenarios.
In order to illustrate this procedures and considerations, we will use the example of a Communications training game that uses real information from terrain maps and 3D models of real elements like towers and radio antennas.
In the next figure, we show a view of a real city, in the Game Engine. This view is based on an ASCII Raster map with a 1m resolution, which is a typical resolution used in Digital

Terrain Maps for Radio Communications (Mobile) Planning. An initial translation from the raster to 3D format, can have more than one million polygons, which is unusable in a Game Engine. Then, it is necessary to apply some techniques that reduce the number of polygons to around 200.000, that is an acceptable number, considering that the 3D scenario will contain other elements like towers, antennas, etc.

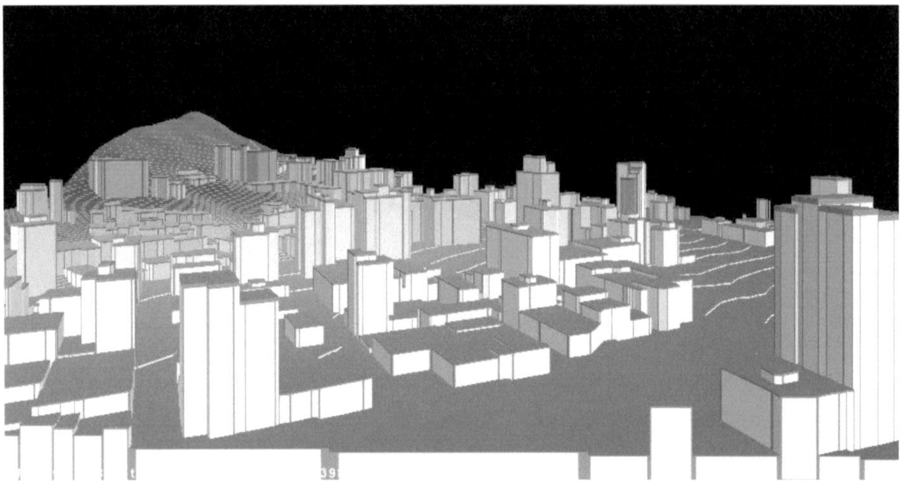

Fig. 4. A 3D map obtained from digital terrain file

There exist many applications for 3D digital city generation. Typically this tools are of the procedural type, meaning that 3D models are created from an automated algorithm instead of been modeled by a designer. This is quite useful where there are not specific requirements for the model, which is common in entertainment games.
One of the most popular open source tools for 3D modeling is Blender. Blender is an open source 3D modeling tool with plug-ins and scripts programmed in Python. Is very useful for 3D modeling and animation and is licensed using the GNU GPL model. For city generation, blender have some scripts like Suicidator City Generator, Suicidator City Engine (SCE) and Blended Cities, which is an evolution of SCE. Suicidator City Engine can use polygons information from an image file (JPEG) in order to generate streets, sidewalks or buildings. Buildings can be modified using the options available in the script. As mentioned before, this tool can be useful for entertainment games, bit for Serious Games this kind of unreal scenarios is not so useful and it is necessary (or desirable) to use real scenarios. In order to use such real scenarios, the most common source is the Digital Elevation Models used in Geographic Information Systems (GIS). This DEM information is represented in formats developed for the GIS requirements and for Cartography requirements, not for 3D game engines. In the next session we explain a procedure for the conversion of a map to a 3D model useful for its implementation on a Game Engine.

6.1 The Source map

It is quite common to have cartographic information in text files in ASCII format, known as ASCII Raster, because well know GIS applications, like ArcInfo, Idrisi or Ilwis use this format. This data included in text file have information about coordinates and height and must be displayed in graphic manner. In Figure 4 we show an example of an ASCII raster file and in Figure 5 the same map is showed using a GIS tool like Google Earth.

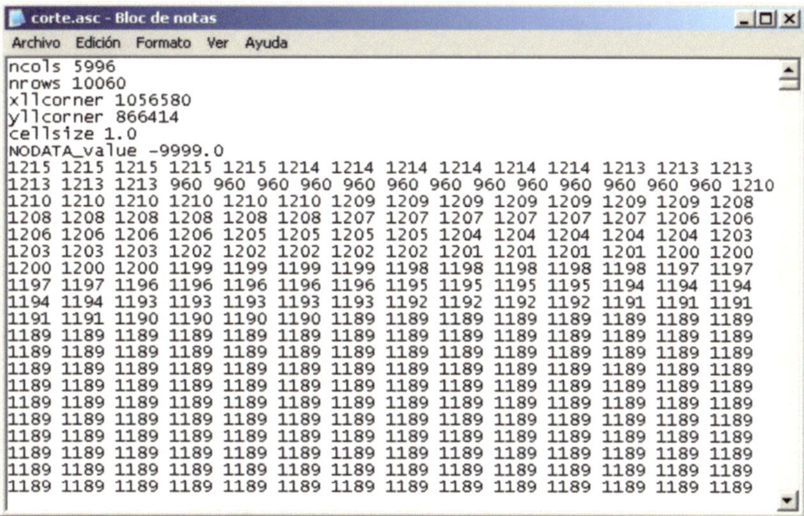

corte.asc - Bloc de notas

Archivo Edición Formato Ver Ayuda

```
ncols 5996
nrows 10060
xllcorner 1056580
yllcorner 866414
cellsize 1.0
NODATA_value -9999.0
1215 1215 1215 1215 1215 1214 1214 1214 1214 1214 1214 1213 1213 1213
1213 1213 1213 960 960 960 960 960 960 960 960 960 960 960 960 960 1210
1210 1210 1210 1210 1210 1210 1209 1209 1209 1209 1209 1209 1209 1208
1208 1208 1208 1208 1208 1208 1207 1207 1207 1207 1207 1207 1206 1206
1206 1206 1206 1206 1205 1205 1205 1205 1204 1204 1204 1204 1204 1203
1203 1203 1203 1202 1202 1202 1202 1202 1201 1201 1201 1201 1200 1200
1200 1200 1200 1199 1199 1199 1199 1198 1198 1198 1198 1198 1197 1197
1197 1197 1196 1196 1196 1196 1196 1195 1195 1195 1195 1194 1194 1194
1194 1194 1193 1193 1193 1193 1193 1192 1192 1192 1192 1191 1191 1191
1191 1191 1190 1190 1190 1190 1189 1189 1189 1189 1189 1189 1189 1189
1189 1189 1189 1189 1189 1189 1189 1189 1189 1189 1189 1189 1189 1189
1189 1189 1189 1189 1189 1189 1189 1189 1189 1189 1189 1189 1189 1189
1189 1189 1189 1189 1189 1189 1189 1189 1189 1189 1189 1189 1189 1189
1189 1189 1189 1189 1189 1189 1189 1189 1189 1189 1189 1189 1189 1189
1189 1189 1189 1189 1189 1189 1189 1189 1189 1189 1189 1189 1189 1189
1189 1189 1189 1189 1189 1189 1189 1189 1189 1189 1189 1189 1189 1189
1189 1189 1189 1189 1189 1189 1189 1189 1189 1189 1189 1189 1189 1189
1189 1189 1189 1189 1189 1189 1189 1189 1189 1189 1189 1189 1189 1189
1189 1189 1189 1189 1189 1189 1189 1189 1189 1189 1189 1189 1189 1189
1189 1189 1189 1189 1189 1189 1189 1189 1189 1189 1189 1189 1189 1189
```

Fig. 5. ASCII Raster file example

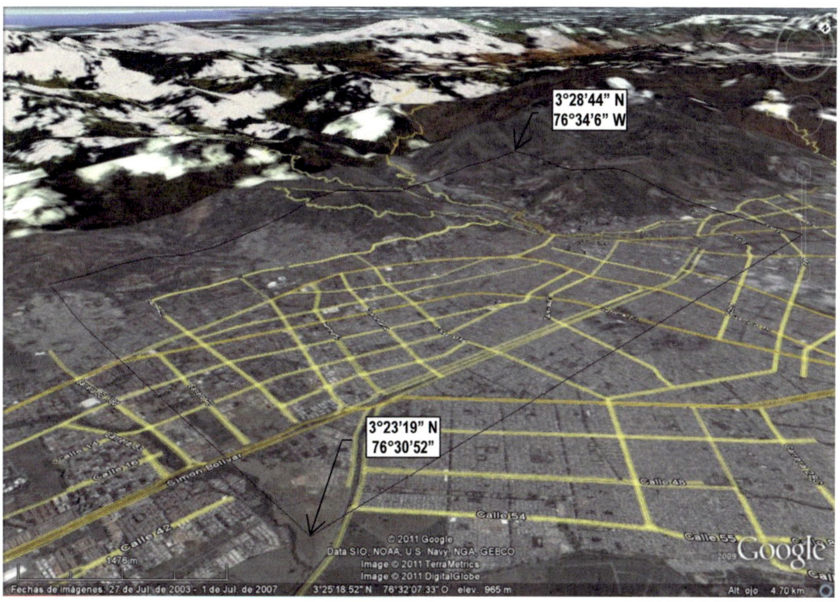

Fig. 6. Same map viewed in Google Earth

There are many open source or free tools for GIS data visualization, as well as different commercial tools for the same purpose. Some Open tools for GIS visualization are MapWindow, GRASS or SAGA. A quite well free tool is OpenEV, which can be sued for 3D visualization and data conversion.

If the map file is available in shape 3D, this kind of file can be exported to Blender almost directly.

6.2 Conversion process

The first step to convert a raster file in to a 3D model is to convert the ASCII file (.asc extension) into a shape file (.shp extension), which is vector file format, more close to most of the 3D format files. For such conversion, tools like MapWindow are adequate, but results do not allow a direct conversion from the shape to 3D tool like Blender. The development of scripts for tools like SAGA or GRASS allows better results.
Other possibility is to use a JPEG file obtained from a GIS visualization tool like OpenEV and use an open source tool like Blender to generate 3D from the gray scale obtained initially. In the Figure 6 is shown a section of a real map in OpenEV.

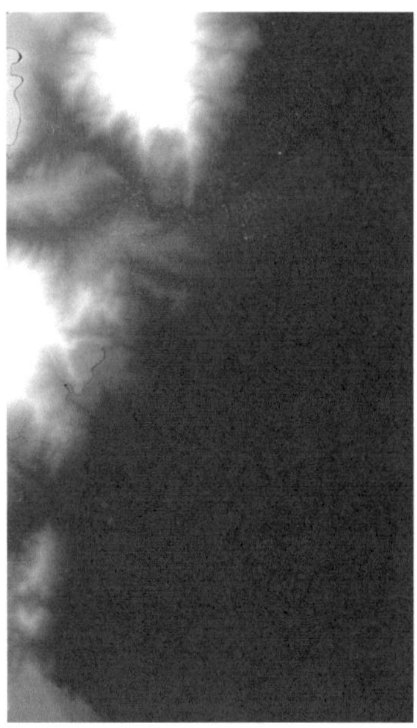

Fig. 7. JPEG image obtained from OpenEV

From this image, it is possible to import the image to Blender, and obtain a 3D model like the one shown in Figure 7. This model can be used in a game engine, just exporting it to an adequate format. However, this model could be improved substantially using additional tools or simple tricks like separating the image of the Figure 3 in two different images that allows separating the terrain from the buildings.

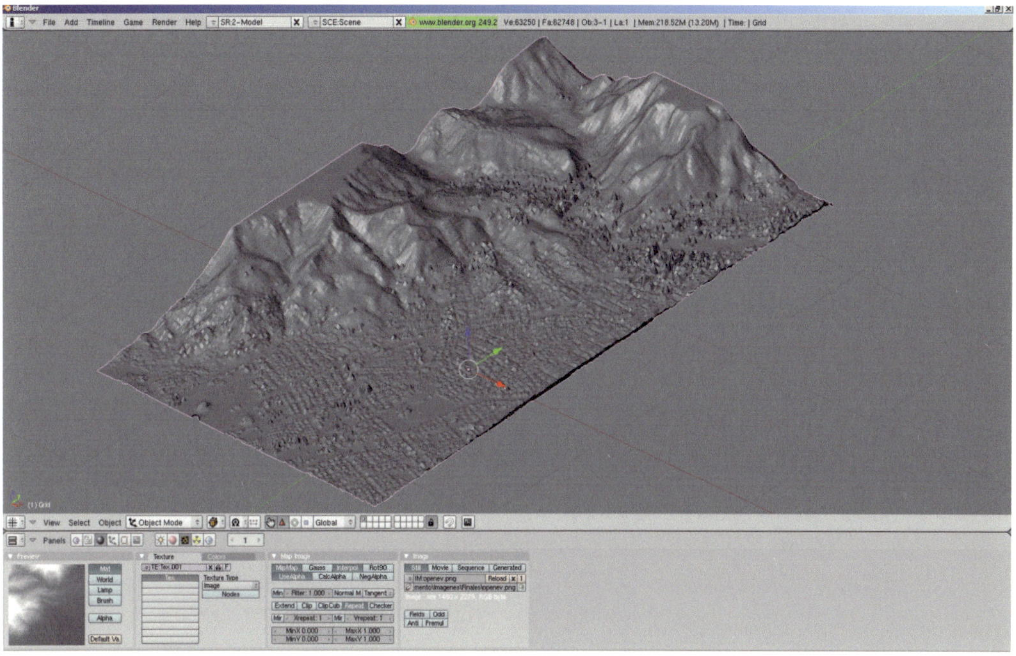

Fig. 8. 3D model obtained in Blender

In Figure 9, two images, one for terrain and the other for buildings are shown. Both images were obtained from the same image of Figure 6, but processed using an image processing tool like Gimp to modify the gray scale and separating buildings from terrain.

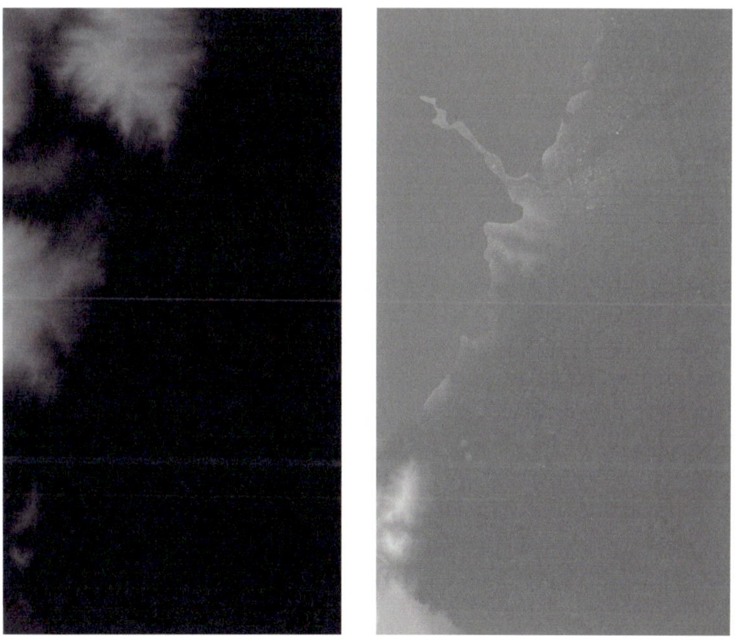

Fig. 9. (a) Image from terrain (b) image for buildings

Additionally and in order to improve the visualization on the game, the 3D map obtained in Blender can be enriched with 3D models obtained from tools like Google SketchUp, and combined with different light sources and renders, finally obtaining a 3D model like the one shown in Figure 10.

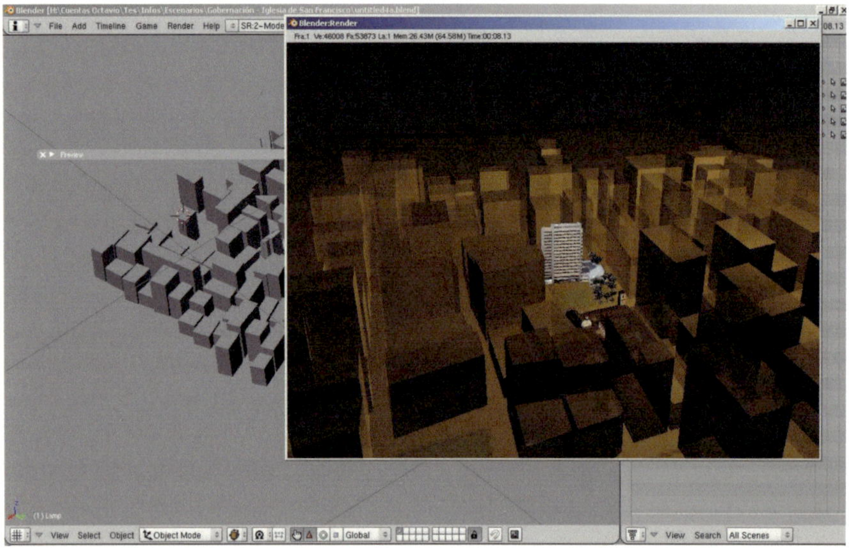

Fig. 10. Buildings 3D model in Blender

6.3 3D modeling tools and its interaction with game engines

In the market exists many 3D modeling tools, like 3D Studio in the commercial world, or Blender in the open source world. However, these tools do not consider the specific needs of a 3D model that will be used in a Game Engine, neither in default formats nor in number of polygons or visualization characteristics. In this section, we will explain how to use such tools in order to model 3D objects for a 3D game with Open Source Game Engines.

In previous section, we explain how to obtain a 3D model from a real map and how to manipulate it in a 3D tool like Blender. The next step is to "optimize" the 3D model in order to load it in the Game Engine and allow a "fluid" navigation in the game. Basically, this process depends on the limitations of the Engine respect to the number of polygons accepted and hardware capacity (RAM, Graphic Card, etc).

The first consideration is the 3D format. There are many 3D formats, but two commonly used are 3ds (originally from 3D Studio Max) and OBJ (is a recent format commonly used in the open source community). For Engines like JMonkey, the better format is OBJ, because it allows preserving the uv coordinates, texture loading and interoperability with alpha channels used in 3D modeling tool. The 3DS format has some problems with alpha channels and iv coordinates in some Engines. Another advantage for OBJ is the preservation of object size. An important consideration when the file is exported from Blender is to export the different 3D layers in different OBJ files, according to the game requirements.

Polygon reduction is perhaps a time consuming task that requires some simplification of the 3D model in Blender. Typically a 3D model obtained from a map like mentioned earlier consist of around 1 to 2 million of polygons and must be reduced to a maximum of 700K polygons, but preferably 200K polygons, like the city shown in Figure 10.

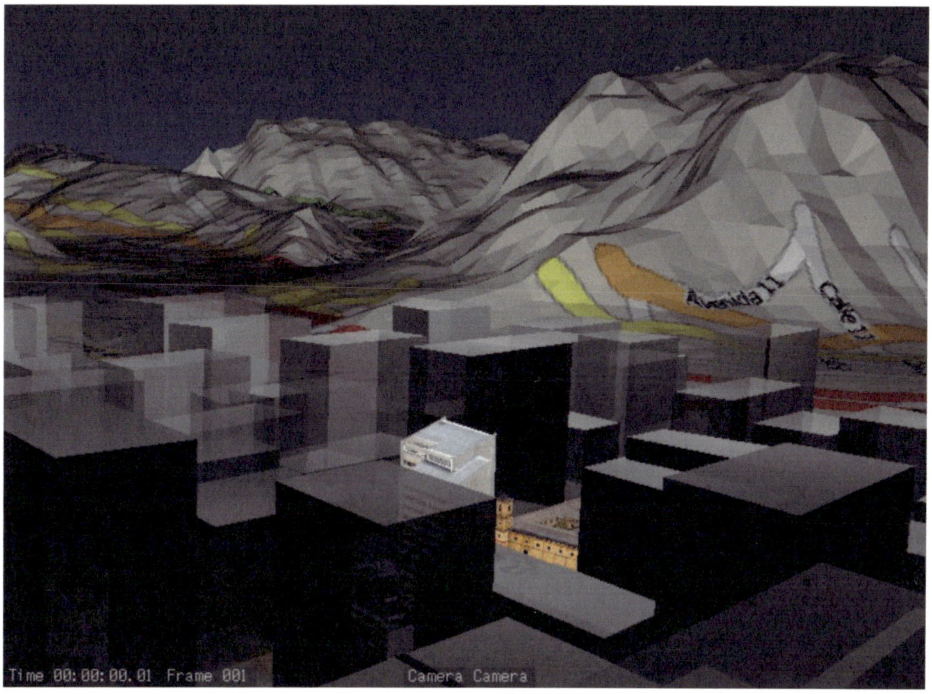

Fig. 11. Final city for Use in Game Engine

7. Conclusions

In this chapter, we have discussed our experience with Digital Terrain Maps conversion to a 3D engine compatible format, using Open Source tools and some considerations about 3D models for Serious Games. We have used Open Source Game Engines with similar performance to a commercial tool.

Special considerations have to be with the polygons number in the 3D map, because the typical conversion process from a DTM to a 3D model generates a huge number of polygons, that makes the Engine unusable.

8. References

Bruner, Jerome (1989). Acción, pensamiento y lenguaje, Madrid: Alianza Editorial.

Caillois, Roger (1986). Les Jeux et les hummens. Los juegos y los hombres : la máscara y el vértigo, México: Ed. Fondo de Cultura Económica.

Huizinga, Johan (1938). Homo Ludens. Madrid: Alianza editorial.

Navarro, Andres; Madriñan, Patricia and Pradilla, Juan Vicente (2010). A 3D Game Tool for Mobile Networks Planning 2010 Second International Conference on Mobile, Hybrid, and On-Line Learning ,Saint Maarten, Netherlands, Antilles February 10-February 16.

Navarro, Andres; Madriñan, Patricia; Londoño, Sebastian and Pradilla, Juan Vicente. (2011). Serious Games: Between Training and Entertainment, *Third International Conference on Mobile, Hybrid, and On-Line Learning*, ISBN: 9781612080031, Gosier, Guadeloupe, France February 2011.

OpenEV, Your Geospatial toolkit. Accessed: June 2011. Available from: http://openev.sourceforge.net/

Map Windows Open Source Project. Accessed: May 2011. Available from: http://www.mapwindow.org/

ESRI, ArcView. Accessed: May 2011. Available from: http://www.esri.com/software/arcgis/arcview/

Modelos Vector Raster (In Spanish). Accessed: January 2011. Available from: http://gemini.udistrital.edu.co/comunidad/profesores/rfranco/vector_raster.htm

Open Street Map. Accessed: January 2011. Available from: http://www.openstreetmap.org/

Blender. Accessed: January 2011. Available from: http://www.blender.org/

Procedural Generation. Accessed: January 2011. Available from: http://en.wikipedia.org/wiki/Procedural_generation

7

Refinement of Visual Hulls for Human Performance Capture

Toshihiko Yamasaki and Kiyoharu Aizawa
The University of Tokyo
Japan

1. Introduction

Generation of dynamic three-dimensional (3D) mesh sequences of human performance using multiple cameras has been actively investigated in recent years (de Aguiar et al., 2008; Hisatomi et al., 2008; Kanade et al., 1997; Kim et al., 2007; Matsuyama et al., 2004; Nobuhara & Matsuyama, 2003; Snow et al., 2000; Starck & Hilton, 2007; Tomiyama et al., 2004; Toyoura et al., 2007; Tung et al., 2008; Vlasic et al., 2008). The topic is drawing a lot of attention because conventional 3D shape measurement tools, such as laser scanners, shape (structure)-from-motion (Huang & Netravali, 1994; Poelman & Kanade, 1997), shape-from-shading (Zhang et al., 1999), etc., are difficult to apply to dynamic scenes. On the other hand, depth cameras, such as time-of-flight (Foix et al., 2011) and structured light (Fofi et al., 2004) cameras can measure depth only from the viewpoint, and they do not measure the entire 3D shape of objects. There are many attractive applications of 3D human performance capture such as movies, education, computer aided design (CAD), heritage documentation, broadcasting, surveillance, gaming, etc.

Shape-from-silhouette (or volume intersection) (Laurentini, 1994) is a fundamental process in generating the convex hulls of the 3D objects. Because the shape-from-silhouette algorithm is directly affected by the foreground/background segmentation, a well-controlled monotone background is often employed (de Aguiar et al., 2008; Kim et al., 2007; Starck & Hilton, 2007; Tomiyama et al., 2004; Toyoura et al., 2007; Vlasic et al., 2008). However, proper segmentation has been a serious problem even in such studios. Therefore, a number of approaches have been proposed for refining the geometrical data of the objects in both the spatial and temporal domains.

This chapter reviews recent works on the refinement of visual hulls and describes our contribution featuring iterative refinement of foreground/background segmentation and visual hull generation.

The rest of this chapter is organized as follows. Section 2 reviews related works for the robust 3D model reconstruction. Section 3 describes our 3D studio and our proposed algorithm. Experimental results are presented in Section 4. Finally, concluding remarks are given in Section 5.

2. Related works

This section summarizes related works on 3D model refinement. The spatial and the temporal domain approaches are orthogonal and are independent of each other. They can be combined to generate more accurate 3D models, although this is out of the scope of this chapter.

2.1 Spatial domain approaches

Spatial domain approaches can be categorized into those that refine the foreground/background segmentation and those that refine the generated visual hulls by additional algorithms.

2.1.1 Refinement of silhouette extraction

One of the straightforward approaches is improving the foreground/background segmentation (Benezeth et al., 2008; McIvor, 2000; Piccardi, 2004) regardless of a 3D modeling context. However, none of the previous algorithms is perfect.

Toyoura (Toyoura et al., 2007) proposed a silhouette extraction algorithm using a random pattern background. By using small patches of a random color pattern, the probability of the foreground color coinciding with that of the background in all viewpoints becomes very small. Even when the color of the background is close to that of the foreground object in a certain view, the background color from a different view is far from that of the foreground object. Therefore, misclassification of the foreground as the background can be suppressed. This approach can reduce the loss of voxels, but on the other hand tends to yield a voxel surplus. In addition, a proper design of a random pattern background depending on the size of the studio is required.

Kim (Kim et al., 2007) introduced a reliability map of foreground/background segmentation. Foreground and background regions were modeled by the stochastic approach, which was named generalized Gaussian family (GGF), and confidence scores were assigned to each pixel. In the modeling process, rule-based error correction was employed to reduce voxel loss because of segmentation errors and occlusions. However, this approach also tends to yield superfluous voxels. In addition, the GGF model needs to be trained in each environment.

An object silhouette extraction method with error detection and correction using multiviewpoint images was proposed by Nobuhara (Nobuhara et al., 2007). In this approach, two constraints were introduced: "intersection," which assumes that the projection of the visual hull on every viewpoint was equal to the silhouette on each viewpoint; and "projection," which implies that projection of the visual hull should have an outline that matches with the apparent edges of the captured image on each viewpoint. This algorithm required several hundreds of iterations and took 0.5–3 days to process only a single frame. Therefore, it was not feasible for our purpose.

2.1.2 Refinement of generated visual hulls

Shape-from-silhouette (or volume intersection) generates a convex hull model and concave parts cannot be modeled properly. The key information to eliminate unnecessary voxels in concave parts is photo consistency.

In (Kutulakos & Seitz, 2000; Seitz & Dyer, 1999; Slabaugh et al., 2001), voxel colorization and photo consistency evaluation was done voxel-by-voxel. When the differences between the voxel color and the corresponding pixel values were above the threshold, the voxel was eliminated. In this approach, the problem was setting the proper threshold value.

Tomiyama (Tomiyama et al., 2004) and Starck (Starck & Hilton, 2007) employed stereo matching to calculate a more detailed shape of the object. The depth search range was restricted by the visual hull model with the assumption that the actual surface point should exist on or inside the visual hull according to the theory of space carving (Kutulakos & Seitz, 2000). By this constraint, the computational cost was reduced and at the same time, the depth estimation error due to mismatching was reduced. A similar idea can also be found in (Fua & Leclerc, 1995), but this work was meant for 2.5D (multiview + depth) model reconstruction.

The graph cuts algorithm was also employed after the shape-from-silhouette for refining the concave part of objects (Hisatomi et al., 2008; Liu et al., 2006; Tung et al., 2008). In (Hisatomi et al., 2008), the constraint term imposed by silhouette edges was introduced to preserve thin parts. Tung (Tung et al., 2008) combined both superresolution and dynamic 3D shape reconstruction problems into a unique Markov random field (MRF) energy formulation and optimized the cost function by graph cuts.

These approaches are used only for removing unnecessary voxels; the loss of voxels deriving from erroneous silhouette extraction cannot be recovered. Therefore, these algorithms should be applied after the shape-from-silhouette processing with perfect foreground/background segmentation to remove only surplus voxels.

2.1.3 Other approaches

An alternative approach to using shape-from-silhouette is using graph cuts in the 3D space (Snow et al., 2000). The difference from (Hisatomi et al., 2008; Liu et al., 2006; Tung et al., 2008) is that this approach does not use the volume intersection. In (Snow et al., 2000), the data term was the sum of the values attached to the voxels, where the value was based on the observed intensities of the pixels that intersect it, and the smoothness term was defined as the number of empty voxels adjacent to filled ones. However, the accuracy of the modeling was not discussed in (Snow et al., 2000). As pointed out in (Hisatomi et al., 2008), combining the shape-from-silhouette and the graph cuts algorithm yields better results for flat color and repetitive color pattern regions.

The probabilistic model (Broadhurst et al., 2001) calculates the photo-consistency energy of the two cases; i.e., whether the voxel exists or not. The probability of the existence of each voxel was calculated by Bayse's rule to choose which case is more likely. Similar stochastic approaches can also be found in (Bonet & Viola, 1999; Isidoro & Sclaroff, 2002).

2.2 Temporal domain approaches

In temporal domain approaches, 3D models are generated by deforming and refining the reference 3D models in different frames. Therefore, the manner of taking the correspondence between the feature points in neighboring frames (models) is important for extracting deformation and refinement parameters. The temporal domain refinement not only generates more accurate shapes of the 3D objects, but also keeps the geometry and the topology of the generated 3D models coherent throughout the frames (i.e., the number of vertices and their connectivity are consistent). This would also facilitate better quality texture mapping, compression, and motion tracking and analysis of the generated 3D model sequences.

Nobuhara (Nobuhara & Matsuyama, 2003) proposed a deformable mesh model taking into account five constraints, such as photo consistency, silhouette, smoothness, 3D motion flow, and inertia. First, intraframe deformation was conducted considering the first three

constraints (this part constitutes spatial refinement) and the 3D model in the previous frame was deformed to match the model in the present frame considering the last two constraints.
In (Vlasic et al., 2008), a skeleton model was used to track the motion of the object and the template model was deformed using linear blend skinning to meet the silhouette fitting constraint. The algorithm depended only on the silhouette and no color information was utilized.
A feature-based tracking in captured 2D images using scale-invariant feature transform (SIFT) features (Lowe, 2004) was proposed by de Aguiar (de Aguiar et al., 2008). The model was then deformed based on the extracted motion. Details were recovered by adjusting the vertices to the silhouette contours and by estimating the depth using multiview stereo. In this work, the initial model was generated using a laser scanner.
In (Luo et al., 2010), a modified annealed particle filtering was proposed to track the motion, and deformation and shape refinement were performed considering the silhouette of the human body.

2.3 Proposed work in this chapter

Most of the algorithms, for spatial refinement in particular, are designed only to eliminate unnecessary voxels, not to recover erroneously removed voxels (exceptions can be found, for example, in (Kim et al., 2007)). Therefore, the misclassification of the foreground object region as background in segmentation is a critical problem, not to mention that the excess number of voxels in the dilation process utilized for solving such a problem is difficult to remove even with the fancy algorithms listed above.
Therefore, we have developed a 3D model generation algorithm with smaller numbers of lost and surplus voxels (Yamasaki et al., 2009), which can be categorized as the spatial domain approach. This algorithm works well even without a monotone background. Our algorithm is based on the iterative feedback between the silhouette extraction and the 3D modeling; namely, the generated 3D models are rendered and used as a seed for the graph cuts algorithm (Boykov & Jolly, 2001; Rother et al., 2008) for better silhouette extraction. The improved silhouette images are used to reconstruct the 3D models. This iterative process is repeated until the geometrical shape of the 3D models converges. As a result, both the voxel loss and surplus can be suppressed drastically compared with conventional algorithms. The difference from (Kim et al., 2007; Toyoura et al., 2007) is that the generated 3D models are improved iteratively, not by a single-shot correction. In addition, the computational cost is not very large because the number of required iterations is quite small, as discussed in 4. Whereas (Nobuhara et al., 2007) updates the silhouette image one by one sequentially, which is therefore time consuming, the proposed method updated all the silhouette images in each iteration.

3. 3D model generation based on iterative feedback between silhouette extraction and geometry modeling

3.1 Studio setup

Our 3D modeling studio is illustrated in Fig. 1. The studio consisted of 12 sets of capturing units: a camera with 1360 $\times$ 1024 resolution and camera-link interface, light, and personal computer (Intel Core2 Duo 2.4 GHz, 4 GB memory, RAID 0 HDD operating at 3 GB/s) attached to a pole. All the cameras were synchronized by an external signal generator. The frame rate was up to 34 fps. The system was built in our laboratory room (Fig. 1(b)). No special background such as a blue sheet was utilized. Only the computers were covered with

cloths because they are shiny and affect the silhouette extraction. Camera calibration was done using Tsai's method (Tsai, 1987).
The system was easy to set up and portable. Disassembling and setting up the studio again can be achieved in a few hours. The size of the studio was about 6 m × 5 m but these dimensions are flexible, depending on the size of the object and the area required for the object to move around.

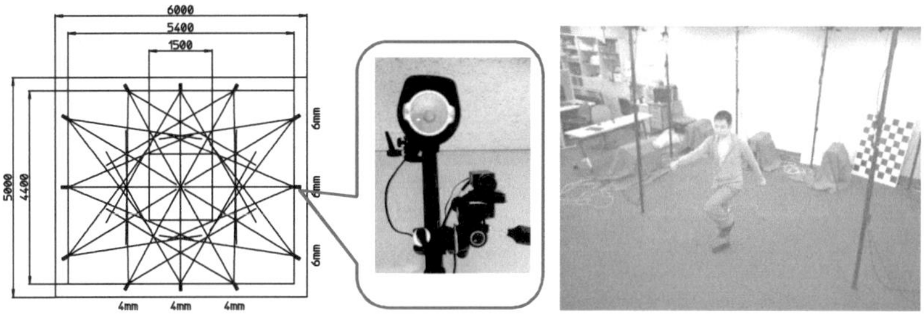

(a) Floor plan (b) A view from a certain camera.

Fig. 1. Studio setup.

3.2 Flow of the algorithm

The flowchart of our 3D modeling algorithm is shown in Fig. 2. In the initial step, we conducted conventional silhouette extraction and 3D modeling. Then, we proceeded to the iterative processing between silhouette refinement using the rendered images and the 3D model reconstruction with error compensation. When the generated 3D model converged and was not very different from that of the previous step, the iteration was terminated and the final 3D mesh was obtained.
For higher-quality modeling, especially for reconstructing concave parts, sophisticated model refinement algorithms are required after the shape-from-silhouette, such as deformable mesh (Matsuyama et al., 2004), stereo matching, (Starck & Hilton, 2007; Tomiyama et al., 2004) and graph cuts in the 3D space (Hisatomi et al., 2008; Tung et al., 2008). However, such a model refinement process is out of the scope of this chapter. Our target was to generate shape-from-silhouette-based 3D mesh models with loss of fewer voxels while suppressing surplus of voxels for such refinement algorithms to work better.

3.3 Shape-from-silhouette with error compensation

The shape-from-silhouette is a 3D modeling algorithm that works by taking the intersections of visual cones of all the cameras surrounding the object, as shown in Fig. 3. In other words, if a voxel is seen from all the cameras, the voxel remains. Otherwise, the voxel is removed. In this manner, the visual hull of the 3D object is estimated. Then, various refinement algorithms are applied for modeling convex parts or smoothing the model. One of the most significant disadvantages of this approach is that when a voxel is invisible from even a single camera due to erroneous silhouette extraction, it is eliminated. On the other hand, the probability of a nonobject voxel to be visible to all the cameras is quite low because the voxel can be labeled as a nonobject by other cameras. Such loss of voxels degrades the visual quality of the model. An example is shown in Fig. 4. In this case, the left arm in camera #10 was missing because of erroneous silhouette extraction and the error significantly affected the generated 3D model. Note that the error in Fig. 4 was an actual result, not a simulation. The refinement algorithms

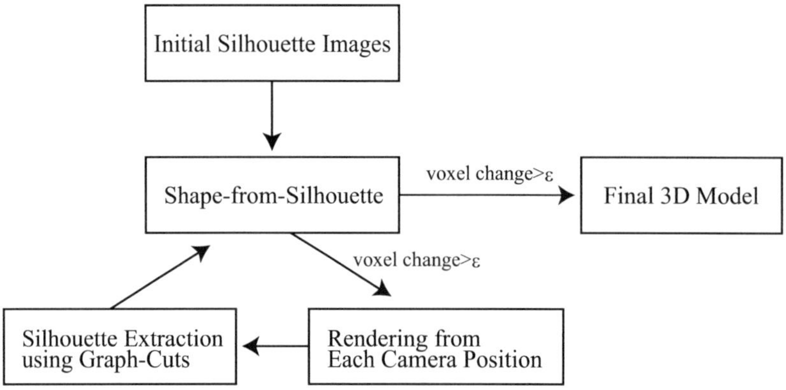

Fig. 2. Flowchart of the proposed algorithm.

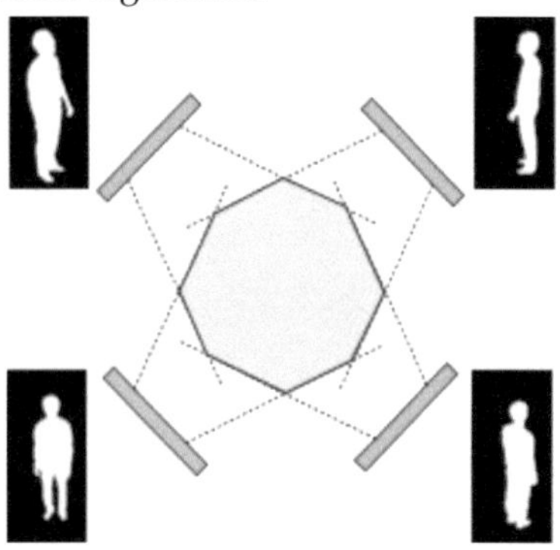

Fig. 3. The shape-from-silhouette algorithm.

(a) Error in silhouette extraction only in camera #10.

(b) Generated 3D model in which the left arm was not reconstructed properly.

Fig. 4. An example of voxel loss.

(Hisatomi et al., 2008; Matsuyama et al., 2004; Tomiyama et al., 2004; Tung et al., 2008) cannot recover such loss of voxels, because they are designed to eliminate unnecessary voxels, not to add necessary ones. Therefore, two kinds of error (loss) compensation algorithms were introduced in this chapter.

One such algorithm is the voting-based modeling method. Here, we assumed the number of cameras in the studio as n, and m was an integer ranging from 1 to $n-1$. If the voxel is visible from $n-m$ cameras, the voxel survives. Typically, m is set as $1-2$ because the probability of a voxel that belongs to an object to be invisible from two or more cameras in the view range is quite low. Therefore, voxels that were deleted due to the erroneous segmentation can be recovered. If we increase m, the generated 3D model would expand more than necessary; namely, the voxels that should be deleted remain in the visual hulls. If the error in silhouette extraction occurs in many camera views, we should reconsider the silhouette extraction algorithm itself. In this approach, one 3D model is generated for a single frame, independent of the value m.

The other approach is modeling with the other $(n-1)$ camera views. When generating the foreground/background seeds for the i-th camera view, the $(n-1)$ camera views, excluding the i-th camera view, are used for the modeling, and the generated 3D model is rendered from the i-th camera position only for improving the i-th silhouette. Therefore, we need to conduct the 3D modeling for all the n camera views. This approach implicitly assumes that the segmentation error does not occur in multiple views at the same time, which is reasonable in most cases. It is important to note here that such an error can occur in multiple parts as long as the condition mentioned above holds. The restriction here is that a voxel is misclassified as a nonobject region by not more than a single camera. Modeling with the other $(n-2)$ camera or fewer views is not reasonable because the number of models to generate becomes quite large: $n \times (n-1)$ for the case of $n-2$.

In the iteration process, 3D model reconstruction is conducted multiple times. In particular, the cost for modeling with the $(n-1)$ camera views approach becomes quite expensive as the number of cameras increases. To save computational cost, the 3D modeling in the iteration can be done with rough spatial resolution and only the final modeling should be carried out with finer spatial resolution. Another option is to iterate the refinement process only once because the modeling accuracy by a single iteration becomes sufficiently high, as demonstrated in Section 4.

3.4 Silhouette extraction and updating

In the initial silhouette extraction, conventional background subtraction with the graph cuts was used. The background and foreground regions with high confidence were generated as follows.

$$\begin{aligned}
\text{if } |Y(x,y) - Y_{BG}(x,y)| > Th1, &\text{ then } (x,y) \text{ is foreground} \\
\text{else if } |Y(x,y) - Y_{BG}(x,y)| < Th2, &\text{ then } (x,y) \text{ is background} \\
&\text{else unknown}
\end{aligned}$$

Here, $Y(x,y)$ is the chroma value of the pixel at (x,y) and $Y_{BG}(x,y)$ is that of the background model. $Th1$ and $Th2$ are predefined threshold values where $Th1 > Th2$ to extract background and foreground regions with high confidence. When $|Y(x,y) - Y_{BG}(x,y)|$ is between $Th1$ and $Th2$, the pixel is left as unknown. Then, the background/foreground maps are fed to the graph cuts algorithms as seeds. The silhouette extraction results are shown in Fig. 4(a).

In the iteration process, we assume that the erroneous loss of voxels is compensated by either of the ways described in 3.2. The silhouette refinement for each camera view was conducted using three images: the original captured image (Fig. 5(a)), the silhouette image in the previous step (Fig. 5(b)), and the rendered 3D image from the camera position (Fig. 5(c)). The background seed was generated by the logical AND operation between the background regions in the previous silhouette image (Fig. 5(b)) and the rendered image (Fig. 5(c)). A similar color region (Fig. 5(d)) between the original captured image (Fig. 5(a)) and the rendered image (Fig. 5(c)) and the eroded silhouette image in the previous step (Fig. 5(e)) were logically summed to form a foreground seed. As a result, the seeds for the background and the foreground for the graph cuts in the next step were generated, as demonstrated in Fig. 5(f). In the figure, the gray, black, and white regions represent the background, foreground, and unknown regions, respectively. The updated silhouette is shown in Fig. 5(g). This procedure was applied to each camera view independently. The updated silhouette images were again utilized for the 3D modeling. An example of the updated 3D model after a single feedback loop is shown in Fig. 5(h).

(a) Original captured image.

(b) Initial silhouette by background subtraction and graph cuts.

(c) The generated 3D model with the error compensation algorithm described in 3.2.

(d) Close-color map between (a) and (c).

(e) Eroded silhouette using (b).

(f) Updated seeds for graph cuts.

(g) Updated silhouette.

(h) Updated 3D model.

Fig. 5. Silhouette updating using the rendered 3D model.

4. Experiments

4.1 Experimental setup

The experiments were conducted using the 3D studio with 12 cameras, as described in Section 3.1. Consecutive $5-10$ frames of video (12 cameras $\times$ $5-10$ frames = $60-120$ images) were recorded for five people in different clothes and poses. The ground-truth data of the silhouettes were generated by hand. Then, ground-truth 3D model sequences were generated by the shape-from-silhouette algorithm. Our shape-from-silhouette program was based on (Tomiyama et al., 2004) (courtesy of Tomiyama and colleagues). The stereo matching in (Tomiyama et al., 2004) was disabled in the experiments to investigate the effect of the iterative silhouette updating only. The accuracy of the model was calculated by comparing the voxels. The voxels in the generated model that did not exist in the ground-truth model were regarded as surplus voxels. On the other hand, voxels in the ground truth that were not observed in the generated model were regarded as lost voxels.

4.2 Evaluation of the five different models

Fig. 6 shows 3D models using only the initial silhouettes, those using the voting-based modeling method, and ground-truth models. In model A in Fig. 6(a), for instance, it is observed that the lost voxels at the back of the head and the missing right hand were compensated correctly. On the other hand, there were still some lost voxels at the right leg in model E. In this case, the color of the trousers was very close to that of the carpet and the assumption that "the probability of the voxel that belongs to the object to be invisible from two or more cameras is quite low" made in Section 3.2 did not hold any more. If the cameras were looking down on the objects, the same region of the floor was observed by multiple cameras. Therefore, the color of the floor should be different from that of the trousers of the performer and vice versa. Otherwise a random pattern can be used only on the floor, as in (Toyoura et al., 2007).

The average errors over the frames for the best (model A) and the worst (model B) cases are summarized in Tables 1 and 2, except for model E that does not hold the assumption. The modeling performance by Toyoura et al. (Toyoura et al., 2007) is also shown in Table 3 for comparison. Note that the experimental setup and the target models were very different from (Toyoura et al., 2007). In Toyoura's approach, the loss of voxels is reduced but at the same time the surplus of voxels is increased and the generated models are "fat" compared with the ground-truth model. On the other hand, in our approach, both the loss and surplus of voxels were suppressed effectively.

	Loss	Surplus	Total Error
Modeling using the initial silhouettes	2.1%	9.4%	11%
Modeling with the other $(n-1)$ camera views	0.90%	0.99%	1.9%
Voting-based with iteration $(n-1$ cameras)	0.73%	1.2%	1.9%

Table 1. Averaged modeling accuracy over the 10 frames of A (the best case among A–D).

	Loss	Surplus	Total Error
Modeling using the initial silhouettes	4.1%	24%	28%
Modeling with the other $(n-1)$ camera views	0.68%	14 %	15%
Voting-based with iteration $(n-1$ cameras)	1.4 %	12 %	14 %

Table 2. Averaged modeling accuracy over the 5 frames of B (the worst case among A–D).

	Loss	Surplus	Total Error
Modeling using the initial silhouettes	58%	3.1 %	60 %
(Toyoura et al., 2007)	2.7%	11%	14%

Table 3. Results in (Toyoura et al., 2007).

(a) Model A.

(b) Model B.

(c) Model C.

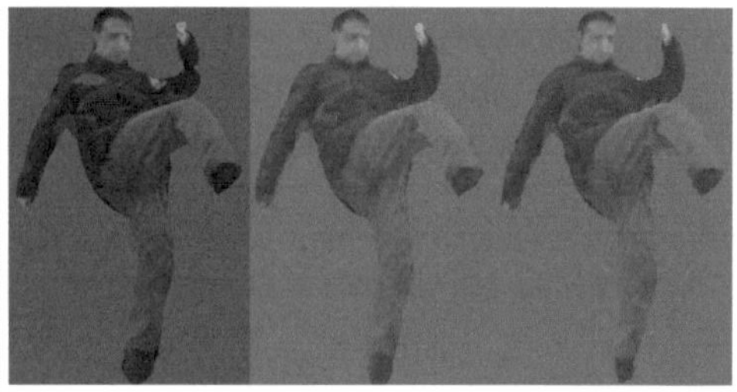

(d) Model D.

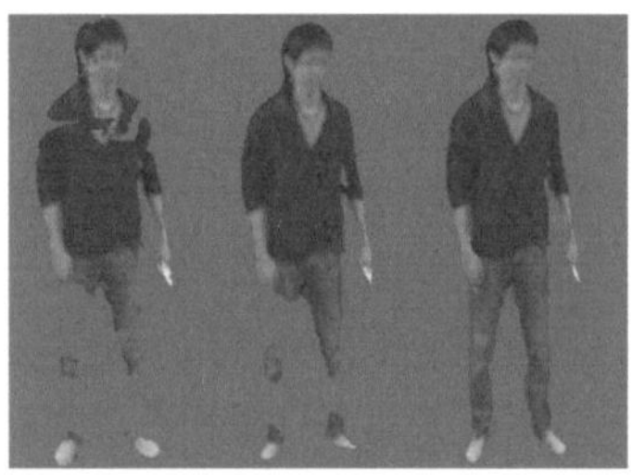

(e) Model E.

Fig. 6. Example of the generated models: (left) models using only initial silhouettes, (middle) refined models using the voting-based method, (right) ground-truth models

4.3 Detailed evaluation over the frames

In this section, we further investigate the performance of the proposed algorithm using model A.

The mean errors over the frames are summarized in Table 4. The modeling errors using six different approaches are compared: modeling using the initial silhouettes, modeling with the other $(n-1)$ camera views, voting-based modeling without iteration (using $n-1$ cameras), voting-based modeling without iteration (using $n-2$ cameras), voting-based modeling with iteration (using $n-1$ cameras), and voting-based modeling with iteration (using $n-2$ cameras). The models without iteration were intermediate models used for silhouette refinement and although they were not the final results, they are listed here for comparison. In modeling using the other camera views, n models were generated. Therefore, the modeling errors of the intermediate models (i.e., modeling without iteration) were difficult to analyze and are not shown in the table. The proposed algorithms yielded a good performance, both in terms of loss and surplus of voxels. The total error was less than 2% for both voting-based modeling by $(n-1)$ cameras and for other $(n-1)$ camera views. When the voting-based modeling method without iteration using $n-1$ camera views was employed, the loss of voxels was quite small. However, generated models contained many surplus voxels, resulting in a larger total error than in the modeling using the initial silhouettes. The region where a major loss of voxels occurred (0.18%) was the region that did not hold the assumption that the probability of a voxel that belongs to the object to be invisible from two or more cameras was quite low. In other words, our assumption was valid for 99.8% of the region.

	Loss	Surplus	Total Error
Modeling using the initial silhouettes	2.1%	9.4%	11%
Modeling with the other $(n-1)$ camera views	0.90%	0.99%	1.9%
Voting-based w/o iteration $(n-1$ cameras)	0.18%	26%	26%
Voting-based w/o iteration $(n-2$ cameras)	0.007%	47%	47%
Voting-based with iteration $(n-1$ cameras)	0.73%	1.2%	1.9%
Voting-based with iteration $(n-2$ cameras)	0.64%	2.0%	2.7%

Table 4. Averaged modeling accuracy for model A over the 10 frames.

It can be observed that the proposed approaches can generate better 3D models than a simple volume intersection method in terms of both loss and surplus of voxels. Namely, the iterative processing between silhouette extraction and 3D modeling can reduce voxel loss while suppressing voxel surplus. Among the lost voxels in the initial model (2.1%), 90% of them (1.9% of the whole model) were invisible only from a single camera and the loss was reduced to 0.73% in the voting-based method using $n-1$ cameras and to 0.90% with the other camera views method. In addition, we can see that modeling with the voting-based method was good at reducing voxel loss and modeling with the other camera views method performed well in reducing voxel surplus.

The modeling errors with the looser assumption that the probability of the voxel belonging to the object to be invisible from three (not two) or more cameras is low is also shown in Table 4 (see voting-based methods using $n-2$ cameras with/without iteration). In the voting-based method without iteration, the loss of voxels was as few as 0.007%, almost negligible. On the other hand, the surplus of voxels increased up to 47%. When the voting-based method with iteration using $n-2$ cameras was employed, voxel loss was at the minimum among the proposed methods. However, the surplus of voxels tended to be somewhat more than in the other approaches and was almost the same as the initial model in some frames (not shown). The optimal number of cameras to use in the iteration should be decided considering the number of cameras, the shape refinement process in the following stage, the required error rate, etc.

Fig. 7 shows the modeling accuracy for model A. It is demonstrated that the error was almost constant throughout the frames independent of the poses of the performer.

In all the frames, the shape of the model converged at the second iteration (the difference between the models in the first and second iterations was smaller than ϵ). To investigate how the errors change in the iteration process, the errors for model A averaged over the 10 frames as a function of the number of the iteration is shown in Fig. 8. In this experiment, the termination decision was disabled. Iteration zero stands for the initial model. Regardless of whether the algorithm was the voting-based method or modeling with the other cameras, the generated 3D model converged quickly and the errors did not improve very much after the first iteration. Therefore, modeling with only a single feedback is enough in most cases. The mean processing time for the voting-based method using $n-1$ cameras was 35 s and that

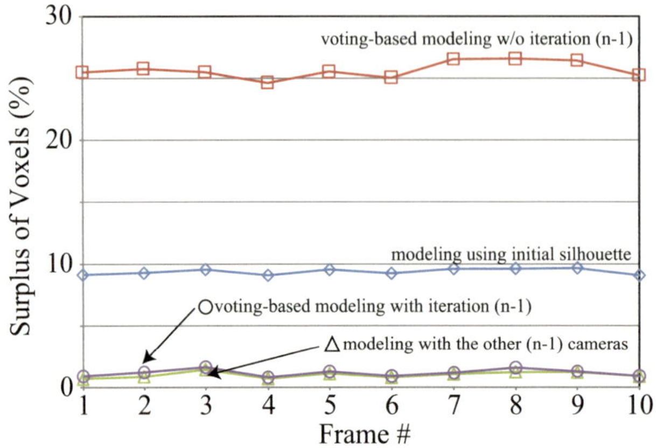

(a) Surplus of voxels.

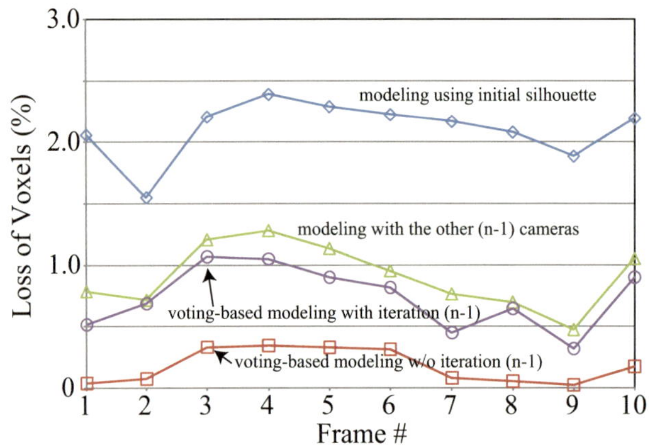

(b) Loss of voxels.

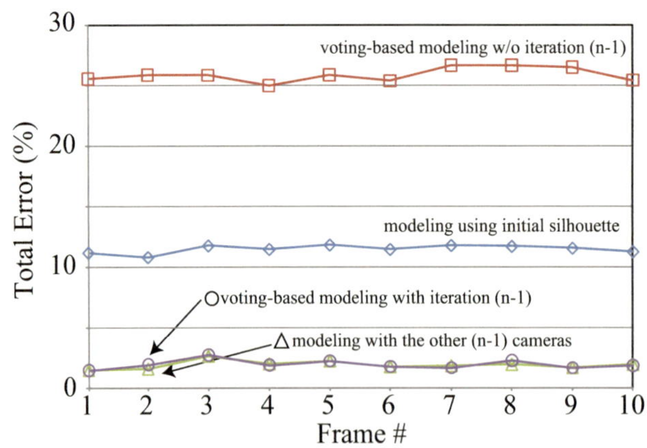

(c) Total error.

Fig. 7. Modeling accuracy for model A.

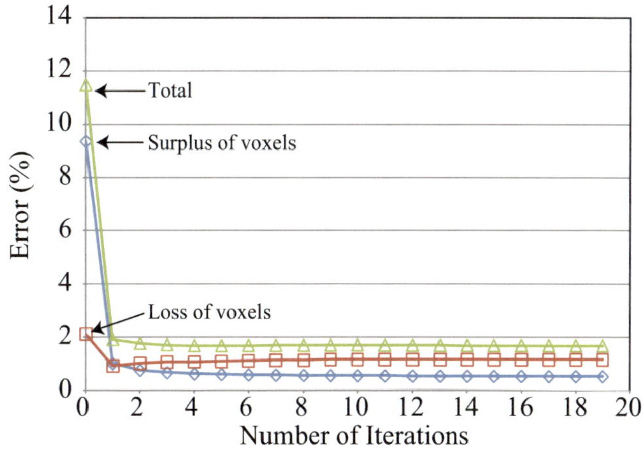

(a) Modeling with the other $(n-1)$ cameras.

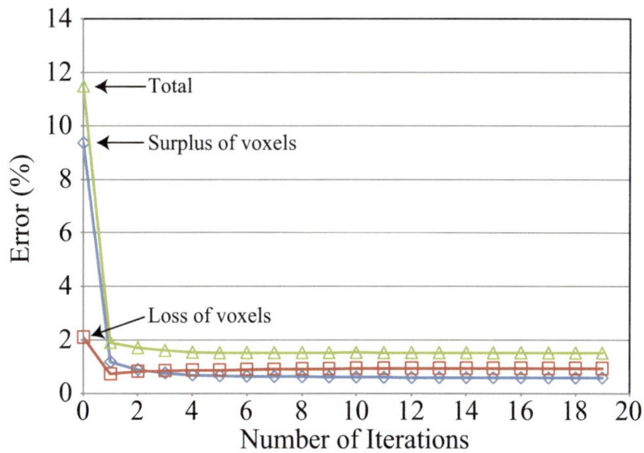

(b) Voting-based modeling by $(n-1)$ cameras.

Fig. 8. Model refinement effects as a function of the number of iterations.

for modeling with the other cameras was 45 s using the Intel Core2 Duo 2.4 GHz and 2.5 GB memory. On the other hand, the simple volume intersection took 2.5 s.

5. Conclusions

In this chapter, we have reviewed visual hull refinement algorithms and presented an iterative refinement algorithm. By the cross-feedback between the 3D model reconstruction with the updated silhouette and the silhouette extraction using the rendered image, the loss and surplus of voxels can be kept very small. We have also proposed two shape-from-silhouette algorithms with error compensation to recover missed segmentation of the background/foreground. Experimental results demonstrated that the loss of voxels was reduced from 2.1% to 0.73–0.90% and the surplus of voxels was reduced from 9.4% to 0.99–1.2%, respectively. Achieving as few a loss of voxels as possible is important because the surplus of voxels can be eliminated by further postprocessing, whereas it is very difficult to recover the erroneously eliminated voxels.

6. Acknowledgments

We would like to thank Mr. Yamada for his contribution and nac Image Technology, Inc. for the studio design. This work is supported by the Microsoft Institute for Japanese Academic Research Collaboration (IJARC). We would like to thank Dr. Tomiyama and colleagues for providing us with their 3D modeling source code.

7. References

Benezeth, Y., Jodoin, P., Emile, B., Laurent, H. & Rosen-berger, C. (2008). Review and evaluation of commonly-implemented background subtraction algorithms, *Proceedings of IEEE 19th International Conference on Pattern Recognition (ICPR 2008)*, pp. 1–4.

Bonet, J. D. & Viola, P. (1999). Roxels: responsibility weighted 3d volume reconstruction, *Proceedings of Eighth IEEE International Conference on Computer Vision (ICCV 2001)*, Vol. Vol. 1, pp. 418–425.

Boykov, Y. & Jolly, M.-P. (2001). Interactive graph cuts for optimal boundary & region segmentation of objects in n-d images, *Proceedings of IEEE International Conference on Conputer Vision (ICCV 2001)*, Vol. Vol. I, pp. 105–112.

Broadhurst, A., Drummond, T. & Cipolla, R. (2001). A probabilistic framework for space carving, *Proceedings of Eighth IEEE International Conference on Computer Vision (ICCV 2001)*, Vol. Vol. 1, pp. 388–393.

de Aguiar, E., Stoll, C., Theobalt, C., Ahmed, N., Seidel, H. & Thrum, S. (2008). Performance capture from sparse multi-view stereo, *ACM Transactions on Graphics (ACM SIGGRAPH2008)*.

Fofi, D., Sliwa, T. & Voisin, Y. (2004). A comparative survey on invisible structured light, *Proceedings of SPIE 5303*, pp. 90–98.

Foix, S., Alenya, G. & Torras, C. (2011). Lock-in time-of-flight (tof) cameras: A survey, *IEEE Sensors Journal* Vol. 11(No. x): xxx–xxx.

Fua, P. & Leclerc, Y. G. (1995). Object-centered surface reconstruction: Combining multi-image stereo and shading, *International Journal of Computer Vision* Vol. 16(No. 1): 35–56.

Hisatomi, K., Tomiyama, K., Katayama, M. & Iwadate, Y. (2008). 3d reconstruction using graph cut with view-dependent polygon texture blending, *5th European Conference on Visual Media Production (CVMP 2008)*, p. 18.

Huang, T. & Netravali, A. (1994). Motion and structure from feature correspondences: a review, *Proceedings of the IEEE* Vol. 82(No. 2): 252–268.

Isidoro, J. & Sclaroff, S. (2002). Stochastic mesh-based multiview reconstruction, *Proceedings of First International Symposium on 3D Data Processing Visualization and Transmission (3DPVT 2002)*, pp. 568–577.

Kanade, T., Rander, P. & Narayanan, P. (1997). Virtualized reality: constructing virtual worlds from real scenes, *IEEE Multimedia* Vol. 4(No. 1): 34–47.

Kim, H., Sakamoto, R., Kitahara, I., Orman, N., Toriyama, T. & Kogure, K. (2007). Compensated visual hull for defective segmentation and occlusion, *Proceedings of the 17th International Conference on Artificial Reality and Telexistence (ICAT 2007)*, pp. 210–217.

Kutulakos, K. N. & Seitz, S. M. (2000). A theory of shape by space carving, *International Journal of Computer Vision (IJCV)* Vol. 38(No. 3): 199–218.

Laurentini, A. (1994). The visual hull concept for silhouette-based image understanding, *IEEE Transactions on Pattern Analysis and Machine Intelligence* Vol. 16(No. 2): 150–162.

Liu, X., Yao, H., Chen, X. & Gao, W. (2006). Visual hull embossment by graph cuts, *Proceedings of 2006 IEEE International Conference on Image Processing (ICIP 2006)*, pp. 2205–2208.

Lowe, D. (2004). Distinctive image features from scale-invariant keypoints, *International Journal of Computer Vision (IJCV)* 60(2).

Luo, W., Yamasaki, T. & Aizawa, K. (2010). Articulated human motion capture from segmented visual hulls and surface re-construction, *Proceedings of 2010 APSIPA Annual Summit and Conference (APSIPA ASC 2010)*, pp. 109–116.

Matsuyama, T., Wu, X., Takai, T. & Wada, T. (2004). Real-time dynamic 3-d object shape reconstruction and high-fidelity texture mapping for 3-d video, *IEEE Transactions on Circuit And System For Video Technology* Vol. 14(No. 3): 357–369.

McIvor, A. (2000). Background subtraction techniques, *Proc. Image Video Comput.*, pp. 147–153.

Nobuhara, S. & Matsuyama, T. (2003). Dynamic 3d shape from multi-viewpoint images using deformable mesh model, *Proceedings of the 3rd International Symposium on Image and Signal Processing and Analysis (ISPA 2003)*, Vol. Vol. 1, pp. 192–197.

Nobuhara, S., Tsuda, Y., Matsuyama, T. & Ohama, I. (2007). Multi-viewpoint silhouette extraction with 3d context-aware error detection, correction, and shadow suppression, *Proceedings of 4th European Conference on Visual Media Production (CVMP2007)*, pp. 1–9.

Piccardi, M. (2004). Background subtraction techniques: a review, *Proceedings of 2004 IEEE International Conference on Systems, Man and Cybernetics*, Vol. Vol. 4, pp. 3099–3104.

Poelman, C. & Kanade, T. (1997). A paraperspective factorization method for shape and motion recovery, *IEEE Transactions on Pattern Analysis and Machine Intelligence* Vol. 19(No. 3): 206–218.

Rother, C., Kolmogorv, V. & Blake, A. (2008). "grabcut":interactive foreground extraction using iterated graph cuts, *ACM Trans. Graphics (SIGGRAPH 2004)* Vol. 23(No. 3): 309–314.

Seitz, S. & Dyer, C. (1999). Photorealistic scene reconstruction by voxel coloring, *International Journal of Computer Vision (IJCV)* 25(1).

Slabaugh, G. G., Culbertson, W. B., Malzbender, T. & Schafer, R. W. (2001). A survey of methods for volumetric scene reconstruction from photographs, *Proceedings of International Workshop on Volume Graphics 2001*.

Snow, D., Viola, P. & Zabih, R. (2000). Exact voxel occupancy with graph cuts, *Proceedings of IEEE Conference on Computer Vision and Pattern Recognition (CVPR 2000)*, Vol. 1, pp. 345–352.

Starck, J. & Hilton, A. (2007). Surface capture for performance-based animation, *IEEE Computer Graphics and Applications* Vol. 27(No. 3): 21–31.

Tomiyama, K., Orihara, Y., Katayama, M. & Iwadate, Y. (2004). Algorithm for dynamic 3d object generation from multiviewpoint images, *Proceedings of SPIE*, pp. 153–161.

Toyoura, M., Iiyama, M., Kakusho, K. & Minoh, M. (2007). Silhouette extraction with random pattern backgrounds for the volume intersection method, *Proceedings of the 6th International Conference on 3-D Digital Imaging and Modeling (3DIM 2007)*, pp. 225–232.

Tsai, R. Y. (1987). A versatile camera calibration technique for high-accuracy 3d machine vision metrology using off-the-shelf tv cameras and lenses, *IEEE Journal of Robotics and Automation* Vol. 3(No. 4): 323–344.

Tung, T., Nobuhara, S. & Matsuyama, T. (2008). Simultaneous super-resolution and 3d video using graph-cuts, *IEEE Computer Society Conference on Computer Vision and Pattern Recognition (CVPR 2008)*, pp. 1–8.

Vlasic, D., Baran, I. & Matusik, W. (2008). Articulated mesh animation from multi-view silhouettes, *ACM Transactions on Graphics (ACM SIGGRAPH2008)*.

Yamasaki, T., Yamada, K. & Aizawa, K. (2009). Time-varying mesh generation based on iterative feedback between silhouette extraction and geometry modeling, *Proceedings of 2009 APSIPA Annual Summit and Conference (APSIPA ASC 2009)*, pp. 502–508.

Zhang, R., Tsai, P.-S., Cryer, J. & Shah, M. (1999). Shape-from-shading: a survey, *IEEE Transactions on Pattern Analysis and Machine Intelligence* Vol. 21(No. 8): 690–706.

Part 2

Virtual Prototyping

8

Analytical Compact Models

Bruno Allard and Hervé Morel
Université de Lyon, INSA Lyon, AMPERE-Lab, Villeurbanne, France

1. Introduction

The virtual prototyping of power electronic converters is considered here. Virtual prototyping is now an important challenge in the context of integration of power systems. If semiconductor devices are considered as the levellers of significant advances in power converters, it is commonly admitted that the next leveller of advances is related to the design methods. The design methods ambition to deliver a satisfying product with the first prototype as a prototype of a power converter is expensive.
Differences in virtual prototyping acceptance may be foreseen depending on the level of integration. On the one hand VLSI power management requires methodologies and models in the framework of integrated circuit tools. The dedicated tools seem to dictate the nature of the models and of the design flow. On the other hand the design of a mechatronic system could rely on a wider range of models and methodologies depending on the background of the involved engineer. In fact the development of virtual prototyping methodologies try to provide a systematic approach to the different steps involved in the emergence of a product. Depending on the complexity of a given system, all or parts of the models and analyses will be solicited.
The idea is that a simple step-down DC/DC converter represents a similar design problem whether a 1 W monolithic IC is required or a 100 W discrete-board converter inside a car mechatronic-item is specified. The common part in the design process of these two seemingly different converters concerns the early stage of virtual prototyping, namely the pre-design. Fig. 1 details the macro-steps in the design flow of a power converter, but the idea is applicable to a mechatronic device. Pre-design covers the early steps in the design flow.
Other steps in the design process will involve hard technology constraints, what will affect the complexity level of some models but design analyses remain essentially the same whatever the level of integration. These intermediate steps in the design process refer to what is practically known as design, what is in essence to choose devices and to optimize circuits. When device and circuits have been globally optimized, next steps concern the geometrical and physical assembly of these devices into a converter. Additional physical phenomena appear that require dedicated tools and models to complete the optimization of the power converter. The final steps in the design process concern the virtual physical verification of the system. The technology constraints and the geometrical size of the system, adding the power level, dictate different approaches for the analyses to be carried out. The latter verification efforts are in relation to the system specifications and receipt.

The early stages of virtual prototyping are the most risky as the possible cost of an error in any choice will continually rise with subsequent design steps. The chapter details several necessary models for the early stages in virtual prototyping, namely the system-level analyses in Fig. 1.

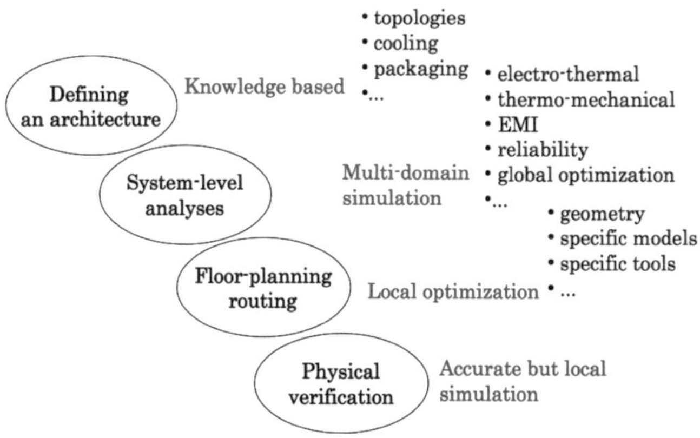

Fig. 1. Schematic of a classical design flow for a power converter with related macro-steps

2. Analytical compact models

Facing the specifications of a power converter, either highly integrated or in relation with a hybrid technology, the electronic engineer has to make a choice of architecture (see Fig. 1). The architecture is a response to the main functionality, i.e. the kind of energy process operated by the required converter. The architecture involves components and operation principles. Unfortunately the specified converter must offer performances in a wide range of operating conditions. Cost, power density, efficiency and reliability are generally the hard performances to address. A satisfying level of trade-off cannot be settled without a proper methodology. The methodology is based on databases, models of components and optimization routines.

When best candidate architectures have been identified, the design goes a step further to confirm various quantities as current, voltage and temperature ratings. Evaluation regarding Electromagnetic compatibility (EMC) is generally a troublemaker. EMC is correlated to some point with efficiency and a second set of optimization against power density and cost will confirm or infirm the possibility of architectures. When one architecture is validated at this step, a practical design-process begins, as it is known for decades. This practical design step depends on the technology and field-related tools are considered. If EMC, efficiency and other considerations do not permit to validate the foreseen architecture from the system elaborated by the pre-design, it is necessary to relax the specifications in any way. It is then mandatory to run the pre-design and the confirmation design step as fast as possible to limit the risk in the subsequent design steps. As a tremendous number of architectures may be considered, it is necessary to provide models dedicated to pre-design and the confirmation design step.

A power converter circuit is made of many devices. Many abstraction models have been developed and detailed in literature (Middlebrook, 1976), (Cùk, 1977), (Krein, 1990), (Lee, 1985), (Sanders, 1991), (Smedley, 1994), (Ben-Yaakov, 1995), (Lai, 1995), (Maksimovic, 1998),

(Xu, 1994), (Olivier, 2000). A functional view of a power converter has been proposed as the so-called average model. The abstraction is to get rid of the switching process. In another way, the goal is to keep only the most significant time-constants in the power converter from control point of view. Fig. 2 gives an idea of the spread of time-constants of physical phenomena in a power converter.

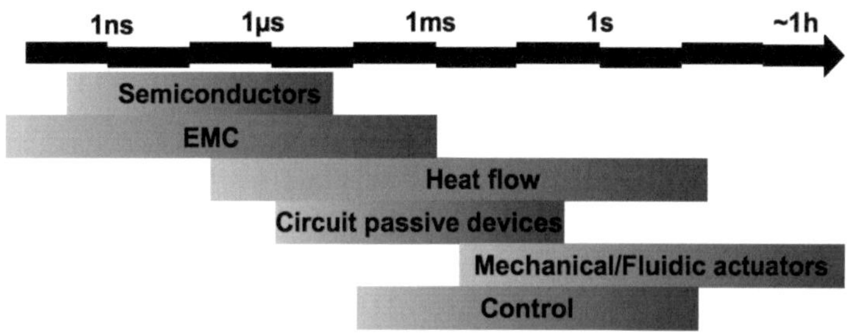

Fig. 2. Repartition of time-constants of physical phenomenon in a power converter

In early 70's appeared most of the power converter architectures as known today. The circuit simulators at the time were sufficiently developed for the field-engineer to detect that basic discrete devices would not be sufficient. The integration time-step in a circuit simulator is dictated by the smallest time-constant. Unfortunately the field-engineer is firstly interested by long-term simulation. The simulation cost is then unaffordable and the necessity for more efficient models of converters emerged. The development of such models has required a tremendous effort and more than hundred thousands of papers have been published on the topic. The name of averaged models comes from the idea to look at the power converter on the basis of the switching period and to eliminate whatever phenomenon exhibiting a time-constant lower than this switching period. Nowadays such models are qualified of "compact models". They are dedicated to system-level analyses.
Fig. 3 lists some of the system-level analyses mentioned in Fig. 1. The figure shows that the compact models useful for a given analysis will cover more than one physical domain and a large spectrum of time-constants.

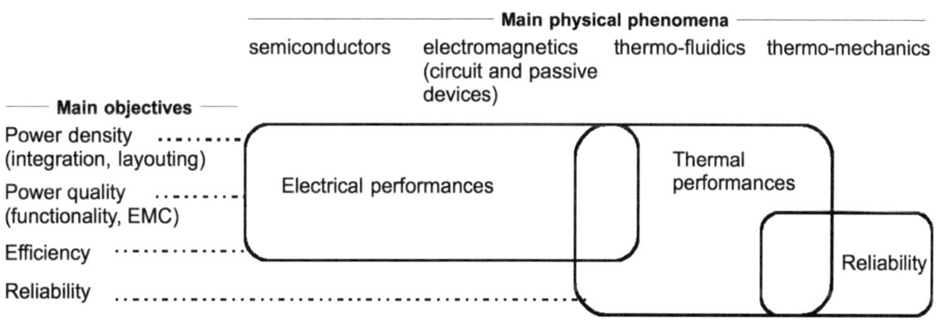

Fig. 3. Relation between system-level analyses and physical phenomena

The average model is mainly used to build feedback loops. One method called the state-space averaging method has been used for decades. Unfortunately the latter method does not apply easily to resonant converters and does not accept non-linear terms as power losses or delays between control signal and power flow. Contribution to EMC is not possible.

Probably this explains that EMC issues are generally considered at the end of the design process and the cost may be significant in additional filters or reduced performances. The power electronic engineer has been dealing with the average model of the converter at hand but he needed to add some view about power losses and temperature. Equivalent electrical models of thermal networks are popular and considered in most approaches. The manufacturer of a thermal system generally gives a practical thermal model of its product or at least an abacus of the so-called thermal impedance of the thermal path. Unfortunately a thermal network is based on the association of thermal effects and/or products and the addition of the practical models - thermal impedances- is not accurate enough. Restricting the analysis to steady-state operation is not sufficient to obtain pertinent evaluations with these practical models. The need for light but accurate models of a thermal network has given rise to methodologies to build so-called compact thermal models. A compact thermal model is a global behavioural model taking power losses in the system as inputs and evaluating specific temperatures inside the systems. These specific temperatures are mostly averaged operating temperatures of the power semiconductor devices and power passive devices. The term of junction temperature is improperly used here.

The chapter wishes to detail methods to build efficiently compact models for the average representation of converters but including power losses. EMC contributions can also be added and compact models of thermal network must be considered to attain electro-thermal simulation.

The proposed compact models come as state-space models and may be used in any simulator providing an entry language. Standard languages are available to distribute such models like VHDL-AMS, IEEE 1076.1.

A hardware description language is unfortunately not a guide for efficient modelling. Alternatively bond graphs are known for decades and have been provided for modelling the dynamics of multi-domain systems. Bond graphs are a framework for graphical representation but implement many methods like the causality analysis. An original extension of the causality analysis was provided to build compact average models. An extension to include power losses is presented here. Contribution to EMC was a recent add-on to the method. Examples will be presented to illustrate the detail of the methods.

Bond Graphs are covered in many books and papers. A short description is provided at the end of the chapter to enable the reader to follow the presentation without pre-requisites.

3. The algebraic causality analysis

This introductory section requires the prior reading of appendices. ACA is a systematic procedure that enhances the causality analysis of a bond graph. It supports then the systematic compact model calculation.

Karnopp and Rosenberg in (Karnopp, 1975, 1990) describe a graphical causality analysis that applies only to bond graphs made of linear elementary components (see section 13). This graphical method is limited in the case of bond graphs that incorporate more complex components. Many electronic devices constitute complex components described with large state-space models including non-linear functions. It must be recalled here that Bond Graphs must be considered as a building framework to derive the constitutive equations of the model of a system. These equations are to be handle by a simulator and nowadays VHDL-AMS is an example of language suitable to perform this task of model handling (Pecheux, 2005). It is presented here an extension of the original causality analysis, called

initially Algebraic Causality Analysis (Allard, 1997a). The purpose is to provide a software-compatible algorithm. ACA considers that state-space models of variable causality represent the components of a bond graph. ACA uses a graphical representation that separates the knowledge of the causality for flow variables and the effort variables.
The graphical representation is listed in Table 6 for non-varying causality components. A power switch with a gate control gives an example of varying causality. When the gate control is not activated (like in a power MOSFET or IGBT), the power switch is in off state and the causality of its power bond is to enforce the flow variable: the switch is a source of null-current. When the gate control is activated, the power switch is equivalent to a source of null-voltage in the ideal case, and the causality is related to the effort variable. This particularity is illustrated in next section.

3.1 Systematic algorithm

The algorithm is applied through the following steps:

1. Apply the causality of sources (Se, Sf) including varying-causality elements
2. Apply the causality of storage elements assuming the integral causality. This also applies to any state-space element.
3. Propagate the causality knowledge through junctions, transformers, gyrators and resistors.
4. Iterate step 3 until the following situation:
   - All causal strokes are drawn without conflict: the bond graph is causal (best case)
   - A conflict of causality appears during the iteration: causality knowledge concerns a variable already known (causal stroke already drawn). It is the case of a redundant equation.
   - It remains a bond without a causal stroke. There is a non-determination of one variable.
   - An example of case (i) above is given by the series RLC circuit in Fig. 28(c). The algorithm application is detailed in Table 4.

3.2 Application to a faulty bond graph

In the example of Fig. 4, the two capacitors connected in parallel lead to a causality fault at the 0-junction. Choosing one of the capacitor in derivative causality solves the causality (see Table 6). The circuit model is then a DAE of index 1.

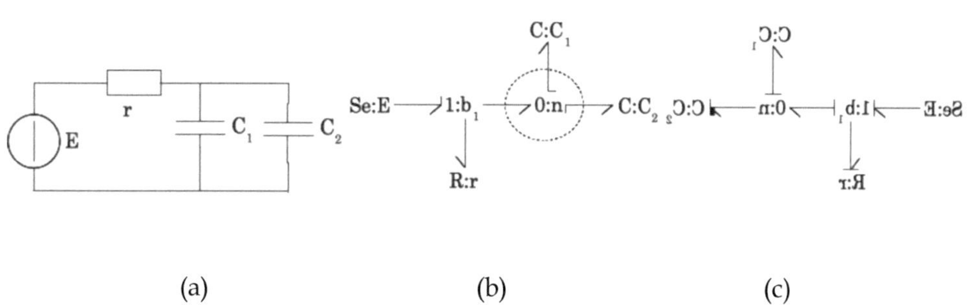

Fig. 4. Simple electrical circuit (a) leading to a causality fault (b), solved by a derivative causality (c).

<table>
<tr><td>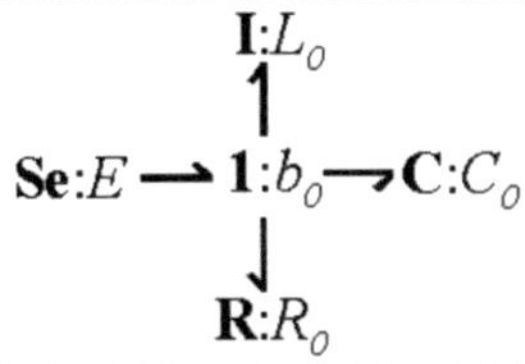
</td><td>Initial bond graph</td></tr>
<tr><td>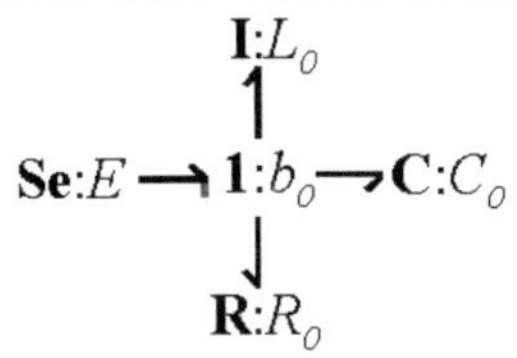
</td><td>1 – Causality of sources
Se: the effort variable is known and the half-stroke for effort variable is added. The half stroke is placed below the half-arrow by convention (see Table 6).</td></tr>
<tr><td>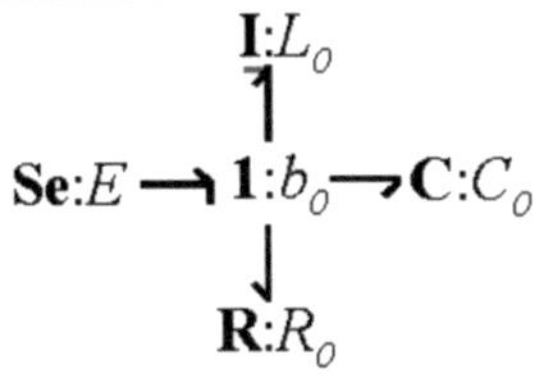
</td><td>2 - Causality of state-space components (C, I ...) in integral causality.
The inductance model yields the value of the current, i.e. the flow variable. A half-stroke is placed on the side of the half-arrow.</td></tr>
<tr><td>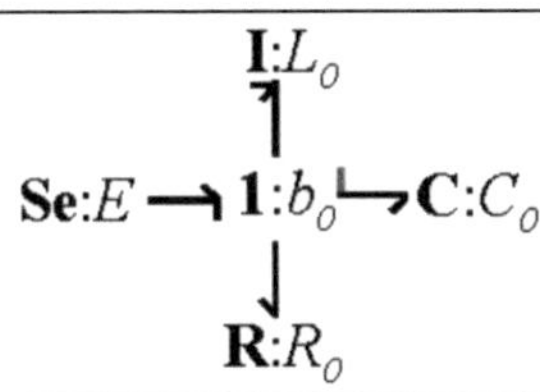
</td><td>2 - Causality of state-space components (C, I ...) in integral causality.
The capacitor model yields the voltage and an half-stroke indicates the effort variable causality.</td></tr>
<tr><td>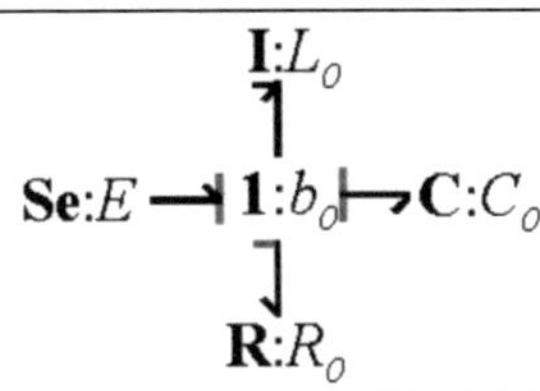
</td><td>3 - Propagate the causality through junctions, transformers and resistors.
The flow variable common to all bonds of the 1-junction is dictated by the inductance. This knowledge is propagated with 3 half-strokes.</td></tr>
<tr><td>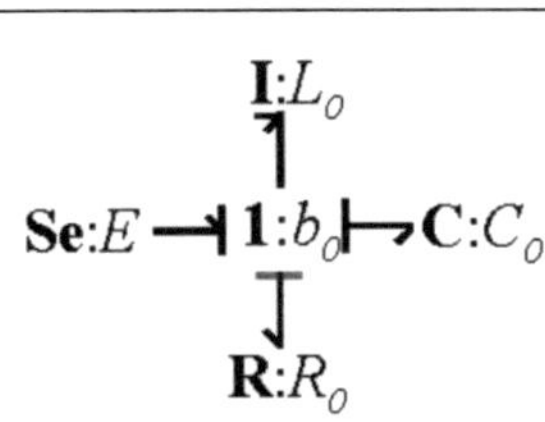
</td><td>3 - Propagate the causality through junctions, transformers and resistors.
The resistor model has two forms. As the flow variable is known, one form dictates the voltage, i.e. the effort variable and a hlf-stroke is added accordingly.</td></tr>
<tr><td>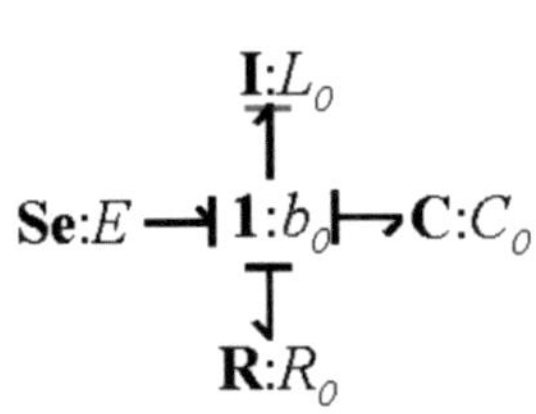
</td><td>4 – iterate step 3
3 - Propagate the causality through junctions, transformers and resistors.
The 1-junction model enables to compute the voltage across the inductance as the other voltage drops are known from the other bonds.</td></tr>
</table>

Table 1. Application of ACA algorithm on a causal bond graph

A second example is a simple chopper circuit as in Fig. 5. The model in Equation 1 represents a power MOSFET and the model in Equation 2 represents a power diode (Morel, 2001).

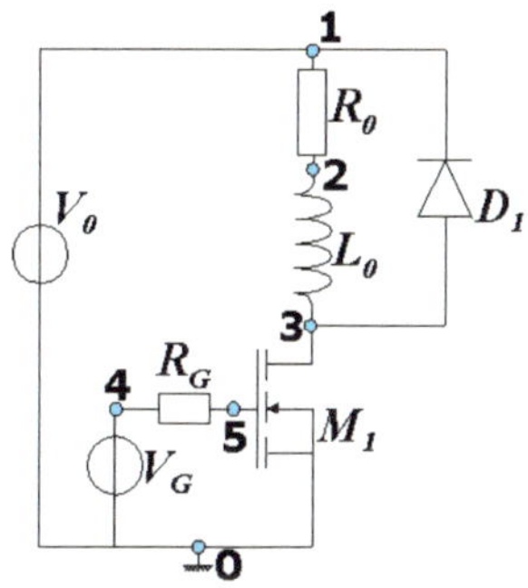

Fig. 5. Simple chopper circuit

ACA is applied step by step (Table 2). ACA terminates with clause (iii) and the current i_A and i_E are not determinate. A circuit simulator gives a result of such a model but experiment does not confirm the result. It is a well-known problem: the model lacks a parasitic inductance at node 1 in Fig. 5 that splits the power supply current between the inductance and the power diode. ACA helps here to exhibit lack in the model that the Nodal Analysis doest not detect.

Bond graph	Comments	Equation
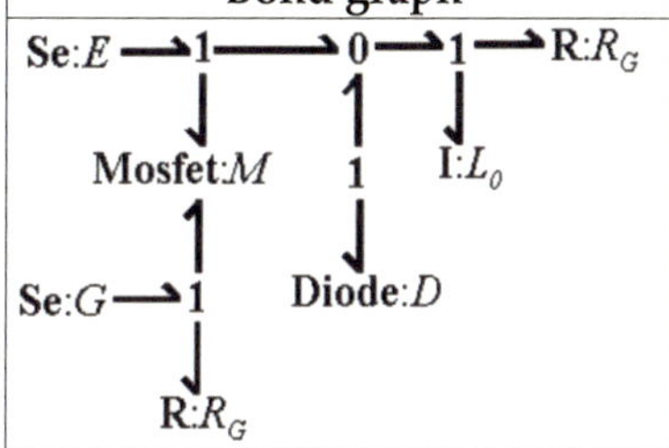	Initial Bond graph	State-variables are Qg, Qj charges in MOSFET. Qd charge in diode junction Φ flux in inductance
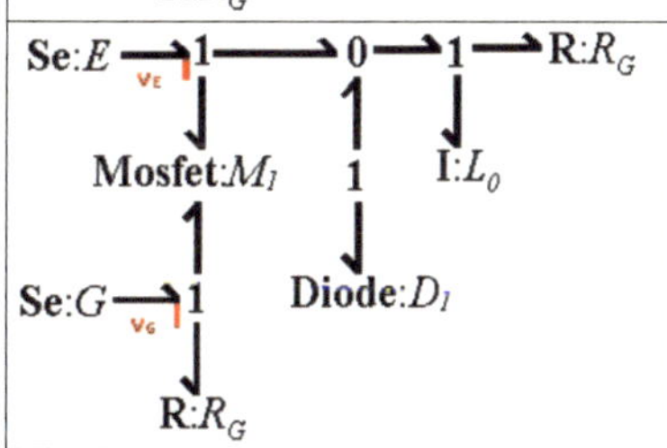	1- causality of sources Se :E and Se :G	$v_E = E, v_G = G(t)$
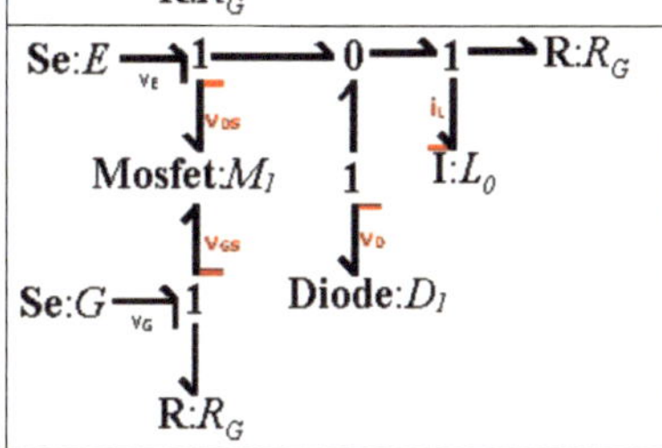	2 – causality of state-space elements I :L₀, MOSFET M and diode D	$i_L = \frac{\phi}{L}$ $v_{DS} = g_4(Q_j, Q_G)$ $v_{GS} = g_3(Q_j, Q_G)$ $v_D = g_1(Q_D)$

Bond graph	Comments	Equation
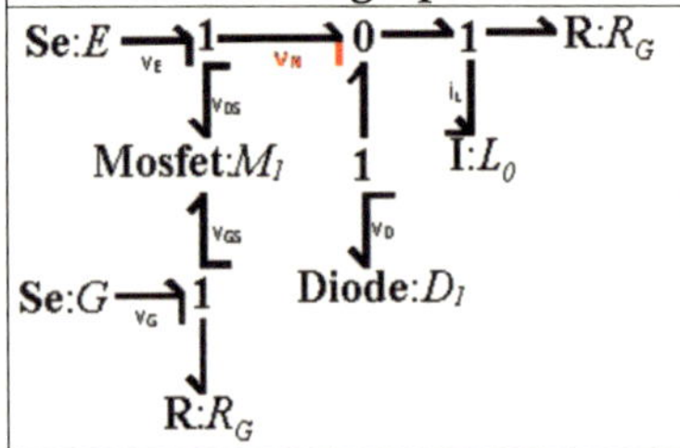	3-Propagation of causality 1-junction linked to MOSFET	$v_N = v_E - v_{DS}$
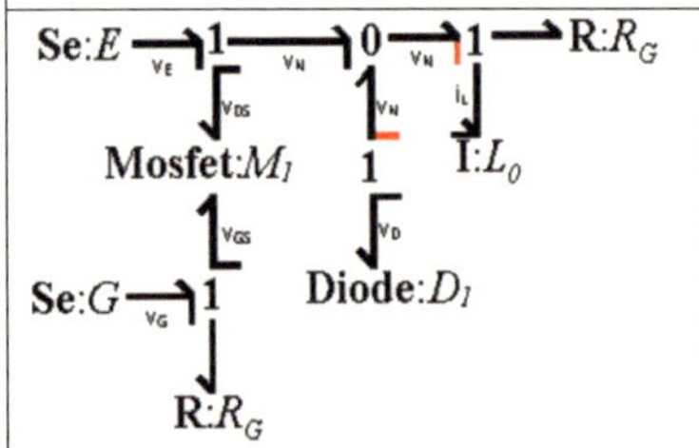	3-Propagation of causality internal 0-junction	Similar voltage drop across all 0-junction bonds
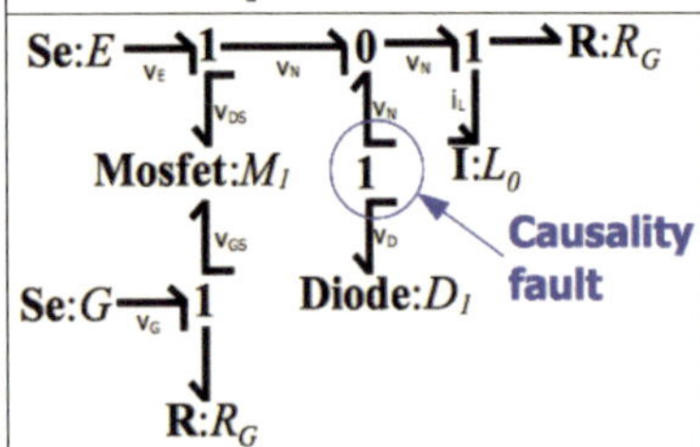	Causality fault at 1-junction linked to diode D clause (ii): variable already known	The causality fault corresponds to the constraint: $v_N + v_D = 0$
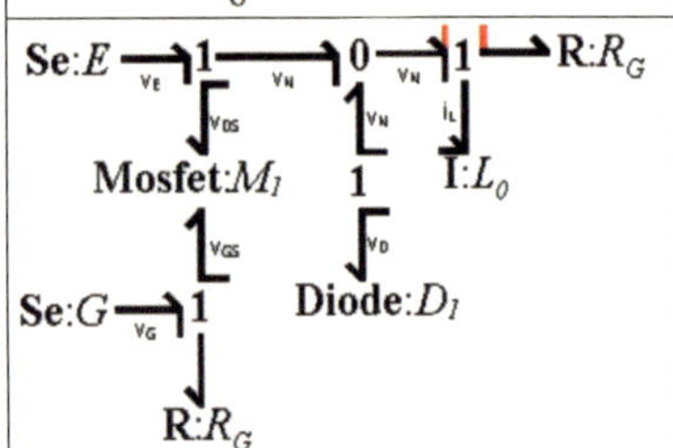	3-Propagation of causality 1-junction linked to L_0 and R	i_L is the current in each bond of the 0-junction
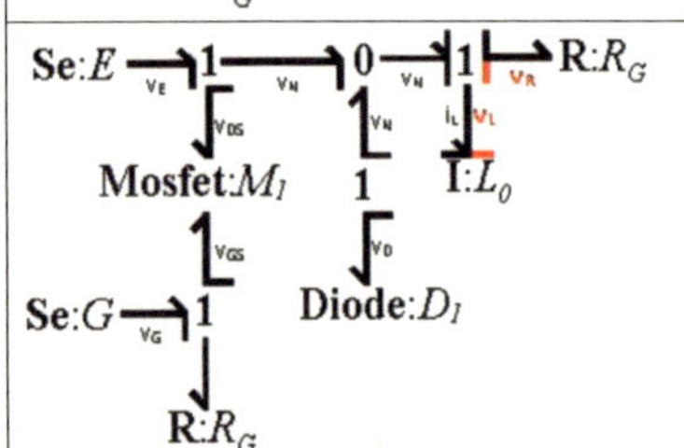	3-Propagation of causality element R	$v_R = R \cdot i_L$ $v_L = v_N - v_R$
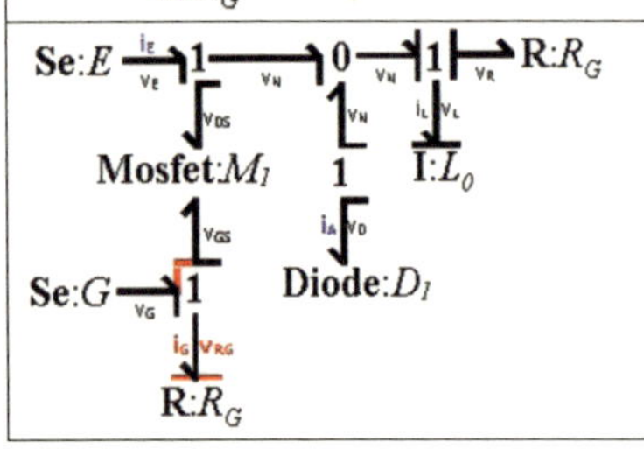	3-Propagation of causality 1-junction linked to Se:G and element R	$v_{R_G} = v_G - v_{GS}$ $i_G = \frac{v_{R_G}}{R_G}$ i_G is the current in each bond of the 1-junction

Table 2. ACA applied to the circuit in Fig. 5

$$\begin{aligned}
&\frac{dQ_G}{dt} = i_G \rightarrow gate\ charge \\
&\frac{dQ_J}{dt} = i_{DS} - g_2(Q_J, Q_G) \rightarrow Miller\ capacitance \\
&v_{GS} = g_3(Q_J, Q_G) \rightarrow gate\ voltage \\
&v_{DS} = g_4(Q_J, Q_G) \rightarrow drain\ voltage
\end{aligned} \tag{1}$$

$$\begin{aligned}
&\frac{dQ_D}{dt} = i - i_D(Q_D) \\
&v_D = g_1(Q_D)
\end{aligned} \tag{2}$$

4. Average models of ideal non-resonant converters

Many methods to build average models of power converters have been published but with two major limitations so far (Allard, 1997b, 1999). On one hand the methods handle only ideal representation of non-resonant converters. On the other hand the methods take the converter as a all and do not differentiate the time-constants to be averaged. The proposed building procedure is then developed on the simplest example of DC/DC converter. The procedure has been translated into a computer program and integrated inside commercial simulators. Results are extrapolated to any non-resonant ideal DC/DC converter.

The building procedure is based on ACA and switching bond graphs, i.e. made of elements of varying causality (Ammous, 2003). The ideal power switches are illustrated in Fig. 6. A power converter that incorporates such ideal switches is affected by the changes in causality: this leads to the so-called topologies of the converter. These are seen here as changes in the assignment of the causality. Fig. 7 illustrates two causality assignments for a basic step-down DC/DC converter.

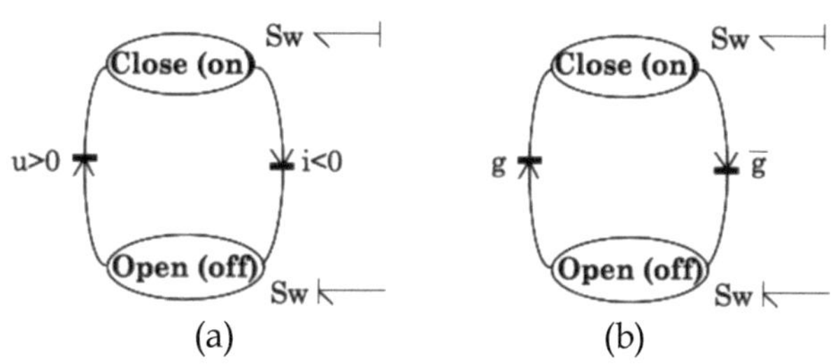

Fig. 6. Ideal natural switch (a) and ideal controlled switch (b)

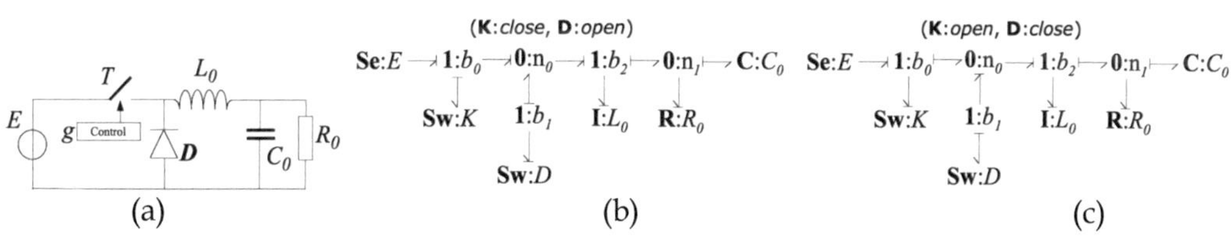

Fig. 7. Ideal step-down DC/DC converter (a) with two causality assignments depending on the state of the power switches (b) and (c).

It is considered now on that the switching period of a DC/DC power converter is always smaller than the time-constants of the passive filter components. The power switches, based on the control signals, define a sequence of causality assignments in the bond graph of the converter. The simplest sequence is generally called the continuous conduction mode (the current never reaches a null value in the inductance in Fig. 7(a)). This sequence comprises two causality assignments. A Petri Network is a convenient tool to picture a sequence. Fig. 8 gives two sequences for the converter in Fig. 7(a).

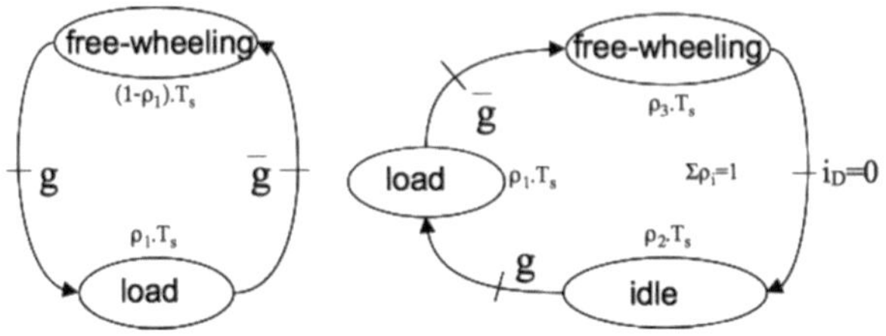

Fig. 8. Two typical causality assignment sequence for a DC/DC converter

The algorithm to build the average model of a DC/DC converter requires knowing the converter architecture (including control signals) and a given sequence of operation. Each sequence of operation requires the derivation of an average model: hence the interest for a systematic method. Six steps have identified.

1. Identification of the switching block: it is made of the all the components which causality changes over the sequence of causality assignment. The resistor connected to an internal junction of the switching block must be included as well.

The bond graph of the ideal buck-boost architecture in Fig. 9 suffers two causality analyses for the continuous conduction mode sequence (Fig. 10). The switching block is then {M, l1, n1, l2, D}

2. Identification of the external variables of the switching block: these are the effort and flow variables of the bonds external to the switching block except the control signals.

Fig. 11 pictures the external bonds to the switching block and the external variables #1(i1, v1), #2(iL, vL) et # (i2, v2)

3. Identification of the input variables to he switching block: these are the variables known from the causality of the components external to the switching block.

As pictured in Fig. 11, the external components of the switching block dictate the following variables: v1 on bond #1, iL on bond #2 and v2 on bond #3.

4. Simplification of the bond graph: the external bonds to the switching variables are replaced by sources of same causality as the input variables.

The external components of the bond #1 are replaced by a voltage source, a current source for bond #2 and a voltage source for bond #3.

5. Expression of the output variables of the switching block

In "free-wheeling" state of the sequence of causality assignment (M: off, D: on), i1=0, vL=v2 and i2=iL. In "load" state (M: on, D: off), i1=iL, vL=E and i2=0.

6. Computation of the average model by the weight-based averaging of the output variables with respect to the duration of the related causality assignment in the switching sequence. Three typical cases appear:
   a. Output variables do not depend on state-variables: immediate result as the variable is independent of time.

The duty-cycle for the power switch M is ρ, *and it comes the average values:* $\langle i_1 \rangle = \rho \cdot I_L, \langle v_L \rangle = \rho \cdot V_1 - (1-\rho) \cdot V_2, \langle i_2 \rangle = (1-\rho) \cdot I_L$. *The bond graph is Fig. 12 may be drawn as the previous equations are related to MTF elements with appropriate ratio (f1=m.f2, see Fig. 25).*

b. Output variables depend on state-variables through inferable functions: an analytical solution is possible
c. Output variables depend on state-variables through non-linear functions: a numerical integration is necessary.

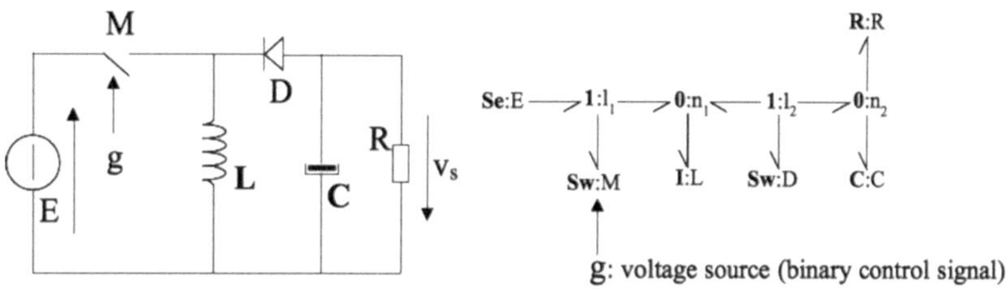

Fig. 9. Ideal buck-boost converter and associated bond graph

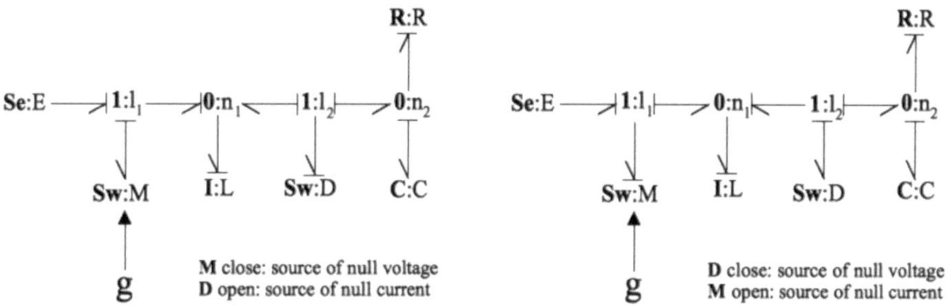

Fig. 10. The two causality assignments in the sequence of in continuous conduction mode of the ideal buck-boost converter

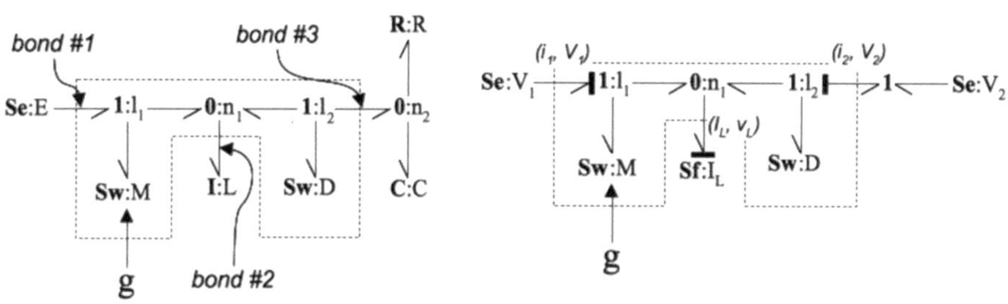

Fig. 11. Steps 3 and 4 of the algorithm

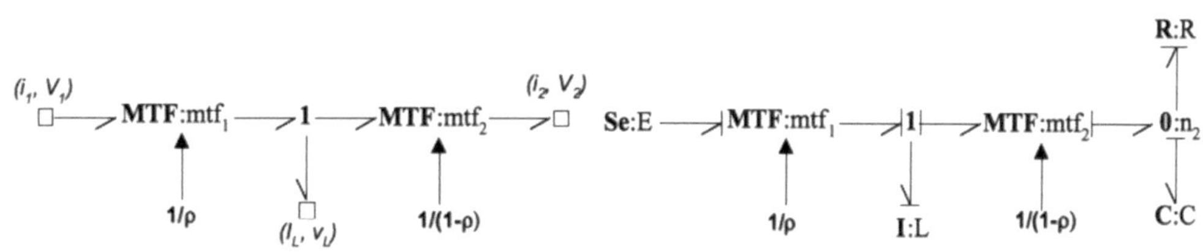

Fig. 12. Average model of the switching block and average model of the ideal buck-boost converter.

Fig. 12 enables to draw the bond graph of the average model of the ideal buck-boost. This model has been obtained in a systematic manner. The EDO of the average-model state-space equation is then obtained in a straightforward manner.

$$\frac{d}{dt}\begin{bmatrix} i_L \\ v_C \end{bmatrix} = \begin{bmatrix} 0 & \dfrac{1-\rho}{L} \\ \dfrac{1-\rho}{C} & -\dfrac{1}{RC} \end{bmatrix}\begin{bmatrix} i_L \\ v_C \end{bmatrix} + E\begin{bmatrix} \dfrac{\rho}{L} \\ 0 \end{bmatrix} \tag{3}$$

5. Average models of ideal resonant converters

The building procedure is now applied to a simple resonant converter. It is a major contribution to the state of the art as none of the previous methods (based on the Generalized Stat-Space Averaging Method) were able to process a change in state-space variables. The above-mentioned algorithm is applied in a straightforward manner. It is considered the example of the ideal ZVS-boost converter (Fig. 13(a)) in continuous conduction mode (Fig. 13(b)).

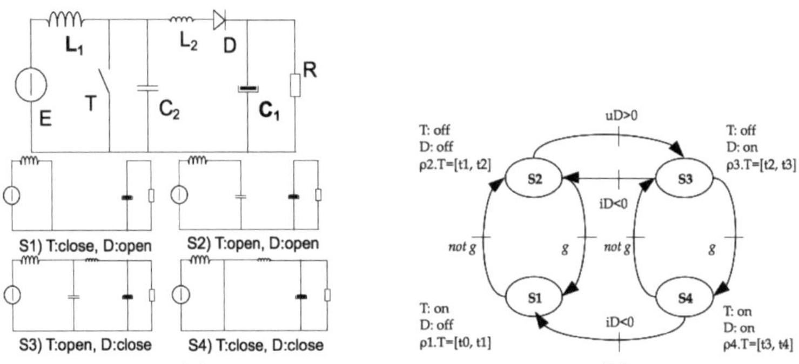

Fig. 13. Ideal ZVS-boost converter in continuous conduction mode (a) and related sequence of causality assignment (b)

At the end of step 4, it comes the simplified bond graph in Fig. 14(b). The switching block is identified as {T, D, C2, L2, n1, l2} with 2 external bonds. The input variables are I1 and V2.

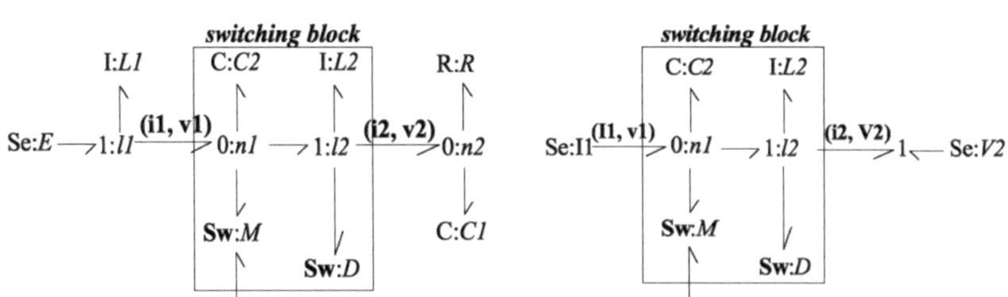

Fig. 14. Title of figure, left justified

Step 5 is to express the output variables of the switching block (v1, i2) in the four cases of causality assignment. The results are summarized in Table 3. The computation of the input variables implies that causal bond graphs be obtained. This leads to consider derivative causality for the inductor L2 in states S1 and S2, and for the capacitor C2 in state S1 and S4. The Algebraic Causality Analysis helps finding systematically the latter considerations. It is this level of details that makes the difference with past methods to build average models and explains their limitations with regard to resonant architectures of power converters.

¶State S1	State S2	State S3	State 4
T: on, D: off L2: derivative[1] C2: derivative	T: off, D: off L2: derivative C2: integral[2] (Q2)	T: off, D: on L2: integral (ϕ2) C2: integral (Q2)	T: on, D: on L2: integral (ϕ2) C2: derivative
$v_1 = 0$ $i_2 = 0$	$v_1 = \frac{Q_2}{C_2}$ $i_2 = 0$ $\frac{dQ_2}{dt} = I_1$	$v_1 = \frac{Q_2}{C_2}$ $i_2 = \frac{\phi_2}{L_2}$ $\frac{dQ_2}{dt} = I_1$ $\frac{d\phi_2}{dt} = \frac{Q_2}{C_2} - V_2$	$v_1 = 0$ $i_2 = \frac{\phi_2}{L_2}$ $\frac{d\phi_2}{dt} = -V_2$

Table 3. Development of step 5 of the algorithm applied to the ideal ZVS-boost converter.

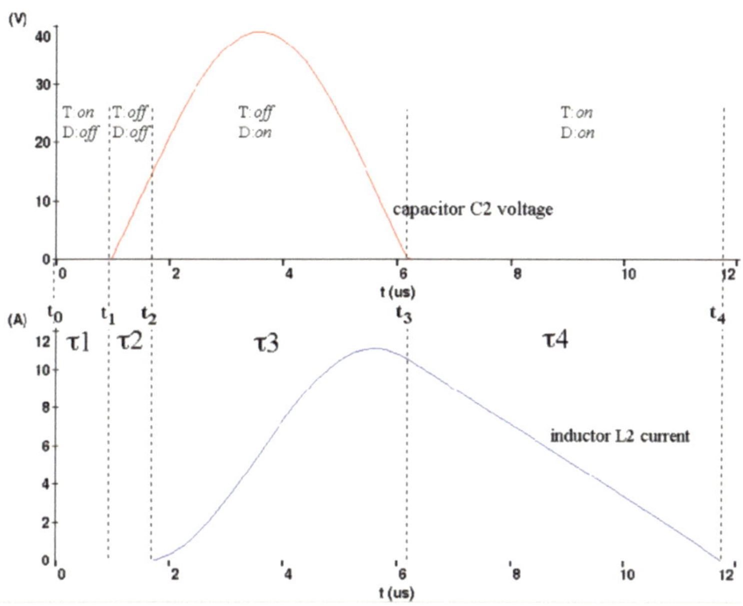

Fig. 15. Simulation of the simplified bond graph in Fig. 14(b)

---

[1] derivative causality: no state variable, i.e. a DAE model, see Table 6

[2] integral causality: normal state variable model (namely the charge Q2 for the capacitor and the magnetic flux ϕ2 for the inductor), see Table 6

Table 3 in fact summarizes the model of the simplified bond graph in Fig. 14(b). A simulation of this model gives the result in Fig. 15. The zero-voltage switching of the converter is clearly illustrated. Step 6 concerns the expression of the average values of the switching block output variables (v1, i2) over the sequence in Fig. 13(b). The respective duration of each state concurs to the switching period Ts. Formal mathematical manipulations leads to Equation 4. The common way to represent this average model is to consider a MTF element which ratio would be in fact ρ_1. The average model of the ideal ZVS-boost converter is obtained when adding the external components of the switching block to the MTF element.

$$\begin{cases} \langle i_2 \rangle = \dfrac{1}{T_S}\left[\dfrac{I_1 \cdot \alpha}{\omega} + C_2 \cdot V_2 + \dfrac{L_2 \cdot I_1^2}{2 \cdot V_2} \cdot (1-\cos\alpha)^2\right] \\ \langle v_1 \rangle = \dfrac{1}{T_S}\left[\dfrac{C_2 \cdot V_2^2}{2 \cdot I_1} + \dfrac{V_2 \cdot \alpha}{\omega} + L_2 \cdot I_1 \cdot (1-\cos\alpha)\right] \end{cases} \text{with} \begin{cases} T_S = \dfrac{1}{1-\rho_1}\left[\dfrac{C_2 \cdot V_2}{I_1} + \dfrac{\alpha}{\omega} + \dfrac{L_2 \cdot I_1}{V_2} \cdot (1-\cos\alpha)\right] \\ \omega = \sqrt{\dfrac{1}{L_2 \cdot C_2}} \\ \sin\alpha = \dfrac{-V_2}{I_1} \cdot \sqrt{\dfrac{C_2}{L_2}} \end{cases} \quad (4)$$

6. Non-linear average models

So far the construction of average model of converters has been applied to ideal architecture. Two contributions have been demonstrated in previous sections: it is a systematic procedure, providing the algebraic causality analysis, and it applies equally to resonant converters. As mentioned in Fig. 1, ideal average models are only useful in early time of the virtual prototyping. It is necessary to incorporate the evaluation of power losses in the average models. Devices in static and transient operations generate power losses. Steady-state power losses are easy to incorporate as they depend only on the current and voltage across the devices. Transient power losses represent here a challenge. The proposed average model wishes to take care of the power switches' non-linear behaviour. An approximation is introduced to substitute the real current and voltage waveforms by ideal signals to enable the formal computation in step 6 of the algorithm. The real buck architecture is taken as an example (Fig. 16(a)). The initial bond graph to be averaged is pictured in Fig. 16(b).

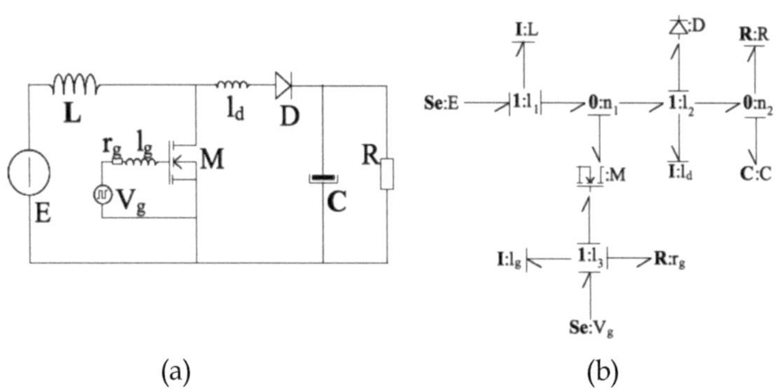

Fig. 16. Real buck converter (a) and related bond graph (b)

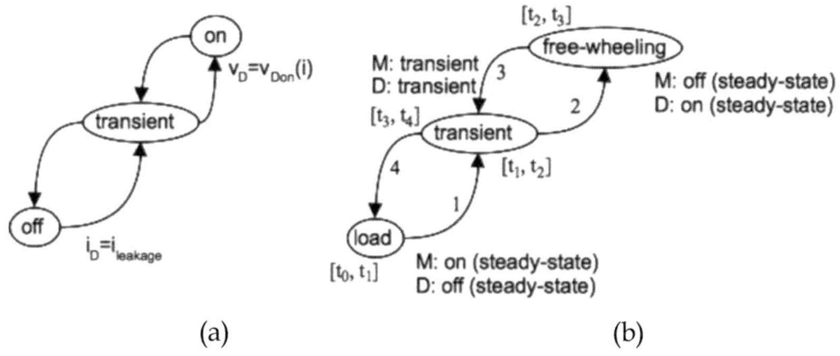

Fig. 17. Petri net of the power diode behaviour (a) and behaviour of the buck converter in Fig. 16(a) in continuous conduction mode (b)

The MOSFET model in Equation 1 is considered and the model in Equation 2 for the power diode. The behaviour of the power switches is pictured in Fig. 17(a) that leads to the buck converter Petri Net of states in Fig. 17(b) for the continuous conduction mode. The algorithm yields the simplified bond graph in Fig. 18. The input variables are I1 and V2, and the output variables are v1 and i2. The variable v1 is related to the MOSFET drain-source voltage while the output variable i2 is related to the diode current. According to the sequence in Fig. 17(b), the step 6 of the algorithm requires the computation of the following average values:

$$\begin{cases} \langle i_2 \rangle = \dfrac{1}{T_S}\left[\displaystyle\int_{t_0}^{t_1} v_{DSon}(I_1)dt + \int_{t_1}^{t_2} v_{DS}(t)dt + \int_{t_2}^{t_3} \left(V_2 + v_{Don}(I_1)\right)dt + \int_{t_3}^{t_4} v_{DS}(t)dt\right] \\ \langle v_1 \rangle = \dfrac{1}{T_S}\left[\displaystyle\int_{t_1}^{t_2} i_D(t)dt + \int_{t_2}^{t_3} I_1 dt + \int_{t_3}^{t_4} i_D(t)dt\right] \end{cases} \quad (5)$$

The proposed method is to substitute ideal signals to $v_{DS}(t)$ and $i_D(t)$ according to Fig. 18(b) and 18(c) respectively. Integrals of the real waveform and the ideal signal must be equal to lead to the same contribution in Equation (4). Virtual delays, $\delta_{v_{DS}}^{off}$, $\delta_{v_{DS}}^{on}$, $\delta_{i_D}^{off}$ and $\delta_{i_D}^{on}$ are introduced that depend on the switching block input variables and the circuit parasitic devices. Tabulation of virtual delay values may be measured or simulated.

The ideal signals and the virtual delays lead to the switching block average model in Equation (6). The bond graph in Fig. 19 is derived. The MTF element represents the average model of the ideal buck converter and the non linearities are reported in the two dissipative elements RS.

$$\begin{cases} \langle i_2 \rangle = I_1 \cdot \left[\rho + \dfrac{\delta_{i_D}^{off} - \delta_{i_D}^{on}}{T_S}\right] \\ \langle v_1 \rangle = \left(V_2 - v_{DSon}\right) \cdot \left[\rho - \dfrac{\delta_{v_{DS}}^{off} - \delta_{v_{DS}}^{on}}{T_S}\right] - v_{DSon} \cdot \left[1 - \rho + \dfrac{\delta_{v_{DS}}^{off} - \delta_{v_{DS}}^{on}}{T_S}\right] \end{cases} \quad (6)$$

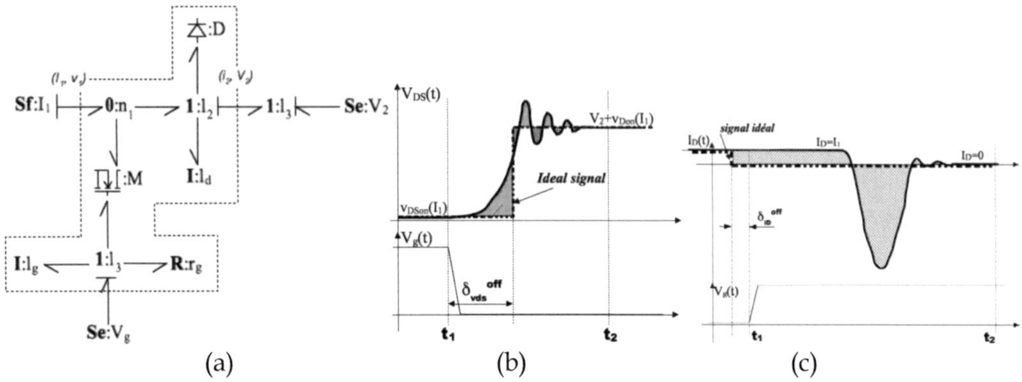

Fig. 18. Simplified bond graph (a) and ideal signal for the MOSFET drain voltage (b) and the diode current (c)

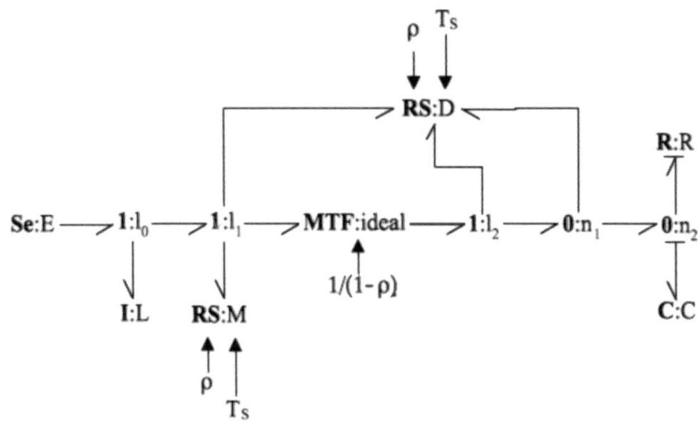

Fig. 19. Average model of the real buck converter in continuous conduction mode.

Many papers have been published to propose formal approximate waveforms for the current and voltages of power switches during transient. The switching power losses can then be calculated in a formal manner. Unfortunately the current and voltage waveforms depend on too many parameters to enable a valid approximation. The substitution proposed here above offers a practical advantage. The same idea of tabulation depending on the switching block parameters has been experimented for the power losses (Allard, 2001), (Ammous, 1998, 2000).

The system in Fig. 20 includes the here above buck converter that feeds a motor fan. The goal of an electro-thermal simulation is to provide an estimation of the power device self-heating behaviour on a long-term duration. This type of simulation requires the average model of the converter including losses. The losses are carried out with RS elements with at least a thermal bond. All thermal bonds are to be connected to a compact model of the system thermal network (like the thermal substrate in Fig. 20). A fast simulation gives results as in Fig. 21 that have been verified experimentally. The left figure compares an accurate device-level simulation of the buck converter to the ideal average model like in Fig. 12 and the buck converter non-ideal average model in Fig. 19. The right figure shows the start-up of the motor fan and the self-heating of the power devices.

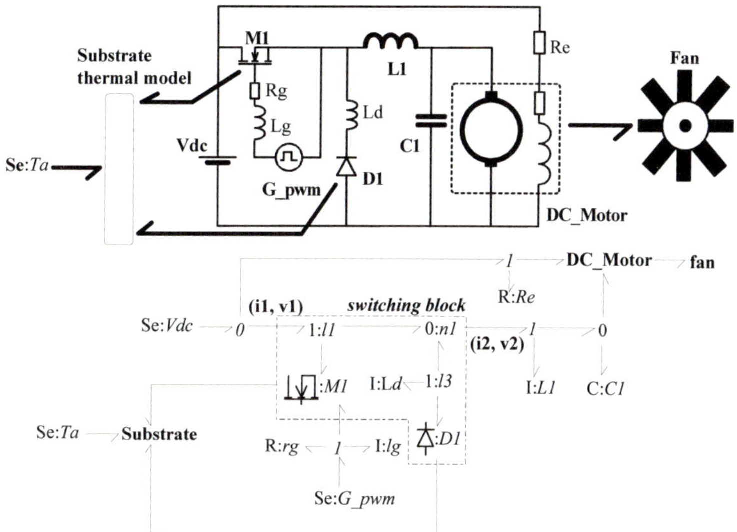

Fig. 20. Example of electro-thermal system

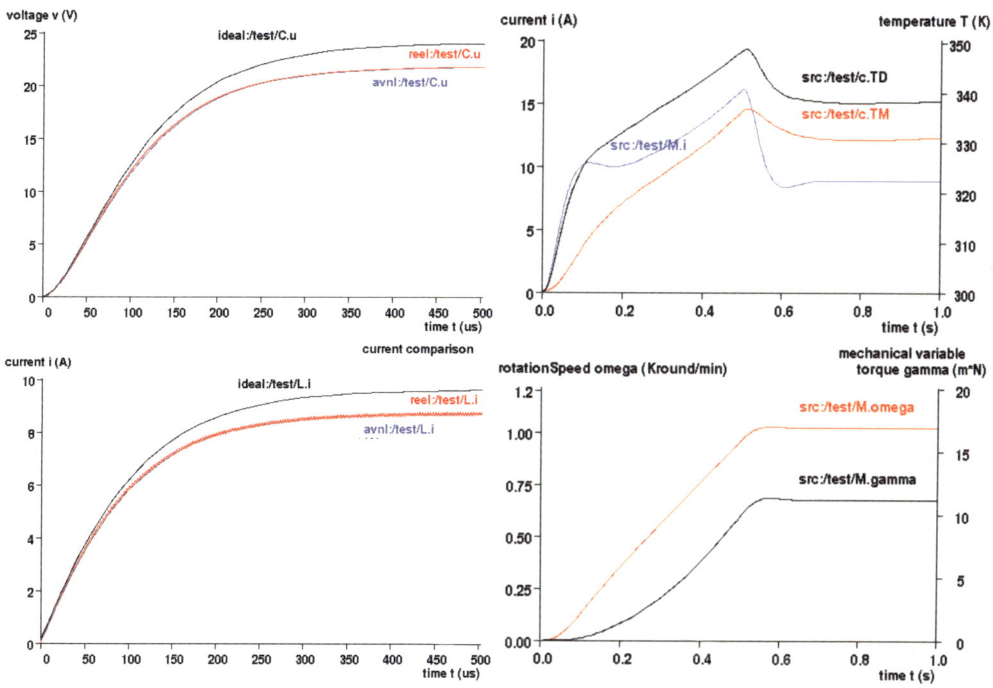

Fig. 21. Example of electro-thermal simulation.

7. Conclusion

This chapter has introduced the interests of compact models for system-level analyses of mechatronic products. Regarding the power converters, the compact models are called average models and a systematic method has been detailed for their building. A simple example is presented at the end. The idea of ideal signals and look-up table of quantities has been applied to take care of EMI contributions.

Bond graphs have been used to build compact models of thermal system behaviour. This kind of compact model appears as the previous ones in the form of state-space models. VHDL-AMS is one example of language to implement easily the state-space models into a system simulator.

8. Annex A: Synthetic presentation of Bond Graphs and related graphical conventions

Bond Graphs is the name given to a framework for the unified modelling of the dynamics of multi-disciplinary systems. It is widely accepted in mechatronic industries like car manufacturers (Radcliffe, 1971), (Margolis, 1974), (Merzouki, 2007). The formalization of the bond graphs as known today is the results by Henry Painter (Painter, 1961). A popular introductory textbook is (Karnopp & Rosenberg, 1975). A rather complete bibliography may be found in (Bosand & Breedweld, 1985).

The First Law of Thermodynamics rules the evolution of a system internal energy that is balanced by heat transfer and external work energy transfer. This Law implies the continuity of energy with respect to time. The Bond Graphs assume also the continuum of micro-systems in the analysis of an engineering system. It is a lumped approach. Energy is then considered locally. Energy then flows into a system with identified boundaries. The system analyses are then valid only within these boundaries. The micro-systems' models are concepts or idealised descriptions of physical phenomena, which are recognised as the dominating behaviour in components (tangible system parts). The Bond Graph framework is a living tool where many ideas have been added since more than 50 years to simplify the modelling approach of dynamic systems. The topic is here to describe the basics of representation and the elementary component (i.e. simple concepts).

8.1 Flow and effort variables

The energy flow between two sub-systems inside the boundary-limited system is carried by a flow of particles, such as mass particles (solid, liquid, gas), electrons and holes, photons, phonons… The Bond Graph framework represents graphically this energy flow as in Fig. 22. The sub-systems A and B are connected through energy ports. In electrical domain, the energy ports are the pins of the devices. The half-arrow indicates the energy flow, directed from A to B.

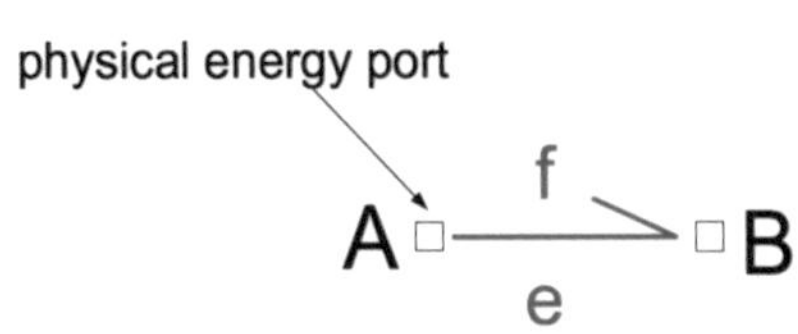

Fig. 22. Graphical representation of an energy exchange between two sub-systems.

The Onsager's theorem[3] has established that the instantaneous power, p, characterizing the energy flow is the product of a flow variable, f, related to the flow of particles, f, by an effort variable, e (Equation 7).

$$P=f.e \tag{7}$$

The flow variable is an extensive variable whereas the effort variable, e, is an intensive variable. Table 4 gives a list of the effort and flow variables in the main physical domains. The graphical convention in Fig. 22 is to write the flow variable on the same side as the half-arrow and the effort variable on the other side. Referring to VHDL-AMS, the energy flow between two devices is defined by the connection of 'terminals'. Quantities of branch are defined such as 'through quantities' and 'across quantities'. The latter quantities may be chosen in essence similar to the flow variables and effort variables respectively.

Domain	Flow	Effort
Electrical	Current, i	Voltage, v
Translation	Velocity, v	Force, f
Rotation	Rotational speed, ω	Torque, Γ
Hydraulic	Volume flow, d	Pressure, p
Thermal	Entropy flow, S	Temperature , t

Table 4. (effort, flow) couples in main physical domains

8.2 Bond Graph linear elements

A Bond Graph of a system is made of sub-systems that can be hierarchically subdivided into elementary components. In a first approach, it has been demonstrated that linear systems can be represented by the components in Table 5 (Breedveld, 1981). The C-element stores potential energy and its state-space model is given in Equation 8 where x is the state-variable.

Energy behaviour	Energetic	Entropic	Creator	None
Storage	C, I			
Irreversible		R, Rs		
Source			Se, Sf	
Constraint				0, 1, TF, MTF, GY, MGY

Table 5. Elements of a linear bond graphs

$$\begin{cases} \dfrac{dx}{dt} = f \\ e = \kappa(x) = x / C \end{cases} \tag{8}$$

An electrical capacitor takes the electrical charge, Q, as the state variable. The I-element in Table 5 is the self-inductor in electrical domain or the inertia in mechanical domain. The R-element is the energy dissipator. This element defines a resistor but also friction or Eddy current effect. The entropic RS-element is a two-port element that transforms the energy into heat (Fig. 23). The entropy flow ($\dot{S}$ or f_s) is the flow variable in the thermal domain is given

[3] Lars Onsager (November 27, 1903 - October 5, 1976). Valid in the case of thermodynamic equilibrium but extended to the case of resonable internal energy

by Equation 9. For convenience, the entropy flow is denoted f_S. The Second Law of Thermodynamics imposes that f_S is strictly positive.

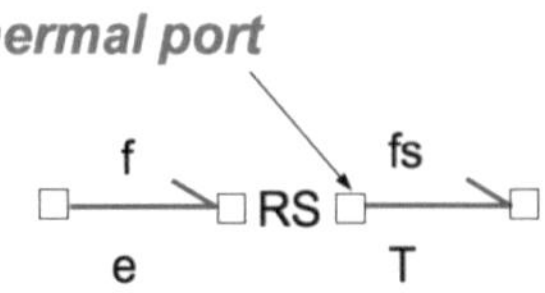

Fig. 23. Two-port, entropic element (RS)

$$f \cdot e = R \cdot f^2 = \dot{S} \cdot T = f_S \cdot T \tag{9}$$

It is said in introduction of this chapter that a system which analysis is considered here, is a limited by boundaries (from geometrical and energetic point of view). The outside world of the system is generally represented by sources: sources of effort, Se, or sources of flow, Sf. The waveform of the source flow or effort may be of various types (continuous, harmonic).
The elements of the system are linked so that they either share a flow of particles or an effort. Two elements are introduced to represent these connection types (Fig. 24). The so-called junction 1 connects the elements that share the same flow variable. It is equivalent to an electrical loop in electrical domain. The 0-junction connects the elements that share the same effort variable. It is equivalent to an electrical node in electrical domain or an iso-thermal connexion in thermal domain.

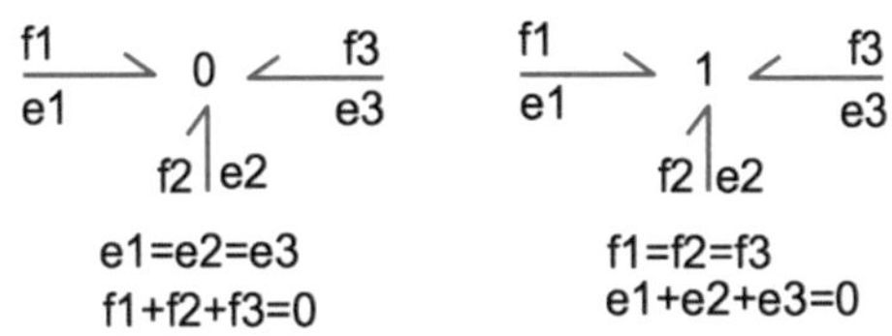

Fig. 24. Representation of junctions (case of 3-ports junctions)

Other constraint elements have been introduced along with junctions to describe other energy transfer and transformation. These constraint elements do not store energy, do not dissipate energy and evidently do not create energy. The most popular element is the transformer, representing the ideal gearbox, an electrical transformer or a pulley. The energy is transformed at equal instantaneous power. The transformer ratio may be different than one as represented in Fig. 25.

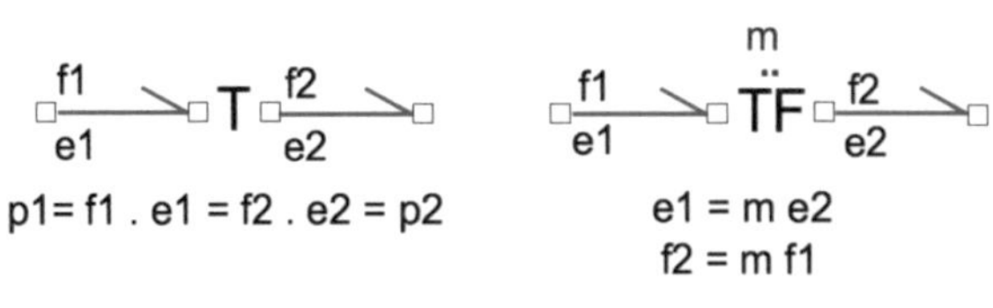

Fig. 25. Transformer elements

The mechanical gyroscope or the electrical coil introduce one final type of energy transformation between flow and effort variables. The gyrator-element has been introduced to take care of this particular energy exchange (Fig. 26). As an example, the electrical coil model represents the electrical energy transformation into magnetic energy. In the magnetic domain, the flow variable is the derivative of the magnetic flux, $\lambda=d\Phi/dt$, and the effort variable is the magneto-motive force, F. The gyrator element is the natural representation for the following equations: $v=N.\lambda$ and $F=N.i$ where v and i are respectively the effort and flow variables of the electrical port and F and λ respectively the effort and flow variables of the magnetic port.

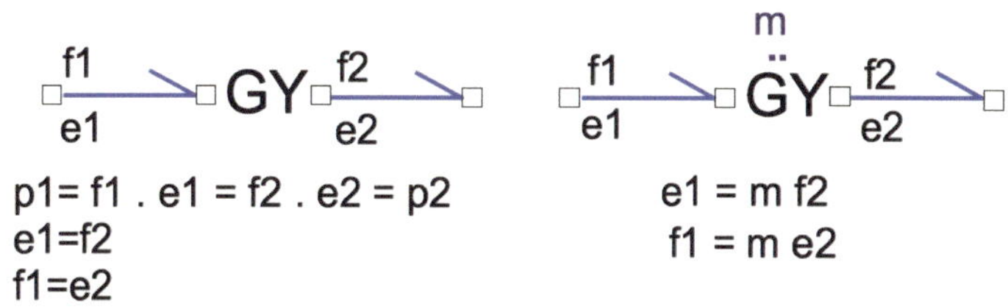

Fig. 26. Representation of the gyrator-element

The transformation ratio of the transformer, TF and the gyrator, GY, may be varying with time. In this case the elements are respectively denoted MTF and MGY but the constitutive equations remain similar.

8.3 Building a bond graph model

A large number of algorithms exist to build a Bond Graph from a pragmatic representation of a system. They are out of the scope of this chapter. Some algorithms deal with the construction of a bond graph from a Kirchhof representation of an electrical circuit (Karnopp, 1990). An advanced algorithm is detailed here after. This algorithm targets the simplification of complex Kirchhof networks. Basically all the nodes of the circuit are transformed into 0-junctions and rules are proposed to simplify the obtained brute bond graph:

1. Replace each component by the bond graph equivalent element and place a 1-junction at each port of each component.
2. Place a 0-juntion between two earlier nodes. Respect the current orientation convention with the half-arrow orientation (Fig. 27).
3. Eliminate one 0-junction and the related half-arrow.
4. Simplify the resulting bond graph:
    a. Eliminate the two-port, well-oriented junctions
    b. Contract into one junction all linked junctions of the same nature
    c. Eliminate the loop between 0- and 1-junctions
    d. Simplify the association of 0-1-0-1 or 1-0-1-0 junctions
    e. Experiment further simplification by inversing the half-arrow to an internal junction

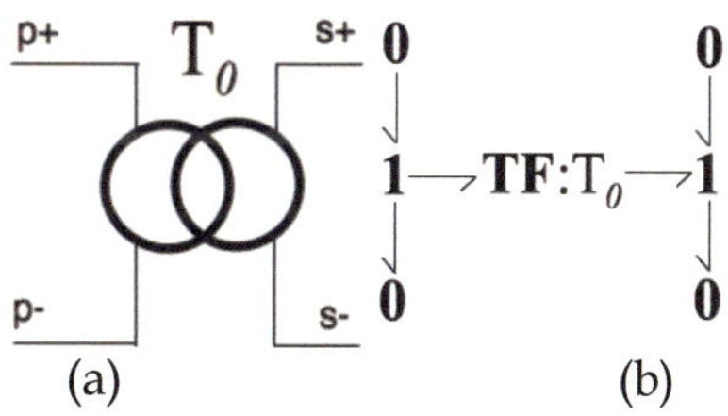

Fig. 27. Application of steps 1 and 2 of the algorithm. Redrawing of a transformer (a) into a bond graph equivalent (b)

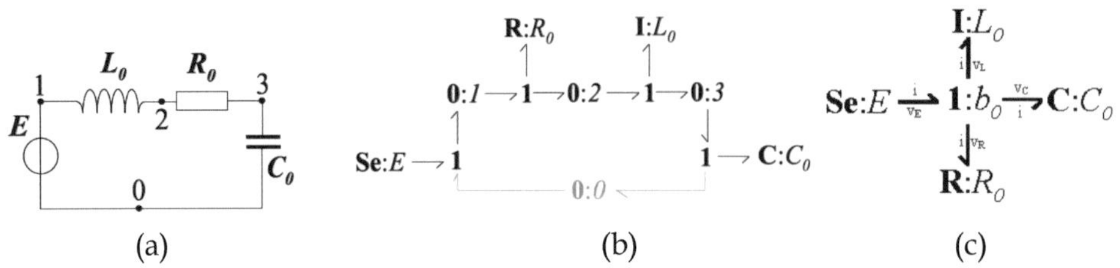

Fig. 28. Application of the algorithm to a simple circuit (a). Bond graphs after step 3 (b) and final bond graph (c).

9. Annex B: Synthetic presentation of the original causality analysis method

Causality or cause-to-effect relation is a philosophical concept since Spinoza in 1670. Physical systems verify that any phenomenon considered as a cause emerges due to another phenomenon considered as the cause and a delay appears between the effect and the caused. Classical mechanics, Maxwell equations or any state-space model verifies this rule, generally implicit.

The causality in the bond graph framework targets a model of the system at hand as an Ordinary Differential Equation. In a state space model like $\dot{x} = G(x,t)$, the Cauchy-Lipschitz theorem indicates that there is one solution given an initial condition if the function G is continuously derivable. It is mostly the case for physical systems. A so-called causal bond graph will then be described as an ODE. A non-causal bond graph will be described as a Differential and Algebraic Equation. The index theory of DAE indicates that only a subset of DAEs describe a deterministic system, i.e. enables a coherent simulation like an ODE (Lakner, 2008).

9.1 Causality of bonds

A bond graph element is meant to influence the system whether by the flow variable or the effort variable. The causality of an energy bond is the indication of the latter preference. The vertical stroke in Fig. 29 indicates that the element A dictates the value of the flow variable in the energy bond to the element B. Conversely the element B dictates the effort variable. It is the case of a causal bond. If both elements dictate the same variable, the causal representation is not possible and the bond is said non-causal: it is a physical impossibility like connecting in series two source of electrical current. Table 6 gives the causality graphical representation of the main bond graph elements. The column called "formal causality analysis" is related to section 3 of this chapter.

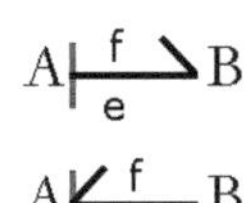

Fig. 29. Causality of an energy bond

If all the bonds of a given bond graph receive a consistent causal stroke, then the bond graph is said causal, i.e. the list of model equations is an ODE. Moreover an explicit list of equations is obtained in opposition of the implicit equation set that the Nodal Analysis Method exhibits in popular circuit simulator like Spice.

symbol	brute	Formal Causality Analysis	Original Causality
Se			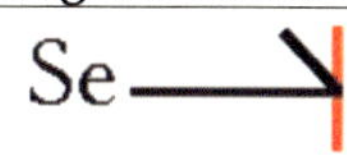
Sf			
C in integral causality $\dot{x} = f, e = \varphi(x)$		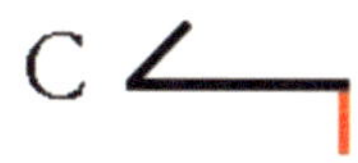	
C in derivative causality[4] $f = \frac{\partial x}{\partial \varphi}\dot{e}$			
I in integral causality $\dot{x} = e, f = \varphi(x)$			
I in derivative causality $e = \frac{\partial x}{\partial \varphi}\dot{f}$		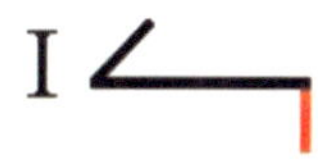	
R		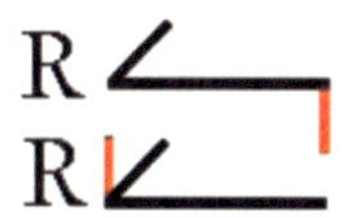	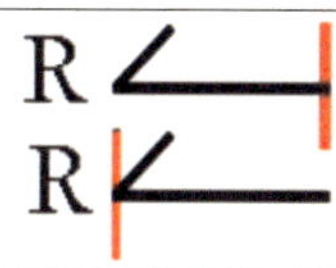
TF or MTF		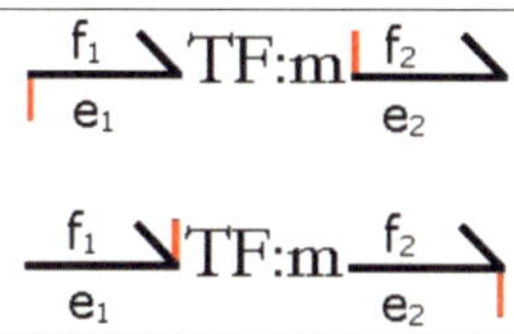	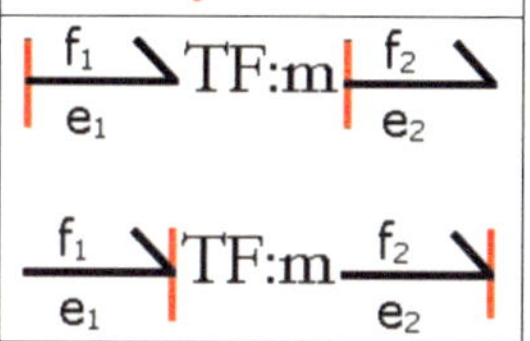
GY or MGY		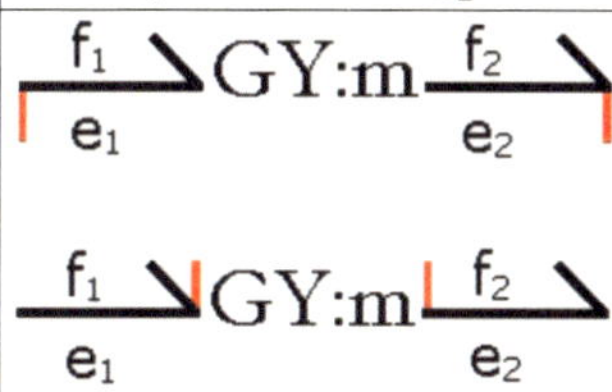	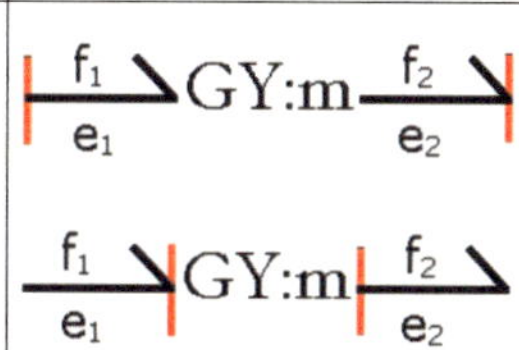
1-junction	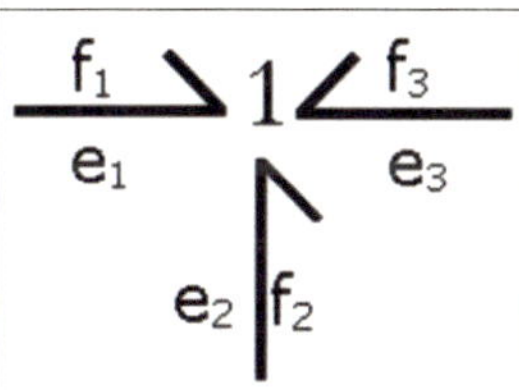	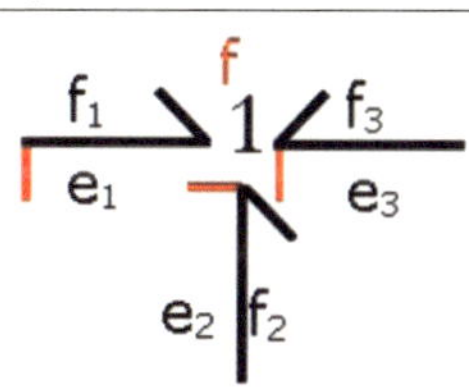	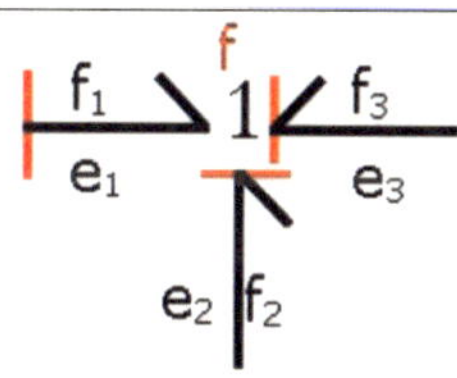

[4] The derivative causality eliminates the state-space variables and leaves a DAE. It is a less favorable case tahn the ODE (integral causality)

symbol	brute	Formal Causality Analysis	Original Causality
0-junction	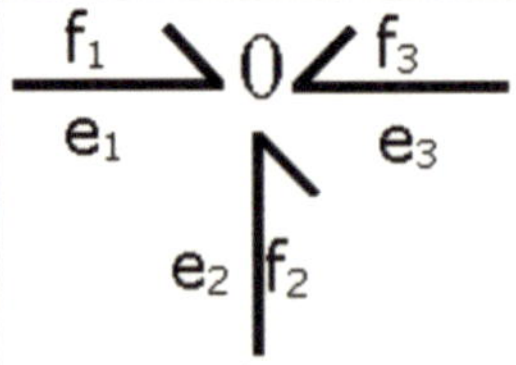	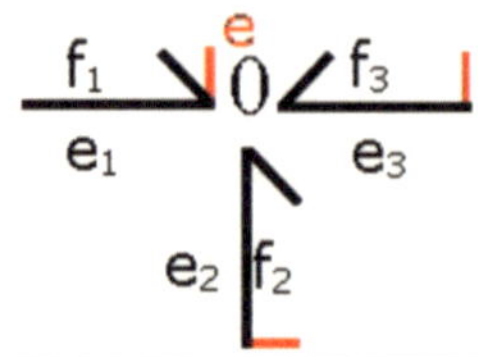	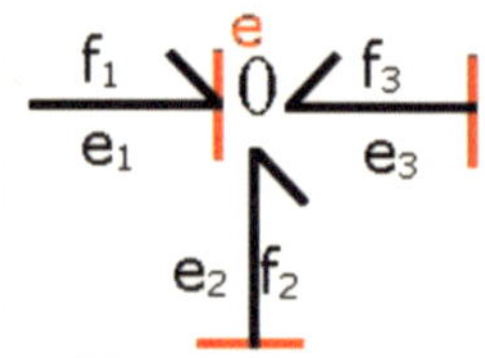

Table 6. Causality of bond graph elementary components

The causality of the bond graph in Fig. 28(c) is given in Fig. 30 along with the list of equations that is an ODE. An example of non-causal bond graph is given in section 3 of the chapter.

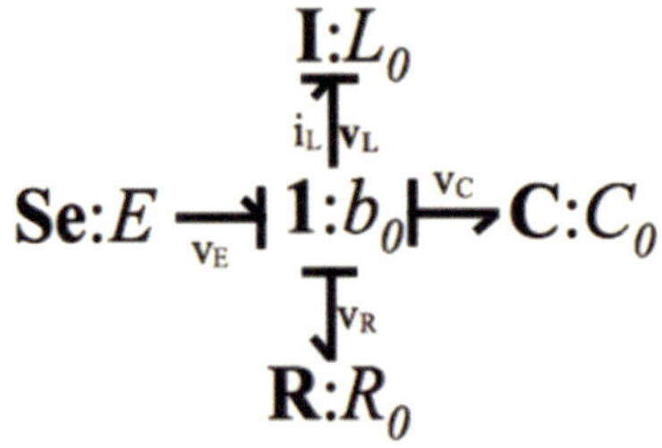

$$\begin{cases} \phi\big|_{t=0} = \phi_0 \\ Q\big|_{t=0} = Q_0 \\ \dfrac{dQ}{dt} = \dfrac{\phi}{L} \\ \dfrac{d\phi}{dt} = E - R\dfrac{\phi}{L} - \dfrac{Q}{C} \end{cases}$$

Fig. 30. Causality of the bond graph in Fig. 28(c) and associated equations

10. References

Allard, B., Morel, H., Ammous, A., Ghedira, S. (1997). Extension of Causality Analysis to Bond Graphs Including State-Space Models, *Proceedings of Society for Computer Simulation, Simulation Series*, Vol. 29, No. 1, pp. 72–78

Allard, B., Morel, H., Lautier, Ph., Retif, J.M. (1997). Bond Graphs for averaged Modeling of Power Electronic Converter, *Proceedings of Society for Computer Simulation, Simulation Series*, Vol. 29, No. 1, pp. 201–206.

Allard, B., Morel, H., Ghedira, S., Ammous. A. (1999). Building Advanced Averaged Models of Power Converters from Switched Bond Graph Representation, *Proceedings of Society for Computer Simulation, Simulation Series*, Vol. 31, No. 1, pp. 331–338.

Allard, B., Bergogne, D., Morel. H. (2001). Experimentally verified electro-thermal simulation of power converters, *Proceedings of SCS Publishing Editor, Simulation Series*, Vol. 33, No. 1, pp. 191-198.

Ammous, K., Allard, B., Morel. H. (2003). Switching-cell as a converter core-representation for analysis, *Proceedings of SCS Publishing Editor, Simulation Series*, Vol. 35, No. 2, pp. 72-78

Allard, B., Morel, H. (1998). Transient Temperature Measurements and Modeling of IGBT's Under Short–Cirtcuit, *IEEE Transactions on Power Electronics*, Vol. 13, No. 1, pp. 12–25.

Ammous, A, Ammous, K., Morel, H., Allard, B., Bergogne, D., Sellami, F., Chante, J.P. (2000). Electrothermal Modeling of the IGBT's: Application to Short Circuit Condition, *IEEE Transactions on Power Electronics*, Vol. 15, No. 4, pp. 778–790.

Ben-Yaakov, S., Wulich, D., Polivka, W.M. (1995). Resolution of an averaging paradox in the analysis of switched-mode dc-dc converters. *IEEE Transactions on Aerospace Electronic Systems*, Vol. 30, N°2, pp. 626-632.

Bosand, A. M., Breedweld, P.C. (1985). Update of the Bond Graph Bibliography, In *University of Twenty*, 20.06.2011, Available from http://doc.utwente.nl/69379/1/Bos85update.pdf

Breedveld, P.C. (1981). *Thermodynamic bond graphs: a new synthesis*, International Jonrual of Modelling and Simulation, Vol. 1, No. 1, pp. 57-61.

Cùk, S., Middlebrook, R.D. (1977). A general unified approach to modeling switching DC-to-DC converters in discontinuous conduction mode, *Proceedings of IEEE Power Electronics Specialists Conference*, pp36-57.

Karnopp, D.C., Rosenberg, R.C. (1975). *System dynamics, a unified approach*, Wiley, New-York

Karnopp, D.C., Margolis, D.L., Rosenberg, R.C. (1990). *System dynamics: a unified approach*, (2nd edition), Wiley-Interscience, New-York.

Krein, P.T., Bentsman, J., Bass, R.M., Lesieutre, B.C. (1990). On the use of averaging for the analysis of power electronics systems. *IEEE Transactions on Power Electronics*, Vol. 5, No. 2, pp. 182-190.

Lai, Y.M., Tse, C.K., Mehta, P. (1995). A computer method for the formulation of averaged models for dc/dc power converter circuits. *Journal of Circuits, Systems and Computer*, Vol. 5, No 3, pp. 373-391.

Lakner, P.R. (2008). Lumped Parameter Model Analysis, In *University of Queensland Hungarian Academy of Sciences*, 20.06.2011, Available from www.dcs.vein.hu/lakner/oktatas/modellezes/chap5b.ppt

Lee, Y.S. (1985). A systematic and unified approach to modeling switches in switch-mode power supplies. *IEEE Transactions on Industrial Electronics*, Vol. 32, pp. 445-448.

Maksimovic, D. (1998). Automated small-signal analysis of switching converters using general purpose time-domain simulator, *Proceedings of IEEE Applied Power Electronics Conference and Exposition*, pp. 357-362.

Margolis, D.L., Tylee, J.L. (1974). Bond graph modelling techniques applied to nonlinear primary and secondary suspensions for high speed ground transportation vehicles, *Proceedings of Simulation Council Series*, Vol. 4, No. 2, pp. 104-131.

Merzouki, R., Ould-Bouamama, B., Djeziri, M.A., Bouteldja, M. (2007). Modelling and estimation of tire–road longitudinal impact efforts using bond graph approach. *Elsevier Mechatronics*, No. 17, pp. 93–108, doi:10.1016/j.mechatronics.2006.11.001

Middlebrook, R.D., Cùk, S. (1976). A general unified approach to modeling switching converters, *Proceedings of IEEE Power Electronics Specialists Conference*, pp. 18-34.

Morel, H., Allard, B., Brevet, O., We, M., Elomari, H., Ammous, K. (2001). Modified nodal approach versus causality analysis, Proceedings of SCS Publishing Editor, Simulation Series, Vol. 33, No. 1, pp. 85-90.

Morel, H., Allard, B., Elomari, H., Ammous, K., Bergogne, D., Ammous, A. (2001). Causality Analysis and State Initialization, *SCS Publishing Editor, Simulation Series*, Vol. 33, No.1, January, pp. 91-97.

Olivier, J.A., Cobos, J.A., Uceda, J., Rascon, M., Quinones, C. (2000). Systematic approach for developing large-signal averaged models of multi-output PWM converters, *Proceedings of IEEE Power Electronics Specialists Conference*, pp. 696-701.

Painter, H. M. (1961). *Analysis and Design of engineering systems*, MIT Press, Cambridge, Mass.

Pecheux, F., Allard, B., Lallement, C., Vachoux, A., Morel, H. (2005). Modeling and simulation of multi-discipline systems using bond graphs and VHDL-AMS, *Proceedings of SCS Publishing Editor, Simulation Series*, Vol. 37, No. 1, pp. 149-161.

Radcliffe, C.J., Karnopp, D.C. (1971), Simulation of nonlinear air cushion vehicle dynamics using bond graph techniques, *Proceedings of Summer Computer Simulation Conference*, Board of Simulation Conference, 5975 Broadway, Denver, Colo., pp. 550-558.

Sanders, S., Noworolski, J., Liu, X.Z., Verghese G.C. (1991). Generalized averaging method of power conversion circuits. *IEEE Transactions on Power Electronics*, Vol. 6, No. 2, pp. 251-258.

Smedley, K., Cùk, S. (1994). Switching flow graph nonlinear modeling technique. *IEEE Transactions on Power Electronics*, Vol. 9, No. 4, pp. 405-413.

Xu, J., Lee, C.Q. (1998). A unified averaging technique for the modeling of quasi-resonant converters. *IEEE Transactions on Power Electronics*, Vol. 13, No. 3, pp. 556-563.

9

Virtual Prototyping for Rapid Product Development

S.H. Choi and H.H. Cheung
Department of Industrial and Manufacturing Systems Engineering
The University of Hong Kong
Hong Kong SAR
China

1. Introduction

Intensifying globalization and market competition has been driving the manufacturing industry to compete on continual reduction in lead-time and cost of product development while assuring high quality and wide varieties. Conventional manufacturing processes are, however, no longer sufficient to speed up product development to meet ever-increasing diversities of customer demands, stringent cost control, and complexity of new products.

In recent years, various technologies have been developed to facilitate rapid product development. Among these technologies, virtual prototyping (VP) and virtual manufacturing (VM) may be regarded as important technological advancements. VP and VM integrate virtual reality (VR) simulation techniques with design and manufacturing processes to fabricate digital prototypes for subsequent stereoscopic visualisation, validation and optimisation of product designs, as well as for evaluation of product assemblability and producability.

As shown in Figure 1, VP and VM together close a design-simulate-improve loop, in which design and production simulation techniques are integrated for visualisation and optimisation of a complete product development process in a VR environment to enhance product maturity. While VP focuses on the design process that digitally fabricates prototypes for evaluation and improvement of a product design, VM facilitates validation and optimisation of all subsequent stages of the downstream manufacturing process, such as facility layout, product assembly, and production scheduling.

This design-simulate-improve loop can be iterated effectively and quickly to shorten the product design and development cycle without incurring much additional costs. Indeed, manufacturers can test all stages of product development in a virtual environment. As such, they will be able to "get it right the first time" to enhance product maturity substantially at an earlier stage, and to deliver quality products to market on time and within budget.

This chapter presents an integrated VP system for digital fabrication of complex prototypes to facilitate rapid product development. The VP system comprises a suite of software packages for multi-material layered manufacturing (MMLM) processes, including multi-toolpath planning, build-time estimation and accuracy analysis, integrated with semi-immersive desktop-based and full-immersive CAVE-based VR technology for digital fabrication and subsequent visualisation of product prototypes. The desktop-based VR system creates a semi-immersive virtual environment for stereoscopic visualisation and quality analysis of a product design. It is relatively cost-effective and easy to operate, but its users may be distracted by environmental disturbances that could possibly diminish their efficiency of product design evaluation and improvement. To alleviate disturbance problems, the CAVE-based VR system provides an enclosed room-like virtual environment that blocks out most disturbances, making it possible for a design team to fully concentrate and collaborate on their product design work.

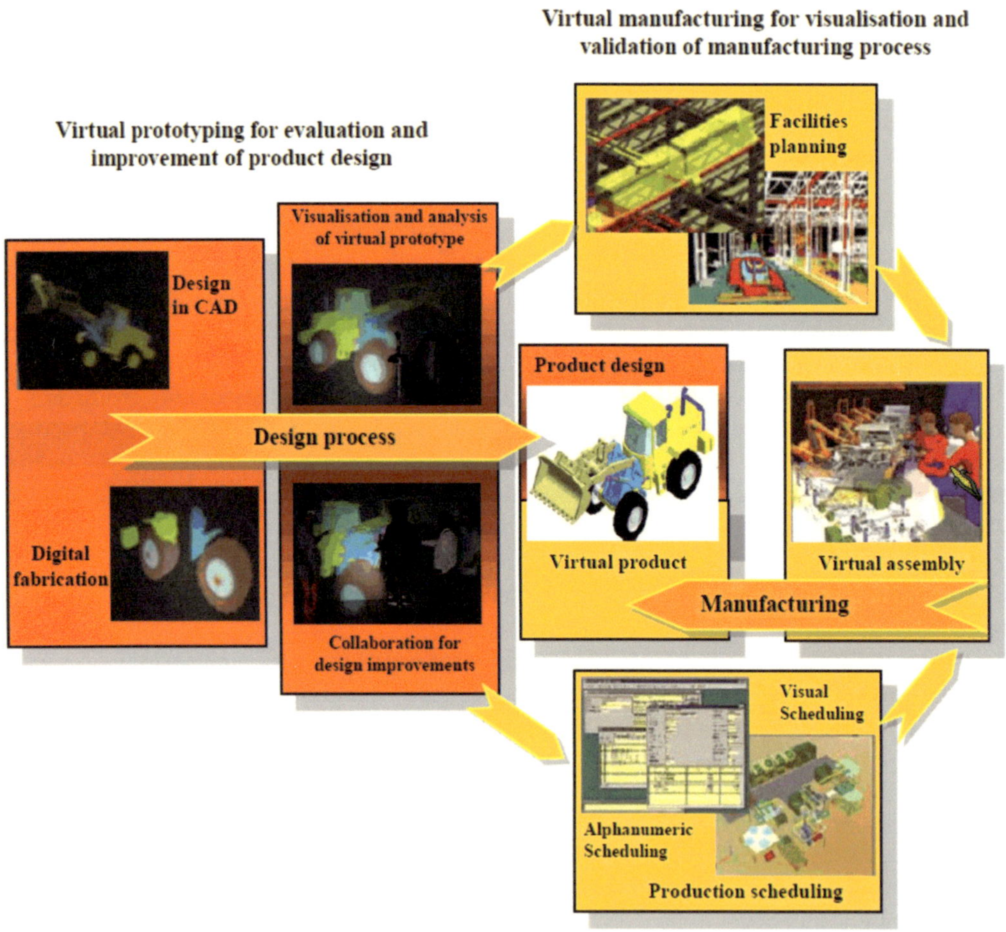

Fig. 1. Integration of virtual prototyping (VP) with virtual manufacturing (VM) for rapid product development

The VP system enhances collaboration and communication between designers working on product development. It provides tools for simulation and visualisation to analyse and improve the design of a product and its fabrication processes. Through simulations, assessment and modification of a product design can be iterated without incurring much manufacturing and material costs of prototypes. Hence, key factors such as product shape and manufacturability that may affect the product maturity and profitability can be optimised quickly. Moreover, the resulting product design can be sent via the Internet to customers for comments or marketing purposes. The VP system therefore facilitates rapid product development and helps reduce time-to-market and cost considerably.

This chapter will first review the background and technologies related to development of VP. The architecture and technical considerations of the proposed VP system will then be discussed in detail. Case studies involving digital fabrication of complex, multi-material objects will be presented to illustrate possible applications of the VP system for product design and development.

2. Review of related works

2.1 Layered Manufacturing and multi-material layered manufacturing

Layered Manufacturing (LM), also called Rapid Prototyping (RP), is an additive manufacturing process that produces a physical prototype from a 3D CAD model layer by layer. The model can be generated from CAD designs or surface data captured from CT, MRI and laser 3D scanning.

LM systems are widely adopted in manufacturing and medical applications to save cost and time. Manufacturers use LM technology to produce prototypes of products for design evaluation, and as master patterns for production tools.

Lopez and Wright (2002) studied the impact of LM on product design and development processes. The study shows that LM may help shorten the product development cycle drastically and enable designers to incorporate mechanical and ergonomic features into new products easily. Tennyson et al. (2006) did a project to promote solid modelling and RP technologies to Idaho's rural manufactures in USA for rapid product development. The result of the project illustrates that the manufacturers adopting such technologies can enhance their capability to bring products to the marketplace more rapidly and with greater success.

Fig. 2. A multi-material bicycle prototype fabricated by Connex500™ multi-material 3D printing system (Object, 2011b)

Multi-material layered manufacturing (MMLM), which evolves from the LM technology, refers to a process of fabricating a prototype or an assembly product consisting of more than one component material from CAD models with material information, layer by layer. Due to the additive characteristics of LM processes, multiple materials can be selectively deposited on the related slice contours.

Object (2011a) created a Connex500™ multi-material 3D printing system that jets multiple model materials simultaneously to fabricate multi-material parts or assemblies with different mechanical or physical properties, all in a single build. Figure 2 shows a printed multi-material bicycle prototype (Object, 2011b).

2.2 Virtual prototyping

VP is an innovative and powerful virtual simulation tool for facilitating rapid product development (Kerttula and Tokkonen, 2001; Mujber et al., 2004), and it has been successfully used in ship-building and car industries (Kim et al., 2002; Wöhlke and Schiller, 2005).

It is a process of using virtual or digital prototypes and simulation techniques, often in a VR environment with innovative input and 3D stereoscopic output, to evaluate and improve a product design and to facilitate validation of its planning and manufacturing processes (Bochenek and Ragusa, 1998; Gomes and Zachmann, 1999; Kerttula and Tokkonen, 2001; Mujber et al., 2004; Patel et al., 2006; Weyrich and Drews, 1999).

Through simulations, key factors such as the shape and the manufacturability of a product may be optimised without committing much to prototypes and tooling. Indeed, virtual simulation reduces the need for physical prototypes and hence minimizes tooling cost and material waste, and it allows manufacturers to "get it right the first time" and helps them deliver quality products to market on time and within budget.

However, the current virtual simulation technique, which often adopts either semi- or full-immersive VR, is not without limitations, particularly with respect to the sense of immersion.

Bochenek and Ragusa (1998) pointed out that it is important to appropriately select a VR system for facilitating product design and development processes. They investigated the use of four commercial VR display systems and found that the sense of immersion plays an important role in improving the design review practices, and that a higher sense of immersion will have better improvement.

In general, semi-immersive VR systems (single-screen or desktop-based) are relatively easy to use, affordable, and of good resolution, though their users tend to be susceptible to environmental distractions. On the other hand, full-immersive VR systems (multi-screen or CAVE-based) can generate a relatively higher sense of immersion that facilitates user interaction and collaboration, but they are generally more expensive, of less resolution and poor portability, and needs special space requirements (Fairen et al. 2004; Hoffmann et al. 2006; Mujber et al. 2004). Hence, it is worthwhile to combine the good features of both semi- and full-immersive VR to enhance the versatility and effectiveness of virtual simulation at affordable cost.

Therefore, it is desirable to develop a VP system for evaluation of product designs and digital fabrication of multi-material prototypes either in a semi-immersive environment or in a full-immersive, disturbance-free environment to facilitate rapid product development.

3. The proposed virtual prototyping system

The proposed VP system consists mainly of a suite of software packages to facilitate and simulate various stages of an MMLM process, including colour STL modelling, slicing, topological hierarchy sorting of slice contours for subsequent process planning, multi-toolpath planning and generation, and build-time estimation (Choi & Cheung, 2005a, 2005b, 2006 & 2007). In particular, these packages are integrated with a set of control modules and VR graphics kernels that drive both desktop- and CAVE-based VR platforms to create semi- and full-immersive visualisation of the MMLM process at the user's choice.

With the proposed VP system, designers can fabricate digital multi-material prototypes, in lieu of costly physical ones, to evaluate product designs and visualise the influences of critical process parameters, such as build-direction, layer thickness, and hatch space, on the MMLM process. The resulting digital prototypes can be sent via the Internet to customers to solicit comments, while the process parameters can be used for optimal fabrication of physical prototypes. This approach can considerably reduce the number of costly physical prototypes needed for rapid product development. As a result, the associated manufacturing overheads and product development time can be reduced substantially, because digital prototypes are mostly used and there is no worry about the cost and the quality of physical prototypes.

Using the resulting set of optimal process parameters, physical prototypes of desirable quality can be made quickly and economically for detailed design evaluation. The physical prototypes can also be used as master patterns for making tools needed by conventional manufacturing processes, such as CNC machining, silicon rubber moulding and injection moulding, for mass production of the final products.

Furthermore, the VP system would be particularly useful for small-batch production of customised products, which cannot be produced with conventional processes economically. Recently, LM has been widely explored for direct manufacture of customised products. It is envisaged that when LM becomes viable for direct manufacture of customised products, it will be vital to validate the accuracy and quality of prototypes before committing to physical fabrication. Therefore, the VP system would be a practical simulation tool for rapid product development.

Figure 3 shows the flow of the VP system. Firstly, a product model created by CAD or captured by a CT/MRI scanner or a laser digitiser is converted into STL format, which is the industry de-facto standard. As STL is monochrome or single-material, an in-house package is used to paint STL models, with each colour representing a specific material.

Secondly, a few steps are undertaken to prepare for subsequent simulation of the MMLM process and visualisation of the resulting digital prototypes: (a) slice the colour STL model into a number of layers of a predefined thickness. If the LM machine supports variable layer thickness, the STL model may be sliced with an adaptive slicing algorithm to increase fabrication efficiency. The resultant layer contours and material information are stored in a modified Common Layer Interface (CLI) file; (b) sort the slice contours with a contour sorting algorithm to establish explicit topological hierarchy; (c) based on the hierarchy information, multi-toolpath planning algorithms are used to plan and generate multi-toolpaths by hatching the slice contours with a predefined hatch space. The hatch vectors are stored in the modified CLI file for fabrication of digital prototypes and build-time estimation.

Thirdly, a versatile VR simulation system is used for digital fabrication of multi-material prototypes. It allows users to choose either a desktop- or CAVE-based VR platform to create a semi- or full-immersive virtual environment, respectively, for stereoscopic visualisation and quality analysis of the resulting digital prototypes, with which product designs can be reviewed and improved efficiently.

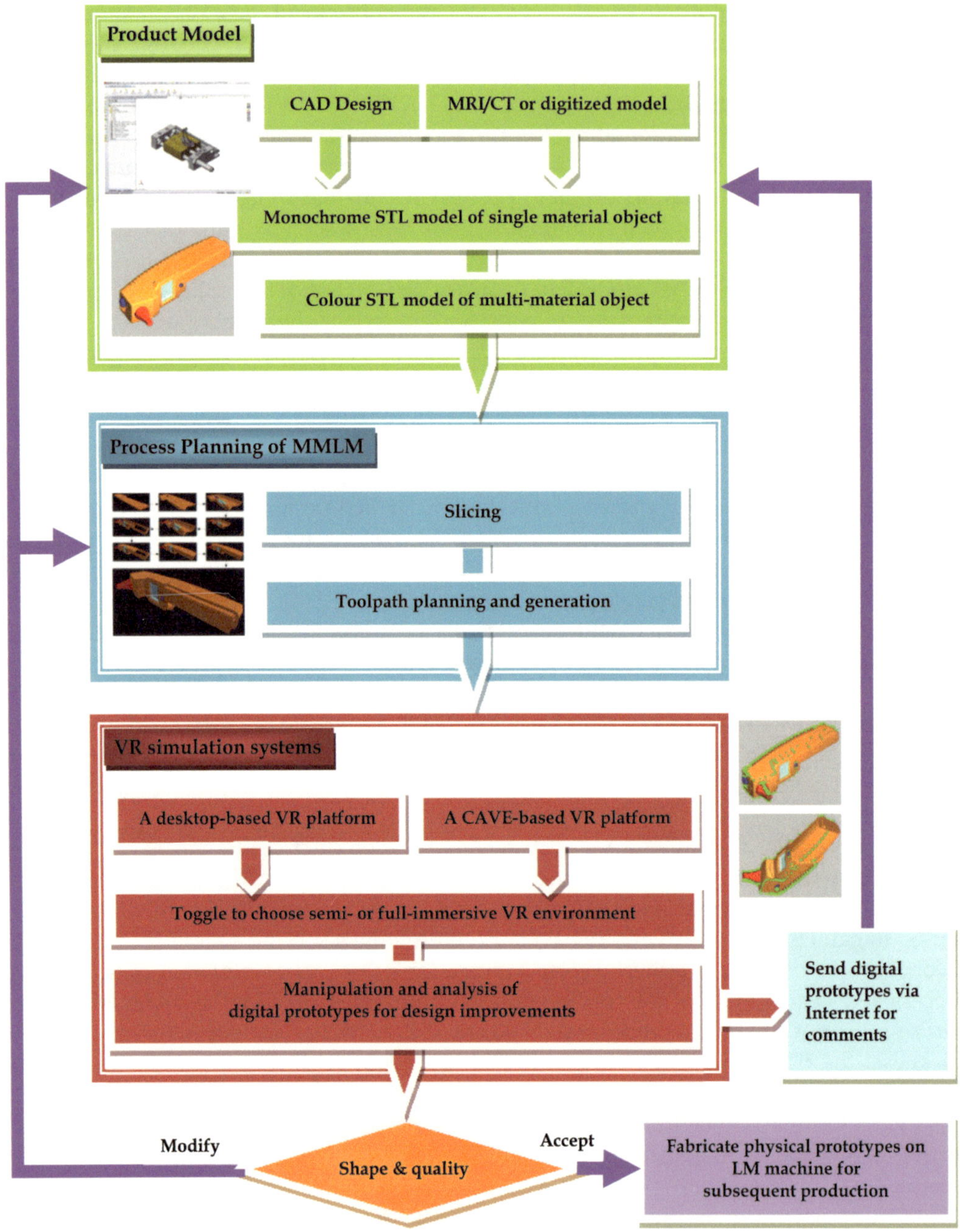

Fig. 3. The flow of the proposed VP system

A suite of algorithms for LM process planning, such as slicing, choice of build-direction, model orientation and layer thickness, generation of sequential and concurrent multi-toolpaths, and build-time estimation, are incorporated in the proposed VP system.
The details of these algorithms have been presented in (Choi & Samavedam, 2001 & 2003; Choi & Chan, 2002; Choi & Kwok, 2002 & 2004; Choi & Cheung, 2005a, 2005b, 2006 & 2007).

This chapter focuses on the development of the VR system. In particular, it addresses the enhancement of versatility and effectiveness of virtual simulation for product design and digital fabrication of multi-material prototypes at affordable cost. The following section describes the desktop- and the CAVE-based VR platforms in detail.

3.1 The desktop-based VR system

The desktop-based VR system consists mainly of a suite of software packages for stereoscopic visualisation of product designs and optimisation of MMLM processes. The software interfaces with commercial desktop-based VR hardware to display a model for stereoscopic visualisation. Using a desktop monitor, which is relatively small but highly portable, a user wears a pair of active shutter glasses that generate stereoscopic feelings by synchronising with the display device to switch on and off the images to the left eye and the right eye alternatively.

This creates a semi-immersive VR environment in which a designer can stereoscopically visualise product designs and perform quality analysis. If a much larger display is needed, a pair of LCD projectors with a large screen as in Figure 4 can be used. The designer wears a pair of oppositely polarised glasses that filter the polarised images for the left eye and the right eye respectively. With this wall-sized screen, a group of designers can participate in stereoscopic visualisation and collaborative review of product designs in the semi-immersive VR environment. This indeed improves exchange of ideas among a design team.

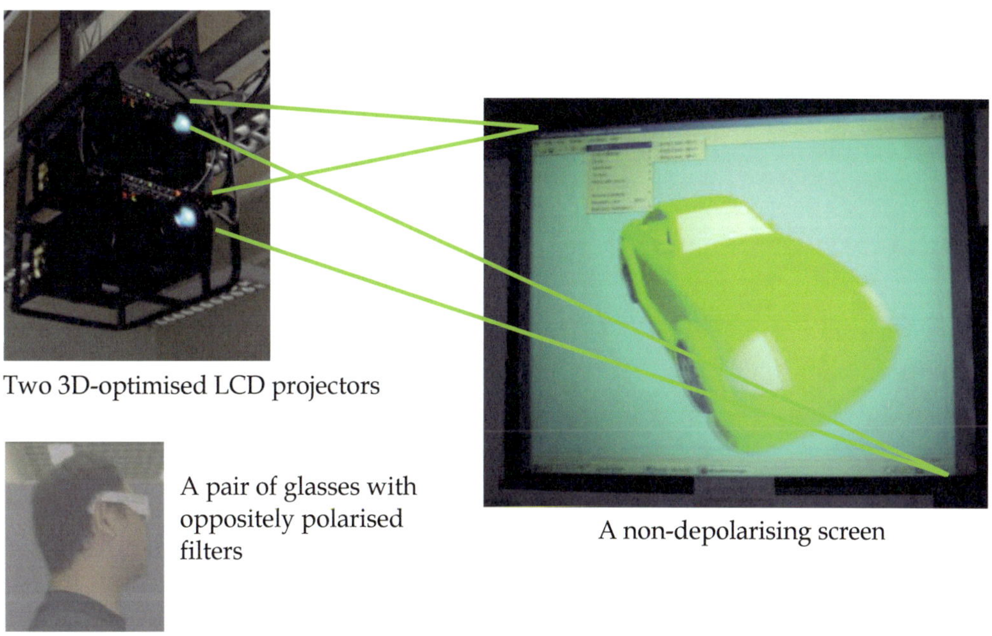

Fig. 4. LCD projectors with a screen for semi-immersive VR display

In addition, the software consists of a Product Viewer module and a Virtual Prototype Fabrication module, based on the WorldToolkit (WTK) graphic libraries, for simulation of MMLM processes.

The Product Viewer module displays a colour product model in a semi-immersive VR environment, in which a small group of designers can work together to study and improve the product design.
The Virtual Prototype Fabrication module can then fabricate digital multi-material prototypes of the product. A dexel-based approach is adopted for digital fabrication of prototypes (Choi & Samavedam, 2001). A dexel is a hatch vector representing the path that a tool has to follow within a contour to build a portion of a layer. By building a volume of a specific height and a width around a dexel, a strip of material is represented. Hence, rectangular solid strips are laid to form a layer, which is subsequently stacked up to form a prototype.
During a digital fabrication process, a designer can observe how a product prototype, such as a toy assembly in figure 5, is fabricated. When it is finished, the resulting digital multi-material prototype can be studied using the utilities provided to visualise the quality of the prototype that the LM machine will subsequently deliver. The designer can navigate around the internal and opaque structures of the prototype to investigate the design. Besides, the colour STL model can be superimposed on its digital prototype for comparison, with the maximum and the average cusp highlighted to indicate the dimensional deviations. A tolerance may be set to highlight locations with deviations beyond the limit. The designer may thus identify and focus on the parts that would need modifications. To improve the accuracy and the surface quality of some specific features of the prototype, the process parameters, such as the build-direction, the model orientation, the layer thickness, and the hatch space, may be tuned accordingly.

Fig. 5. Two perspectives of a toy assembly prototype

After the visualisation process, the colour STL model of the toy assembly is sliced, for example, into 60 layers with a thickness of 3.310 mm, because most current LM machines support only uniform layer thickness during a prototype fabrication process. If the LM machine to be simulated supports variable layer thickness, the model may be instead sliced with an adaptive slicing algorithm. The resulting layer contours are then sorted to establish the topological hierarchy for generation of multi-toolpaths with a hatch space of 0.100mm. Subsequently, the Virtual Prototype Fabrication module fabricates a digital prototype by depositing the rectangular solid strips one by one at an appropriate z-height, as shown in Figure 6.

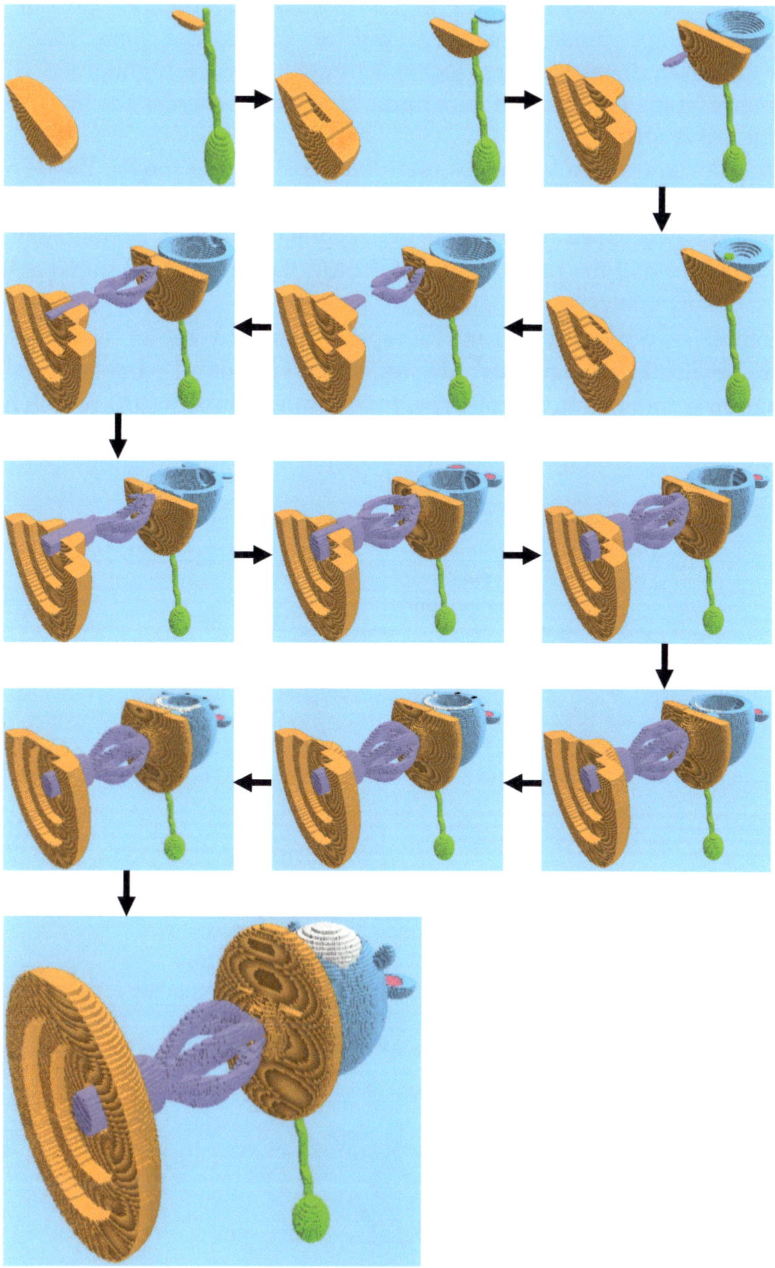

Fig. 6. Digital fabrication of a multi-material toy assembly

The resulting virtual prototype of the toy assembly can be manipulated for visual inspection, as in Figure 7. Furthermore, it can be superimposed on its STL model to highlight the surface texture and the dimensional deviations. The system also calculates the cusp heights to evaluate the overall dimensional deviations. In this example, the average and the maximum cusp heights are 2.001mm and 0.992mm, respectively. Suppose that any deviations more than 1.990mm are considered unacceptable, the designer may choose to highlight the areas which are out of the design limit for subsequent investigation of these critical features. Excessive deviations are highlighted with red or green pins. The red pins point to the maximum deviations whereas the green ones point to unacceptable deviations.

If unsatisfactory deviations are located at important parts of the model, the designer may choose either to change the model orientation to shift the deviations or to reduce the layer thickness and the hatch space to improve the accuracy. When it is necessary to assess detailed assembly fitness of the various parts of the toy, the parts can be stored as individual STL models for quality analysis and digital fabrication.

Digital fabrication of a prototype can be repeated until a set of acceptable process parameters are obtained. Subsequently, physical prototypes of all parts are produced and assembled to form a complete toy prototype. Furthermore, the physical prototypes can be processed and used as master patterns to make tools for mass production of the product.

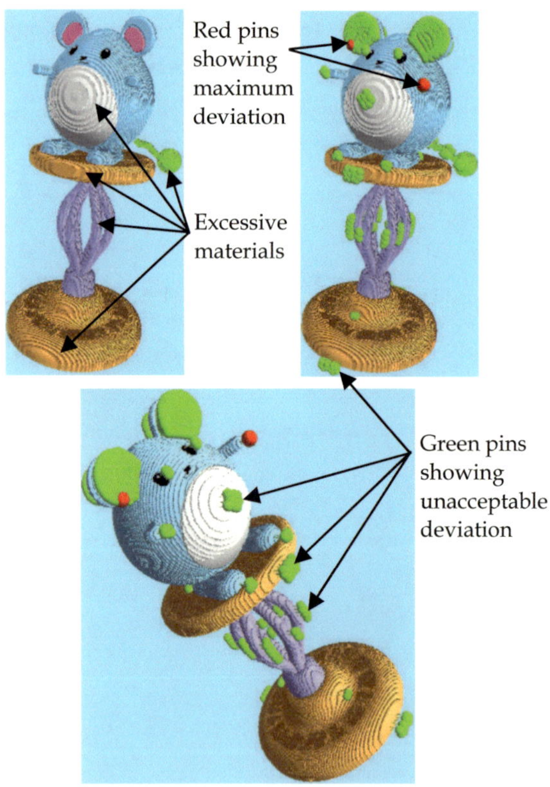

Fig. 7. Superimposition of the toy assembly prototype on its STL model

Therefore, the proposed desktop-based VR system is an easy-to-use and cost-effective tool for visualisation and digital fabrication of multi-material prototypes to facilitate review and improvement of product designs. However, the semi-immersive VR environment may be susceptible to environmental disturbances, diminishing the designers' true feeling and concentration and hence their efficiency in the design process.

To address this problem, the level of immersion is enhanced by integrating the VP system with a CAVE-based VR system with multiple screens to provide a full-immersive virtual environment for vivid stereoscopic visualisation and interaction in a natural way. As such, a design team can fully immerse in exploration, study, and improvement of a product design, including assemblies, sub-assemblies, and components, well before they ever exist physically in reality. Hence, the time and cost of product development can be further reduced.

3.2 The CAVE-based VR platform

The CAVE-based VR platform consists of a cluster of PCs with a cubicle of three walls on a floor. An immersive virtual environment is created by projecting stereoscopic images on three 10ft x 8ft screens on the walls, namely the front, the right, and the left, respectively, and on a 10ft x 10ft screen on the floor. Figure 8a and Figure 8b show respectively the architecture and the physical construction of the PC-based CAVE system, called imseCAVE, in the IMSE Department at the University of Hong Kong.

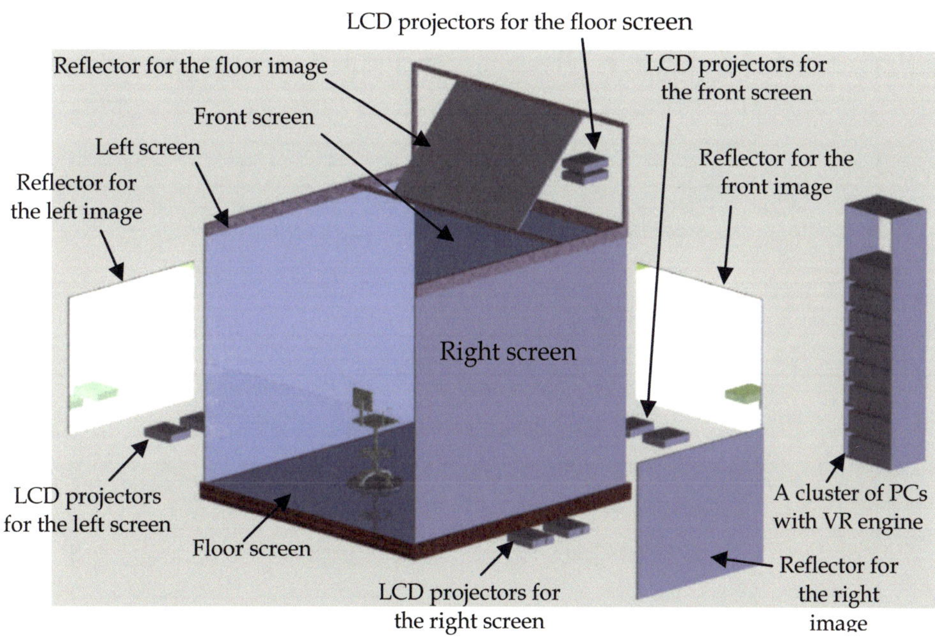

Fig. 8a. The architecture of the imseCAVE

Each projection screen has a reflector and two LCD projectors controlled by two related PCs. The LCD projectors are specially designed with polarising lenses to produce high-resolution stereoscopic images. A VR engine, consisting of a cluster of network PCs, coordinates the projectors to project images on the related screens to create an immersive virtual environment. This configuration forms a relatively low-cost, configurable, and flexible CAVE-based VR system, which can be conveniently integrated to form the proposed versatile VP system to facilitate product development. The hardware is controlled by a software package, which can be separated into three layers, as shown in Figure 9.

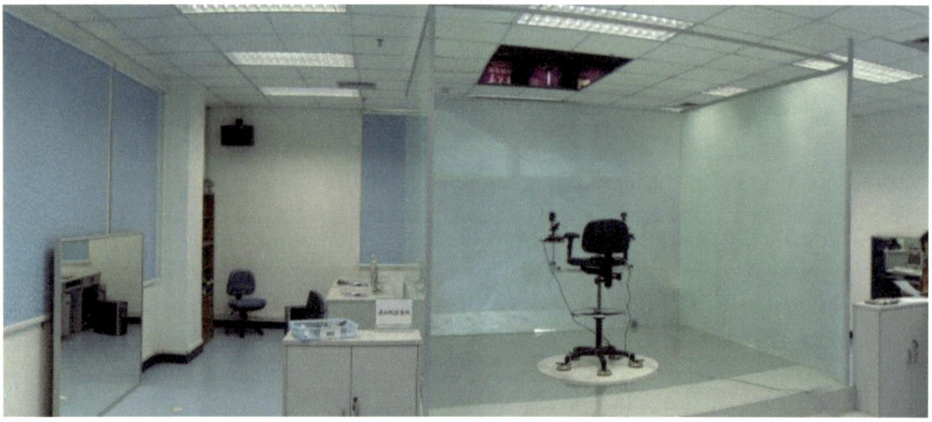

Fig. 8b. Physical construction of the imseCAVE

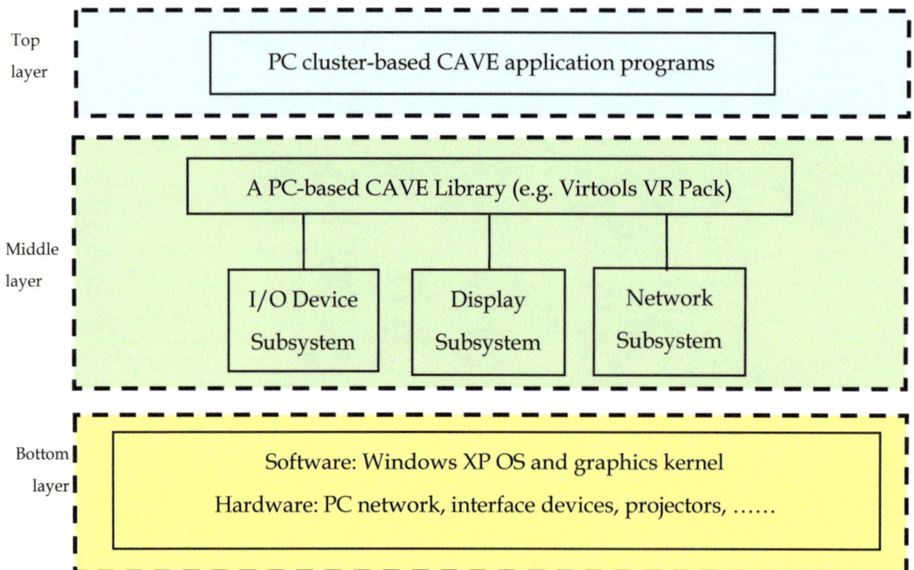

Fig. 9. Software architecture of the PC cluster-based CAVE system

The bottom layer includes basic system software and hardware, such as Windows XP OS and graphics kernel for control of the PC network, interface devices, and projectors.

The middle layer is a PC cluster-based library that coordinates all operations of the CAVE system. It synchronises all the devices to create correct perspective for each screen, keeps track of which screens are in use, and provides the applications with the current states of all the CAVE elements. It consists of three sub-systems: (i) I/O device sub-system for controlling I/O devices; (ii) display subsystem for projecting images on the corresponding screens; and (iii) the network subsystem for keeping communication and synchronisation between all clustering PCs.

The top layer is a package of tailor-made application programs, developed with the PC cluster-based CAVE library, for immersive visualisation and simulation in the CAVE system. This application package is implemented in an object-oriented programming tool, called the Virtools Dev, and its add-on library, called Virtools VR Pack (Virtools, 2006). The Virtools Dev contains a suite of algorithms to help programmers create, visualise, manipulate, and track objects in the virtual environment. Besides, the Virtools VR Pack allows users to tailor applications for producing full-immersive, life experiences using the PC-based distributed computing.

The application package for the PC cluster-based CAVE system contains two modules, namely, Product Viewer and Virtual Fabricator, similar to those for the desk-based system.

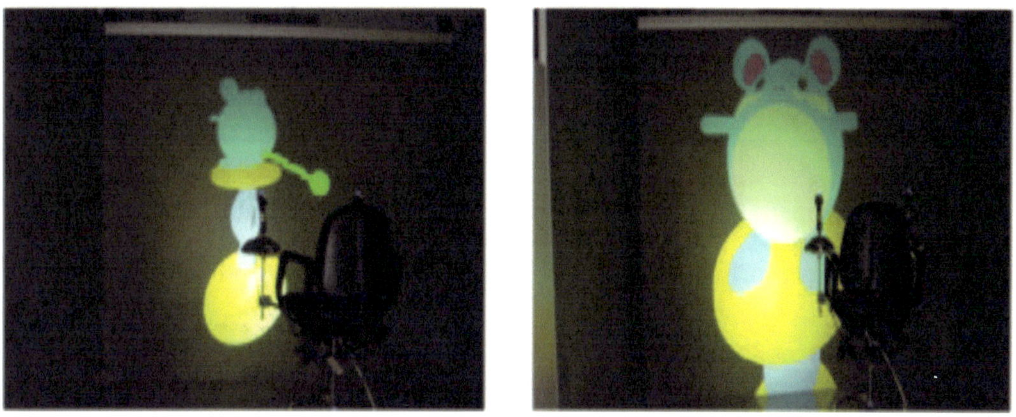

Fig. 10. Study of a toy design in the CAVE VR environment

The Product Viewer displays a virtual product in a CAVE virtual environment, in which users can fully immerse to manipulate and study the design, as in Figure 10. It also facilitates manipulations of a virtual product, including rotation, and scale up/down, toggling visibility/invisibility of a component, using wireless I/O devices, such as a mouse, a keyboard, and a joystick. The designer can hide the external toy body to study the assembly from different perspectives.

In addition, the Virtual Fabricator, similar to that in the desktop-based system, is created with the Virtools Dev for digital fabrication of multi-material prototypes, as in Figure 11. When the fabrication completes, designers can fully immerse in the CAVE virtual environment for stereoscopic visualisation and quality analysis of the resulting multi-material virtual prototype. This full-immersive environment blocks out most disturbances and hence enhances the efficiency of the design review and improvement process.

It can be seen that the PC cluster-based CAVE system above is relatively convenient and flexible, making full-immersive VR a versatile and affordable tool for small-and-medium sized companies to develop products.

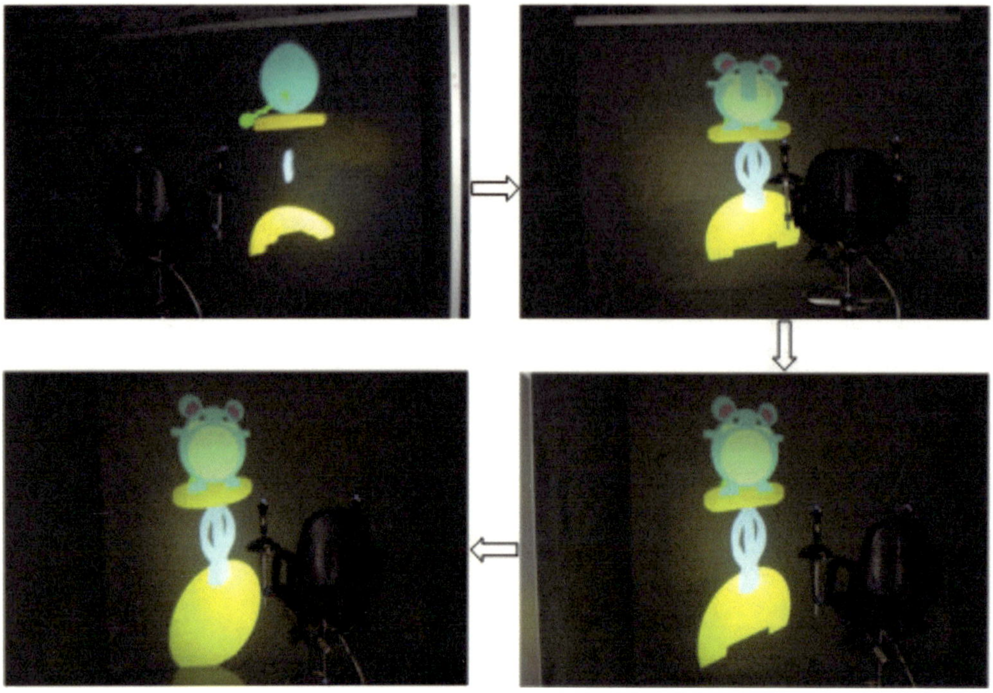

Fig. 11. Digital fabrication of a multi-material toy assembly in a CAVE VR environment

4. Case studies

4.1 A thermometer casing

Figure 12 shows an infrared thermometer commonly fabricated by a manufacturer in Hong Kong. Such products have become very popular as a result of heightened awareness of personal hygiene due to recent outbreaks of infectious diseases. The thermometer is assembled with several components of different materials. Using the MMVP system, multi-toolpaths can be efficiently planned to fabricate a digital prototype of the thermometer casing. Subsequently, the prototype quality can be evaluated by stereoscopic visualisation and superimposition of the prototype on its STL model.

Figure 13 shows the complete multi-material digital prototype, while Figure 14a superimposes it on the STL model for visual analysis. It can be seen that there are excessive materials on the prototype. The overall accuracy of the prototype was evaluated by calculating the average and maximum cusp heights, which are 0.027mm and 0.060mm, respectively. In Figure 14b, green pins and red pins are used to highlight unacceptable deviations exceeding 0.055mm and the maximum deviations, respectively. Therefore, using the MMVP system, the MMLM process may be conveniently iterated with new sets of process parameters without incurring much extra cost. Hence, an optimal combination of process parameters can be obtained for subsequent fabrication of physical prototypes of satisfactory quality.

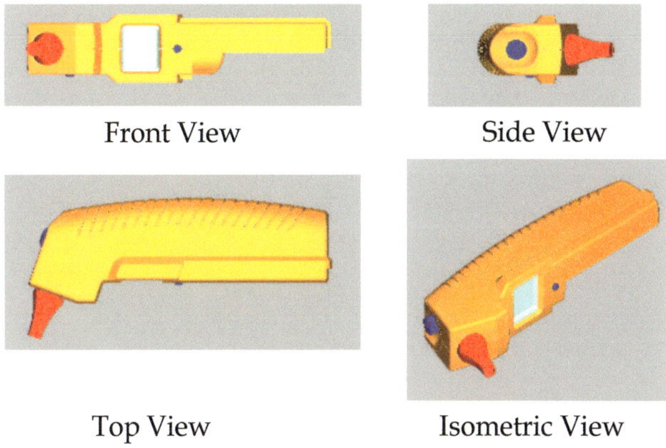

Fig. 12. A colour STL model of an infrared thermometer casing

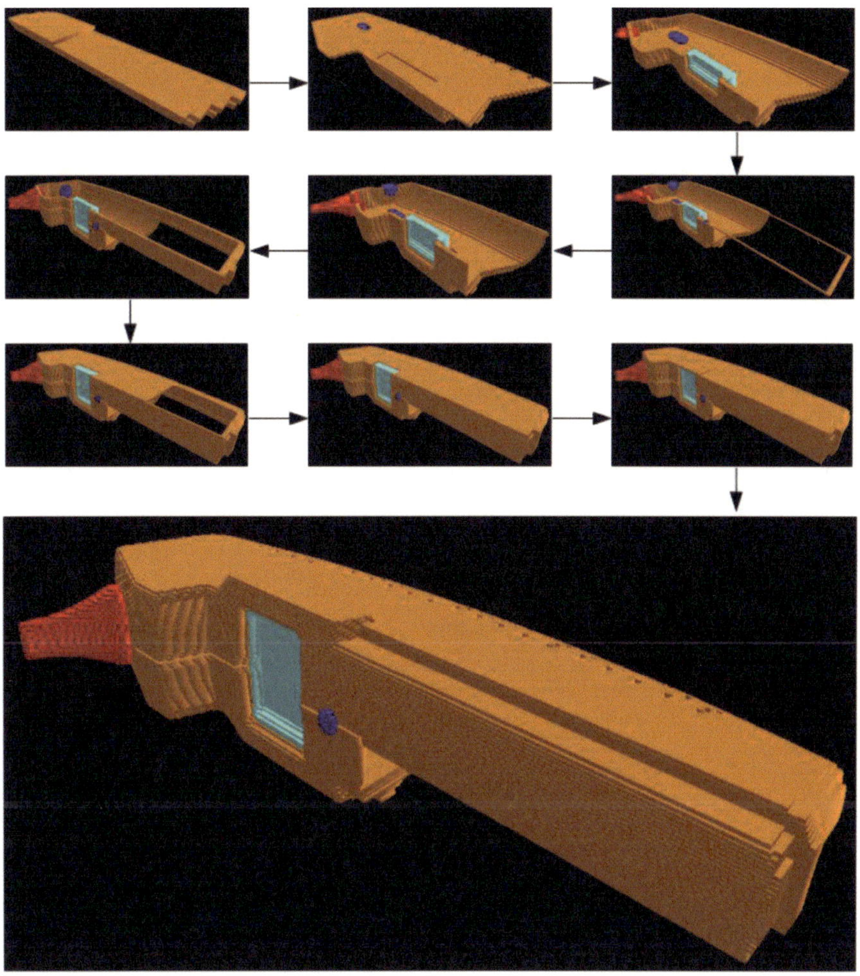

Fig. 13. Digital fabrication of the thermometer casing

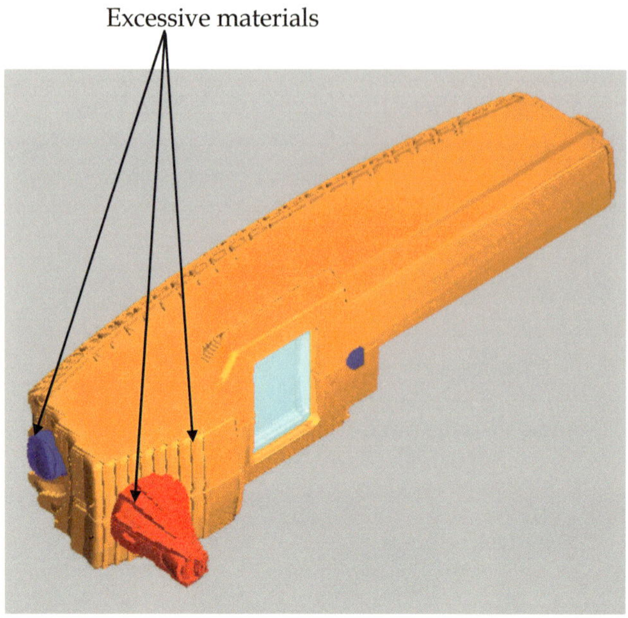

Fig. 14a. Digital multi-material thermometer casing and superimposition on its STL model

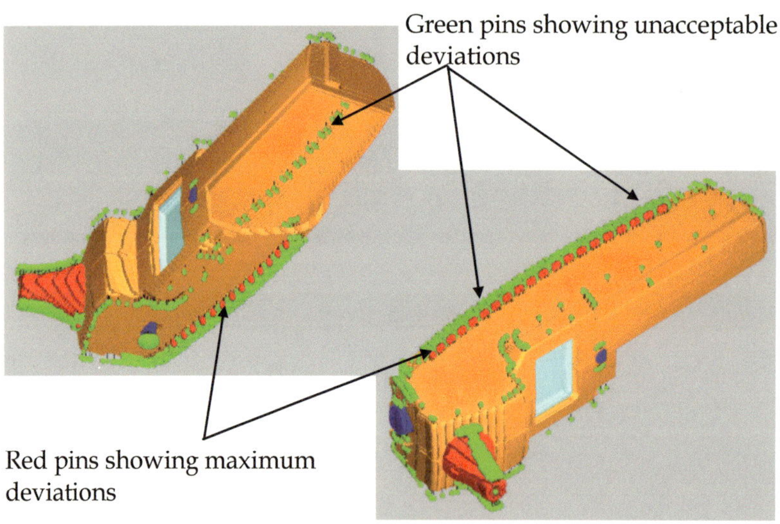

Fig. 14b. Areas of the thermometer casing with dimensional deviation beyond design limits

4.2 A jewellery product – a necklace

Hong Kong is a leading exporter of jewellery products. As such products get more fashion-oriented, innovative designs become more important. Local jewellery manufacturers have realised that they should not only rely on the skills of individual craftsmen. Some have recently adopted LM technology to develop high value-added jewellery items. Hence, the proposed multi-material virtual prototyping system will be particularly useful for building digital multi-material prototypes to help improve designs and shorten development cycles of jewellery products at competitive costs. Designers can view and evaluate their designs with digital prototypes instead of physical ones, at minimal costs and time possible. Furthermore, digital prototypes may be conveniently transmitted over the Internet to facilitate global manufacturing.

Fig. 15. A multi-material necklace

Figure 15 shows an example of a fashion necklace, and the MMVP system is used to produce digital prototypes of such products. Figure 16 shows the digital fabrication process and the complete multi-material digital prototype, which can be stereoscopically visualised for quality analysis, as in Figure 17a. The necklace prototype can also be superimposed on its STL model to highlight the excessive materials, as shown in Figures 17b and 17c. The average and maximum cusp heights of the prototype, which are 0.260mm and 0.554mm, respectively, are calculated for evaluation of the overall accuracy of the prototype. In Figure

17c, green pins and red pins are used to highlight unacceptable deviations exceeding 0.550mm and the maximum deviations, respectively. Therefore, using the MMVP system, the designers can conveniently perform quality analysis and iterate the MMLM processes. Thus, an optimal combination of process parameters such as, the build direction, layer thickness, and hatch space can be obtained for subsequent fabrication of physical prototypes.

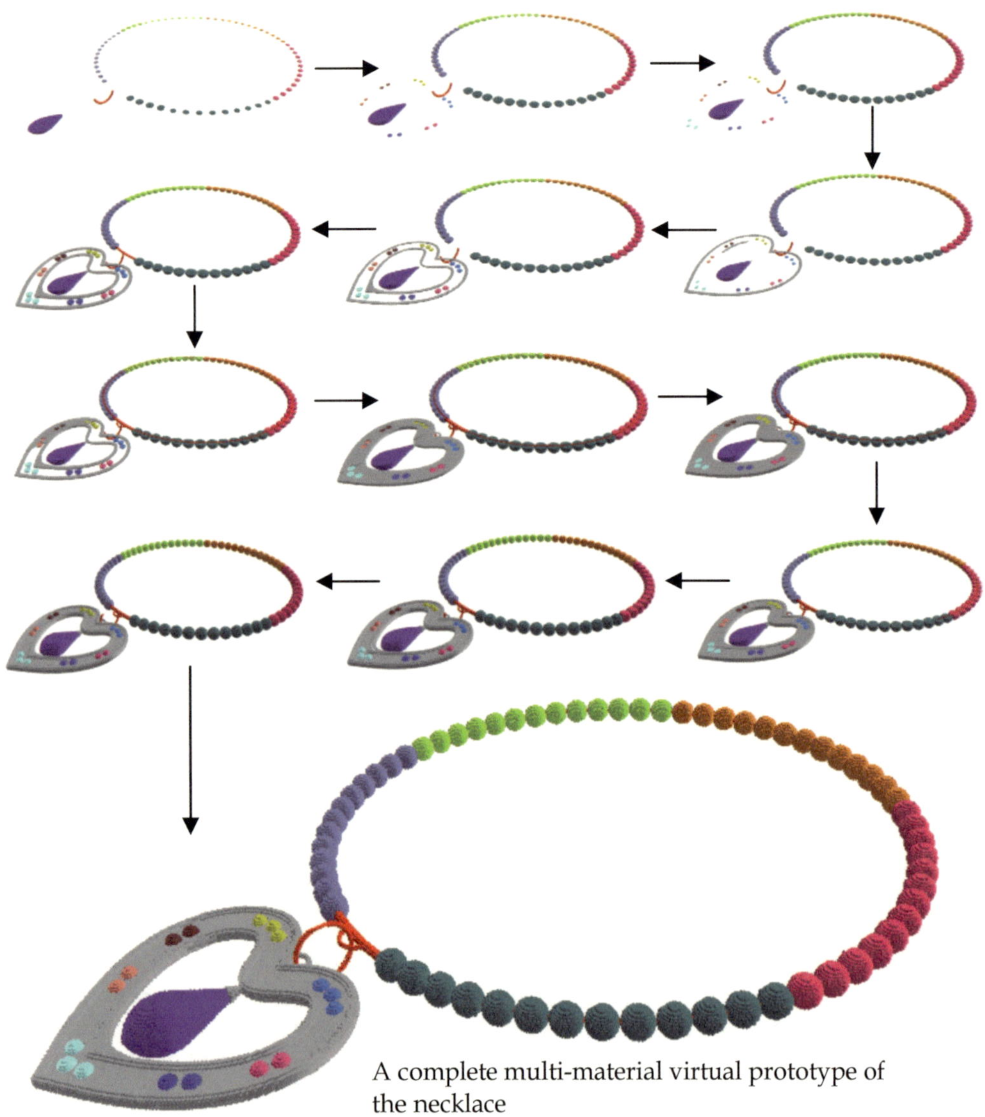

Fig. 16. Digital fabrication process of a multi-material prototype of the necklace

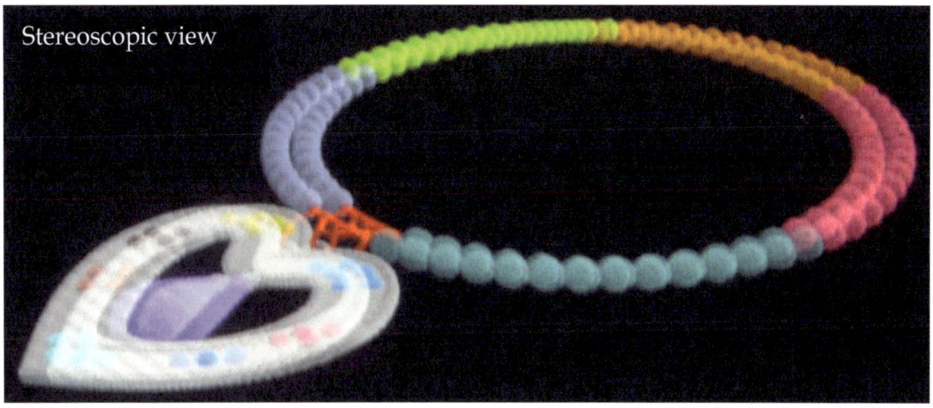

Fig. 17a. Stereoscopic view for visualisation of the necklace prototype

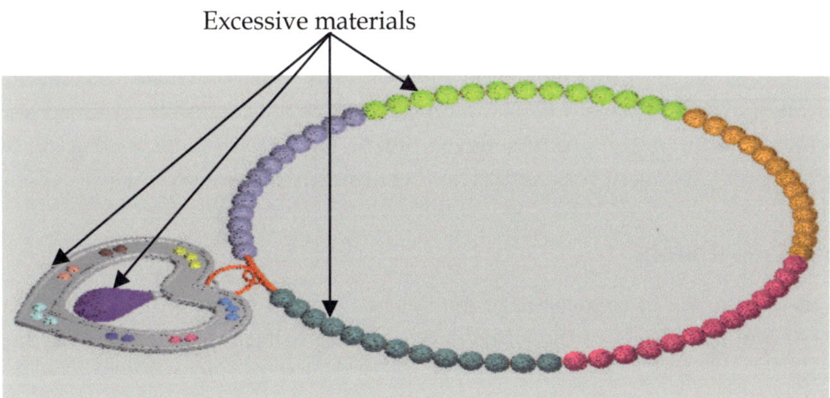

Fig. 17b. Superimposition of the necklace prototype and on its STL model

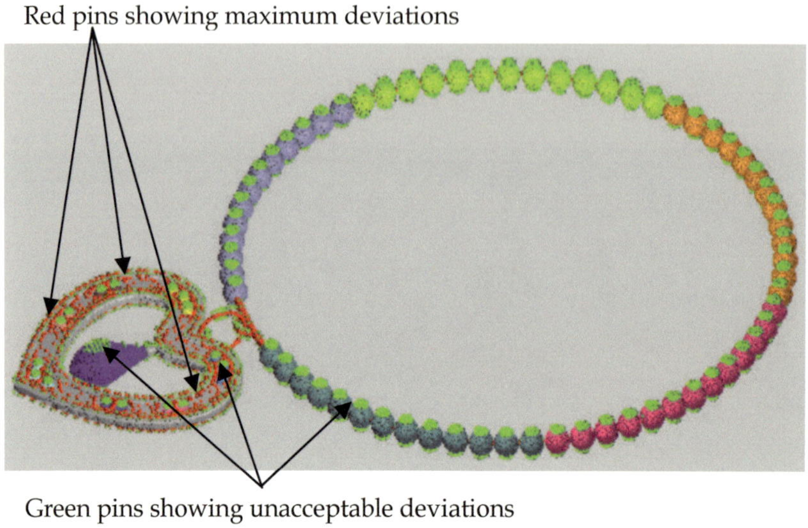

Fig. 17c. Areas of necklace prototype with dimensional deviations beyond design limits

5. Conclusion

This chapter proposes a VP system which integrates the good features of semi- and full-immersive VR to enhance the versatility and effectiveness of virtual simulation for product design and digital fabrication of multi-material prototypes at affordable cost.

The VP system comprises mainly a suite of software packages for simulation of MMLM processes, including multi-toolpath planning, build-time estimation, and accuracy analysis. It can drive a desktop-based VR system with either a monitor or a large non-depolarising screen to generate a semi-immersive VR environment, which is cost-effective, portable, and easy to operate, for review and improvement of product designs. To minimise disturbances and to enhance the level of immersion, the VP system can control a PC cluster-based CAVE system to create a full-immersive VR environment that enhances collaboration and communication of a design team working on product development. It is indeed an effective and versatile tool for rapid product development to meet ever-increasing diversities of customer demands, stringent cost control, and complexity of new products.

6. Acknowledgements

The authors would like to acknowledge the Research Grant Council of the Hong Kong SAR Government and the CRCG of the University of Hong Kong for their financial support for this project.

7. References

Bochenek, G.M. & Ragusa, J.M. (1998). Study results: the use of virtual environments for product design. In: Proceedings of IEEE International Conference on Systems, Man, and Cybernetics, Hyatt Regency La Jolla, San Diego, California, USA, 11-14 October, 1998. p. 250-1253.

Choi, S.H. & Chan, A.M.M. (2002). A dexel-based virtual prototyping system for product development. *Rapid Prototyping Journal*, Vol.8, No.5, 300-314.

Choi, S.H. & Cheung, H.H. (2005a). A multi-material virtual prototyping system. *Computer-Aided Design*, Vol.37, No.1, 123-136.

Choi, S.H. & Cheung, H.H. (2005b). A multi-material virtual prototyping system for product development and biomedical engineering. *Computer-Aided Design and Applications*, Vol.2, No.1-4, 329-338.

Choi, S.H. & Cheung, H.H. (2006). A topological hierarchy-based approach to toolpath planning for multi-material layered manufacturing. *Computer-Aided Design*, Vol.38, No.2, 143-156.

Choi, S.H. & Cheung, H.H. (2007). Multi-material virtual prototyping for product development and biomedical. *Computers In Industry*, Vol.58, No.5, 438-452.

Choi, S.H. & Kwok, K.T. (2002). A tolerant slicing algorithm for layered manufacturing. *Rapid Prototyping Journal*, Vol.8, No.3, 161-179.

Choi, S.H. & Kwok, K.T. (2004). A topological hierarchy-sorting algorithm for layered manufacturing. *Rapid Prototyping Journal*, Vol.10, No.2, 98-113.

Choi, S.H. & Samavedam, S. (2001). Visualisation of rapid prototyping. *Rapid Prototyping Journal*, Vol.7, No.2, 99–114.

Choi, S.H. & Samavedam, S. (2003). Modelling and optimisation of rapid prototyping. *Computers in Industry*, Vol.47, No.1, 39-53.

Gomes de Sá, A. & Zachmann, G. (1999). Virtual reality as a tool for verification of assembly and maintenance processes. *Computers & Graphics*, Vol.23, No.3, 389-403.

Kerttula, M. & Tokkonen, T. (2001). Virtual design of multiengineering electronics systems. *IEEE Computer*, Vol.34, No.11, 71-79.

Kim, H.T., Lee, J.K., Park, J.H., Park, B.J. & Jang, D.S. (2002). Applying digital manufacturing technology to ship production and the maritime environment. *Integrated Manufacturing Systems*, 13(5):295-305.

Lopez, S.M. & Wright, P.K. (2002). The role of rapid prototyping in the product development process: a case study on the ergonomic factors of handheld video games. *Rapid Prototyping Journal*, Vol.8, No.2, 116-125.

Mujber, T.S., Szecsi, T. & Hashmi, M.S.J. (2004). Virtual reality applications in manufacturing process simulation. *Journal of Materials Processing Technology*, 155-156:1834-1838.

Object, (2011a). http://www.objet.com/3D-Printer/Objet_connex500/.

Object, (2011b). http://www.objetblog.com/2011/05/23/objet-to-demonstrate-unique-multi-material-3d-printing-applications-at-rapid/.

Patel, H., Sharples, S., Letourneur, S., Johansson, E., Hoffmann, H., Lorisson, L., Saluaar, D. & Stefani, O. (2006). Practical evaluations of real user company needs for visualization technologies. *International Journal of Human-Computer Studies*, Vol. 64, No.3, 267-279.

Tennyson, S., McCain, G., Hatten, S. & Eggert, R. (2006). Case study: promoting design automation by rural manufacturers. *Rapid Prototyping Journal*, Vol.12, No.5, 304-309.

Virtools, (2006). http://www.virtools.com.

Weyrich, M. & Drews, P. (1999). An interactive environment for virtual manufacturing: the virtual workbench. *Computers in Industry*, Vol.38, No.1, 5-15.

Wöhlke, G. & Schiller, E. (2005). Digital planning validation in automotive industry. *Computers in Industry*, Vol.56, No.4, 393-405.

10

Oriented Multi-Body System Virtual Prototyping Technology for Railway Vehicle

Guofu Ding, Yisheng Zou, Kaiyin Yan and Meiwei Jia
Institute of Advanced Design & Manufacturing, School of Mechanical Engineering, Southwest Jiaotong University, People's Republic of China

1. Introduction

1.1 Railway vehicle virtual prototyping

In recent years, knowledge-based new product competition has become the mainstream of manufacturing competitiveness. As an important way to simulate various problems of complex mechanical systems, virtual prototyping technology is being widely used. It supports concurrent engineering and emphasizes the overall product performance, and strives to simulate the product function and behavior. Based on considering the overall product performance in three-dimensional CAD and its following function modules, virtual prototyping does the innovative design and informs a digital prototyping which do not depends on the physical prototype.

Virtual Prototyping (VP) is a new product design method generated in the recent 20 years. Based on computer simulation, VP embodies not only the product's innovative design but also the product's risk-free digital test, especially suiting for high cost trial production of complex mechanical system development. The main elements of VP are: virtual prototype model - virtual test analysis - virtual prototype evaluation (qualitative and quantitative). VP embodies the global optimization process which is based on computer simulation and aims to get more realistic products. It supports "Top-to-Down" design approach. The main techniques of VP ---- CAX, multi-body system modeling and analysis, simulation, optimization, visualization and VR technology are used to get a digital prototype with optimized performance, thereby the development costs and the reliance on physical prototypes are reduced, product qualities are improved, and time-to-market is accelerated.

Railway vehicle system which belongs to complex mechanical system areas is composed of mechanical, electrical, active control and drive systems (power distributed EMU), and its main part is mechanical systems. The quality of vehicle performances is the key problem of the vehicle product development. Based on the railway vehicle product design, especially the design results of the whole product machine, the performances include: dynamic performance, operational safety, aerodynamics, air-condition, strength and fatigue reliability. Therefore, it is inevitable to research and develop the railway vehicle virtual prototyping for advanced manufacturing technology.

It is also inevitable to research the railway vehicle virtual prototyping technique for the railway transportation equipment, especially for the high-speed, heavy haul train. The past railway vehicle product development mainly takes the following forms:

1. For the research methods, the traditional design embodies the serial, over-reliance on physical prototypes and over-focuses on local optimization of product characteristics, over-emphasizes on the structure itself, less stresses on the whole design features. As the increasing of railway vehicle speeds, these traditional design methods can not meet the performance requirements of high-speed vehicle, so a new performance design concept must be adopted which particularly emphasizes on the overall performance requirements under the high-speed conditions.
2. For the research process, the traditional design methods do not form a complete innovative product development system. Different railway vehicle models were designed by different research institutes, followed by the related performance analysis carried out by other different research units, then they were produced by relevant companies and tested to form the product at last. This has led to no systematicness in the product development process and a serious gap between design, performance analysis, manufacturing and testing. And analysis platforms and analysis models which impact the product performance are different. For example, the structural strength analysis did not use dynamic load spectrum from dynamics study to fatigue strength analysis for key components and structure, and did not consider the impact of railway vehicle movement and structure vibration from the air flow disturbance, and so on. So there are differences between research results and actual operating conditions which lead to railway vehicle running accidents. According to this situation, based on improving the various functional softwares of railway vehicles to establish integrated and intelligent performance design software platform, and form a unified computing methods and standards, combing traditional mechanical design, part strength analysis and product performance analysis in a design analysis platform to do visual design and overall performance design is very urgent.

Improving the speed of railway transport will not only bring issues such as safety, comfort, economy and environmental protection, but also result in a number of major scientific and technological problems. The most typical scientific and technical issues with speed are as follows:

- Air resistance problem - in the dense atmosphere, the aerodynamic drag is the cubic relationship to the rate of growth, so there is a reasonable speed value in terms of the track on the ground. Then, how to break this resistance barrier to further improve the ground speed of rail transport? Under the high-speed conditions, there are serious basic scientific problems to be solved, such as railway vehicle and air-coupled dynamic problem, air compressibility characteristics problem, and so on.
- Running noise problem - the main problem of high-speed railway vehicle is noise. Both the wheel-rail noise and aerodynamic noise need to be explored from the noise generation mechanism to the transmission mechanism. Vibration and noise reduction are the eternal scientific and technical issues.

With the increasing railway vehicle speed, safety, comfort, economy and environmental protection for high-speed railway vehicle are more and more important. Building the virtual prototype high-speed railway vehicle platform will provide strong technical support for researches arising from high speed.

Therefore, based on comprehensive analysis of related research fields, railway vehicle virtual prototype engineering research is carried out; the development and testing platform of railway vehicle virtual prototyping is established. Combined with the existing railway vehicle rolling test experiment bench, a hardware and software platform is formed which can make scheme decision and be easy to deal with three-dimensional CAX / DFX intelligent optimization design, a variety of integrated performance analysis (vehicle dynamics, aerodynamics, strength, fatigue reliability, etc.) and l dynamic running simulation of mutual behaviours. In the end, So it can enhance the innovative design for high-speed railway vehicle to a new level.

1.2 Research status of the railway vehicle virtual prototyping

At present, there are two levels in the virtual prototyping study. The first level is the development and manufacturing of the virtual prototype platform, i.e. the development of various software. There are three software development modes. First is the development of various functional modules software, such as Pro-E, Solidwork, Catia, UG, CAXA, etc; railway vehicle dynamics software: ADAMS/Rail, SIMPACK, NUCARS, VAMPIRE, DADS/Rail, etc; strength and fatigue analysis software: Ideas, ABAQUS, ANSYS, Fatigue, etc; fluid analysis software: FLUENT, StarCD etc; the work mainly depends on software companies to develop. The second is integrating various modeling and analysis software based on PDM, through the interfaces and PDM management (such as using collaborative management platform of Pro-E) to realize the concept of virtual prototyping-based software process, and design the experience and knowledge library, prototype library, model library, physical experimental data and analysis data repository. There has been some work on the re-development of existing software, but the analysis software itself has not been studied. The third level is developing a truly virtual prototyping platform to complete design and analysis in one software that does not need data transmission and conversion which is seamless connectivity. Such as Virtual-Lab from LMS company which co-operates with physical design software of Catia, mergers dynamics software of DADS, is seamlessly connected with ABAQUS, ANSYS (only finite element solver), and finally joins the advantages of fatigue and acoustic computing from LMS's own company to achieve a complete virtual prototype platform.

According to these studies, three main virtual prototyping platforms at present are as follows:

1. Virtual prototype platform architecture research based on simulation framework, mainly for spacecraft.
2. The core is CAX/DFX which is combined with other virtual prototyping platform analysis software, typically for Virtual-Lab from LMS which is a more versatile platform for virtual prototyping.
3. According to the industry needs and the concept of the virtual prototype, various analysis software were integrated based on PDM; some re-developments for acquiring the product solution are done. There are many such systems.

2. Layout of railway vehicle virtual prototyping

2.1 Overall plan

Complying with virtual prototyping technology, railway vehicle virtual prototyping intends to establish a digital development platform for railway vehicle products. According to the railway vehicle characteristics, the following factors should be considered:

1. Establish the railway vehicle product digital model. Based on three-dimensional CAD, establish the innovative design platform for railway vehicle products.

2. Integrate multi-domain prototype model. Based on three-dimensional CAD model, consider basic data of various characteristics of railway vehicle, such as physical information, assembly information, etc.
3. Take into account the integrality of the prototype model. Integrate seamlessly the multi-body dynamics environment and integrated model based on CAD, make dynamic automatic modeling and solving according to the CAD model, and build railway vehicle multi-body system with nonlinear dynamics simulation and computation.
4. Take into account the integrality of the prototype mode. Integrate seamlessly the integrated model and CAE analysis environment; analyze and simulate the structures, fatigue and the reliability performance for railway vehicle; simulate and calculate the model of airflow field and temperature field outside and inside the train.
5. Combine the virtual reality technology and build a virtual prototype test platform. Considering the simulation of human factor and hardware in the loop, the assessment analysis of railway vehicle virtual prototype should be built
6. Build the design platform of key components for railway vehicle, comprehensively evaluate the manufacturability to achieve the aim of railway vehicle virtual prototype based on CAX / DFX and optimize the design of railway vehicle virtual prototype.
7. In accordance with PDM principle, establish the data management platform of the entire system to build the system simulation management platform, and make the system an organic whole.

According to the specific case of railway vehicle virtual prototype, the program of establishing the "railway vehicle virtual prototype research and development platform" is shown in Fig. 2-1. The core part of the whole project should be achieved in high-speed local area network platform which supports concurrent engineering methodology and is composed of high-performance PC. The platform should be the overall situation to solve problems related to the global system. Considering the relationship of various parts of the virtual prototype, it can regulate and coordinate the running of various sub-systems, and share the information and resources to achieve the overall goal of railway vehicle virtual prototype.

Different constrained work is carried out concurrently on the basis of the management platform. There are mainly five major modules according to the product development process: PDM module, product research module, product performance analysis module, product virtual manufacture modules and product running simulation module, as shown in Fig. 2-1.

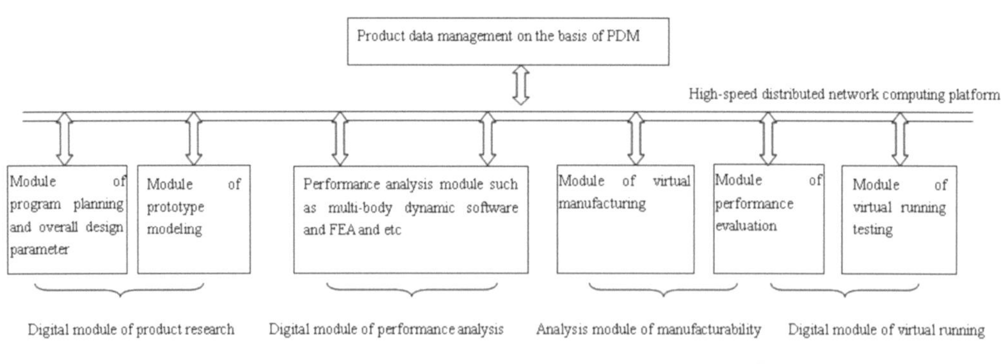

Fig. 2-1. Digitization process of the product research and manufacturing

In accordance with the above ideas, the concept of the platform for railway vehicle virtual prototype is shown in Fig. 2-2. Structure of this part is divided into four main sections:

1. Product digital design and simulation basis system
   This part is composed of distributed network running software and hardware, virtual prototype concurrent design and simulation systems, distributed database servers, clusters computer group and etc.
2. Product innovation design system based on three-dimensional CAD
   Around the mainstream 3D CAD software, a railway vehicle product innovation design platform which includes four major parts is built:
   a. Model design of product digitization
      This model is the basis for subsequent design and analysis. This section includes: product scheme design, design automation, serialization and modularization and optimization design, different model library for railway vehicles;
   b. Product modeling based on physical properties
      Interface the following performance and simulation, establish the interconnected middleware of CAD and CAE platform to achieve the model unity;
   c. Design oriented manufacturing
      This section is mainly designed for cost, assembly, processing techniques and other manufacturing characteristics. Evaluate the economy, manufacturability, assembly ability of products according to a comprehensive perspective to reduce the risk of trial and trial times for the final product optimization services. This section mainly includes: virtual assembly and virtual manufacturing;
   d. Product data management (PDM)
      This part mainly completes the integration management of the design and analysis of manufacturing data from database server.
3. Digital prototyping-oriented performance analysis
   Based on the above product digital description, mainly simulate the function, behavior and running environment of the products: railway vehicle multi-body dynamics analysis, multi-field coupling dynamic analysis and simulation, strength and fatigue reliability analysis of key parts, analysis and simulation of railway vehicle structural vibration noise, simulation of mode, brake and shock response, analysis and simulation of aerodynamics and air noise, co-simulation of multi-field coupling and etc.
4. Railway vehicle running simulation
   Combining with the digital model and various performance analysis results, the mixed digital simulation of the railway vehicle dynamic, which is a multi-domain environment coupled simulation, includes: railway vehicle running simulation and etc based on virtual reality technical.

Those four parts above form a more complete railway vehicle virtual prototype development platform. On this platform, PDM, concurrent simulation tools and platform are the linkage to achieve these functions. Fig. 2-3 is the data flow analysis for railway vehicle virtual prototyping engineering.

The part with thin red line means that exchange data is needed before data processing. From this it can be seen that the three-dimensional model is the entire data center of the system. The key processes of this part are: establish a reasonable railway vehicle database model and the database structure of the whole vehicle model, open the system to all data format; establish the database coordinating relationship between various databases; deal with concurrency control and collaboration issues between various database.

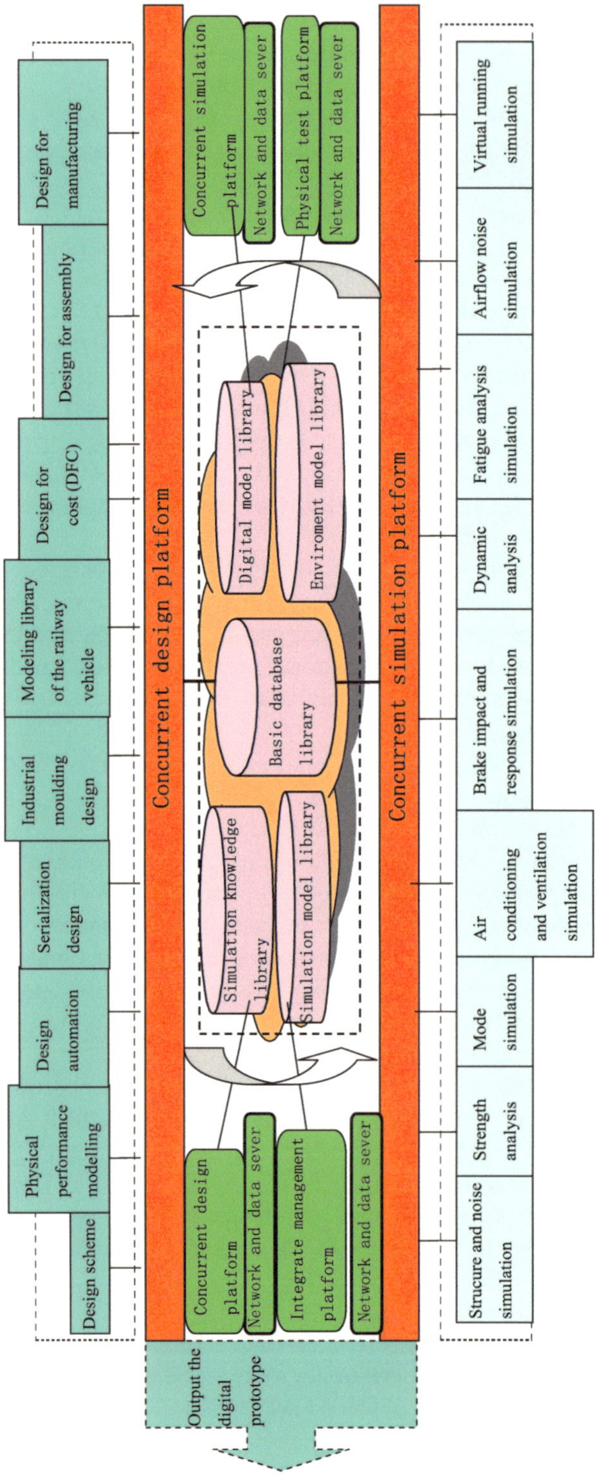

Fig. 2-2. Innovation system of railway vehicle virtual prototype

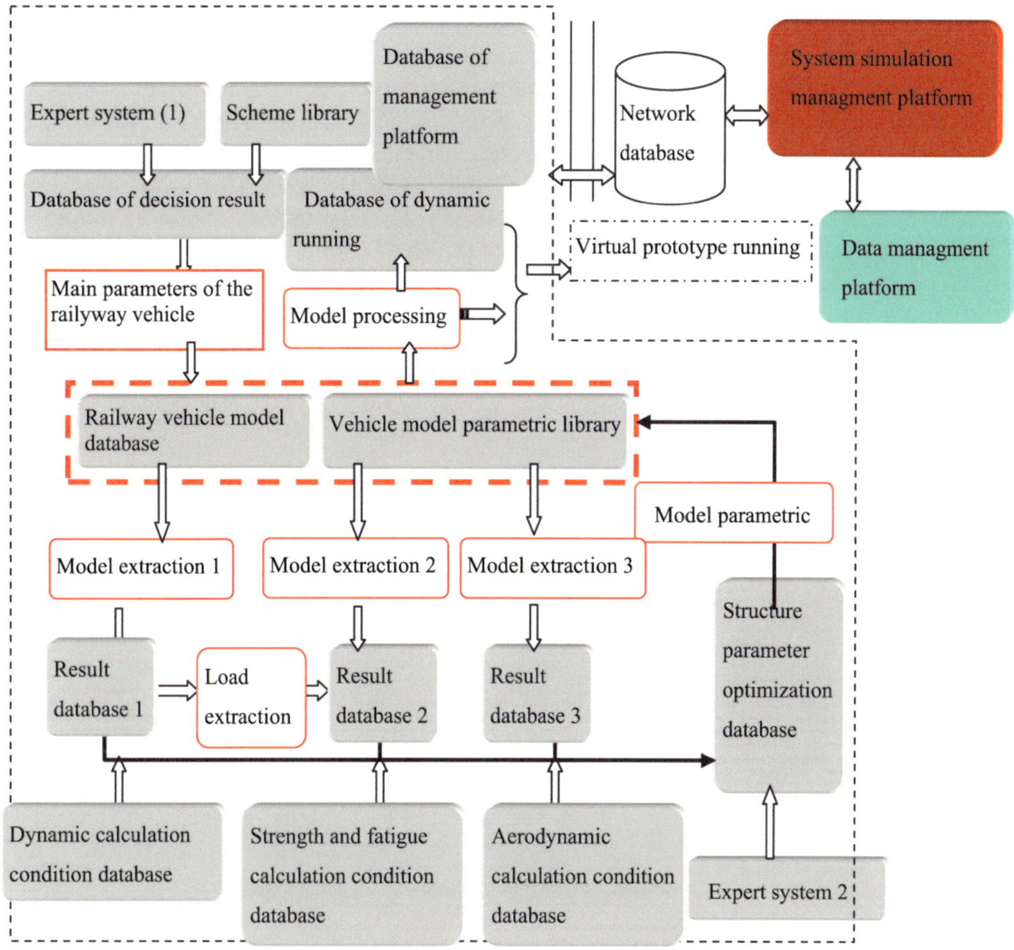

Fig. 2-3. Data flow analysis for railway vehicle virtual prototyping engineering

2.2 Innovative design platform for railway vehicle virtual prototyping

From Fig. 2-4, it can be seen that establishing a reasonable, reliable and adequate information model is the core of the entire system data processing. The model database is a complete virtual prototype model. The work will be done by the product design platform. This section can rely on the function of three-dimensional solid modeling such as CAXA to improve itself, the specific functional requirements are:

1. Have all functions of generating three-dimensional solid model;
2. Generate the physical model and simplified model (simplified according to the requirements of the mechanical model) corresponding with three-dimensional solid model; plan the model according to the actual performance including materials, quality, mass center, surface area, volume, inertia moment, mechanical properties curve function, stiffness, composite calculation of main/sub-section and etc; classify the entities with performance characteristics in accordance with the similar principle.
3. Have the part assembly function, it is design for assembly (DFA) ,and can be combined in accordance with the model tree to generate a separate entity model, so that it has its

own physical property performance, for example: the change of the mass center, surface area, volume, inertia moment, materials composition and etc.

4. Establish constraint models of all kinds of components in accordance with the constraints. It should have the function of kinematics analysis which be able to detect interference, moreover can simulate the deformed elastic components.
5. Have parametric function which has both features and structural parametric characteristic to generate the parts automatically, and can modify the entity parameter manually or automatically according to the optimized result.
6. Geometric model must support the STEP standard and support design for manufacturing (DFM) to expand the virtual manufacturing;
7. Have the management function for all model databases and the whole vehicle database. Each component has a physical (including the simplified model) and geometric model sub-database. All model databases should be opened to all, and should have the function of automatic indexing.
8. All geometric and physical models must support the conversion with kinds of software interface and a strong re-development based on VC interface;

The architecture and data flow of this platform is shown in Fig. 2-4.

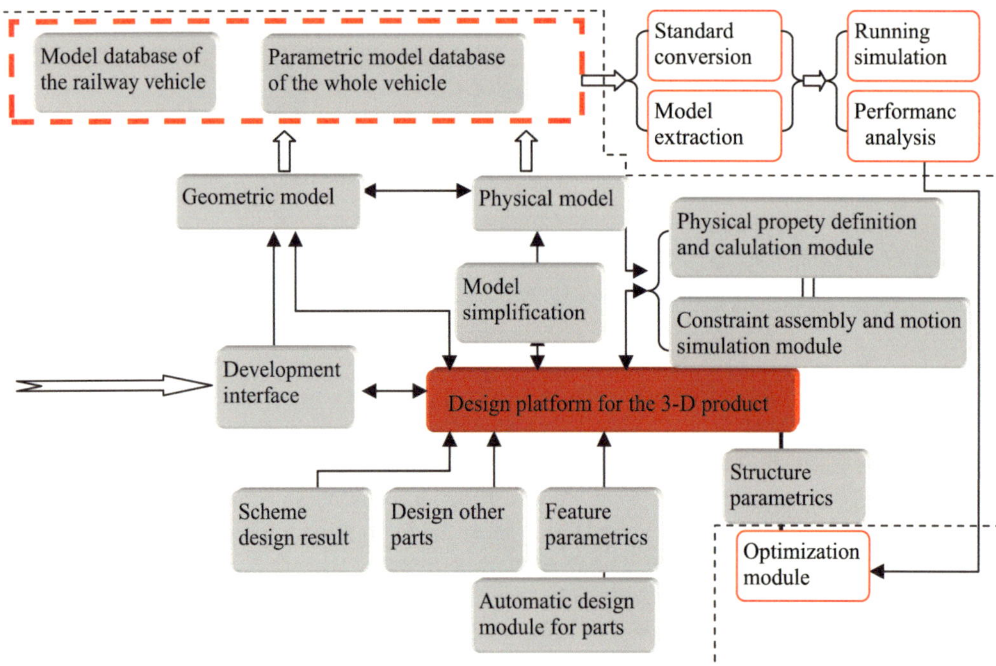

Fig. 2-4. 3-D design platform for railway vehicle oriented virtual prototyping

2.3 Performance analysis platform for railway vehicle virtual prototyping

Railway vehicle performance analysis is mainly composed by dynamics, intensity and fluid analysis, with the core dynamics based on meshing analysis. They are established on the basis of three-dimensional CAD digital model. The main ways to analyze railway vehicle are shown in Fig. 2-5.

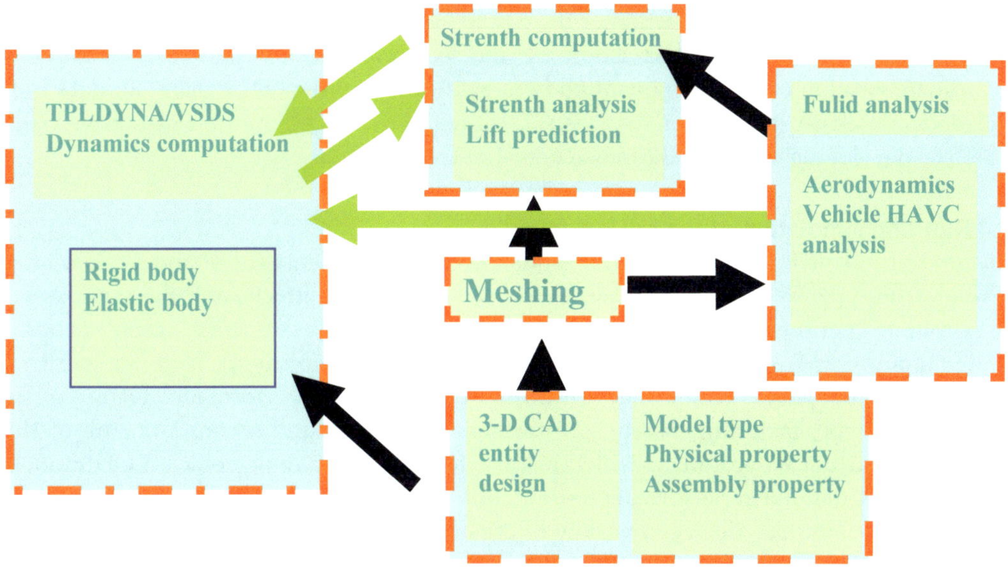

Fig. 2-5. Main ways to analyze railway vehicle

This platform integrates the railway vehicle parametric design and vehicle dynamics computation. Based on the railway vehicle dynamics simulation software, using multi-body system dynamics computation method and model database from entity CAD design, settle the model first, which includes error checking, feature and parameter identification and extraction to form the dynamic computation model. According to the simulation run line conditions, do simulation solution and analyze the three elements(safety, stability, comfortability) of the railway vehicle to obtain the critical instability speed, ride comfort, dynamic wheel-rail forces and other targets. The dynamic load and dynamic stress from simulation can be used for strength and fatigue reliability analysis. Send the result database is transferred to optimization design module to do parameters and structure optimization. The dynamic computational platform for railway vehicle is shown in Fig. 2-6.

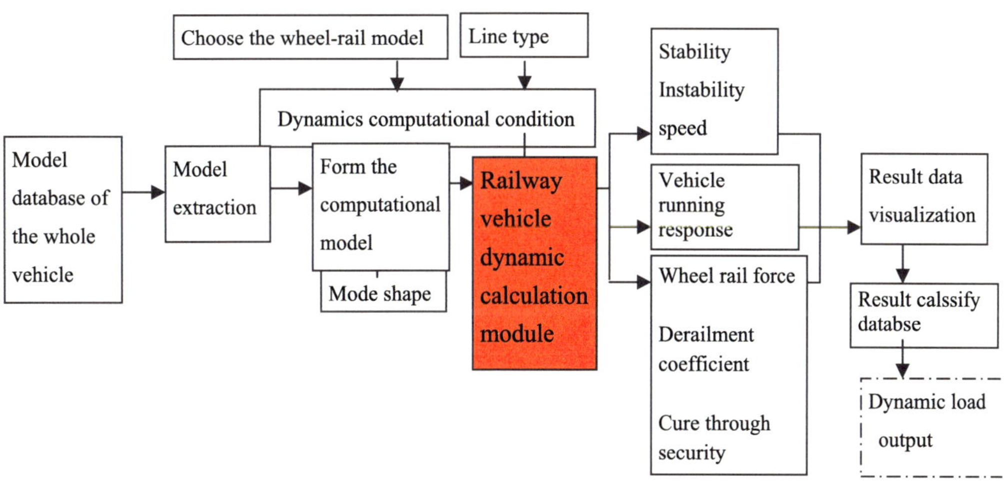

Fig. 2-6. Dynamic computational platform for railway vehicle

The key of this part is the extraction of the whole vehicle model database including entities simplification, combination, extraction of the physical properties, and extraction of coordinate location of the component and etc, with the requirement of using all data from the model database; In addition, data visualization and classification of the results also need interface development. This is the main context of this chapter.

2.4 Running simulation of the railway vehicle

The platform does the final integrated simulation of comprehensive test and evaluation to virtual prototype. Related tools are used to produce various effects, and the main task is to simulate various operating conditions of the vehicle to make clear people's understanding and awareness of the vehicle in the simulation loop. In other words, it means to regard people as an intelligent individual to do all performance testing of the virtual prototype, including: safety, comfortability, stability and so on. The core of this platform is virtual environment which has the following contents: vehicle LOD models, various result data form performance simulation computation, vehicle kinematics model, virtual reality interface device, a variety of effects tools (all kinds of dynamic simulation tools, brake tools, control simulation tools, etc.), virtual scene (bridges, tunnels, rail, the distance light scenes, etc.), control mathematical model, traction model, braking model and etc.

The key of this part is how to integrate these multi-dimensional information as a whole and simulate various properties of the railway vehicle virtual prototype, saving the dynamic test database as a certain prototype database ultimately. Running simulation of the railway vehicle is shown in Fig. 2-9.

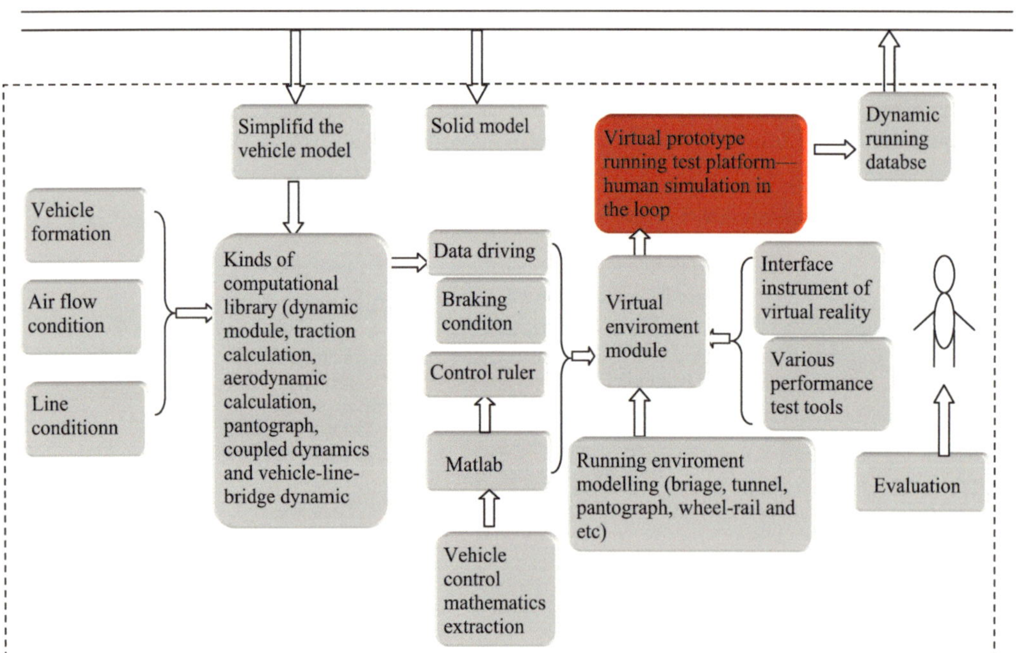

Fig. 2-9. Running simulation of the railway vehicle (virtual test)

3. Design model of the railway vehicle digital prototype-take bogie for an example

In the virtual prototyping, the first is to get the virtual prototype model which must rely on three-dimensional CAD software. How to get the virtual prototype model fast and accurately is the basic part for speeding up product design. According to the parts that can be parameterized, prototype model automated design ideas and methods are proposed. Take the bogie design for an example, this approach is detail studied. The following process of this method is shown in Fig. 2-9.

Around the bogie design automation, its implementation framework is shown in Figure 3-1. In object-oriented development environment, the automatic design of the bogie parts with user-friendly interface is completed, the data management library is established, and the changes and assembly of the bogie vehicle model (mainly for the wheelset and spring components) are implemented. At the same time, the extraction of bogie performance attribute parameters is completed, generated bogie model is saved as sel-definied file automatically, and the bogie component model and corresponding data are reproduced in the file browser. Thus, the data for dynamics calculation platform and finite element analysis platform are subsequently provided.

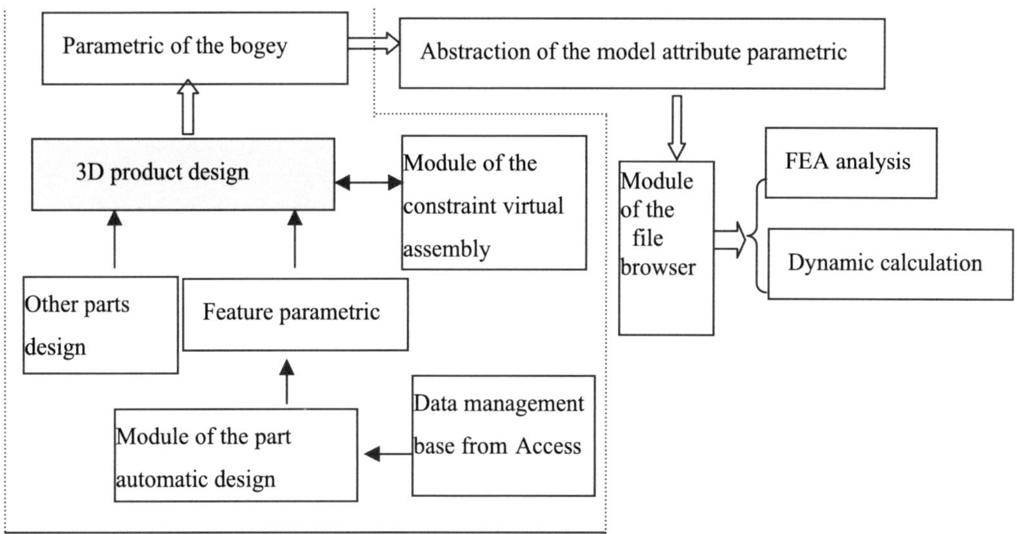

Fig. 3-1. Structure graph of the system framework

Since there are many parts in the bogey, the secondary stiff spring is taken here for an example. First, the basic design flow is obtained according to the design requirement. According to the design results, based on the technical support of COM component interface, API, CAD environment and database under three-dimensional CAD re-development environment, drive 3D rendering engine and draw out different specification three-dimensional model of the secondary stiffness spring to get the virtual model. The design results are shown in Fig. 3-2.

With the same process, other parts of the bogie can also be designed. 3-D figure of the wheelset and wheel axle which was obtained from automatic design is shown in Fig. 3-3 and 3-4.

The automatic assembly process of the bogie is shown in Fig.3-5 (some small parts omitted). Through this automatic process, it only takes less than one minute to complete bogie assembly in SolidWorks. With the parameters of the previous parts, a different type of bogie can be designed easily which speeds up the design rate and efficiency.

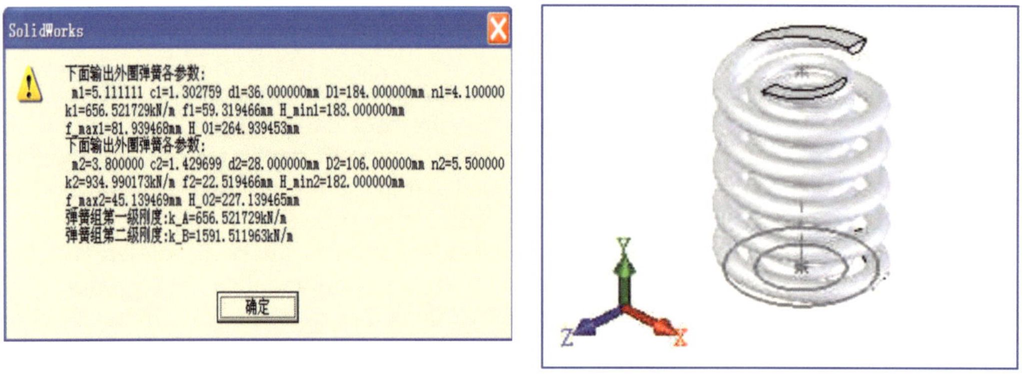

Fig. 3-2. Design automation of the secondary stiffness spring

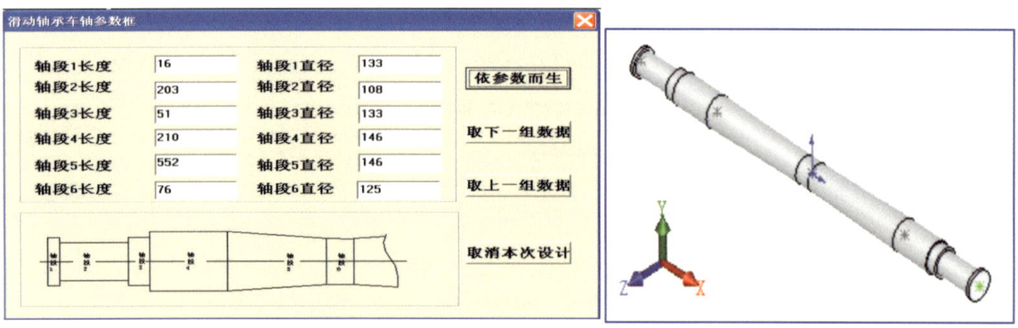

Fig. 3-3. Design automation of the axle

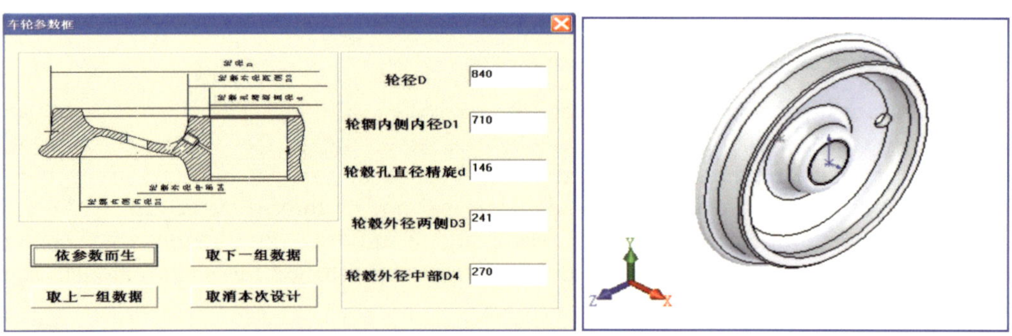

Fig. 3-4. Design automation of the wheelset

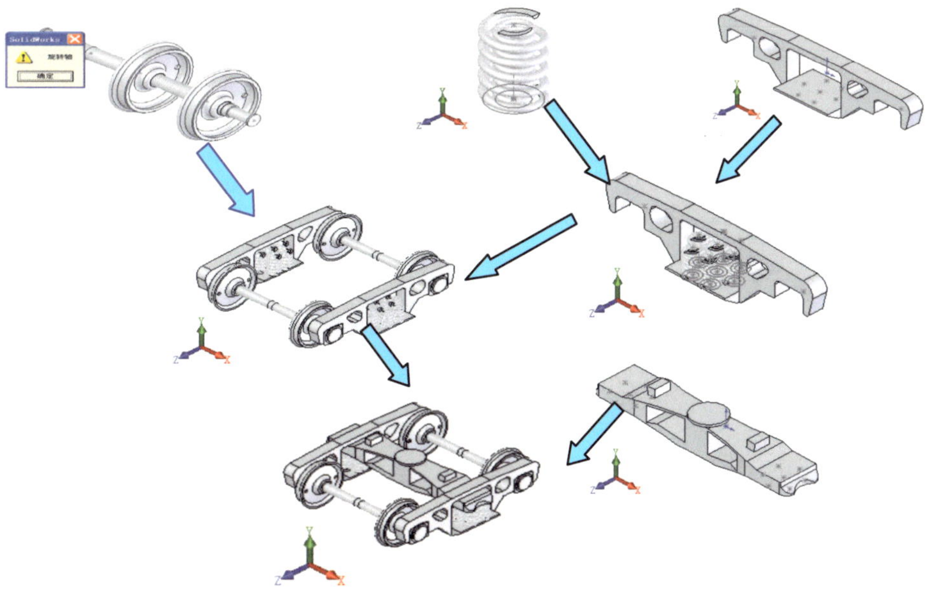

Fig. 3-5. Automatic assembly process of the bogie

4. Performance extraction of railway vehicle digital prototype oriented multi-body system

4.1 Method

Existed CAD software has been able to get a very complete product configuration and can get the relationship between the product and components in its design space, but it is mainly designed for manufacturing. Therefore, functionality and output data provided by CAD rarely faces to the subsequent performance analysis which has been confirmed in the analysis of many product cases. In the subsequent product performance analysis which includes multi-body dynamic analysis, strength and reliability analysis and other performance analysis, CAD still only provides a preliminary physical model which can not get its own performance properties from the entity itself. So the attribute data of product components need to be obtained by physical experiment. The difficulties of data collection, the investment of testing equipment and the cost of product development are enlarged. Moreover, with the perspective of practical effect, in the following process of passing the performance analysis function, due to precision, algorithm, solving model and other reasons, CAD models will lose some information that may lead to too much human intervention and waste a lot of human and material resources. Even a small mistake can result in the fact that the prototype analysis can not keep going normally. So, a lot of virtual prototype analysis at present still do their own studies. CAD is only responsible for the design. The model is re-modeled after being simplified according to the product function in dynamic analysis. The model is carried out according to the initial design scheme in finite element analysis. So these lead to serious gap between analysis software and CAD, also lead to no unification of the analytical results from different analysis software. Enterprise even does not know which algorithm is correct, so they still choose the conservative design approach such as raising the safety factor and so on. This makes people misunderstand the virtual prototyping technology.

The real reason for this misunderstanding is only considering the geometric modeling in the CAD, but not considering modeling of product components and the full machine. By putting the extraction of the product model's performance data in performance analysis module artificially, the integrity of the CAD model itself is ignored. In fact, the product CAD model provides geometric model and physical properties of the products and components simultaneously, so the physical properties should be modeled in CAD and property definition should be considered in CAD design to provide a complete integrated model for the following performance analysis which will unify the model. These two ideas are summarized in Fig. 4-1.

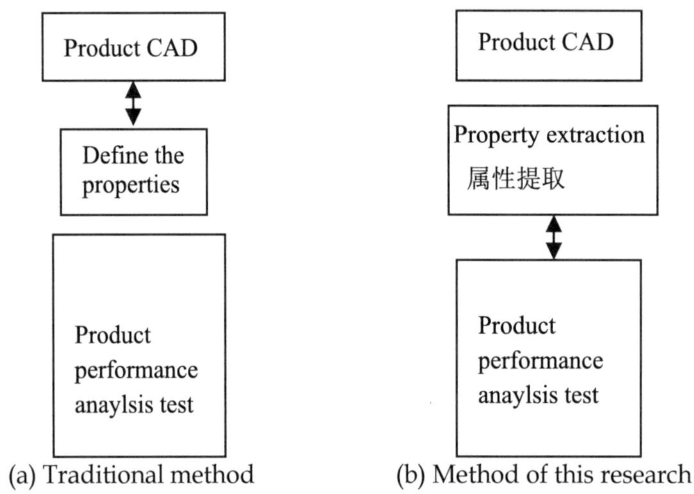

Fig. 4-1. Two different methods to definite the property

The proposed method provides an abstraction layer between CAD and prototype performance analysis in order to obtain a satisfactory virtual prototype model.

4.2 The requirements of virtual prototype model for product performance analysis under multi-body system

The ultimate virtual prototype not only depends on the completeness of the design, but also depends on the correctness of prototype analysis, which will replace the product physical prototypes to achieve product performance analysis, testing and evaluation. For mechanical system virtual prototyping, the main performance analysis tools are: strength analysis, life prediction, multi-body dynamics, fluid analysis (gas, fluid dynamics) and so on.

The basic data of the analysis are from the three-dimensional CAD design itself. Take multi-body systems analysis for example, the following performance data should be provided by the system:

For rigid body: identification number, quality, geometry shape, mass center, moment of inertia, location coordinates, position coordinates, degree of freedom, material density, etc.

For kinematic pair: identity, type, location of hinge points and associated two rigid, position coordinates of the hinge point, location coordinates of the hinge point, the number of degrees of freedom. In general, kinematic set are: rotating set, sliding set, planar joint, cylindric pair, cardan joint, spherical pair, gear pair, etc.

For the elastic body: identification number, quality, geometry shape, mass center, moment of inertia, location coordinates, freedom, material density, modulus of elasticity, mode, damping, etc.
For element force: serial number, coordinate position which connects two rigid bodies (location of the up and down points), physical definition of the force element type (stiffness, damping, friction and other characteristics).
The data are given by their own characteristics of the product components such as quality, geometry shape, mass, inertia, density, modulus of elasticity, stiffness, damping, etc. Some are obtained from product assembly relationship and space movement characteristics such as: position, location, connection relationship of hinge and multi-body, position coordinates. Many of these properties can be extracted from the CAD model, but all current CAD systems do not provide this function. So the building of an abstraction layer between CAD and prototype performance analysis is proposed to obtain a satisfactory virtual prototype model as shown in Fig. 3-6.
In theory, the second defined data is directly from the CAD design model. It should be more accurate and more reasonable, but the difficulty of CAD may increase. If taken as a separate function layer designed by design and analysis staff, this difficulty can be simplified. In the first approach, manufacturing are mainly considered after the CAD model is designed, without considering the definition of products and component attributes. Most are obtained by analyzing the functions supplied by analysis tests tools to do re-modeling.

4.3 Virtual prototype performance design solutions based on CAD

From Fig. 4-1 (b), in order to achieve the aim of extraction from CAD directly or attributes definition, higher requirements are needed on CAD functions. However, the current CAD can not meet this requirement obviously, so its function should be extended. For a variety of CAD software, they have re-development functions, such as ToolKit of Pro-E, SDK API (Application Programming Interface) of SolidWork, SDK (Software Development Kit) of CAXA. This study is based on three-dimensional CAD of CAXA.
Prototyping can be obtained from three-dimensional solid model design, Extend Data Object (EDO), internal and extended Catalogs (a pixel classification function of CAXA software) and the second development. The model attribute definitions can be defined through an external interface or SDK development of CAXA platform to obtain an extended IGES file. The so-called extensible IGES files are to keep the original model data interface and format unchanged, increase the special format data in the end of the file system which is mainly used to define the properties of the model data. This file can interface the common application software and can be used for the system which has both specialization and generality. Therefore, the obtained data are data blocks based on IGES that can describe model properties. Those data blocks form the whole data model are for the platform.
Obviously, the prototype model is actually a combination of a space abstracted physical prototype and the entity model. Entity model is obtained from the CAD design and attached to the physically abstracted model. The abstracted model not only defines the properties of the product components, but also maps to the graph-like model structure according to their functions and relationships, reducing the functionality according to the follow-up requirement. In order to overcome the model data consistency, several key issues must be solved, and they are: define and extract the data directly in the solid

model, mesh finite element in the solid model automatically in accordance with the requirements of FEA, extract model directly to do visualization of functional analysis subsequently and so on. The relationship of the model and performance analysis based on CAXA is shown in Fig. 4-2.

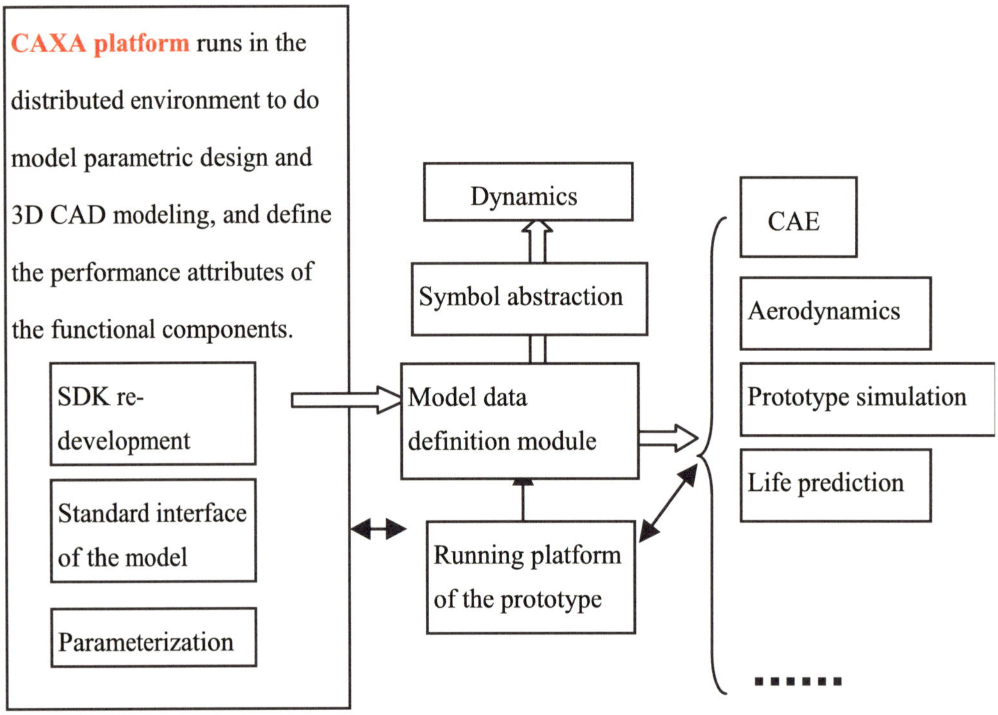

Fig. 4-2. Relationship of the model and performance analysis based on CAXA

Property definition for the performance analysis can be achieved by several re-developments such as EDO, API, Catalog and so on.

4.4 Extraction of the virtual prototype performance attribute based on CAXA

Railway vehicle system is a typical complex mechanical system. in the view of multi-body dynamics, this system is a complex system which interacts with a multi-body system. It can be simplified as: rigid body (soft body), hinge, force element, force, and etc. It can be defined as following:

1. Relative to the suspension system, the stiffness of the car, bogie, wheelset and other qualities is much great, so they can be defined as rigid body without considering their flexibility.
2. Define the suspension as force element;
3. Define the force and force couple of the rigid body as the external force.

For the body in the mechanical systems virtual prototyping, the most important is to describe its geometric and physical relationship in space. The architecture process of the performance and attributes obtained system for the entire multi-body system is shown in Fig. 4-6.

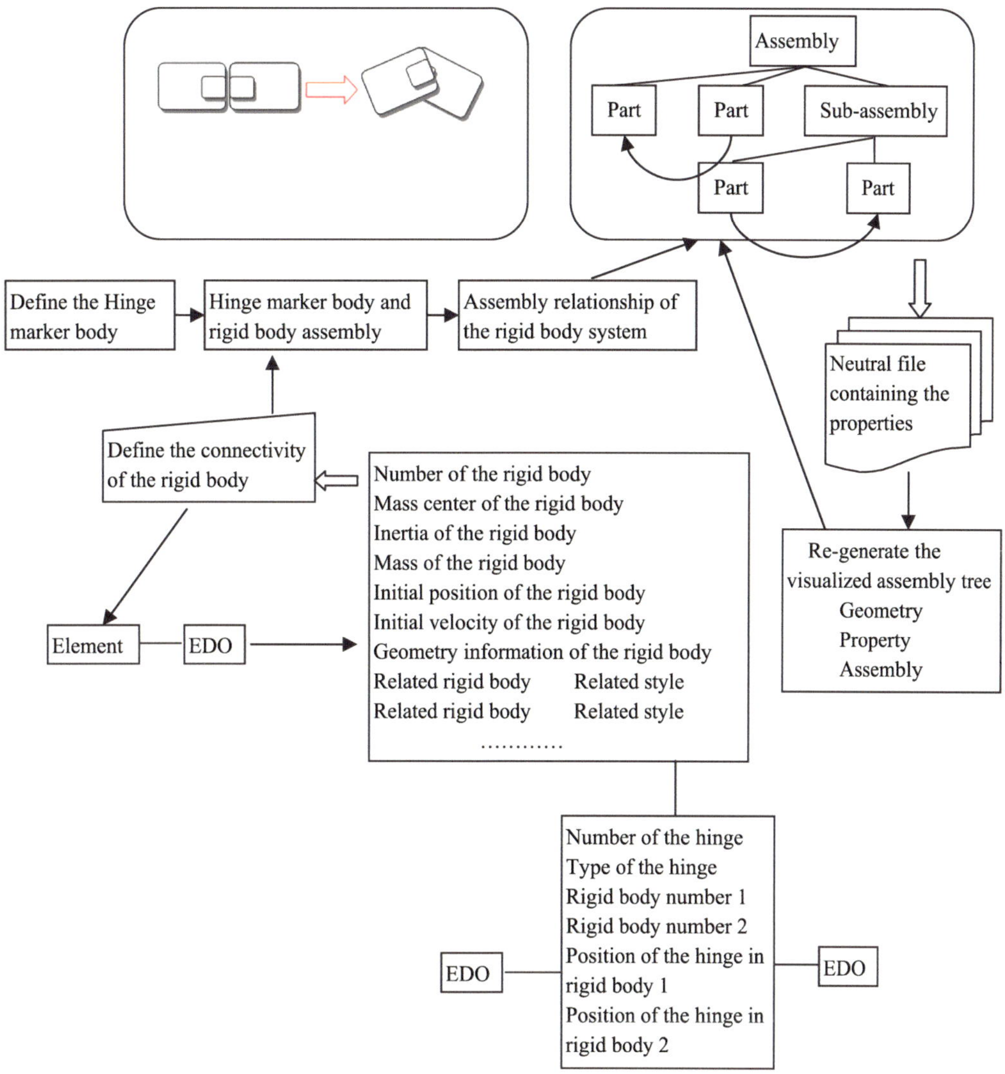

Fig. 4-6. Property extraction of the multi-body system based on CAXA

In the extracted process, coordinate transformation of design space, assembly space and feature space of the part is used in CAXA. Various properties of abstract defined bodies based on the geometric topological core are obtained. For unabstracted properties, the rich re-development interface function is used for extension, more suitable methods are: EDO, Catalog, AttributeSet, embedded database and etc.

Once the model is defined and extracted, the virtual prototype based on CAD with unified regulations and property definition can be obtained, and pass to the performance analysis module.

Physical abstracted model corresponds with entity model through the marker and serial number. It strictly reflects the space topology construct relationship between various bodies. Their mapping forms an integrated digital model which has CAD features and physical features of product components to the following performance analysis.

Property extraction in CAXA is shown in Fig. 4-8.

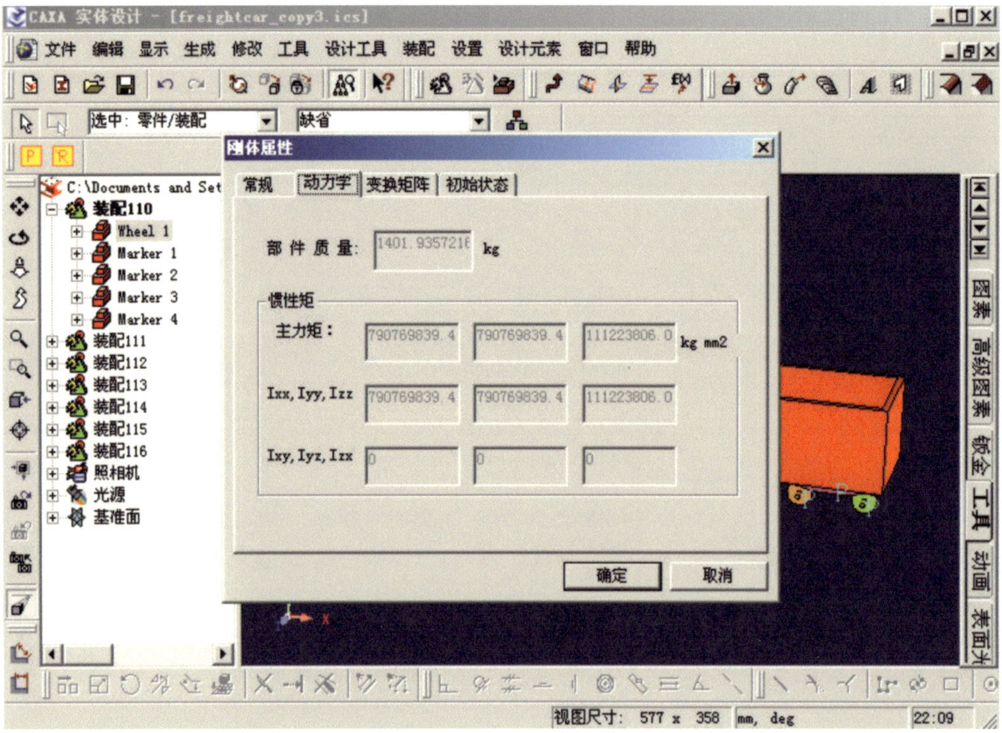

Fig. 4-8. Property extracted in CAXA

5. Topology construction of railway vehicle virtual prototype oriented to multi-body system --physical model abstraction

5.1 Transition of design prototype model to multi-body system analysis model based on virtual prototype-- the establishment of topology structure

Mapa topology structure of multi-body system in CAD environment through property modeling, and store it in a neutral file format. This format retains the defined topology of the multi-body system including assembly location relationship, position and orientation relationship of the space coordinate, constraint relations and constraint definitions between bodies and etc. Output a corresponding geometric model simultaneously which strictly corresponds to the part or assembly in the neutral file. The initial data for multi-body system modeling abstracted from the CAD modeling are obtained. The transition from virtual prototype model to the multi-body analysis model is achieved.

Decode the neutral file first. Obtain the rigid body, marker body, constraint, element force, applied force and etc according to established formats. Resume the space topology of the multi-body system according to the defined property. For example, rigid body a, b, c, has marker i, j, k, and force d, e, f, respectively, and the associated relationships ii, jj, kk, ee have been defined. The space topology structure can be resumed which is shown in Fig. 5-1.

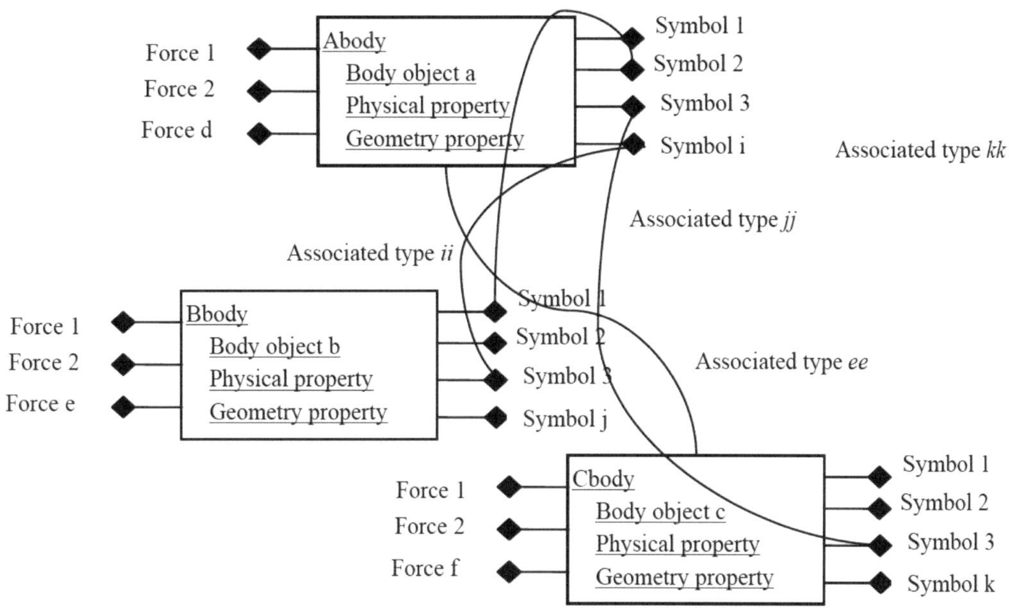

Fig. 5-1. Rebuild multi-body system structure

Although the physical models based on multi-body system are obtained, it has not been attached to the geometric solid model. In order to obtain a visual model, it needs to output the neutral file model in CAXA. In accordance with the decoded format, it can be IGES, STL, OBJ, 3DS, etc. In this study, 3DS model is adopted. The way to obtain the geometric model of the prototype is shown in Fig. 5-2.

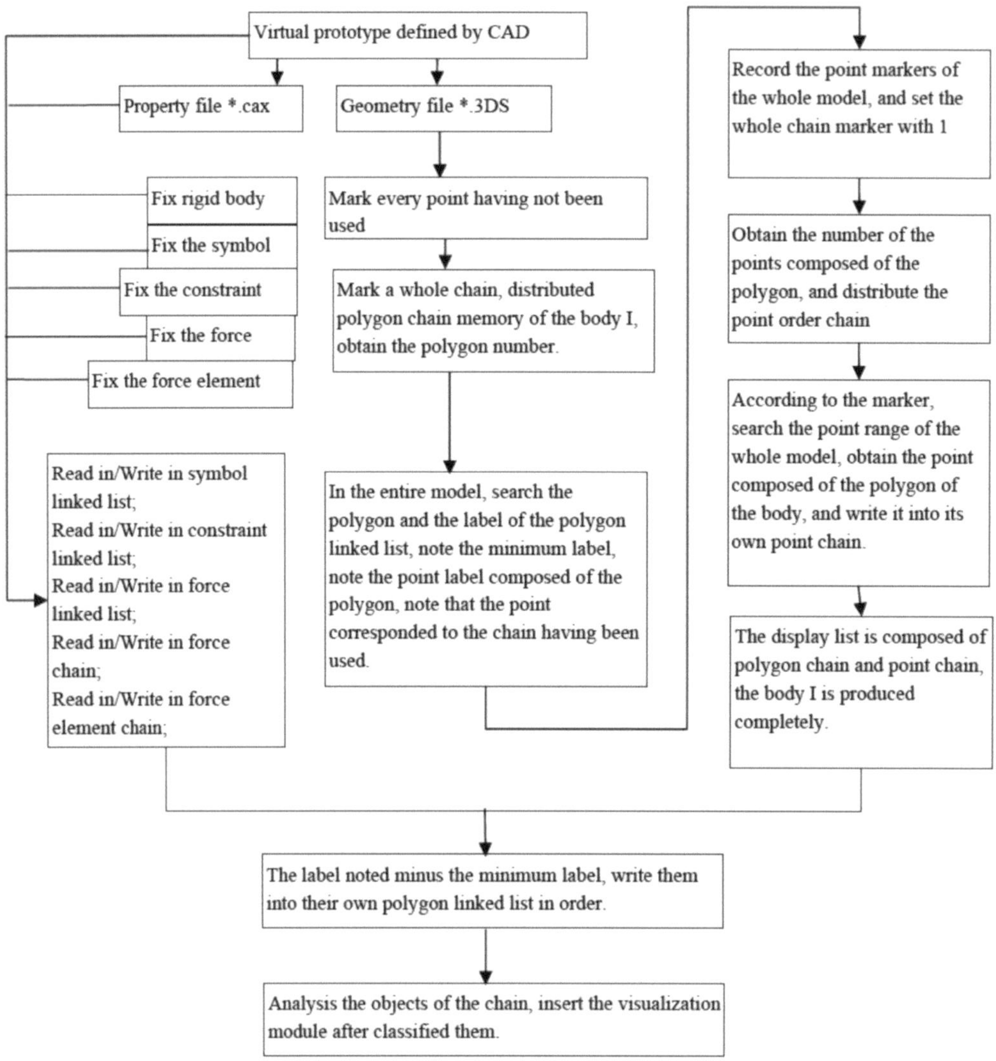

Fig. 5-2. Transition of virtual prototype of analysis model

From the figure above, multi-body description of the physical model corresponds to the objects given by geometric entities exactly. These objects determine to give which solid through classifying the point, line and surface. According to the assembly sequence of virtual prototype in CAD and marker body of the neutral file, their position relation is mapped. Properties such as transformation relation between the fixed coordinate system and the inertial coordinate system, transformation relation between the marker coordinate system and the fixed coordinate system, Euler angle corresponded to the rigid body, position and orientation of the marker coordinate system, the relationship of the defined constraints (restriction of the degree freedom), position and orientation corresponded to the force, have been strictly defined in the neutral file. Finally it is located by mapping the coordinate system of virtual prototype and space coordinate system of the visualization module to obtain the satisfactory model of multi-body system.

In accordance with the virtual prototype form CAD, describe them as objects with multi-body meaning using object-oriented idea, map them into 5 linear chains, and form a space topology model of visualized multi-body system. This model is also built on the principle of framework based on OpenGL and object oriented graphics. The existed relationship of this model in three-dimensional visualized space is shown in Fig.5-3.

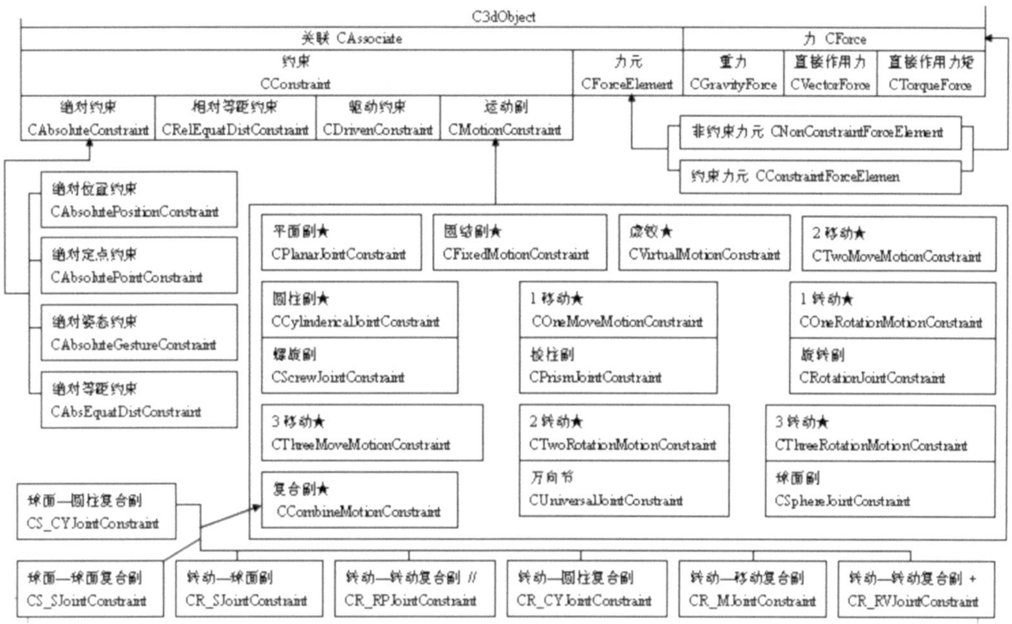

Fig. 5-3. Existed relationship of this model in three-dimensional visualized space

5.2 Topology construction of the railway vehicle multi-body system

The above visual model suits for not only mechanical multi-body system, but also railway vehicle. Considering the particularity of the railway vehicle multi-body system solution, according to the given multi-body system analysis software, the special object is established as shown in Fig. 5-4. The visualized model can be defined in the system or imported form the CAD model directly.

These objects include: Car, Bogie, Wheelset, Track, Damper, Rod, Spring and Friction plate, which complete vehicle component modeling, simulate for vehicle model running, and prepare for the dynamic calculation.

Create the solid model according to the associated sign of the given two ends. If the relative marker position changes, the shape and position or orientation of the model can be adjusted. It has basic functions of three-dimensional simulation.

Four categories have their own "dynamic" property pages. Every category has its corresponding variable receiving and data transformation which prepare initial data for dynamics solver.

Components of four categories are stress-carrying parts and are built by inheriting the CForceElement in the virtual prototype system. In order to facilitate the unified management of data, four categories created by this module are added to the CForceElementList chain, and also to the ObjectList chain for the visualization need.

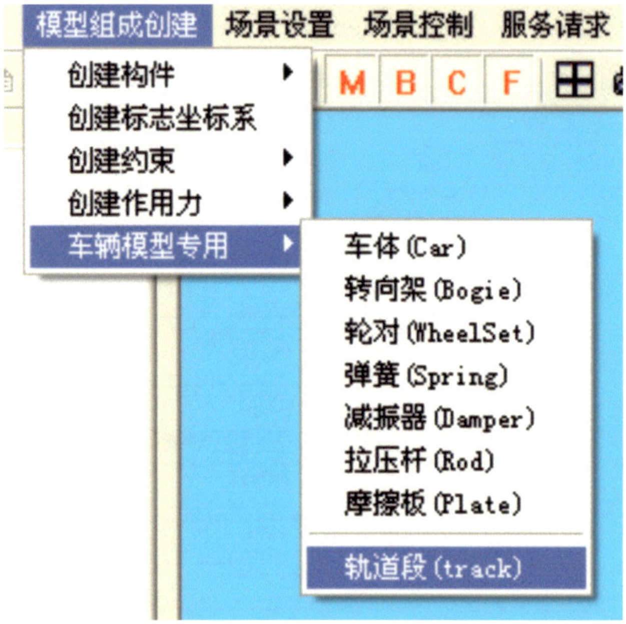

Fig. 5-4. Define railway vehicle model

Associated structure layers are shown in Fig. 5-5.

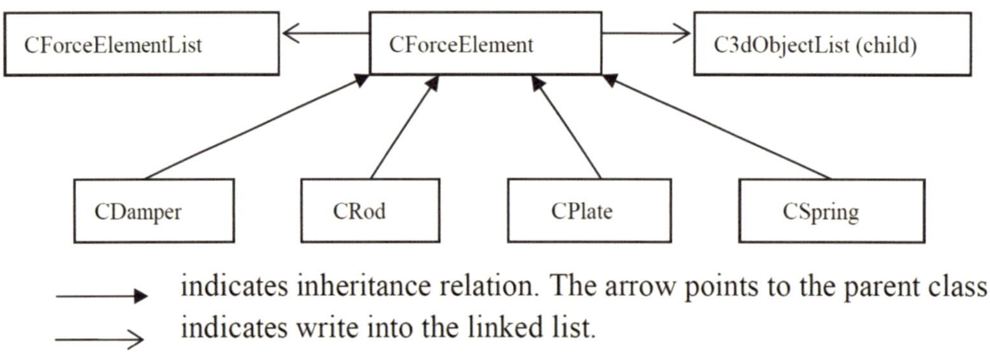

Fig. 5-5. Associated structure of the railway vehicle

A railway vehicle multi-body system model can be generated rapidly according to the above description. The defined model is shown in Fig. 5-6, which is a simplified model. Fig. 5-7 shows that import models from the design.

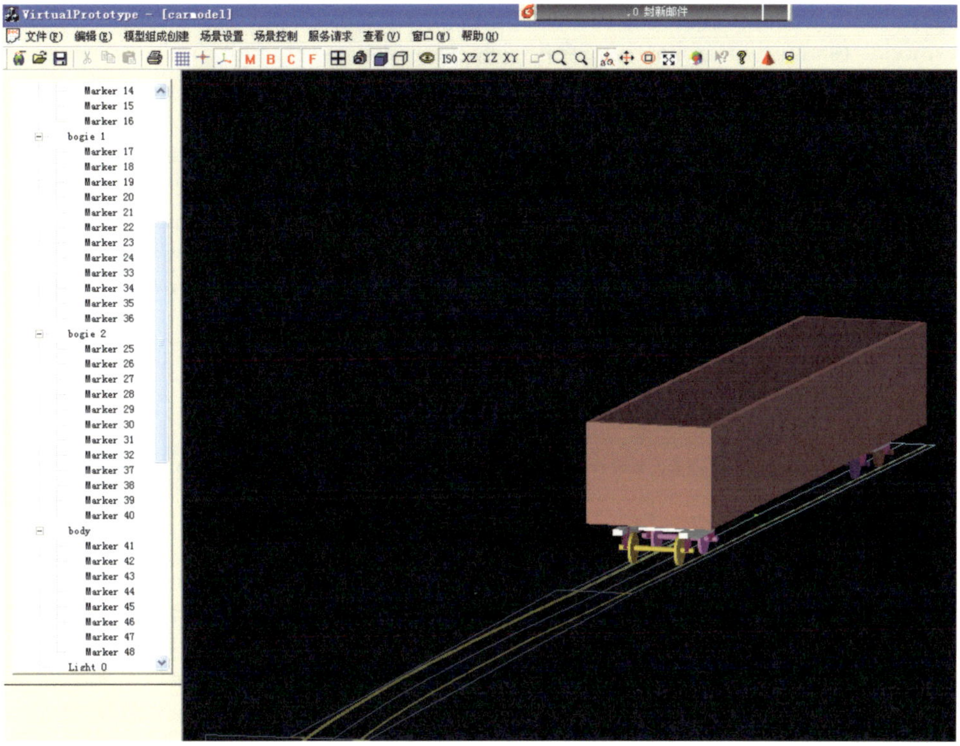

Fig. 5-6. Model the railway vehicle (simplified model, import model)

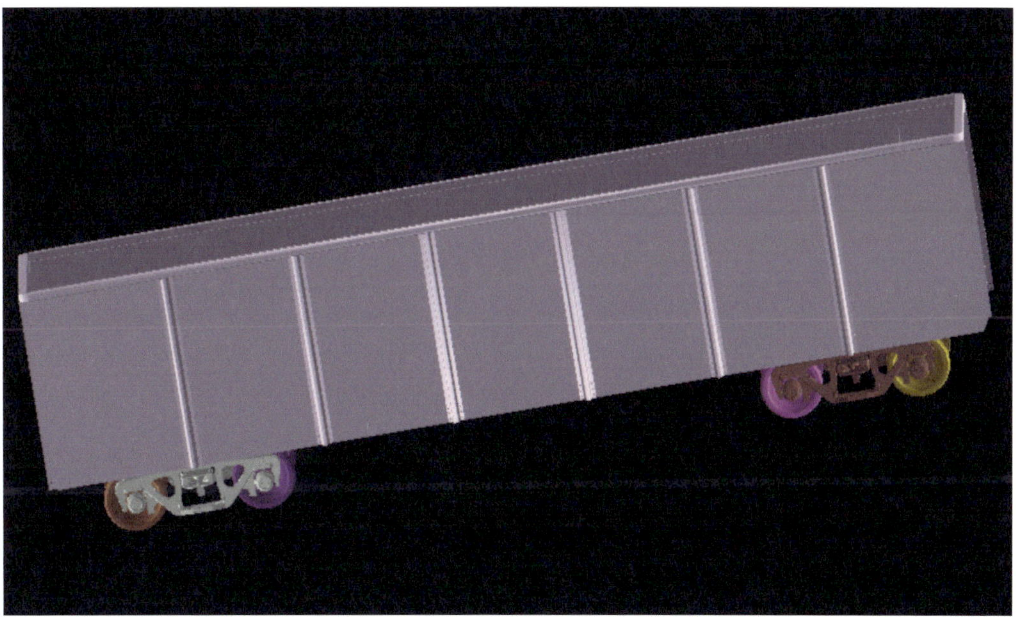

Fig. 5-7. Model the railway vehicle (obtained from the design drawing, import the model with 1:1)

5.3 Multi-body system analysis

The model established includes variety data for analysis of multi-body systems. After transiting to analysis model, multi-body analysis will be done by analysis module. Since the universality of the model and plug-in nature of the multi-body analysis module, many solvers can be used to compute for common mechanical multi-body system, such as Adams, Simpack, etc. For railway vehicle multi-body system, because of the field specialization, a specialized analysis module is needed to do analysis, such as Adams / Rail, railway vehicle part of Simpack. A software system is self-developed such as TPLdyna, VSDS. TPLdyna is developed by State Key Laboratory of Power Traction of Southwest Jiaotong Universtiy. VSDS is developed by Dr. Jue Wang of SWJTU. They both have multi-body system features but have different solvers. This study supplies the model interface to them. Here especially supports Dr. Jue Wang'VSDS, see Fig.6.10-14.

6. A case study of railway vehicle virtual prototype oriented to the multi-body system

6.1 Analysis idea

According to the modeling method above, space topology structure of the railway vehicle is shown in Fig. 6-1. B1 is car, B2 and B3 are frameworks, B4-B7 are wheelsets, B8 is track, FE1-FE6 are force elements, F1-F4 are wheel-track contact forces. Defining the force element, hinge and external force as directional has two aims: First, defining one of two adjacent objects as a reference object is to describe the relative movement of another. Second, it aims to define the positive direction of applied force and reacted force between the adjacent objects.

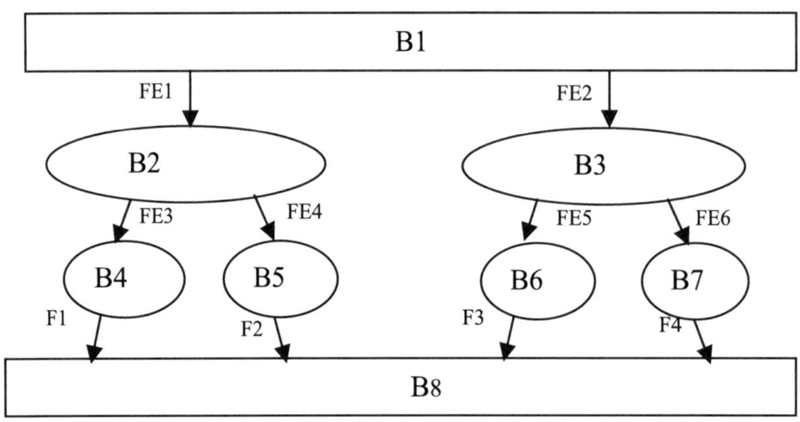

Fig. 6-1. Topology description of the railway vehicle multi-body system

To accomplish the railway vehicle virtual prototype analysis, take multi-body system analysis as an example, the processing description is shown in Fig. 6-2.

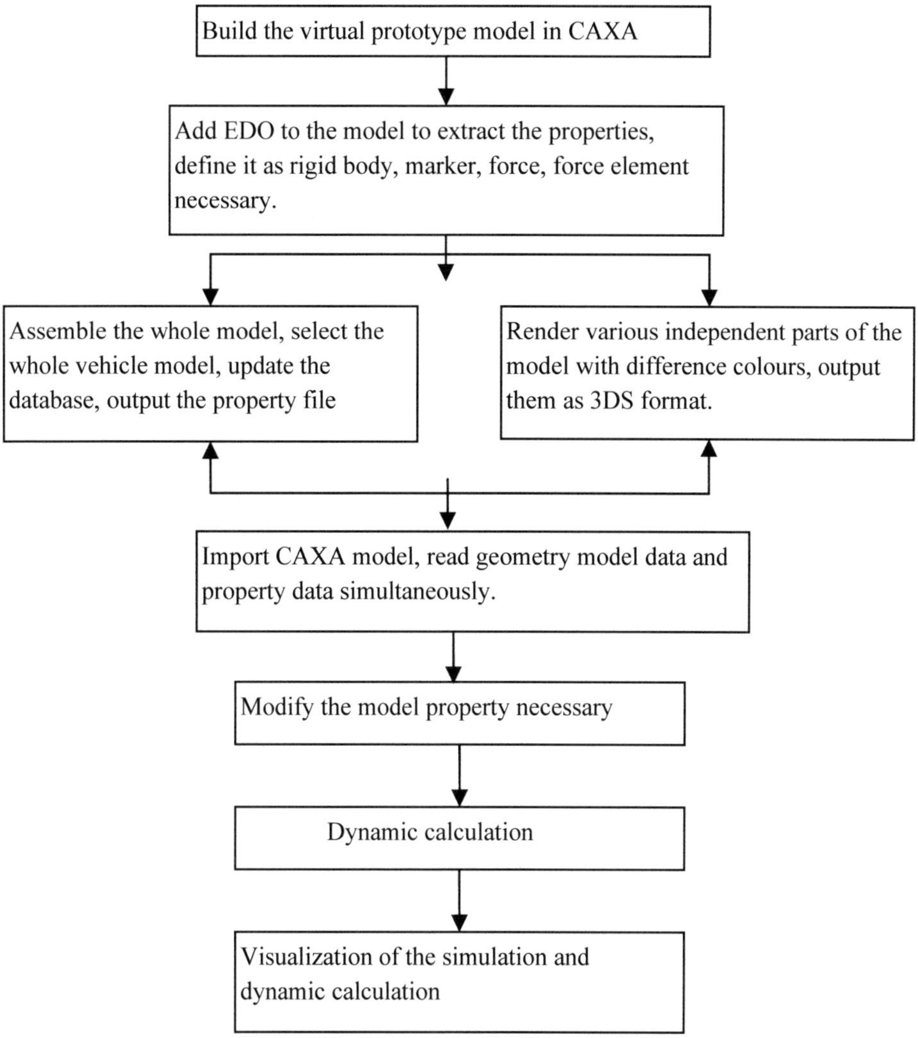

Fig. 6-2. Analysis flow of the railway vehicle virtual prototype

The process is actually obtained directly from the virtual prototype → properties extraction of the multi-body system model →transition of geometrical and physical model of multi-body systems → multi-body systems visualization modeling and mathematical modeling building → kinematics and dynamics solving of the multi-body system. This process is like mechanical system product development process, reflecting the integrated process from design model to analysis model, then to solve model, and reflecting the cycle iteration in product design process. This process supplies a theoretical and practical basis for study of product optimization process and intelligent design process.

6.2 A case process study of railway vehicle virtual prototype

Since the system is more complex, in order to obtain more significant technical route, the railway vehicle design model is simplified. The railway vehicle virtual prototype process is achieved.

1. Build the railway vehicle virtual prototype model in CAXA as shown in Fig. 6-3 and Fig. 6-4.

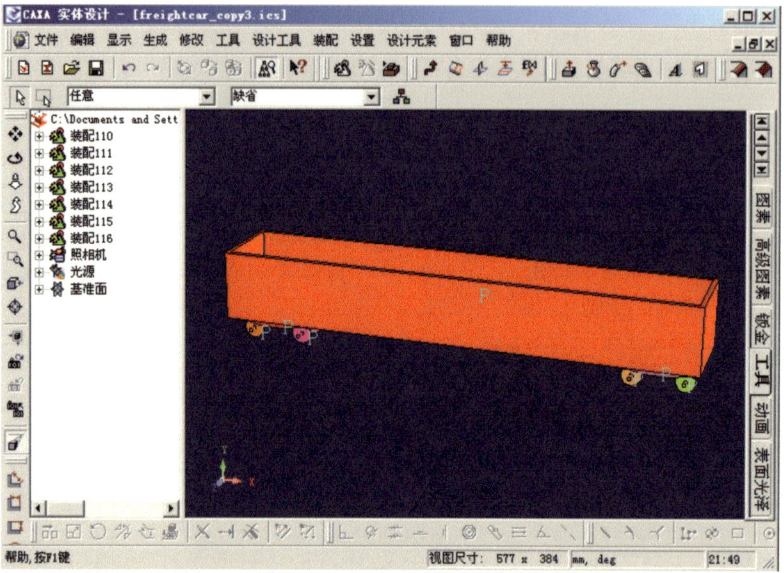

Fig. 6-3. Design model in CAXA

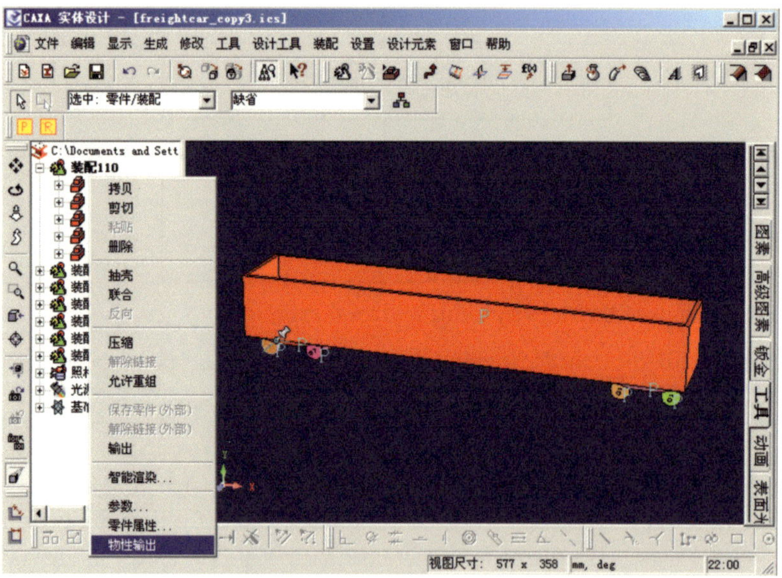

Fig. 6-4. COM interface added design model

2. Add EDO on the model to extract the model property. Then click the right key → "physical property output", to view or add properties.
3. For components, it is required to extract attribute mass, inertia, coordinate transformation matrix, space location and etc. For initial state such as initial

displacement, velocity, etc. it should be entered manually. The physical property extraction is shown in Fig.6-5.

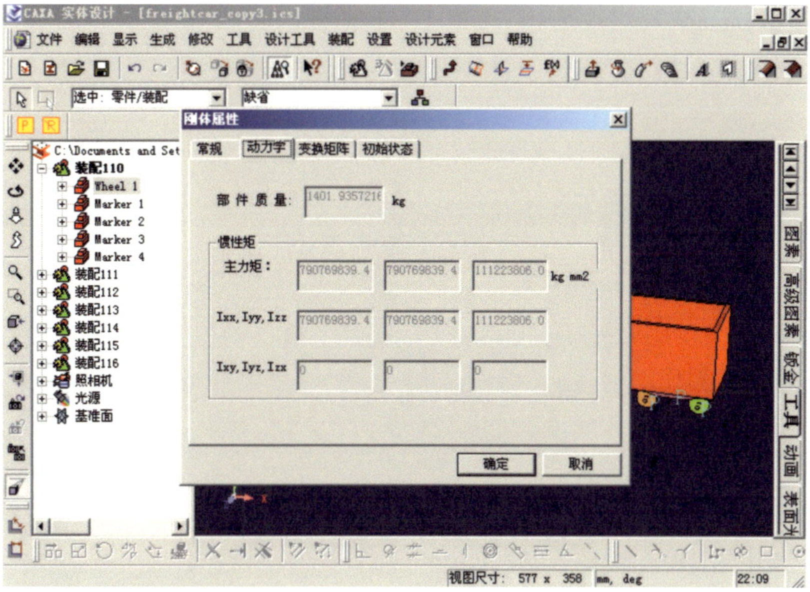

Fig. 6-5. Physical property extraction

4. For marker, the extracted information includes components, location and relative coordinate transformation matrix of the component coordinate system. Achievement of the marker information is shown in Fig. 6-6.

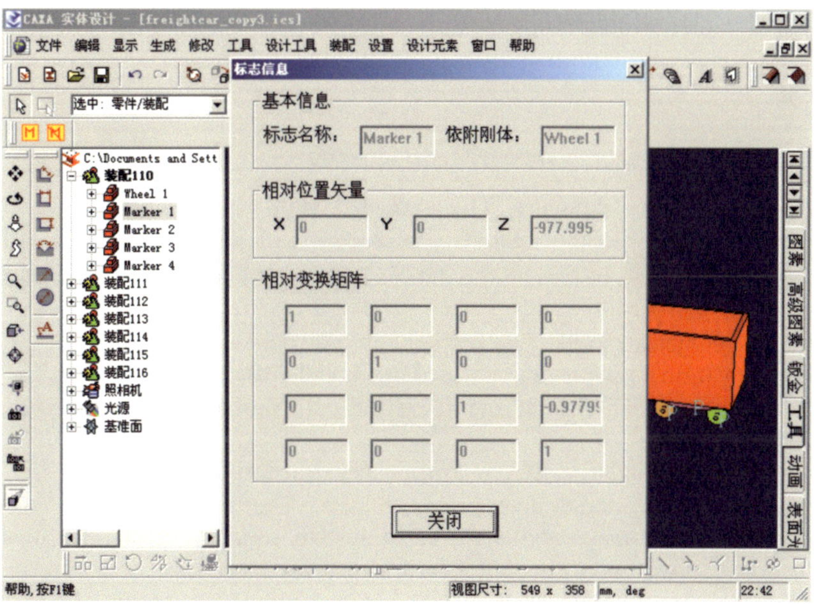

Fig. 6-6. Obtain the marker information

5. For force element (spring, damper, friction plate and rod), extracted information includes connected components and marker point which is to fix the position and orientation of the component. Multi-body topology relation from design model is shown in Fig. 6-7.

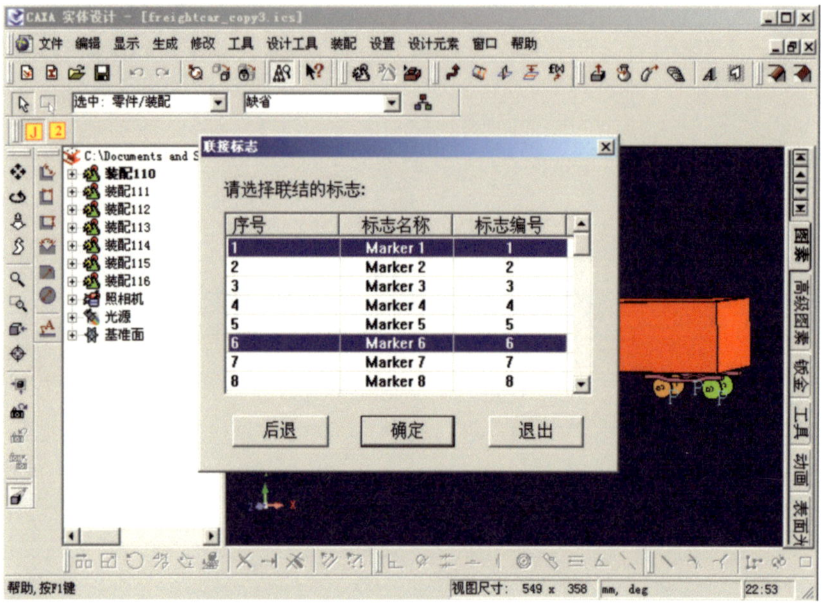

Fig. 6-7. Multi-body topology relation from design model

6. Output the property database. The extracted property has been written into the database after the operation above. The subsequent job is to assemble the whole prototype, clicking  to update the database, then clicking  to output the property data to the certain position.
7. Output the geometric model. Two points should be paid attention to:
   a. Render various independent parts of the model with difference colors.
   b. Output files as 3DS format! file name and path should be the same with property data.

By operations above, model in CAXA and property extraction has been finished.

8. Import the CAXA model and property data. The model can be recovered in VirtualMBS, and it maps the multi-body system topology relationship of railway vehicle. The catalog tree in the left clearly expresses space layer structure and mutual dependence of multi-body system. The model resuming and checking in analysis view is shown in Fig. 6-8.

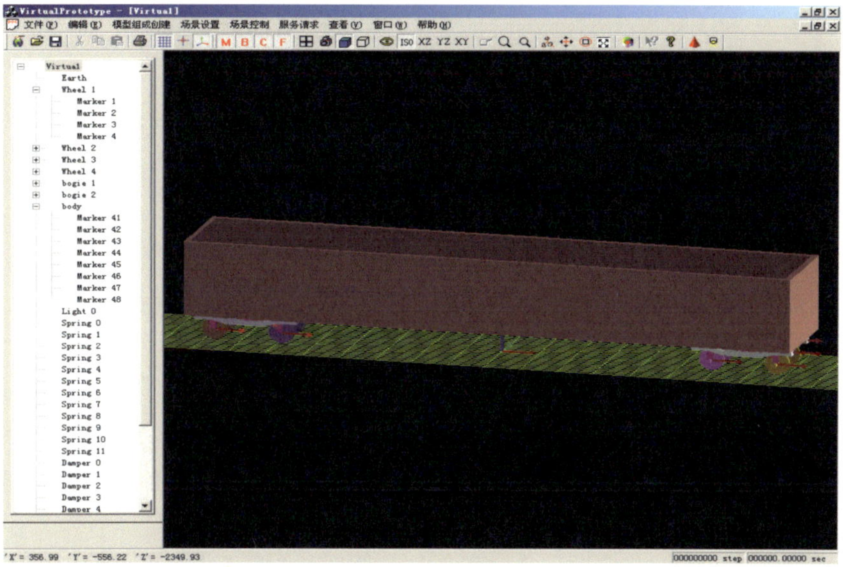

Fig. 6-8. Model resuming and checking in analysis view

9. Check the accuracy of the data imported, perfect some incomplete information. Test results show that the model is resumed completely and property data is right. The data meets the dynamics and simulation requirements. Then transition of model to performance analysis module is shown in Fig.6-9.

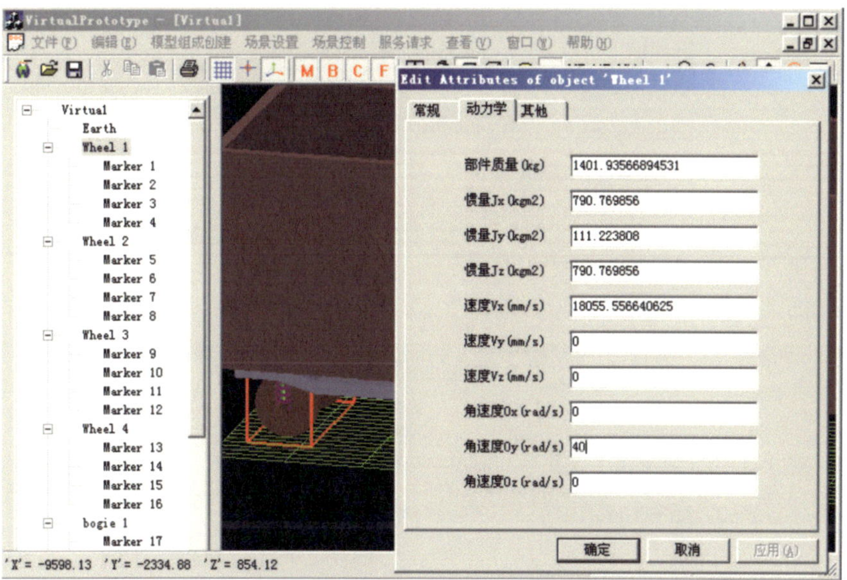

Fig. 6-9. Transition of model to performance analysis module

10. Load the track, set the measure variables and simulation parameters, and prepare for the dynamics calculation and simulation. Post-processing of the analysis module is shown in Fig.6-10.

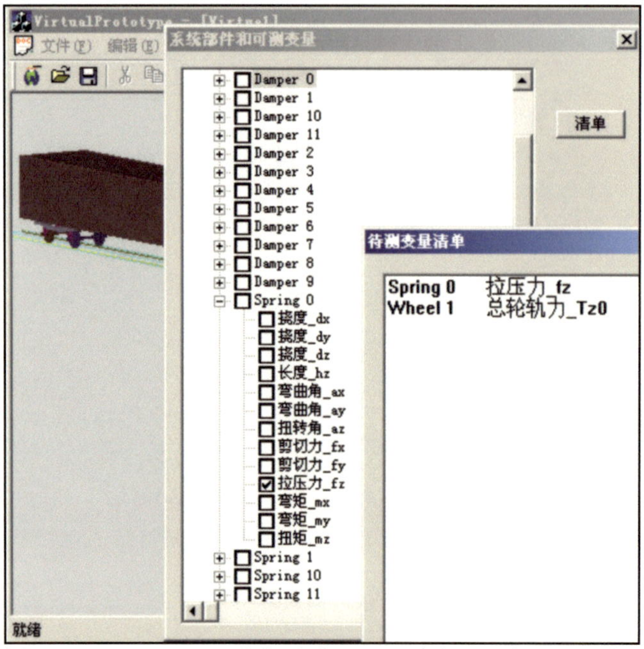

a) Post-processing module definition of the analysis module
(two-dimensional data visualization)

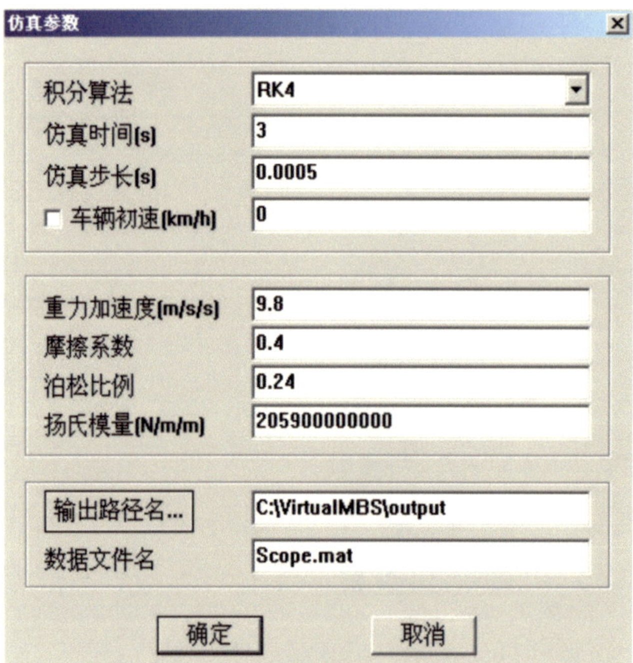

b) Simulation parameter definition
of the analysis module

Fig. 6-10. Post-processing of the analysis module

11. Dynamics calculation results and simulation. Given speed is 65km/h and straight length is 30.78m, when the simulation period is 0.389s, vehicle enters the curve segment, and runs stably. Realtime simulation of the railway vehicle dynamics based on 3-D visualization is shown in Fig.6-11.

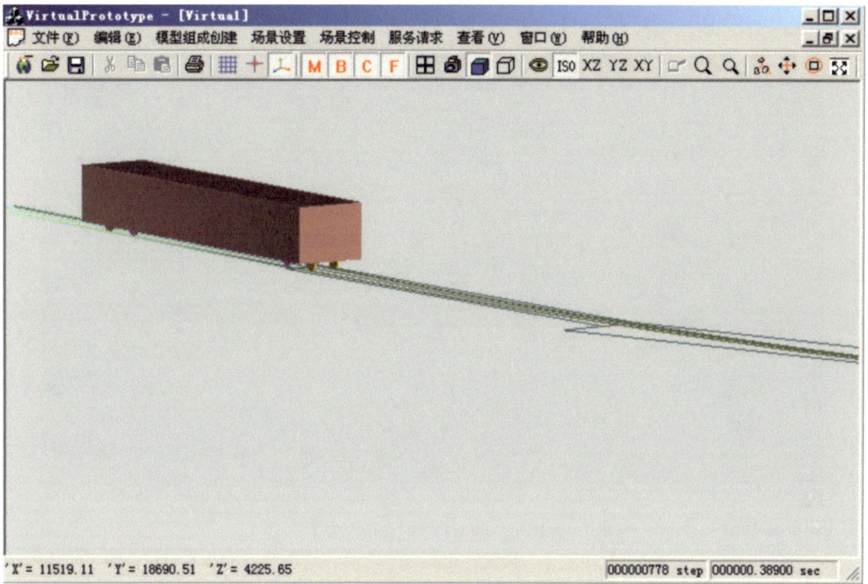

Fig. 6-11. Realtime simulation of the railway vehicle dynamics based on 3-D visualization

During the process the tension and pressure fz of the measured variable Spring0 and the total wheel force Tz0 are shown in Fig. 6-12. The red is for fz, the green is for Tz0.

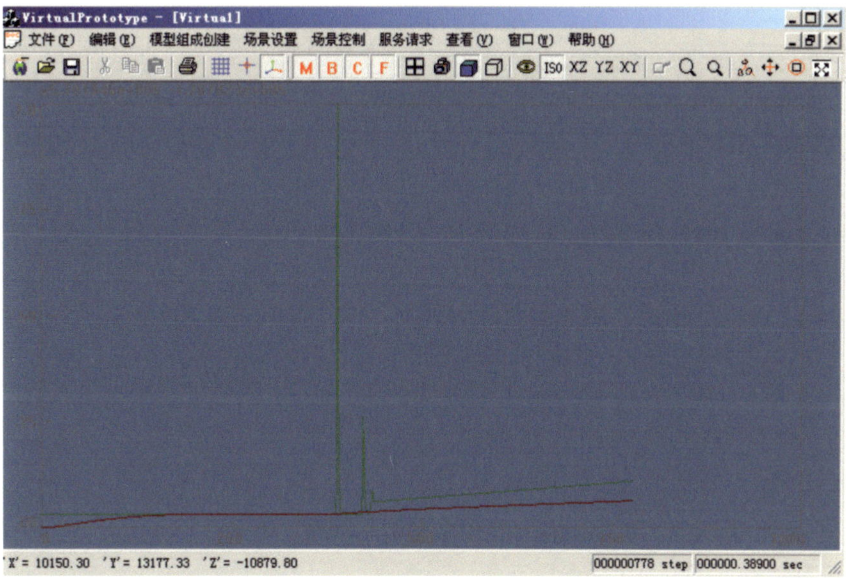

Fig. 6-12. Calculation results

Other visualized results of this system are as follows:

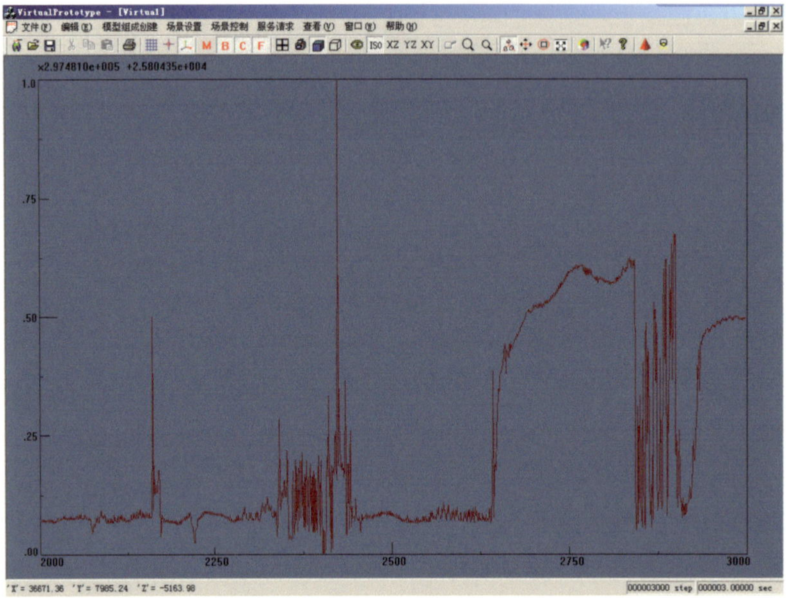

Fig. 6-13. Wheel-track force of left wheel of the wheelset 2

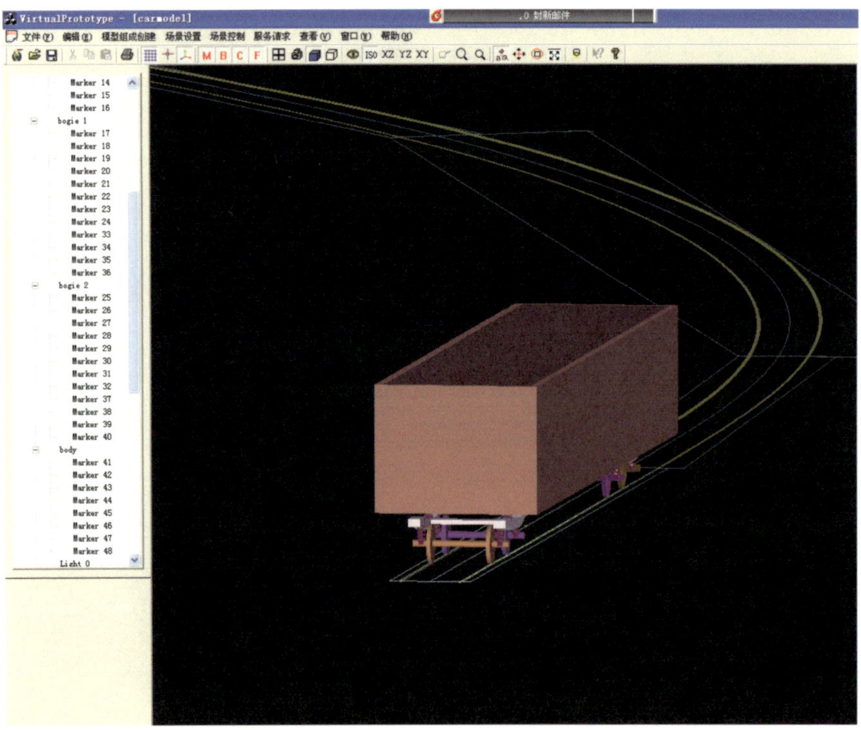

Fig. 6-14. Analysis space scene

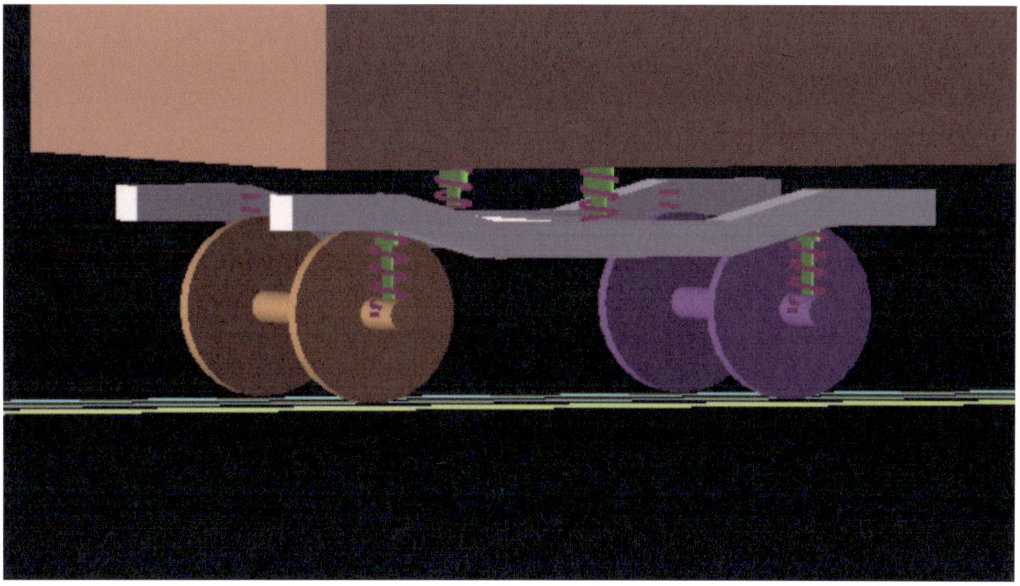

Fig. 6-15. Partial view

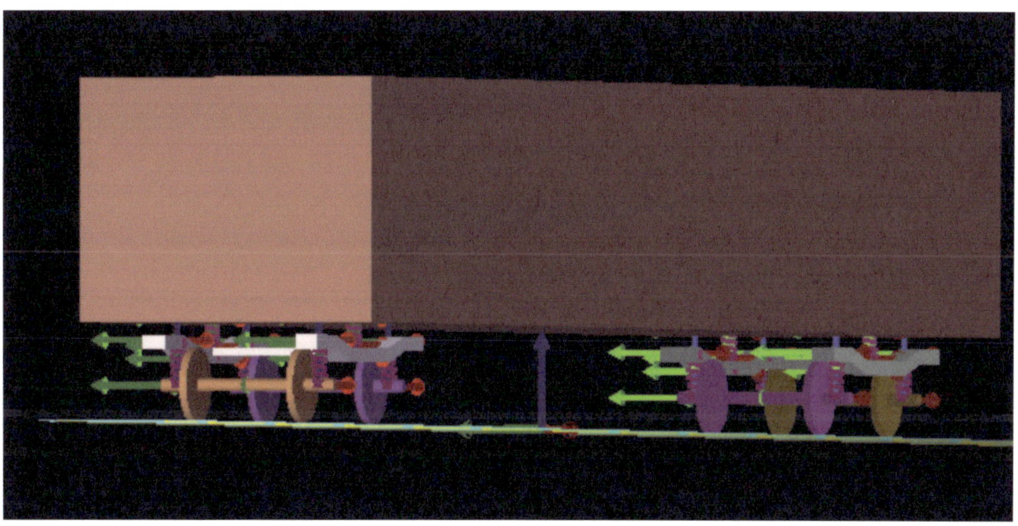

Fig. 6-16. Model with coordinate system

7. Summary

1. Through analyzing the current virtual prototyping patterns, the framework of railway vehicle virtual prototype platform is proposed.
2. The follow-up property extraction of analysis module is put into the three-dimensional CAD environment to ensure the uniformity of analysis model and prototype model.
3. The whole process of transition form prototype model to analysis model for virtual prototype is proposed and studied.
4. In order to check the series theory proposed, take a certain railway vehicle model design as an example, a case study is done in the developed software to check the research results well.

According to the study above, the technology from virtual prototype design-prototype property extraction-analysis model established based on the multi-body system-transition from multi-body system design model to multi-body system analysis model, analysis solution of multi-body system-data visualization, is initially proved, which embodies the product design process. It can be promoted to other CAE analysis module, and it supplies detailed basic research theory and techniques for railway vehicle virtual prototype platform independent researches.

8. Acknowledgment

This work is supported by the National Natural Science Foundation of China (NSFC) under Grant 50975240 and by the Youth Fund of Sichuan Province under Grant 09ZQ026-003 and the Fundamental Research Funds for the Central Universities under Grant SWJTU09ZT06, and New Century Excellence Plan Grand NCET-09-0665. In this works, VSDS computation module is used for testify the procedure, which is developed by Dr. Jue Wang. Thanks for his work.

9. References

R-S, Lossack.; Y, Umeda & T, Tomiyama. (1998). Requirement, function and physical principle modelling as the basis for a model of synthesis, In Computer-Aided Conceptual Design, *Proceedings of the 1998 Lancaster International Workshop on Engineering Design*, pp. 165-179. Lancaster University, May, 1998.

P.J, Bentely & J.P, wakefield. (1997). Conceptual Evolutionary Design by Genetic Algorithms. *Engineering Design and Automation*, Vol.3, No.2, pp. 119-131.

C.J, Moore; J.C, Miles & D.W.G, Rees. (1997). Decision support for conceptual bridge design. *Artifical Intelligence in Engineering*, No.11, pp. 259-272.

Marco, Farina; Kalyanmoy, Deb & Paolo Amato. (2004). Dynamic Multi-objective Optimization Problems: Test Cases, Approximations, and Applications. *EVOLUTIONARY COMPUTATION*, Vol. 8, No. 5, pp. 425-442.

Antonio, St & Clair Lloyd, Williams. (2000). Multidisciplinary Design Optimization of Optomechanical Devices, PhD thesis, University of Rochester, pp. 1-214, U.S.A.

A, Wymyslowski; K.J, Urbanski & T.M, Berlicki. (2005). Numerical Simulation and Optimization of the Vacuum Micro-sensor, 6th Int. Conf. *on Thermal Mechanical and*

Multi-Physics Simulation and Experiments in Micro-Electronics and Micro-Systems, pp. 576-583.

Weihua, Zhang; Guofu, Ding & et al. (2004). *Research on General Virtual Prototype Platform of Vehicle System*, ICFDM, Xi'an, China, June.

Wei, Zhang; Bao-chun, Lu & Hui-zhong, Wu. (2002). Modeling and Simulation Approach for Multi-disciplinary Virtual Prototyping, *Proceedings of the 4th World Congress on Intelligent Control and Automation*, pp. 1586-1590.

Weihua, Zhang; Guofu, Ding ; Kaiyin, Yan & et al. (2004). Study on Virtual Prototype Platform of Vehicle, *The 6th International conference on frontiers on Design and Manufacturing*, XJU, Xi'an, China.

Walid, Tizani & Robert, Smith. (2003). Incremental Virtual Prototyping as an IT Tool for CE Projects. *Information Technology*, pp. 1-9.

Kyo Chul, Kang; Moonzoo, Kim; Jaejoon, Lee; Byungkil, Kim; Youngjin, Hong; Hyoungki, Lee & Seokwon Bang. (2005). 3D Virtual Prototyping of Home Service Robots Using ASADAL/OBJ, *Proceedings of the 2005 IEEE International Conference on Robotics and Automation Barcelona*, pp. 2903-2908.

Young-Ran, Lee; Sang-Young, Cho & Jeong-Bae, Lee. (2005). The Design A Virtual prototyping based on ARMulator, *Proceedings of the Fourth Annual ACIS International Conference on Computer and information SCIENCE.*

Qing, Shen; Michael, Grafe; Jochen, Bauch & Radkowski. Interdisciplinary Knowledge Sharing in Solution Elemeng Based Virtual Prototyping of Mechatronic Systems, *The 9th International Conference on Computer Supported Cooperative Work in Design Proceedings*, pp. 1171-1176.

G, Wachutka; G, Schrag & R, Sattler. (2004). Predictive Simulation of Microdevices and Microsystems: The Basis of Virtual Prototyping, *24th INTERNATIONAL CONFERENCE ON MICROELECTRONIC*, pp. 71-78.

P.F, Lister; P.L, Watten; M.R, Lewis; P.F, Newbury; M, White; M.C, Bassett;

B.J.C, Jackson & V, Trignano. (2004). Electronic Simulation for Virtual Reality: Virtual Prototyping, Proceedings of the Theory and Practice of Computer Graphics.

Mingwu, Fan; Shiqi, Li; Tiaoqin, Yu; Dezhi, Chen & Yongqian, Xiong. (2003). Applying virtual prototyping to the innovative design of low energy accelerators, *Proceedings of the Particle Accelerator Conference* , pp. 1560-1562.

Liwen, Guan; Jinsong, Wang & Liping, Wang. (2003). Integrated Approach for Parallel Machine Tool Conceptual Design, *Processing of International Conference an Robotics Intelligent Systems and Signal*, pp. 456-461.

Thorsten, Scher; Christian, Müller-Schloer & Siemens AG. (2004). Design, Implementation and Validation of a Generic and Reconfigurable Protocol Stack Framework for Mobile Terminals, *Proceedings of the 24th International Conference on Distributed Computing Systems Workshops.*

K.L, Cartwright; L. A, Bowers; A.D, Greenwood; C.A, Fichtl; J.W, Luginsland & J J, Watrous. (2003). Virtual Prototyping of Directed Energy Weapons, *Proceedings of the 2003 User Group Conference.*

Marcelo, Kallmann1; Patrick, Lemoine1; Daniel, Thalmann1; Frederic, Cordier2; Nadia, Magnenat-Thalmann2; Cecilia, Ruspa3 & Silvia, Quattrocolo. (2003). Immersive

Vehicle Simulators for Prototyping, Training and Ergonomics. *Proceedings of the Computer Graphics International.*

Ronald, D. Williams & Robert, H. Klenke. (2003). Teaching Computer Design Using Virtual Prototyping. *IEEE Transactions on education*, Vol. 46, No. 2.

11

Enabling and Analyzing Natural Interaction with Functional Virtual Prototypes

Frank Gommlich, Guido Heumer, Bernhard Jung,
Matthias Lenk and Arnd Vitzthum
Technical University Bergakademie Freiberg
Germany

1. Introduction

Functional validations of virtual prototypes are a promising application area of immersive Virtual Reality (Moehring & Froehlich, 2011). Through the interactive simulation of operating procedures such analyses aim at providing insight about virtual prototypes, e. g. concerning visibility aspects, reachability of control elements, and ergonomics. A key requirement is the enabling of *natural interaction* defined by Zachmann as *"interaction which imitates that same interaction in the real world as close as possible"* (Zachmann & Rettig, 2001). In immersive VR, natural interaction can be realized through data gloves and motion tracking devices.

However, a challenging task remains in the modeling and simulation of interactions with dynamic control elements such as sliders, switches etc. (Moehring & Fröhlich, 2010). We have devised and implemented a framework that not only aims at simplifying the specification of such *control actuators* for interactive virtual environments but also facilitates the recording, automated classification, and analysis of natural interactions with such control actuators. The presented approach builds on the European Standard EN 894-3 (DIN894-3, 2006) and covers all types of control actuators defined therein. This standard defines systematic guidelines for the choice and configuration of control actuators to ergonomically design machinery.

A characterizing feature of control actuators in the real world is given by their function: Controlling the behavior of machines and other appliances. In order to model the triggering of changes of environment objects in the simulation, our framework allows to associate control actuators with *interaction events*. Interaction events may be fired continuously, e. g. during movement of sliders, or when discrete states are reached, e. g. switches. Besides making interactive simulations more realistic, interaction events can also be recorded to allow later playback and analysis of the interaction. For this, detailed timing information is stored in the interaction events. For example, interaction events may be used for the animation of virtual humans that imitate the user interactions when operating virtual prototypes.

Contributions of our research include an XML-based modeling language for control actuators that can be seen as both an abstraction layer and an extension to lower-level rigid body physics modeling capabilities provided e. g. by Collada (Khronos Group, 2008) and X3D (International Organization for Standardization, 2008). Further, we produce a reference implementation of control actuators with direct object manipulation, an interaction database for analyzing interaction events including recognizing basic interactions and grasp classification, and a powerful graphical analysis tool. Through this, the process of adding interactive elements to virtual prototypes can be drastically simplified.

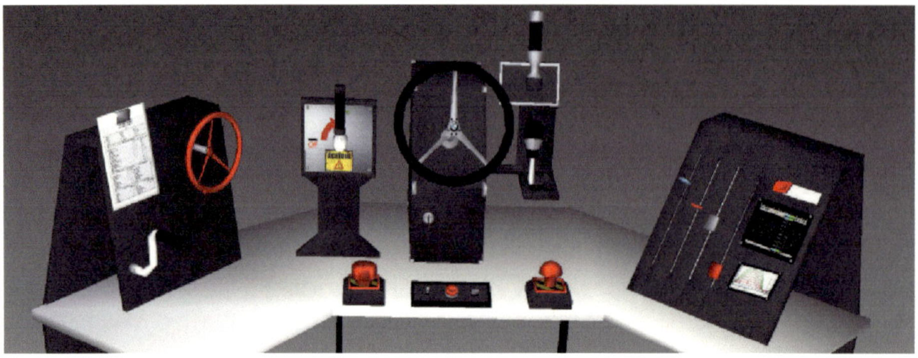

Fig. 1. Selection of control actuators defined in the European standard EN 894-3.

2. Control actuators

This subchapter introduces the concept of control actuators, our XML based modeling language and a reference implementation of control actuators. An easy way to include different control actuators into a dynamic environment is to use an extended version of annotated objects (Weber et al., 2006). They are declared and managed in an XML-based representation structure, which combines all information about types of scene objects in a common database. Such information includes graphical model, type, component references, physical parameters, joint definitions, etc. Annotated objects are similar to the concept of smart objects (Kallmann & Thalmann, 1999). In contrast to smart objects, they do not contain any form of behavior description, neither for object nor for actor behavior. The object behavior of annotated objects is totally dependent on their physical simulation.

2.1 Concept

Structurally, control actuators are compound objects where a movable part can change its position or orientation w.r.t. a static part, the fitting. The relative movement is constrained by the degrees of freedom (DOFs) of a joint connecting the static and the movable part. Here, the composition of both is called control actuator. In Figure 2 an emergency button is shown. In this example the button takes the role of the actuator. Multiple actuators with the same fitting are also conceivable and are used, e. g., in the case of cockpit instruments, keyboards or other operational controls. Thus, control actuators share many similarities with rigid bodies from the Collada and X3D specifications. However, the definition of control actuators requires additional capabilities not available in basic Collada or X3D. In particular, many types of control actuators such as switches and gear shifts exhibit lock states which correspond to discrete values along a continuous DOF of joints. A control actuator will snap to a discrete state when no further force is exerted on the actuator.
Our concept of control actuators covers all types of control actuators and guidelines defined in the European standard EN 894-3 (see fig. 1).

2.2 Declaration

Annotated objects with their attributes are represented in a compact and easy to use XML structure. To check the correct syntax of annotated objects and their actuators there is an XML schema. To ensure extensibility of the format, all object attributes are denoted by an all-purpose parameter format consisting of name, type and value, represented by the *param* element.

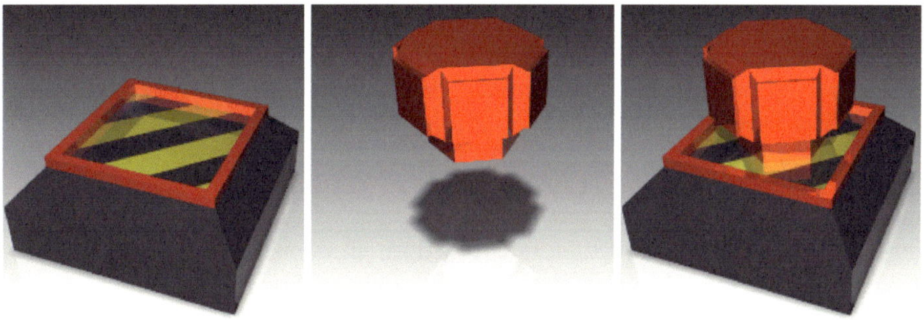

(a) Fitting (b) Actuator (c) Control Actuator

Fig. 2. Composition of a control actuator. Each control actuator consists of a fitting and at least one actuator.

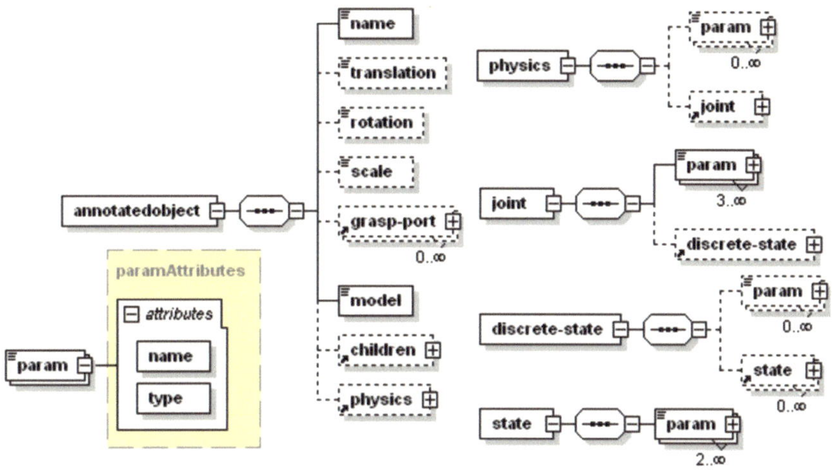

Fig. 3. The XML schema for annotated objects within our framework.

The element *physics* and its subelement *joint* (see figure 3) contains the major characteristics of control actuators regarding their representation in the dynamics simulation. The fitting references one or more actuators with the *children* element. These actuators are also annotated objects with the difference that they have specified information about *joint*s and their constraints. A joint definition contains at least the joint type (e. g. DoubleAxisHinge for a joystick, or Slider for a volume control), the specification of the DOF axes and the constraints along these axes.

In case of discrete actuators it is necessary to define at least one discrete state which is represented by an angular or translational offset from the neutral position. Additional it is possible to specify unsteady intermediate states. When a control actuator reaches an unsteady state, it will automatically move to a defined successor state. This is useful for realizing complex actuator movements, e. g. a gear shift. Figure 4 shows the gears of a car with steady gear states and intermediate discrete states. States Ⓐ and Ⓑ are unsteady with ⑤ as the successor state. Listing 1 shows an example for discrete states of an actuator definition.

It proved possible to implement all presented control actuators in the European standard EN 894-3 with at most two DOFs for either translation or rotation. A combination or mixture of translation and rotation is not intended by the standard. Therefore it was effectual to divide the standard actuators into four different types according to their DOFs. We called these four joint types *Slider*, *Hinge*, *DoubleAxisSlider* and *DoubleAxisHinge*. The slider and the hinge type have one DOF each whereas the DoubleAxisSlider and the DoubleAxisHinge type have two DOFs.

2.3 Implementation

The implementation of control actuators is based on an open-source physics engine called Newton Game Dynamics (Jerez & Suero, 2011).

In order to effect an actuator manipulation by a VR user, forces are calculated from the user's hand movements and applied to the actuator (see Section 3). The actuator can be continuously moved within its degrees of freedom, constrained by its joint limits and subject to possible collisions with other geometries. When the actuator is released by the VR user, the engine realizes a snap to the closest discrete lock state. The flow of this automatic snap mechanism is shown in Figure 5 and is realized with the help of forces applied to the actuator to reach the calculated position. This results in a smooth and continuous movement to the new position.

Finally, if the reached position is unsteady, then the cycle starts again and the force for the following state will be calculated. This action will be repeated until the first steady state is reached or until the actuator is grasped again.

In order to restrict the actuator movements, e.g. to special tracks in a two dimensional layer (see figure 4, left column) we used the automatic collision response mechanism of the dynamics engine. This mechanism ensures a realistic movement of the stick inside the tracks of the fitting, without explicitly modeling the permissible pathways.

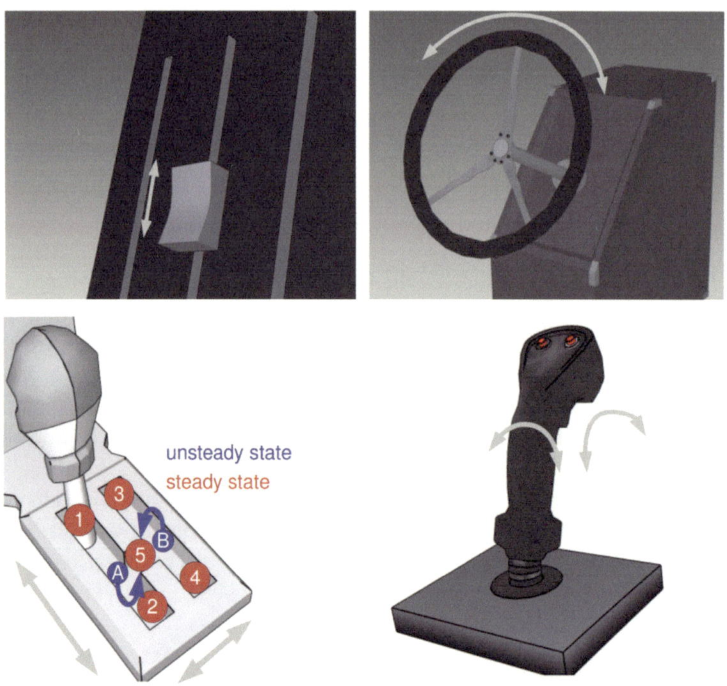

Fig. 4. Overview of the different joint types. first row: Slider and Hinge. second row: DoubleAxisSlider and DoubleAxisHinge.

```
<annotatedobject>
    <name>emergencyFitting</name>
    <model>emergencyFitting.iv</model>
    <children>
        <child type="string">emergencyActuator</child>
    </children>
</annotatedobject>
<annotatedobject>
    <name>emergencyActuator</name>
    <model>emergencyActuator.iv</model>
    <physics>
        <joint>
            <param name="jointtype" type="string">slider</param>
            <param name="pinDir" type="array3">0 0 -1</param>
            <param name="minValue" type="double">0</param>
            <param name="maxValue" type="double">0.1</param>
            <discrete-state>
                <state>
                    <param name="name" type="string">deactivated</param>
                    <param name="value" type="double">0</param>
                </state>
                <state>
                    <param name="name" type="string">activated</param>
                    <param name="value" type="double">0.05</param>
                </state>
            </discrete-state>
        </joint>
    </physics>
</annotatedobject>
```

Listing 1. XML code example of an emergency button, shown in figure 2.

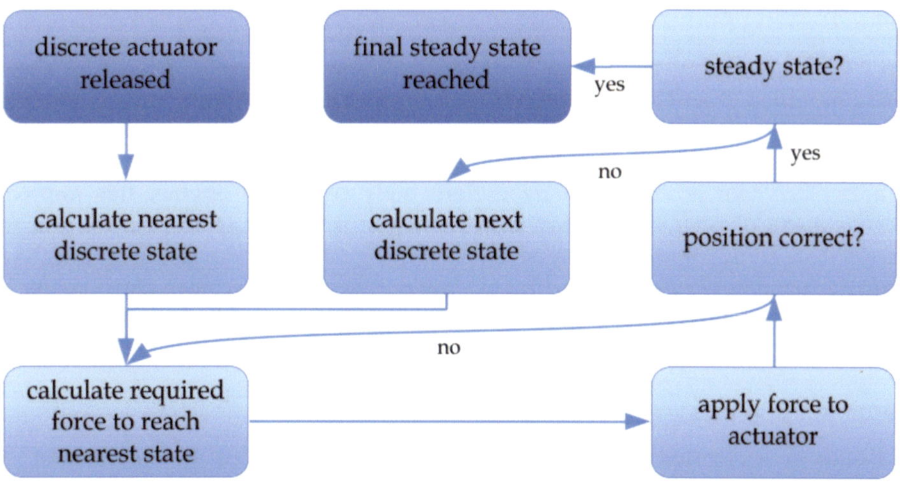

Fig. 5. Flowchart for the snap in behavior of control actuators. If the user releases the actuator, the system moves them to the nearest discrete state.

3. Direct object manipulation

The simulation of realistic manual object manipulation by a user in virtual environments is an important feature in virtual prototyping, ergonomics analysis and virtual training scenarios. To differentiate this kind of natural interaction from other, more commonly used types of object manipulation where the user either selects, grabs and moves an object by help of a pointing geometry (akin to a 3D mouse pointer) or picking ray we refer to it as "direct object manipulation". The discriminating factor is that a user directly controls virtual models of his hands that (more or less) exactly follow his real arm and finger movements (isomorphic control). With the help of these hand models, which act as the representations of the user's real hands in the virtual world, the user is able to touch, push, pick up and drop objects as he would in reality.

Clearly, the functional hand model is an important feature in this kind of interaction technique. The properties of contacts – their location, direction and forces – that exist between a hand and an object determines which kind of manipulation is taking place. E. g. mere touching vs. forceful pushing, prehensile (grabbing) vs. non-prehensile (pushing, dragging, sliding) manipulation, the various types of grasping an object, etc.

To be able to discriminate which parts of the hand are in contact with the object, we work with a setting that uses virtual sensors fitted on the finger segments of the hand model (see figure 6 left). These sensors can detect collision with annotated objects, including the control actuators described in the previous section. Each phalanx (finger segment) is represented by four box-shaped sensors (one on the top, the bottom, the left and the right side) allowing for discrimination of which part of the phalanx collides with the object. Similarly, the palm is represented by differently shaped collision primitives. This approach in constructing the hand model has two advantages. First, it allows for a rather close approximation of collision geometry to the real anatomical shape of the hand while still enabling efficient collision detection by only using convex collision primitives which are supported by many modern implementations of dynamics engines. Second, it provides information about possible contact configurations and whether they form a valid grasp or not, e. g. it is not possible to form a grasp with the inside of the palm and the upside of the thumb. Further, knowing which segment of the hand touches the object helps inform the classification of grasp types (see section 4.2). The sensors themselves are mere collision detectors and have no simulated physical properties. To effect real manipulations on the object, resulting forces are calculated, based on collision centers, collision normals and penetration depths of the sensors and applied to the physical simulation of the annotated objects (see figure 6 right).

Since object behavior is simulated by a rigid body dynamics engine, this approach to implement direct object manipulation simulation enables the user to pick up and release objects and to manipulate them in prehensile and non-prehensile ways.

This allows for *natural interaction* with functional virtual prototypes. Our approach also supports the integration of haptic devices into the hardware setup for an even more realistic interaction experience (Abate et al., 2009; Zorriassatine et al., 2003).

4. Interaction analysis

To be useful in interactive VR applications, a mere simulation of the behavior of control actuators and their interaction with a virtual hand model is in many cases not enough. Additionally, information about interactions of the user with virtual objects and the resulting state changes need to be processed. An important first step is to record all interaction data that is generated during direct object manipulation.

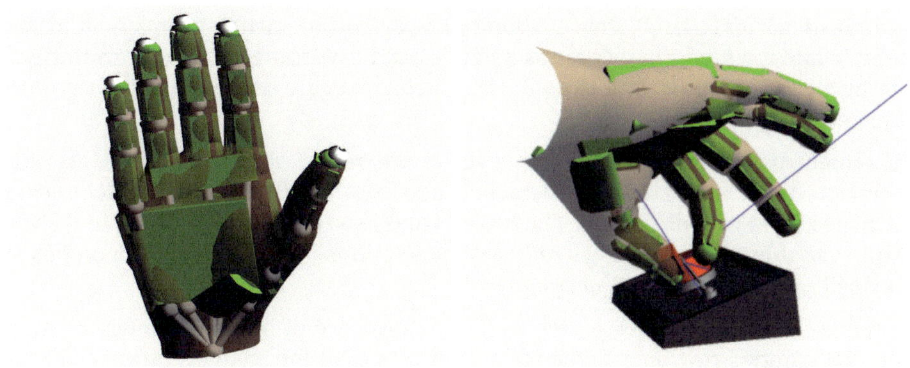

Fig. 6. left: Articulated virtual hand model fitted with collision sensors (depicted in green). right: Sensors of hand model detecting collisions with object and generating respective forces for physical simulation (blue lines).

4.1 Interaction recording

Most importantly, *arm trajectory*, *hand posture* and *collision* data during grasping is recorded. In our system all interaction data is stored persistently in an interaction database organized by recording sessions. Recording sessions are subdivided into channels each of which represents a certain single stream or constituent of the interaction data (see figure 7). This could be an input device like an optical tracker or a data glove, or motion data of a certain part of the body like hand postures or hand trajectories.

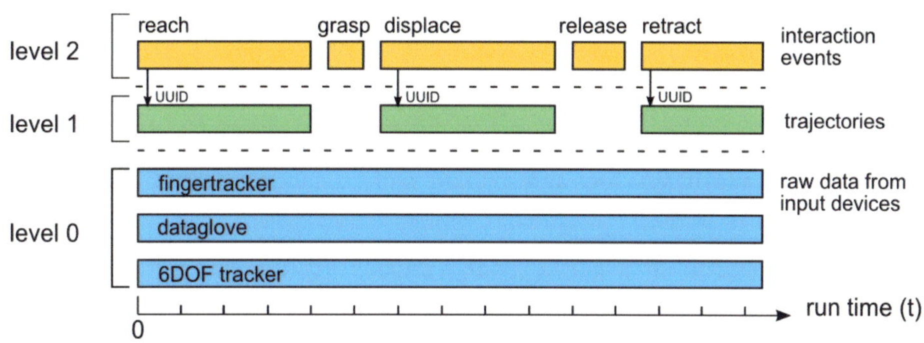

Fig. 7. Examples for channels of the interaction database and their division into to different levels.

Recording channels are organized into different levels, based on the type of data they contain:

Level 0 - Raw data: This level contains the raw data, captured from the different input devices at certain sampling times denoted by timestamps. This data is *continuous* and *homogeneous*, i.e. each input device sends the same amount of data at a time step and continues producing data from the start of the application till the end.

Level 1 - Motion data: On this level, each channel contains motion data of a specific part of the user's body, e. g. hand trajectory, elbow swivel angle, gaze direction, etc. This data also contains time stamps but is additionally segmented into intervals of motion, separated by pauses or by object contact. Each interval can be referenced by higher levels of data via a unique identifier (UUID), thus enabling playback of interaction events with high visual fidelity while the motion intervals as a whole can be rearranged in time arbitrarily. Thus, in terms of the structure of this data, level 1 channels are described as *homogeneous* and *interval-based*.

Level 2 - Interaction data: Data on this level is the result of detection and classification processes. These are primarily interaction and control actuator events (see section 4.3) which are stored in XML format. The amount and length of data contained in these events is quite variable and they always refer to certain points in time. Thus, data on this level is described as *selective* and *nonhomogeneous*.

Through this multi-level database architecture, persistence of the whole interaction session, from the fine-grained raw data to the abstracted results of the analysis process, is achieved. Further, the data captured in the interaction database can be played back in a modular way. It is possible to play back only a selection of channels, depending on the purpose of the playback. This is where the subdivision into channels and levels becomes valuable. If only level 0 rawdata is played back, the interaction can be simulated again and also the analyses process can be repeated. This allows for training and testing of e. g. the involved classification algorithms. Conversely, if only data from higher levels is played back, animations can be generated reproducing the recognized interactions *in effect*, that is, they can be flexibly adapted to changed scenes or different body model proportions.

4.2 Grasp classification

Hand posture data during hand-object contact is automatically classified w.r.t. its grasp type (Heumer et al., 2008).

During the course of the virtual workers project several grasp taxonomies from the medical, e. g. (Schlesinger, 1919), and robotics literature, e. g. (Cutkosky, 1989), have been explored. Since some significant shortcomings in relation to applicability in virtual environments have been identified, additionally a new taxonomy has been proposed in (Heumer, 2010) which as a unique feature provides support for different types of non-prehensile grasps. The latter play an important role in the operation of control actuators in application domains like virtual prototyping, ergonomics evaluations and simulation of machine operation procedures.

4.3 Recognition of basic interactions

Fed by a multilayer classification and recognition scheme, thoroughly described in (Heumer, 2010), the continuous stream of body movements and scene interactions is segmented and analyzed. As a result, *interaction events* are generated which contain information about smallest semantically meaningful constituents called *basic interactions*, e. g. grasp, touch, push, reach, etc. All basic interactions are characterized by one specific aspect that is modified by the respective type of interaction, such as hand-object distance, hand-object contact, forces, prehension, and object position or orientation. Besides its distinct type or category, a basic interaction is further qualified by a type-specific set of parameters. Figure 8 shows the different types of basic interactions that are currently distinguished. Regarding implementation, the interaction events are realized as observer pattern, so arbitrary other parts of the system can subscribe as listeners to these events such as storage, visualization, action recognition, etc.

A subclass of interaction events are control actuator events (CAEs). These are generated under certain conditions when a control actuator changes its state. The exact condition of generation and the granularity of information contained in the events is configurable. Generally, CAEs are fired when the user interaction with a control actuator ends (see figure 9 for an example).

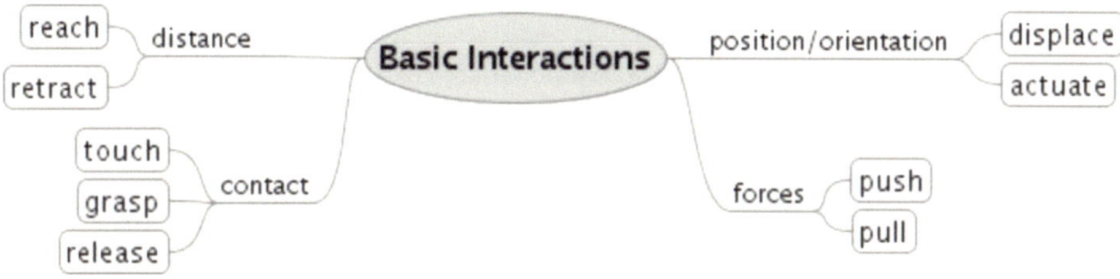

Fig. 8. Taxonomy of basic interactions.

In this case, the event contains the state (rotation around rotational DOFs, translation along translational DOFs) quantified between a minimum and a maximum value. For control actuators with discrete states, the name of the final state is also included. Furthermore, intermediate states during the interaction can also generate events when they are passed before the interaction ends. All state names and DOF information is referenced as specified in the XML actuator declaration (cf. 2.2) thus rendering the event format also human-readable. See listing 2 for an example.

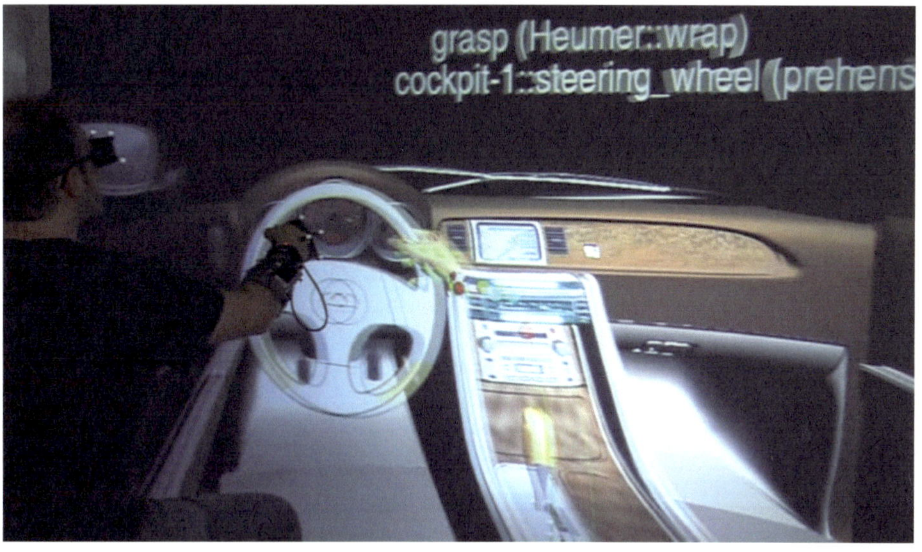

Fig. 9. Automatic recognition of basic interactions while manipulating the control actuators of a virtual car interior.

For full detail of the interaction, a complete history can be recorded (current state in every frame). This history is stored globally under a unique ID and is referenced by this ID in the interaction event fired at the end of the interaction. This enables the reproduction of either the outcome of the interaction (just final state), a reproduction of the state change order (intermediate discrete states) or an exact reproduction of the whole interaction (history). By the latter a replay in a purely graphical scene can be realized without the further need for an active dynamics simulation.
The result of the complete interaction analysis process is a stream of basic interactions which are persistently stored and also propagated to other application parts via the event system. There, they can be analyzed and processed further with automatic methods (action recognition and animation generation) or by hand.

4.4 Visual analysis tool

In order to monitor and improve the classification processes for interaction events (described in the previous section), we implemented a graphical tool that allows us to visualize, analyze and easily edit the recorded interaction data from a database or from local files. We implemented our tool VisuAnIA (Visualizing and Analyzing tool for InterAction data) by using a plug-in architecture, to easily extend the application and to provide different views, e. g. a 3D trajectory view or an animated hand view.

A graphical browser for the different channels (see section 4.1) offers a generic overview with a timeline (see fig. 10, left view). According to the layers in the interaction database (fig. 7) this view is separated into three levels. The top level contains the interaction events which are referring to the segmented hand trajectories in the second level, as well as to the raw data in the third level that has been captured from various input devices such as motion trackers, data gloves, etc. Following the FacetZoom metaphor as described in (Dachselt et al., 2008), the navigation through the three hierarchical levels can be done by clicking on a desired level, at which adjacent levels will be represented smaller and remain in context. The interval-based data (that contains a start and end time) is drawn in a box-like manner along the timeline and is enriched with generic textual information, such as the type of an interaction event or the exact time values. Furthermore the user can select one or more of these interval-boxes to analyze them by using special views. Similar to an audio editing tool, the current position of the cursor determines a time value that will be used in other plug-ins. To enable the analysis even for very short or long datasets, this view also provides a linear zooming option along the timeline.

For a more specific visualization of the hand trajectories we implemented another plug-in that provides a 3D view (fig. 10, middle view). Next to rotating and zooming, this view allows the examination of smaller parts of the trajectories. This is done by defining an interval in the timeline view. Only those parts of the trajectories are displayed which are inside the interval, what is useful in particular when a recorded action is very local and a hand trajectory occludes parts of itself. In order to illustrate the timing of the hand movement during the interaction, on the segmented trajectories a little sphere is shown. This sphere indicates the position of the hand according to the currently selected time value

A further view shows an animated 3D hand model to visualize the data from a dataglove (fig. 10, right view). Again using the timeline, the user can access the recorded postures of

```
<event type="actuator" start-time="11.1374" duration="0.2058" id="CAE-2">
    [...]
    <actuator-states object-id="cockpit-1::steering_wheel">
      <start-data>
        <state dof="rotational1" value="-0.0094"/>
        <discrete-state value="center"/>
      </start-data>
      <goal-data>
        <state dof="rotational1" value="3.3676"/>
        <discrete-state value="right"/>
      </goal-data>
    </actuator-states>
</event>
```

Listing 2. Code example of a control actuator event.

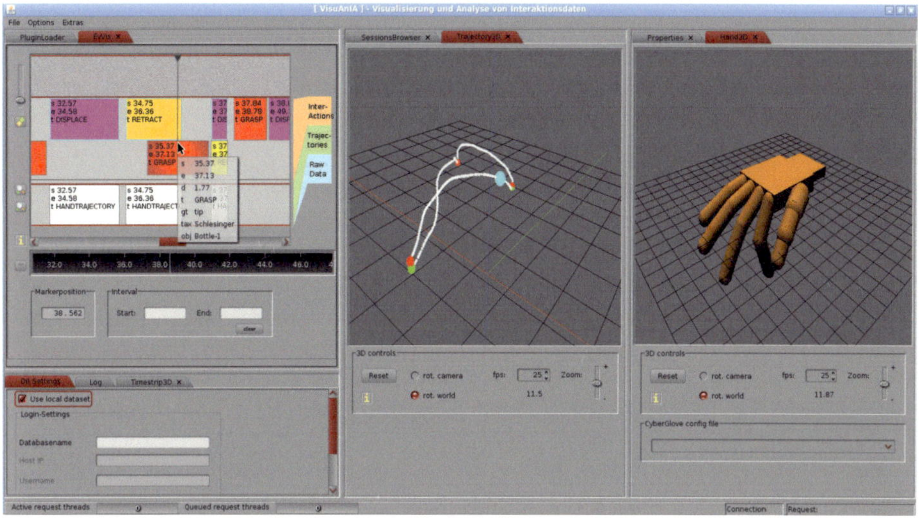

Fig. 10. VisuAnIA: The generic timeline view on the left is used to browse the data that gets visualized in special 3D views.

the hand and compare them to the types of the recognized interaction events or to the objects which have been used.

A plug-in with a commonly known generic properties view (fig. 11, right view) allows the listing of all the recorded values as they are stored in the database. This view also permits the modification of important attributes, such as timing values or the type of an interaction event. Due to the linear zooming option in the basic timeline view, all interval-boxes outside the focused area will disappear from the context so that large datasets may not be adequately examined. Therefore we implemented a conceptual 3D timeline plug-in (*Timestrip3D*) that only shows a small fraction from the basic timeline (fig. 11, lower view). To indicate the relation between the two timelines a small box, that defines the interval for the second timeline and marks the area of interest, is drawn in the basic timeline view. By using these two timelines it is possible to examine a focused area of the dataset without losing context. Additionally, the timestrip offers a fisheye like zooming option, that carries on the focus-plus-context representation and thus supports the user during analysis. The 3D strip actually consists of several Bézier surfaces that will be modified to achieve the zooming effect. Since the textual information on the timestrip is generated by using different font sizes, different zooming degrees implicate varying levels of detail of the presented information.

To keep both of the timelines synchronized, e. g. while using the generic timeline view to browse and analyze a dataset and the timestrip to obtain additional information, we implemented a new tool we call *Foculyzer*. The aim of the tool is to apply the currently examined (focused) area around the cursor from one timeline view automatically to a second timeline view. That means that a user does not need to set the area of interest (red box in fig. 11) by hand, as necessary e. g. in the TimeSearcher 2 tool (Buono et al., 2005). The tolerance range in which the cursor can be moved without shifting the area of interest can be freely adjusted in our tool. Thus, e. g. depending on the kind of analysis or length of the dataset, the user can customize the tool according to the current needs. Two sliders on the focused area are provided for such adjustments (fig. 11). The sliders are hidden during analysis so that the timeline itself won't be occluded. With our tool we overcame the two drawbacks: The first one occurs when the area of interest is centered exactly around the cursor, which means

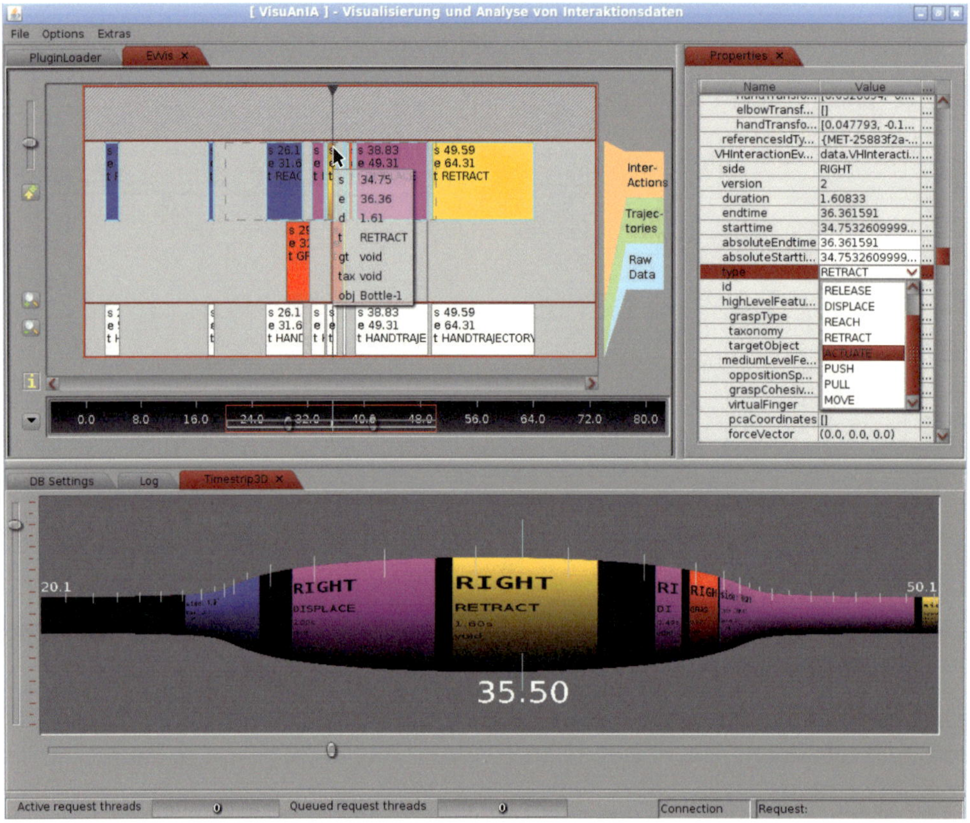

Fig. 11. While the user analyzes interaction events in the upper timeline view, the focused area is automatically applied to the timestrip where more information and a fisheye like zooming is provided. The range of tolerance for the cursor is controlled by the sliders on the red box. On the right, a generic properties view shows the values of the selected interval-boxes and allows the modification of important values.

that every little movement of the cursor causes the area to shift as described in (Bederson, 2000). A second drawback found in some systems results, when the area of interest is shifted only upon the collision of the cursor with the area bounds. Thus, in order to effect a focus change the cursor has to be moved to the borders explicitly which can be annoying. The adjustable tolerance range allows for a more flexible interaction instead. Our tool Foculyzer is not restricted to interaction events, but can also be used to synchronize various other views, e. g. in audio or video editing programs to analyze different channels or different views of one channel.

Future versions of our tool VisuAnIA will provide plug-ins for data filtering, e. g. to recognize wrongly tracked trajectories. Furthermore, we will implement a player to reproduce the recorded interaction data in various speeds.

5. Application scenarios

Due to its universal and extendable nature, the framework for control actuators presented here can be used in many different types of interactive VR prototyping applications where movable parts with physically believable behavior are called for. In our particular area of research - which has virtual prototyping as application domain - we use the framework to simulate parts of machinery or other virtual prototypes. The operation is done manually by a VR user. The aim is to demonstrate manipulation sequences that are repeated by an animated character, i.e. a virtual human, see Figure 12. This type of animation is closely related to *Programming by Demonstration* in the field of robotics and is referred to as *Action Capture* in (Jung et al., 2006).

Fig. 12. Control actuators contained in the virtual prototype of a car cockpit.

Apart from our research scenario many different use cases are conceivable. Such applications can include virtual prototyping and construction, ergonomics studies, instructional animations, etc. The only prerequisite is a mechanism to determine forces and torques exerted on the actuators. A simple mechanism would be to translate 6DOF input from e. g. a Spaceball or a tracking device and translate its output to appropriate forces and torques.
Furthermore, interactive scene functionality can be realized by subscribing and reacting to interaction events. For example, a car radio sound can be played when the car radio button is pressed. The volume can be adjusted, when the knob is turned, etc.
In this section, we discuss the benefits of our approach for two typical application domains (virtual training, ergonomic studies with virtual prototypes) on the basis of two scenarios we have (partially) implemented.

Scenarios

The first scenario is a control panel on which different actuators are located (see fig. 1). These VR objects represent reference implementations of the fundamental types of control actuators specified in (DIN894-3, 2006). Among these control actuators are a steering wheel, different knobs and sliders.
The second scenario is a car driving application (fig. 13). In this scenario, the user sits in a virtual cockpit and manipulates control actuators in order to drive the car. Control actuators are a steering wheel, a gear shift, radio knobs and the ignition key. The user's interactions trigger certain functionalities and animations.

Fig. 13. A user manipulates the gear shift in our car driving scenario.

Virtual training and functional prototypes

An important use case of our approach is virtual training. Our first prototype serves the purpose to improve the user's fundamental skills in operating virtual control actuators. The user can change the state of an actuator in order to explore its behavior.

In the second scenario, the user can learn how to start and drive a car or he can improve his driving skills. By connecting the manipulation of an actuator with a certain functionality using the event mechanism described before, functional prototypes can be realized. For example, the user can hear the sound of the car's engine after starting it and while driving; he can hear music from the radio after turning it on and he can navigate the car through the virtual environment by rotating the steering wheel. By providing physically correct behavior of actuators in combination with functional prototypes, the degree of realism and the feeling of immersion can be dramatically improved. In this way, the training scenario becomes a very realistic user experience which facilitates the transfer of learned skills from a virtual to a real environment.

Ergonomic studies

A main application domain of our approach is ergonomic evaluation of virtual prototypes. The evaluations can be conducted with real VR users and virtual humans. An example of a virtual prototype suitable for ergonomic studies is a virtual car as described in the second scenario. The car prototype provides a set of actuators which are typically required for driving. A user performs different actions, such as turning the ignition key, turning the radio on, switching the gears and turning the steering wheel. These actions can be imitated by virtual humans with different body proportions. Ergonomic problems occur, e. g., if a (virtual) human's arm collides with an obstacle while trying to grasp a target object or if the human cannot even reach the target object. Such problems can be identified and analyzed by observing the real VR user performing the actions required to reach a certain goal (e. g. starting the car's engine) or by watching animations of virtual humans synthesized from captured action sequences. In this context, realistic actuator behavior is important, since a state change of an actuator can influence ergonomic conditions. For instance, if there were no collisions with the gear shift lever, such collisions can suddenly occur after changing the lever's state (orientation/position). In addition, by using an event serialization mechanism, it is not only possible to reproduce the motions of the involved control actuators exactly (even without virtual humans), but also to visualize the generated events for a more thorough analysis (e. g., in order to identify unwanted collisions). This is an important use case for our VisuAnIA tool (see 4.4) that offers the required analysis functionality.

6. Conclusion

We presented a comprehensive approach for enabling and analyzing natural interactions with functional virtual prototypes. Compared to more generic languages such as X3D or Collada, a domain-specific XML-based language simplifies the specification of virtual control actuators. In immersive VR settings, control actuators can be manipulated using natural interaction techniques based on data gloves and motion tracking devices. During on-going user interactions, the current state of the control actuator is continuously monitored and made available to other components of the overall VR-system by means of an event mechanism. A continuously moving control actuator may snap to predefined discrete states, e. g. on/off positions of a switch, and special events are fired when the actuator reaches such a discrete state. For instance, this allows to simulate functional effects of control actuators in the VR system. The described approach covers all control actuators described in the European standard EN 894-3.

True functional validation of virtual prototypes, in our opinion, should include but not be restricted to live experiences of VR users. Therefore, our approach comprises several concepts and tools for recording and offline analysis of operating procedures performed on virtual prototypes in immersive VR. For this, various aspects of user interactions can be stored in an interaction database, from low-level sensor data, over trajectory data, up to high-level interaction events containing e. g. the classifications of user grasps w.r.t. a grasp taxonomy. A graphical tool that builds on state-of-the-art as well as newly designed information visualization methods serves to analyze and, if appropriate, edit the recorded interactions. The power of our approach is demonstrated by an implemented application where animations of virtual humans are generated from the recorded interaction data. We believe that several application settings, such as VR-based training systems, could benefit from the presented approach.

7. References

Abate, A. F., Guida, M., Leoncini, P., Nappi, M. & Ricciardi, S. (2009). A Haptic-Based Approach to Virtual Training for Aerospace Industry, *J. Vis. Lang. Comput.* 20: 318–325.
URL: *http://portal.acm.org/citation.cfm?id=1598095.1598605*

Bederson, B. B. (2000). Fisheye Menus, *Proceedings of the 13th annual ACM symposium on User interface software and technology*, UIST '00, ACM, New York, NY, USA, pp. 217–225.
URL: *http://doi.acm.org/10.1145/354401.354782*

Buono, P., Aris, A., Plaisant, C., Khella, A. & Shneiderman, B. (2005). Interactive Pattern Search in Time Series, Vol. 5669, SPIE, pp. 175–186.
URL: *http://link.aip.org/link/?PSI/5669/175/1*

Cutkosky, M. (1989). On Grasp Choice, Grasp Models and the Design of Hands for Manufacturing Tasks, *IEEE Transactions on Robotics and Automation* 5(3): 269–279.

Dachselt, R., Frisch, M. & Weiland, M. (2008). Facetzoom: A Continuous Multi-Scale Widget for Navigating Hierarchical Metadata, *CHI '08: Proceeding of the twenty-sixth annual SIGCHI conference on Human factors in computing systems*, ACM, New York, NY, USA, pp. 1353–1356.

DIN894-3 (2006). Safety of Machinery - Ergonomic Requirements for the Design of Displays and Control Actuators - part 3: Control Actuators, en 894-3.

Heumer, G. (2010). *Simulation, Erfassung und Analyse direkter Objektmanipulationen in virtuellen Umgebungen*, PhD thesis, TU BA Freiberg.
URL: *http://nbn-resolving.de/urn:nbn:de:bsz:105-qucosa-70518*

Heumer, G., Ben Amor, H. & Jung, B. (2008). Grasp Recognition for Uncalibrated Data Gloves: A Machine Learning Approach, *Presence: Teleoperators and Virtual Environments* 17: 121–142.
URL: *http://portal.acm.org/citation.cfm?id=1362509.1362512*

International Organization for Standardization (2008). *ISO/IEC FDIS 19775-1:2008: Information technology – Computer graphics and image processing – Extensible 3D (X3D) – Part 1: Architecture and base components, 2. Edition.*

Jerez, J. & Suero, A. (2011). Newton Game Dynamics. Open-Source Physics Engine .
URL: *http://newtondynamics.com*

Jung, B., Amor, H. B., Heumer, G. & Weber, M. (2006). From Motion Capture to Action Capture: A Review of Imitation Learning Techniques and their Application to VR-based Character Animation, *Proceedings VRST 2006 - Thirteenth ACM Symposium on Virtual Reality Software and Technology*, pp. 145–154.

Kallmann, M. & Thalmann, D. (1999). Direct 3D Interaction with Smart Objects, *Proceedings ACM VRST 99, London.*

Khronos Group (2008). *Collada - Digital Asset Schema Release 1.5.0 Specification.*

Moehring, M. & Froehlich, B. (2011). Natural Interaction Metaphors for Functional Validations of Virtual Car Models, *IEEE Transactions on Visualization and Computer Graphics (TVCG), accepted manuscript .*
URL: *http://dx.doi.org/10.1109/TVCG.2011.36*

Moehring, M. & Fröhlich, B. (2010). Enabling Functional Validation of Virtual Cars Through Natural Interaction Metaphors, *Proceedings of IEEE Virtual Reality Conference, VR 2010*, pp. 27–34.

Schlesinger, G. (1919). Der Mechanische Aufbau der Künstlichen Glieder, *in* M. Borchardt et al. (eds), *Ersatzglieder und Arbeitshilfen für Kriegsbeschädigte und Unfallverletzte*, Springer-Verlag, Berlin, Germany, pp. 321–661.

Weber, M., Heumer, G., Amor, H. B. & Jung, B. (2006). An Animation System for Imitation of Object Grasping in Virtual Reality, *Proceedings of Advances in Artificial Reality and Tele-Existence, 16th International Conference on Artificial Reality and Telexistence, ICAT*, Springer, pp. 65–76.

Zachmann, G. & Rettig, A. (2001). Natural and Robust Interaction in Virtual Assembly Simulation , *Eighth ISPE International Conference on Concurrent Engineering: Research and Applications (ISPE/CE2001)*, pp. 425–434.

Zorriassatine, F., Wykes, C., Parkin, R. & Gindy, N. (2003). A Survey of Virtual Prototyping Techniques for Mechanical Product Development, *Journal of Engineering Manufacture* 217.

12

Fluid Pressurization in Cartilages and Menisci in the Normal and Repaired Human Knees

LePing Li and Mojtaba Kazemi
University of Calgary
Canada

1. Introduction

Computer simulation has found extensive applications in biomedical engineering. In particular, finite element methods have been used in orthopaedic biomechanics to help design prostheses and implants and understand joint injuries and diseases. We are interested in the mechanics of the knee joint that is associated with the fluid pressure and flow in the articular cartilages and menisci. This section presents a brief review of current status of computer mechanical modeling of the human knee and the cartilaginous tissues. The background of our present research will be understood in this section.

1.1 Mechanical structure of the knee

The human knee joint is a complex mechanical structure. It connects the two major bones of the lower limb together: the femur and tibia. Femoral and tibial cartilages, which are hydrated soft tissues, cover the ends of the femur and tibia respectively (Fig. 1, finite element model). These articular cartilages together with menisci, another hydrated soft tissue, provide smooth articulating surfaces that redistribute the joint loading and reduce stress concentrations in the bones. The lubrication in the knee is provided by the synovial fluid and low stiffness of the cartilaginous tissues, including cartilages and menisci. During daily activities such as walking and running, a normal knee experiences minimum frictions and virtually no wear (Callaghan et al., 2003; Swanson, 1979). The femoral cartilage has a curved shape while the tibial cartilages are almost flat. The two menisci locate between the femoral and tibial cartilages and provide the shape congruency in the knee joint. Each meniscus has a crescent-like form, and is connected to the tibia plateau at the both ends by meniscus horns. The wedge-shape cross-section of the menisci minimizes the direct contact of the femoral and tibial cartilages. In the case of healthy menisci, the direct contact can be as low as 10% of the cartilage surfaces (Walker & Erkman, 1975). By improving the joint congruency, the menisci support and redistribute the joint load, increase the joint stability and facilitate lubrication (Fithian et al., 1990; Kurosawa et al., 1980; Walker & Hajek, 1972). Ligaments are fibrous tissues with fibers mainly aligned in the longitudinal direction. Four ligaments connect the femur and tibia or fibula. They are Medial Collateral Ligament (MCL), Lateral Collateral Ligament (LCL), Anterior Cruciate Ligament (ACL) and Posterior Cruciate Ligament (PCL). Among the main roles of ligaments is to stabilize the joint and support a portion of the applied load (Daniel et al., 1990). Other important mechanical components include tendons and muscles, which are beyond the scope of this chapter.

The main constituents of the cartilage and menisci are fluid, collagen fibers (mainly type II in cartilages and type I in menisci) and proteoglycan matrix. The fluid is the most abundant component of these tissues. It takes 68-85% of the weight of cartilage and 60-70% of the menisci (Mow & Ratcliffe, 1990). Hydrated tissues such as cartilages and menisci are viscoelastic: they exhibit stress relaxation when the strain is held constant and creep when the stress is held constant. The viscoelastic behavior is mainly due to the interstitial fluid flow and the intrinsic viscoelasticity of the collagen fibers. In general, cartilaginous tissues appear very soft to facilitate joint movement when they are not pressurized. However, under fast knee compressions, these tissues can be highly pressurized to support and redistribute loadings (Mow et al., 1980; Spilker et al., 1992).

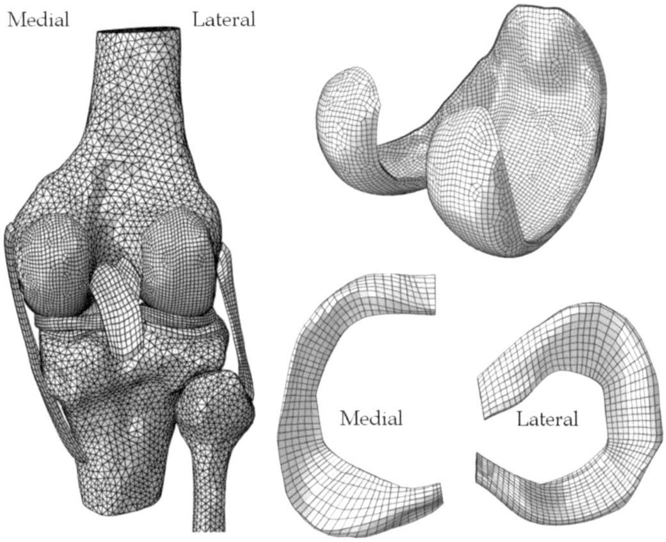

Fig. 1. Finite element model of the knee joint. Top right: femoral cartilage (posterior view); bottom right: menisci (top view). The model was obtained from a young male's right knee (the patella was not modeled)

The mechanical function of the knee joint is partially performed through mechanical contacts between several contacting pairs of cartilaginous tissues. The major contact pairs are the femoral cartilage–tibial cartilage, femoral cartilage–menisci and menisci–tibial cartilages. Understanding the contact mechanics of the individual knee tissues as well as the whole joint assembly may lead to better prevention, diagnosis and treatment of joint injury and diseases. The changes in the health state of the cartilages or menisci can alter the contact mechanics of the knee and therefore affect its normal functioning. For instance, partial meniscectomy, which is a surgical operation to remove the injured part of the meniscus, can alter the stress and pressure distributions in the cartilaginous tissues and may initiate or advance osteoarthritis.

1.2 Finite element modeling of the knee

Finite element methods have been extensively used to investigate the mechanics of the knee joint or its individual tissues. The advantages of using finite element simulations compared to the experimental studies include convenient control of load and boundary conditions, easy evaluation of stress and strain fields, time and cost efficiency and capability of parametric studies. However, each finite element study is associated with numerous simplifications in geometrical modeling, material definition, constitutive behavior, etc. In recent two decades, new finite elements have been proposed to improve modeling and eliminate some limitations. Simplified or experimental explants geometries have been widely used to validate the complex constitutive relationships of the knee tissues. Earlier joint modeling was also based on axisymmetrical or plane-strain geometries: two pieces of tissues in two dimensional geometries were often used to represent a knee joint contact (Adeeb et al., 2004; Wu et al., 1998). More recently, anatomically accurate knee models become increasingly popular for the investigation of realistic joint contact in different loading conditions and health states. These real knee geometries are normally reconstructed from the Computer Tomography (CT) or Magnetic Resonance Imaging (MRI). The constitutive modeling used for the hydrated soft tissues may be classified into three main categories: *single-phase* solid models, *poroelastic* or *biphasic* models (with additional fluid phase) and *fibril-reinforced* models (fluid phase and fibril-reinforced solid phase). Due to time cost and convergence difficulties associated with the anatomically accurate models, simpler constitutive behaviors (commonly single-phase) have been used in these studies as compared to the cases with simplified geometries.

1.3 Constitutive modeling of the knee tissues

The finite element studies of articular cartilage and menisci have been quite comprehensive with experimental tissue testing geometries (Ateshian et al., 1994; Li et al., 2003; Mow et al., 1980). The constitutive models used in these studies have been evolved from that for single-phase materials, i.e. from that for a structural steel (Coletti et al., 1972; Hayes et al., 1972; Kempson et al., 1971). Since only elastic properties were considered in the single-phase material, the time dependent load response resulted from the fluid flow could not be described by these early models. Linear elasticity, homogeneity and isotropy were often assumed (Armstrong et al., 1980; Hayes et al., 1972). Some single-phase models featured viscoelastic behavior using dashpots and springs (e.g. Kelvin-Voigt-Maxwell models). They had the potential to describe the time dependent responses (Coletti et al., 1972; Hayes & Mockros, 1971; Parsons & Black, 1977). However, the fluid flow relative to the tissue matrix could not be described by such modeling. Another limitation was associated with the use of effective modulus, when a single-phase elastic model was employed. Instead of the real Young's modulus of the tissue matrix, a greater effective modulus accounting for the stiffness of the pressurized tissue had to be used, in order to match the stress measured experimentally. This effective modulus is generally pressure-dependent, resulting in uncertainties in its appropriate determination and thus uncertainties in the results (Li and Gu, 2011).

Poroelastic/biphasic models for biological tissues were proposed to capture the time dependent response of the tissues (solid + fluid phases). Poroelastic models were based on the soil consolidation theory (Biot 1941, 1962), while the biphasic theory was initially proposed by Mow et al. (1980) using the theory of porous media. It was believed that these two theories yield similar results if the fluid was assumed as inviscid (Simon, 1992). In fact, it was shown that the linear poroelasticity was essentially equivalent to the linear theory of porous media, although some inconsistencies were observed in correlating the material properties (Schanz and Diebels, 2003). The early poroelastic models were developed to investigate the mechanics of bones (Nowinski, 1971, 1972; Nowinski and Davis, 1970, 1972). The biphasic models have been improved substantially from its initial linear version (Mow et al., 1980), e.g. variable permeability (Lai et al., 1981) and large deformation have been formulated (Suh et al., 1991). Many independent formulations were also developed (e.g. Lanir, 1987). The biphasic models were found to be able to account for the mechanical response of articular cartilage at low strain-rates only (Brown and Singerman, 1986; Miller, 1998).

The load response of articular cartilage is highly transient. Given a compression, the stress in the tissue can be an order higher at a high compression rate than that at a low compression rate (Oloyede et al., 1992). Fibril-reinforced models were proposed to capture this high-ratio of fast versus slow compressions. In a fibril-reinforced model, the solid phase was separated into two constituents: the fibrillar and non-fibrillar matrices. The non-fibrillar matrix defines the proteoglycan matrix, and the fibrillar matrix models the collagen network (Soulhat et al., 1999). It was found that the nonlinear fibrillar properties must be considered in order to account for the strong transient responses of articular cartilage (Li et al. 1999b). In a finite element procedure, the fibrillar matrix could be represented by discrete spring elements (Li et al. 1999b; Soulhat et al., 1999) or continuum elements (Li & Herzog, 2004; Wilson et al., 2004). A fibril-reinforced model was used for the soft tissues in the present study.

1.4 Anatomically accurate knee modeling

Poroelastic and fibril-reinforced models have been extensively used to describe the tissue mechanical behavior for the problems with simple geometries. However, these studies have not been extended to the anatomically accurate knee models until our recent work (Gu and Li, 2011). Single-phase material models have been commonly used in the joint finite element modeling. The geometrical data of these models were commonly obtained from CT and MRI. A typical finite element model of the tibio-femoral joint is illustrated in Fig. 1. In many three-dimensional models, bones are considered as rigid due to their higher stiffness compared to the soft tissues (3 orders in difference). The fluid pressure in the soft tissues is normally ignored to avoid the numerical difficulties resulted from complicated mechanical contacts and time-dependent responses (Bendjaballah et al., 1995; Li et al., 1999a; Peña et al., 2005). Articular cartilages were often simplified as single-phase, linear elastic, homogenous and isotropic materials (Haut Donahue et al., 2002; Peña et al., 2006). Menisci were modeled as isotropic (Peña et al., 2005, 2006, 2008), transversely isotropic (Haut Donahue et al., 2002) or fiber-reinforced linearly elastic solid (Penrose et al., 2002; Shirazi et al., 2008). Example case studies are: knee joint under compression (Bendjaballah et al., 1995; Shirazi et al., 2008), knee joint in combined loading (Peña et al., 2006; Shirazi & Shirazi-Adl, 2009), effect of meniscectomies (Peña et al., 2005, 2008; Yang et al., 2009; Zielinska & Donahue, 2006) and effect of ligament reconstruction on the knee joint biomechanics (Shirazi & Shirazi-Adl, 2009; Suggs et al., 2003).

Although fluid flow is believed to play a substantial role in the load response of the knee, little information is known about the fluid pressurization in cartilages and menisci in the real knee contact configuration. By modeling the fluid flow in the soft tissues, the time dependent response of the knee joint can be described, i.e. the creep and relaxation behaviors can be predicted. Further important information may be obtained. For instance, not only the magnitude, but also the distribution of contact pressure between the articular surfaces was found to be different when the fluid pressure was modeled (Li and Gu, 2011). The location of the maximum contact pressure may also change with creep or relaxation, which cannot be predicted by a single-phase elastic model. Mechanical response associated with fluid pressurization in the tissues may play important roles in the scenarios previously studied, which might not have been understood because the fluid pressure was ignored. Considering the difficulties associated with in-situ measurements of fluid pressure in cartilage and menisci, a three-dimensional computational model is a good option for the determination of the fluid pressurization in these tissues. The fluid flow has been successfully modeled in a three-dimensional fiber-reinforced model of the temporomandibular joint (Perez del Palomar & Doblare, 2007). More recently, a three-dimensional anatomically accurate knee model has been proposed to capture the stress relaxation and creep behaviors of the healthy and meniscectomized knee joints (Gu & Li, 2011; Kazemi et al., 2011, Li and Gu, 2011). We will consider some complementary results here.

2. Methods

The mechanical responses were simulated for the intact knee, as well as six cases of partial meniscectomy at different sites. The finite element modeling developed in our previous studies will be briefly reviewed in this section. The meshes, material properties and loading conditions for the present study will be particularly discussed.

2.1 Geometry and finite element mesh

The joint geometry was obtained using the Magnetic Resonance Imaging (MRI) of a healthy male's right knee in full extension (Cheung et al., 2005). The commercial finite element software ABAQUS v6.8-2 (Simulia Inc., Providence, RI, USA) was used to generate the mesh (Fig. 1). The model consisted of the distal femur, tibia, fibula, articular cartilages, menisci and the four major ligaments (ACL, PCL, MCL and LCL). Bones were considered as rigid and triangular elements were used to mesh their surfaces (triangles normally describe a curved surface better). In total, 12,829 surface elements were used for the bones (Table 1).

Tissue	Femur	Tibia	Fibula	Femoral cartilage	Tibial cartilage	Menisci	ACL	PCL	LCL	MCL
Number of elements	5668	5385	1776	18432	637	3423	288	306	456	516
Number of nodes	2836	2709	891	89689	1482	5117	513	540	780	924

Table 1. Nodes and elements for individual tissues in the finite element mesh of the knee

Articular cartilages, menisci and ligaments were meshed using hexahedral elements. Porous elements with linear variation of fluid pressure and quadratic variation of displacement were chosen for the femoral cartilage (20 nodes). Porous elements with linear variation of displacement were used for the menisci and tibial cartilages (8 nodes). Solid elements with linear displacement were used for the ligaments. In total, 24,058 elements and 99,045 nodes were used to mesh the soft tissues of the healthy knee (Table 1).

In order to model the total and partial meniscectomized knees, the elements corresponding to the resected meniscus were removed from the intact element assembly. Here, the total meniscectomy refers to the complete removal of both medial and lateral menisci. For the partial meniscectomy, two sites of resections in the avascular zone (inner peripheral meniscus) were considered. One resection was in the lateral and one in the medial meniscus. They were thus referred as to the extended lateral meniscectomy and extended medial meniscectomy, respectively. Meniscectomies in this zone are more common because lesions there have very low chance of natural healing due to absence of blood supply in the zone. The resection is often longitudinal or in the circumferential direction (Dandy, 1990; Greis et al., 2002). An extended meniscectomy encountered longer resection in the longitudinal direction.

2.2 Material properties

Cartilages, menisci and ligaments were modeled as fibril-reinforced materials. The fiber orientation in the femoral cartilage was assumed based on the split line patterns (Below et al., 2002). For the menisci, the primary fibers were oriented circumferentially (Aspden et al., 1985). The fibers in the tibial cartilage were oriented randomly due to lack of information about the primary fiber direction in this tissue. In the case of ligaments, the fibers were aligned in the longitudinal direction. The initial strains in ligaments were ignored since only small deformation was considered in the current study. The reported initial strains of the ligaments are normally beyond the small deformation range (Grood & Hefzy, 1982).

The non-fibrillar matrix of the soft tissues was considered as linearly elastic and isotropic. The viscoelasticity of collagen fibers was formulated previously (Li et al., 2009) but omitted here in favor of brevity. In short, the following relation was used for the fibrillar stiffness in the primary fiber direction, x:

$$E_x^f(\varepsilon_x) = E_x^0 + E_x^\varepsilon \varepsilon_x \tag{1}$$

where ε_x is the tensile strain, and E_x^0 and E_x^ε are elastic constants in x direction. The same equations, but with different values for coefficients, were used for the y and z directions. The compressive stiffness of the fibrillar matrix was ignored.

The fibrillar properties of different tissues were determined from previous fibril-reinforced modeling and experimental data from the literature (Hirokawa & Tsuruno, 2000; Li et al., 2003; Shirazi et al., 2008; Woo et al., 1976). The numerical values of material properties are listed in Table 2. More details and references about the material properties can be found in our recent papers (Gu and Li, 2011; Kazemi et al., 2011).

2.3 Contact interactions

Cartilaginous tissues in the knee are in multiple mechanical contacts between the mating surfaces. These contacts require particular attention for a successful simulation. For each contact pair, one surface is selected as the master surface and the other one as the slave surface. A master surface may penetrate the mating slave surface, but the other way is not permissible. The surface discretization can be node-to-surface or surface-to-surface. The contact constraint can be enforced with different methods. The efficiency of a contact enforcement method is usually determined by the type of surface discretization. In the present study with the existence of fluid pressure in three-dimensional geometries, surface-to-surface discretization was selected and the linear penalty method was found to be the most efficient approach for the contact enforcement.

Tissues	Fibrillar elastic moduli (MPa), Eq. (1)				Non-fibrillar solid matrix			
	Primary fiber direction x		Directions y & z		Young's modulus (MPa)	Poisson's ratio	Permeability (mm⁴/Ns)	
	E^0	E^ε	E^0	E^ε			Direction x	Directions y & z
Femoral cartilage	3	1600	0.9	480	0.26	0.36	0.002	0.001
Menisci	28	0	5	0	0.50	0.36	0.002	0.001
Tibial cartilage	2	1000	2	1000	0.26	0.36	0.002	0.001
Ligament	10	14000	0	0	1.0	0.30	0	0

Table 2. Material properties of the soft tissues used in the finite element simulation

For the intact and partially meniscectomized knees, six contact pairs were defined (three on the medial and three on the lateral side): femoral cartilage-tibial cartilage, femoral cartilage-menisci and menisci-tibial cartilage. Obviously, for the total meniscectomy, only contacts between the femoral and tibial cartilages remained (2 pairs). Frictional contact with a coefficient of 0.02 (Mow et al., 1993) was considered for all the contacts.

The ends of the ligaments and menisci were TIED (fixed) to the bones at the insertion sites. This is obviously in agreement with the actual attachment of the ligaments to the bones. The ends of meniscus are actually fixed to the tibia through meniscus horns. The horns were not particularly modeled in the present study.

2.4 Loads, boundary conditions and solution methods

A stress relaxation protocol was used for the study of the intact, partial and total meniscectomized knees. For the purpose of comparison, the loading and boundary conditions were chosen to be as close as possible to that of similar experimental studies. In all cases, a ramp knee compression of 0.3 mm was applied in one second and remained constant thereafter. The displacement was applied to the femur in proximal-distal direction. Femur was free in all translations but fixed in all rotations. In all cases, the knee joint was assumed in full extension and the tibia and fibula were constrained in all directions.

A complete description of the solution methods is beyond the scope of this chapter. The overall procedure is presented here briefly. More details can be found in our recent papers (Gu and Li, 2011; Kazemi et al., 2011) and the ABAQUS manuals. The implicit finite element method with transient *Soil Consolidation* option available from ABAQUS/Standard was used for the current study. The Newton method was chosen to solve the nonlinear equations. In each iteration of a typical time increment, the convergence of force and volumetric flux was checked at first. In an iteration with converged force and volumetric flux, the convergence of displacement and fluid pressure was assessed. If the convergence of force, volumetric flux, displacement and fluid pressure was satisfied, the final convergence was accepted when the largest increment in fluid pressure was less than a given value (5 kPa in all cases presented here).

The computer simulations were done on the high performance computers at the University of Calgary (Westgrid) and on our Dell workstations (4 CPUs with 16 GB RAMs). It took a week or two to complete one simulation.

3. Results

Most of the results were plotted for the times 1 and 2000 seconds. The knee compression reached its maximum of 0.3 mm at 1 second followed by relaxation. At 2000 second, the fluid pressure was greatly reduced for the relaxation loading protocol considered (this time may not be long enough for substantial pressure reduction in other cases).

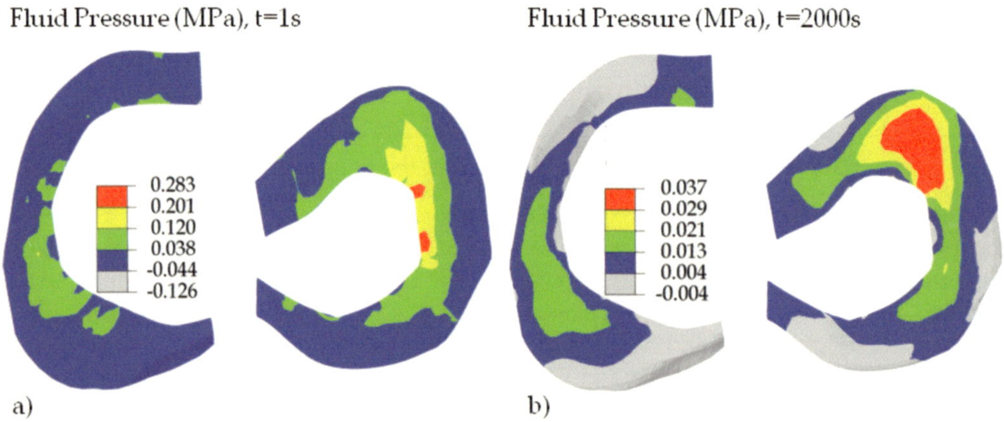

Fig. 2. Fluid pressure in the menisci of an intact right knee. The pressure was obtained for the centroids of the elements. The lateral meniscus is on the right with the posterior side shown in the lower part in each figure (top view)

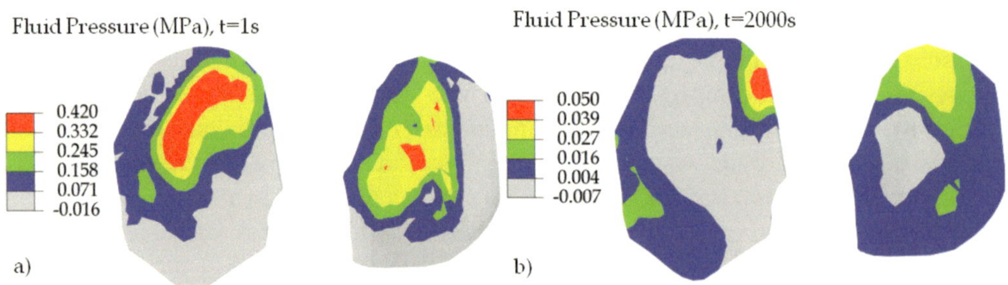

Fig. 3. Fluid pressure in the tibial cartilages of the intact knee. The pressure was obtained for the centroids of the elements. The lateral side is on the right (top view)

NORMAL KNEE – Selected results for the intact joint are shown in Figs. 2-6. The lateral meniscus, which is on the right in Fig. 2a or 2b, was more pressurized than the medial one. The high-pressure region moved toward the anterior side with relaxation (Fig. 2b). The tibial cartilage, on the other hand, was more pressurized on the medial side (Fig. 3). The short-term contact pressure on the articular surface of the tibial cartilage, which could be in contact with the femoral cartilage and menisci, was consistent with the fluid pressure (Figs. 4a vs 3a). A bigger difference in pattern between the fluid and contact pressures was observed at 2000 second (Figs. 4b vs 3b), because the fluid pressure was less significant at later times.

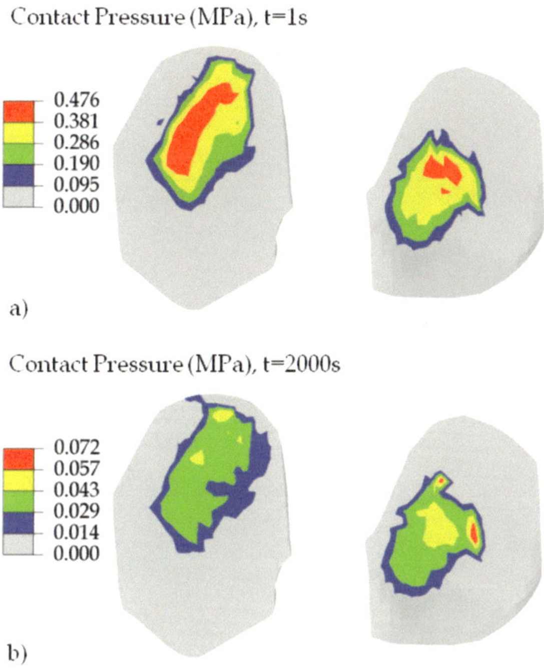

Fig. 4. Contact pressure on the articular surface of the tibial cartilages for the intact knee. The lateral side is on the right (top view)

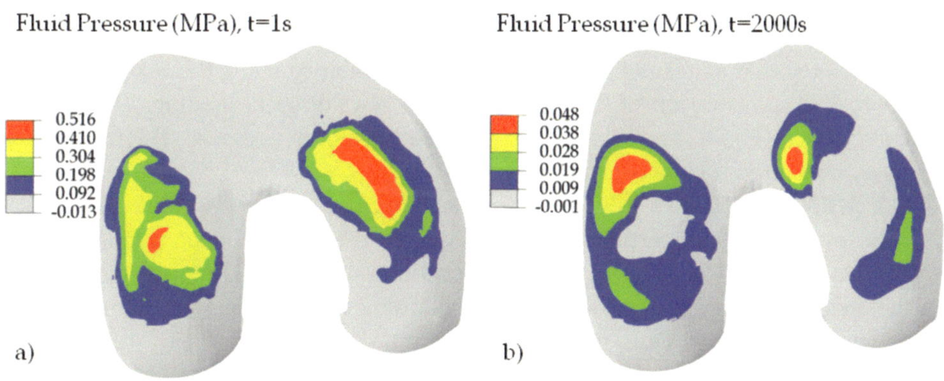

Fig. 5. Fluid pressure in the deep layer of the femoral cartilage for the intact knee. The pressure was obtained for the centroids of the elements that were located approximately 3/4 of the depth from the articular surface. The medial condyle is on the right (inferior view)

The fluid pressure contour for the deep layer of the femoral cartilage (Fig. 5) shows a more regular pattern than that for the menisci (Fig. 2), possibly indicating better results. This was probably because the mesh for the femoral cartilage was more refined, and the mesh for the menisci was mostly irregular due to the wedge shape of the menisci. The contact pressure on the articular surface of the femoral cartilage (Fig. 6) had some similarities with the fluid pressure (Fig. 5), but the differences in distribution are clearly seen. One can also see that the contact pressure in the knee was mainly contributed by the fluid pressurization, because it was decreased substantially with relaxation (Fig. 6b vs 6a).

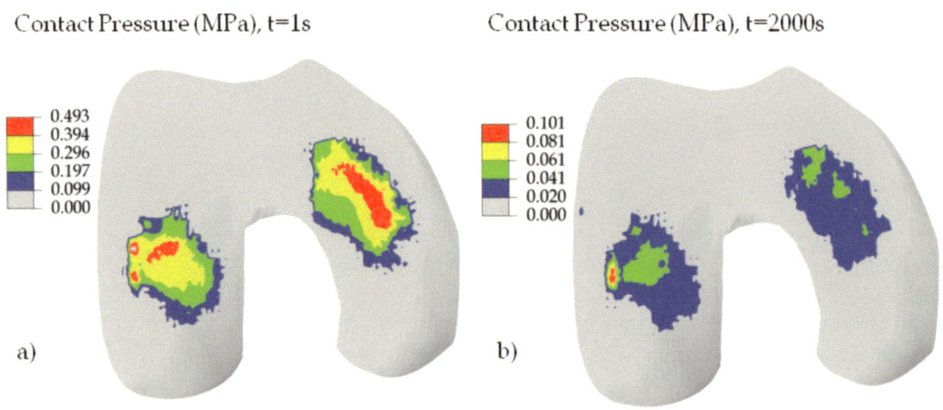

Fig. 6. Contact pressure on the articular surface of the femoral cartilage for the intact knee. The medial condyle is on the right (inferior view). The colors do not show the contact areas exactly, because each color stands for a range of contact pressure. In particular, the color grey does not mean precisely zero pressure there.

It should be noted that all results presented here were obtained using the small deformation assumption. The compression of 0.3 mm was not a physiological loading. The maximum pressures shown in Fig. 6 is merely 10% of possible maximum pressure. The high-pressure regions may be altered if large compression is applied.

PARTIAL MENISCECTOMY – The contact mechanics of the knee was also investigated previously for six cases of partial meniscectomies. In that study (to be published), creep loading protocols were considered. We consider the relaxation loading here for two cases only, the extended lateral and medial meniscectomies. The effect of partial meniscal resections on joint mechanics was more significant in these two cases (Figs. 7-10).

The fluid pressures in the menisci for the two cases of partial meniscectomies were preliminary (Fig. 7). No substantial differences were observed for the two cases (although some small differences are shown in Fig. 7, as comparing Figs. 7a with 7c and 7b with 7d). It was not clear whether this was due to the inaccuracy of the mesh for the menisci or due to small compression applied to the knee. For the same two cases, however, significantly different fluid pressures were observed in the tibial cartilages (Fig. 8). The higher fluid pressure occurred at the side where the meniscus was partially removed. Furthermore, the maximum fluid pressure was much greater in the case of extended medial meniscectomy (Fig. 8c,d) than that in extended lateral meniscectomy (Fig. 8a,b). This was the case because the higher pressure should have occurred on the medial side even for the intact knee. Now, the meniscectomy on this side made it worse with higher pressurization (Fig. 8, lower figures compared to the upper figures respectively).

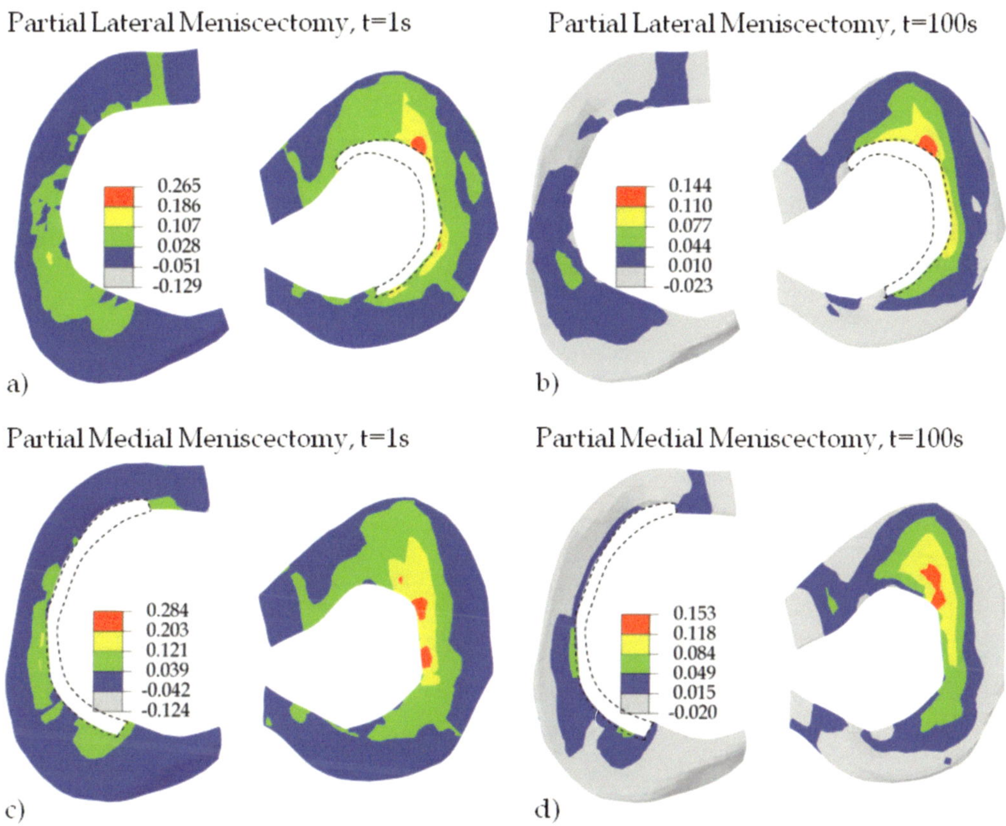

Fig. 7. Fluid pressure (MPa) in the menisci of partial meniscectomized knees. (a) and (b) extended lateral meniscectomy; (c) and (d) extended medial meniscectomy. The lateral meniscus is on the right with the posterior side shown in the lower part in each figure (top view). The sites of resection are indicated with the dashed lines.

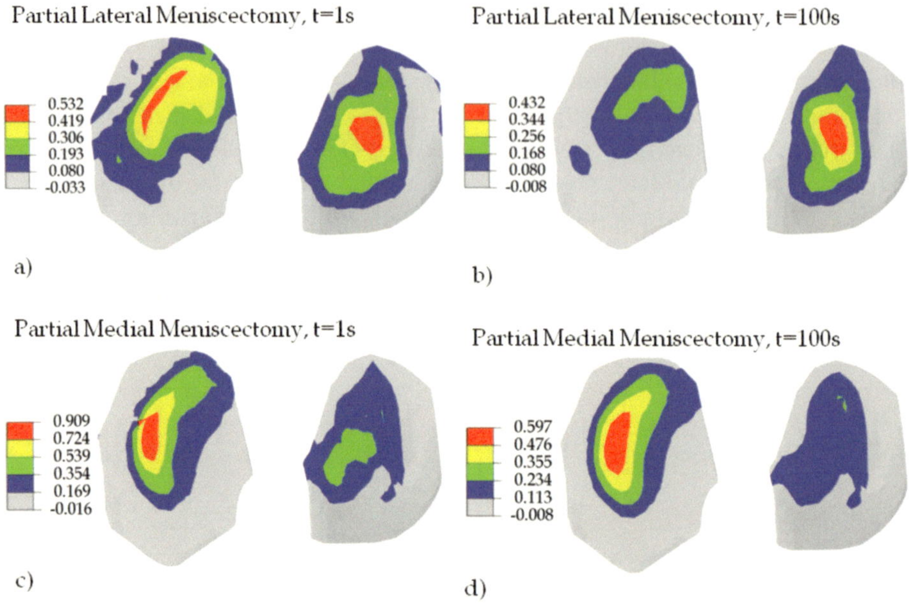

Fig. 8. Fluid pressure (MPa) in the tibial cartilages. (a) and (b) extended lateral meniscectomy; (c) and (d) extended medial meniscectomy. The pressure was obtained for the centroids of the elements. The lateral side is on the right (top view)

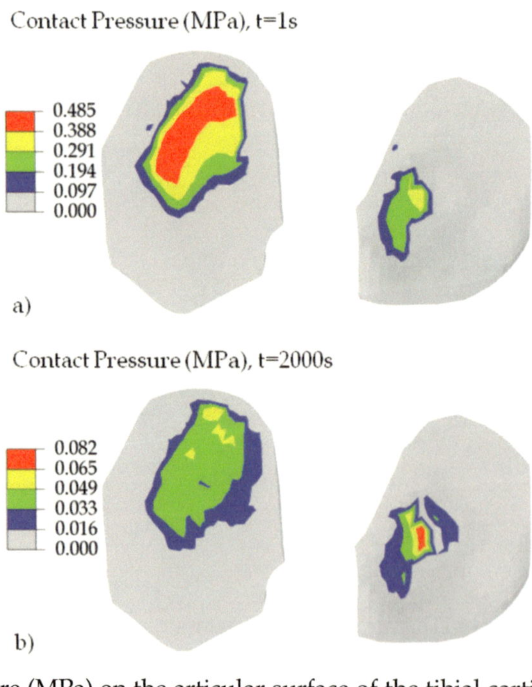

Fig. 9. Contact pressure (MPa) on the articular surface of the tibial cartilages for the case of extended lateral meniscectomy. The lateral side is on the right (top view)

The contact pressures on the articular surfaces are shown in Fig. 9 for the tibial cartilages and Fig. 10 for the femoral cartilage, both for the case of extended lateral meniscectomy. Again, the contact pressures were very low at later stage of relaxation (Figs. 9b and 10b). It was not clear why the maximum contact pressures on the surface (Fig. 9a) were not greater than the maximum fluid pressure within the tissue shown in Fig. 8a. However, it was most likely due to the coarse mesh for the tibial cartilages. There was only one layer of elements for the tibial cartilages, comparing to four layers of elements for the femoral cartilage.

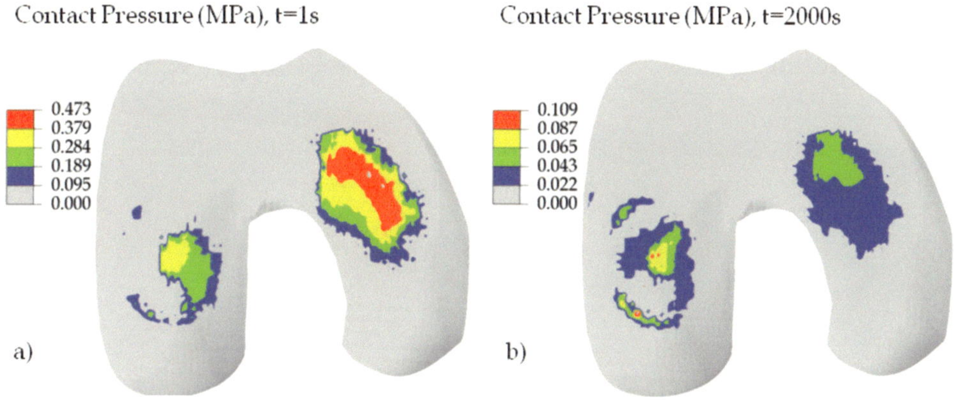

Fig. 10. Contact pressure on the articular surface of the femoral cartilage for the case of extended lateral meniscectomy. The medial condyle is on the right (inferior view)

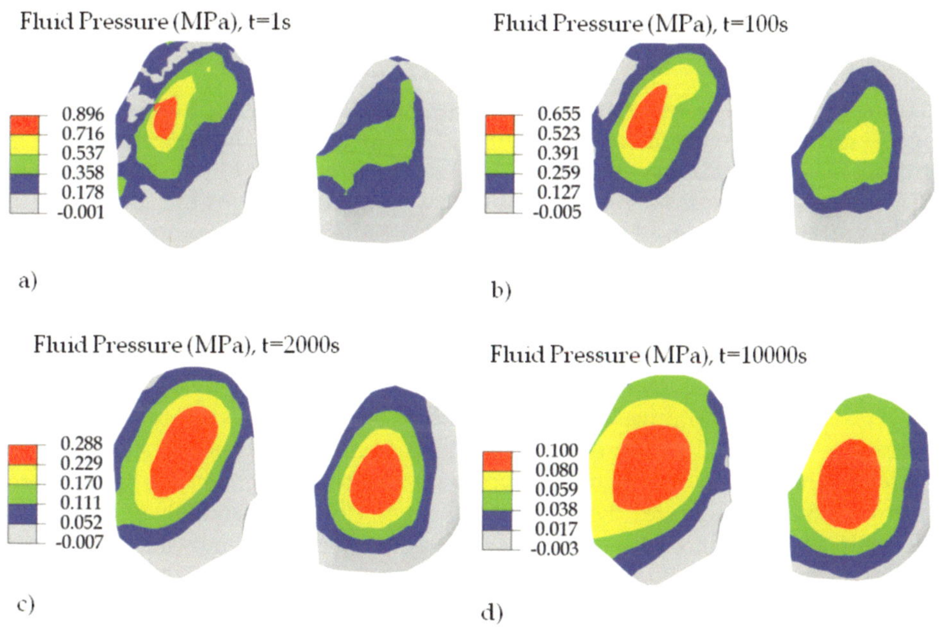

Fig. 11. Fluid pressure in the tibial cartilages for the case of total meniscectomy. The lateral side is on the right and posterior side below (top view)

TOTAL MENISCECTOMY – The fluid pressures in the tibial and femoral cartilages are shown in Figs. 11 and 12, respectively, for the case of total meniscectomy, i.e. when both menisci were removed. The contours here look more in regular shape, possibly because the poorly-shaped meniscal elements were removed. The dissipation of fluid pressure was substantially slowed down by total meniscectomy (Figs. 11 and 12). The peak fluid pressure was the maximum at 1 second. The maximum fluid pressure was still at 32% and 11% of the peak value, respectively, even at 2000 and 10000 seconds (Fig. 11). The medial condyle was more pressurized than the lateral one at 1 second, but the loading was more balanced between the two condyles at 2000 seconds (Fig. 12).

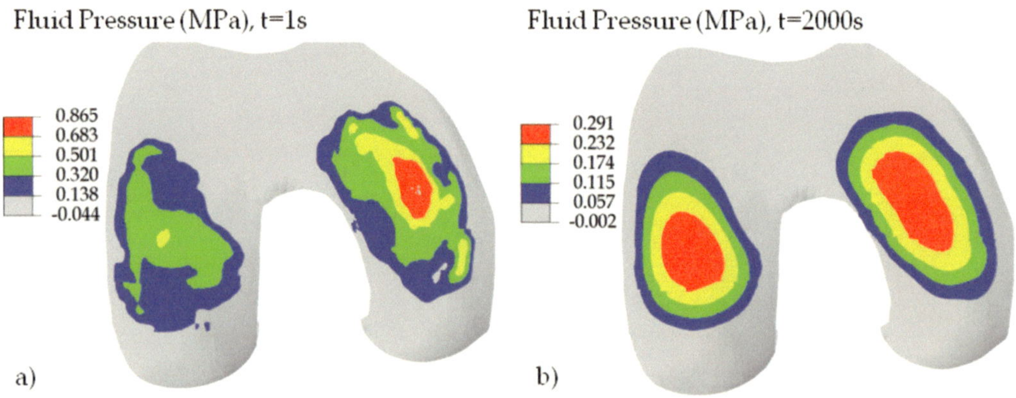

Fig. 12. Fluid pressure in the deep layer of the femoral cartilage for the case of total meniscectomy. The pressure was obtained for the centroids of the elements that were located approximately 3/4 of the depth from the articular surface. The medial condyle is on the right (inferior view)

Comparing to the intact knee, a greater fluid pressure gradient was produced by meniscal removal and it was significant for at least 100 seconds (Fig. 11a,b). Note this was the case of relaxation loading: the maximum compression was constant after 1 second. It was possible that part of the 0.3mm-compression was absorbed by the menisci for the case of the intact knee. The greater pressure gradient was more likely produced by stress concentration.

4. Discussions

The fluid pressures in the cartilaginous tissues and contact pressures between the articulating surfaces were obtained for the normal, partial and total meniscectomized human knees. The constitutive law for the soft tissues was previously developed and numerically incorporated in the commercial finite element software ABAQUS (Li et al., 1999b, 2009). The present results complemented our recent studies, when we simulated 0.1-mm compressive relaxation for the intact knee (Gu and Li, 2011) and 300-N creep loading for the total meniscectomized knee (Kazemi at al., 2011). There were indications that some of our previous results were compatible with limited experimental data available from the literature. Here, we were not able to validate the computational results with more experimental data. However, we saw that the fluid pressure in Fig. 3a was compatible with the contact pressure in Fig. 4a: they had similar distributions but the contact pressure, which was contributed from both the fluid pressure and the tissue matrix, was greater than the fluid pressure. We also observed that both the maximum fluid and contact pressures occurred at the medial-anterior side (Figs. 3a, 4a, 5a and 6a) (note that Figs. 3 and 4 are top view, while Figs. 5 and 6 are inferior view). These observations indicated reasonable results.

4.1 Significance of fluid pressurization in contact mechanics

In agreement with previous studies, the contact pressure between two articulating surfaces in the knee was predominantly contributed from the fluid pressurization in the cartilaginous tissues, and thus highly time-dependent when joint loadings were applied quickly. The high-pressure regions in the tissues also moved with time (Figs. 2-6, a vs b respectively). These results have not been available from the literature, when the knee joint is modeled as elastic solid (while the fluid phase is not considered).

The fluid pressurization was even more significant in meniscectomized knees. Note that the pressure was also dependent on the types of loadings that were applied on the knee. The fluid pressure lasted much longer with creep loading, as observed in the experiments with tissue explants (Li et al., 2008) and also found in our previous knee modeling (Kazemi et al., 2011).

According to published fibril-reinforced modeling of articular cartilage *in vitro*, the strong fluid pressurization was produced by the nonlinear collagen fiber-reinforcement in the tissues (Li et al., 2003). The collagen fiber orientation and fibrillar properties were particularly considered in the present modeling, which was an important feature of the simulations presented here. These pressure results for the cartilaginous tissues *in situ* may provide additional information on the injury and pathomechanics of the knee joint. For example, collagen degeneration is believed to trigger osteoarthritis. We may use similar modeling to investigate the alteration of the fluid pressure in the knee initiated by collagen generation at a particular site in order to understand the progression of osteoarthritis.

4.2 Effect of meniscectomy on contact mechanics

Meniscectomy caused the pressure increase in the joint (Figs. 12 vs 5), and also slowed down the fluid pressure dissipation during relaxation: the maximum fluid pressure at 2000 second was reduced to 9.3% of the peak value at 1 second for the intact knee (Figs. 5b vs 5a), but to 33.6% for the case of total meniscectomy (Figs. 12b vs 12a). This result may explain the clinical observation that meniscectomy caused stiffness in the knees. However, the alteration in pressure was very minor in the cases of partial meniscectomies, as compared to the total meniscectomy (Figs. 3a, 8a & 11a). This was because the relaxation loading was considered. The effect of partial meniscectomy was more significant in creep than in relaxation as we found in another study using the same computer modeling.

A partial meniscectomy may change the load balance in the knee joint. For the intact knee, the medial side was more pressurized than the lateral side before relaxation (Figs. 3a, 4a, 5a & 6a). A meniscectomy increased the fluid pressure from the normal level. Therefore, the fluid pressure became much higher in the medial side than the lateral side after medial meniscectomy (Fig 8c).

The total meniscectomy was studied previously for the case of creep loading (Kazemi et al., 2011). In that case, the peak fluid pressure in the femoral cartilage at 1 second was at the same level as it here. However, the maximum fluid pressure at 2000 second was only reduced by 20% from the peak pressure in the case of creep, as compared 66% for the present case of relaxation (Fig. 12). Therefore, the clinical implication of total meniscectomy was more significant than the present results have shown, because creep is closer to the physiological loadings than relaxation.

4.3 Numerical convergence, limitations and challenges

In spite of careful control of the solution procedure within the commercial software, there were indeed indications of possible numerical problems. For example, the maximum contact pressure was not greater than the maximum fluid pressure in the femoral cartilage (Figs. 5a vs 6a). This might have been caused by the errors in mesh, especially the coarse meshes for the menisci and tibial cartilages. However, it was also possible that the maximum fluid pressure in the deep layer of the femoral cartilage (Fig. 5a) was supposed to be greater than the maximum contact pressure on the articular surface (Fig. 6a). We did not plot the fluid pressure in the surface layer, because the results there did not precisely agree with the actual contact boundary due to the incapability of applying accurate zero pressure boundary condition around the contact area. This was because the closest boundary applied was determined by the corner nodes of the elements that were closest to the actual contact boundary. These closest nodes did not precisely describe the actual contact boundary due to the coarse mesh used in the simulations. The numerical accuracy of such results can be improved and confirmed later with better meshes when more powerful computers are used. The fluid pressures shown for the deep layers should have negligible influence from the inaccurate fluid pressure boundary conditions.

The main limitations of the present study were the small deformation assumption and the use of non-physiological loadings. The small compression used might not have been sufficient to minimize the influences of the geometrical errors that were introduced by meshing or by the reconstruction of the knee model from MRI data. The simulations were time-consuming even for these simple cases, because of the multiple mechanical contacts involved in the time-dependent problem. We chose these simple cases to start with the research, and will validate these results later with a formulation of large deformation.

Other issues existed such as the poor element aspect ratios and some distorted elements used in the simulations, in order to limit the number of nodes and speed up the solutions. The cartilaginous tissues are very thin (articular cartilage 1-5mm), especially at the inner edge of meniscus (where the thickness is close to zero). Therefore, the 3D finite elements must be very thin and several times wider in other two directions. The issue with aspect ratio can be solved in the future using more computer power, e.g. using computers with dozens of CPUs. However, the issue with distort elements can only be improved. Some distorted elements are unavoidable in order to match the geometry of the tissue, such as the inner edge of the meniscus. Special finite elements could be developed to address this tissue.

It would be challenging to simulate physiological loadings in walking. The computer power never seems to be sufficient. Currently, using a new 6-core computer with 24 GB RAMs, it takes hours to a full day (depending on the meshes used) to run the first second simulation in the loading phase (up to hundreds of times faster in later relaxation and creep phase). Numerical difficulties would also be expected when the contact in the knee is dynamic.

Accurate surface reconstruction is essential for correct modeling of the mechanical contact in the knee joint. For this purpose, we have obtained new MRIs using the 3-Tesla facility at the University MR research centre. Images in both sagittal and coronal planes were obtained for the same knee and will be used to construct precise surfaces and tissue boundaries. We will also determine and minimize the geometrical errors introduced by finite element meshes. We should be able to obtain new results soon.

It is always important to validate the computational results with experimental data. We plan to test the modeling in a few different settings, such as measuring the tissue deformation with MRI under static compression and cadaveric knee mechanical tests. This is beyond the scope of this chapter.

5. Summary and conclusions

The computer simulations on the mechanical response of human knee joint have been mostly based on the single-phase elastic modeling of the soft tissues. The fluid pressure in the tissues *in situ* has not been available from the literature until our recent publications (Gu and Li, 2011; Kazemi et al., 2011), although the fluid pressurization is believed to play an important role in the mechanical functioning of the joints, and has been studied both theoretically and experimentally for decades at the tissue level. Our recent studies extended the previous fibril-reinforced modeling at the tissue level to the joint level. Compared to most existing knee models from the literature, two major features were added in the present modeling: the fluid flow/pressurization in articular cartilages and menisci, and realistic site-specific fiber orientations in the femoral cartilage and menisci.

The tissue model was previously validated against experimental data under several loading conditions. The constitutive law was numerically incorporated in the commercial software ABAQUS using the option of user-defined material. The meshes for the femoral cartilage were more refined and the fiber orientations there were incorporated using measured split-line pattern from the literature (Below at al., 2002). Coarse meshes (one layer only) were used for the tibial cartilages because our previous focus was on the femoral cartilage. The meshes for the menisci were difficult to be refined because of the wedge shape. Converged solutions were obtained that satisfied desired criteria. However, the pressures in the deep layer of the femoral cartilage might be more reliable than other results.

The present study has shown the importance of the fluid pressurization in the mechanical functions of the normal and repaired human knees. The remainder of the normal tissues can be more pressurized with injuries or repairs in the knee. The site of the repair and the amount of tissues that were lost in injury may be important parameters for the altered mechanical functions of the knee. The present results were obtained for small knee compression which might have been compromised by small errors in surface geometries. However, the modeling can obviously be used to study site-specific cartilage degeneration and injury after large deformation is incorporated.

The present study may also indicate the limitation of previous elastic modeling that did not consider the fluid pressure, which was not explored in the chapter. An independent study, however, showed that the results predicted by elastic models were compromised but could provide certain useful information if the results were interpreted correctly.

6. Acknowledgments

The present study was partially supported by the Natural Sciences and Engineering Research Council (NSERC) of Canada. The second author also received a scholarship from the NSERC Create training program. The knee geometry was reconstructed using MRI data by Drs. Ming Zhang and Jason Cheung at the Hong Kong Polytechnic University in China.

7. References

Adeeb, SM., Ahmed, EYS., Matyas, J., Hart, DA., Frank, CB. & Shrive, NG. (2004). Congruency Effects on Load Bearing in Diarthrodial Joints. *Computer Methods in Biomechanics and Biomedical Engineering*, Vol.7, No.3, pp. 147-157, ISSN 1025-5842

Armstrong, CG., Bahrani, AS. & Gardner DL. (1980). Changes in the Deformational Behavior of Human Hip Cartilage with Age. *Journal of Biomechanical Engineering*, Vol.102, No.3, pp. 214-220, ISSN 0148-0731

Aspden, RM., Yarker, YE. & Hukins, DW. (1985). Collagen Orientations in the Meniscus of the Knee Joint. *Journal of Anatomy*, Vol.140, No.3, pp. 371-380, ISSN 00218782

Ateshian, GA., Lai, WM., Zhu, WB. & Mow, VC. (1994). An Asymptotic Solution for the Contact of Two Biphasic Cartilage Layers. *Journal of Biomechanics*, Vol.27, No.11, pp. 1347-1360, ISSN 0021-9290

Below, S., Arnoczky, SP., Dodds, J., Kooima, C. & Walter, N. (2002). The Split-Line Pattern of the Distal Femur: a Consideration in the Orientation of Autologous Cartilage Grafts. *J Arthroscopic and Related Surgery*, Vol.18, No.6, pp. 613-617, ISSN 0749-8063

Bendjaballah, MZ., Shirazi-Adl, A. & Zukor, DJ. (1995). Biomechanics of the Human Knee Joint in Compression: Reconstruction, Mesh Generation and Finite Element Analysis. *The Knee*, Vol.2, No.2, pp. 69-79, ISSN 0968-0160

Biot, MA. (1941). General Theory of Three Dimensional Consolidation. *Journal of Applied Physics*, Vol.12, No.2, pp. 155-164, ISSN 0021-8979

Biot, MA. (1962). Mechanics of Deformation and Acoustic Propagation in Porous Media. *Journal of Applied Physics*, Vol.33, No.4, pp. 1482-1498, ISSN 0021-8979

Brown, TD. & Singerman, RJ. (1986). Experimental Determination of the Linear Biphasic Constitutive Coefficients of Human Fetal Proximal Femoral Chondroepiphysis. *Journal of Biomechanics*, Vol.19, pp. 597-605, ISSN 0021-9290

Callaghan, JJ., Rosenberg, AG., Rubash HE., Simonian, PT. & Wickiewicz, TL. (2003). *The Adult Knee.* (Vol.I), Lippincott Williams & Wilkins, ISBN 0781732476, Philadelphia

Coletti, JMJ., Akeson, WH. & Woo, SL. (1972). A Comparison of the Physical Behavior of Normal Articular Cartilage and the Arthroplasty Surface. *Journal of Bone and Joint Surgery - Series A*, Vol.54, No.1, pp. 147-160, ISSN 0021-9355

Cheung, JTM., Zhang, M., Leung , AKL. & Fan, YB. (2005). Three-dimensional Finite Element Analysis of the Foot During Standing – A Material Sensitivity Study. *Journal of Biomechannics*, Vol.38, pp. 1045-1054, ISSN 0021-9290

Daniel, DM., Akeson, WH. & O'Connor, JJ. (1990). *Knee Ligaments: Structure, Function, Injury and Repair.* Raven Press, ISBN 0881676055, New York

Dandy, DJ. (1990). The Arthroscopic Anatomy of Symptomatic Meniscal Lesions. *Journal of Bone and Joint Surgery - Series B*, Vol.72, No.4, pp. 628-633, ISSN 0301-620X

Fithian, DC., Kelly, MA. & Mow VC. (1990). Material Properties and Structure-Function Relationships in the Menisci. *Clinical Orthopaedics and Related Research*, Vol.252, pp. 19-31, ISSN 0009-921X

Greis, PE., Bardana, DD., Holmstrom, MC. & Burks, RT. (2002). Meniscal Injury: I. Basic Science and Evaluation. *The Journal of the American Academy of Orthopaedic Surgeons*, Vol.10, No.3, pp. 168-176, ISSN 1067-151X

Grood, ES. & Hefzy, MS. (1982). An Analytical Technique for Modeling Knee Joint Stiffness. Part I: Ligamentous Forces. *Journal of Biomechanical Engineering*, Vol.104, No.4, pp. 330-337, ISSN 0148-0731

Gu, KB. & Li, LP. (2011). A Human Knee Joint Model Considering Fluid Pressure and Fiber Orientation in Cartilages and Menisci. *Medical Engineering and Physics*, Vol.33, No.4, pp. 497-503, ISSN 1350-4533

Haut Donahue, TL., Hull, ML., Rashid, MM. & Jacobs, CR. (2002). A Finite Element Model of the Human Knee Joint for the Study of Tibio-Femoral Contact. *Journal of Biomechanical Engineering*, Vol.124, No.3. pp. 273-280, ISSN 0148-0731

Hayes, WC., Keer, LM., Herrmann, G. & Mockros, LF. (1972). A Mathematical Analysis for Indentation Tests of Articular Cartilage. *Journal of Biomechanics*, Vol.5, No.5, pp. 541-551, ISSN 0021-9290

Hayes, WC. & Mockros, J. (1971). Viscoelastic Properties of Human Articular Cartilage. *Journal of applied physiology*, Vol.31, No.4, pp. 562–568, ISSN 0021-8987

Hirokawa, S. & Tsuruno, R. (2000). Three-Dimensional Deformation and Stress Distribution in an Analytical/Computational Model of the Anterior Cruciate Ligament. *Journal of Biomechanics*, Vol.33, No.9, pp. 1069-1077, ISSN 0021-9290

Kazemi, M., Li, LP., Savard, P. & Buschmann, MD. (2011). Creep Behavior of the Intact and Meniscectomy Knee Joints. *Journal of the Mechanical Behavior of Biomedical Materials*, Vol.4, No.7, 1351-1358, doi:10.1016/j.jmbbm.2011.05.004, ISSN 1751-6161

Kempson, GE., Freeman, MAR. & Swanson, SAV. (1971). The Determination of a Creep Modulus for Articular Cartilage from Indentation Tests on the Human Femoral Head. *Journal of Biomechanics*, Vol.4, No.4, pp. 239-250, ISSN 0021-9290

Kurosawa, H., Fukubayashi, T. & Nakajima, H. (1980). Load-Bearing Mode of the Knee Joint: Physical Behavior of the Knee Joint with or Without Menisci. *Clinical Orthopaedics and Related Research*, Vol.149, pp. 283-290, ISSN 0009-921X

Lai, WM., Mow, VC. & Roth, V. (1981). Effects of Non-Linear Strain-Dependent Permeability and Rate of Compression on the Stress Behaviour of Articular Cartilage. *Journal of Biomechanical Engineering*, Vol.103, No.2, pp. 61-66, ISSN 0148-0731

Lanir, Y. (1987). Biorheology and Fluid Flux in Swelling Tissues. II. Analysis of Unconfined Compressive Response of Transversely Isotropic Cartilage Disc. *Biorheology*, Vol.24, pp. 189-205, 0006-355X

Li, LP., Buschmann, MD. & Shirazi-Adl, A. (2003). Strain Rate Dependent Stiffness of Articular Cartilage in Unconfined Compression. *Journal of Biomechanical Engineering*, Vol.125, No.2, pp. 161-168, ISSN 0148-0731

Li, LP, Cheung, JTM., & Herzog W (2009). Three-dimensional Fibril-Reinforced Finite Element Model of Articular Cartilage. *Medical & Biological Engineering & Computing*, Vol.47, pp. 607-615, ISSN 0140-0118

Li, G., Gil, J., Kanamori, A. &Woo, SL. (1999a). A Validated Three-Dimensional Computational Model of a Human Knee Joint. *Journal of Biomechanical Engineering*, Vol.121, No.6, pp. 657-662, ISSN 0148-0731

Li, LP. & Gu, KB. (2011). Reconsideration on the Use of Elastic Models to Predict the Instantaneous Load Response of the Knee Joint. *Proceedings of the Institution of Mechanical Engineers, Part H: Journal of Engineering in Medicine*, ISSN 0954-4119. In press, DOI: 10.1177/0954411911412464

Li, LP. & Herzog, W. (2004). Strain-Rate Dependence of Cartilage Stiffness in Unconfined Compression: The Role of Fibril Reinforcement versus Tissue Volume Change in Fluid Pressurization. *Journal of Biomechanics*, Vol.37, No.3, pp. 375-382, ISSN 0021-9290

Li, LP., Korhonen, RK., Iivarinen, J., Jurvelin, JS. & Herzog, W. (2008). Fluid Pressure Driven Fibril Reinforcement in Creep and Relaxation Tests of Articular Cartilage. *Medical Engineering & Physics*, Vol.30, No.2, pp. 182-189, ISSN 1350-4533

Li, LP., Soulhat, J., Buschmann, MD. & Shirazi-Adl, A. (1999b). Non-Linear Analysis of Cartilage in Unconfined Ramp Compression Using a Fibril Reinforced Poroelastic Model. *Clinical Biomechanics*, Vol.14, No.9, pp. 673-682, ISSN 0268-0033

Miller, K. (1998). Modelling Soft Tissue using Biphasic Theory – A Word of Caution. *Computer Methods in Biomechanics and Biomedical Engineering*, Vol.1, pp. 261-263, ISSN 1025-5842

Mow, VC. & Ratcliffe, A. (1990). *Biomechanics of Diarthrodial Joints.* Springer, ISBN 0387973796, New York

Mow, VC., Kuei, SC., Lai, WM. & Armstrong CG. (1980). Biphasic Creep and Stress Relaxation of Articular Cartilage in Compression: Theory and Experiments. *Journal of Biomechanical Engineering,* Vol.102, No.1, pp. 73-84, ISSN 0148-0731

Mow, VC., Ateshian, GA. & Spilker, RL. (1993). Biomechanics of Diarthrodial Joints: A Review of Twenty Years of Progress. *Journal of Biomechanical Engineering,* Vol.115, No.4B, pp. 460-467, ISSN 0148-0731

Nowinski, JL. (1971). Bone Articulations as Systems of Poroelastic Bodies in Contact. *AIAA Journal,* Vol.9, pp. 62-69, ISSN 0001-1452

Nowinski, JL. (1972). Stress Concentrations Around a Cylindrical Cavity in Bone Treated as a Poroelastic Body. *Acta Mechanica,* Vol.13, pp. 281-292, ISSN 0001-5970

Nowinski, JL. & Davis, CF. (1970). A model of the Human Skull as a Poroelastic Spherical Shell Subjected to a Quasistatic Load. *Mathematical Biosciences,* Vol.8, pp. 397-416, ISSN 0025-5564

Nowinski, JL. & Davis, CF. (1972). The Flexure and Torsion of Bones Viewed as Anisotropic Poroelastic Bodies. *International Journal of Engineering Science,* Vol.10, pp. 1063-1079, ISSN 0020-7225

Oloyede, A., Flachsmann R., & Broom ND. (1992). The Dramatic Influence of Loading Velocity on the Compressive Response of Articular Cartilage. *Connective Tissue Research,* Vol.27, pp. 211-244, ISSN 0300-8207

Parsons, JR. & Black J. (1977). The Viscoelastic Shear Behavior of Normal Rabbit Articular Cartilage. *Journal of Biomechanics,* Vol.10, No.1, pp. 21-29, ISSN 0021-9290

Peña, E., Calvo, B., Martínez, MA. & Doblaré, M. (2008). Computer Simulation of Damage on Distal Femoral Articular Cartilage after Meniscectomies. *Computers in Biology and Medicine,* Vol.38, No.1, pp. 69-81, ISSN 0010-4825

Peña, E., Calvo, B., Martínez, MA. & Palanca D, Doblaré M. (2005). Finite Element Analysis of the Effect of Meniscal Tears and Meniscectomies on Human Knee Biomechanics. *Clinical Biomechanics,* Vol.20, No.5, pp. 498-507, ISSN 0268-0033

Peña, E., Calvo, B., Martínez, MA. & Doblaré, M. (2006). A Three-Dimensional Finite Element Analysis of the Combined Behavior of Ligaments and Menisci in the Healthy Human Knee Joint. *Journal of Biomechanics,* Vol.39, No.9, pp. 1686-1701, ISSN 00219290

Penrose, JM., Holt, GM., Beaugonin, M. & Hose, DR. (2002). Development of an Accurate Three-Dimensional Finite Element Knee Model. *Computer Methods in Biomechanics and Biomedical Engineering,* Vol.5, No.4, pp. 291-300, ISSN 1025-5842

Pérez del Palomar, A. & Doblaré, M. (2007). An Accurate Simulation Model of Anteriorly Displaced TMJ Discs with and Without Reduction. *Medical Engineering and Physics,* Vol.29, No.2, pp. 216-226, ISSN 1350-4533

Schanz, M. & Diebels, S. (2003). A Comparative Study of Biot's Theory and the Linear Theory of Porous Media for Wave Propagation Problems. *Acta Mechanica,* Vol.161, pp. 213-235, ISSN 0001-5970

Shirazi, R., Shirazi-Adl, A. & Hurtig, M. (2008). Role of Cartilage Collagen Fibrils Networks in Knee Joint Biomechanics Under Compression. *Journal of Biomechanics,* Vol.41, No.16, pp. 3340-3348, ISSN 0021-9290

Shirazi, R. & Shirazi-Adl, A. (2009). Analysis of Partial Meniscectomy and ACL Reconstruction in Knee Joint Biomechanics Under a Combined Loading. *Clinical Biomechanics,* Vol.24, No.9, pp. 755-761, ISSN 02680033

Simon, BR. (1992). Multiphasic Poroelastic Finite Element Models for Soft Tissue Structures. *Applied Mechanics Riviews*, Vol.45, No.6, pp. 191-218, ISSN 0003-6900

Soulhat, J., Buschmann, MD. & Shirazi-Adl, A. (1999). A Fibril-Network-Reinforced Biphasic Model of Cartilage in Unconfined Compression. *Journal of Biomechanical Engineering,* Vol.121, No.3, pp. 340-347, ISSN 0148-0731

Spilker, RL., Donzelli, PS. & Mow, VC. (1992). A Transversely Isotropic Biphasic Finite Element Model of the Meniscus. *Journal of Biomechanics,* Vol.25, No.9, pp. 1027-1045, ISSN 00219290

Suggs, J., Wang, C. & Li, G. (2003). The Effect of Graft Stiffness on Knee Joint Biomechanics After ACL Reconstruction- a 3D Computational Simulation. *Clinical Biomechanics,* Vol.18, No.1, pp. 35-43, ISSN 0268-0033

Suh, JK., Spilker, RL. & Holmes, MH. (1991). A Penalty Finite Element Analysis for Nonlinear Mechanics of Biphasic Hydrated Soft Tissue under Large Deformation. *International Journal for Numerical Methods in Engineering,* Vol.32, No.7, pp. 1411-1439, ISBN 1097-0207

Swanson, SAV. (1979). Friction, Wear and Lubrication. In: *Adult Articular Cartilage*, MAR. Freeman, (Ed.), 415-457, Pitman Medical, ISBN 039758248X, London, UK

Walker, PS. & Erkman, MJ. (1975). The Role of the Menisci in Force Transmission Across the Knee. *Clinical Orthopaedics and Related Research,* Vol.109, pp. 184-192, ISSN 0009-921X

Walker, PS. & Hajek, JV. (1972). The Load-Bearing Area in the Knee Joint. *Journal of Biomechanics,* Vol.5, No.6, pp. 581-589, ISSN 0021-9290

Wilson, W., van Donkelaar, CC., van Rietbergen, B., Ito, K. & Huiskes, R. (2004). Stresses in the Local Collagen Network of Articular Cartilage: a Poroviscoelastic Fibril-Reinforced Finite Element Study. *Journal of Biomechanics,* Vol.37, No.3, pp. 357-366, ISSN 0021-9290

Woo, SL., Akeson, WH. & Jemmott, GF. (1976). Measurements of Nonhomogeneous, Directional Mechanical Properties of Articular Cartilage in Tension. *Journal of Biomechanics,* Vol.9, No.12, pp. 785-791, ISSN 0021-9290

Wu, JZ., Herzog, W. & Epstein, M. (1998). Evaluation of the Finite Element Software ABAQUS for Biomechanical Modelling of Biphasic Tissues. *Journal of Biomechanics,* Vol.31, pp. 165-169, ISSN 0021-9290

Yang, N., Nayeb-Hashemi, H., & Canavan, PK. (2009). The Combined Effect of Frontal Plane Tibiofemoral Knee Angle and Meniscectomy on the Cartilage Contact Stresses and Strains. *Annals of Biomedical Engineering,* Vol.37, No.11, pp. 2360-2372, ISSN 00906964

Zielinska, B., & Donahue, TL. (2006). 3D Finite Element Model of Meniscectomy: Changes in Joint Contact Behavior. *Journal of Biomechanical Engineering,* Vol.128, No.1, pp. 115-123, ISNN 01480731

Other Related Publications From the Authors

Li, LP., Soulhat, J., Buschmann, MD. & Shirazi-Adl, A. (1999). Non-Linear Analysis of Cartilage in Unconfined Ramp Compression Using a Fibril Reinforced Poroelastic Model. *Clinical Biomechanics,* Vol.14, No.9, pp. 673-682, ISSN 0268-0033

Li, LP., Buschmann, MD. & Shirazi-Adl, A. (2000). A Fibril Reinforced Nonhomogeneous Poroelastic Model for Articular Cartilage: Inhomogeneous Response in Unconfined Compression. *Journal of Biomechanics,* Vol.33, No.12, pp. 1533-1541, ISSN 00219290

Li, LP., Buschmann, MD. & Shirazi-Adl, A. (2001). The Asymmetry of Transient Response in Compression vs Release for Cartilage in Unconfined Compression. *ASME Journal of Biomechanical Engineering,* Vol.123, No. 5, pp. 519-522, ISSN 01480731

Li, LP., Buschmann, MD. & Shirazi-Adl, A. (2002). The Role of Fibril Reinforcement in the Mechanical Behavior of Cartilage. *Biorheology*, Vol.39, Nos. 1-2, pp. 89-96, ISSN 0006355X

Li, LP., Shirazi-Adl, A. & Buschmann, MD. (2002). Alterations in Mechanical Behavior of Articular Cartilage due to Changes in Depth Varying Material Properties - A Nonhomogeneous Poroelastic Model Study. *Computer Methods in Biomechanics and Biomedical Engineering*, Vol.5, No. 1, pp. 45-52, ISSN 10255842

Li, LP., Shirazi-Adl, A. & Buschmann, MD. (2003). Investigation of Mechanical Behavior of Articular Cartilage by Fibril Reinforced Poroelastic Models. *Biorheology*, Vol.40, Nos. 1-3, pp. 227-233, ISSN 0006355X

Li, LP., Buschmann, MD. & Shirazi-Adl, A. (2003). Strain Rate Dependent Stiffness of Articular Cartilage in Unconfined Compression. *Journal of Biomechanical Engineering*, Vol.125, No.2, pp. 161-168, ISSN 0148-0731

Li, LP., & Herzog, W. (2004). Strain-Rate Dependence of Cartilage Stiffness in Unconfined Compression: The Role of Fibril Reinforcement versus Tissue Volume Change in Fluid Pressurization. *Journal of Biomechanics*, Vol.37, No.3, pp. 375-382, ISSN 0021-9290

Li, LP., & Herzog, W. (2004). The Role of Viscoelasticity of Collagen Fibers in Articular Cartilage: Theory and Numerical Formulation. *Biorheology, Vol.*41, Nos. 3-4, pp. 181-194, ISSN 0006355X

Li, LP., Herzog, W., Korhonen, RK. & Jurvelin, JS. (2005). The Role of Viscoelasticity of Collagen Fibers in Articular Cartilage: Axial Tension versus Compression. *Medical Engineering & Physics*, Vol.27, No.1, pp. 51-57, ISSN 13504533

Li, LP., & Herzog, W. (2005). Electromechanical Response of Articular Cartilage in Indentation - Considerations on the Determination of Cartilage Properties during Arthroscopy. *Computer Methods in Biomechanics and Biomedical Engineering*, Vol.8, No.2, pp. 83-91, ISSN 10255842

Li, LP., & Herzog, W. (2006). Arthroscopic Evaluation of Cartilage Degeneration using Indentation Testing - Influence of Indenter Geometry. *Clinical Biomechanics*, Vol.21, No. 4, pp. 420-426, ISSN 02680033

Li, LP., Korhonen, RK., Iivarinen, J., Jurvelin, JS. & Herzog, W. (2008). Fluid Pressure Driven Fibril Reinforcement in Creep and Relaxation Tests of Articular Cartilage. *Medical Engineering & Physics*, Vol.30, No.2, pp. 182-189, ISSN 1350-4533

Li, LP, Cheung, JTM., & Herzog W (2009). Three-dimensional Fibril-Reinforced Finite Element Model of Articular Cartilage. *Medical & Biological Engineering & Computing*, Vol.47, pp. 607-615, ISSN 0140-0118

Gu, KB. & Li, LP. (2011). A Human Knee Joint Model Considering Fluid Pressure and Fiber Orientation in Cartilages and Menisci. *Medical Engineering and Physics*, Vol.33, No.4, pp. 497-503, ISSN 1350-4533

Kazemi, M., Li, LP., Savard, P. & Buschmann, MD. (2011). Creep Behavior of the Intact and Meniscectomy Knee Joints. *Journal of the Mechanical Behavior of Biomedical Materials*, Vol.4, No.7, 1351-1358, ISSN 1751-6161

Li, LP. & Gu, KB. (2011). Reconsideration on the Use of Elastic Models to Predict the Instantaneous Load Response of the Knee Joint. *Proceedings of the Institution of Mechanical Engineers, Part H: Journal of Engineering in Medicine*, Vol.225, pp. 888-896, ISSN 0954-4119